S0-BIY-819

THE BLUE GUIDES

Countries **Austria**
Belgium and Luxembourg
Channel Islands
China
Corsica
Crete
Cyprus
Czechoslovakia
Denmark
Egypt
England
France
France: Burgundy
Germany
Greece
Holland
Hungary
Ireland
Northern Italy
Southern Italy
Malta and Gozo
Morocco
Portugal
Scotland
Sicily
Spain
Switzerland
Turkey: the Aegean and Mediterranean Coasts
Wales
Yugoslavia

Cities **Athens and Environs**
Barcelona
Boston and Cambridge
Florence
Istanbul
Jerusalem
London
Moscow and Leningrad
New York
Oxford and Cambridge
Paris and Versailles
Rome and Environs
Venice

Themes **Churches and Chapels of Northern England**
Churches and Chapels of Southern England
Gardens of England
Literary Britain and Ireland
Museums and Galleries of London
Victorian Architecture in Britain

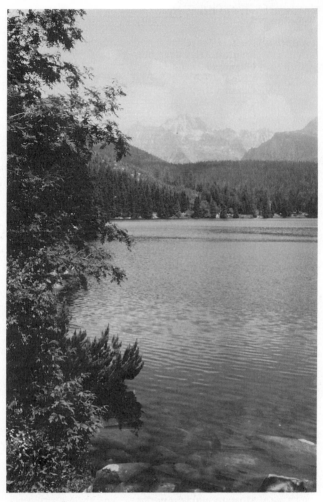

The lake at Štrbské Pleso, looking towards the snow-capped peaks of the High Tatras

BLUE GUIDE

CZECHOSLOVAKIA

Michael Jacobs

Maps and plans by John Flower

A & C Black
London

W W Norton
New York

First edition 1992

Published by A & C Black (Publishers) Limited
35 Bedford Row, London WC1R 4JH

© A & C Black (Publishers) Limited 1992

ISBN 0–7136–3230–5

A CIP catalogue record for this book
is available from the British Library

Published in the United States of America by
WW Norton & Company, Incorporated
500 Fifth Avenue, New York NY 10110

Published simultaneously in Canada by
Penguin Books Canada Limited
2801 John Street, Markham, Ontario L3R 1B4

ISBN 0–393–30840–5 USA

The publishers and the author have done their best to ensure the
accuracy of all the information in Blue Guide Czechoslovakia;
however, they can accept no responsibility for any loss, injury or
inconvenience sustained by any traveller as a result of information or
advice contained in the guide.

Michael Jacobs was born in Genova, Italy, in 1952. He studied at the
Courtauld Institute of Art in London, where he received a Ph.D. in
1982 for his researches into eighteenth-century Italian art and
architecture. A full-time author, he has written numerous books on
art and travel, including *The Phaidon Companion to Art and Artists
in the British Isles* (1980; with Malcolm Warner), *The Good and
Simple Life: Artist Colonies in Europe and America* (1984), *The Road
to Santiago de Compostela* (1991), guides to *Provence* (1988) and
Andalucia (1990), and the forthcoming *Blue Guide Barcelona*. He is
currently writing a travelogue on Spain.

Photographs by Michael Jacobs.

Typeset by CRB Typesetting Services, Ely, Cambs.

Printed and bound in Great Britain by
William Clowes Limited, Beccles and London

PREFACE

Neville Chamberlain, allowing Hitler in 1938 to appropriate a large portion of Czechoslovakia, notoriously referred to the place as a 'far-away country' populated by a 'people of whom we know nothing'. Today there is far less excuse for revealing such ignorance about Czechoslovakia. Prague is becoming one of the major tourist destinations in Europe, while modern Czech writers are among the most popular of all foreign authors in translation. An added glamour has been given to the country by the presidency of Václav Havel, who has drawn the attention of the world to Bohemia's long-standing humanist tradition.

For all this attention, however, Czechoslovakia still remains a little-known place, and the extraordinary wealth of the architectural and artistic treasures that await the tourist outside of Prague is still not widely appreciated. There are few countries of its size in Europe that can boast such a remarkable concentration of castles and country houses, so many well-preserved town squares, and such a magnificent range of monuments from the late Gothic period up to the 1930s. Unfortunately, until only recently, Czechoslovakia has been poorly served by guide and travel books, and not even the old Baedekers contain much useful information on the country as a whole. The present book is the first on Czechoslovakia in the Blue Guide series, and though it is intended as the most comprehensive cultural guide to the country as yet available in English, I can only claim to have laid the foundations for some fuller work of the future. I appreciate that Czechoslovakia has been changing so rapidly since I first began my research for this book (in the last months of the Communist regime), and that so much new material is now coming to light, that anything which is written on the country today will soon need revising.

The itineraries that make up the bulk of this book have been divided into separate sections dealing with Slovakia, Moravia and each of the main administrative districts comprising Bohemia. Apart from Prague and its environs, the Bohemian regions of greatest interest to tourists are those of West and South Bohemia, the former offering the evocative spa towns once known as Karlsbad and Marienbad, and the latter the so-called Rose Country, with its haunting landscape of vast fish-ponds, and its outstanding group of Renaissance towns and villages. The appeal of Moravia lies essentially in its southern half, where you will find palatial sixteenth to eighteenth-century residences rivalling those of Bohemia, as well as much pioneering architecture of the 1920s and 1930s, above all in Brno and Zlín; North Moravia, as with North and East Bohemia, is heavily industrialised, though with numerous architectural and even scenic rewards for those who put up with the pollution.

Whereas Moravia, both geographically and culturally, is little different from Bohemia, Slovakia should really be considered as a separate country. The gently undulating expanses of pine forests alternating with towns that cover so much of Bohemia and Moravia, give way in Slovakia to mountainous scenery of a wild and spectacular kind. The Tatra mountains have always been Slovakia's main tourist attractions, but the region's cultural treasures, though more scattered than they are elsewhere in Czechoslovakia, deserve far more attention than they have hitherto received. As you would expect from a relatively underpopulated region, with a traditionally rural-based economy, Slovakia is particularly rich in folk architecture. However, its culture has also been enormously enhanced by its German settlers and Hungarian rulers. The German settlements of the Spiš district are atmospheric medieval survivals comparable to the German towns of Transylvania. As for the Hungarians, they created in Bratislava and Košice two of Czechoslovakia's most exciting cities, and also left a series of splendid castles that in their present ruined state, on rocky outcrops rising above dense forests, have a particularly romantic appeal.

My greatest debt in the writing of this book is to the staff of the Čedok office in London, who arranged sponsorship for a lengthy stay in Czechoslovakia in 1989. Peter Biely, the office's Deputy Managing Director, managed with humour and exceptional efficiency the feat of co-ordinating the help of at least twenty administrative bodies in Czechoslovakia, ranging from youth to spa organisations, and was admirably nonplussed when a radical revamping of the country's tourist structure led to the disappearance of most of these. Since then numerous other changes have occurred, and it is unlikely that in the present economic climate of the country that I would have been provided—as I was in 1989—with a car, chauffeur and guide to take me wherever I wanted to go. Jaroslav Spišek, my principal guide in Bohemia, made a wonderful companion throughout the region, enlightened me with his numerous tales and recollections, and diffused the solemnity of many an official occasion with his delightful informality and sense of the absurd; in our more improvised and unscrupulous attempts to get in to places, he delighted in referring to ourselves as 'partisans'. The section on Slovakia would scarcely have been possible without the assistance of Ľudovít Haeberle, who accompanied me almost to every corner of his native region, and openly shared with me his unrivalled knowledge of its culture, history and landscapes. Daniel Lukač, of the Slovakian Ministry of Commerce and Tourism, was another major debt in Slovakia, and to him I owe above all my introduction to the lighter side of Slovakian life. Among the many other individuals I would like to thank from my 1989 visit to Czechoslovakia are Jan Kolařík, V. Holub and Josef Vacl from Čedok in Prague; Irena Bulířová from the advertising department of Jablonex in Jablonec nad Nisou; Jindřich Rasche from Pilsner Urquel in Plzeň; Lev Novobilský from the Grand Hotel Pupp in Karlovy Vary; the golf champion Tunkl Boris; Ladislav P. Černý, director of the spa at Třeboň; and Emil Baniari, Ján Šavel and Mariana Zuberová, who organised an especially enjoyable stay at the spa of Trenčianské Teplice, and arranged to dress me up as a doctor to enable me to have a more intimate tour of the spa buildings than would otherwise have been possible. Dr David Cockerill, a friend from England, showed me round the Academy of Sciences at Bechyně, and assisted me with my researches into Brno night-life. More recently in Czechoslovakia I am grateful to the hospitality of Jan Maisler, to the staff of the Barrandov Film Studios, to Dr Marketa Hallová of the Dvořák Museum in Prague, and to the wonderful actress Mahulena Bočanová of Prague's Činoherní Klub. Jaroslav Celeryn, the Vice General Manager of Wolff Ost-Reisen in Prague, kept me up to date with recent developments in Czechoslovakia's tourism, while Sidarkat Kahri, the knowledgeable author of the Cadogan Guide to Prague, made numerous helpful suggestions during my last stay in that city.

The Blue Guide staff and associates, in particular my editor Gemma Davies, have sustained me with their remarkable kindness, efficiency, and patience. Ian Chilvers, as usual, has generously lent me books from his eccentric private library, and I have enjoyed my many discussions on Czechoslovakia with Dr Adam Yamey, who has supplied me with much information on music. Finally, I must thank the long-suffering Jackie Rae for putting up once again both with my long absences from home, and my many hours absorbed at the word-processor.

Publisher's Note. Please write in with your comments, suggestions and corrections. Writers of the best letters will be awarded a free Blue Guide of their choice.

Acknowledgements

For permission to use extracts in this book the publishers would like to thank the following: Penguin Books Limited for *A Guide to Central Europe* by Richard Bassett, Jonathon Cape for *Utz* by Bruce Chatwin, Penguin Books Limited for *We the People* by Timothy Garton Ash, John Murray (Publishers) Limited for *A Time of Gifts* by Patrick Leigh Fermor, Andre Deutsch Limited and Dilia Agency for *The Selected Poetry of Jaroslav Seifert*, William Heinemann Limited for *War and Peace* by Leo Tolstoy, Faber and Faber Limited for *Disturbing the Peace* by Václav Havel.

A NOTE ON BLUE GUIDES

The Blue Guides series began in 1915 when Muirhead Guide-Books Limited published 'Blue Guide London and its Environs'. Finlay and James Muirhead already had extensive experience of guide-book publishing: before the First World War they had been the editors of the English editions of the German Baedekers, and by 1915 they had acquired the copyright of most of the famous 'Red' handbooks from John Murray.

An agreement made with the French publishing house Hachette et Cie in 1917 led to the translation of Muirhead's London Guide, which became the first 'Guide Bleu'—Hachette had previously published the blue-covered 'Guides Joanne'. Subsequently, Hachette's 'Guide Bleu Paris et ses Environs' was adapted and published in London by Muirhead. The collaboration between the two publishing houses continued until 1933.

In 1931 Ernest Benn took over the Blue Guides, appointing Russell Muirhead, Finlay Muirhead's son, editor in 1934. The Muirheads' connection with Blue Guides ended in 1963 when Stuart Rossiter, who had been working on the Guides since 1954, became house editor, revising and compiling several of the books himself.

The Blue Guides are now published by A & C Black, who acquired Ernest Benn in 1984, so continuing the tradition of guide-book publishing which began in 1826 with 'Black's Economical Tourist of Scotland'. The Blue Guide series continues to grow: there are now more than 40 titles in print with revised editions appearing regularly and many new Blue Guides in preparation.

'Blue Guides' is a registered trade mark.

CONTENTS

Maps and Plans

Map of Czechoslovakia   *at the back of the book*

Town Plans

Ground Plans

BACKGROUND INFORMATION

Historical Summary

Anyone who has known Czechoslovakia before and after the Revolution of November 1989 will have observed at close hand how quickly history can be rewritten, and how absurd this process can be. Milan Kundera's novel, *The Book of Laughter and Forgetting* (1979), opens with an image of the Communist leader Klement Gottwald stepping out onto a balcony in Prague's Old Town Square to proclaim to a vast crowd the coming of the Communists to power. 'It was', Kundera noted, 'a crucial moment in Czech history—a fateful moment of the kind that occurs once or twice in a millennium.' Standing behind Gottwald was one of his close associates, Clementis, who, as it was cold and Gottwald was bare-headed, solicitously gave the new president his own fur cap. The photograph of the balcony scene became an image known to every Czech schoolboy, with the difference that in later versions of the picture Clementis could no longer be seen, the man having been accused of treason and hung only four years after it was taken. 'All that remains of Clementis', wrote Kundera, 'is the cap on Gottwald's head.'

Today it is Gottwald's turn to be erased from history, and his name, which was once to be found in streets and squares throughout Czechoslovakia, was rapidly removed in the course of 1990, as was that of almost every other Czechoslovak Communist, including the brave journalist Julius Fučík, who was killed by the Nazis. In the place of the old heroes a new mythology is being created, dominated by the figure of Jan Palach, who set fire to himself in January 1969 as a protest against the Soviet invasion of the country, and whose name has now been given to the large Prague square which once commemorated the Soviet 'liberation' of Czechoslovakia in 1945.

The vision of history which the Communists promoted will take longer to disappear than the names of their leaders, and visitors to Czechoslovakia today will almost certainly find themselves reading turgid accounts of the revolutionary and working-class traditions of the Czech and Slovak nations. Yet underlying all interpretations of Czechoslovakia's history are the nationalist myths that gained a wide currency in the nineteenth century, and gave particular emphasis to the period of Hussite domination, and to the country's distant past, where fact and fiction can more freely be allowed to mingle.

The **early history** of the present-day territory of Czechoslovakia is scantly documented, and the first Czech chronicler, Cosmas, was himself to admit in c 1120 that he had been unable to find much firm information dating from before the ninth century AD. Greek and Roman sources refer to the Celtic tribe of the Boii, who came here probably around 400 BC and from whom the name 'Bohemia' almost certainly derives. The Boii were subjugated in about 10 BC by the Teutonic tribe of the Marcomanni, and by the second century the Romans had penetrated as far as the Slovakian town known today as Trenčín. The Slavs only began moving into this part of Europe from about AD 450, those among them who ended up in Bohemia being led, according to legend, by a certain Čech, who decided to settle here after surveying the fertile countryside to be seen from the top of the hill of Říp. No less mythical a person than Čech was his descendant Princess Libuše, who ruled the Bohemians until about AD 800, when they tired of being subject to a woman and provoked her into marrying a ploughman (přemysl).

Following the mythical emergence of the **Přemysl dynasty** at the beginning of the ninth century, Bohemia was eclipsed in importance by its Slavonic neighbour Moravia, which, after subduing the non-Aryan tribe of the Avars, was to forge alliances with the Slavs in both Bohemia and the County of Nitra (Slovakia) to form the Great Moravian Empire. The greatest threat to the Slavs at this time came from the north, where Charlemagne and the subsequent rulers of Germany coveted Bohemia and Moravia not simply for political reasons but also in the cause of spreading Christianity. Christianity did take root in these lands during the ninth century, but it was in an attempt to lessen the influence from Germany that the Moravian leader Prince Rostislav turned in 863 towards the Church in the East, and appealed to the Emperor Michael at Byzantium to send here clergy capable of expounding the Christian faith in the language of the Slavs. The Emperor responded by sending over the brothers Cyril and Methodius, whose enormous success at the Court of Moravia was doubtlessly facilitated by their apparent invention of the Cyrillic alphabet, a Greek-based script adapted to suit certain Slav peculiarities.

Rostislav was later deposed by his treacherous nephew Svatopluk, who has often been portrayed romantically as a Slavonic champion, though in fact he plotted with Charlemagne's grand-son, Louis the German, and was responsible for the brief imprisonment of Methodius in Germany. Methodius was later summoned by the Pope to Rome, where he was able successfully to defend the Slav liturgy; none the less Moravia and Bohemia were soon to enter definitely into the sphere of Rome, and the Slav liturgy and script to be driven eastwards. The collapse of the Great Moravian Empire, however, was brought about not by religious strife but by a completely unforeseen eventuality, which was to lead the Germans to side with the Slavs. Shortly after the death of Svatopluk in 894 hordes of Magyars began arriving in Europe and were crushingly to defeat the combined forces of the Slavs and Germans at a battle which took place near Posonium (Bratislava). The southern part of the Empire, Slovakia, came to be incorporated into the new country which the Magyars created, and was to remain a part of Hungary until 1918. The Slavonic unity which the Empire had fitfully represented was in later centuries to fuel the dream of Panslavism.

Moravia, which has never been separated from Bohemia by firm geographical boundaries, became absorbed after the collapse of its empire into Bohemia, which from the early tenth century onwards began developing into an important power of its own. The history of Bohemia after c 860 was marked at first principally by the consolidation of Christianity in the country. Prince Bořivoj, the first documented member of the Přemyslid dynasty, was converted to Christianity probably by Methodius, and Bořivoj's widow, Ludmila, provided Bohemia with its first saint and martyr after she was murdered by her daughter-in-law in 874. Ludmila's grandson was the equally pious Wenceslas, who was made Prince of Bohemia in 921, and was later to be immortalised by the popular Christmas carol which wrongly designates him as 'Good' *King* Wenceslas. Politically the reign of Wenceslas was characterised by successful efforts to improve relations with Germany, and it was around this fact that certain nineteenth-century historians, aware of the necessity of a German orientation for Bohemia, promoted him as one of the greatest of all Czech heroes. His reign was to be short one, however, for in 929, when he was only 22, he was murdered by his brother Boleslav, who became in consequence Boleslav I or the Cruel. Boleslav broke off the cordial relations that his brother had established with Germany, but later in life sided with the German ruler Otto the Great, and shared in the latter's decisive victory over the Magyars at Lechfeld (near Augsburg) in 955. Germany played an increasingly important role in Bohemia's development in the Middle Ages, and growing numbers of German merchants came to settle here, receiving particular encouragement to do so from Soběslav II, who in 1178 granted them fiscal privileges and exemption fom military service. A later ruler, Přemysl Otakar I, played a skilful game of shifting allegiances during Germany's Civil War of the early thirteenth century, and thereby won constant concessions for his country, culminating in 1212 when he extracted from the Emperor a Golden Bull granting to him and his descendants the title of king. The thirteenth century saw Bohemia rapidly gaining both in political and economic power, and was the period when most of its major towns were founded: a particular boost was the discovery of silver mines in Kutná Hora and elsewhere, a discovery which was to make the Bohemian court one of the wealthiest in Europe.

The Přemyslids, like the Hungarian dynasty of Arpád, died out at the beginning of the fourteenth century, their last king, Wenceslas III, being murdered in 1306. As Wenceslas had no heir, the German King Henry VII, of the House of Luxemburg, managed to secure the throne of Bohemia for his own family by arranging that his son John marry the second daughter of Wenceslas II, Elizabeth. John, who became known as 'the Blind' after being wounded in the eye and treated by a quack doctor, showed little interest in Bohemia, and in 1344 entrusted its government to his son Charles, a small and ugly man whose rule was to bring about what is generally described as **'the Golden Age of Bohemia'**. King of Bohemia in 1346, King of Germany in 1347, and Holy Roman Emperor in 1355, Charles IV made Bohemia the capital of his empire, and in so doing managed to place the country at the forefront both of European politics and culture. He enlarged the boundaries of his kingdom, reorganised the country's legal and administrative system, founded both the city of Carlsbad (Karlovy Vary) and the New Town of Prague, built Prague's magnificent Charles Bridge and the enormous castle at Karlštejn, established the first University in Central Europe, and attracted to his court at Prague many of the leading artists, architects and intellectuals of the day. Though brought up in France and equally fluent in French, German and Czech, his particular preference was for Czech, and he refused official appointments in Bohemia to all Germans who could not speak this language. In addition he secured from the pope permission to use Czech in all ecclesiastical services in certain monasteries. More importantly he gave support to a generation of reformist preachers—including Milíč of Kroměříž, Matthew of Janov and Tomáš of Štítný—whose advocacy of the Czech language over Latin, and call for a return to the pious simplicity of the early Christians, were to pave the way for one of the greatest figures in the early history of Çzech thought and literature, Jan Hus.

Charles died in 1378, and his son and successor, the quarrelsome and impulsive Wenceslas IV, inherited little of his father's greatness, succeeding in losing the crown of Germany to his brother Sigismund in 1400, and leading Bohemia into a great social and religious crisis, out of which the **Hussite movement** was to emerge. Jan Hus, who was to give his name to this movement, was born in 1373 of peasant parents in the South Bohemian village of Husinec. After studying at Prague University, he entered the Church, and rapidly earned for himself such a reputation as a priest that he was selected as confessor to Queen Sophie. He was at first unwavering in his devotion to the Church of Rome, but the papacy's corruption at the time of the Schism—as exemplified in its selling of indulgences in the streets of Prague—was to turn Hus into one of its most violent opponents. In 1402 he began denouncing the morals of the clergy from Prague's Bethlehem Chapel, a place which had been founded ten years earlier by a Czech patriot who had insisted that the preaching of the word of God be done in the mother tongue; two years later Hus was to find support for his views following the arrival in Prague from England of two disciples of the English reformer John Wycliffe, James and Conrad of Canterbury.

The preachings of Hus soon won him an enormous following among the Czech people and led to a great rift developing at Prague University between the Czechs and the Germans, the latter all taking the side of the Church of Rome. In 1409 a major victory was scored for Hus after he managed to persuade Wenceslas IV to impose the Decree of Kutná Hora, whereby the voting system in the University was changed greatly in favour of the Czechs, a decision which led to an exodus from Prague of 2000 German students and many professors, who went on subsequently to found the University of Leipzig in Saxony. The success of the Czech reform movement incited the new pope at Rome, Alexander V, to authorise the archbishop of Prague to destroy all the writings of Wycliffe and to punish those who read and preached his doctrines. When Hus persisted in his preachings, he was excommunicated, and all those who supported him were threatened with the same fate, even if they only offered him food and drink; it was further stipulated that all religious services were to be suspended in every town which he entered. Wenceslas IV persuaded Hus to leave Prague for a while, in the hope that his absence from the city would help to calm the situation. In his 20 months of voluntary exile Hus produced most of his finest writings, but also continued to preach, finding his congregations in the villages and farms around his native Husinec. In the meantime Wenceslas' brother Sigismund induced the church authorities to call a Council at Constance to settle the dispute between the rival pontiffs. Sigismund also suggested that Hus should attend this council to refute the charges of heresy, promising him a safe-conduct and a free return to Bohemia whatever the outcome. Hus was burnt at the stake at Constance on 6 July 1415.

The enormous popular support which Hus had enjoyed during his lifetime was vastly to increase after his death: many Czech historians have interpreted this support in terms of a great 'humanist' tradition in Bohemia, while Communist apologists have shown it as an example of the socialist and revolutionary tendencies of the Czech people. The Hussites did not in fact represent a united front, and came to be divided after Hus's death into two main camps, moderate and radical. The symbol common to both parties was the Chalice, a reference to the Hussite belief that the Holy Communion should be administered to the laity both with bread and wine, an ancient practice which had been preserved in the Greek Orthodox Church,

from which Bohemia had received Christianity. The moderate Hussites, drawn mainly from the Bohemian nobility and the more
conservative nationalists, are sometimes referred to as the 'Calixtines' (after the Latin for chalice), though they are more usually
known as the Utraquists (from the Latin phrase *sub utraque specie*).
The more popularly based radical wing of the Hussites went far
further in their views than the Utraquists, maintaining that the Holy
Bible was the sole authority in all matters of religious belief, and
rejecting the doctrine of the existence of Purgatory, all the Sacraments with the exception of Baptism and Communion, and many
other of the teachings of the Church. The radicals enjoyed the
leadership of one of the greatest of Bohemia's military commanders,
Jan Žižka, a man whose early background is little known other than
that he came from a family of the lesser nobility in South Bohemia,
and had held a post at the court of Queen Sophia; he and his
followers, the Taborites, were to establish as their principal base a
stronghold in South Bohemia which they named Tábor after the
Biblical hill where Christ had been transfigured.

The widespread unrest resulting from Hus's death came to a head
in 1419 when Wenceslas attempted to check the Hussite movement
by allowing the return of all priests who had opposed Utraquism and
granting the Utraquists the use of only three churches in Prague. On
29 July of that year, only one week after Taborites from all over the
country had gathered in South Bohemia, a procession of Utraquists
led by Jan of Želivský marched through the Prague streets, being
greeted with stones as they passed underneath the New Town Hall.
In anger the Utraquists stormed the building, and flung the Mayor
and several of his councillors out of the window and onto the square,
where they were torn apart limb by limb. This was to be the the first
of the two so-called 'Defenestrations' in Bohemia's history, incidents
that on both occasions were to bring the country into war. The news
of what had happened at the Town Hall had the immediate effect of
making Wenceslas so annoyed that he died of apoplexy; as he was
heirless, this in turn led to the thorny problem of succession. The
principal claimant to the throne was his brother Sigismund, a man
widely hated in Bohemia, particularly after his treacherous
behaviour to Jan Hus; his only supporters were the Roman Catholics,
most of whom belonged to the country's German communities. In the
absence of a king, Queen Sophia was appointed Regentess of the
country, but shortly afterwards a Papal Bull was issued proclaiming a
crusade against the heretics of Bohemia. By June 1420, Sigismund, at
the head of crusading forces drawn from almost every European
country, reached the outskirts of Prague, where he was defeated in
battle by Jan Žižka, whose forces knelt upon the field of victory and
intoned the Te Deum. Before fleeing to Moravia, Sigismund had
himself crowned in Prague's St. Vitus's Cathedral, but the ceremony
was such a hurried and reduced one that his opponents considered it
to be invalid. It was in any case to be a further sixteen years before he
would be able to take possession of his kingdom.

Jan Žižka died of plague in 1424, and was succeeded as Taborite
leader by Prokop, a married priest who was to earn himself the
nickname of 'the Great' and prove himself almost as formidable a
soldier as Žižka. He and his well-disciplined soldiers were to hold out
as late as 1434 when, on 30 May, they were brutally crushed at the
Battle of Lipany near Kolín; this day was one of the many later to be
described by Czech historians as 'the saddest in Bohemian history'.
Sigismund, by now an old man, was only to reign over Bohemia

between 1436 and 1437, after which came the equally brief rule of his detested son-in-law Albert of Austria (1347–49). A period of confusion then followed, Albert's only heir being born after his father's death, hence his nickname of Ladislav the Posthumous. A strong Regent was clearly required during the minority of Ladislav, and, following much fighting between the Utraquists and the Catholics, the young Utraquist leader **George of Poděbrady** was recognised by Ladislav's guardian—the Emperor Frederick III—as *de facto* ruler in Bohemia. Ladislav was crowned in 1453, but power in the country continued to remain in the hands of George of Poděbrady, who, after Ladislav's death from plague in 1457, was elected by the Bohemian Diet as King of Bohemia: to mark this triumph of Utraquism, a resplendent Chalice was placed on the west façade of Prague's Týn Church. Another important moment in the religious history of Bohemia was the formal organisation, ten years later, of the Bohemian Brethren, whose true founder was Peter Chelčický. Chelčický, the most remarkable of George of Poděbrady's Czech contemporaries, carried the doctrines of Wycliffe and Hus one stage further and condemned the use of force in religious matters, emphasising the Christian teachings of humility and the equality of all men.

George of Poděbrady, the most popular of Bohemia's kings after Charles IV, died in 1471, and his throne was sought by a number of candidates, including Matthias of Hungary, Albert of Saxony and George's own two sons, the Dukes of Münsterberg. In the end Prince Vladislav Jagiello of Poland was elected, partly because he was George's own designated candidate, and partly because of his maternal descent from the Luxemburg and hence Přemyslid dynasties. He proved to be a weak ruler, and was soon called King All-Right owing to his habit of saying *Dobře* or 'Good' to everything that was said to him by his powerful barons; he was also a Catholic, and his reign was one of compromise between the rival Utraquist and Romanist factions. On the death of Matthias of Hungary in 1490, Vladislav inherited the throne of Hungary, and thereafter transferred the capital of his by now vast domains to Buda. The fates of Bohemia and Hungary were to be linked from this moment right up to 1918. Shortly before his own death in 1516, Vladislav had signed with the Habsburg Emperor Maximilian what has been described as one of the most momentous marriage contracts in history. The outcome of this was that Vladislav's daughter Anne was married to the Emperor's second grandson, Archduke Ferdinand, while his young son Louis became the husband of Ferdinand's second sister Mary; in the event of Louis dying childless, it was agreed that the Crown of Bohemia should pass to Anne's descendants. In 1526 the 20-year-old Louis drowned in a swamp while fleeing from the Battle of Mohács, where the Hungarian army was virtually wiped out by the Turks. This was effectively the year when the Habsburg monarchy was born, a monarchy which would control the destinies of Bohemia and Hungary for the next 400 years.

The religious tensions that had beset Bohemia during the fifteenth century were intensified in the course of the sixteenth century with the rapid spread of **Lutheranism**, a religion which was brought into Bohemia, ironically, by German merchants. Utraquists, Bohemian Brethren and Lutherans came easily to outnumber the Catholics in the country, but the Catholics had the support of the Habsburgs, who ruthlessly introduced the Counter-Reformation into Bohemia, beginning with the invitation of the Jesuits to Prague in 1556, the year that Ferdinand I inherited the additional office of Emperor of

Germany. Ferdinand's son, Maximilian, prevaricated at first between Catholic and Protestant causes, but placed his allegiance firmly on the side of the former as soon as he succeeded to his father in 1564. In contrast, Catholic hopes were to be greatly disappointed by Maximilian's own son and successor, Rudolph II, who had been brought up in the fanatical environment of Spain and had been expected to pursue the intransigent policies of his grandfather Ferdinand. Rudolph turned out to be a suspicious and withdrawn man who was so incapable of coming to decisions that he even hesitated for twenty years over whether to marry Philip II's daughter, Isabella, and decided in the end to remain a bachelor.

His interest in matters of state was minimal, but he had in compensation a mania for art, astrology and astronomy which was to result not only in his amassing one of Europe's finest art collections, but also in the transformation of his court at Prague into a haven for many of the controversial thinkers and scientists of the day such as Giordano Bruno, Tycho de Brahe and Johannes Kepler. Clearly he had inherited a streak of madness from his Spanish great-grandmother Juana la Loca, and this streak was to encourage Habsburg plans to limit his power and eventually depose him. Under attack from his cousin Leopold and his brother Matthias he turned for help to the Bohemian Estates, and in return was obliged to sign in July 1609 the momentous 'Letter of Majesty', whereby he surrendered the absolutist pretensions of the Crown, and assured the freedom of religion in Bohemia. In May 1611 he was forced finally to surrender the throne of Bohemia to Matthias, but he was allowed to retain the imperial title and the possession of the castle in Prague; during the remaining eight months of his life he actively intrigued with the Protestant Union.

Controversy over the interpretation of the 'Letter of Majesty' was to lead to the **Thirty Years' War**, which was sparked off when a group of Protestants marched on 23 May 1618 into Prague Castle and threw out of the window two Councillors whom they had accused of influencing the anti-Protestant bias of Matthias' successor, Ferdinand II. The Protestant nobility were encouraged afterwards to rise up in rebellion against the Habsburgs, and in the following year they succeeded in deposing Ferdinand and replacing him with the Elector Frederick V of the Palatinate, a man whose short-lived rule was to earn him the name of the 'winter king'. At the Battle of the White Mountain, which took place outside Prague on 8 November 1620, Ferdinand, with the assistance of the Catholic League and Maximilian of Bavaria, managed in the space of a few hours to put Frederick to flight and demolish the Bohemian army. This definitely put an end to Bohemian independence, and initiated a series of terrible reprisals against the Protestants, including, in 1621, the execution on Prague's Old Town Square of twenty-seven leading members of their nobility. Ferdinand consolidated the Habsburg cause in Bohemia in 1624 by moving the Bohemian Court Chancellery to Vienna and by instituting four years later an Imperial Ordinance re-establishing the hereditary right of the House of Austria to the throne of Bohemia and making Catholicism the only permitted religion. Czech schools were closed, the Czech language was suppressed, the University at Prague was turned into a Jesuit College, and thousands of Czech books were destroyed, one Jesuit priest, Andrew Koniáš even boasting of having himself burnt 60,000 of them.

As with Czechoslovakia in 1938, the misfortunes of Bohemia after the Battle of the White Mountain heralded a tragedy on a much larger scale when Ferdinand II was dragged into the protracted war between Protestant and Catholic factions in Northern Europe, where many of the Bohemian exiles had taken refuge. The excellently equipped armies of the Swedish ruler Gustavus Adolphus seemed certain to come to the aid of the struggling German Protestants, and threatened to jeopardise Ferdinand's Counter-Reformation policies. Ferdinand had to enlist the support of the brilliant but devious Duke of Wallenstein, a man who had benefited enormously from the confiscation of property from exiled and executed Czechs. Wallenstein drove back the Swedes from Bohemia in 1631, but his constant treacheries led to his murder by British mercenaries at Cheb in 1634. By 1648, when peace was finally declared, the Swedes had occupied Prague's Little Quarter. The Treaty of Westphalia, which had brought about the end of the war, represented a further blow to Bohemian hopes, for it excluded the return to Bohemia of those exiles who had fought with the Swedes; such had been the damage incurred by the war that neither party was willing to fight further over this issue. Bohemia had been decimated over these 30 years, its economy and political importance destroyed, its towns razed, and its population reduced to a fraction of what it had previously been. A symbol of Bohemia's loss during these years was the exile of one of its most outstanding intellectual figures, the pioneering pedagogue Jan Ámos Komenský (Comenius), who was to be described by the French historian Michelet as 'the Galileo of Education'. Comenius's concern for the plight of his nation was expressed most poignantly in his appeal of 1650 entitled *Bequest of the Dying Mother of the Unity of Czech Brethren*; the words of this appeal were to provide succour to a Czech exile of a much later generation, Tomáš Masaryk.

In the wake of the Thirty Years' War **opposition to Habsburg rule** was to be concentrated in Hungarian lands, Slovakia playing an important part in the rebellions led in the late seventeenth and early eighteenth century by the Hungarian aristocrats István Bocskay, Gábor Bethlen and Ferenc Rákóczy II: among those who fought with Rákóczy was Juraj Jánošík, a Robin Hood figure who was one of Slovakia's earliest and greatest popular heroes. Bohemia itself was not to become involved in any major conflict until 1750, when Frederick II of Prussia waged war on the new Habsburg Empress Maria Theresa, accusing her Jesuits of wrongly persecuting the Silesian Protestants (who, according to the terms of the Treaty of Westphalia, should have been allowed freely to practice their religion). In 1757 the Prussians were laying siege to Prague when Frederick's troops were defeated at the nearby town of Kolín; the outcome of the Seven Years' War was further devastation of Bohemia. Maria Theresa finally decided to expel the Jesuits from Bohemia in 1773, and further major reforms were to be carried out by her successor Joseph II, who in 1781, a year after his mother's death, abolished serfdom, introduced a decree of religious tolerance, and suppressed seven hundred monasteries. The rule of Joseph II is often described as one of 'enlightened despotism', and another of his acts was to try and introduce compulsory education while insisting that all teaching be conducted in German; he vainly hoped by this to bring unity to his vast empire and diminish the many cultural and linguistic barriers that divided it. In 1809, four years after massively defeating the combined Russian and Austrian forces near the Moravian town of Slavkov (Austerlitz), Napoleon made a stirring appeal to the Bohemian people to rid themselves once and for all of the

Austrian tyranny. The appeal was for the moment unheeded, and the Bohemians continued to support the Austrians during the Napoleonic wars. None the less the early years of the nineteenth century saw also the beginnings in both Bohemia and Slovakia of a great cultural and intellectual renaissance.

A key moment in the revival of Czech culture was the foundation in 1818 of the **Society of the Bohemian National Museum**, a society whose members comprised a remarkable group of both Bohemian and Slovakian intellectuals, including Josef Dobrovský ('the patriarch of Slavonic studies'), Josef Jungmann (the founder of the modern Czech literary language) and the Slovak philologist Pavel Šafařík. Perhaps the most important member of all was the historian, poet and politician František Palacký, who was fundamental in the founding of a Bohemian national party and whose enormous *History of the Czech Nation* led to his being called 'the Father of the Nation': in this pioneering work, the first volume of which was published in 1836, Palacký saw the Czech history in terms of 'the constant contact and conflict between the Slavs on the one hand and Rome and the Germans on the other'. Palacký declined an offer to become Minister of Education at Vienna, and in 1848 turned down an invitation to appear as one of six delegates to be sent by the Habsburgs to a meeting of the Germanic Federation at Frankfurt: he based his refusal on the grounds that he was 'not a German but a Bohemian belonging to the Slav race'.

As an impressive counterblast to the Frankfurt meeting, Palacký and his friends convoked in Prague that same year a Congress of all the Slav races under the monarchy. The opening speech was made by Šafařík while another Slovak, Ľudovít Štúr—the only Slovak representative in the Hungarian Parliament—made an impassioned appeal in favour of common action between Slovaks and Czechs. Rioting ensued in the streets of Prague at the end of the Congress, and rebellion was brutally suppressed by the military commander Prince Windischgrätz, a believer in the return of absolutist rule in Bohemia.

In the second half of the century tensions greatly increased not only between Germans and Czechs but also between Slovaks and Hungarians, particularly in the wake of the Dual Compromise of 1867, an agreement between Austria and Hungary which snubbed Bohemia and led to a policy of brutal 'Magyarisation' in Slovakia. Yet the nationalist movement continued to grow and found its expression not only in a great surge of patriotic works of art, architecture, literature and music, but also in the foundation of numerous nationalist schools, cultural organisations and other institutions. Notable among these were the Slovakian cultural organisation known as Matica Slovenská—which was founded in Martin in 1867—and the Sokol movement, a gymnastic society which spread rapidly throughout Bohemia and Slovakia from the 1860s onwards, and had as its aim the 'revival of the fatherland, by the education of the body and the spirit, by physical energy, by art and science, by all moral means...'

A curious phenomenon of Czech history this century, and one which was to lead in recent times to a positive superstitious mania, is the way in which most of the key events in this history have taken place in years containing the figure 8. The most significant of what Václav Havel was to call 'the years of 8' was 1918, when the breakdown of the Austro-Hungarian Empire resulted in the creation of the **Czechoslovak Republic**. The new country was made up of three sections, the largest comprising the so-called 'Lands of the Crown of St. Wenceslas' (Bohemia, Moravia and Silesia); next in size came Slovakia, and finally there was Ruthenia, which was composed of the districts of North-East Hungary populated by Ruthenians or Ukranians. Inevitably the Republic experienced numerous racial tensions not to mention political ones, but under the enlightened rule of the former professor of history at Prague University, Tomáš Masaryk, Czechoslovakia became one of the most progressive European countries between the wars, as well as the only long-lasting democracy in a part of Europe falling increasingly under the shadow of fascism. It was thus particularly inexcusable when in 1938, three years after Masaryk had been succeeded as president by Edvard Beneš, the Allies signed the **Munich Agreement** and thereby allowed the German-settled territories of northern Bohemia (the Sudetenland) to be taken over by Nazi Germany, and parts of eastern Slovakia to be reclaimed by fascist Hungary. Explaining to the British public the reasons for this fatal decision, Neville Chamberlain made the famous pronouncement: 'How terrible, fantastic, incredible it is that we should be digging trenches and trying on gas masks here because of a quarrel in a far-away country between people of whom we know nothing ...'

It was not long after the signing of the Munich Agreement that Hitler seized the whole of Bohemia and Moravia, touring it into a Nazi Protectorate on the preposterous historical grounds that it had belonged to the German Reich for over a thousand years; the greater part of Slovakia meanwhile was made an independent country, ruled by the fascist priest Jozef Tiso, who acted as a puppet to Hitler. After November 1941 75,000 Bohemian Jews were taken to the specially created ghetto town of Terezín in northern Bohemia, and out of these only 9000 were to survive; following the assassination in 1942 of the Nazi 'Protector of Bohemia and Moravia' Reinhard Heydrich, the whole country was to suffer reprisals that make those experienced after the Battle of the White Mountain seem minor in comparison. In the freeing of Czechoslovakia from Nazi rule a major role was played by Slovakian partisans and soldiers, though in later accounts of this liberation the emphasis was to be on the Soviet army, which entered Slovakia in November 1944 and reached Prague on 5 May of the following year.

The third of the fateful 'years of 8' was 1948, when the Communists came to power and created the **People's Republic of Czechoslovakia**. The general mood was at first one of optimism, and most Czechs believed that Communism would assume in this traditionally enlightened country a much milder form than that which it had taken in Russia. The mysterious death later that year of Jan Masaryk, the son of the former President, provoked certain misgivings, as did the first of the great wave of purges that took place from 1950 onwards. A powerful account of these years of terror is given in *Prague Farewell* (1988), the autobiography of Heda Margolius-Kovály, a Jewish woman who survived Auschwitz only to see her husband—an idealistic and conscientious government worker—executed along with ten other Jews as a result of the notorious Slánský Trial of 1951. Klement Gottwald died in 1953, ironically as a result of catching a cold while attending the funeral of his beloved Stalin; it was also rumoured that his health had been undermined by a combination of syphillis and excessive drinking habits. The victims of the Slánský trial were later 'rehabilitated', and in the 1960s there were signs of renewed optimism that were to culminate in the **'Prague Spring'** of 1968, when the Party's First Secretary Alexander Dubček tried to introduce 'Socialism with a human face'. The arrival of Soviet troops in August of that year brought these developments to a spectacular end, with Soviet tanks and soldiers being taunted by motorcyclists, flag-waving students and mini-skirted women. When the scenes of anarchy had finally cleared Czechoslovakia found itself depleted of many of its most talented figures, who opted for exile rather than staying on in the country to an increasingly uncertain fate. One of the later exiles was Milan Kundera, who described the Russian invasion as not only a tragedy but also 'as a carnival of hate filled with a curious (and no longer explicable) euphoria'.

Czechoslovakia remains to this day a deeply divided country, and the principle division—that between the Czechs and the Slovaks—was to intensify after 1968. Shortly after the Russian invasion the country was turned into a federal state, the government being divided between Prague and the Slovakian capital of Bratislava; this development was greatly welcomed by most Slovaks, and helps largely to explain the relatively positive mood experienced in Slovakia at a time when the rest of the country was suffering from the deep sense of hopelessness described by Václav Havel in his auto-biographical reflections, *Disturbing the Peace* (1990). A further division is the continuing one between Protestants and Catholics, which has taken on a new dimension in recent times, the former group becoming associated with post-1948 collaboration, the latter with post-1948 resistance.

For all these differences there emerged from Czechoslovakia in 1977 the most sustained charter of human liberties in the history of Communist Europe, **Charter 77**. This document, representing the first open challenge to the rule of the Soviet-appointed President Husák ('the President of Forgetting'), had come about directly as the result of the banning of a rock group called 'Plastic People'. One of its first and most famous signatories was the dramatist Václav Havel, who later helped to found, as an offshoot of the Charter, the Committee for the Defence of the Unjustly Prosecuted (VONS); in 1979 he himself was to join the ranks of those he was defending, being sent to prison for the next four years. In the late 1980s, when Gorbachev's reforms in Russia were leading to a mellowing of conditions elsewhere in eastern Europe, the Czech Government remained as intransigent as ever. Out of respect for the 'years of 8' tradition, hopes for major change were placed on 1988, though all that happened that year was a petition for freedom of the Catholic Church signed by no less than 440,000 people and organised, no less remarkably, by a Moravian peasant called Augustin Navrátil, who cleverly exploited a loophole in the law. Fortunately the Czechs did not have to wait until 1998 for the much-awaited political break-through. It came in November 1989, and with such speed and ease that it was called afterwards the **'Velvet Revolution'**. On 17 November a gathering of people commemorating a student killed by the Nazis was transformed into a massive demonstration which ended up at Prague's Wenceslas Square; a new political party, Civic Forum, was hastily formed afterwards, and in the following days the Square was continually filled with growing crowds. On 22 November Václav Havel appeared on a balcony in the company of Alexander Dubček, and on 3 December a call for a general strike finally toppled the crumbling government. Havel was appointed acting President, and in June 1990 was the overwhelming victor in Czechoslovakia's first democratically held elections for over sixty years.

In September 1990 Václav Kraus, a convinced monetarist, was elected Finance Minister, an appointment which signified a swing to the right in Civic Forum. By December of that year, the euphoria of 1989 had given way to a cautious mood, as people prepared for rapidly increasing unemployment, a rising crime rate and grave economic recession.

Art and Architecture

The sentimental traveller to Czechoslovakia, confronted by this country's extraordinary wealth of little spoilt towns, might well reflect nostalgically on what the rest of central Europe must have been like before the Second World War. Yet, in comparison, say, to the towns of pre-war Germany, the towns of Czechoslovakia have retained relatively few intact examples of their medieval architecture. The religious wars of the fifteenth and seventeenth centuries brutally interrupted the course of this country's art and architecture, and devastated its medieval legacy. Furthermore, much of what has survived from the Middle Ages has been hidden under successive layers of remodelling and rebuilding, work which in many cases was carried out with the conscious intention of papering over a heretical past.

The Medieval Period. Among the earliest and most distinctive survivals of Czech architecture are a number of heavily restored rotundas scattered throughout Bohemia and Moravia, and ranging in date from c 900 to c 1225. Probably the oldest is that of Levý Hradec near Prague, which appears to have been founded by Prince Bořivoj, the first of the Přemyslid princes to be converted to Christianity. Of particular interest is the Rotunda of St. Catherine at Znojmo, a late eleventh-century structure which was covered in 1134 with a remarkable fresco cycle containing scenes representing the lineage of the Přemyslids. Other rare remains of Romanesque painting in Czechoslovakia are to be found in the early twelfth-century Basilica of St. George in Prague, a building in the shape of a Roman basilica but with heavy walls and small openings that suggest the influence of Ottonian Germany. A French style of art and architecture was introduced into Bohemia and Moravia with the arrival later in the century of the Cistercians, whose abbey church at Tišnov features one of the finest medieval portals in the country, the so-called Porta Coeli (1260): the jambs and voussoirs of this unmistakably French portal are richly carved with vegetal motifs, while in the tympanum is a representation of Christ in Glory flanked by the Virgin and St. John the Baptist, and the kneeling figures of Přemysl Otakar I and his wife, Constance.

The thirteenth century was the age when most of the large Czech towns were founded, many being laid out on regular grid-plans that have been kept to this day. A common feature of these plans is a central market square lined on all sides with arcaded houses, the actual arcading being generally all that has survived of the original buildings. The largest of the many outstanding town squares to be seen in Czechoslovakia is that of České Budějovice, which measures 133 square metres, and was designed in 1265 by the engineer to

Přemysl Otakar II, Hrz of Zvíkov. As for the ecclesiastical architecture of this period, this is characterised by a stubborn persistence of a Cistercian Gothic style, and a resistance to the French High Gothic, which was to have only a moderate influence here. Beginning with the enormous churches of St. Bartholomew at Plzeň, St. Nicholas at Kutná Hora, and St. Nicholas at Znojmo—all of which were founded in the 1320s—the predominant medieval church plan in Czech lands was to be derived from the German hall church (in which the aisles are the same height as the nave).

It was during the reign of Charles IV that Bohemia was to experience the first great flowering of its art and architecture. Charles had been brought up in France, and it was thus not surprising that for the first major commission of his rule—the rebuilding of St. Vitus's Cathedral in Prague—he should have called in a French architect, Matthew of Arras (?–1352). Matthew, who had previously worked at Avignon under Charles's friend Clement VI, produced a plan with radiating chapels in the ambulatory which was closely based on the French cathedral at Narbonne. However, Matthew died only eight years after work had begun on the building, and in 1352 Charles summoned to Prague an architect of a very different background, Peter Parler (1330–1405/6). Parler, one of the outstanding architects of the Middle Ages, had been born to a family of architects in Cologne in 1330, and had probably received most of his training in the Rhineland. Within the limits imposed by Matthew of Arras's plan, Parler introduced into St. Vitus's cathedral elements that look ahead to the German *Sondergotik* or late Gothic. Among his achievements here was the creation of a bold, openwork staircase which was to be copied in the cathedrals at Ulm and Strasbourg; but his principal contribution was his exceptionally inventive vaulting, which included a dazzling star-shaped formation and a system of free-standing ribs spread out like a fan.

The age of Charles IV saw the development of an important local school of painting, to which much impetus was given by Charles's large collection of French and Italian illuminated manuscripts, and by the numerous foreign artists who were attracted to his court, such as the Italian painter Tommaso di Modena. Italian and in particular Sienese influence can be felt in many of the early Bohemian artists, for instance in the Master of Vyšší Brod and in the anonymous painter of the Votive Panel of Jan Očko of Vlašim, a work which shows the Virgin and Child flanked by the donor and Charles IV in a way which recalls an Italian *Sacra Conversazione*. The leading and most idiosyncratic painter in Charles's circle was Master Theodoric, who is best known for a series of 129 panels painted between 1357–65 for the Holy Rood Chapel at Karlštejn Castle: his solid but softly modelled figures are set here against a background studded with semi-precious stones, an unusual feature—also to be found in the Wenceslas Chapel in St. Vitus's Cathedral—which reflects Charles's passionate love of jewellery. At the end of the century, during the reign of Charles's successor Wenceslas IV, the dominant Bohemian painter came to be the Master of the Třeboň Altarpiece, whose art, with its strong sense of colour and feeling for linear rhythm, turned not to the south but to the west, and has strong affinities with contemporary Burgundian artists such as Melchior Broederlam.

The intense period of building and cultural activity which Charles IV had initiated was cut short in 1420 with the outbreak of the Hussite Wars, and was not to be renewed until the end of the century, when the kingdoms of Bohemia, Hungary and Poland were united under the rule of Vladislav Jagiello I. Vladislav's rule saw some of the more spectacular achievements of the late Gothic style, as well as a budding influence from Renaissance Italy. Exuberant late Gothic ornamentation can be seen in the fantastical Royal Oratory in St. Vitus's Cathedral, and in the structures associated with Matěj Rejsek (c 1450–1506), for instance the Public Fountain at Kutná Hora and the Powder Tower in Prague.

Towards the Renaissance. Later in his life Vladislav was to move his court to Buda and surround himself with Italian artists and architects, but before doing so he invited to Prague in around 1480 a German architect of extraordinary originality, Benedikt Ried (c 1454–1534). Ried, who came probably from South Germany and soon came to supersede all other architects in Bohemia, was given the monumental task of extending the fortifications of Prague Castle and rebuilding the Royal Palace there. For the latter he constructed in 1493 the vast Ladislav Hall, in which Renaissance features (in the doors and windows) are to be found in Bohemia for the first time, but combined eccentrically with late Gothic vaulting of a fantasy and complexity virtually unparalleled in the rest of Europe. Similarly elaborate vaulting was created by him in St. Barbara's Cathedral at Kutná Hora, which he took over in 1515 from Matěj Rejsek, whose own vaulting here, though complex, lacks the flowing energy of Ried's. Another style of vaulting, no less idiosyncratic, was evolved at this time in provincial Bohemia, the earliest documented example being in the Deanery Church at Soběslav (1499–1501). This style, known usually as 'diamond vaulting', reached its apogee in the Franciscan Church at Bechyně (c 1515), where an elaborate, whitewashed vault is composed solely of faceted recesses, the overall effect resembling a cross between a stiffly pleated skirt and an Expressionist film set.

The main painter at Vladislav's court in Prague was The Master of the Litoměřice Altarpiece, who is sometimes identified with the German artist Hans Elfelder; he was at any rate someone who had clearly been brought up in South Germany and might also have had a first-hand knowledge of North Italian art. The altarpiece from which he derives his name was painted around 1500 for the chapel adjoining the Ladislav Hall, and is characterised by its lively and detailed realism. Artists from his workshop are often said to have been responsible for the frescoes of c 1509 on the upper walls of the Wenceslas Chapel, which reveal an Italianate sense of composition and perspective, as do the slightly earlier frescoes in the Smíšek chapel at Kutná Hora. The outstanding sculptor of this period was another German, Master Pavol of Levoča, who was active not in Bohemia but in an area of Central Slovakia known as the Spiš. This region, which had been colonised by Germans in the late thirteenth century, experienced during the reign of Vladislav Jagiello the greatest period in its cultural life, culminating in the great Wing Altar which Master Pavol executed between 1508 and 1517 for the Church of St. James in Levoča. Within a gilded late Gothic framework of breathtaking intricacy, Master Pavol created scenes of a most powerful naturalism, which is evident above all in the predella panel of the Last Supper, the faces in which are said to have been based on members of the town's council.

With the coming to power of the Habsburgs in 1526, the art and architecture of Bohemia and Moravia came to be dominated by Italians, most of whom were from the Como region. From the time of Benedict Ried classical detailing had sometimes been applied to

Gothic structures, but it was not until the 1530s that work was begun in Prague on a truly Italianate building. This, the so-called Belvedere in the Hradčany, was commissioned by Ferdinand I from Paolo della Stella, and is surrounded by a most elegant arcaded loggia decorated with exquisitely carved mythological and classical scenes. The only feature which singles the building out as a work executed outside of Italy is its bizarre copper roof in the form of an upturned hull of a ship, an addition of the mid-sixteenth century by the Bohemian court architect Bonifác Wohlmut (?–1579). Wohlmut's architecture represents a curious synthesis of Italian and Czech elements, and indeed he created for the same Belvedere an upper floor inspired by Bramante's Tempietto in Rome; another work of his is the organ loft in St. Vitus's Cathedral, which seems at first wholly in the spirit of the High Renaissance and yet conceals Gothic vaulting behind its classical arches. Such a synthesis was to typify the spirit of the Czech Renaissance, and even the many Italian architects and craftsmen who were to come to Bohemia in the wake of Paolo della Stella were to adapt to local building traditions.

Pietro Ferrabosco, Baldassare Maggi (Maio da Vomio) and Giovanni Battista and Ulrico Aostalli (Avostallis) are among the better known of this later generation of Italian Renaissance architects, and were responsible for a whole series of monumental country residences, most of which featured courtyards with three tiers of classical arcading. Of these houses, the one at Bučovice (designed by Ferrabosco in 1567) has a particularly fine interior, and contains one room where you will find—surrounded by classical grotesque work—a gilded and exuberantly ornate stucco figure of Charles V which seems to have come straight from some medieval pageant. Also remarkable are the Renaissance interiors at Telč, which include richly polychromed carvings attached to classical coffered ceilings. Telč was one of several imposing buildings commissioned by the powerful Lords of Hradec, a Moravian family whose favourite architect was Baldassare Maggi. One of the last and most original works that Maggi designed for them was a round and enormous garden pavilion at Jindřichův Hradec (1591): to an otherwise wholly Italianate structure Maggi lent a touch of Bohemian fantasy through the addition of an extraordinary conical roof ringed by gabled dormer windows.

Dormer windows, as well as fantastical parapets and stepped gables of every conceivable shape and size, are among the main distinguishing characteristics of the Czech Renaissance, as is the tendency to cover the exteriors of buildings with what are known as sgraffito decorations: the latter, created by incising into the plaster, are generally of scenes from classical history and mythology, but are sometimes wholly ornamental. This style of architecture was applied as much to grand palaces such as the magnificent Šternberk Palace in Prague's Hradčany as to modest burghers' dwellings, and was to be current in Czechoslovakia right up to the late seventeenth century.

The last great period of court patronage in Bohemia took place under Rudolph II, at the turn of the sixteenth century. Rudolph's mania for art, and his habit in later life of shutting himself up in his *Schatzkammer* to contemplate obsessively the accumulated treasures therein, gave him much in common with his Spanish cousin Philip II, with whom he also shared a taste for the bizarre and the erotic. However, unlike Philip II, the artists whom Rudolph admired tended to be precious and ultra-refined, the eroticism of Correggio's

Io, for instance, being apparently preferred to the more full-blooded sensuality characteristic of Titian's mythologies. His favourite sculptor was the Flemish-born Italian Mannerist Giambologna, in whom he showed an interest which was one-sided and hardly subtle: after amassing almost all this artist's statuettes of Venus he wrote to him to ask for 'another naked female figure of the same size'. Rudolph tried unsuccessfully to lure Giambologna to Prague, but succeeded instead in attracting here from Italy the latter's pupil Adriaen de Vries (1546–1626), as well as two other Flemish-born artists, the painters Hans van Aachen (1552–1615) and Bartolomaeus Spranger (1546–1611), both of whom could combine precious eroticism with the sort of allegorical subject-matter which appealed to Rudolph's love of the esoteric.

As for Rudolph's taste for the bizarre, this was amply satisfied by the Milanese artist, Giuseppe Arcimboldo (1527–93), who had been first summoned to Prague in 1566 by Ferdinand I, and who was so admired by Rudolph that he was given in 1592 the title of Count Palatine. Arcimboldo, who worked at Prague not only as a painter but also as an organiser of lavish festivities, developed a speciality in 'visual punning' which was to be dismissed after his death as a mere curiosity but to be greatly appreciated this century by the surrealists: he portrayed members of the court with appropriate still-life objects, thus turning the royal gardener into a composite of flowers, or the Court historiographer Wolfgang Lazius into an accumulation of books. In comparison to Rudolph's patronage of the visual arts, relatively little has been written about the architectural commissions associated with him, though these were in fact considerable. Mention, above all, should be made of the Italian Chapel in Prague's Klementinum, which was designed in 1590 by Ottaviano Mascharino and was the first church in Bohemia with an oval ground-plan, a form which was to be much used by Bohemian architects of the baroque period.

The Baroque. It is ironical that a country with such strong Hussite and Protestant traditions as Bohemia should have ended up as one of the great baroque centres of Europe. The devastation caused by the Thirty Years' War led to a rebuilding campaign on a vast scale, and most of Bohemia's old towns today, in particular Prague, have a predominantly seventeenth-and eighteenth-century look. A vital role in the artistic and architectural renewal of the country was played by the Jesuits, who were determined to create resplendent buildings and works of art that would embody the spirit of the triumphant Catholic Church. In many ways their propaganda was quite subtle, for in their attempts to give a fresh image to the country, they turned to Bohemia's past and formed out of this a new national mythology which they hoped would counteract the Protestant one. A particular stroke of genius was to have discovered an obscure prelate called John of Pomuk who had fallen foul of Wenceslas IV in 1393 and been thrown into the Vltava. In the course of the seventeenth century legends began circulating about him—that he had refused to betray the queen's secrets in the confessional, that a constellation of stars had hovered above his floating body—and eventually in 1693 he was canonised as St. Jan Nepomucký, thus inspiring the consecration of many new churches, and providing the subject of much of the religious statuary to be seen around Czechoslovakia.

A truly baroque style of architecture was slow to develop in Bohemia, and was not in fact to emerge until the arrival of the Dientzenhofers towards the end of the seventeenth century. The majority of the seventeenth-century architects continued to be from the Como region, and were for the most part deeply conservative. Shortly after the Catholic victory at the Battle of the White Mountain, a former Lutheran church in Prague's Lesser Quarter was transformed into Our Lady of Victory, which was little more than a gloomy, impoverished version of the Mannerist Jesuit Church in Rome. During the same decade the Duke of Wallenstein commissioned for himself a building misleadingly referred to as Prague's 'first baroque palace', though which is actually a structure wholly in the spirit of the Florentine High Renaissance.

The two leading Como architects of the middle and late years of the century were Carlo Lurago (1615–84) and Francesco Caratti (?–1677/9), both of whom largely achieved their effects of splendour through the unsubtle means of repeating the same elements over enormously long façades, the masterpiece in this style being Caratti's façade of the Čzernín Palace in Prague (1679–88). The main architect to break the Comasque hegemony at this time was Jean-Baptiste Mathey (c 1630–c 1695), a Burgundian by birth who had trained in Rome not as an architect but as a painter. The elegance and low relief of much of the detailing of his work are very French, and at the Troja Country House, on the outskirts of Prague, he broke away from the block-like or quadrangular Italian villa through the introduction of a French pavilion system and projecting wings. An admirer of Mathey was the outstanding Viennese architect Fischer von Erlach, whose own work none the less was essentially Italian in inspiration. Though active mainly in Austria, he executed in this country two of his greatest works, the earliest being the Hall of Ancestors at Vranov (1683), a grand Bernini-inspired oval which brilliantly exploited a peculiarly dramatic cliff-top situation; the last of his Bohemian buildings was the Clam-Gallas Palace in Prague (1713), which reveals the influence of Palladio while at the same time accommodating statuary by the most dynamic of Bohemia's baroque sculptors, Matthias Braun.

The major architects of the Bohemian baroque were virtually all of foreign origin, and it seems possible that nationalist tensions within Bohemia led to difficulties being put in the way of indigenous Czech architects, whether Czech or German-speaking. Significantly, the greatest of these indigenous architects, Balthasar Neumann (who was born in 1687 in the Bohemian town of Cheb) worked entirely in Germany, while the foremost German architects active in Bohemia, Christoph and Kilian Ignaz Dientzenhofer, originated from Bavaria. Remarkably little is known about Christoph Dientzenhofer (1655–1722), other than that he settled in Prague at some time in the late 1670s, married there in 1685 and died there in 1722, at the age of sixty-seven; there is also a document of 1689 which refers to him as someone who 'understood his art very well ... despite an inability either to read or write'. It is not always easy to distinguish his works from those of his extraordinarily prolific son, Kilian Ignaz (1689–1751), but it is generally agreed that he was the more brilliant and innovative of the two. The two architects can at any rate claim together to have popularised in Bohemia a dynamic architectural style indebted to the work of both Francesco Borromini and, above all, Guarino Guarini, who himself had produced a design in 1692 for Prague's Theatine Church of Our Lady of Perpetual Succour. The hallmarks of the Dientzenhofer style include undulating façades and interiors, plans based on intersecting ovals, a rich play of convex and concave surfaces, piers that project diagonally into the nave, and

Gothic-inspired cross-vaulting such as Guarini had advocated. The supreme expression of this style is the Church of St. Nicholas in Prague's Lower Quarter (1703–55), the most dominant landmark in this city after the Castle, and as such a particularly eloquent assertion of resurgent Catholicism.

Though Guarini and in turn the Dientzenhofers had revived the use of a Gothic system of vaulting, it was left to Bohemia's most original baroque architect, Johann Santini-Aichel (1677–1723), to devise a new style of church architecture which was later christened as 'baroque Gothic'. This represented only one aspect of Santini's work, and indeed he produced numerous churches in a wholly baroque manner, as well as a vast number of palaces; however, it is the aspect by which he is best remembered today. Born in Prague in 1677, Santini was the crippled grand-son of an immigrant mason from Como, whose family later added the name Aichel. As with Mathey, under whom his father had worked, Santini's training was as a painter, and he seems to have had no building to his credit when in 1702 he was chosen to replace the architect P.I. Bayer in the rebuilding of the Cistercian Abbey Church at Sedlec. Santini's adoption of a Gothic style for this and the later Bohemian monasteries that he was to rebuild can be linked to the same motifs which had led the Jesuits to create the cult of St. Jan Nepomucký. Sedlec had been burnt down by the Hussites, and by reconstructing it in a medieval manner Santini was looking back to a past as yet uncontaminated by Utraquism and later heresies. The brilliance of Santini's work at Sedlec lies above all in the vaulting, which was certainly inspired by that of Benedikt Ried at nearby Kutná Hora, and combines the latter's elegance and complexity with baroque dynamism. An even more remarkable interpretation of a late Gothic manner can be seen in Santini's reconstruction of the Benedictine Abbey Church at Kladruby (1712–16), a building which had been razed first by the Hussites and then during the Thirty Years' War. In this building, dominated on the exterior by a crossing dome in the shape of the Bohemian Crown, baroque frescoes by the Assam brothers blend happily into a setting which features star-shaped vaulting of dazzling complexity, altars that burst into a forest of crocketed pinnacles, and, for the High Altar, a pinnacled open-work framework supporting agitated baroque marble statuary. No wonder that the abbot of the time remarked that the 'building was in a hitherto unseen Gothic style'. The bizarre climax of Santini's career, however, was reached not in this work but in a pilgrimage chapel which was commissioned from him by the abbot of Žďár in 1720, and intended to commemorate the miraculous rediscovery the year before of the tongue of St. Jan Nepomucký in an undecayed state. Every detail of this extraordinary five-side building is replete with symbolical significance: Nepomucký's tongue, the five stars that hovered above his dead body, and his steadfastness in the confessional, are everywhere referred to, the resulting structure being unlike any other building in Bohemia.

The great surge of building activity in Bohemia from the late seventeenth century onwards was accompanied by a renascence of the local schools of painting and sculpture. Few artists of interest were active in the first half of the century, with the exception of Karel Škréta (1610–74) who, though not the genius that is often claimed by Czech art historians, was a painter of great energy and versatility, who led also an intriguing early life. Born to a Protestant family in Záborice in 1610, he and his mother fled to Freiburg in Saxony in

1628. From there he went to Italy, and spent time in Venice and Bologna before completing an artistic training in Rome, where he met and did a portrait of the French painter Poussin in 1634. Whether out of genuine conviction or a longing to return to his native Bohemia, he converted to Catholicism shortly after leaving Italy, and eventually settled in Prague, becoming there a prolific painter of altarpieces. As a painter he owes nothing to Poussin, but embraces a whole spectrum of Italian baroque artists from Caravaggio to Guercino and Annibale Carracci. His dark and dramatic canvases sometimes display an impressive realism, which is particularly evident in his portraits, of which the most famous is a lively and informal group portrait of the *Gem-cutter* Dionisio Miseroni and his family. Two painters of a slightly later generation are Michael Willman (1630–1706) and the latter's stepson and pupil Jan Liška (c 1650–1712), the former working in a strongly Rubens-inspired manner, the latter evolving a loosely handled and vividly coloured style which is sometimes described as proto-rococo.

The leading painter active in Bohemia at the beginning of the eighteenth century was Peter Brandl (1686–1735), who, like the sculptor Matthias Braun, enjoyed the patronage of the eccentric and visionary Count Sporck. Brandl was an artist as varied in his style and subject-matter as Škréta, painting portraits in an heroic French manner one moment and the next dark religious canvases in which the paint is handled with an agitation reminiscent of the sculptural effects of Braun. A contemporary of Brandl was the portraitist Jan Kupecký (1667–1740), in many ways the greatest of all Bohemian painters, but who neither studied nor worked in his native Bohemia. An active member of the Moravian Bethren, he was born in Prague, but was forced to emigrate with his Protestant parents to Pezinok, in western Slovakia. When he was fifteen he ran away from home to avoid being apprenticed to a weaver, and entered a painter's workshop in Vienna before going on to Italy. After suffering years of hardship he was finally able to establish a workshop in Rome and stayed there until 1729, when he accepted an invitation from Prince Adam von Liechtenstein to settle in Vienna. His friend the portraitist Johann Caspar Füssli (the father of the Swiss-born English painter Henry Fuseli) described Kupecký's portraits as combining 'the power of Rubens, the delicacy and spirituality of Van Dyck, the sombreness and magic of Rembrandt'. Another contemporary, Anton Graff, gave a better idea of Kupecký's pictures when he wrote that you found in them 'true nature, life itself'. The realism of his portraits is certainly remarkable and gave much inspiration to the Bohemian artists at the end of the century who were trying to get away from the pleasing but shallow rococo manner of painters such as Norbert Grund (1717–60).

The great specialists in large-scale decorative painting in Europe were the Italians, but relatively few of these worked in Bohemia. At the end of the seventeenth century two obscure Italians, Francesco and Giovanni Marchetti, were invited to decorate the Troja Château near Prague but they suffered the humiliation of being replaced there by the Dutch artist Abraham Godyn, who covered its main hall with one of the most spectacular examples of Italian-inspired illusionistic painting to be seen in this country. One of the main Italian exponents of this heavily architectural style of decorative painting was Padre Pozzo, who moved in later life to Vienna, where he influenced a number of Bohemia's artists, for instance Johann Hiebel (1681–?) and the prolific V.V. Reiner (1689–1743). A more painterly and colourful style of ceiling painting was practised by the great

Austrian decorators, all of whom were active at some stage in Bohemia and Moravia, including Rottmayr, Troger and and above all Maulbertsch, whose ceiling in the Philosophical Hall at Prague's Strahov Monastery (1796) is one of the culminating works of the Bohemian baroque. Among the indigenous decorators to be influenced by the Austrians were Franz Xavier Karl Palko (1727–67) and Johann Lucas Kracker (1717–79), the latter being responsible for the masterly ceiling paintings in the Church of St. Nicholas in Prague's Little Quarter.

Few countries in Europe have such a wealth of public statuary as Bohemia, and much of this was the creation of the baroque period, when palace façades were embellished with struggling giants and atlantes, bridges such as Prague's remarkable Charles Bridge lined with gesticulating saints, and almost every town square in the country adorned with tapering piles of statuary that offered thanksgiving to the Virgin for protection during a plague. The earliest of the great baroque sculptors working in Bohemia was Johan Georg Bendl (c 1620–80), who is sometimes thought of as the sculptural equivalent of Škréta, combining as he does baroque drama with powerful realism; though intimate with the sculpture of the Roman baroque, he seems to have been trained in his native South Germany, which perhaps explains his particular genius for limewood carving. All the other main sculptors of the Bohemian baroque took part in the decoration of the Charles Bridge, including Jan Brokoff (1652–1718) and Matěj Václav Jäckel (1655–1738), both of whom were influenced by Bernini. Brokoff's son, Ferdinand Maximilian Brokoff (1688–1731), began his career collaborating with his father on Charles Bridge, but soon surpassed him both in technique and imagination, evolving a heavy monumental style enlivened with vivid touches of realism.

Brokoff would have been without equal in Bohemia if his career had not coincided with that of Matthias Bernard Braun (1684–1738), one of the most brilliant sculptors of the European baroque. Born in the Oetz Valley in North Tirol and trained probably in Italy, Braun came to Prague in about 1710. The Vision of St. Luitgard, which he executed that year for the Charles Bridge, is a dynamic sculptural group of astonishing technical virtuosity, and so painterly in its approach to stone that you can well believe the tradition which ascribes its design to the painter Petr Bendl. In later years the agitated, almost hysterical energy of his art was to make the work of Bernini seem quite restrained in comparison. Fortunately he was to benefit from the enlightened patronage of Count Šporck, who gave him a freedom far greater than that enjoyed by most other sculptors of the day. Šporck's vision and Braun's genius came together at Šporck's county estate at Kuks to produce among the most exciting sculptures to be seen anywhere in Europe, culminating in the works in the Bethlehem Wood, where, in the last years of his life, Braun carved biblical scenes directly onto great boulders scattered in the middle of a dark forest.

Braun had a large workshop, but his influence on the Bohemian sculptors of the late eighteenth century was slight. The leading sculptor of this later generation was Ignác František Platzer (1717–87), whose art owes less to Braun than to the more classical art of Austria's foremost eighteenth-century sculptor, Georg Raphael Donner (1693–1741). Donner deserves a brief mention in an account of the arts in Czechoslovakia, owing to his having spent much of the 1720s and 1730s in the Slovakian capital of Bratislava. His main work there, a bronze group of St. Martin and the Beggar (1733–35) is remarkable for showing the saint dressed as a Hungarian Hussar, a feature which invests this heroic baroque group with a character which looks ahead to the Romantic era.

The late eighteenth century brought with it major changes in the structure of patronage in Bohemia. The expulsion by Maria Theresa of the Jesuits in 1775 and Joseph II's dissolution of most of the country's monasteries in the course of the 1780s greatly diminished the political and economic power of the Church. The country's artists and architects could thus no longer depend on what had once been their most stable source of income, and were forced to rely more on the nobility, who came to be based for much of the year in Vienna, and would come to Bohemia principally for summer stays on their country estates.

Neo-classicism. An elegant neo-classicism of French derivation became the dominant architectural style in Bohemia and Slovakia from the 1770s onwards, to be followed after about 1800 by an Empire style inspired, not so much by France as its name would suggest, but by Viennese architects such as Georg Fischer. Bratislava was transformed in the late eighteenth century into one of Central Europe's smartest and most fashionable towns, owing to the long periods in residence there of Maria Theresa and her court. In Bohemia meanwhile much of the building activity was centred on the many newly founded spa towns, which attracted a growing aristocratic clientele from all over Europe. Some of these places, such as Mariánské Lázně (Marienbad) and Karlovy Vary (Carlsbad), were extensively rebuilt in the late nineteenth century, but others—in particular Teplice and Františkovy Lázně (Franzensbad)—have remained to this day showpieces of neo-classical and Empire architecture, filled with simple and elegant structures in pastel colours, with a predominance of the vivid yellow once known, evocatively, as *Kaisergelb* or 'imperial yellow'. The greatest Bohemian patrons of this period were the Chotek family, one of whom, Rudolf, had become in 1760 Austria's first Supreme Chancellor. Rudolf's son, Jan Rudolf, after having supervised the laying out of Prague's first boulevard, Na Příkopě, commissioned in 1802 for his estate at Kačina one of the grandest of Bohemia's Empire style houses. He also shared the passion of his father and other members of his family for gardens, and not only provided Prague with the large public park of Letná, but also created in his estates at Kačina and Veltrusy magnificent gardens in an English Romantic style. Romantic gardens, adorned with extraordinary follies ranging from minarets to fantastical Gothic chapels, indeed constitute one of Bohemia's greatest attractions during this period, other notable examples being at Krásný Dvůr, and Lednice.

A remarkable eclecticism characterises the architecture of Bohemia in the late nineteenth century, some of the historical pastiches being wholly fantastical both in their scale and style, such as the Schwarzenberg's country house at Hluboká, an Austrian-designed building said to be in an 'English Windsor' style but in fact more reminiscent of 'Mad King' Ludwig's Neuschwanstein in Bavaria. A virtual monopoly of the neo-baroque was enjoyed by the Vienna-based architects Ferdinand Fellner (1847–1916) and Hermann Helmer, who produced monumental opera houses and theatres all over the Habsburg Empire, including at Karlovy Vary, Bratislava and Prague. Nationalist sentiments found a partial expression in the neo-Gothic, of which one of the principal Czech

exponents was Josef Mocker (1835–1899), Bohemia's answer to
Viollet-le-Duc, and a man known for his drastic restoration and
rebuilding of many of this country's medieval monuments, including
Karlštejn. The major buildings of this period associated with the
Nationalist revival were in a neo-Renaissance style, which was
initiated in Bohemia by Josef Zítek (1832–1909). Zítek was trained in
Vienna under the architects of the Vienna Opera House, E. van der
Nüll, and A. von Sicardsburg, and devoted much of his life to the
building of Prague's National Theatre (1867–81); his style was
perpetuated by his one-time collaborator Josef Schulz (1840–1917),
who was the author of this city's equally grandiose, if rather less
eloquent, National Museum (1881–83). A variant of the style was the
neo-Czech Renaissance, which, at the turn of the century, brought
back a fashion for stepped gables and sgraffito decorations. Neither
Bohemia nor Slovakia can boast Art-Nouveau architects of the same
calibre, say, as Hungary's Ödön Lechner or Austria's Otto Wagner,
but there are numerous fanciful buildings in this style to be seen
here, most notably Prague's Municipal House, which was built
between 1903–11 by Antonín Balšánek, Osvald Polívka and Josef
Chochol. The later development of Art Nouveau, when decorative
exuberance gave way to more rationalist tendencies, is represented
in Bohemia principally by Jan Kotěra (1871–1923), a pupil of Otto
Wagner and the Viennese Secessionists, and whose works helped
pave the way for the remarkable generation of pioneering architects
active in Bohemia in the early twentieth century.

The Nationalist Revival of the 19C, both in Bohemia and Slovakia,
provided a great rallying point for painters and sculptors, and gave
them a necessary encouragement at a time when the conditions for
producing art here were generally unfavourable. The situation for
Bohemia's artists at the end of the eighteenth century could in fact
hardly have been worse, thanks to a combination of the Church's
diminished role as a patron, and Prague's decline into a provincial
backwater. Concern with the provincial nature of Prague's cultural
life led finally in 1796 to a group of Bohemian nobles and rich Prague
citizens founding The Society of Patriotic Friends in Art. To help
compensate for the loss to Vienna of Prague's imperial collections,
this Society began amassing a collection of paintings and sculptures
which would later form the basis of the Czech National Gallery. Of
more immediate consequence to the city's art life was the foundation
by the Society in 1796 of the Prague Academy of Fine Arts, an
institution at which most of Bohemia's leading artists of the nineteenth century were to receive their basic training. The majority of
Bohemia's painters in the early years of the nineteenth century were
highly conventional, including the Academy's first director, Josef
Bergler (1753–1829)—who painted stiff mythologies and baroque-
style portraits—and its first Professor of landscape painting, Karel
Postl (1769–1818), an artist in the Claude tradition. The portraitist
Antonín Machek (1775–1844) delicately portrayed the leading figures associated with the Nationalist Revival, while the landscapist
Antonín Mánes (1784–1843)—the father of a great dynasty of
painters—is notable principally for his romantic landscapes of sites
associated with Bohemia's past. A more remarkable painter than
either of these was Josef Navrátil (1798–1865), who painted still-lifes
of extraordinary freshness and realism that only came to light long
after his death. But by far the most important painter of the first half
of the century was Mánes's son, Josef Mánes (1820–71), an artist of
great versatility, equally adept at portaiture, landscape painting,

nudes, romantic historical works, and classical allegories. His central position in Czech art is also due to his fascination with Slavic country-folk, and close involvement with the Nationalist Revival. A tour around Silesia in 1846 first aroused his interest in traditional rural life, and this interest was further stimulated in the course of numerous stays after 1849 with the Silva Tarouca family in their estate in the Haná region, a region of Moravia known for its strong folk culture; in 1854 he undertook a long journey through Moravia, Slovakia and Silesia with the specific aim of recording folk costumes and traditions. He designed banners for patriotic organisations, and, in the last years of his life, ensured his lasting popularity in Bohemia through his delightful scenes of the Czech and Slovak countryside for the Astronomical Clock on Prague's Old Town Square.

Vienna and Munich were the principal art centres to which Bohemian artists were attracted in the first half of the nineteenth century. By the middle of the century, however, Paris had super-seded these places in popularity, and a number of the leading artists of this generation spent a long period of their lives there, including the Courbet-inspired portraitist and still-life painter Karel Purkyně (1834–68), the landscapist and genre painter Soběslav Pinkas (1827–1901) and Viktor Barvitius (1834–1902), who abandoned an early career as a history painter to devote himself to the portrayal of urban life. The only painters of this period to gain an international reputation was Jaroslav Čermák (1830–78), who painted scenes from Czech history in a style indebted to French artists such as Delacroix and Fromentin; as well as spending many years in France, he travelled extensively around Dalmatia, and produced a large body of work documenting the struggle of the Montenegran people against Turk-ish domination.

From the 1870s onwards, the situation for artists wishing to work in Bohemia itself was greatly improved, and, following a pattern wide-spread throughout Europe, many of the artists who had lived for a long time in France began returning to their home country. The ambitious buildings that were erected in Prague in the last years of the century such as the National Theatre involved the collaboration of virtually all the country's important artists, and indeed this whole generation is referred to today as the National Theatre Generation. Two of these painters, František Ženíšek (1849–1916) and Vojtěch Hynais (1854–1925) produced spirited interpretations of often ridiculous classical subject-matter, involving numerous female nudes; another, Václav Brožík (1851–1901), after specialising in quiet landscape studies in France, made a name for himself in Bohemia with two large canvases representing Jan Hus before the Council of Constance, and The Election of George of Poděbrady as King of Bohemia (1898). The major landscapists to have worked in the National Theatre were Julius Mařák (1832–1899), famous for his romantic woodland scenes, and Antonín Chitussi (1847–91), who spent much of his early life working in and around the Fontainebleau forest near Paris, and later applied a Barbizon School manner to the depiction of his native Czech-Moravian Highlands. The central figure of this generation was Mikoláš Aleš (1852–1913), whose works can be paralleled with the historical novels of his contemporary Alois Jirásek. He endlessly depicted scenes from Bohemian history and folk-tales, and, at the National Theatre, collaborated with Ženíšek on a great patriotic cycle entitled *My Country* (now in Moravský Krumlov). Lively and very decorative, his style was ideally suited to book illustration, and, after 1882, virtually abandoned oil painting to devote himself to graphic work, a move which also be connected with his constant financial difficulties.

Aleš today is little known outside Czechoslovakia, in contrast to his contemporary Alfons Mucha (1860–1939), whose life was spent largely in Paris, where he gained enormous fame for his luxuriously flowing Art Nouveau posters, in particular a series of the 1890s featuring the actress Sarah Bernhardt. Though an essentially decorative artist he worked in fact in many different fields, and was sponsored by a Chicago industrialist and Slavophile, Charles Richard Crane, to paint a series of 20 enormous canvases entitled Slav Epic. An immensely wealthy and celebrated artist, he settled permanently to Czechoslovakia in 1922, taking up residence in a Renaissance palace in Prague's Little Quarter, and continuing his varied career through such activities as designing stamps and banknotes. To the end Mucha's art remained deeply rooted in the world of the turn of the century, as did that of the later artist Max Švabinský (1873–1962), another highly successful figure working in many fields, from oil painting to the design of stained-glass windows and mosaics. The strong Symbolist elements in Švabinský's paintings are also evident in those of J. Preisler (1872–1918), who executed decorative works reminiscent of those of Puvis de Chavannes, and designed mosaics for a number of Art Nouveau buildings in Prague. The principal exponent in Bohemia of an Impressionist style of landscape painting was Antonín Slavíček (1870–1910), while Post-Impressionist tendencies can be seen in the work of Jakub Schikaneder (1855–1924), whose highly subtle paintings mark the transition between Czech art of the nineteenth century and the experimental generation of the early years of this century. Schikaneder began his career painting peasant genre scenes in the tradition of the French painter Bastien-Lepage, but ended it with haunting and almost abstract evocations of dusk scenes in Prague.

Bohemian sculpture, after a period of decline in the late eighteenth century, was to enjoy during the following century a gradual renewal in vitality which was to lead eventually to one of the livelier periods in its history. The Prague Academy of Fine Arts was not to have its own sculpture school until 1896, but a number of aspiring sculptors went there to study drawing from the Antique, including Václav Prachner (1784–1832), who evolved a robust classicism. Romantic historical subjects were the speciality of the brothers Josef Max (1804–55) and Emanuel Max (1810–1901), artists of German origin who, while often portraying scenes from Czech history, did so in a stiff and linear manner which owes more to German rather than Czech sculptural traditions. A very sensual modelling, which was to be one of the main characteristics of later Czech sculpture, was shown instead in the early works of Václav Levý, whose bronze of the legendary Czech bard Lumír (1848) in the Klatovy Museum is sometimes regarded as one of the first eloquent manifestations in sculpture of Czech national consciousness. However, Levý was unable successfully to compete in Prague with the Max brothers, and in 1854 settled in Rome, where he fell under the cold and sterile influence of the religious art of the Nazarenes.

The second half of the century was dominated by Josef Václav Myslbek (1848–1922), a sculptor whose richly worked bronzes were to be admired by Rodin. In Myslbek's work a romantic Slavonic fervour vied with a strong neo-Renaissance element, and in the course of the slow evolution of his Wenceslas Monument in Prague (1888–1923), a wild and romantic portrayal of the saint gave way to a statelier and more sober one. One of the greatest of Myslbek's pupils was Stanislav Sucharda (1866–1916), who displayed particular brilliance as a sculptor of Symbolist metal reliefs, and was also responsible for one of the most exciting of Prague's monuments, the Palacký Monument (1898–1912), a work with a pictorial verve worthy of Matthias Braun. The other outstanding monument from turn-of-the-century Prague was the Hus Monument (1900–15) by Ladislav Jan Šaloun (1880–1946), one of the few sculptors of this period to have developed independent of Myslbek. This much neglected and misunderstood work revealed a painterly approach to bronze which was anathema to Myslbek, who had instilled in his pupils a rigorous tectonic approach to sculpture and had encouraged them to avoid the more extreme forms of Art Nouveau. A comparably isolated artist who had rejected both Myslbek's training and principles was František Bílek (1872–1941), the author of elongated Art Nouveau works of great expressive power. The more mainstream Czech sculptors at the turn of the century were heavily influenced by Rodin, including two of Myslbek's more important later pupils, Josef Mařatka (1874–1937) and Bohumil Kafka (1878–1942). The former organised a major exhibition of Rodin in Prague in 1902, while the latter entered Rodin's studio in Paris in 1904; in later years Kafka was to devote himself to romantic historical works, culminating in his statue of Jan Žižka on Prague's Žižkov Hill, which is claimed to be the largest statue in the world. Another of Myslbek's pupils was Jan Štursa (1880–1925), who achieved particular notoriety for his exceptionally sensual female nudes, executed in a great range of styles, from the very classical to the highly realistic.

Before summarising the great developments in Czechoslovak art and architecture in the early twentieth century, mention should briefly be made of the situation in nineteenth-century Slovakia. The awakening of Slovakian national consciousness at the beginning of the nineteenth century, though encouraging a literary revival in Slovakia, was in fact slow to have any impact on the visual arts here. The indigenous Slovakian artists who remained in their native region were of purely local significance, including the painter Jozef Czauczik (1780–1857), whose charmingly naïf landscapes and portraits are reminiscent of some of the early examples of the nineteenth-century American school. Scarcely more sophisticated are the portraits of Peter Michal Bohún (1822–1879), who is sometimes regarded as one of the father figures of a native Slovakian school of painting, not least because of his involvement in the revolutionary activities of 1848–49. Right up to the end of the nineteenth century the story of Slovakian art was to remain inseparable from that of Hungarian art, and several of the Slovakian artists of this period were to be appropriated by the Hungarians. Such is the case with two of the finest painters of the turn of the century, Baron Ladislav Mednánský (1852–1919) and Dominik Skutecký (1849–1921). The former, after a training as an engineer, studied art in Munich and Paris, and subsequently set up studios in Vienna and Budapest. A strange and restless man, who wrote his diary in a secret code and was fascinated by Oriental mysticism, Mednánský was the author of expressive and often anguished landscapes and figure studies, executed mainly in sombre tonalities and with hasty, but suggestive brushstrokes. Skutecký, a slicker and more straightforward painter than Mednánský, had a cosmopolitan training, but returned to his native Slovakian town of Banská Bystrica in the 1880s, and spent there the rest of his life, drawing his inspiration largely from local life, in particular scenes from the town's smithies. From about 1900 onwards the art life of Slovakia became incresingly more integrated with that of Bohemia,the region's growing number of artists, including the group refered to as 'the Generation of 1909', veering more towards Prague than to Budapest.

The vital role which Czechoslovakia has played in the art and architecture of the twentieth century has come to be recognised only recently, and is still not widely appreciated. The towering genius of the early years of the century was František Kupka (1871–1957), one of the pioneers of abstract painting in Europe, but someone whose work was grealy neglected in Czechoslovakia after the Second World War. After studying at the Prague Academy of Fine Arts, and later in Vienna, Kupka settled in Paris in 1895, and was thereafter to live mainly in France. In his early years he painted a number of vividly coloured Symbolist canvases, but worked principally as a satirical artist and book illustrator. From the start he had been fascinated by spiritualism and the occult, and from this had grown an interest in the spiritual symbolism of colour. Soon he began experimenting with linear rhythms and colour schemes that attempted to approximate to the effects of music, and even started to call himself a 'colour symphonist'. Inspired by high-speed photography after 1909, he went on to portray effects of movement,and this was to lead in 1912 to the pure abstraction of *Amorpha: Fugue in Two Colours* (now in the National Gallery of Prague), which created a sensation at the Salon d'Automne of that year. The lyrical abstraction of these years, which can closely be related to the work of Delaunay and the Orphists, gave way in the 1920s to a more geometric abstract style. In 1923 he published in Prague an influential theoretical work entitled *Creation in Plastic Art* (Tvoření v Umění výtvarném), and in 1931 was one of the founder members of the French-based Abstraction-Création Group.

The Twentieth Century. In the years immediately before the First World War, when Kupka had been engaged in his experiments in Paris, Prague had emerged as one of the main centres of the European avant-garde. The more modern tendencies in Czech art had been represented for many years by the Mánes Association of Artists, which had been founded in 1887 in opposition to the Prague Academy of Arts, and had organised several highly influential exhibitions in the early years of this century. One of these was an exhibition in 1905 of the Norwegian artist Edvard Munch, which had been derided by both the public and critics alike and yet had been a decisive influence on the formation in 1907 of Czechoslovakia's first avant-garde group of artists, the Eight ('Osma'). Four years later members of the short-lived Eight were to found The Association of Plastic Arts, the membership of which included all the painters, sculptors and architects who were to be associated with Czech Cubism. A knowledge of French Cubism among the Czech artists was derived to begin with largely from visits to Paris, but an important part in its dissemination here was also played by the art historian and future director of the National Gallery, Vincenc Kramář, an avid collector of the works of Picasso and Braque. The main Cubist painters in Czechoslovakia were Vincenc Beneš (1893–1979), Josef Čapek (1887–1945), Emil Filla (1882–1963), Antonín Procházka (1882–1945), Václav Špála (1885–1946), and the appropriately named Bohumil Kubišta (1884–1918); most of these artists were to remain faithful to the principles of Cubism for the rest of their lives. Filla, the principal spokesman of this group, made two attempts at Cubist sculpture, but the leading sculptor in this style was Otto Gutfreund (1889–1927), perhaps the most outstanding Czech sculptor this century. After evolving an idiosyncratic 'Analytical Cubist' manner by 1911, Gutfreund moved later in the decade closer to 'Synthetic Cubism' before abandoning Cubism altogether after 1920 and producing works in a style which came to be known as 'Objective Realism.' In these last years Gutfreund devoted himself to the realistic but dignified portrayal of the everyday world, which he represented with simple, stately forms, often making use of colour and terracotta; these works were to have an enormous influence on Czech sculptors of the 1920s, including Karel Dvořák (1893–1950), Jan Lauda (1898–1959), Karel Pokorný (1891–1962) and Bedřich Stefan (1892–1982).

A phenomenon unique to Czechoslovakia was the impact of Cubism on architecture. Believing that the ever more severe brick and concrete structures of the Secessionist architect Jan Kotěra had become far too rationalist, a group of architect members of the Association of Plastic Arts attempted to create a more self-consciously artistic architecture, using a simplified ornamental vocabulary comparable to the forms employed by Cubist painters such as Braque and Picasso. Pavel Janák (1882–1956) was the leader of this group, but some of the finest buildings in the style were those created between 1911–14 by Josef Chochol (1880–1956) at the foot of Prague's Vyšehrad: the façades of these structures were covered in faceted diamond-shaped forms that owe a debt not only to Cubism but also to the diamond or 'cellular' vaulting of the Bohemian architects of the late Gothic period. Another of the Cubist architects was Josef Gočár (1880–1945), who was inspired instead by the ordering of Bohemian façades of the Empire period, and came to evolve in the 1920s an academic Cubist style made up of cylindrical forms, most notably in the former Legio bank in Prague.

The optimism and excitement following the creation of the Republic of Czechoslovakia in 1918 led to a period of quite exceptional cultural vitality and experimentation. Thanks to its situation at the heart of Europe, Czechoslovakia became a meeting-point for all the conflicting cultural fashions of the time, and appropriated and transformed such influences as Constructivism and Productivism from Russia, Dadaism from Zürich and Berlin, Futurism from Italy, the Bauhaus from Weimar and Dessau, and Purism and Surrealism from Paris. The great focal-point of the Czech avant-garde of this period was a left-wing group which was formed in Prague's Union Café in 1920, and given the mysterious name of Devětsil, which is both the name of an obscure flower and a composite of two words meaning 'nine' and 'forces', the forces in question being probably the nine muses of Parnassus. It was a group which experimented with most of the 'isms' of the 1920s, and included progressive figures active in all cultural fields, from architecture and the fine arts to design, poetry, music, drama, and film; honorary memberships were even given to Charlie Chaplin and Douglas Fairbanks, though it is unlikely that these two figures would have been aware of this honour. Its leader was the witty and charismatic Karel Teige, an experimental poet and collage artist, who believed in the integration of all the arts, and whose theoretical writings included an article on the work of art in the age of mechanical reproduction which anticipated by some ten years Walter Benjamin's famous essay on this subject. Teige's aesthetic was based essentially on the reconciliation of the opposing extremes of utilitarianism and lyrical subjectivity, a dichotomy which he described in terms of 'Constructivism and Poetism': 'Constructivism', he wrote, 'is a method with rigorous rules, it is the art of usefulness. Poetism, its living accessory, is the atmosphere of life … the art of pleasure.' The Marxist utopianism of Devětsil was not to survive the growing totalitarianism of the 1930s, but when the group finally folded, in 1931, it had managed to maintain its delicate unity longer than all the other European avant-gardes of the 1920s.

One of the principal ideals behind Czech avant-garde architecture of the inter-war years was a belief in the beauty of the industrial age, and it is significant that several of the Devětsil architects, such as Jaromír Krejcar (1895–1949), were inspired by transatlantic steamers and other modern forms of transport, incorporating into their buildings such elements as portholes, the rounded windows of express trains, and terraces balustraded with railings as on a ship's deck: such conceits were typical of Devětsil, the geometry of the architecture being invested with a strong element of poetry, in this case derived from the glamorous associations of long distance travel. However, with the rapid growth of Devětsil's architectural membership, the poetry of the buildings was made increasingly subservient to their utilitarian, and purely abstract elements, Constructivism becoming replaced by an international Functionalism of a type promoted by Le Corbusier, Gropius and Mies van der Rohe: an important example of such a building was Prague's Social Insurance Building of 1929–34, a gaunt concrete structure by Josef Havíček (1899–1961) and Karel Honzík (1900–60).

Outside of Prague the main centre of Czech Functionalism was the Moravian capital of Brno, where modernist architecture was promoted by the town's enlightened Jewish industrialists, and included Mies van der Rohe's pioneering Villa Tugendhat as well as numerous structures by Bohuslav Fuchs (1895–1972). Another Moravian industrialist, the visionary and megalomaniac shoe-manufacturer, Tomáš Baťa, sought the assistance of Le Corbusier in the creation at nearby Zlín of a revolutionary modern township for his workers, a task which eventually befell the local architect František L. Gahura (1891–1958). An architect of these years whose work ran contrary to all the prevailing modernist trends was Jozef Plečník (1872–1957), a Slovenian architect who had been invited to Prague by Jan Kotěra in 1911 to teach at the School of Decorative Arts. Later Plečník had formed a close friendship with the President Tomáš Masaryk, who commissioned from him in the 1920s the restoration of Prague's Castle. His interest in the architecture of the past, as well as in traditional craftsmanship and materials, has led him to be hailed in recent years as a precursor of post-modernism, though in reality his work was so idiosyncratic as to defy rigid categorisation. His Prague Church of the Sacred Heart is certainly one of the more bizarre masterpieces of Czech architecture between the wars, taking elements from such diverse sources as an Early Christian Basilica and an Egyptian Temple, and treating them with a boldness which is thoroughly modern.

The artists of Devětsil, in common with the Dadaists, rejected the notion of high art, though in their case they expressed this disdain at first through taking an interest in popular culture, devoting themselves at the beginning of the 1920s to what they termed 'Poetic Naivism'. Inspired by ex-votos and anonymous shop signs, but also by Henri Rousseau, the Czech Cubists, and the child-like figures in the paintings of the Czech artist Jan Zrzavý (1890–1977), several of the Devětsil members, such as the painter and art historian Adolf Hoffmeister (1902–73), created self-consciously naïf works. Soviet-style Constructivism had little impact on the painters of this generation, though it did influence one of the most original of the Devětsil sculptors, Zdeněk Pešánek (1896–1965), who experimented with kinetic art and also made a number of works involving electric light. Constructivism was also an important force behind the works of the pioneering photographers, Jaroslav Rössler (1902–90) and Jaromír Funke (1896–1945), both of whom were technically adventurous and flirted with pure abstraction. Two other outstanding photographers of these years were František Drtikol (1883–1961) and the one-armed Josef Sudek (1896–1976), the former specialising in female nudes in disturbing, geometrical settings, the latter concentrating on the abstract qualities of everyday scenes and objects, and also creating some of the most evocative images ever produced of Prague. The Devětsil leader Karel Teige employed photographs in his spirited and mysterious collages, which he described as 'Pictorial Poems'. The free rein given to the poetic impulse and to the subconscious in the work of Teige and other Devětsil members created effects of pure Surrealism, which was perhaps the lasting legacy of the Devětsil artists. Not surprisingly, when Devětsil eventually closed, many of its members went on to found the Czech Group of Surrealists. The French Surrealist, André Breton, described Prague as 'the magic metropolis of old Europe', and it was only fitting that this city should have become between the wars one of the main European centres of Surrealism. The Czech Surrealists included the sculptor Ladislav Zívr (1909–80), who devised a number of strange assemblages, and Zdeněk Rykr (1900–40), an artist remarkable above all for his delicate collages made out of thread, tissues and other ephemeral materials. Among the other Surrealists were the versatile Jindřich Štyrský (1899–1942), and the morphological painters Josef Šíma (1881–1971) and Toyen (1902–1980). Another of the painters was Kamil Lhoták (1912–), who was to be one of the most interesting Czech artists active in the 1940s and 1950s, executing strange and sinister landscapes that beautifully evoked the uncertainty of the war years and their aftermath.

As a whole the art and architecture in Czechoslovakia since 1945 has been unmemorable, and certainly cannot be compared in quality to the literature, theatre and cinema of these years. The revolutionary Functionalism of the 1920s and 1930s led under Socialism to the drabbest of housing schemes and civic buildings, while the visual arts of this period suffered from a lack both of imaginative patronage and of a true spirit of communal endeavour. Some of the finer examples of Socialist patronage are to be seen in Slovakia, a region which has never been a major centre of the avant-garde, but has produced this century a number of charming and colourful painters of local life and landscape, most notably Ľudovít Fulla (1902–80) and Martin Benka (1888–1971). The remarkable Slovakian monuments of the post-war period are the numerous war memorials scattered throughout the region, often occupying the most beautiful sites. Among the powerful if conservative sculptors who have collaborated on these structures are Július Bártfay (1888–1979), Frano Stefunko (1903–) and Rudolf Pribiš (1913–), all of whom were involved in the creation of the most imposing monument of them all, the Soviet memorial on top of Bratislava's Slavín Hill. This austere, classical-inspired structure of soaring proportions is a very impressive if chilling expression of the totalitarian spirit.

Literature and Cinema

The recent elevation of a dramatist to the presidency of Czecho-slovakia has highlighted the vital role which literature has played in the history of this country, a country where the search for a national cultural identity has gone hand in hand with the political struggle.

One of the oldest written documents in the Czech language is the hymn 'Lord have mercy on us' ('*Hospodine, pomiluj ny*'), which is known to have been sung at the installation of Bishop Dietmar of Prague in 973, and has been sometimes attributed to Cyril and Methodius. However, the first major work of prose in Bohemia was a Latin chronicle written by Cosmas of Prague (1045?–1125), 'the father of Bohemian history'. Probably of noble descent, he became first a canon and then a Dean of the Chapter of Prague, though did this not stop him from marrying at the age of forty-one to one Božetěcha. It was not until after Božetěcha's death in 1117, when he was already in his seventies, that Cosmas embarked on his *Chronica Boëmorum*, a record of Bohemian history from the earliest times up to the present, written with immense learning but also with objectivity and wit; its success is attested by the numerous manuscript copies in existence. Nearly two centuries later a rather more fanciful version of this history was given by an obscure nobleman from North Bohemia called Dalimil (c 1312), who wrote not only in verse but also in Czech, thus earning for himself the distinction of being Bohemia's earliest known poet.

The first important body of Czech prose took a more serious form than Dalimil's Chronicle and comprised the theological works of the famous reformist preachers active in Bohemia from the late four-teenth century onwards, including Milíč of Kroměříž (1330?–74), Tomáš of Štítný (1330/1–1401) and Matěj of Janov. The adoption of Czech rather than Latin, the normal language of the clergy, was part of their reform programme and at least one of them, Tomáš of Štítný—the author, among other works, of a moralising tract entitled *Of Virgins, Of Widows, and Of Married People*—was heavily crit-icised for doing so. These thinkers prepared the ground for Jan Hus (1371?–1415), whose literary achievement rests both on his sermons and on a series of letters written mainly in captivity at Constance, and addressed, modestly, 'To the whole Bohemian nation': thus was initiated a Czech tradition of prison writing which was to be perpetuated in recent years by Václav Havel in his *Letters to Olga* (1983). One of the more interesting thinkers in the wake of Hus was Petr Chelčický (c 1390–c 1460), a pacifist whose writings were to be much admired by Tolstoy. A man of modest background who knew no Latin, Chelčický wrote in a direct and colourful style which was to have a great influence on the future development of Czech prose.

From the time of Jan Hus right up to the outbreak of the Thirty Years' War in 1620, literature flourished in Bohemia, at least in terms of quantity, and received particular encouragement from the late fifteenth century onwards with the spread of the humanist movement and the growing strength of the Bohemian Brethren. One of the main humanist poets of the sixteenth century was Šimon Lomnický (1552–1623?), a man of little religious or political idealism, but a self-confessed 'lover of sweet venus', who brought sexuality into a number of his works, including the unpromisingly titled *Advice to a Landowner*, the best known of his longer poems. A great opportunist, he made a living writing poems flattering the nobility, and was so successful in this that he was even awarded a noble title himself by Rudolph II. Later he welcomed in verse the brief accession to the throne of the Protestant Frederick of the Palatinate, and saved his neck afterwards by writing a poem praising the execution in 1621 of the Protestant nobility who had taken part in the Battle of the White Mountain. Among his contemporaries were two writers of spirited travel accounts, Václav Vratislav of Mitrovic (1576–1635), and Krištof Harant (1564–1621). The former, a Catholic, was sent at the age of fifteen on a mission to the Turkish Sultan in Constantinople, and was subsequently imprisoned by the Turks and forced to serve for four years on the galleys; he published an account of his experiences on his return to Bohemia in 1599. Krištof Harant, Lord of Polžice and Bezdružice, spent several years working as a diplomat for Rudolph II before deciding in 1598, after the death of his first wife, to fulfil his desire to see the Holy Land. Accompanied by his friend Heřman Černín and only one servant, he set off from Plzeň to the Holy Land by way of Venice, and later moved on to Egypt. His account of his journey, published in Bohemia in 1608, is long-winded and excessively learned in parts, but is filled with vivid descriptions of landscapes and of the people he met. After surviving all the many dangers which he relates in this work, Harant ended up as one of the Protestant nobles executed on Prague's Old Town Square in 1621. He himself seems to have been aware of this irony, for he is reputed to have said on the way to his death: 'Oh my dear God, through how many lands have I travelled, how many dangers have I encountered, for how many days have I no seen bread; once I have been buried in the sands. From all these perils God has rescued me, and now I must die guiltless in my own dear land.'

The writer who movingly recorded Harant's last moments was the greatest of the many historians active in Bohemia at this time, Pavel Skála of Zhoř (1583–c 1640), a man whom Palacký was to describe as 'not only the most voluminous but also the most valuable historian of Bohemia'. Educated at the Protestant university of Wittenberg, Skála held a government office during the reign of Frederick of the Palatinate, and later joined Frederick in exile before settling in the Saxon town of Freiburg. His major work is the colossal *History of the Church* (preserved in ten enormous volumes of manuscript), which, despite its name, deals as much with political as ecclesiastical history; of especial interest is his lively and exceedingly graphic account of Bohemian history from the Defenestration of 1618 up to the tragic aftermath of the Battle of the White Mountain.

The most famous and influential of this generation of Bohemian exiles was Jan Ámos Komenský (1592–1670), who is better known under his Latinised name of Comenius. Born in Moravia, he was educated at the Universities of Herborn and Heidelberg, and in 1616 was ordained a priest of the Bohemian Brethren. In the year following the White Mountain his house and library at the north Moravian town of Fulnek were burnt down by Catholics, and he led an increasingly precarious existence before finally deciding to leave his native country in 1628. The rest of his life was spent travelling around Europe, staying for long periods in both London and Amsterdam, and gaining an international reputation for his revolutionary theories of education. His main literary achievement, however, is not well known outside of Czechoslovakia, and indeed was not translated into English until as late as 1901. This, *The Labyrinth of the World and the Paradise of the Heart* (1631), is an account of the author's pilgrimage through a city symbolising contemporary society. Everyone whom he encounters in his journey only convinces him of the vanity and futility of human endeavour, and in the end he turns to Christ as the sole haven of security in the universe. The ravages of the Thirty Years' War undoubtedly prompted Comenius in these reflections, and in one passage of the book he gives a harrowing description of a meeting with fighting soldiers: 'Then suddenly the drums beat, the trumpet resounds, noisy cries arise. Then, behold, all rise up, seize daggers, cutlasses, bayonets, or whatever they have, and strike unmercifully at one another till the blood spurts out. They hack and hew at one another worse than the most savage animals.'

The Czech language continued to be widely spoken in Bohemia after the Thirty Years' War, and when Peter the Great came here in 1697, he was able to speak to the Bohemian nobility in his own language, which was so close to theirs. However, the massive book-burning campaign which the Jesuits had initiated as part of their reprisals against the Protestants had devastating effects on the development of a native literary language, and, after the death of Comenius, there was virtually no one writing in Czech. The beginnings of a revival in the literary language only took place at the end of the eighteenth century, during the reign of Joseph II, who though excluding Czech from all schools and institutions, allowed books and even a newspaper in Czech to be issued as an expression of his Enlightenment views. A key role in the rehabilitation of Czech culture was played by Josef Dobrovský (1753–1829), who both codified the modern literary language, and reappraised Czech literature of earlier periods. He wrote exclusively in German and Latin, and was apparently only interested in Czech for academic rather than nationalistic reasons. In contrast his younger contemporaries who were associated with the Czech National Revival studied the literature of their forebears with patriotic fervour, and many of them became actively involved in nationalist politics. One of these figures was the author and philologist Josef Jungmann (1773–1847), who brought out a Czech-German dictionary between 1835–39, and translated numerous books into Czech, including Chateaubriand's *Atala* in 1805 and Milton's *Paradise Lost* in 1811.

The other protagonists of this pioneering generation include two Slovaks writing in Czech, Ján Kollár (1793–1852) and Pavel Josef Šafařík (1795–1861). The former, a close friend of Jungmann and the prominent Panslavist of the time, was the author of a cycle of sonnets entitled *Daughter of Sláva*, which was first published in 1824 and increasingly enlarged in subsequent editions. These poems, which bring together a wide range of themes, from the erotic to the patriotic, feature such stirring lines as 'Slavia, Slavia! Thou name of sweet sound but of bitter memory; hundred times divided and destroyed, but yet more honoured than ever.' Safarik was a philologist and archaeologist, who published several learned works on early Slavic history, in one of which he collaborated with the historian František Palacký (1798–1876). Palacký became the leading force behind the National Revival, first as a writer and editor of the important *Journal of the Bohemian Museum*, and then as the Chairman of the Slavonic Congress in Prague in 1848. Between 1836–67 he published the major work of his career, a nine-volume history of Bohemia, which, though only covering the period from 1526 onwards, has had an enormous influence on his compatriots, both through its stress on the liberating role of the Hussite movement, and its conception of Czech history as one of 'contact and conflict' with the Germans.

A consequence of the enormous interest in Czech history and culture which had been generated by Dobrovský and his learned followers was the creation of a literary hoax comparable to the contemporary Ossian forgeries by Macpherson. The main perpertrator was the future librarian of the National Museum Václav Hanka (1791–1861), who 'discovered' in 1817 a manuscript which was claimed to be the work of a Czech Homer active at the very dawn of Bohemia's history. Hanka was himself a poet, but the works published under his own name had none of the impact of his forgeries, which were translated into many languages, and became models for those writers who were beginning to revive Bohemia's literary tradition; they were not to be exposed until the 1880s. A scholar and poet of more honest leanings than Hanka was Karel Jaromír Erben (1811–70), the son of a farmer who graduated in law and philosophy to become archivist of the city of Prague. Erben was primarily important for promoting an interest in Czech folk-songs and Slavonic folk-tales, which he avidly studied and collected; the influence of such works is very evident in his own poems. Karel Hynek Mácha (1810–36), though relatively little appreciated during his own life and sometimes dismissed as a Czech imitator of Byron, was the author of the one truly outstanding Czech poem of the first half of the nineteenth century, *May*. This lyrico-epic work, full of Romantic pessimism and metaphysical anguish, was to make Mácha so popular with later generations of Czechs that when the Germans took over the Sudetenland in 1938 the Czechs were successfully to apply for permission to have his corpse exhumed from there and brought in ceremony to Prague.

Czech drama was to have little encouragement until the opening of the city theatre in Prague in 1859, but the first half of the century saw none the less the emergence of the influential Czech dramatist and theatre director Josef Kajetán Tyl (1808–56), one of whose plays contained the song which would later be adapted as the Czech national anthem, 'Where is my home?' (*Kde domov můj?*).

One of the earliest Czech novelists was Božena Němcová (1820–62), who was also the first eminent Czech woman writer. She was born in Vienna in 1820 to parents who worked in the domestic service of the Duchess of Zaháň, the owner of a large estate near Náchod in North Bohemia; a significant and memorably happy part of Božena's childhood would be spent with her peasant grandmother at Ratibořice, a hamlet on the edge of the Duchess's estate. Forced by her father into a marriage with a much older custom's officer, she and her husband lived at first in Kostelec and then at Domažlice, where she contracted consumption in 1845. After further changes of abode, the husband was forced to retire in 1853 as a punishment for having allegedly taken part in the political activities of 1848–49. They settled subsequently in Prague, where they tried ineffectively to scrape a living through writing. A respite from poverty seemed to be offered in 1861, when a publisher from Litomyšl invited her to come to his town, where she was promised twelve florints for every three pages of manuscript, as well as free lodging. After she had moved on her own to Litomyšl, however, she was not to receive the agreed fees, and was to find furthermore that the publisher had ordered the hotel-keeper not to provide her with any food. Making do with bread and water before receiving financial assistance from her husband, she soon returned to Prague, where she was to die shortly afterwards, a destroyed woman physically and emotionally. She published numerous folk- and fairy-tales but is best remembered for her autobiographical novel, *Grandmother* (1855), which is essentially a portrait of the village where she had spent the happiest days of her childhood, and features characters based on her grandmother, on her childhood self (under the name of Barunka) and on the Duchess of Zahan, who is referred to as the Princess. This book, combining a romantic vision of country life with realistic observation, was to have such an international reputation after the author's death that 'The Ladies of the American Club' in Prague were even to erect a monument to Němcová over her grave in the Vyšehrad. Though largely forgotten today outside Czechoslovakia, she continues to inspire here a reverence which is reserved for few other writers.

Jan Neruda (1834–91), one of the greatest Czech writers of the late nineteenth century, enjoyed much more recognition than Němcová in his lifetime, but suffered from a very sad personal life, remaining a bachelor after experiencing several emotional disappointments. The son of a tobacconist and a charwoman, he lived all his life in Prague, and was brought up among the city's poor. After graduating at university, he worked as a teacher before joining the staff of the foremost Czech newspaper, *Národní listy*, where he was to be employed as a writer and editor up to the time of his death. His literary achievement is one of great variety, and includes poetry which ranges from intimate lyrics of a reflective and analytical kind to the visions of an ardent nationalist. He was also an outstanding writer of short stories, basing his tales on a realistic portrayal of contemporary society, for instance in his *Tales of the Little Quarter* (1878), which describe the area of Prague where he lived. The remarkable concision and ironic humour of these stories is a reflection of his work as a journalist, in which the limitations both of Austrian censorship and of having to write to the length of a *feuilleton* compelled him to rely heavily on satire, aphorism and allusion. Many other Czech writers, right up to the present day, have also worked as journalists, and have likewise developed a concisely ironic style as a way of exploiting restrictions both in length and freedom. One such writer was Neruda's immediate precursor, Karel Havlíček Borovský (1821–56), who had founded in 1848 the Czech newspaper *Národní noviny* and after a spell in prison for his Panslavist views, had died young of tuberculosis. His most original work was *The Conversion of St. Vladimir* (which was unfinished and only published in 1874), a brilliant satire on the two institutions which he most hated, the absolutist regime and the established Church.

A very popular satirist of Neruda's generation was Svatopluk Čech (1846–1908), whose most famous creation was a man called Matěj Brouček, who, under the influence of the beer served in the Vikárka ale-house in Prague Castle, undertook fantastical exploits, including to the moon and back to the fifteenth century. Yet Čech was also a poet who wrote such romantic and nationalist works as his long allegorical poems *Evropa* (1878) and *Slávie* (1884). Two other neo-Romantic writers of this period were Julius Zeyer (1841–1901) and Alois Jirásek (1851–1930). The former, a poet, novelist and dramatist of Jewish and French German origins, was a writer of a very cosmopolitan outlook, and yet in many of his works he gave a glamorous treatment to Bohemia's history and legends, for instance in his celebrated epic cycle, *Vyšehrad* (1880). Jirásek, a history teacher by profession, took up the writing of historical novels at a time when the genre was in decline, and wrote works inspired by

Bohemia's glorious past—in particular the Hussite period—which were to win him a wide readership and have great political influence.

Tomáš Garrigue Masaryk (1850–1937), the most important political and philosophical writer of his day, rose from being the son of a former serf to become Professor of Philosophy at Prague University and eventually first President of the Czechoslovak Republic. His philosophy was one of rationalist humanism, and two of his greatest heroes were Comenius and František Palacký. Another of his mentors was the journalist Havlíček, whom he admired for having rejected the uncritical idealisation of the past which had characterised many of the writers of the Romantic era. Sentimental nationalism was falling out of favour generally with the Czech writers who came to fruition at the turn of the century, many of whom were signatories in 1895 of a manifesto declaring that 'Gloomy auspices have presided at the growth of the present generation. Suffocated by empty phrases, nauseated by Slavic mottoes and patriotic anthems, we have opened our eyes. With scepticism we have looked upon our fathers. A sorry sight.'

One of the most original of this Decadent, rebellious generation was the poet Karel Hlaváček (1874–98), who died young of tuberculosis and was the author of the gloomy epic, *Song of Vengeance* (1898), an ironic tale of revolt set in sixteenth-century Holland and written with a precise, musical style which was to have a great influence on later Czech poetry. The reclusive school-teacher Otakar Březina (1868–1929) turned for inspiration for his metaphysical dream world to Baudelaire, Indian sacred writings and the Christian mystics, while Josef Svatopluk Machar (1864–1942) expressed his abhorrence of contemporary society through the taking up of themes from classical antiquity. An almost violent streak of hatred runs through the poetry of Petr Bezruč (1857–1958), who in several of his works posed as a rough and ugly miner speaking on behalf of the oppressed 70,000 Czechs from his native Silesia. Stanislav Kostka Neumann (1875–1947), a rebel from an old Prague family, was to graduate from Decadence and anarchy to naturalism and Marxism.

Whereas in Bohemia by 1900 a remarkable body of literature had evolved in a relatively short period of time, in Slovakia literature was still in its infancy. A written Slovak language had barely existed before the nineteenth century, and right up to 1918 was to be used largely by doctors and the judiciary. The first person to codify a Slovak literary language was the philologist Anton Bernolák (1762–1813), whose *Grammatica slavica* of 1790 was based on the dialects of western Slovakia. A number of writers employed this language in the early nineteenth century—such as the poet Ján Hollý—but it was to be superseded after 1846 by a Slovak language which had been constructed from the dialects of central Slovakia. The leading personality in the development of this new literary language was Ľudovít Štúr (1815–56), who was not only a philologist but also a poet and statesman who was untiring in his efforts to publicise his creation, despite much opposition on the grounds that it would endanger the common political struggle of Bohemia and Slovakia. Two of the earliest important poets to write in the new language were Andrej Sládkovič (1820–72) and Janko Kráľ (1822–76). The former was the author of the lyrical, Pushkin-inspired epic *Marína*, while the latter, a political radical, wrote ballads and lyrics that express Panslavonic enthusiasm in a style which echoes popular verse; mention should also be made of Ján Botto (1829–81), whose main achievement was a romantic lyrical epic of 1862 based on the gruesome death of one of Slovakia's most popular heroes, Juraj Jánošík, the Slovak Robin Hood.

A prolific and sophisticated writer who did much to raise Slovak literature from its provincialism was Pavol Orszagh (1849–1921), a professional lawyer who wrote poetry and drama under the name of Hviezdoslav; one of the main advocates of Czech-Slovak co-operation, his work is marked both by patriotism and the principles of his Evangelical faith. The founder of the Slovak novel was Svetozár Hurban Vajanský (1847–1916), a great fighter for Slovak rights, and a man imprisoned several times by the Austrian authorities; he idealised contemporary Slovak life in his novels, and urged the Slovaks to turn towards Russia rather than the decadent West. Martin Kukučín (1860–1928), another novelist, spent most of his adulthood as an emigré doctor in Chile and Dalmatia, but continued to draw inspiration for many of his works from Slovak village life.

One of the greatest poets to have written in the German language this century, Rainer Maria Rilke, was born in Prague and spent here an important part of his youth, though he has as much claim to be regarded as Czech as have Sigmund Freud or Gustav Mahler, both of whom also came from what is now Czechoslovak territory. However, a different case is presented by a remarkable group of German-speaking Jewish writers who were central to Prague's literary life in the early years of this century, and without whom any account of literature in Bohemia would be incomplete. Indeed the best known writer of this group, Franz Kafka (1883–1924) has become in the eyes of most foreigners one of the most significant of all 'Czech' writers. The depressing facts of Kafka's life are well known, and lend themselves only too easily to Freudian interpretation. The only son (he had three sisters) of a dominating self-made businessman, Kafka developed a life-long obsession with his parents which was reflected both in his writings and in his inability to marry, despite several engagements. Trained unwillingly in the law, he worked at first for the Prague branch of the Trieste-based Assicurazioni Generali, from which he resigned in 1908 on the grounds of 'nervousness and cardiac instability'. From 1908 he was based at a fifth-floor office in the Workers' Accident Insurance Institute, but from 1917 spent an increasing amount of time in sanatoria. In 1922 he was forced finally by ill health to leave his job, dying of tuberculosis two years later.

An obsessive diarist, and a prolific writer of letters, above all to his father, and to Felice Bauer (fiancée) and Milena Jesenská (mistress), Kafka unflinchingly analysed in these writings his every mood, action and physical sensation, and was equally honest in his ever changing assessment of his family and friends. The rest of his literary output, however, was relatively small, and all that he published in his lifetime was a number of short stories that can easily be contained in a single, modestly sized volume; as for his three novels, *America*, *The Trial* and *The Castle*, these were not completed to his satisfaction and were only to be published after his death. Kafka was a stylistic perfectionist, but it would seem that his talent was best-suited to the short story, for as that other master of concision, Jorge Luis Borges, has perceptively noted, Kafka was primarily interested in atmosphere, and not in the convolutions of story or in creating a psychological portrait of the hero. The meaning of his works has been the subject of much dreary analysis, but some idea of the general character of his fiction is given by the word 'Kafkaesque', which is used today mainly by people who have never read anything by him. The innocent individual caught up inexplicably in a night-marish situation which is beyond his power to control recurs again and again in his work, as for instance in his story *Metamorphosis*, which has one of the most memorable of his opening lines: 'Gregor Samsa woke from uneasy dreams one morning to find himself changed into a giant bug.' The claustrophobia of his family life deeply affected his perception of the world as did the labyrinthine bureaucracy of the Austrian Empire, of which he had close experience as an insurance clerk. A Czech edition of *The Castle* did not appear until 1938, and had little success, but perhaps the book's impact would have been far greater had it been brought out during the Stalinist years, the terrors of which it seems to prophesy. As it happens, all Kafka's works would be banned in Czechoslovakia for much of the period of Communist rule.

One of the main meeting-places in Prague for Kafka's literary circle was the Café Arco, which reached the height of its popularity just before the First World War. Its leading associates called themselves the 'Arconauts', and represented for the Viennese writer Kaul Kraus a Jewish cabal besmirching the purity of the German language: Kraus named these associates in his untranslatable line describing the café: '*Es werfelt und brodet und kafkat und kischt.*' Franz Werfel (1890–1945) began his literary career writing Symbolist dramas of ideas and lyrical Expressionist poetry, but progressed to historical and political realism, both in drama and fiction; he escaped on foot to Spain in 1940 and died five years later in Beverly Hills, California. Max Brod (1884–1968), who emigrated in 1939 to Tel Aviv, was a novelist and critic, but is best known as an editor and biographer of Kafka, to whom he was deeply devoted. Kafka for his part came to the conclusion that Brod had little understanding of him, but none the less entrusted him with the job of being his literary executor, a job which entailed as its main duty the destruction of all his unpublished manuscripts: Brod had sufficient understanding of Kafka not to fulfil this duty, realising that anyone who genuinely wished his works to be destroyed would not hand them over to a devotee. Egon Erwin Kisch (1885–1948) was in many ways the most 'Czech' of these German writers, working all his life as a journalist, and wittily commenting on lesser aspects of Prague life, as in his *Tales from Prague's Streets and Nights*. A highly individual German novelist in Prague who separated himself from Kafka's circle was Hermann Ungar (1893–1929), a Moravian-born Jew who worked after 1921 as a commercial attaché at the Czechoslovak Embassy in Berlin; hypochondria forced him eventually to leave his job, but he died shortly afterwards in Prague of acute appendicitis. His master-piece is *The Mutilated* (1923), a novel about a mediocre bank clerk enslaved by a young widow; one of the work's great admirers was Thomas Mann, who thought that it revealed a 'deep understanding of vice, shame and misery'. Completely forgotten after his death, the works of Ungar are beginning again to attract attention, though they still await an English translator.

The German literary world in Prague was rigidly separated from the Czech one, and the Czech journalist Milena Jesenská infuriated many of her compatriots by her fascination with Kafka and his circle. A writer who belonged to neither of these worlds, and yet high-lighted through both his personality and writings the enormous differences between the Czech and German character, was *Jaroslav Hašek* (1883–1923). Certainly few greater contrasts can be imagined than that between Kafka and Hašek, both in terms of their lives and their works. The picaresque life of Hašek is almost as entertaining as what he wrote, and has been the subject of a superb biography by the former British ambassador in Prague, Sir Cecil Parrot (*The Bad Bohemian*, London, 1978). The son of an impoverished school-teacher who drank himself to death, Hašek was brought up in Prague and studied there at the recently founded Czechoslovak Commercial Academy, where he acquired his life-long tastes for writing and vagrancy. Interrupting his studies periodically to wander penniless around different parts of Central Europe, he was eventually expelled from the Academy, and decided to devote himself full-time to writing, having already managed to have accounts of his wanderings published in *Národní listy*. For a while he was a member of a literary club called Syrinx, which used to hold rowdy meetings at Prague's U Fleků ale-house and later at St. Thomas's cavern, but even these proved too intellectual for Hašek. He took an increasingly active part in anarchist activities, and committed the ultimate anarchist act when he bartered for drink the office bicycle of the particular anarchist group to which he belonged. At the same time he developed a notorious line in practical jokes, attempting on one occasion to commit suicide from the same spot on the Charles Bridge from where St. John of Nepomuk had been thrown, and on another signing himself in a Prague hotel as a spy, an act which was to lead to the hotel being surrounded by the Austrian militia. In 1909 he became editor of the serious natural history magazine called *Animal World*, and perplexed its readers by his invention of several new species. His most sustained escapade, however, was his creation in 1912 of a new political party called *The Party of Moderate and Peaceful Progress Within the Limits of the Law*, the meetings of which gave ample scope for Hašek's exhibitionism, and also helped bolster the ailing finances of the pub where they were held.

Hašek's varied career in the First World War, from which he returned a bigamist after serving a spell in Russia as a deputy commandant in the Red Army, provided him with the material for the book which was to secure his future reputation, *The Good Soldier Švejk*. Published in instalments together with illustrations by his friend Josef Lada, the book was composed largely in pubs, where Hašek would write hastily at the corner of a table, sending off every so often one of his companions to deliver the newly completed parts of the manuscript to the publisher. Hašek's health, after a lifetime of bodily abuse, was now failing him, and he moved from Prague to a village in the Czech-Moravian Highlands, but died shortly afterwards, leaving his book unfinished; few of his old friends and none of his family attended the funeral. Despite the enormous and immediate popular success of the *Good Soldier Švejk*, the book was not taken seriously as literature for many years, and few people of the time would have predicted its importance for later Czech writers. Švejk himself may not represent the archetypal Czech as some foreigners insultingly like to believe, but the way that this little man is used by Hašek to reduce global events to human proportions can be singled out as a characteristically Czech device. To Hašek the outwardly insignificant Švejk was in his own way no less of a hero than Alexander the Great, for in his simplicity and congenital idiocy he succeeded in exposing the absurdity of all those around him, just like Hašek himself had done.

The Czech writer who best encapsulates the spirit of the First Czechoslovak Republic was Karel Čapek (1890–1938), who came to literary prominence at the Republic's onset, and died just before its demise. A humanist, a pragmatist and a man of moderate political views, he had an enormous amount in common with President Masaryk, to whom Čapek was to become both a close friend and a sort of Boswell, recording the president's life and thoughts over a long series of interviews carried out from the mid-1920s onwards. The son of a country doctor, Čapek was born in a village in the Giant Mountains of North-East Bohemia, and studied philosophy in Prague, Berlin and Paris before finally taking up a career in writing. His first stories were published in 1916, and in the following year he began practising journalism, which he would continue to do for the rest of his life, believing, as numerous Czechs have done, that this was a good way of fulfilling a writer's duty to a nation. His literary activities proliferated in the course of the 1920s and came to include essays, novels, children's stories, travel writing, and even a humorous book on gardening. But he made his reputation above all in the theatre, both as a director, and as a writer of such famous works as *R.U.R.* (1921), *The Macropolous Affair* (1922) and the witty morality play *From the life of the Insects* (1921), which he wrote in collaboration with his painter brother Josef. A strong science fiction element runs through his work, and in *R.U.R.* ('Rossum's Universal Robots'), he was to give international currency to the Czech word 'Robot'; two years later he was to write a novel, *Krakatit*, in which, prophetically, an atomic bomb was invented. In these and other works he expressed his fear of man being dominated by the machines he invents, but he treated such a weighty theme with a complete lack of pretentiousness. Even when dealing with the strange and the exotic, he never lost his characteristically Czech common sense and interest in ordinary life: his robots were given the failings of normal human beings, as were the newts in his famous novel *The War of the Newts* (1936). By 1936 Čapek was a strong contender for the Nobel Prize, but the Swedish Academy was wary of offending Nazi Germany by honouring an outspoken anti-fascist. The Academy reputedly asked Čapek to write some new, blandly inoffensive work, but Čapek replied with his typical wit that he had already submitted his doctoral dissertation. He died two years later, literally heart-broken by Chamberlain's betrayal of Czechoslovakia.

The great centre of Czech literary and artistic life between the wars was Prague's Union Café, where there gathered a particularly brilliant galaxy of poets. At the very beginning of the 1920s the dominant poetic fashion was for realistic, socially committed verse, of which one of the earliest exponents was Josef Hora (1891–1945), a member of the Communist party until 1929, and a journalist by profession. František Halas (1901–1949), the self-educated son of a textile worker, was another poet associated in his early years with this so-called 'proletarian phase'. But the most prominent advocate of the style among the Union Café poets was Jiří Wolker (1900–1924), who was also the least likely candidate for 'proletarianism', being a trained lawyer from a privileged background who arrogantly prided himself on his supposed English descent, believing that his surname was a corruption of Walker. 'ENOUGH OF WOLKER!' was to be the battle cry of the advocates of Poetism, which became the new fashion after 1923 and one of the main forces behind the avant-garde group known as Devětsil. Devětsil, which had been founded at a meeting at the Union Café in October 1920, was made up of leading figures in all the arts, and even Wolker had been one of its members until his disagreement with its orientation towards Poetism. The leader of Devětsil was the versatile Karel Teige (1900–51; see Art and

Architecture), who defined Poetism as 'the rule of pure poetry', an expression of joy in which ideas and images freely mingle, unconstrained by the normal continuities such as narrative and a rigid ideological viewpoint; ultimately Poetism, with its belief in free association and the impulse of the subconscious, was to give way to Surrealism. Vítězslav Nezval (1900–1958), who in 1934 was to be a founder member of the Czech Group of Surrealists, was Poetism's most significant poet, and the author in 1924 of what could be described as the movement's manifesto, *Pantomime*. With a layout and graphics by Teige, illustrations by J. Styrský (see Art and Architecture), and numerous photographs, this was a book in which the visual presentation was as important as the text itself, and where you could find such diverse concepts as a 'photogenic poem', a film script in book form, a libretto for a mime show, and a picture poem. Devětsil, and Poetism in particular, aimed to break down the barriers between the various arts, and its literary associates were all people of a strong visual imagination, some, such as Nezval, even practising painting.

Quite apart from its impact on poetry, art and architecture, Devětsil had a major influence on the development of Czech theatre between the wars. In 1926 a group of Devětsil members including the directors Jindřich Honzl (1894–1953) and Jiří Frejka (1904–1952), and the actors Jiří Voskovec (1905–1981) and Jan Werich (1905–1980) founded The Liberated Theatre, which soon became one of the main avant-garde venues of Europe. Employing many of the techniques of the circus, music-hall and cabaret, it put on plays, ballets and dramatised poems by Devětsil authors, as well as numerous Futurist, Dada and Surrealist works by foreign authors such as Marinetti, Alfred Jarry, André Breton and Jean Cocteau. These fantastical and lyrical works were always enacted against simple, functional and anti-illusionary stage sets of the tradition of Soviet directors such as Meyerhold, thus successfully realising Devětsil's programme of reconciling Poetism with a more utilitarian Constructivism.

The cinema, which was then in its infancy in Czechoslovakia, was another potentially ideal medium to express the theories of Devětsil, and in 1925 Karel Teige published a pioneering treatise of film aesthetics entitled *Film*, in which he put forward a case for 'pure cinematography', arguing that cinema should be an independent art with a self-sufficient poetic language of its own. His ideas, sadly, were not to be put into practice between the wars, but, in compensation, the avant-garde poetic humour and satire of the Liberated Theatre were to be taken up in the medium of film by the actors Voskovec and Werich. These two actors, whose partnership came to be known as as 'the duo V & W', were associated in the 1930s with a number of films that greatly helped to raise the Czechoslovak film industry from its provincialism. Their second and best film, *Your Money or Your Life* (1932), represented the birth of the Czech film comedy, while later works of theirs took a more political direction, following a general trend in the arts in Czechoslovakia at the time of Hitler's rise to power. These latter films were directed by the prolific Martin Frič (1902–68), whose film *Jánošík*, based on the life of the Slovak Robin Hood, was one of the first works of the Czechoslovak cinema to gain international recognition.

Dada, slapstick and films were a great influence on the writings of the principal novelist associated with Devětsil, Vladislav Vančura (1891–1942), a virtuoso and experimental stylist who combined boundless fantasy with humour and satire, as in his story *Capricious Summer* (1926), which was to be the subject of one of the greatest Czech films of the 1960s. He evolved a more realistic style of novel in the 1930s, exploring social and political themes, but his involvement with left-wing politics led to his execution by the Nazis in 1942. Perhaps the best loved and most widely known writer to emerge out of Devětsil was the poet Jaroslav Seifert (1901–86), who was only narrowly to escape Vančura's fate during the Second World War. One of the few genuinely proletarian writers of this generation, Seifert was the son of a factory blacksmith from the Prague district of Žižkov, a strong working-class area of which Seifert was always to be intensely proud. His first volume of poetry, *Town in Tears* (1921), is considered one of the most 'proletarian' of all Czech works of poetry, but his subsequent collection, *Nothing but Love* (1923), marked the beginning of a long 'modernist' phase, and has references to the circus, the cinema, skyscrapers and other subjects so typical of Devětsil. The euphonic, densely compressed and incantatory manner of his 'modernist' works was to intensify from 1929 onwards, but in the last two decades of his life he developed a more 'conversational' style, directly addressing the reader in simple and unadorned free verse. Though his style changed, certain themes of his verse, such as his dual obsession with Prague and women, remained constant, and though his verse is at times intensely nostalgic and preoccupied with death, it is never morbidly introspective, and always retains a semi-humorous quality and a concern with the joys and pleasures of life.

Few other writers were so ideally suited to serve as spokesmen for the Czech nation, which is what Seifert virtually became from the late 1930s onwards, when he came to enjoy a popularity on a scale which no modern British or American poet could ever hope to achieve. From 1938, when Seifert mourned in verse the death of Masaryk, right up to the aftermath of 1968, the Czech public were anxiously to await his every word, whether expressed in poetry, or, as was the case with much of his writings during the war years, in journalism. Death nearly came to Seifert in 1945, when he was captured by the Germans and lined up against a wall to be shot, being reprieved only at the last moment. His later account of this Dostoyevsky-like experience typifies not only the particular mentality of Seifert but also the approach to history of many of the finest Czech writers of a later generation: instead of dwelling on the horror and heroism of these potential last moments, Seifert relates how his mind was largely preoccupied with speculation about what the inhabitants of a neighbouring block of flats were cooking, and with a childhood memory of a nearby sidewalk toilet which had been defaced with a picture of a naked woman in a compromising position.

An ironic humour and a sense of the absurdity underlying even the most tragic and oppressive situation were to provide Czech writers with the best means of coping with the limitations of freedom imposed by Communist rule. However, during the worst years of Stalinism, individuality of any sort was a dangerous commodity, and a number of writers who had fought against Fascism now found themselves accused of anti-State activities, for instance the Slovak poet Laco Novomeský (1904–), and the son of the artist Alfons Mucha, Jiří Mucha (1915–1991), who was later to write an account of this period in his *Living and Partly Living* (1967). Seifert maintained a silence for much of the 1950s, but other contemporaries of his such as Nezval compromised their artistic integrity through writing sycophantic poems to the new regime, Nezval even managing on one occasion to write a beautiful poem praising the distinctly unappealing wife of Klement Gottwald. Certain novelists, in particular the Slovak writer František Hečko (1905–60), fulfilled the demands of 'socialist realism' through detailed descriptions of village life; but the principal theme of Czechoslovak writing from 1945 right up to the end of the 1950s was the Second World War and the immediate period leading up to it, with especial emphasis on the heroic role of the Czech and Slovak partisans, and of the Soviet army.

Among the main novelists writing during this period were three Slovaks, Petr Jilemnický (1901–49), Milo Urban (1904–), and the die-hard Stalinist Ladislav Mňačko (1919–), all of whom wrote novels about the Slovak involvement in the war. As for the Jewish experience of the war this was dealt with memorably in the stories of Arnošt Lustig—which were based on life in the concentration camp at Terezín, and in an outstanding novel by Jiří Weil, *Life with a Star*, which was published during the period of relative freedom just before the Communist take-over, and was later denounced by the Communists as a 'decadent' example of 'pernicious existentialism.' Weil (1900–59), a journalist and former member of Devětsil, was expelled from the Czech Writers' Union early in the 1950s, but, through the intervention of Seifert, later managed to be appointed as director of the Jewish State Museum in Prague, only one year before dying of cancer. *Life with a Star* is a highly autobiographical work, dealing with how a humble Jewish citizen of Prague copes with the increasingly tyrannical and ridiculous measures imposed on his race by the Nazis. Living in a house which has been stripped of everything, not allowed even to use public transport or enter certain shops, the protagonist is sustained in his loneliness through memories of his long departed mistress and through the companionship of a stray cat, but eventually the memory of the former fades and the latter is killed by a German soldier. The novel is saved from unrelenting bleakness by the author's ability to perceive the absurdity of the whole situation, and the conclusion is a curiously optimistic one, with the hero unafraid of anything else which might befall him.

The gradual improvement in the political and social situation in Czechoslovakia, leading in 1962 to the demolition of the monumental statue of Stalin which dominated Prague's Letná Hill, prepared the ground for a great literary renascence. The writers who emerged in the decade between 1958–68 have gained for modern Czech literature an enormous international popularity, though it has to be said that foreigners continue to be ignorant of such interesting Slovak writers of this period as Ladislav Ballek, Jan Johannides and Pavel Vilikovský. Ballek is the author of epic novels set in southern Slovakia, while Jan Johannides made his name as an existentialist writer, many of whose works are preoccupied with guilt and the meaning of distinct national identity. Vilikovský wrote in the late 1960s one of the funniest novels in Slovakian literature, *Ever Green is...*, a book which poked fun at Slovakian nationalists and at everything which was held sacred in Slovakia under Communist rule; though accepted (with alterations) for publication in 1969, it was only issued twenty years later. Of the new Czech generation of writers, one of the best known is Josef Škvorecký (1924–), who was born and brought up in the North Bohemian town of Náchod, and acquired there a life-long passion for American literature and jazz. During the war years he was lucky enough to be able to remain in his home town through obtaining a job as an auxiliary worker in the local Messerschmitt engineering works: as with many Czech writers who were later obliged to take on factory and other manual jobs, the experience of working here was a formulative one in his future development as a writer, for it enabled him to write sympathetically about Czechs from every walk of society. Of more immediate consequence, he met at the factory a working-class girl who deprived him of his virginity, and also spurred him on to try and sabotage one of the planes, a would-be act of heroism which was fortunately interpreted as incompetence. Shortly after the war he moved to Prague, where he worked for a while in a publishing house and became involved in one of the few circles of underground literature in the early 1950s. In 1958 he committed what he described as artistic suicide by publishing a novel which he had written immediately after the war and had wisely decided to hold on to throughout the Stalinist years. Even in the marginally more tolerant climate of the late 1950s, this novel, *The Cowards*, was savagely denounced by the Communist party and later banned, thus greatly increasing the book's popularity; however, a new edition was to be allowed in 1962, which was to make Škvorecký one of the most fêted of Czech novelists.

The Cowards was intended as a work of 'magic' as opposed to 'socialist realism', a work in which Škvorecký set out to write about events in his past life so that they would be 'etherialised by distance'. In contrast to the customary tales of Nazi atrocities and Soviet heroism, *The Cowards* gives a humorous and almost idyllic portrayal of life in a Czech town at the very end of the war, and centres around a group of youngsters whose primary interests are in girls and jazz rather than in the forthcoming glorious revolution. The work is almost completely autobiographical and would initiate a series of novels in which Náchod is referred to as Kostelec, and the young Škvorecký as Danny Smiřický. The girl known as Irene, the principal object of Danny's unrealised sexual fantasies, apparently never spoke to Škvorecký again after the publication of the first Kostelec novel, even though, as Škvorecký said, he had straightened out in his book her bandy legs; in later works her bandy legs were to return. The enormous popularity which Škvorecký enjoyed in Czechoslovakia following the second edition of *The Cowards* was much enhanced later in the 1960s with a series of droll and witty detective stories featuring the mournful-faced Lieutenant Borůvka. His critical reputation, however, was enhanced principally by his experimental novella *The Bass Saxophone* (1967), which is set in war-time Kostelec, and adopts a prose-style which brilliantly emulates the rhythms of jazz, a form of music which was considered decadent first by the Nazis and later by the Communists. The last work which Škvorecký published in Czechoslovakia before becoming a banned author in 1969 was the delightful *Miss Silver's Past* (known in Czech as *The Lion Cub*), a tale of love set against the complexities of life in a Czech publishing house, influenced by Jewish experience in the Second World War.

Milan Kundera (1929–) was the first Czech novelist to have a large international success, though his popularity in his native country has never been as great as authors such as Škvorecký, not least because most of what he has written dates from after he went into exile in 1975. Born in Brno, his early career included work as a labourer, a jazz musician, and—in the mid 1960s, at the height of the Czech New Wave in film—a professor at the Prague Institute for Advanced Cinematographic Studies. His first and only novel published in

Czechoslovakia before 1968 was *The Joke* (1967), the protagonist of which commits the grave error as a Communist student of sending a teasing postcard to his earnest Stalinist girlfriend containing the lines: 'Optimism is the opium of the people! The healthy atmosphere stinks! Long live Trotsky!' The humour was not appreciated by those who intercepted the card, and, despite the hero's protestations that 'it was only a joke', he is expelled from university and spends seven years consigned to an army penal corps, where he works in the coal mines. The novel contains in embryo most of the themes that Kundera was to explore in his later works, most notably the interconnected themes of 'lightness' and 'forgetting'. The 'burden of lightness' refers in this book's case to the way in which a joke deprives the hero 'of the right to tragedy', and condemns him to triviality. The absurd, inconsequential nature of history is further illustrated in Kundera's works by the process of 'forgetting', whereby the past, both personal and political, is rewritten; this theme was to have particular resonance after 1968, during the rule of President Husák, 'the president of forgetting'. *The Joke* was once described as a 'major indictment of Stalinism', but Kundera was quick to interject on this occasion, 'Spare me your Stalinism, please. *The Joke* is a love story!' An erotic element has always been central to Kundera's fiction, and the many graphic scenes of physical love that have featured in his works have been justified by him as a way of bringing out the essence of a character or a situation. These scenes have doubtless contributed to the vast sales of Kundera's works, sales that show him in Britain at least to be the most popular of all modern foreign authors.

Eroticism of a more playful and less pretentious kind features in the novels and stories of Bohumil Hrabal (1914–), who is thought of in Czechoslovakia itself as the grand old man of Czech letters, and has in many ways been the most influential of all Czech writers since the war. Though he graduated in law at Prague University, he was never able to practise as a lawyer after 1939, and worked from 1948 onwards in an astonishing variety of jobs, including as a clerk, a railway lineman, a train dispatcher, a stage-hand, a postman, a steel-worker, a travelling salesman, and as a dealer in scrap paper: it was while working in the latter capacity that he first came to know Škvorecký, whose duties at a publishing house included delivering obsolete galley proofs to the scrap-paper salvage centre. Hrabal, whose first novel was not be published until 1963, was to remain in Czechoslovakia after 1968, though many of his works had to be adapted to meet the requirements of the censor. Notorious even today as a habitué of Prague's pubs, he married a waitress who could have come straight out of one of his works, and prefers to refer to himself as a reporter of pub stories than as a writer. His down-to-earth humour, use of slang, and love of pubs have led to comparisons with Hašek, but his extraordinary fantasy, taste for 'Chaplinesque' slapstick, and special, almost untranslatable way of using Czech, make him closer in spirit to Vančura. Fame and a devoted readership came to him with the publication in 1965 of his novella, *Closely Observed Trains*, which, though a much tamer version of an earlier story of his called *The Legend of Cain*, displayed an irreverence towards war which far surpassed Škvorecký's. Set in a provincial railway station, it deals with an adolescent boy whose euphoria at overcoming a problem of premature ejaculation leads him to commit an unpremeditated act of patriotism. Perhaps Hrabal's greatest achievement to date is his novel, *I Served the King of England*, which was the only one of his works which he resolutely refused to have altered in any way. To try and escape the attentions of the censor, he sneakily, and with typical 'Hrabalian' wit, allowed the work to be published as a special bulletin of the Jazz Section of the Czech Musicians's Union. Dedicated to the 'Readers of the Jazz Section so that they might have some fun', the work is a humorous and grotesquely distorted view of Czech history from the 1920s onwards as seen through the eyes of a diminutive waiter with a preternatural gift for survival and the giving of sexual pleasure. After distinguishing himself in the course of an extravagant banquet put on in a grand Prague hotel for the Emperor of Ethiopia, the waiter then goes on to marry a German woman who ends the war with her head blown off but still clutching to her hands a precious stamp album confiscated from a wealthy Jew. The sale of this album turns the protagonist briefly into a millionaire, but he finishes his life clearing remote forest roads in southern Bohemia, possessing little more than his memories of the past, and an ability to contemplate the world with serene detachment.

The 1960s were a golden age not only for Czech fiction, but also for Czech theatre and cinema. The exciting theatrical life of this period was concentrated on the many small theatres that grew up from the 1950s onwards and included such places as Semafor, The Theatre on the Balustrade, The Činoherní Klub and the Theatre beyond the Gate, the latter being run by the charismatic actor and present director of Prague's National Theatre, Otomar Krejča. The actor, singer, poet and writer Jiří Suchý (1931–) joined forces with the composer Jiří Šlitr to form the 'S & S' duo, which carried on the tradition of 'V & W' and the Liberated Theatre; another major theatrical figure of this time was Ivan Vyskočil (1929–), a writer of experimental prose who displayed eccentric brilliance but complete impracticality during his period as a director of The Theatre on the Balustrade. Semafor, under the creative domination of 'S & S', was the most popular and influential of the small theatres, but the Theatre of the Balustrade is today the most famous of these places owing to its associations with Václav Havel (1936–). The son of a distinguished civil engineer whose brother had been one of the creators of Prague's Barrandov film studios, Havel worked initially as an apprentice and later a laboratory technician at the Czech Technical High School at Prague. He published his first works of journalism in 1955, and was to continue writing for a number of periodicals, mainly literary and theatrical, up to 1969. From the start he showed a strong political bent, and made his first public appearance with a highly critical address given at a working party of new authors at the Dobříš Writers' Home near Prague. Hindsight has led some Czechs to suggest that Havel subsequently became involved in the theatre principally as a way of entering into politics. After being turned down as a student at both the Film and Drama Faculties of Prague's Performing Arts Academy, Havel joined the Theatre at the Balustrade in 1960, working initially as a stage-hand and later as a literary adviser and assistant producer; his first play, *The Garden Party* was performed here in 1963. In common with the Liberated Theatre of the 1920s, The Theatre at the Balustrade developed a speciality in the drama of the Absurd, and in the course of the 1960s put on important productions of works by both Alfred Jarry and Samuel Beckett. Havel's own plays maintained this absurdist vein, but used it to comment on life under totalitarianism.

International interest in the great cultural developments that were taking place in Czechoslovakia from the late 1950s onwards was stimulated above all by the cinema of this period. The promising tendencies that had emerged in Czech cinema in the late 1930s had still been very much in evidence in the years immediately after the war, with Czech directors continuing to show poetic lyricism and an ability to transpose good literature to the screen. One of the more important films of these years was *The Strike* (1946), which was the first and only Czech film to win a Golden Lion award at the Venice Film Festival; this adaptation by Karel Steklý (born 1903) of a popular novel about a miner's life by Marie Majerová (1882–1967) combined social pathos with avant-garde poetics. The Second World War— which was to be the main theme of Czech and Slovak films right up to the end of the 1950s—was the subject of two other outstanding films of these years, *Silent Barricade* (1948) by Otakar Vávra (1911–), and *Stolen Frontier* (1947), which was the story of a Czech frontier village after the Munich agreement, and the first full-length work by Jiří Weiss (1913–). Alfréd Radok (1914–76), for whom Havel was to work in the 1960s at the Theatre of the Balustrade, was one of the more interesting directors to emerge during the Stalinist years, and made in 1953 the first Czechoslovak musical, *The Magic Hat*; another pioneering work of his, *The Distant Journey* (1950), was an expressionistic tale of the Terezín ghetto inspired to a large extent by surrealist poetics, but was immediately banned for being 'existentialistic'. One of the main outlets for the visionary and avant-garde imagination during this repressive period was the medium of animated film, the greatest practitioners of which were Jiří Trnka (1912–70) and Karel Zeman (1910–), both of whom worked at the celebrated animated studios that had been established in the 1930s by Tomáš Baťa at Zlín. The relaxation of censorship after 1956 saw the beginnings of a renascence in Czech cinema, as well as the emergence of the first major work of Slovak cinema, *Forty-four* (1957), a powerful work by Palo Bielik (1910–) based on a suppressed revolt of Slovak soldiers during the First World War. The attention of the world, however, was directed to Czechoslovakia at this time not by any one film but by a revolutionary new art form devised by Alfréd Radok in 1958 and involving a mixture of cinema and theatre. Known as *The Magic Theatre*, it enjoyed a great success at the Brussels World Exhibition of 1958, and introduced the world to one of the future protagonists of the Czech New Wave, Miloš Forman (1932–).

From the time of Devětsil, literature in Czechoslovakia had been closely associated with the cinema, but this was particularly true of the 1960s, when leading writers such as Škvorecký, Kundera and Hrabal played an important role in the history of the New Wave. The main characteristics of the films of this period were those that had informed some of the greatest works of Czech literature, notably a concentration on scenes of ordinary life and a transformation of reality through elements of fantasy and whimsical humour. Another feature of the New Wave was the extensive use of non-professional actors, a feature which had been common to British and Italian realist films of the post-war period, but had been frowned upon, curiously, by the advocates of 'socialist realism', who demanded both professional actors and theatrical acting: Jiří Weiss, in his film *The Last Shot* (1950), which showed the end of the war in a large steel mill, had been criticised for a lack of pathos and for giving leading roles to amateurs. The first key film of the New Wave was *Sunshine in a Net* (1963) by the Slovak director Štefan Uher (1930–), a work which did away with dramatic conventions of plot and with political opportunism to concentrate instead on the inner life of ordinary people and to show on the screen aspects of the true face of economic reality. Other Slovak directors of this decade included Elo Havetta (died 1975), a former graphic artist whose best known film was *Party in the Botanical Garden* (1969), a joyful and anarchical protest against pettiness, filled with surreal images inspired by rural life in the Slovakian hill country. The creation of the New Wave, however, was essentially the work of Czech directors, one of whom was Jan Němec, whose *Report on the Party and the Guests* (1966) was a morality play dealing with the way 'ordinary' people can become indifferent to the fate of others and even willingly accept force and violence: this parable, set at a large outdoor banquet, and culminating with a pack of dogs chasing the one guest who decides to make his escape, was not allowed to be shown in Czechoslovakia until the Prague Spring of 1968, after which it was immediately banned once more.

The two Czech film directors of this period with the greatest international reputation were Miloš Forman and Jiří Menzel (1938–). Forman's first feature film was the story of a boy informer *Black Peter* (1963), but he came to international prominence with *A Blonde in Love* (1965), a charming comedy of small town life. The town in question, featuring a shoe factory employing hundreds of women, has a serious shortage of men, and asks the army to supply the missing 'male element', but, instead of receiving young soldiers, is sent a unit of middle-aged reservists. This witty satire on bureaucracy's absurd ways of coping with emotional human needs, is full of vivid observations of everyday life, as, for instance, in a famous scene when an idyllic erotic encounter between the eponymous blonde and a touring piano player is constantly interrupted by a malfunctioning blind. Forman returned to the absurdities of provincial life in the last film which he was to make in Czechoslovakia, *The Fireman's Ball* (1967), which, taking as its subject a dance and beauty competition organised by the dignitaries of a fire brigade, hilariously shows up bureaucratic stupidity, incompetence and dullness.

Fantasy, surreal comedy, and a poetic obsession with the absurd minutiae of everyday life, come together in the work of Menzel, one of whose most famous films, *Capricious Summer* (1967) is based on Vančura's novel about a circus troupe in the country. But of all the authors whom Menzel adapted, the one whose vision most closely corresponded to his own was Bohumil Hrabal. Menzel's version of *Closely Observed Trains* (1966), which Hrabal claimed to prefer to his own novella, was the most successful Czech film of this period, and won an Oscar for the Best Foreign Film. Its accumulation of detail builds up to a remarkably evocative picture of a provincial Czech railway station, but each of these details is loaded with suggestions, as for instance the waiting-room sofa which is torn in the course of the boy's momentous first sexual encounter. Or again, the bilingual rubber stamps of the stationmaster, which are pressed on one notorious occasion on a girl's naked bottom, a moment which is not only intensely erotic but also serves to ridicule bureaucracy, for the man who has used the stamps in this way is later accused not of a sexual offence but of abusing the German language; furthermore a pun was also intended, the Czech expression 'heading for the arse' meaning 'heading for disaster', a reference in this case to the German armies. Menzel, an actor who directed plays as well as films, was very keen to take on the part of the boy in *Closely Observed*

Trains, though, as Škvorecký noted in his short book on the making of this film, this was probably less for artistic reasons than to have an excuse to go to bed with the girl, if only in the studio; in the end he had to content himself with the Freudian role of doctor-confessor. Škvorecký's own work provided Menzel with the subjects of two of his films, and in 1968 preparations were going ahead for Menzel's projected film version of *The Cowards*, which would have featured the daughter of bandy-legged Irena playing her own mother. The arrival of Soviet troops in August of that year sadly interrupted these whimsical plans.

The impact of the Soviet invasion of 1968 on the cultural life of Czechoslovakia was scarcely less dramatic than that of the Battle of the White Mountain in 1620, though fortunately the effects were not to be so long-lasting. Virtually all the main films of the Czech New Wave were immediately banned, as were most of the writers who come to prominence in this decade. Škvorecký emigrated in 1969 to Canada, where his wife was to found *Sixty-Eight Publishers*, which brought out much of the Czech and Slovak literature to be written during the 1970s and 80s. Kundera remained in Czechoslovakia until 1975, deprived of his post as a teacher, and seeing all his books removed from public libraries; eventually he settled in Paris, where his combination of intellectual and sexual concerns, together with the mystique of being a banned writer, were soon to turn him into a hero for the French. One of those who stayed resolutely on in Czechoslovakia was Jaroslav Seifert, and Škvorecký was later to write that the one good consequence of the Soviet invasion was to have 'put the incapacitated old poet back on his feet'. The arrival of Soviet tanks so incensed him that he made his way soon afterwards on crutches to the Writer's Club on the Old Town Square and had himself elected the union's chairman, in the place of someone who had had to flee the country; he vigorously promoted the cause of writers for the remaining nine months of the union's existence, and was later to become a signatory of Charter 77. He was to cause further embarrassment to the government when in 1984 he was awarded the Nobel Prize for Literature.

Václav Havel, after suffering from bleak depression in the early 1970s, when he spent long periods of isolation in his country cottage in northern Bohemia, took an increasingly active part in underground resistance after 1975, eventually becoming one of the main organisers of Charter 77, for which he was later to be sentenced for four years in prison. While in prison he was allowed to write one four-page letter a week to his wife Olga, but these had to refer only to 'family matters' and to conform to such other absurd rules as not having any deletions, underlinings, or quotation marks; these limitations forced Havel to write in a cryptic and abstract style which is at times barely comprehensible but was none the less to enhance his reputation as a thinker. The letters, which were eventually published in English as *Letters to Olga* (1988), circulated in Czechoslovakia in what is known as a *samizdat* edition, a typewritten edition of about twelve copies which were passed on secretly from one person to another. This form of publishing, born in this country at the beginning of the 1970s, had acquired a remarkably wide currency in the wake of Charter 77, and was the principle means by which the principal Czech and Slovak writers continued to function within Czechoslovakia. The main *samizdat* organisation was *Padlock Editions*, which published the circle of the most strictly forbidden authors, among whom were Pavel Kohout (1928–), Ludvík Vaculík

(1926–) and Ivan Klíma (1931). All these authors were associated with the revival of the *feuilleton*, but it was Vaculík who perfected the genre, writing essays that are models of irony, wit and concision, as for instance in his collection *A Cup of Coffee with My Interrogator*, 1986). However, the 'Padlock' author who is at present enjoying the most popularity is Klíma, a former journalist whose novels and short stories bring together that characteristically Czech mixture of amorous intrigue, ironic reflection, and a sense of the poetry and absurdity of everyday life. His most recent novel is *Love and Garbage* (1986), which, adopting a narrative technique similar to that of Jiří Weil in *Life with a Star*, blends memories of a passionate, adulterous affair with philosophical reflections, and descriptions of a writer working as a refuse collector. Another author who was banned for many years after 1968 is Miroslav Holub (1923–), a practising immunologist who is also the greatest Czech poet working today. Associated at one time with a literary group called Poetry of Everyday, he uses frequent medical analogies in his work and dissects human experience with the economy and precision of a pathologist.

The inauguration of Václav Havel as president of Czechoslovakia has been seen by some as this playwright's culminating achievement as a dramatist of the Absurd. Havel's writings now dominate the bookshops, and an old script of his has just been filmed by Jiří Menzel, who is making his comeback to the cinema after an enforced absence of over twenty years. The future of the arts in Czechoslovakia would seem assured, and yet the irony is that in this time of both freedom and economic recession, financial rather than cultural matters have assumed a more pressing importance. The main theatres are half full, the film studios at Barrandov have been reduced to the making of only five films a year, and publishing houses have of necessity become very commercially-minded. There is at least the consolation that the absurdities, contradictions and reversals of fortune within the new Czechoslovakia must surely be providing abundant material for the Czech and Slovak writers of the future.

Bibliography

General and History

Bailey, Anthony, *Along the Edge of the Forest: An Iron Curtain Journey*, London, 1983
Brook, Stephen, *The Double Eagle: Vienna, Budapest, Prague*, London, 1988
Buber-Neumann, Margarete, *Milena*, London, 1988
Evans, R.J.W., *Rudolf II and his World: A Study in Intellectual History, 1576–1612*, Oxford, 1973
Frankland, Mark, *The Patriots' Revolution: How East Europe won its freedom*, London, 1990
Garton Ash, Timothy, *The Uses of Adversity: Essays on the Fate of Central Europe*, Cambridge 1989
Garton Ash, Timothy, *We The People: The Revolution of '89*, Cambridge, 1990
Glenny, Misha, *The Rebirth of History: Eastern Europe in the Age of Democracy*, London, 1990
Granta 30: The New Europe!, Cambridge, 1990
Havel, Václav, *Letters to Olga*, London, 1988

Havel, Václav, *Living in Truth* (ed. by Jan Vladislav), London, 1987
Havel, Václav, *Disturbing the Peace*, London, 1990
Humphreys, Rob (ed.), *The Rough Guide to Czechoslovakia*, London, 1991
Jirásek, Alois, *Stories and Legends of Old Prague*
Leigh Fermor, Patrick, *A Time of Gifts*, London, 1977
Lützow, Count Francis, *Master John Hus*, London, 1909
Lützow, Count Francis, *Bohemia*, London, 1896
Margolius Kovaly, Heda, *Prague Farewell*, London, 1988
Magris, Claudio, *Danube: A Sentimental Journey from the Source to the Black Sea*, London, 1989
Masaryk, Tomáš, *The Meaning of Czech History*, University of North Carolina, 1974
Mucha, Jiří, *Living and Partly Living*, London, 1968
Muir, Edwin, *An Autobiography*, London, 1980
Renner, Hans, *A History of Czechoslovakia since 1945*, London, 1989
Seton-Watson, R.W., *The History of the Czechs and Slovaks*, London, 1943
Seton-Watson, R.W. (ed.), *Slovakia Then and Now*, London, 1931
Shawcross, William, *Dubček and Czechoslovakia (1918–1990)*, London, 1990
Zeman, Zbyněk, *Prague Spring: A report on Czechoslovakia 1968*, Harmondsworth
Zeman, Zbyněk, *The Masaryks: The making of Czechoslovakia*, London, 1990
Wiskemann, Elizabeth, *Czechs and Germans*, London, 1985
Young, Edgar, *Czechoslovakia*, London, 1938

Art and Architecture

Bachmann, Erich, *Gothic Art in Bohemia: Architecture, Sculpture and Painting*, London
Baroque in Bohemia, Exhibition Catalogue, Victoria and Albert Museum, London, 1969
Bialostocki, Jan, *The Art of the Renaissance in Eastern Europe: Hungary, Bohemia, Poland*, London, 1976
Blažíček, Oldřich, *Baroque Art in Bohemia*, London, 1968
Cannon-Brookes, Peter, *Czech Sculpture, 1800–1938*, London
Czech Functionalism, Exhibition Catalogue, Architectural Association, London, 1987
Czech Modernism, 1900–1945, Exhibition Catalogue, Phoenix, Arizona
Denkstein, V., and Matous, A., *Gothic Art of South Bohemia*, Prague, 1955
Denkstein, Vladimír (ed.), *Great Centres of Art: Prague*, London, 1979
Devětsil: Czech avant-garde architecture and design of the 1920s and 30s, Exhibition catalogue, Museum of Modern Art, Oxford, 1990
Hempel, E., *Baroque Art and Architecure in Central Europe*, Harmondsworth, 1965
Hořejší, Jiřina, et al, *Renaissance Art in Bohemia*, London, 1979
Knox, Brian, *The Architecture of Prague and Bohemia*, London, 1962
Laing, Alastair, 'Central and Eastern Europe' in Blunt, Anthony (ed.), *Baroque and Rococo: Architecture and Decoration*, London, 1978
Mencl, Václav, *Czech Architecture of the Luxemburg Period*, Prague, 1955

Mucha Jiří, *Alphonse Mucha*, London, 1966
Teige, Karel, *Modern Czechoslovak Architecture*, London, 1947

Literature and Film

Čapek, Karel, *Toward the Radical Center: A Karel Čapek reader* (ed. Peter Kussi), New Jersey, 1990
Comenius, *The Labyrinth of the World and the Paradise of the Heart* (1631), trans. Lützow, Count F., 1950
Hašek, Jaroslav, *The Good Soldier Švejk and His Fortunes in the World War*, London, 1973
Hašek, Jaroslav, *The Red Commissar*, London, 1983
Havlíček Borovský, Karel, *The Conversion of St. Vladimir* (1876), tr., Altschul, E., Cleveland, 1930
Holub, Miroslav, *Vanishing Lung Syndrome*, London, 1990
Hrabal, Bohumil, *A Close Watch on the Trains*, London, 1968
Hrabal, Bohumil, *The Death of Mr Baltisberger*, London, 1990
Hrabal, Bohumil, *I Served the King of England*, London, 1989
Hrabal, Bohumil, *Too Loud a Solitude*, London, 1991
Kafka, Franz, *Stories, 1904–1924*, London, 1981
Kafka, Franz, *The Collected Novels of Franz Kafka*, Harmondsworth
Klíma, Ivan, *My Merry Mornings*, London, 1986
Klíma, Ivan, *My First Loves*, London, 1986
Klíma, Ivan, *A Summer Affair*, London, 1987
Klíma, Ivan, *Love and Garbage*, London, 1990
Kundera, Milan, *The Farewell Party*, London, 1977
Kundera, Milan, *The Book of Laughter and Forgetting*, London, 1982
Kundera, Milan, *The Joke*, London, 1983
Kundera, Milan, *The Unbearable Lightness of Being*, London, 1984
Kundera, Milan, *Life is Elsewhere*, London, 1986
Kundera, Milan, *The Art of the Novel*, London, 1988
Kundera, Milan, *Immortality*, London, 1991
Liehm, Antonín and Mira, *The Most Important Art: Soviet and Eastern European Film after 1945*, University of California Press, 1977
Lustig, Arnost, *Diamonds of the Night*, London, 1989
Lützow, Count Francis, *A History of Bohemian Literature*, London
Mňačko, Ladislav, *The Taste of Power*, London
Mňačko, Ladislav, *Death is Called Engelchen*, Prague, 1961
Němcová, Božena, *The Grandmother: A story of country life* (1855), trans. by Gregor, Frances, Chicago, 1891
Němcová, Jeanne W. (ed.), Czech and Slovak Short Stories, London, 1967
Neruda, Jan, *Tales of the Little Quarter* (1878, trans., Pargeter, E., Prague, 1957
Parrott, Sir Cecil, *The Bad Bohemian: the extraordinary life of Jaroslav Hašek, author of The Good Soldier Švejk*, London, 1978
Pavel, Ernst, *The Nightmare of Reason: A Life of Franz Kafka*, London, 1988
Pynsent, Robert, *Modern Slovak Prose: fiction since 1954*, London, 1991
Seifert, Jaroslav, *The Selected Poetry of Jaroslav Seifert* (ed. Gibian, George), London, 1986
Škvorecký, Josef, *The Cowards*, London, 1958
Škvorecký, Josef, *The Mournful Demeanour of Lieutenant Borůvka*, London, 1973
Škvorecký, Josef, *Miss Silver's Past*, London, 1974
Škvorecký, Josef, *The Bass Saxophone*, London, 1978

Škvorecký, Josef, *The Swell Season: A Text on the Most Important Things in Life*, London, 1983
Škvorecký, Josef, *Dvořák in Love*, London, 1989
Škvorecký, Josef, *The Engineer of Human Souls*, London, 1985
Škvorecký, Josef, *Talkin' Moscow Blues*, London, 1989
Škvorecký, Josef, *The Miracle Game*, London, 1991
Vaculík, Ludvík, *A Cup of Coffee with my Interrogator*, London, 1987

Language

By *Elizabeth Brimelow*

Czech and Slovak. There is no such language as Czechoslovak. There is Czech, and there is Slovak: two distinct languages, though very closely related. Both are members of the western Slavonic group of languages. Czech is the language of Bohemia and Moravia. Slovak is the language of Slovakia.

Czech speakers easily understand Slovak, and vice versa. Visitors do not need to struggle with both, and therefore these notes on language deal only with Czech.

Czech grammar is complex, in the manner of other highly inflected Indo-European languages. Nouns and adjectives decline in seven cases; adjectives agree with nouns in number, case and gender; verb forms reflect both tense and aspect. However, no-one will expect a visitor, using a phrase-book, to have got to grips with all this.

Czech spelling and pronunciation. Czech uses the Latin alphabet. The orthography, reformed by Jan Hus at the start of the fifteenth century, provides admirable consistency in spelling and pronunciation. To English eyes it appears dense and prickly, but it is not as difficult as it looks.

The following is a simplified guide. Approximate transliterations of Czech words are given in square brackets.

Vowels

a	Southern English 'u' as in 'cup', or Northern English short 'a' as in 'grass'.
	e.g. ano [u-no], yes
á	a as in 'half'
	e.g. dáma [dah-ma], lady
e	e as in 'mend'
	e.g. den [den], day
é	no real equivalent in English: roughly like the first part of the vowel sound in 'there' or 'pear'
	e.g. léto [leh-to], summer
ě	ye as in 'yet'
	e.g. pět [pyet], five
i	i as in 'pit'
	e.g. pivo [pi-vo], beer
í	ee as in 'need'
	e.g. víno [vee-no], wine
o	o as in 'not'
	e.g. okno [ok-no], window

ó	aw as in 'claw'
	e.g. móda [maw-da], fashion
u	southern English u as in 'put' or oo as in 'book'
	e.g. ruka [ru-ka], hand
ů or ú	oo as in 'school'
	e.g. dům [doom], house
	údolí [oo-do-lee], valley
y, ý	exactly the same as i, í

The letters l and r can do duty as vowels and form a syllable when standing between two other consonants:

> e.g.   Brno [Br-no], the chief city of Moravia
> vlk [vlk], wolf

(cf. American pronunciation of 'missile' or 'turn')

Diphthongs

Unlike in English, both letters of a diphthong are pronounced equally clearly.

au	ow as in 'now'
	e.g. auto [ow-to], car
ou	o as in a Northern English 'oh'
	e.g. houska [hoh-ska], bread roll
eu	does not occur in any single English word; rather like the vowels in Northern English 'Eh up'
	e.g. pneumatika [pneoo-ma-ti-ka], tyre

Consonants

Generally the same or nearly the same as in English, but there are exceptions:

c	ts as in 'oats'
	e.g. co [tso], what
č	ch as in 'child'
	e.g. český [che-skee], Czech
g	always hard as in 'get', never soft as in 'general'
	e.g. guma [goo-mah], rubber
j	y as in 'you'
	e.g. jak [yak], how
	kraj [krai], region (rhymes with 'try')
	olej [o-lei], oil (rhymes with 'pray')
ch	Scottish ch as in 'loch'
	e.g. chléb [khlehb], bread
r	Rolled Scottish r as in red
	e.g. ryba [ri-ba], fish
ř	No equivalent in English; combines a rolled Scottish *r* with the zh sound as in 'pleasure'
	e.g. řeka [rzhe-ka], river
š	sh as in 'she'
	e.g. šest [shest], six
ž	the zh sound in 'pleasure'
	e.g. žena [zhe-na], woman

d, t, and n, if followed by i or í, are softened, i.e. pronounced as though there was an (English) y after the consonant:

> e.g.   divadlo [dyi-va-dlo], theatre
> titulek [tyi-tu-lek], headline, caption
> není [ne-nyee], it isn't, there isn't

These consonants may also occasionally be softened other than when followed by i or í; this is indicated by an apostrophe after the consonant or, for the letter n, a háček above it

    e.g. loď, boat
          zbraň, weapon

Stress and intonation. The main stress in Czech always falls on the first syllable of the word.

Stressed syllables can be either long or short. So can unstressed ones. The idea of unstressed long syllables may seem odd, but they occur in English too: try saying 'always', or 'for his part' with the stress on 'his'.

Unstressed syllables don't get reduced and distorted as they do in English; e.g. in the word 'matka' [mat-ka] (mother) the second letter 'a' is pronounced in exactly the same way as the first. The word is not pronounced 'Maht-ker' as it probably would be in English.

Intonation is roughly like English: down at the end of a sentence for a statement, up at the end for a question.

Some useful phrases

Mluvíte anglicky? [mloo-vee-te ang-glits-ki] Do you speak English?

Nerozumím Česky. [ne-ro-zoo-meem che-ski] I don't understand Czech.

Rozumíte? [ro-zoo-mee-te] Do you understand?

Jsem Angličan(ka) [Y-sem An-gli-chan(ka)] I am English (the 'ka' ending is used if the speaker is a woman).

Ano [a-no], Yes

Ne [ne], No

Prosím [pro-seem], Please

Děkuji (mockrát) [dye-koo-yi mots-kraht], Thank you (very much)

Díky [dyee-kil], Thanks

Dobrý den [do-bree den], How do you do (lit. 'good day', general purpose greeting)

Na shledanou [na-skhle-da-noh], Goodbye, au revoir

Dobrou noc [dob-roh nots], Goodnight

Kdy? v kolik hodin? [gdi? fko-lik ho-dyin?], When? At what time?

Jak dlouho? [yak dloh-ho], How long (i.e. time)

Kde? [gde], Where?

Kde mohu koupit...? [gde mo-hu koh-pit], Where can I buy...?

Co? [tso], What?

Jak? [yak], How?

Jak se dostanu k...? [yak se do-sta-nu k], How do I get to...?

Smím...? [smeem], May I...

Máte...? [mah-te], Have you got...?

Chtěl bych (chtěla bych)... [khytyel bikh/khtye-la bikh], I would like... (the 'a' on the end is used if the speaker is a woman)

Kolik (stojí...)? [ko-lik sto-yee], How much (does it cost)?

Prosím napište... [pro-seem na-pish-te], Please write (may be helpful if you are getting an answer in Czech which is an address, a number, a date or time of day)

Promiňte [pro-min-te], Excuse me (as in English, this can be used either when accosting or interrupting someone, or as a mild apology.)

Je mi (velice) líto [ye mi ve-li-tse lee-to], I'm (very) sorry

Není zač [ne-nyee zatch], Not at all (lit. 'there is nothing for which', a polite response to thanks or apologies)

Pane, Paní, Slečno [pa-ne, pa-nyee, sletch-no] Mr, Mrs, Miss. Like 'Monsieur' or 'Madame' in French, they can be used with or without a proper name following. They are given here in the vocative case, which is used when you are talking *to* someone rather than about them.

Signs and notices

Pozor, Attention, warning, mind out for…
Vchod, Entrance
Východ, Exit
Otevřeno, Open
Zavřeno, Closed
Zakázán, Forbidden
Vstup zakázán, No admittance
Kouření zakázano, No smoking
Nešlapte (nevstupujte) po trávě, Keep off the grass
Vlevo, Left, to the left
Vpravo, Right, to the right
Záchod, WC
Muži, Men
Páni, Gentlemen
Ženy, Women
Dámy, Ladies
Informace, Information
Zvoňte, Ring
Volný, Free (i.e. vacant, not taken)
Obsazeno, Reserved (table), full up (bus), taken (seat)
Pitná voda, Drinking water
Pokladna, Cash desk, booking office
Platte u pokladny, Pay at the desk
Samoobsluha, Self-service
Šatna, Cloakroom
Objížďka, Diversion
Silnice v opravě (se opravuje), Roadworks, Road up
Letiště, Airport
Nádraží, Railway Station
Nástupiště, Platform
Odjezd, Departure
Příjezd, Arrival
Občerstvení, Refreshments, snack-bar
Čekárna, Waiting room

Simple food and drink

(Bílé/červené) Víno [bee-leh/cher-ve-neh vee-no], (red/white) wine
Pivo [pi-vo], beer
Káva [kah-va], coffee
Čaj [chai], tea
Mléko [mleh-ko], milk
(minerální) voda [mi-ne-rahl-nyee vo-da], (mineral) water

Zmrzlina [zmrz-li-na], ice cream
rohlík, houska [ro-hleek, hoh-ska], bread roll
máslo [mahs-lo], butter
šunka [shoon-ka], ham
sýr [seer], cheese
salát [sa-laht], salad
ovoce [o-vo-tse], fruit

Máte lístek v angličtině? (mah-te lees-tek van glitch-ti-nye]. Have
you got a menu in English?

Prosím, platit [pro-seem pla-tyit], The bill please (lit. 'please, to pay')

Tourist glossary

Ulice, Street
Ulička, Alley
Náměstí, Square
Třída, Avenue
Silnice, Road
Cesta, Path
Kostel, Church
Chrám/katedrála, Cathedral
Kaple, Chapel
Klášter, Monastery
Svatý, Saint
Most, Bridge
Křižovatka, Cross-roads
Nábřeží, Embankment
Trh, Market
Tržiště, Market-place
Kašna, Fountain
Hrad, Castle
Zámek, Château
Palác, Palace
Věž, Tower
Radnice, Town hall
Město, Town
Vesnice, Village
Staré město, Old town
(Historická) Čtvrť, (Historic) quarter
Památky, Monuments, historic buildings
Hřbitov, Cemetery
Zahrada, Garden
Sad, Garden
Muzeum, Museum
Galerie, Gallery
Výstava, Exhibition
Národní, National
Knihovna, Library
Divadlo, Theatre
Opera, Opera
Socha, Statue
Obrazy, Pictures
Lesy, Woods, forest
Hory, Mountains
Kopec, Hill
Vrch, Hill
Důl, Mine

Řeka, River
Pramen, Spring
Mlýn, Mill
Jezero, Lake
Ostrov, Island
Rybník, Man-made lake, fish-pond
Staviště, Landing-stage
Loď, Boat
Průvodce, Guide (either a person or a guidebook)
Kavárna, Café
Restaurace, Restaurant
Hospoda, Inn, tavern
Pošta, Post office
Známky, Stamps
Noviny, Newspapers
Koruna, Crown (Czechoslovak currency)
Haléř, one-hundredth of a Crown
Porucha, Breakdown
Nehoda, Accident
Lékář, Doctor
Policie, Police
Pas, Passport

Numbers

        0 nula [nu-la]
        1 jeden [ye-den]
        2 dva [dva]
        3 tři [trzhi]
        4 čtyři [chti-rzhi]
        5 pět [pyet]
        6 šest [shest]
        7 sedm [se-dum]
        8 osm [o-sum]
        9 devět [de-vyet]
       10 deset [de-set]
       11 jedenáct [ye-de-nahtst]
       12 dvanáct [dva-nahtst]
       13 třináct [trzhi-nahtst]
       14 čtrnáct [chtr-nahtst]
       15 patnáct [pat-nahtst]
       16 šestnáct [shest-nahtst]
       17 sedmnáct [se-dum-nahtst]
       18 osmnáct [o-sum-nahtst]
       19 devatenáct [de-va-te-nahtst]
       20 dvacet [dva-tset]
       30 třicet [trzhi-tset]
       40 čtyřicet [chti-rzhi-tset]
       50 padesát [pa-de-saht]
       60 šedesát [she-de-saht]
       70 sedmdesát [se-dum-de-saht]
       80 osmdesát [o-sum-de-saht]
       90 devadesát [de-va-de-saht]
      100 sto [sto]
     1000 tisíc [tyi-seets]

Intermediate numbers work like English, or, more precisely, like
American English: 127 is said as 'one hundred twenty seven', sto
dvacet sedm (no 'and').

Czechs may however reverse the order of tens and units when saying or writing the words, e.g. 'seven-and-twenty', sedmadvacet (the same words in reverse order, with an 'a' in the middle) as this avoids some grammatical complications. You may therefore hear 'sto sedmadvacet' for 127. If in doubt, ask for the number to be written down.

Days and months

Sunday, neděle [ne-dye-le]
Monday, pondělí [pon-dye-lee]
Tuesday, úterý [oo-te-ree]
Wednesday, středa [strzhe-da]
Thursday, čtvrtek [chtvr-tek]
Friday, pátek [pah-tek]
Saturday, sobota [so-bo-ta]

January, leden [le-den]
February, únor [oo-nor]
March, březen [brzhe-zen]
April, duben [du-ben]
May, květen [kvye-ten]
June, červen [cher-ven]
July, červenec [cher-ve-nets]
August, srpen [sr-pen]
September, září [zah-rzhee]
October, říjen [rzhee-yen]
November, listopad [lis-to-pad]
December, prosinec [pro-si-nets]

Note. Days and months do not have capital letters in Czech.

Food and Drink

Many people visit Czechoslovakia for no better reason than to drink its excellent beer, though it is unlikely that anyone would wish to come here simply for its food. Magdalena Dobromila Rettigová (1785–1845), Bohemia's answer to Mrs Beeton, was a key figure in the Czech National Revival, and saw food as playing an important role in the renewal of her country. However, the food of Bohemia and Moravia did not emerge from centuries of Austrian dominance with an exciting and distinctive character of its own; nor did the food of Slovakia overcome the pervasive influence of Hungary. In the composite country that is Czechoslovakia Slavic, Austrian and Hungarian influences have been blended together to form an amorphous cuisine, a process greatly assisted by the years of Communist rule, when lack of fresh produce and private initiative significantly lessened the scope for regional flair. The cuisine of Czechoslovakia has strong peasant roots, though not in a way which would make it appeal to the fashionable, health-conscious tastes of today: its essential simplicity is frequently disguised by over-rich dressing, and there can be few national cuisines quite as fattening as this one. In contrast to countries such as Italy, Spain or France, a rather hurried attitude to food predominates in Czechoslovakia today, and eating in itself is undertaken less for pleasure than for filling the stomach, or as a means to maintain long bouts of drinking. Heartiness is the key note of Czech and Slovak food, and this is evident even in the breakfasts here, which normally comprise large quantities of ham, eggs, sausages or cheese, and often feature more substantial dishes such as goulash, washed down by large glasses of beer. It is perhaps significant that in Czechoslovakia, as in other Eastern European countries, restaurant menus usually state the exact weight of the food on offer, just as the pubs here always advertise the alcoholic content of the beer they serve. In short this is a country where food is best enjoyed on a cold winter's day, fuelled by considerable quantities of alcohol. Under those circumstances the lavish descriptions of food with which the great drinker and gastronome Jaroslav Hašek larded his *Good Soldier Švejk* begin to sound appetising.

Bacon and above all caraway seed are the ubiquitous flavourings of both Czech and Slovak food, and, as in Russian and Hungarian cooking, soured cream is an accompaniment to numerous dishes. However the first thought which comes to mind at the very mention of Czech food is of dumplings (*knedlíky*), which have the same role in Bohemia and Moravia as chips do in other countries. There are several types of dumplings, including potato dumplings (*Bramborové knedlíky*), plum dumplings (*Švestkové knedlíky*) and, most common of all, a type of dumpling known as *Houskové knedlíky*, which is made in the shape of a Swiss roll from a mixture of flour, eggs and cubes of white bread, and is served in slices that are invariably, though unintentionally, stale; some of the better restaurants will even provide you with a separate tray piled high with a selection of all of these. One of the pleasures of coming to Slovakia from Bohemia and Moravia is that dumplings are not so common here, boiled potatoes and rice being the more usual substitutes. The differences between Czech and Slovak food are otherwise not so great, though the latter tends to be spicier, with a liberal use of paprika as in Hungary. Many of the Slovakian dishes of Hungarian origin such as goulash (*Segedinský guláš*), stuffed peppers (*Plnené papriky*) and paprika chicken (*Kuře na paprice*) have today been incorporated in milder form into Czech cuisine.

Shortly after you sit down in some of the fancier restaurants in Czechoslovakia you are likely to be offered aperitifs from a trolley (see below) followed by a tray of unappealing canapés, for which you will be charged individually; the canapés, of glazed, artificial appearance, invariably feature cream or cream cheese, one of the more popular ones being a ham roll filled with cream cheese and gherkin slices; others are coated with hard lumps of jelly, and should be avoided at all costs. A normal Czech meal, however, begins with a soup, two common soups being potato soup (*Bramborová polévka*) and a thick white soup known as *Kmínová polévka*, both of which are heavily flavoured with caraway seed; a popular clear soup is *Polévka s játrovými knedlíčky*, which is beef broth with little dumplings made from liver, garlic, lemon rind, eggs and breadcrumbs.

The most typical main dish you can eat in Bohemia and Moravia is pork or Frankfurter-style sausage accompanied by dumplings and sauerkraut. Meat is consumed in vast quantities all over Czechoslovakia, and tends to be tough and overcooked. Pork is often served with eggs and ham on top, and, like veal, is frequently dipped in a mixture of flour, breadcrumbs and eggs to form an escalope or *řízek*; a tastier dish is *Vepřová pečené*, or pork roasted with caraway seeds.

Thick fillets of beef piled high with cream and cranberries can be found in the more pretentious establishments, but beef is more commonly served as braised slices in a brown onion sauce (*Dušená rošťenka*) or else as boiled slices in a delicious dill-flavoured white sauce known as *Koprová omáčka*. There are far fewer poultry than meat dishes in Czechoslovakia, and the most usual one is roast chicken (*Pečené kuře*); goose is becoming less common but is traditionally served roast with sauerkraut (*Pečená husa se zelím*). Not even Mrs Rettigova, in her standard book on Bohemian food, could find much to write on fish, which is little eaten here. The best places for finding fish are the Slovak capital of Bratislava—where a number of the restaurants serve pike and trout fished straight from the polluted Danube—and South Bohemia, which abounds in huge ponds where carp is bred. Carp is by far the most popular fish in Czechoslovakia, but even so tends to be eaten mainly as a traditional Christmas Eve dish, when it is served with a near indigestible black sauce made from fish stock, raspberry juice, beer, lemon rind, sugar, honey cake, raisins and almonds (*Kapr na černo*). The great joy of Czechoslovak cuisine, if such an extreme term can be used, is its game, which is the particular speciality of Slovakia and is sometimes roasted over a wood fire and flavoured with juniper berries. Especially good, though difficult to find in restaurants, are the roebuck and—if you can overcome ecological principles and childhood memories of favourite toys—the brown bears.

'A smaller selection is usually possible when it comes to fresh vegetables (sterilised ones are often served even in summer)', writes one of the authors of a government-sponsored guide to Czechoslovakia published in 1989. Fresh fruit and vegetables are now far more widely available than before, but for some reason are still only rarely found in restaurants, where tinned fruit (often served as a mixed compote known as a *Míchaný ovocný kompot*), sauerkraut (*zelí*) and pickled vegetable salads such as *Okurkový salát* (cucumber salad) predominate. Cheese tends to be processed and served in dried-out slices, though in Slovakia you can still find a delicious brine cheese called *brynza*, which is comparable to the Greek *feta*. Puddings are of the hearty kind such as *Povidlový koláč* (plum jam cake) or, more commonly, *palačinky*, pancakes that are usually heaped with mountains of cream and chocolate sauce, and occasionally flambéd. The legacy of Austria is fortunately still apparent in the delectable range of cakes and pastries to be found in the country's cafés and bakeries. The coffee itself, however, is mainly *turecká káva* or Turkish coffee, while the so-called espresso—regarded by many as a more refined alternative—is more often than not tepid instant coffee of insipid flavour.

Drinks. Spirits and liquors tend to be drunk neat as an aperitif or as a beer chaser, one of the most famous being the greenish, herb-flavoured liquor known as *becherovka*, a speciality of the Bohemian spa town of Karlovy Vary (Carlsbad) and reputedly far more beneficial to the health than the town's waters. Most of the Czechoslovak spirits, however, come from Moravia and Slovakia and include plum brandy or *slivovice* (one of the more renowned brands being *jelenec*), and a juniper-flavoured gin known as *borovička* (a particular speciality of the Slovakian town of Trenčín): according to popular tradition a glass of *borovička* drunk half an hour before eating is a considerable aid to the digestion, though its potential beneficial effects are sometimes lost as a result of the hors-d'oeuvres that often come with it. The largest wine-producing area in Czechoslovakia is in southern Slovakia and includes a small part of the famous Tokay vineyard, where Hungary's sweet Tokay and Furmint wines come from; the other Slovakian wines also use the same grapes as those of northern Hungary, for instance Muscat Otonel, Ezerjó, Veltiner, Müller-Thurgau, Italian Riesling and Leányka. The adjoining Moravian vineyards, all of which are to be found south of Brno, are smaller in extent but have a reputation for slightly better wines and excellent Ruländer, Sauvignon, Traminer and Spätburgunder wines are made in places such as Velké Pavlovice, Mikulov, Musov, Znojmo and Pavlovice. Bohemia's small number of wines are grown mainly around Mělník, an area which was planted with Burgundy grapes during the reign of Charles IV. Wines throughout Czechoslovakia are drunk principally in the setting of a *vinárna* or Wine Bar (see below), but there is a pleasant tradition common to both Slovakia and Moravia (in particular in Brno, Bratislava and Nitra) of friends and families coming together for bouts of intensive drinking in small private cellars. However, wine here is less commonly drunk than beer, which is by far the most popular drink in Czechoslovakia, and the usual accompaniment to meals. When it comes to discussing Czech beer, superlatives can at last be used with complete honesty, for it is generally agreed to be the best in the world, and has a reputation going back to the Middle Ages. Beer is made throughout the country, and dark as well as light beer can be found here, as can a number of small breweries, some of which are attached to their own pubs. However the general consensus of opinion is that the finest are the light and creamy ones from the Bohemian towns of České Budějovice (the original Budweiser) and, above all, Plzeň, where the *Prazdroj* or *Urquell* brew served as the prototype for Pils-style beers throughout the world; the most famous of the Slovak Beers is *Zlatý Bažant* (Golden Pheasant) from the small town of Hurbanovo.

A few words should finally be said about the actual places where you can eat and drink in Czechoslovakia. The smartest of the restaurants, bars and night-clubs here prefer their clients to be formally dressed (this is particularly true outside of Prague), and all of them have cloakrooms, where you are obliged to leave your coats immediately on entering; booking is advisable in the large towns, and essential in Prague, particularly in the summer, when you often have to reserve a table up to one week in advance. Many of the principal restaurants in the cities, and virtually all of those in the villages and small towns, are attached to dreary modern hotels, but these places are often animated in the evenings by local bands that will appeal to lovers of Czech films such as *The Fireman's Ball* (see Literature and Cinema). The wine-bars or *vinárna* are smart establishments generally situated in historic cellars, and always providing food, though they will never serve you with beer. The modest restaurants, pubs and beer-cellars are invariably the liveliest and friendliest of all the eating and drinking establishments here, and their smoke-filled atmosphere, dirty walls and floors, and portly waiters or waitresses who will slam a large glass of beer on to your table often without your asking for it, are an intrinsic part of their charm; food is served at most of the pubs and beer-cellars and is usually no worse, and certainly far cheaper, than in the more pretentious establishments. The hurried tourist could snatch a bite at a *bufet*, a self-service establishment where you are generally obliged to eat standing up; an *automat* is the same but with cold rather than hot food. Even more time could be saved at one of the many outdoor kiosks, which specialise in *bramborák* (a type of potato pancake) and Frankfurter-style sausages (*klobása*), the latter served on a paper plate together with a mountain of mustard. A *cukrárna*, which is only open during the day-time, is a café specialising in cakes and pastries. An eating establishment which originated in Slovakia in the early 1960s, but is now also found to a lesser extent in Bohemia and Moravia, is the *Koliba*, a cosy wooden hut usually situated in a bosky setting and supposedly inspired by bandits' encampments of the last century. The gastronomic speciality here is meat grilled or barbecued over a wood fire, most notably 'Robber's steak', which comes accompanied with onions and peppers; to complete the whole macho experience you should drink *hriato*, a warm mixture of alcohol, caramelised sugar and spices served with diced smoky bacon. Unique to Slovakia, and a more genuinely modest establishment than the *Koliba* is the *Salaš*, an imitation of a shepherd's hut and specialising in sheep products, in particular *Bryndzové pirohy s máslom* and *Bryndzové halušky*. These two simple but magnificent dishes, both of which are made from ewe's cheese and sprinkled with diced smoky bacon, feature respectively *tortellini*-like pasta and *gnocchi*-like dumplings; the traditional drink to accompany them is sour sheep's milk.

Menu

Polévky, Soups
Boršč, Beetroot soup
Bramborová, Potato soup
Čočková, Lentil soup
Fazolová, Bean soup
Hovězí, Beef soup
Hrachová, Pea soup
Slepičí, Chicken soup
Rajská, Tomato soup
Zeleninòvá, Vegetable soup

Chléb, Bread
Máslo, Butter
Vejce, Eggs
Niva, Soft blue cheese
Oštěpek, smoked curd cheese
Pivný sýr, Beer-flavoured cheese
Tvaroh, Curd cheese

Maso, Meat
Čevapčici, Spiced meat balls
Hovězí, Beef
Játra, Liver
Kachna, Duck
Klobásy, Sausages
Kuře, Chicken
Salám, Salami
Sekaná, Meat loaf
Slanina, Bacon
Šunka, Ham
Telecí, Veal
Vepřové, Pork

Ryby, Fish
Kapr, Carp
Makrela, Mackerel
Pstruh, Trout
Zavináč, Herring

Zelenina, Vegetables
Brambory, Potatoes (Hranolky, Chips)
Cibule, Onion
Česnek, Garlic
Houby, Mushrooms
Hrášek, Peas
Květák, Cauliflower
Kyselé zelí, Sauerkraut
Lečo, Ratatouille
Mrkev, Carrot
Rajče, Tomato
Špenát, Spinach
Zelí, Cabbage
Žampiony, Champignons

Ovoce, Fruit
Banán, Banana
Broskev, Peach
Citrón, Lemon
Víno, Grapes
Hruška, Pear
Jablko, Apple
Meruňka, Apricot
Pomeranč, Orange
Třešně, Cherry

Nápoje, Drinks
Čaj, Tea
Káva, Coffee
Koňak, Brandy
Minerální voda, Mineral water
Mléko, Milk
Pivo, Beer
Víno, Wine

PRACTICAL INFORMATION

Getting to Czechoslovakia

By *Guy Dixon and Emily Hill*

Information. Čedok, The Czechoslovak Travel Bureau, provides information, and also specialises in all types of holidays and travel in the country. Čedok is at 17–18 Old Bond St, London W1X 4RB (tel. 071-629 6058); 10 East 40th Street, New York NY 10016 (tel. 212/ 689-9720).

By Air. Numerous airlines fly regularly to Prague from most major European airports. ČSA (the Czechoslovakian National Airline) and British Airways operate daily flights between London and Prague (flying time approximately two hours).

ČSA, 12a Margaret St, London W1 (tel. 071-255 1898 for reservations and 071-255 1366 for information). British Airways, 156 Regent St, London W1 (tel. 071-434 4700; for bookings 081-897 4000). Pan Am fly three times a week from the USA.

Prague Ruzyně Airport is situated 20km outside the city centre, connected to two regular bus services. There is a ČSA bus to the centre, which runs from 5.30am to 19.00 and a public transport bus No. 119 (4.30am–23.00) which goes to Dejvická metro station. The journey takes 25 minutes. There is also a taxi-rank immediately outside the airport building.

Passport control takes no longer than in Western airports and customs control is the standard red/green system. The normal airport services are on offer (currency exchange, accommodation office, Post office, car rental and duty-free shop). Porters and trolleys are also available.

By Rail. Prague Hlavní Nádraží is linked to many international railways. The greatest number of Express trains run north to south: Berlin–Prague–Bratislava–Vienna–Budapest. There are also regular trains from the West: Paris–Frankfurt–Prague. A daily London–Prague train (changing in Paris) takes 24 hours. British Rail International, International Rail Centre, Victoria Station, London, SW1V 1JY (tel. 071-834 2345). Eurotrain, 52 Grosvenor Gardens, London SW1W 0AG (tel. 071-730 8518).

At Hlavní Nádraží there is an accommodation office, where a map of the city can be obtained, as well as a currency exchange office. Inter-Rail tickets are now valid in Czechoslovakia.

By Bus. Eurolines, 52 Grosvenor Gardens, London SW1 (tel. 071-730 8235).

By Car or Private Vehicle. Czechoslovakia can be entered at 32 border crossings from all five neighbouring countries: Germany, the USSR, Hungary, Poland and Austria. Most crossings are open 24 hours a day, and petrol and diesel coupons can be purchased here. Third party insurance, a national driving licence and vehicle registration documents are compulsory.

Visas, Customs and Currency

Visas. Visas are no longer required by British and American passport holders to enter Czechoslovakia. British people should note that the one-year Visitors' passport is not valid.

Registration. Visitors must register with the police within 48 hours of arrival. If you are staying at a hotel, botel or campsite registrations will be done for you. The bureaucracy for registration is notoriously slow, and in practice many people do not bother.

Customs. Czechoslovakia has strict regulations on what you can take out of the country, due to the number of visitors from both the West and the East who come to stock up on items that are more expensive or unobtainable in their own country.

The main regulations are: visitors can take out duty-free: food and drink for consumption while travelling, not exceeding 1 litre of spirits, 2 litres of wine, 3 kilos of food and 250 cigarettes (or the equivalent amount in tobacco products); gifts of up to 1000 Kčs in value, provided they are not items subject to export permission, and items bought in the hard-currency duty-free Tuzex shops.

Export permission must be paid on some goods, including leather, sports equipment, electrical household appliances and musical instruments.

The export of the following items is totally prohibited: all foodstuffs, shoes, antiquities, gold and silver products and children's clothes.

Dogs and cats may be imported on production of a veterinary certificate, issued within the previous 48 hours, at the border. It must also have a vaccination certificate.

For customs enquiries, contact the Central Customs Office at Havlíčkova 11 (tel. 232 22 70), or at the airport.

Currency. There is no compulsory currency exchange. There are an increasing number of places to change money, especially in Prague, and a flourishing black market to which the usual warnings apply. The unit of currency is the Czechoslovak crown (Kčs) which contains 100 hellers. There are notes of 10, 20, 50, 100, 500 and 1000 Kčs. Two types of 20 and 50 Kčs notes are in circulation, and it should be noted that the 20 Kčs note is very similar to that for 1000 Kčs.

The use of credit cards is still very limited, apart from hotels and car hire firms, only Tuzex shops and a handful of shops and restaurants accept them. The bank at Na Příkopě 20 will give cash advances on most major credit cards.

Re-exchanging money. This is only possible at banks, and you must have a receipt to prove that you changed money into crowns. You can only take 100 Kčs out of the country.

Where to Stay

Until more hotels are established, it is advisable to book your accommodation well in advance, particularly in the case of Prague. Tour operators include Čedok (tel. 071-629 6058), Regent Holidays UK Ltd (tel. 0272 211711), Explore Worldwide Ltd (tel. 0252 333031), TK Travel (tel. 081-699 8065) and Czechbook Agency (tel. 081-853

1168). Austro Tours (tel. 0727 38191) and Austrian Holidays (tel. 071-439 7108) offer holidays in Prague.

Recently, the shortage of hotel places has been met by a large increase in the availability of private accommodation. Local tourist offices are not yet in a position to supply detailed information on accommodation.

Hotels in Czechoslovakia are converting to the international star system, though many still maintain the old grading system. A one-star hotel is a C grade, two-star is B grade, three-star is B*, four-star is A*, and five-star A* de luxe.

Tourist-class hotels. New commercial agencies offer accommodation in the lower grade hotels. These hotels do not have private facilities, and they charge extra for the use of showers.

Private rooms/flats. These are usually with Czechoslovak families, though you are guaranteed your own key and freedom of movement. They are obtainable through agencies, though you may get a better deal from people letting rooms independently. Look out for the *Zimmer frei* signs on private houses.

Hostels. CKM (Cestovní kancelář mládeže) run a chain of Junior Hotels (for all ages) with excellent basic B grade facilities with additional temporary, hostels during the summer months. YHA card-holders should get a reduction. Pressure on places is high, so it is wise to book in advance.

Botels. These are boats on the Vltava in Prague and on the Danube in Bratislava which have been converted into hotels. Botels sound more romantic than they actually are.

Camping. Autokemping campsites are usually only open over the summer. There are two grades—A and B—and both are basic. The minimum facilities are toilet and washroom. Food can often be bought on the site, although cooking facilities are rare.

Useful Addresses. For information on hostels: CKM, Žitná 12, Praha 1; for camping: Sportourist, Národní 33, Praha 1.

Getting Around

Czechoslovakia has an extensive railway and bus network. Travel is cheap and efficient. Generally speaking travel by bus is faster, although slightly more expensive.

By Rail. The railway network, connecting all the country's main centres, is operated by the Czechoslovakian State Railways (ČSD; Československé státní dráhy) connecting all the country's main centres. *Expres, Rychlík* and *Osobní* are the different categories of trains. Expres trains are the fastest, but you have to pay a surcharge. It is advisable to avoid the much slower Osobní trains, unless you have plenty of time to spare.

There is an information office where English is spoken at Hlavní Nádraží, the main station in Prague (tel. 23 64 441). Tickets are normally purchased at the station, but you can book in advance at Čedok, and other travel agencies, for a surcharge. Reservations are required for international train journeys, and these can be made at the station. You must also book in advance for couchettes.

The four main stations in Prague are Hlavní Nádraží and Holešovice (for international trains and most long-distance national routes), Smíchov and Masarykovo Nádraží. All four stations are on metro lines.

By Bus. Regional buses are operated by the Czechoslovak State Bus Company (ČSAD, Československá státní automobilová doprava). Tickets are normally bought from the driver as you get on; however, on more popular routes (e.g. Prague–Karlovy Vary) and at weekends it is advisable to buy tickets in advance at the station. International and long-distance buses go from the central bus station at Florenc (metro lines B and C). There is an information office here, but little English is spoken.

By Air. ČSA operate flights from Prague to the main provincial centres, which can be booked through ČSA or Čedok.

Motoring. Although roads are more basic than in the West, and the surfaces not always good, the road network is extensive and the volume of traffic low. The country's only motorways connect the three major cities of Prague, Brno and Bratislava. There is no toll.

Most road signs follow the international system.

Documentation. A valid national driving licence is sufficient, although an International Driving Licence is safer. You also need vehicle registration and proof of insurance. Always carry your passport.

Traffic regulations. The wearing of seatbelts in the front seat is now compulsory at all times. The speed limit in urban areas is 60kmph (37mph); on open roads it is 90kmph (56mph), and on motorways 110kmph (68mph). There are frequent police radar checks. Motorcyclists should keep their headlights on dip during daylight hours, and must wear helmets and goggles.

There is a total ban on alcohol while driving. Drinking and driving is regarded as a very serious offence.

Accidents. Accidents should be immediately reported to the nearest police station to determine damages and liability. All damages must be reported to the Czechoslovak State Insurance Company, Spálená 14, Praha 1 (tel. 214 81 11). The AA provide a Five-Star insurance scheme that protects against the cost of repairs and any other emergencies.

Fuel. Foreigners cannot pay for fuel in crowns. Petrol and diesel can only be obtained with special coupons, sold at border crossings, exchange offices and hotels. For visitors with convertible currencies the price of fuel is based on the average prices in Austria and Germany. Petrol stations are less frequent than in the West, so it is advisable to fill up. The three types of petrol available are Super (96 octane), Special (90 octane) and normal (80 octane). Lead-free petrol is becoming more widely available—look for the sign 'Natural' at petrol stations. A list of stations selling lead-free petrol can be obtained from Automotoclub (see below).

Breakdown. Automotoclub (Mánesova 20, Praha 2; tel. 02/123 or 154) operates a national emergency service. The Prague office also provides a list of offices throughout the country. Spare parts are not easily found in Czechoslovakia, but Prague now offers repair services for the following makes: Austin, BMW, Fiat, Ford, Chrysler, Simca, Mercedes, Renault, Seat, Toyota and Volkswagen.

Car Hire. Hertz, Avis and Europcar operate in Czechoslovakia, along with the local Pragocar (Praha 1, Štěpánská 42; tel. 02 352 825) and Czech Auto Rent. Westerners can only rent cars for hard currency, Travellers' cheques and credit cards. Cars can be ordered in advance from abroad. The minimum age for car hire is between 18 and 21, depending on the type of car. An International Drivers' Licence is not essential.

Parking. The centre of Prague is largely kept free of traffic and parking can be a problem. Hotel guests have free priority parking in the centre; otherwise, it is advisable to park outside the centre and use the excellent public transport system. Illegally parked cars are towed away to Hostivař, Černostotecka, Praha 10.

Hitch-hiking is popular with young Czechoslovaks and comparatively safe. It is legal everywhere except on motorways.

Cycling. Outside the cities, empty roads and a great variety of scenery make cycling an attractive means of transport. It is possible to take bicycles on trains.

During the summer bicycles can be rented from Old Town Square in Prague. Heart Adventures Travel Agency (P.O. Box 16, 11121, Praha 1) offer one-day bike trips around Prague and mountain-biking in the High Tatras.

Cycling is illegal on motorways.

Public Transport in Prague

The public transport system is cheap, clean and efficient, with interconnecting metro, tram and bus services. Tickets must be purchased in advance from the yellow machines in metro stations, or at newsagents, hotels, and some shops and restaurants. There is only one type of ticket and a uniform fare for all forms of transport. Tickets must be validated in the machines at the entrance to the metro, and on buses and trams. One ticket is good for 90 minutes' travel after being validated, but if you change to a different form of transport you must use a new ticket. Checks by 'plain clothes' inspectors are quite frequent, with an on-the-spot fine of 500Kčs. One-day travelcards can be bought from red machines in the metro, and two to five-day cards from newsagents, hotels and travel agencies.

Note. The names of many of the metro stations were changed in 1989, so beware of older maps of the city.

Bus. The validating machines are just inside the doors of the buses. Insert the ticket and pull the handle forward until it clicks. Buses stop at every stop: the main stops are displayed in the windows of the bus. They run from approximately 05.00–23.00. There are few buses in the centre of the city (Praha 1).

Tram. As with buses, validating machines are inside the doors and main stops are displayed in the window. The trams also run from approximately 05.00–23.00.

A night tram and bus service that runs through the night though not very frequently. The night service numbers all begin with a 5— shown on a blue background to distinguish them from the daytime services.

Taxis. There are plenty of taxis in Prague. Check that the meter is on before your journey starts, as overcharging foreigners is standard practice. To avoid being cheated, you can ask for a receipt, which the driver is obliged to give you, showing the start and finish point of your journey and the price paid. Alternatively, you can agree a reasonable price beforehand, which, though probably too much, will still be cheap by Western standards.

Taxi stands are in Wenceslas Square, the railway stations and in Old Town Square.

For round-the-clock booking, tel. 202951-60 or 203941-50; for advance booking: tel. 2365875; 2352611.

Other transport. There is a funicular railway up Petřín Hill which takes the same tickets as other public transport. Horse-drawn carriage rides are on offer in Old Town Square.

Useful Addresses

Tourist Information Offices. Czechoslovakia lacks a good network of tourist information offices. Tourist information services are still geared towards package holidays and good disinterested information is hard to come by.

In Prague, PIS (Prague Information Service) will help with basic orientation. The main office is situated near Můstek metro station at Na Příkopě 20 (tel. 54 44 44) and there is another on Old Town Square. PIS will provide a free map of the city, addresses for accommodation and car hire as well as a 'what's on' guide. A similar service is offered in Bratislava at BIPS, Leningradská 1 (tel. 33 44 15). The American Hospitality Center, just off Prague Old Town Square at Malé náměstí 14 (tel. 236 7486) is a private concern which offers all the usual tourist office services as well as a parcel services and a café.

Outside Prague and Bratislava, Čedok (the state-owned travel agency) and Autotourist are the only sources of tourist information. English is spoken in most of their offices, though German is more usual.

Čedok offices
Banská Bystrica, Nám. V.I. Lenina 4, 974 75 Banská Bystrica. Tel. 22231, 23696. Telex. 070232
Bratislava, Štúrova 13, 813 83 Bratislava. Tel. 55280, 52002, 55274. Telex. 092233
Brno, Divadelní 3, 662 46 Brno. Tel. 23303, 23923. Telex. 062257
České Budějovice, Hroznova 21, 370 21 České Budějovice. Tel. 32381, 34050. Telex. 0144407
Gottwaldov, Kvítkova 80, 760 43 Gottwaldov. Tel. 25822, 24071. Telex. 067233
Hradec Králové, Leninova tř. 63, 501 39 Hradec Králové. Tel. 32586, 32321-5. Telex. 0194263
Karlovy Vary, Tržiště 23, 360 34 Karlovy Vary. Tel. 27798, 24378, 26705. Telex. 0156267
Kladno, náměstí Revoluce 4/5, 272 67 Kladno. Tel. 3436-8. Telex. 0132271
Košice, Rooseveltova 1, 043 08 Košice. Tel. 20764, 23123. Telex. 077276
Liberec, Revoluční 66, 460 34 Liberec. Tel. 21046-9. Telex. 0186226
Mladá Boleslav, Tř. Lidových milicí 1009, 293 27 Mladá Boleslav. Tel. 25991, 3057-9. Telex. 0136330
Nitra, LeninovaTř. 72, 949 75 Nitra. Tel. 28250, 28248. Telex. 098305

Olomouc, Náměstí Míru 2, 771 03 Olomouc. Tel. 28831. Telex. 066245
Ostrava, Dimitrovova 9, 729 92 Ostrava. Tel. 231424, 234287. Telex. 052204
Piešťany, Pavlovova 38, 921 70 Piešťany. Tel. 21506, 22215. Telex. 071210
Plzeň, Prešovská 10, 303 21 Plzeň. Tel. 37216, 36776, Telex. 0154330
Starý Smokovec, 060 12 Starý Smokovec V/22. Tel. 2417, 2710. Telex. 078268
Trutnov, Gottwaldovo nám. 120/21, 541 41 Trutnov. Tel. 3862, 3886. Telex. 0194392
Ústí nad Labem, Hrnčířská 9/3, 400 75 Ústí nad Labem. Tel. 26251-5. Telex. 0184254
Žilina, Hodžova 9, 011 09 Žilina. Tel. 23347, 23093. Telex. 075202

Autotourist offices

Praha, 120 00 Praha 2, Ječná 40. Tel. 290956, 295096, 293733. Telex. 122606
České Budějovice, 370 21 České Budějovice, Kanovnická 11. Tel. 37860, 35260. Telex. 144408
Pelhřimov, 393 01 Pelhřimov, Mírové nám. 33. Tel. 5885
Plzeň, 301 24 Plzeň, Nejedlého sady 3. Tel. 220006. Telex. 154545
Karlovy Vary, 360 01 Karlovy Vary, Vitězná 17. Tel. 25314
Ústí nad Labem, 400 01 Ústí nad Labem, Pařížská 10. Tel. 23639, 27219. Telex. 184626
Liberec, 460 01 Liberec, Jablonecká 16. Tel. 27498. Telex. 186612
Teplice, 419 26 Teplice, Zámecké nám. 7. Tel. 2003
Most, 434 00 Most, Josefa Skupy, blok 218. Tel. 794235
Hradec Králové, 500 00 Hradec Králové, Mýtská 4. Tel. 24748. Telex. 194648
Pardubice, 523 36 Pardubice, Jindřišská 2039. Tel. 38676
Harrachov, 512 46 Harrachov, Dům služeb, Sídliště Nový svět. Tel. 929448
Brno, 602 00 Brno, Pekařská 24. Tel. 333745, 334672, 337413. Telex. 63090
Zlín, 760 01 Zlín, Majora Murzina 4228. Tel. 22916. Telex. 67316
Ostrava, 701 00 Ostrava, Husova 9. Tel. 236223, 235642. Telex. 52714
Olomouc, 772 00 Olomouc, Školní 4. Tel. 29901
Opava, 746 01 Opava, Masarykova třída 10. Tel. 216129
Karviná, 735 06 Karviná, Dvořákova 1634. Tel. 45327
Bratislava, 811 02 Bratislava, nám. L'. Štúra 1. Tel. 330695, 330716, 333471-4
Nitra, 949 01 Nitra, nám. Osloboditeľov. Tel. 28629
Trenčín, 911 01 Trenčín, Štúrovo nám. 10. Tel. 33505. Telex. 72573
Banská Bystrica, 974 00 B. Bystrica, Partizánska 65. Tel. 23062. Telex. 70296
Žilina, 010 01 Žilina, 30. apríla 24. Tel. 33535. Telex. 75448
Prešov, 080 01 Prešov, Slovenská 67. Tel. 23304
Košice, 040 01 Košice, Thälmannova ul. Tel. 24066. Telex. 77558
Poprad, 058 01 Poprad, n. Duklianskych hrdinov 65. Tel. 22663. Telex. 78365

Embassies and Consulates

Austria, Praha 5 Smíchov, Viktora Huga 10. Tel. 546550
Belgium, Praha 1 Malá Strana, Valdštejnská 6. Tel. 534051
Bulgaria, Praha 1 Nové Město, Krakovská 6. Tel. 264306
Canada, Praha 6 Hradčany, Mickiewiczova 6. Tel. 3120251-4

China, Praha 6 Bubeneč, Majakovského 22. Tel. 326141
Denmark, Praha 2 Vinohrady, U Havlíčkových sadů 1. Tel. 254715
France, Praha 1 Malá Strana, Velkopřevorské nám. 2. Tel. 533042
Federal Republic of Germany, Praha 1 Malá Strana, Vlašská 19. Tel. 532351
Greece, Praha 6 Střešovice, Na Ořechovce 19. Tel. 354279
Great Britain, Praha 1 Malá Strana, Thunovská 14. Tel. 533347
Holland, Praha 1 Malá Strana, Maltézské náměstí 1. Tel. 531368
Hungary, Praha 6 Hradčany, I.V. Mičurina 1. Tel. 365041
India, Praha 1 Malá Strana, Valdštejnské 6. Tel. 532642
Italy, Praha 1 Malá Strana, Nerudova 20. Tel. 530666
Japan, Praha 1 Malá Strana, Maltézské náměstí 6. Tel. 535751
Portugal, Praha 7 Holešovice, Bubenská 3. Tel. 878472
Poland, Praha 1 Malá Strana, Valdštejnská 8. Tel. 536951
Romania, Praha 1 Malá Strana, Nerudova 5. Tel. 533059
Spain, Praha 6 Pevnostní 9. Tel. 327124
Switzerland, Praha 6 Střešovice, Pevnostní 7. Tel. 320406
United States of America, Praha 1 Malá Strana, Tržiště 15. Tel. 536641
USSR, Praha 6 Bubeneč, Pod Kaštany 1. Tel. 381940
Yugoslavia, Praha 1-Malá Strana, Mostecká 15. Tel. 531443

General Information

Churches. Access to churches, apart from when services are in progress, is generally not a problem in Prague, though outside the capital they are not usually open for more than a couple of hours a day.

Church services held in English in Prague:
Anglican, St. Kliment's, Klimentská ul., Nové Město, Praha 1. Sunday 11.00am. Eucharist.
Roman Catholic, St. Joseph's Church, Josefská 4, Malá Strana, Praha 1. Sunday 10.30am. Mass.
Interdenominational, Vrázova 4 (off Svornosti) Praha 5. Sunday 11.30am.

Climate. The Czechoslovakian climate is typically continental, with warm summers and cold winters. Average temperatures for July and August are over 20°C, though it can get much hotter, especially in Slovakia. Winters are harsh, with temperatures often dropping well below zero. July is the rainiest month.

Electric current. The standard voltage in Czechoslovakia is 220, though there are plans to increase it to 250 in the near future. 240V western appliances function normally. Sockets usually contain an earth pin, and take two-pin plugs, with a hole for the earth pin. 13amp square pin plug adaptors should be bought before travelling.

Emergencies
Ambulance—155
Fire Brigade—150
Police—158

Prague has recently seen a large increase in street crime. Care should be taken in the city centre, especially along Wenceslas

Square. Thefts can be reported at any police station, although the Police headquarters at Konviktské náměstí is the best place for English speakers. Emergency telephone boxes can be found at all metro stations.

English Language publications and broadcasts. The BBC World Service is now broadcast from Prague and can be received clearly on FM. The following English language newspapers are usually available at news-stands in the centre of Prague: *The International Guardian, The Financial Times, The European, The Wall Street Journal, USA Today* and *The Herald Tribune. Prognosis* is a newspaper written by local teachers and journalists. It contains a tourist section as well as a guide to the best pubs, clubs and wine bars.

Health and Medical Care. Foreigners are entitled to use the emergency services in case of an accident or sudden illness. Payment depends on individual countries' agreements with Czechoslovakia: the emergency service is free for British citizens, as Britain has a reciprocal agreement with Czechoslovakia, but American citizens must pay.

Pharmacies (Lékárna) are reasonably well stocked with common medicines. There is a 24-hour service at Na Příkopě 7, Praha 1, and at selected pharmacies in other districts and cities. Look for the sign 'Pohotovostní služba'.

There is a fully-equipped hospital for foreigners in Prague, at Na Homolce 724, Praha 5 Motol (tel. 5292 2146). Both English and German are spoken here, and the hours are 07.30–16.00 (after hours, tel. 5292 2191 or 5291 1111). The hospital also has a dental clinic.

Medical Aid: tel. 155
Dental Service: Vladisova 22, Praha 1, tel. 269374
24-hour pharmacy: Na Příkopě 7, Praha 1 (turn right at the bottom of Wenceslas Square), tel. 220081.

The tapwater is drinkable but overloaded with chemicals and unpleasant to taste.

Lost Property. The central office for all lost property in Prague is at Bolzanova 5, near Hlavní Nádraží.

Museums and Galleries. Opening times are usually from 09.00–10.00 to 17.00–18.00 six days a week, though there are a number of exceptions. The smaller places often close for an hour at lunch-time. Most museums, galleries and castles are closed on Mondays. Entrance charges are low and there are often discounts for students.

Orientation in Prague. Prague is divided into ten districts. The central district, Praha 1, has the Vltava running through it and contains the five historical towns of Prague. On one side of the Vltava are the Old and New Towns, and Josefov (the Jewish Quarter) and on the other, Hradčany (the Castle District) and Malá Strana. Although the city of Prague now extends over a large area, the historical centre is very compact. Confusingly, all houses have two numbers; keep to the blue and white ones, which have odd numbers on one side of the street and even on the other. The European system of numbering the building rather than individual premises is followed.

There is detailed map of the city in every metro station, and street maps can be obtained from most tourist offices and bookshops.

Photography. Various brands of western film are now available in Czechoslovakia, as well as an increasingly wide range of photographic equipment. There are a number of developing and printing services, and in Prague a 1-hour service is available. Passport photos can be obtained at 35 Wenceslas Square and in Můstek metro station.

Post Office Services. Post offices are usually open Monday to Friday 08.00–18.00, on Saturdays 08.00–12.00. Prague's main Post Office (Hlavní Pošta) is situated near Václavské náměstí, at 14 Jindřišská, and is open 24 hours a day throughout the week. Faxes can be sent from here and it provides Czechoslovakia's best international telephone service.

Mail sent *post restante* should be addressed—name, Post Restante, name of post office, post code, town, post district.

Stamps can also be purchased at tobacconists. Letters to the UK usually take under a week and a stamp costs five crowns (six crowns to the USA).

Public Holidays.
1 January—New Year's Day
March/April—Easter Monday
1 May—Labour Day
9 May—Liberation from Fascism (1945)
5 July
6 July—Jan Hus

(Bohemia and Moravia)
28 October—National Day—creation of the Czechoslovak state in 1918
24 December—Christmas Eve
25 December—Christmas Day
26 December—Boxing Day

Public Toilets. Public toilets in reasonable condition can be found at all Prague metro stations (open 08.00–22.00; cost two crowns). Outside Prague the best facilities are to be found in wine bars or hotels. All *hospodas* (pubs) have toilets, though they are not always of the highest standard.

Shopping. Department stores open 08.00–18.00 and general food shops 07.00–20.00. The opening times of the new private shops vary, but 09.00–18.00 is the norm. State shops open at 08.00 and close at 18.00, with a two-hour break for lunch between 12.00 and 14.00. In self-service supermarkets you must collect a basket before entering; this often means queuing at the entrance.

Tuzex shops sell goods, duty-free, that are not available in normal shops. Payment here is only in hard currency or by credit card. Opening times are from 10.00–18.00 Monday to Friday and 08.00–12.00 on Saturdays. The best food market is on Října, at the bottom of Wenceslas Square.

Telephoning. International calls can be made from the large grey telephones found in the centre of Prague and in metro stations, though you will have to keep feeding in five crown coins. International calls can be booked at any post office or hotel. For inquiries about telephone numbers abroad and international and national codes dial 0149. The code for the UK is 0044 and 001 for the USA. At the time of writing, the charge for a local call from a call-box is one crown.

The code for Czechoslovakia from abroad is 0042. For telegrams by phone the number is 127.

Theatre and Concert Tickets. You can book tickets in advance at IFB (Institute for Educational Travels). They have two offices in Prague— one on Wenceslas Square next to the Hotel Europa, which is open every day of the week, and one on Na Příkopě next to Čedok. IFB will also book trips and sightseeing tours.

Tickets can also be obtained from the appropriate theatre or concert hall. There is a high demand for all performances during the summer so it is advisable to book as far in advance as possible. During the winter tickets are sometimes available on the door half an hour before the performance.

Time. Czechoslovakia lies within the Central European Time Zone, i.e. GMT+ one hour in winter. Summer time is in effect from the end of March until the end of September: GMT+ two hours.

Tipping. In *hospodas* (pubs) it is usual to round off the bill to the nearest couple of crowns. In restaurants it is customary to tip the cloakroom attendant. Elsewhere tip as you would in the West, i.e. in taxis, hotels, etc.

Wheelchair access. There are virtually no special provisions for wheelchair users.

PRAGUE AND CENTRAL BOHEMIA

1 Prague

Prague, a city spread over wooded hills on either side of the Vltava, is a place that has always inspired superlatives and effusive prose. Spared by bombing in the Second World War, and, as yet, scarcely defaced by billboards, brash neon and other attributes of the western city, the old centre of Prague is so uncannily well preserved that at times the visitor appears to be walking not in a real place but in a stage-set or fairy-tale illustration. Few dispute that Prague is a city unrivalled in its beauty in central Europe, but there are also many who would agree with Milan Kundera's assessment—reached in the course of a stroll one day up a deserted Petřín Hill—that Prague was 'the most beautiful city in the world'.

Evocations of Prague inevitably stress how the physical beauty of the city is matched by a haunting, almost disturbing quality. The British writer Patrick Leigh Fermor, whose indigestibly rich prose has conjured up images of a wholly fantastical Prague, is by no means alone in considering the city not just as one of the most beautiful he has known but also as the strangest. The word 'magical', so misused by travel writers, is literally applicable to Prague, a city where the Habsburg emperor Rudolph II immersed himself in alchemy and the occult to the extent that he was eventually deposed as insane, where

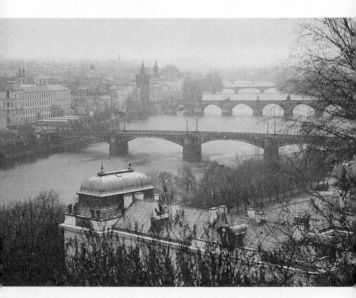

View of Prague from Letná Gardens

Doctor Faustus sold his soul to the devil, and where the Surrealist poet André Breton discovered his 'magic metropolis of old Europe'. Few cities have so secretive a character, and none in Europe has so many covered passages, as Erwin Kisch pointed out in his curious book *Monograph of the Covered Passage*: here is, Kisch claimed, a city which you can cross without hardly touching a street. There exists an immensely sinister Prague, a city of dark and empty streets, of distorted gables from some Expressionistic nightmare, of crows hovering around the black silhouette of a medieval tower.

The writings of Franz Kafka might come to mind as you wander around the streets of Prague, and yet those of the contemporary author Bohumil Hrabal perhaps more faithfully convey the true flavour of the city. Hrabal is someone who combines an imagination which has been referred to as 'baroque' with earthiness and coarse humour: his is a mind nourished by the rough and dirty drinking establishments where many of the ordinary townspeople interrupt even their mornings downing great glasses of beer.

The beauty and 'magic' of Prague should not make you lose sight of the more down-to-earth place which exists beneath the often fantastical façade. The city so frequently described as 'Golden' is also a city of terrible pollution, blackened plaster and peeling paintwork, and where the vast number of buildings shrouded in apparently permanent scaffolding is the subject of continual outrage in the local press. The same view from the Petřín Hill which so enthused Kundera was described in the 1920s by the Scottish poet Edwin Muir as 'intensely dismal', the air filled even on the sunniest days with a 'fine, impalpable dust'.

Tourism has made its own unattractive contribution to Prague, and the situation is becoming increasingly worse, as rapidly growing numbers of western visitors have led to the congestion of present hotel facilities, the necessity of booking good restaurants sometimes at least a week in advance, and even to queues forming to walk across the incomparably beautiful Charles Bridge. In the spring and summer months the centre of the city rings with foreign and not Czech voices, and the streets are crowded with tourists ravenously collecting souvenirs at what for them are bargain prices, and getting drunk on the excellent and ridiculously cheap beer.

The tourist vision of Prague is an extremely limited one, and much of the tourism of the city is fortunately contained in and around the so-called 'Royal Road' which leads from the Powder Tower in the Old Town up to the Royal Castle on the Hradčany. Many of the buildings along this route have been renovated in recent years and have that pastel-coloured doll's house appearance which is to be found in many of the old town centres of present-day Germany. It is easy to come away from Prague with a nostalgic vision of an essentially medieval and Renaissance city overlaid with baroque and rococo tinsel. Yet there is much more to Prague than this, and you should be wary of seeing the place simply as a museum of the past. You should pay a visit to one of Prague's many small theatres to experience something of the city's continuing vitality as a cultural centre; and you need to wander into the side streets and suburbs to understand the vital role which Prague has played in the development of 20C architecture. Ideally too, you should come here both in the summer and winter, so as to see a city which can at one moment be greener than almost any other major city in Europe, and the next frighteningly and unforgettably monochrome. Prague makes an immediate impact on the first-time visitor, but its lasting appeal is only slowly appreciated, for it lies in the city's remarkable complexity.

History. Appropriately for a city of such fairy-tale appearance, there is a legend connected with the founding of Prague. In around AD 800. Princess Libuše, a woman with great powers of divination, sent her henchmen into the forest with the instructions to found a town at the spot where they saw a ploughman (*Přemysl*) constructing the threshold (*práh*) of a house. She married the ploughman (thus establishing the Přemyslid dynasty), and, from her palace at Vyšehrad, situated on a rocky outcrop above the right bank of the Vltava, predicted that the new town, later to be called Praha or Prague, would have a future so glorious that its fame would reach the stars.

The real origins of Prague are rather more prosaic and are connected with Slavic settlers occupying the left bank of the Vltava (to the N of Vyšehrad) at about the beginning of the 6C AD. The citadel which was established here at the end of the 9C by the first documented member of the Přemyslid family, Prince Bořivoj, became the first seat of the Přemysl dynasty, and not Vyšehrad, as legend would have us believe. Prague was made a bishopric in 973, during the reign of Boleslav II, the Pious. In the course of the same century, numerous Jewish, German, Italian and French merchants settled on the right bank of the Vltava, at the meeting-place of several trade routes, and directly opposite the Slavic settlement on the left bank; the two areas were connected by a wooden bridge at the end of the century. Prince Vratislav II (from 1085 King Vradislav I) transferred his residence to Vyšehrad, which was to remain the seat of the Czech rulers until 1140, when the seat was moved back to its original location. The importance of Vyšehrad Castle greatly declined thereafter, but the area of the right bank to the N of it, where the merchants had settled, became an increasingly bustling commercial centre, particularly from the 1170s onwards, when the wooden bridge across the Vltava was replaced by a stone one (the so-called Judith's Bridge), and special privileges were granted by Prince Soběslav II to encourage further Germans to stay here. This commercial settlement, featuring a walled merchant's court known as the Týn, formed a separate township which was granted a municipal charter in around 1230 and is called today the Staré Město or Old Town; the extensive Jewish community was contained from the early 13C within their own walled ghetto attached to the northern side of this settlement. Meanwhile on the left bank of the Vltava, in the sparsely populated outer bailey of the castle, King Přemysl Otakar II founded in 1257 the township later to be called the Malá Strana or Little Quarter, the population of which was originally made up largely of German colonists summoned by the king. In the early 13C the district of Hradčany was founded just to the W of the castle, and Prague emerged as one of the most important and densely populated cities in Europe. But the highpoint of Prague's medieval development was to be reached during the reign of Charles IV (1344–78), who was to turn the city in 1355 into the capital of the Holy Roman Empire.

Under Charles IV Prague became the 'Rome of the North', attracting scholars and artists from all over Europe, including the Italian poet Petrarch. Elevated to archbishopric in 1344, Prague became in 1348 the seat of the first university in central Europe, an institution which bears to this day the name of Charles University. In that same year Charles greatly increased the size of Prague by founding yet another township, the Nové Město or New Town, which incorporated the former Horse and Cattle Markets (respectively today the Wenceslas and Charles Squares) and came even-utally to extend from the Vyšehrad all the way to the north-eastern corner of the Old Town. Numerous churches and other monuments were founded by Charles, most notably the Gothic cathedral of St. Vitus, on which there worked one of the outstanding medieval architects of Europe, Peter Parler, who was summoned to Prague by Charles in 1353. In 1357, in replacement of the Judith's Bridge, another of Prague's great landmarks was created, the Charles Bridge.

With the succession of Wenceslas IV to the throne in 1348, social and religious tensions led to a period of cultural and economic decline. Urged by the religious reformer Jan Hus, Wenceslas curtailed the rights of the Germans at the Charles University, thus leading to the exodus of 2000 students and many professors. The peculiarly Czech tradition of throwing people to their deaths from high places—initiated by Wenceslas with the ejection of the prelate Jan Nepomucký from the Charles Bridge in 1379—continued with the shoving of two Catholic councillors in 1419 out of the window of the New Town Hall, an event which sparked off the Hussite Wars and was later dignified with the absurd and pompous name of First Defenestration. Renewed stability and building activity set in with the reign of George of Poděbrady (1458–71), but Prague's importance as a trading centre continued to decline. George's successor, Vladislav II Jagiello (1471–1516), brought the Renaissance to Prague by inviting here the outstandingly original architect Benedikt Ried, whose idiosyncratic Vladislav Hall in the Prague Castle is the earliest example in Bohemia of the influence of contemporary Italian architecture. However Vladislav also consolidated the political decline of Prague by transferring his court in 1490 to the Hungarian capital of Buda.

Through most of the period of Habsburg rule, which began in 1526, Prague continued to play a secondary role in European politics, the city being now subservient to Vienna. However it experienced a brief political and cultural revival during the rule of the Emperor Rudolph II (1576–1612), who established his court at Prague, and indulged here his passions for collecting, lavish festivities, astronomy and the occult. He attracted here artists associated with the so-called Mannerist style (most notably Bartolomaeus Spranger, Adriaen de Vries and Giuseppe Arcimboldo), as well as such leading and controversial European scientists as the astronomers Tycho Brahe and Johannes Kepler, the alchemist Edward Kelley, the surgeon Jan Jesenius (who conducted the first public dissection in Prague), and the mathematician Jost Bürgi, the inventor of logarithms. In 1612 he was forced to abdicate in favour of his brother Matthias, who brought back the court to Vienna in 1617. On 23 May 1618 over a hundred members of the Bohemian nobility rose up in revolt against the Habsburgs and made their way to Prague Castle, where they perpetuated the Second Defenestration, an incident giving rise to the Thirty Years' War. After the defeat of the Protestants at the Battle of the White Mountain in 1620—which took place on the western outskirts of Prague, near the star-shaped hunting lodge of Hvězda—twenty-seven of the Protestant leaders were executed on the Old Town Square. Occupied by Saxons between 1631–32, Prague was later besieged by the Swedes, who managed to take possession of the Little Quarter just before peace was declared in 1648.

As with the rest of Bohemia, Prague was left in a state of devastation at the end of the Thirty Years' War. Yet the process of rebuilding the city (beginning with the reconstruction from 1630 onwards of the Malá Strana), together with the spectacular reassertion of the Catholic Church following years of religious strife, led to the transformation of Prague into one of the great baroque centres of Europe. The highpoint of the city's baroque development was reached during the early 18C, during the period of architectural supremacy of the prolific K.I. Dientzenhofer, who was responsible for the vast Clementinum, and countless palaces and churches, most notably that of St. Nicholas in the Little Quarter, which is comparable to Longhena's Church of the Salute in Venice in dominating the skyline of the city. This same century saw the burgeoning of palace gardens in the Little Quarter, the creation of the wooded parks of Letná, Troja and Petřín, and the extension, between 1753–75 of Prague Castle into the complex of buildings and courtyards that is to be seen today. In place of the medieval fortifications around the Old Town there was laid out between 1760–81 Prague's first boulevard, comprising Na Příkopě and its continuation, Národní třída. Prague's development into a bustling modern city was consolidated in 1784 with the bringing together into a single administrative unit of the four hitherto separate townships of the Old Town, New Town, Little Quarter and Hradčany.

The rapid industrialisation of Prague in the 19C, and the increase in the city's population from 80,000 to well over 200,000 went hand in hand with a mood of growing Czech nationalism, and ever greater tensions between the Czechs and Germans in the city. In 1848 a Czech national uprising centred on Prague was crushed, but in that same year there also took place here the first Panslavic Congress. Germans lost their majority in the Prague municipal Parliament for the first time in 1861, and in 1882 the Charles University was divided up according to nationality. In the latter years of the century the city's skyline was enriched by two massive neo-Renaissance buildings that expressed the aspirations of the Czech people: one was the National Theatre at the western end of Národní třída, the other was the National Museum, situated above what was now emerging as the new focal point of Prague life, the Wenceslas Square. Other major urban changes were occurring in Prague at this time, including the demolition of the city's remaining ramparts between 1874–76, and the destruction of the Jewish quarter through the creation in the 1890s of a long street named after the city of Paris and lined, as its name would suggest, with pompous apartment blocks and fashionable shops. An important Industrial Exhibition held in Prague in 1891 confirmed the city's position as one of the main industrial and commercial centres of the Habsburg Empire.

Already by the early years of the 20C, Prague was becoming a leading European centre of the avant-garde, and the visionary achievements of a writer such as Kafka were matched by the construction of exceptionally original 'cubist' buildings by the likes of Gočár and Chochol. However, it was the establishment of the Czech Republic in 1918 which led to one of the richest and liveliest periods in the cultural history of Prague. Pioneering poets, painters, designers, photographers and architects were all brought together by the Prague-based group Devětsil, which was closely associated with the city's developing reputation as the European centre of Constructivism and Functionalism. Uncompromising structures in concrete and glass grew up in the very centre of the city, while suburbs such as Podbaba and Barrandov became showpieces of modernist architecture.

The German occupation of 1939–45, followed by the repressive years of Communism, drove the city's cultural life underground, but by no means extinguished it, as became evident in the great burst of literary, cinematic and theatrical talent in the 1960s, culminating in the 'Prague Spring' of 1968. World attention was drawn once again to Prague, but admiration turned to horror in August of that year, when television cameras showed Soviet tanks marching into Prague's Old Town Square. On 16 January 1969, at a spot near the Wenceslas Square, the student Jan Palach set fire to himself in protest against the Soviet invasion. The subsequent years, up to the signing in 1977 of Charter 77, were among the greyest in the city's history, though they were also ones of rapid urban growth: in 1974 the city's underground railway system was opened, and the city boundaries were greatly increased by the incorporation within them of 74 outlying communities, bringing the total population of Prague up to 1,200,000 inhabitants. The new architecture was generally drab and mediocre, reducing the exciting functionalism of the 1920s to unimaginative uniformity; a lively literary culture, however, continued to exist in the city, thanks principally to *samizdat* publishing, typewritten articles and books that circulated from hand to hand within a wide illicit network. Leading dissident meeting-places included jazz clubs, the Café Slavia (opposite the National Theatre), and the backrooms of the Magic Lantern, the latter coming to play a vital role in the 'Velvet Revolution' of November 1989, a revolution which had begun on 17 November with a large student demonstration making its way from the Vltava down Národní třída and eventually settling in the Wenceslas Square. Among the first acts of the Civic Forum Government led by the playwright president Václav Havel was to rename, in January 1990, the Red Army Square after Jan Palach. The renaming of numerous other squares and streets in Prague gathered momentum in the course of 1990, and in October of that year the remains of Jan Palach were brought back to Olšanské Cemetery in the Prague district of Vinohrady.

Among the famous natives of Prague are Václav Hollar (1607–77), Jan Neruda (1834–91), Rainer Maria Rilke (1875–1926), Jaroslav Hašek (1883–1923), Franz Kafka (1883–1924), Max Brod (1884–1968), Franz Werfel (1890–1945), Egon Erwin Kisch (1855–1948), Jaroslav Seifert (1901–86), Karel Teige (1900–51), Václav Havel (1936–) and Ivan Klíma (1931–). The principal cultural event of the Prague year is the Music Festival known as the 'Prague Spring', which is held in late May and June. Every five years Prague's vast Strahov Stadium becomes the scene of an internationally renowned gymnastics event called the spartakiáda (the next one is supposed to be held in the summer of 1995).

The CENTRE of Prague, though relatively small in size, has an extraordinary concentration of attractions, and at least a week is needed to begin to do justice to these; visitors, with only two or three days to spare, should largely devote their attention to the streets and monuments along the so-called Royal Road, most notably the Powder Tower, Celetná Street, Old Town Square, Karlova Street, Charles Bridge, St. Nicholas in the Little Quarter, Nerudova Street and Prague Castle; additional sights that should certainly not be missed are the Jewish Museum in the Josefov, the Týn Church, the Municipal House, the Loreta, the Library of the Strahov Monastery, the gardens of the Wallenstein Palace and the National Gallery in the Sternberg Palace. By far the best means of touring the city is on foot, though visitors should be warned that the comparatively short

TROJA

VLTAVA

tromovka • Lapidarium
Park of Culture & Rest

HOLEŠOVICE

Trades Fair
Building
Inat Gall.

Vltavská Ⓜ

BUBENSKÉ NÁBŘEŽÍ

Praha-Expo 58
ady Restaurant

KARLÍN

NABŘ. KPT. JAROŠE

VLTAVA →

Invalid War
Veterans Home

Křižíkova Ⓜ

SOKOLOVSKÁ

OSEFOV

ee larger scale plan for Central area

STAROMĚSTSKÉ NÁM.

KŘIŽÍKOVA

MALÉ NÁM.

Powder Tower

HYBERNSKÁ

HUSITSKÁ

Jan Žižka Monument

KONĚVOVA

STARE MESTO

NÁM. PŘÍKOPECH
WINSTON
CHURCHILL

SEIFERTOVA

ŽIŽKOV

VÁCLAVSKÉ NÁMĚSTI

Riegrovy
Sady

Mahlerovy
Sady

Olšany
Cemetery

Fleku New Town National
Hall Mus

JAGELLONSKÁ

VINOHRADY

Ch. of the
Sacred Heart

Flora Ⓜ

Cyrila a
Metoděje
KARLOVO
NÁM. Ⓜ

Rotunda

ŽITNÁ

ANGLICKÁ

P. Pavlova Ⓜ

•Theatre

VINOHRADSKÁ

SLEZSKÁ

Jiřího z
Podebrad Ⓜ

NOVÉ MĚSTO

JEČNÁ

Faust Ho. sv
Kateřiny

Villa America

RUMUNSKÁ

NÁM.
MIRU Ⓜ

KORUNNÍ

Ch.of St John
on the Rock

naus Botanical
nast Garden

FRANCOUZSKÁ

RUSKÁ

Our Lady
Na Slupi

Karlov

BĚLEHRADSKÁ

Havlíčkovy
Sady

sv. Václav

VRŠOVICE

HORSKÁ

SEKANINOVA

SBORU

NÁRODNÍ

BEZPEČNOSTI

VYŠEHRAD

AVOVA

Peter & Paul

šehrad Rotunda Vyšehrad Ⓜ

Leopold
Gate

NA BUČANCE

Pal. of
Culture

CIKLOVA

MUGELSKA

Tábor
Gate

**PRAGUE
GENERAL**

0 metres   800

Ⓜ Metro Stations

N

New Jewish Cemetery & Vinohrady Cemetery

distances are made up for by the numerous hills to be negotiated as soon as you leave the Staré Město. Travelling beyond the central districts of Prague 1 and 2, you should make use of Prague's excellent bus, tram and metro systems (tickets for these—valid for all three forms of transport—can be obtained at newspaper kiosks, hotel lobbies and the automatic vending machines at the metro stations themselves). There is transport running from 5 o'clock in the morning up to 12 o'clock at night. For those arriving at Prague by air and wishing to travel to the centre by public transport, you should take Bus 119 to its last stop, Dejvické náměstí (square), and from there continue the journey by metro. Taxis are extremely cheap, but foreign tourists should make sure that the drivers set their meters.

A.   Staré Město (Old Town)

The Staré Mešto, or Old Town, is bordered to the N and W by the river Vltava, and to the S and E by a long thoroughfare (comprising Národní třída, Na Příkopě and Revoluční), marking the line of the medieval fortifications. The **Powder Gate** (Prašná brána) stands on the náměstí Republiky, which divides the pedestrian Na Příkopě from its northern continuation Revoluční.

Originally known as the New Tower, the dark and sinister Powder Gate, 65m tall, was commissioned in 1475 by Vladislav Jagiello on the site of one of the 13 gates forming part of the Old Town's defensive system, a system which had been made redundant following the founding of the New Town in 1348. The Gate, adjoining at one time the building which served from 1383 to 1484 as the seat of the Royal Court of Bohemia, was intended purely as a monumental entrance to the Old Town, and marked the beginning of the processional route used by the Czech kings on their way to be crowned in St. Vitus's Cathedral. When in 1484 Vladislav Jagiello moved the Royal Court back to Prague Castle, work on the Gate was abandoned, and the incomplete structure was given a temporary roof and put to use—until the end of the 17C—as a storehouse for gunpowder. Heavily damaged during the Prussian siege of Prague in 1737, it was left in a ruined state until the late 19C. Its present appearance is due largely to reconstruction work carried out between 1875–86 by Josef Mocker, who provided the structure with its turreted upper gallery, steeply pitched roof and flamboyant Gothic decoration. The writer Max Brod recalled how every afternoon at 2 o'clock he would wait at the foot of the newly restored tower for his friend Franz Kafka, who invariably would arrive late: 'My anger', wrote Brod, 'at his lateness would rapidly dissolve as soon as the tall, thin figure appeared, who, more often than not, would be wearing an embarrassed smile'.

The profuse neo-Gothic ornament which covers the Powder Gate contains, alongside late 19C statues of Czech kings and other pseudo-medieval figures, fragments of the original sculptural decoration carried out by Matěj Rejsek of Prostějov after 1478; during the summer months you can climb up to the tower's upper gallery, the best point from which to study the layout of Prague's Old Town. Before entering the Old Town, you should take a look at two of the other monuments on the náměstí Republiky. Facing the gate, at the eastern end of the square (No. 3), is the 'U hybernů' House, which occupies the site of a former church and monastery belonging to the Hybernian Order (Franciscans of Irish origin). The monastery building, erected in 1637–52, is a simple structure now used for offices; far more impressive is the adjoining former church, which was transformed by Georg Fischer in 1810 into a grandiose Customs House, inspired in its design by the former Mint in Berlin, and constituting one of the finest examples in Prague of the Empire style (the building now serves as a space for ambitious art exhibitions). Meanwhile, flanking the northern side of the Powder Gate, and indeed dominating the whole square, is the most outstanding Art Nouveau building in Czechoslovakia, **THE MUNICIPAL HOUSE** (Obecní dům).

The Municipal House stands on the site originally occupied by the Royal Court of Bohemia, a building dating back to the late 14C and later converted first into a seminary, then into a barracks, and finally into a cadets' school, which was pulled down between 1902–03. The idea of erecting the Municipal House was that of the Czech Patriotic Society, which envisaged a building which would serve as a social and cultural centre for the Czech community in Prague, complete with café, restaurant, concert hall, and rooms for civic functions and assemblies. The architects chosen for the task, after a public competition which closed in 1905, were Antonín Balšánek and Osvald Polívka. Work on the building was undertaken between 1906–12, and involved the collaboration of many of the leading Czech painters and sculptors of the turn of the century, including Ladislav Šaloun (the sculptor of the Hus Monument in the Old Town Square), Max Švabinský (who created the stained-glass windows in St. Vitus's Cathedral), and Alfons Mucha, who had accepted the commission in the mistaken belief that he had been asked to carry out all the decoration of the House (a protracted and heated correspondence in the press concluded that it would not be fitting for a single artist to assume responsibility for the whole work). The most important meetings to have taken place in the building were held at the end of the First World War, concluding with the proclamation here, on 28 October 1918, of the independence of Czechoslovakia, and the issuing of the New Republic's Constitution. As for the Concert Hall, this continues to be one of Prague's most important cultural venues, hosting each year the inauguration concert of the Prague Spring Musical Festival; among the famous musicians to have performed in the hall are Sviatoslav Richter, David Oistrakh, Yehudi Menuhin, Mstislav Rostropovitch and Pablo Casals.

The exterior of the large, irregularly-shaped building is impressive above all for its central ironwork canopy, which is coloured with stained-glass and topped by bronze figures of lamp-bearers executed by K. Novák. Above the canopy is a large lunette decorated by Karel Špillar with a mosaic Homage to Prague; crowning this is a cupola, while on either side are sculptural groups by Ladislav Šaloun representing respectively the Humiliation and Rebirth of the Czech Nation. Numerous other sculptures adorn the exterior, including a statue by Čeněk Vosmík of the main architect of the adjoining Powder Gate, Matěj Rejsek, and a relief by Šaloun commemorating the first assembly in 1918 of the National Committee of the Czechoslovak Republic. Inside the building you find yourself in a vestibule adorned with bronze statues of Flora and Fauna by Bohumil Kafka. To the right a door leads into a *Restaurant*, with large views of Prague by Josef Tomec and Antonín Záhel, and paintings by Josef Wenig representing Hop-Growing, Viticulture, and Prague welcoming its Visitors; to the left of the vestibule is the similarly elegant *Café*, featuring at one end a niche containing a statue of a nymph made of white Carrara marble by Josef Pekárek. A further restaurant and a late night bar are situated in the basement, where you will find coloured drawings by Mikoláš Aleš and a folkloric fantasy by Jakub Obrovský entitled Harvest Time. The Concert Hall and Civic Rooms are to be found on the first floor, and can be visited during the day only in the course of occasional guided tours (enquire at the concert ticket office in the lobby). The large, ochre-coloured **Concert Hall**, named after the composer Smetana, has a central section domed in stained-glass, and two wide balconies flanked by large murals by Karel Špillar representing Music, Dance, Poetry and Drama. In between the stage and two prominent boxes at the front of the hall

PRAGUE CENTRE

M Metro Stations

0 metres   400

Letenské Sady

Hanavský Pavilion

Čechův most

NÁBŘ. KPT. JAROŠE

NA FRANTIŠKU

St Agnes
Nat. Gall. 19
Czech Printin

KOŽI

NÁM. EL. KRASNOHORSKÉ
CURIEOVÝCH
PAŘÍŽSKÁ TŘÍDA

SS. Simon
& Judas

U MILOSRDNÝCH

DUŠNÍ

KLAROV

KOSÁRKOVO

DVOŘÁKOVO

JOSEFOV

Malostranská

M

Span Syn.

MOSTECKÁ

Rudolfinum

17 LISTOPADU

Ceremonial
Ho.

MASLOVA

HŘBITOVA

Old-New
Syng
High
Syng
Jewish Town
Hall

Ch. of the
Holy Ghost

KOŽI

DLOUHÁ

Vojanov
Sady

Mus. of
Decor. Arts

Klaus
Syng.

Cemetery
Pinkas
Syn.

ŠIROKÁ

PAŘÍŽSKÁ

St Salvator

MASN

Mánesův
most

JAN PALACH
NÁM.

Maîs
Synagogue

MAISLOVA

U drou Šdri

KAPROVA

Staroměstská

M

DLOUHÁ

sv. Mikuláš

Jan Hus
Mon.

Goltz-Kinsky
Pal.

KŘIŽOVNICKÁ

NÁM. PRIM. DR. V. VACKA
(MARIÁNSKÉ NÁM.)

STAROMĚSTSKÉ
NÁM.

Týn
Church

U RADNICE

Sch

Staroměstská
radnice

Clock

MALÉ
NÁM.

ŽELEZNÁ

Clam-Gallas
Pal.

Clementinum

KARLOVA

Carolinum

SEMINÁŘSKÁ

KŘIŽOVNICKÉ NÁM.

St Salvator

Tower

KARLOVA

KARLOVA

Charles Bridge
(Karlův most)

Smetana
Museum

NOVOTNÉHO NÁBŘ.

LÁVKA

ANENSKÁ

LILIOVÁ

ŘETĚZOVÁ

JALOVCOVÁ

sv. Jilji
(St Giles)

HUSOVA TŘÍDA

ZLATÁ

MICHALSKÁ

HAVELSKÁ

Týn
Theat

sv. Havla

RYTÍŘSKÁ

VLTAVA

SMETANOVO NÁBŘ.

Divadlo
Na Zábradlí

Bethlem Chapel

BETLÉMSKÁ

SKOŘEPKA

VODIČKOVA

STARE
MESTO

Mu

Náprstek Mus.

NÁPRSTKOVA

28 ŘÍJNA

PERLOVÁ

Rotunda

Holy Rood

KAROLINY

DIVADELNÍ

SVĚTLÉ

KONVIKTSKÁ

sv. Bartoloměje

PERŠTÝNE

BARTOLOMĚJSKÁ

NÁRODNÍ TŘÍDA

JUNGMANNOVO

JUNGMANNOVA NÁM.

K. Panr
Marie

STŘELECKÝ
OSTROV

MASARYK NÁBŘEŽÍ

Mon.

KROČÍNOVA

Adria
Palace
(Magic Lantern)

SPALENA

Most Legii

Cafe Slavia

NÁRODNÍ

TŘÍDA

VORŠILSKÁ

Národní
třída

M

PALACKÉH

sv. Voršily

National Theatre
(Národní divadlo)

MASARYK

OSTROVNÍ

OSTROVNÍ

KŘEMENCOVA

Studio Ypsilon

SPALENA

VLADISLAVOVA

SLOVANSKÝ
OSTROV

OPATOVICKÁ

Diamond
Ho.

Holy Trinity

New Town Hall
(Novoměstská radnice)

NOVÉ MĚST

U Fleků

ience Museum

Expo 58
Restaurant

TENSKÝ TUNNEL

NÁBŘ. KPT. JAROŠE

VLTAVA

Švermův most

Hlávkův most

TĚŠNOVSKÝ TUNNEL

KEŠTVANIC

NÁBŘ. LUDVIKA SVOBODY

WILSONOVA

KLIMENTSKÁ

ASTALSKÁ

PETRSKÉ NÁM.

PETRSKÉ

allus

SOUKENICKA

+ St Peter na
Poříčí

REVOLUČNÍ

TRUHLÁŘSKÁ

ZLATNICKA

BISKUPSKA

NA POŘÍČÍ

Florenc
Švermovy
Sady

M

RYBNÁ

NA POŘÍČÍ

Legio
Bank

City of
Prague Mus.

sv.Jakub
KUBSKA

KRÁLODVORSKÁ

NA FLORENCI

U PRAŠNÉ

NÁM.REPUBLIKY

Municipal
Ho.
(Obecnídům)

M

Náměsti Republiky

Kinský

HAVLÍČKOVA

Prague
Central Station
(Nádraží Praha-střed)

WILSONOVA

CELETNÁ

Powder Gate
(Prašná brána)

HYBERNSKÁ

of the
k Virgin

NA PŘÍKOPĚ

SENOVÁŽNÁ

DLÁŽDĚNÁ

Cafe Arco

BOLZANOVA

HUSITSKÁ

+sv.Kříže

NEKÁZANKA

Belfry

JINDŘIŠSKÁ

sv.Jindřicha

JERUZALÉMSKÁ

OPLETALOVA

Sylva-Taroucca
Pal.

PANSKÁ

runna Pal.

RUŽOVA

Vrchlického Sady

Hlavní nádraží

M

POLITICKÝCH VĚZŇŮ

Central Station
(Hlaví nádraží)

istek

M

VÁCLAVSKÉ NÁM.

Grand Hotel
Europa

Hotel
Esplanade

OPLETALOVA

WASHINGTONOVA

WILSONOVA

SPANĚLSKÁ

KOVA

ŠTĚPÁNSKÁ

JÁME

Hotel
Alcron

VE SMEČKÁCH

sv.Václava
Mon.

M

Smetana Theatre

Federal Assembly

Cinoherní
Klub

KRAKOVSKÁ

Národní
Museum

LEGEROVA

(the box on the left is that used by President Havel), are two dynamic stucco groups by Ladislav Šaloun portraying scenes from Dvořák's Slavonic Dances and Smetana's Opera Vyšehrad. Among the other first-floor rooms are the small and exquisitely tasteful neo-classical pastiche called the *Sweetshop*, the rather brasher *Oriental Room*, and the *Němcová Salon*, decorated all over with stuccowork inspired by folkloric themes. Other rooms on this floor have ambitious large-scale paintings, for instance the *Rieger Hall*, which has two long painted panels by Max Švabinský (Czech Spring) containing portraits of leading Czech writers, artists and musicians such as Jan Neruda, Božena Němcová, Josef Mylsbek, Josef Mánes, Mikoláš Aleš, Bedřich Smetana and Antonín Dvořák. Pride of place among the Civic Rooms must go to the **Hall of the Lord Mayor**, the windows of which occupy the central position on the building's façade. All the furniture and furnishings, and every detail of the decoration of this circular room are by Alfons Mucha, including allegorical murals on the walls and shallow ceiling, the pale blue stained-glass windows, the Lord Mayor's chair, and the elaborately embroidered curtains.

After leaving the Municipal House, turn left and then left again into the narrow side-street U Obecního domu, which flanks the northern side of the building. On the right-hand side of this street is another fine building of the turn of the century, the recently restored *Hotel Paris*, which was built in 1907 by Jan Vejrych and illustrated as a model of Art Nouveau architecture in a group of old photographs in the Musée des Arts Décoratifs in Paris. There are colourful figurative decorations on the corner façade of its gabled, Gothic-inspired exterior, while inside are an attractively panelled café, and a mirrored restaurant with blue mosaics. A fantastical description of this hotel—now a moderately priced institution—appears in Bohumil Hrabal's novel, I Served the King of England (first published in England in 1989): 'The Hotel Paris was so beautiful it almost knocked me over. So many mirrors and brass balustrades and brass door handles and brass candelabras, all polished till the place shone like a palace of gold.' It was here that the picaresque narrator of the novel meets the head waiter who 'served the King of England', and where he himself makes his reputation by serving Haile Salasse at a Gargantuan banquet centred around a stuffed and roasted camel.

At the end of U Obecního domu turn left into the short U Prašné brány, where you will pass at No. 1 an Art Nouveau apartment block built by Bedřich Bendelmayer between 1903–04, and featuring inside an elegant semi-circular staircase. The street brings you back to the Powder Gate and to the eastern end of Celetná. Celetná, the pedestrian street at the start of the Royal Route, is one of the showpiece streets of the Old Town, and lined principally with recently restored houses of medieval origin that were given pastel-coloured façades during the baroque period. At No. 31, on the right-hand side of the street, is a palace built in 1750 by K.I. Dientzenhofer for the Master Minter Josef Pachta of Rájov; the Mint itself was situated up to 1784 in the palace on the opposite side of the street (at No. 36), a building which Pachta erected in 1759 on the site of the medieval Mint, and featuring atlante figures of miners by the baroque sculptor I.F. Platzer. At No. 34 Celetná, is one of the more interesting modern buildings in the Old Town, the corner department store known as the *House of the Black Virgin* (Dům U černé Matky Boží). Built in 1911–12 by Josef Gočár, this corner house is one of the masterpieces of Czech Cubism, and has two prominent cornices as well as heavy prism-shaped forms painted a dark maroon; a curious survival of the baroque building which it replaced is the baroque statue of the Virgin in the corner niche. Opposite the building, at No. 23 Celetná, is to be found another statue of the Virgin, this one by a pupil of Matthias Braun and attached to the undulating baroque façade of the palace built for the Schönpflok family.

Continuing to walk on the right-hand side of Celetná, turn right just after No. 17 and walk through the covered passage leading towards the Malá Štupartská, on which stands the former monastery church of **St. James** (Sv. Jakub), which was founded by Minorites in 1232, and completely remodelled by Jan Šimon Pánek between 1689–1702. The tall twin-towered west façade has rich stuccowork by O. Mosto, executed in 1695 and featuring representations of SS. James, Francis and Anthony of Padua. The enormously long and imposing interior, which has retained the medieval three-aisled plan and tall, Gothic proportions, is profusely white-washed and gilded, and contains ceiling frescoes of the Life of the Virgin by F. Voget (1736), and 22 altars. The main altarpiece, supported by an exuberant gilded framework of angels high above the chancel, is a painting by V.V. Reiner of the Martyrdom of St. James. Three of the altars on the right-hand side of the nave are by P. Brandl, and executed around 1710; another work by Brandl (the St. Joseph Altar of 1708) is on the left-hand side of the nave, where can also be found an altar by J.K. Liška representing St. Valburg. The latter side of the nave also boasts one of Prague's grandest funerary monuments, the *Monument to Jan Vratislav of Mitrovice*, designed by Fischer von Erlach in 1721 and containing sculpted figures by F.M. Brokoff. The church is famous for its acoustics, and the sung high mass on Sundays is well worth attending, as is the annual Christmas day service featuring the Christmas Mass by the Czech composer Ryba.

Return to Celetná through the same covered passage, and you will find yourself directly in front of the smart beer cellar (at No. 22) known as *At the Vulture* (U Supa), which is housed on the ground floor of a pale green late 18C building with a German inscription dating back to the days when the royal jeweller Gindle had his shop here. Continuing W on the left-hand side of Celetná, you will come, at No. 12, to the elegant Hrzán Palace, a building of Romanesque origin remodelled to a design by G.B. Alliprandi in 1702, and with sculptural decorations on the façade by pupils of F.M. Brokoff; the father of Franz Kafka, Hermann, had a haberdashery shop on the premises after 1882. Further down the street, at No. 2, is the house where the Kafka family lived between 1888–89, and where Albert Einstein is said to have first explained his Theory of Relativity. Between 1896–1901 the Kafka family lived on the opposite side of the street, at No. 3, where there is now to be found Prague's only Vegetarian Restaurant. At the adjoining No. 5 is the 17C Týn Presbytery, occupying the site of a 12C hospice for foreign merchants; a short and narrow alley between the two houses leads to the south portal of the Church of Our Lady before Týn (see below). Celetná Street comes to an end at the spacious **OLD TOWN SQUARE** (Staroměstské náměstí), one of Europe's most beautiful squares.

Situated at what was formerly the junction of several trade routes, the Old Town Square served as the market-place of the Old Town in the 11C and 12C centuries. An important point on the traditional processional route of the Bohemian kings, and overlooked by the former Hussite Church of Our Lady before Týn, the square was later to witness some of the most significant—and tragic—events in the history of Prague, and came almost to symbolise the struggles and aspirations of the Czech people. Jan Želivský—the Hussite leader whose storming of the New Town Hall in 1419 had sparked off the Hussite Wars—was executed here in 1422; 56 other Hussites, including the officer Jan Roháč of Dubé, were executed on the square 15 years later. At the Old Town Hall George of Poděbrady was elected King of Bohemia in 1458, and in 1621, 27 of the Protestant leaders who had taken part in the Battle of the White Mountain were beheaded outside the building. One of these was the pioneering surgeon Jan Jessenius, an ancestor of Kafka's great love, Milena Jesenská. Before his tongue had been taken out prior to the execution he had said, 'You are treating us shamefully, but I want you to know that others will come who will bury with honour our heads, which you have desecrated and put on show.' In 1945 large crowds welcomed the arrival here of Soviet troops, and three years later Klement Gottwald proclaimed from the balcony of the Kinský Palace the accession of the Communists to power. A rather different response to the Soviet army was shown in 1968, when, at the end of the 'Prague Spring', Soviet tanks advanced on the square, their arrival being greeted not by applause but by Molotov cocktails.

The square is surrounded by a picturesque jumble of medieval to baroque buildings, to which recent restoration has given a toy-like cleanliness and cheerful range of light and vivid colours. Though most of the square is now traffic-free, it is the tourist heart of Prague, and you would be best advised to come here early in the day to appreciate the place before it fills up with a vast and noisy crowd in which buskers, street vendors and money-changers now jostle with the foreigners. Rising up on steps near its centre and dominating the whole space, is the extraordinary bronze **Monument to Jan Hus**, a disgracefully undervalued work of the early years of the century, considered by some to be completely out of place in the square, but which is surely one of the most powerful public monuments in any European city, and one which brilliantly complements its surroundings.

The Monument to Jan Hus was the masterpiece of the idiosyncratic sculptor Ladislav Šaloun, who began planning the work as early as 1898, and struggled with it for the next 17 years, making constant changes throughout this period of gestation. The monument was intended to be unveiled in 1915, on the occasion of the 500th anniversary of the burning of Jan Hus for heresy. The unveiling went ahead as planned, but few worse moments could have been chosen for the completion of a highly emotive monument symbolising the Czech national consciousness and the fight for Czech independence. The Austrian authorities did not permit any speech or unveiling ceremony of any kind to take place, but within a few days the work was completely covered with flowers, and all that showed of it was a solitary finger pointing menacingly to the sky. At this time there still stood next to the monument a Marian Column erected in 1650 to commemorate the 'Peace of Westphalia'—the Treaty which brought the Thirty Years' War to an end. In 1918, only five days after the declaration of independent Czechoslovakia, this symbol of Catholic and Habsburg dominance, with its sculpted angels trampling over devils, was pulled down, leaving only Jan Hus to preside over the square. The continuing power of the latter monument is attested in the wake of the Soviet invasion of August 1968, when it was shrouded in black drapes.

Šaloun's monument to Hus, which bears at its base the preacher's words 'The truth will prevail', features the figure of Hus rising above a struggling sea of gesticulating figures in a defiant posture reminiscent of one of Rodin's Burghers of Calais; the power of this detailed yet unified composition lies to a large extent in the way in which—even on the brightest of days—it forms against the light and cheerful background of the square a dark and menacing profile, vividly reminding the spectator of the bleaker moments in Czech history.

The eastern end of the square is overshadowed by the most prominent building in the Old Town, and one of those most closely associated with the Hussite cause, **The Church of Our Lady before Týn**. As with most medieval churches in Bohemia it does not rise directly above the square, but is set back behind a row of arcaded houses, comprising in this case a house of Romanesque origin with a tall late 18C façade (No. 15, at the south-eastern end of the square), and the attractive *Týn School* (No. 14), which has a late 14C ground floor and a pair of stepped 16C gables recalling those of the Scuola Grande di San Marco in Venice; the architect Matěj Rejsek of Prostějov was a teacher at the school in the late 15C. Walking through the second of the school's four arches will take you to the west portal of the church (alternatively you could enter the church through its south portal by following the alley alongside the Týn Presbytery at No. 5 Celetná; see above). For many years much of the exterior of the Týn has been encased by scaffolding, and access to its very restricted site has been extremely limited; entry to the building can only be guaranteed at times of services, and this situation is likely to persist for many more years.

The origins of the Týn church are in a Romanesque building first mentioned in 1135 as the property of the foreign merchants' hospice in Celetná. Work on the present structure was begun in 1365, and by the 1380s the north portal, the side aisles, the walls of the nave and much of the east end had been completed. The reformist preachers K. Waldhauser and Milič of Kroměříž were already preaching in the building by the end of the 14C, and early in the following century the place was to become the main Prague church of the Hussites; it was to remain associated with the followers of Jan Hus until 1621. The nave was vaulted by 1457, a year before the accession to the throne of the Ultraquist monarch George of Poděbrady, who was to be one of the church's greatest benefactors. Under George the northern of the west façade's twin towers was erected (the southern one dates from the early 16C), as was this façade's tall gable. The gable was adorned with a statue of George and a gold chalice symbolising the Ultraquist cause, but these were removed after the Battle of the White Mountain in 1620, and replaced with an image of the Virgin, whose halo was made from the gold of the chalice. A severe fire in 1679 led to the rebuilding of the nave vault and extensive remodelling of the interior.

The twin-towered exterior of the church is a gloomy pile of exposed masonry, the principal decoration being concentrated on the north portal, where there is a late 14C tympanum of the Crucifixion from the workshop of Peter Parler (the original is now in the National Gallery in Prague Castle). The north portal can be reached along the narrow Týnská, which runs along the northern side of the Týn School, and off which there is a gateway (just to the E of the church) leading into the merchants' courtyard which gave this area its name ('Týn' means 'enclosure'); the courtyard, used from the 11C to 18C for the stocking and selling of goods, and as a custom's house, retains only the ground-plan of the medieval structure, the oldest surviving part being the mid 16C loggia of the Granovský House. The interior of the Týn church, greatly in need of restoration, is a dark three-aisled hall space with crumbling, unadorned plaster from the baroque period. At the western end of the north aisle is a Gothic baldachin by Matěj Rejsek (1493) which was originally situated above the tomb of the Hussite bishop A.L. Mirandola. The outstanding work of art in the building is the intricately carved Baptism of Christ by the Monogramist I.P. (c 1526) on the pier immediately to the right of the south portal. Attached to the south aisle pier directly in front of the main apse is the red marble tombstone of the Danish astronomer Tycho Brahe (d. 1601). The high altar of the Ascension (1649) is by Karel Škréta.

Returning to the Old Town Square, and continuing walking N along its eastern side, the next building which you will come to after the Týn School is House at the Stone Bell (No. 13; Dům U kamenného zvonu), a narrow-fronted structure, the baroque cladding of which was recently removed to reveal its original late 14C stonework; the interior, now used for concerts and small exhibitions, features a small chapel with fragments of 14C murals. Adjoining it, at No. 12, is one of the most elegant of the city's 18C palaces, the **Goltz-Kinský Palace** (1755–65), which was built by Anselmo Lurago to a design supplied by K.I. Dientzenhofer, and richly stuccoed by C.G. Bossi. The twin pediments of the façade are a clever solution to the

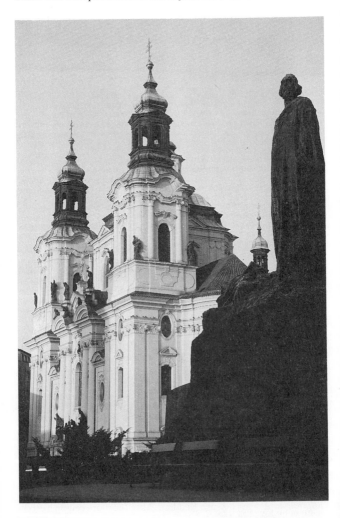

The Church of St. Nicholas on Prague's Old Town Square; in the foreground is the monument to Jan Hus by Ladislav Šaloun

building's position at the corner of the square, and show how the architects were anxious not to destroy the unity of the multi-gabled square by providing a single enormous pediment. One of the many distinguished visitors to have stayed in the palace was the Swedish dynamite magnate Alfred Nobel, who was enamoured of Bertha Kinský, a radical member of the family and a great pacifist, whose ideas may have been influential in determining Nobel's decision in later life to found the Nobel Peace Prize. It was from the balcony of the palace that on 21 February 1948 Klement Gottwald proclaimed to an assembled crowd of thousands the coming to power of the Communist regime. At his side, and later airbrushed from all the many photographs of the scene, was a man called Clementis who was executed four years later for high treason; this incident is recalled in the opening passages of Milan Kundera's novel, The Book of Laughter and Forgetting (1st English edition, 1980). The building later served to house the Print Room of the Prague National Gallery, but is at present closed, pending a decision to be taken about its future use.

The northern side of the square was radically altered at the end of the 19C, at around the same time that the pompous Pařížská avenue was built. At the north-eastern corner of the square, adjacent to the Goltz-Kinský Palace, is the late 17C former Pauline Monastery (Klášter paulánů), but the space between here and Pařížská is now taken up by the enormous, neo-baroque building housing the Ministry of Domestic Trading. The **Church of St. Nicholas** (sv. Mikuláš) was once tucked away at the very corner of the square, at the junction of Pařížská and U radnice, but, since the destruction in the last war of the eastern wing of the Town Hall, has now a prominent, exposed position, and indeed is one of the square's great glories.

The original Church of St. Nicholas was founded by merchants in the late 13C, and served until the building of the Týn church as the parish church of the Old Town. The reformist preacher Jan Milíč gave sermons here in the 1360s, and, in the following century, the building was taken over by the Utraquists, who were to keep it for over two centuries. In 1635 the church was presented to the Benedictines, who had it rebuilt between 1650–60. During the rule of Abbot Anselmo Vlach it was demolished and replaced by the present structure, which was built between 1732–35 by K.I. Dientzenhofer. The monastery was abolished in 1787, and for a while the church was used as a concert hall before being handed over to the Russian Orthodox Church in 1871. Since 1920 it has been the property of the Czechoslovak Hussite Church, which was founded in that same year. A thorough restoration of the building was completed in 1990.

The church, which has recently been given a dazzling coat of white paint, is a centrally planned structure with an unusual design which was determined to a large extent by the once cramped nature of the site. Dientzenhofer, wishing to create a structure which would powerfully reaffirm the Catholic faith in the wake of the building's Ultraquist past, was forced by the restricted site to put the emphasis on verticality. The twin-towered southern façade of the church, adorned with sculptures from the school of Braun, has an arrangement recalling that of Borromini's Sant' Agnese in Rome, but the architectural elements have been elongated in the creation of soaring proportions. The spectacular interior, now also a brilliant white, is dominated by the enormously tall central dome, and gives you the impression of being inside a wedding cake. There are ceiling frescoes by the Bavarian artist P. Assam of scenes from the Old Testament and the lives of SS. Nicholas and Benedict, but—unusually for Dientzenhofer—the painting decorations are subservient to the exceptionally rich stucco framework (by Bernard Spinetti).

Adjacent to the west façade of St. Nicholas, on Maislova, is the site of the house where Franz Kafka was born on 3 July 1883 (bronze plaque). The house, known as At the Tower ('U Věže'), originally belonged to the Benedictines, but by Kafka's day had been turned into a warren of small apartments, at the southernmost end of the Jewish ghetto; demolished at the end of the 19C (but retaining the original baroque portal), the building is currently being restored, and a small Kafka museum is planned. Immediately to the S of St. Nicholas is a small garden laid out on the site of the demolished east wing of the Old Town Hall. The heavily restored **Old Town Hall** (Staroměstská radnice), which projects out into the south-western corner of the Old Town Square, is the square's principal tourist attraction. Its history is a complex one, the place being an assemblage of several buildings, the earliest of which dates back to the beginning of the 14C.

To understand the Town Hall's genesis you should walk slowly around the exterior, beginning with the eastern end, which incorporates part of the ground floor of the original building—a private house which the civic authorities purchased from one Wolflin of Kámen in 1338. A tower was added to this in 1364, and a chapel—with an oriel window projecting east—built on its first floor by 1381; on the wall underneath the oriel is a plaque bearing the names of the 27 Protestants executed on the square in 1621, the exact place of the execution being marked on some nearby paving stones. The block which was attached to the northern end of Wolflin's house was a late 15C addition, rebuilt in the late 18C, and again in the early 19C; it was burnt down by the Nazis on the penultimate day of the last war, and plans to put up a modern extension on its site seem to have been abandoned. Walking the length of the southern side of the Town Hall, from E to W, you will come immediately to the famous **Astronomical Clock**, which was added to the south façade of Wolflin's house in 1410.

Installed originally by the master clocksmith Mikoláš of Kadaň in 1410, it was rebuilt in 1490 by a teacher at the Charles University, Master Hanuš of Růže. According to legend Hanuš was blinded to prevent him from creating another such marvel in Prague, but the blind man then climbed up the tower and stopped the clock. The true story is that the clock's mechanism was not to be perfected until Jan Táborský repaired it between 1552–60, after which it required no further alterations. Only its decorations have been changed, the painted calendar on the lower level being executed by J. Mánes in 1865 (the original is in the National Gallery at St. Agnes Convent), and the coloured figurines on all three of its levels being carved by V. Sucharda in 1948. The middle level comprises the clock proper, which both tells the time and gives the position of the sun and moon. Just before the striking of each hour a large crowd gathers in front of the clock to watch an impressive spectacle which begins with a skeleton (on the upper right corner of the clock) raising an hour glass and pulling a funerary bell; windows subsequently open on the upper level, and a macabre procession of Apostles and allegorical figures (such as a miser gloating over a sack of gold) files past.

W of the clock is a portal of 1470–80, attributed to Master Rejsek, and constituting the main entrance to the building. Further W is the former Kříž House, purchased by the civic authorities in 1360 and featuring a fine Renaissance window of 1520 bearing the Latin inscription 'Praga caput regni' (Prague, capital of the kingdom). In 1458 the Town Hall was extended by the purchase of the now attached house to the W, a property belonging previously to Mikeš the Furrier and which was to be remodelled in a neo-Renaissance style in 1878 by the architect A. Baum. The complex was enlarged yet further in 1835 with the purchase of the adjoining house called At the Cock, an originally Romanesque structure given an Empire façade in 1830. Finally, in 1896, the Town Hall bought the splendid property adjacent to the western end of At the Cock, **At the Minute** (Dům U minuty), a house where the Kafka family had lived from 1889 right up to the time of its purchase. The exterior of the house is covered with among the finest sgraffito decorations in Prague; these monochrome works, representing classical and biblical scenes and allegorical figures of the Virtues, were executed around 1611, and restored in 1919 by none other than J. Čapek, the brother of the writer Karel (they were to be restored again after the 1945 fire).

The interior of the Town Hall can only be visited with a guided tour, and these take place at irregular intervals throughout the day, and attract great crowds of tourists. Though it has been much altered over the centuries and was badly gutted in 1945, it retains on the second floor the late Gothic Council Chamber of 1470. The late 19C Assembly Room on the same floor was dominated until recently by two large canvases by V. Brožík, Jan Hus at the Council of Constance, and The Election of George of Poděbrady as King of Bohemia (these are now in the Troja Château); the Gothic vaulting in the vestibule of the building has a mosaic decoration of 1937, executed after designs by M. Aleš, and representing the story of the mythical Princess Libuše. A visit to the Town Hall is complemented by a climb up its 70m-high tower, from where an excellent view can be had.

Before leaving the Old Town Square, you should walk along the southern side of the square, which is lined with an especially attractive row of arcaded houses. The neo-Gothic one at No. 16 (at the entrance to Celetná) has sgrafittoed decorations by M. Aleš, most notably a representation of St. Wenceslas on horseback. Further W, at No. 20, is the *House at the Golden Unicorn* (Dům U zlatého jednorožce), which has an 18C façade with a Gothic portal; the cellar is a Romanesque structure of the 13C, while the late Gothic vaulting in the vestibule was designed by Master Rejsek in 1496. A plaque on the outside of the building records that in 1848 the composer Bedřich Smetana established here his first music school.

The Old Town Square leads at its narrow south-eastern corner into the quieter and triangular-shaped **Small Square** or Malé náměstí, which is centred around a small fountain surrounded by a Renaissance ironwork grille of 1560. One of the oldest spaces in the Old Town, this was inhabited in the 12C by French merchants; fruit markets were held here during the Middle Ages. Though a number of the houses have Romanesque cellars, the present appearance of the square is due mainly to 18C and 19C remodelling. One of the most prominent of the buildings is the one at No. 3, which was rebuilt in a neo-Renaissance style in 1890 for the ironmongery firm of V.J. Rott; the name of Rott appears on the wonderful if rather faded painted façade, which is covered all over with figurative and ornamental motifs based on designs supplied by M. Aleš. An excellently preserved neo-baroque pharmacy of the last century is incorporated into the late 18C house at No. 13, adjoining which, at the southwestern corner of the square, is the recently opened American Reception Centre, a meeting-place for American tourists, and a rather brash and incongruous addition to the Old Town; this is the place to buy T-shirts inscribed with the words, 'Prague. Czech it out'.

Continuing to follow the processional route of the Bohemian kings, turn left at the American Reception Centre, and then immediately right into Karlova street, which is as much of a showpiece as Celetná,

Neo-Renaissance façade designed by Mikuláš Aleš for the ironmongery firm of Rott; Prague, Malé náměstí

but narrower and more winding, with houses that are picturesquely askew; come here at dusk, in particular during the winter months, and the impression of entering some fairy-tale is intensified. At the junction of Karlova and Husova, the first street which you cross, are three interconnected buildings forming the *Central Bohemian Gallery*, where temporary art exhibitions are put on. The part of the gallery on Karlova is an elegant 18C structure, but the building where the gallery's main entrance is situated, at No. 19 Husova, is a Renaissance house crowned by an attractive pair of stepped gables;

the interior of the gallery, featuring a Romanesque cellar, successfully incorporates the surviving medieval elements into a bright modern setting. Just to the S of the entrance, at No. 19 Husova, is the beer cellar called *At the Golden Tiger* (U zlatého tygra), a popular haunt of the writer Bohumil Hrabal, and mentioned in several of his writings, for instance in a short piece entitled The Magic Flute (1989): 'And I was at the Golden Tiger, deep in thought, saying to myself, as I always do, that if the Gods loved me I would expire in front of a glass of beer...'

Deviating N from Karlova along Husova you will come after a few metres to one of the most celebrated of Prague's baroque palaces, **The Clam-Gallas Palace**. Built between 1713–19 for Count J.W. Gallas, it was the work of the great Viennese architect Johann Bernard Fischer von Erlach, aided by two of the leading artists of his day, the sculptor Matthias Braun and the Italian painter Carlo Carlone. The main façade, hemmed in on the narrow Husova Street, is in many ways remarkably classical, with its large central pediment, simple fenestration, and largely undecorated walls. At the same time, however, it is given a dynamic baroque quality through Braun's sculptural additions—the row of figures (replaced mainly by copies) along the attic, and, above all, the powerful, struggling **atlantes** who support the two portals, which are situated, unusually, at the sides of the façade. The dramatic elements of the exterior are continued inside in the exciting *Grand Staircase*, where there are further works by Braun in addition to sumptuous stuccowork by Santino Bussi and an exhilarating ceiling painting by Carlone representing The Triumph of Apollo. The whole building, boasting a number of other ceilings by Carlone, was beautifully restored in the 1980s, and now houses the *Print Room* of the Prague National Gallery, which puts on temporary exhibitions of prints and drawings.

The northern side of the palace abuts into the náměstí primátora dr. Vacka, where you will find, immediately on turning right into the square, a fountain attached to the palace's garden wall. Within its niche is a famous sculpture executed in 1812 by the Romantic artist Václav Prachner (the original has now been taken to the National Gallery at Zbraslav): entitled Vltava but popularly called Terezka, it is a vigorous portrayal of a female nude, and tradition has it that an old man living in the neighbourhood fell in love with this image, and left all his money for her in his will. The rest of the square is taken up by the north-eastern corner of the vast Clementinum (see below), the grim Municipal Public Library (1924–28), and, on the eastern side of the square, the New Town Hall. The latter, built in 1908–11 by O. Polívka, is a grey and heavy Art Nouveau structure enlivened by some fine and prominent statuary: the allegorical figures and reliefs around the main portal are by S. Sucharda and J. Mařatka, while the niche figures at the two corners of the façade are by L. Šaloun, and include a wonderful sandstone representation of Rabbi Löw (1910).

The short Seminářská, at the south-western corner of the square, will take you back to Karlova, passing at the junction of the two streets (No. 3 Karlova) the toy-like corner house known as *At the Golden Well* (Dům U zlaté studně), a Renaissance structure later adorned with stucco figures of saints by Ulrich Mayer; the latter were added in 1701, shortly after an outbreak of plague, and include two saints normally invoked at times of plague, SS. Anthony and Roch. Continue walking W along Karlova and you will find, at the junction with the next street, Liliová, a pink Renaissance house named At the Golden Serpent (U zlatého hada) (No. 18), with a 19C plaque of a snake on the outside. In the early 18C the house was occupied by the Armenian coffee-merchant Deodatus Damajan, who sold coffee in the streets of Prague before opening here the first coffee-shop in Prague (later he opened another shop at the Three Ostriches (U tří pštrosů) on the other side of the river); the place today still functions as a café, but has a chic modern décor in questionable taste. Further W along the southern side of Karlova, at No. 4, is a plaque marking the house where the German astronomer J. Kepler lived between 1607–12, formulating during this period his first two laws concerning the movement of the Earth around the sun; the tower within the courtyard of the house is said to have been used by Kepler as an observatory.

The whole northern side of the Karlova, from Seminářská right up to the end of the street, is lined by the former Jesuit College of the **Clementinum**, the largest complex of buildings in Prague after the Castle, and covering an area of two hectares.

As part of his campaign to strengthen the Catholic faith in Bohemia, the Habsburg Emperor Ferdinand I summoned the Jesuits in 1556 to Prague where they took over the former Dominican church and monastery of St. Clement. At the western end of Karlova, overlooking the Square of the Knights of the Cross (Křižovnické náměstí), the Jesuits began building in 1593 the Church of the Holy Saviour, the construction of which was later to involve two of the leading architects of the early baroque in Bohemia, Anselmo Lurago and Francesco Caratti. By the middle of the 17C the teaching establishment which the Jesuits had founded alongside the church had been turned into a university college, endowed with an important library. From 1653 onwards F. Caratti began work on the university buildings, a task which was to entail the pulling down of much of the Old Town and was not to be completed until 1748, under the direction of F.M. Kaňka. With the expulsion of the Jesuit order in 1773, the Clementinum was given over to the Charles University, which shortly afterwards transferred here its own library. This library has now been amalgamated into the National Library of Czechoslovakia, which takes up most of the complex and boasts such precious works as the Vyšehrad Codex of 1085.

Walking down Karlova from Seminářská you skirt the southern side of the former Dominican church of *St. Clement*, which is incorporated into the southern walls of the Clementinum. The church was rebuilt in 1711–15 by F.M. Kaňka, and is now used by the Greek Catholic Church. The recently restored interior, which is rarely open, is covered with ceiling paintings of the life of St. Clement by J. Hiebel, who was also responsible for the illusionistic framework in the chancel, a work clearly inspired by the Italian quadratura specialist Padre Pozzo. More remarkable are the outstanding and emotionally charged series of statues of the Evangelists and Fathers of the Church by Matthias Braun and his workshop, decorating the niches of the piers. Adjacent to the western end of St. Clement, and attached to the apse of the Holy Saviour, is the *Italian Chapel*, the rounded exterior of which affects the course of Karlova, and gives drama to the street; built around 1590 (but with an interior redecorated in the 18C), it is the earliest example in central Europe of an elliptically planned structure. The grandest of the churches associated with the Clementinum is that of *St. Salvator*, which was begun in 1593 and not completed until 1714. The Italianate west façade, facing the Knights of the Cross Square, is inspired by that of the Jesuit's mother church in Rome, but has a three-arched portico which was added by Francesco Caratti in 1653–59; the sculptures on the portico's balustrade, as well as those on the pediment above, were executed by Jan Bendl in 1659. The interior, with alterations by both C. Lurago and F.M. Kaňka, has rich stucco decorations by Bendl, and also a ceiling painting of the Four Continents by K. Kovář (1748); among the furnishings is a confessional (1675) which Bendl decorated with sculptures of the Apostles.

Running N of the church of St. Salvator along Křižovnická is the earliest and most grandiose of the Clementinum's façades, begun by F. Caratti in 1653 and featuring stucco medallions of Roman emperors by Antonio Cometa. An arch by the side of the church will lead you inside the complex, where you will find four large and greying courtyards, one of which has a statue by Emmanuel Max of a Prague Student (1847), a work commemorating the role played by students in defending the Charles Bridge during the Sack of Prague by the Swedes in 1648; in another of the courtyards is an 18C observatory tower crowned by a bronze of Atlas (1722). The interiors of the Clementinum, which can only be visited with special permission, are remarkable for their rococo rooms by F.M. Kaňka, most notably the **University Library** of 1727, a sumptuous gilded space with a ceiling painting by J. Hiebl of The Temple of Wisdom, and walls enlivened by salomonic columns.

The small and busy Knights of the Cross Square (Křižovnické náměstí) derives its name from the hospice brotherhood to which was entrusted in the 13C the protection of the Judith's Bridge, the predecessor of the Charles Bridge. The former monastery and church of St. Francis which once belonged to this Order stand adjacent to the church of St. Salvator, and were rebuilt in the late 17C. Designed by Jean-Baptiste Mathey, and carried out by Carlo Lurago, the centrally-planned church has a dome based closely on that of St. Peter's in Rome. The interior is ringed with dark Slivenec marble altars, and adorned with a ceiling painting of the Last Judgement by V.V. Reiner (1722–23); in the crypt are the foundations of the original three-aisled structure of the 13C. Just outside the church is a cast-iron memorial to Charles IV, designed by A. Hähnel in 1848 to commemorate the fifth centenary of the foundation of the Charles University. The western end of the square is marked by the **Tower of the Old Town Bridge**, a late 14C structure which served as a model for the Powder Tower, and has rich sculptural decorations from the workshop of Peter Parler, including, above the gate, representations of St. Vitus (the bridge's patron saint) flanked by St. Wenceslas and Charles IV; the structure was heavily restored and considerably embellished by Josef Mocker in the 1870s. The view from the top is in many ways the finest in all Prague, embracing the Old Town, the Little Quarter and a grand sweep of the Vltava.

The arch of the tower leads on to the Charles Bridge (see Route C), along which the coronation processions would pass on their way to St. Vitus. Leave the Royal Route and head S from the square along the Smetana Embankment (Smetanovo nábřeží) to visit the southern half of the Old Town. The first turning to the right is the short Novotného Lávka, which takes you on to a tiny spit of land jutting out into the Vltava and dominated by the former municipal water tower (a structure of 1489 reconstructed at the end of the 19C). The furthermost building, originally a part of the municipal waterworks, was built in 1885 in a Czech Renaissance style, and is covered with sgraffito decorations representing the Siege of the Old Town by the Swedes, and executed after designs by M. Aleš, F. Ženíšek and J. Koula. Inside is a hall where concerts and lectures are given, and a drably modern display of exhibits relating to the life and work of the composer *Bedřich Smetana*, of whom there is a statue by J. Malejovský (1984) in front of the building. Across the Smetana embankment from Novotného lávka is Anenská, which leads after a few metres into the intimate Anenské náměstí. Immediately to your right on entering the square (at No. 4) is a rococo palace built in c 1765 by Jan Josef Wirch for Count Hubert Karel Pachta of Rájov; the Pachtas were great patrons of music, and Mozart and his wife Constance, and Beethoven were among those who have stayed here. Attached to this building, at No. 5, is an early 19C building which was transformed in the late 1950s into one of Prague's most influential small theatres, *The Theatre on the Balustrade* (Divadlo Na zábradlí).

The Theatre on the Balustrade rose to prominence in around 1960 under the directorship of the visionary, dictatorial and totally impractical director Ivan Vyskočil, whom Václav Havel recalls in his book *Disturbing the Peace* (1990): 'Sometimes his behaviour was outrageous: for example, he'd say, 'Tomorrow we're going to try out whatever comes into our minds', but then he wouldn't come to the rehearsal, although he was the only person in the troupe capable of that kind of creativity.' Leon Grossman took over the directorship of the theatre shortly afterwards, and it was under him that it experienced its greatest years, putting on acclaimed productions of Jarry's Ubu Roi, Beckett's Waiting for Godot, and a dramatisation of Kafka's The Trial. The theatre is perhaps best remembered today for its associations with Václav Havel, who worked here between 1960 and 1968, establishing himself as a playwright through such works as The Garden Party, The Memorandum and The Increased Difficulty of Concentration. Since the events of November 1989, Havel's plays and those of his banned contemporaries have returned to the repertory here, and alternated for a while with the mime productions of Fialka and his troupe. Fialka's internationally renowned Pantomime, which acquired in later years the status of a tourist attraction, was housed in this theatre from the time the place was founded up to Fialka's death in the spring of 1991.

On the opposite side of the square to the theatre is the former Convent of St. Anne (Klášter sv. Anny), which was founded by Dominican nuns in 1313 inside a monastery which had belonged up to then to the Order of the Knights Templar. The nuns built after 1330 a Gothic church on the site of the Templars' Romanesque rotunda, the foundations of which were excavated between 1954–57; the convent itself was rebuilt in the late 17C, and has an imposing main façade of 1676. The church—where Christoph Willibald Gluck used to play the organ in the early 18C—survives to this day, though has been put to other uses since the abolition of the convent in 1782; the whole complex, for many years the centre of the printing works of Schönfeld, is used today partly as lithographic studios, and partly as rehearsal rooms for the National Theatre. The former convent extends E of the square all the way to the continuation of Anenská, Řetězová, on which stands, at No. 3, the *House at the Stork's* (Dům U Čápa), one of the more remarkable survivals in Prague of Romanesque domestic architecture, containing as it does a ground floor which has remained little changed since around 1200; the building, which can be visited, belonged in the 15C to George of Poděbrady.

Return along Anenská to the Smetana Embankment, and walk S by the side of the Vltava. Shortly you will come to a small garden containing Prague's answer to London's Albert Memorial—a neo-Gothic *monument to the Emperor Franz I*, who died in 1846. Erected in 1844–46 by J.O. Kranner, it features at its base a series of allegorical figures by Josef Max, executed in a style which owes nothing to Czech art, but much to German sculpture and engravings of the late 15C and early 16C; the equestrian statue of Franz I which once crowned the monument, was taken down in 1918, and now languishes in that sculptural mortuary comprising the Lapidarium of the National Museum. Due E of the garden, along Konviktská, is the tiny *Rotunda of the Holy Rood* (Rotunda sv. Kříže), one of Prague's oldest buildings. Dating back to the early 12C, it was well restored by Vojtěch Ullmann in 1862–65, and ringed by an attractive iron-work grille designed by Josef Mánes; the interior, restored again in the late 1970s, contains fragments of 14C wall-paintings, including a scene of the Coronation of the Virgin.

Head S from the Rotunda down Karolíny Světlé and turn left along Krocínova into Bartolomějská. Towards the end of the latter street, you will pass on your left the former Jesuit church of *St. Bartholomew* (sv. Bartoloměje), which was built by K.I. Dientzenhofer in 1726–31, and has a richly decorated west façade, and ceiling paintings by V.V. Reiner; next to it is a former Jesuit College intended for young noblewomen, and built in 1660 on the site of a centre for reformed prostitutes. Turn left at the end of the street into Průchodní, which leads into the Betlémské náměstí. On the western side of the square (at No. 1) is the House at the Hálaneks, which was formed of three 15C houses that were remodelled at the end of the 16C.

In the middle of the 19C the House at the Hálaneks came into the hands of Vojta Náprstek (1826–94), a manufacturer and academic who was responsible, among other things, for introducing to Prague such modern appliances as the refrigerator, the washing machine and the sewing machine. An enthusiast of anthropology, he arranged lectures on the subject in his house, and opened here first a library and then a museum of anthropology. Thanks to numerous bequests from Czech travellers, Náprstek was soon able to build at the back of his house a large modern extension to this museum, designed in 1886 by A. Baum and B. Münzberger.

Náprstek's institution, subsequently administered by the National Museum, is known today as the *Náprstek Museum of Asian, African and American Cultures*, and is housed in its entirety in the extension of 1886. This grand red-brick block forms a complete contrast to the intimate arcaded courtyard which precedes it. The collections are clearly displayed, and, in the case of those on the top floor dedicated to Australasia, with considerable imagination.

The north side of the Betlémské náměstí is dominated by the austere twin-gabled chapel which gives the square its name.

In 1391 followers of the reformist preacher Milíč of Kroměříž decided to build a church where the Mass would be said in Czech. The Catholic authorities agreed only to the construction of a chapel, which, however, turned out when completed in 1394 to be large enough to contain a congregation of 3000. Jan Hus preached here between 1402–13, and the place—called the Bethlehem Chapel—was to remain the spiritual centre of his followers long after his death. His friend, Master Jakoubek of Stříbro, succeeded him as preacher here from 1414–29, and in 1521 the German peasant leader Thomas Münzer proclaimed from the chapel's pulpit his Utopian social views; from 1609 up to the Battle of the White Mountain in 1620, the chapel belonged to the Union of Czech Brethren, one of whose preachers was the future father-in-law of Comenius, J.A. Komenský. Taken over subsequently by the Jesuits, the building was destroyed three years after the expulsion of the Jesuit Order in 1773, and a private dwelling put up in its place. In 1919 part of the chapel was unearthed under the house, and further archaeological excavations in 1949 revealed that all except the southern wall of the chapel had been used in the construction of the later building. The decision was then taken to reconstruct the Bethlehem Chapel in its original state, the idea being to create a memorial to the Hussites, who, according to remarks made at this time by Klement Gottwald, were already 'fighting for communism' 500 years ago.

The box-like interior of the chapel, which was reconstructed in 1950–52 by Jaroslav Fragner, has pseudo-medieval wall-paintings and wooden furnishings, and is focused on the pulpit rather than the altar. A door on the eastern side leads into the house where Jan Hus and other preachers lived: inside you will find a partial recreation of a domestic interior of the early 15C, and displays relating to the Hussite movement.

After leaving the building turn left and then left again into Husova, on which stands—shortly to the N on the right-hand side—the church of *St. Giles* (sv. Jiljí). Founded in the 13C and rebuilt between 1310–71, this church has a sturdy, twin-towered west façade which has been little altered since the 14C, when the building was the principal base of the reform preacher Milíč of Kroměříž; the tall interior, however, was remodelled by F. Špaček after 1733, and has been cloaked with massive gilded capitals, rich stucco decoration by B. Spinetti, and ceiling frescoes by V.V. Reiner comprising a central panel of the Celebration of the Dominican Order, and two flanking ones representing the Legends of St. Giles and St. Thomas Aquinas.

Head E of the church along the tiny Zlatá, turn right into Jilská, and then immediately left into Vejvodova; this will take you into Michalská, where you turn right again, and then first left into Havelská. At its north-eastern end Havelská widens into a narrow square, enlivened today by market stalls, and dominated by the church of *St. Gall* (sv. Havla). The latter, a 13C foundation, was remodelled around 1722 by Pavel Bayer and Jan Santini-Aichel, who gave the church its powerful, undulating façade. The building has been under restoration for many years, as has indeed a large area to the E embracing the Tyl Theatre, the Carolinum, and the former Fruit Market (Ovocný trh). The *Tyl Theatre*, situated on Železná, in between St. Gall and the Fruit Market, is an elegant neo-classical building designed by Antonín Haffenecker in 1781.

The oldest theatre in Prague, the Tyl Theatre opened in 1783 with a performance of Lessing's play Emilia Galotti. Four years later the first ever performance of Mozart's opera Don Giovanni took place here, and early in the following century the place acquired further musical renown when the German composer K.M. Weber was director of its operatic ensemble. The property after 1799 of the Czech Estates, the theatre was known up to 1945 as the Estates Theatre, after which it was renamed in honour of the Czech dramatist J.K. Tyl (1808–56), whose comedy Fidlovačka—from which the song and future Czech national anthem, Where is my Home, is taken—had been premiered here in 1834.

Adjoining the Theatre, at No. 9 Železná, is the *Carolinum*, the original building of the oldest university in central Europe. Founded by Charles IV in 1348, the university building is also claimed to be the oldest still in use in Europe, though in fact very little of the medieval structure survives, the principal survival being the charming oriel window on the southern side, facing the Fruit Market. The structure was extensively rebuilt by F.M. Kaňka after 1718, at the time when the University was in the hands of the Jesuits; further major reconstruction took place after the war. Continue N up Železná, and turn left into Kožná, where, at No. 1, is a house with a beautiful Renaissance portal featuring two bears. A plaque indicates that the house was the birthplace of the journalist Egon Erwin Kisch (1885–1948), who devoted much of his writing to accounts of his native Prague, including *Prague Adventures* and *Tales from Prague's Streets and Nights*. Another of his works was dedicated to the city's covered passages, and it is singularly appropriate that from No. 10 Kožná you can walk through such passages all the way back to Jilská. Kisch's birthplace stands at the corner of Melantrichova, where you turn right to rejoin the southern side of the Old Town Square.

Walk to the opposite side of the square and enter Pařížská, a good starting-point for a tour of the northern half of the Old Town. This long straight avenue, built at the end of the 19C, is lined with large oppressively ornamented blocks, featuring fantastical corners composed of irregularly shaped balconies and openings piled up one on top of each other. Its creation consituted one of the few major plans of urban renewal within the Old Town of Prague, cutting as it did a great swathe through a slum area crammed with picturesque but decayed old houses inhabited largely by the city's Jewish population. Before reaching the main monuments of Jewish Prague, take the first turning to the right, and then turn right again into Salvátorská, on which stands, at No. 8 an innovative brick building constructed for the *Stenc Publishing House* by Otakar Novotný 1908–11. Return to Pařížská, and continue walking N, crossing at the end of the next block the large intersecting street of Široká. At No. 9 Široká, just to the W of the junction of this street with Pařížská, is an Art Nouveau apartment block, built by Karel Mašek in 1908, and boasting a magnificent portal flanked by sculpted female allegories; adjoining this, at No. 11, is a neo-Gothic apartment of 1906 by Matěj Blecha, with an oval Art Nouveau staircase well. Continuing N along Pařížská, you will find at the end of the next block to the left the *U Velké Synagogy*, a beer hall and modest restaurant with a little spoilt turn-of-the-century interior (the place is another of the haunts of the writer Bohumil Hrabal). Immediately beyond this establishment there is a sudden interruption in the line of Pařížská's turn-of-the-century blocks to reveal incongruously, just below the pavement level on the left-hand side, three of the main survivals of Jewish Prague—the Jewish Town Hall, and the High and Old-New Synagogues. These and several other neighbouring monuments form part of **THE STATE JEWISH MUSEUM**, the tickets for which have to be bought outside the Old Jewish Cemetery (from Pařížska take the turning to the left in between the Town Hall and the Synagogue, cross Maislova, and continue walking W, following for 50m U starého hřbitova).

Jews began settling in Prague from at least the 10C onwards, though it was not apparently until the mid 13C that they began forming a ghetto in the district around the Old-New Synagogue; in accordance with the Third Lateran Council of 1179 this ghetto was separated from its Christian surroundings by a wall. Despite fires, pogroms and even a law of 1541 banishing Jews from the whole of Bohemia, the ghetto flourished, and by the 17C an estimated 7000 people were crowded into the area. Two of its most influential figures were active during the reign of Rudolph II, one being the Emperor's finance minister, Mordechaj Markus Maisel, who was responsible for the paving of the ghetto, and the building of the Maisel Synagogue and the Jewish Town Hall. The other great Jew of this period was the Rabbi Löw, a man much respected by Rudolph II and the leading aristocratic families of the time, and under whose influence the Jewish community in Prague enjoyed the most privileged period in their history. A prominent theologian, Löw was the author of many writings that became an inherent part of Hasidic teaching, such as his homily On the Hardening of Pharaoh's Heart. But Löw was to be remembered above all for his reputed supernatural powers, a reputation doubtless enhanced by his being a passionate devotee of the Cabbala, whereby he believed that the whole of human history, past, present and future, could be read in the Torah. Numerous fanciful tales are told of Löw, but none more famous than that of his creation—from the mud of the Vltava—of Yossel the Golem a prototype of the robot.

The law requiring the Prague Jews to be contained in the ghetto was abolished during the rule of Maria Theresa, and in 1850 the area was turned into a district of Prague called Josefov in honour of the Emperor Joseph II. Much of this district was a slum, without water-supply or drainage, and in 1893 the whole area was razed, leaving only the buildings of historical interest still standing. Later the Nazis, far from wishing to destroy these surviving monuments, planned to turn them into a 'Museum of Jewry', so as to record for posterity the culture of what they believed would soon be an extinct race. A museum of Jewish art had existed since the beginning of the century, but, as a result of the Nazis' confiscation of Jewish property, the collections were swelled to become the largest in the world of synagogical art. The museum's growth coincided with the dwindling of the Jewish population of Bohemia and Moravia to a tenth of its former size: a memorial in one of the Prague synagogues (the Pinkas Synagogue) records the names of 77,297 Jews killed during the Nazi occupation of the country. Today only a small community of Orthodox Jews remains in the traditional Jewish quarter of Prague.

The former Jewish ghetto has always held a strong fascination for visitors to Prague, and a number of foreign writers have evoked the place in their works, for instance the popular American novelist of the last century, Marion Crawford. In her novel, The Witch of Prague (1882), Crawford evokes the ghetto with an unsavoury mixture of romantic fascination and deep repellence: 'Throngs of gowned men, crooked, bearded, filthy, vulture-eyed, crowded upon each other in the narrow, public place ... a writhing mass of humanity, intoxicated by the smell of gold, mad for its possession, half hysteric with the fear of losing it, timid, yet dangerous, poisoned to the core by the sweet sting of money, terrible in intelligence, vile in heart, contemptible in body, irresistible in the unity of their greed—the Jews of Prague two hundred years ago.' More recently the former ghetto provided the main setting for the English novelist Bruce Chatwin's compelling novella, Utz (1988), which deals with a collector of Meissen porcelain figures living in the same district where the Rabbi Löw had fashioned his Golem.

The Josefov is today one of the city's obligatory tourist sights, and the throngs of visitors who descend upon this restricted area leads to unpleasant congestion and long queues to enter some of the monuments. One of the main attractions is the **OLD JEWISH CEMETERY** (Starý židovský hřbitov), where over 20,000 tombstones are jumbled together among trees in a manner which at times echoes the visiting conditions. Though established in the late 15C, it contains tombs transferred from an earlier cemetery, the oldest being that of the Rabbi Abigdor Kar (d. 1389); the last person to be buried here was Moses Beck in 1787. The tall, cracked and often perilously leaning stones are engraved with symbolical reliefs referring either to the occupation or the name of the deceased, for instance a stag in the case of someone named Hirsch, or a pair of scissors in the case of a tailor. One of the most richly decorated stones is that of Heudele Bassevi (d. 1628), who was the wife of the first Prague Jew to be raised to the nobility; among the graves of other distinguished Jews are those of Mordechaj Maisel (d. 1601), the astronomer David Gaus (d. 1613), the scientist Josef Delmedigo (d. 1655) and the bibliophile David Oppenheimer (d. 1736). Pebbles are often thrown on the graves as a gesture of respect towards the dead. The grave with the greatest accumulation of these is that of the most famous Jew of all to be buried here, the Rabbi Löw, on top of whom visitors also throw bank notes in the hope that this man with supernatural powers will grant them their wishes. A beautiful description of the cemetery appears in Bruce Chatwin's novella, Utz (1988): 'It was now early evening and we were sitting on a slatted seat in the Old Jewish Cemetery. Pigeons were burbling on the roof of the Klausen Synagogue. The sunbeams, falling through sycamores, lit up spirals of midges and landed on the mossy tombstones, which, heaped one upon the other, resembled seaweed-covered rocks at low tide.'

Flanking the entrance to the cemetery are the Klaus Synagogue and former Ceremonial Hall. The former, dating back to 1694, has a stuccoed, barrel-vaulted interior containing today a large collection of Hebraic manuscripts and prints; the latter, designed by F. Gerstl in 1906 in the form of a tiny neo-Romanesque castle, features a display of children's and other drawings depicting conditions at the Terezín ghetto and concentration camp (see Route 7). After seeing these

you should return to the **OLD-NEW SYNAGOGUE** (Staronová syn-
agoga), which is architecturally the most interesting of the synagogues, as well as the only one still in use today. One of the oldest
synagogues in Europe, it dates back to the middle of the 13C, and
owes its unusual name to the fact that it was originally called the
'New' Synagogue until another 'New' one was built in the vicinity.
The most striking features of the exterior are the unusually tall
stepped brick gable on the western side (a 15C addition), and the
13C entrance portal on the southern side, adorned with delicate
carvings of vine leaves and grapes. The narrow barrel-vaulted
vestibule which you come to on the other side of this portal was
originally the main hall of the synagogue until the present one was
added after c 1270; in the 17C metal boxes were placed in this
vestibule for the collection of Jewish taxes. The actual main hall, one
of the finest examples in Prague of the Cistercian Gothic style, is a
double-aisled space with numerous references, both in its decoration
and plan, to the figure 12, symbolising the twelve tribes of Israel. 13C
leaf ornament decorates the tympanum of the shrine on the east wall
containing the Torah (a parchment scroll of the five Books of Moses,
or Pentateuch). In the middle of the hall stands a pulpit, surrounded
by a beautiful Gothic grille of the late 15C; the benches lining the
walls are early 19C, while on the walls themselves are traces of
medieval frescoes and inscriptions of 1618 recording certain sections
of the Psalms.

Directly facing the south portal of the building is the entrance to
the *High Synagogue*, which was built in 1568, extended at the end of
the following century, and remodelled and given its present façade
in the 19C; on the ground floor is a display of synagogical textiles,
while in the tall, stuccoed hall above is a collection of metalwork.
Adjoining the synagogue, and connected to it up to the 19C by a
door, is the picturesque *Jewish Town Hall*, founded by Maisel in the
late 16C, but completely rebuilt in 1763 and given then its toy-like
wooden turret, complete with a Hebraic clock which tells the time
backwards. Its main entrance, at No. 18 Maislova, leads into Prague's
only kosher restaurant, a once simple establishment which has
recently been given a candle-lit elegance so as to attract greater
tourism.

Heading N along Maislova from the Old-New Synagogue you will
find at the end of the street (at No. 21) an elegant and beautifully
decorated Art Nouveau apartment block, built by František Weyr
and Richard Klenka in 1911; facing its northern side, at No. 2
Břehová, is another fine building of this period, designed by Bedřich
Bendelmayer. Walking instead S down Maislova you will come at
No. 10 to the *Maisel Synagogue*, which was commissioned and paid
for by Maisel in 1590, later rebuilt in a baroque style, and then given
a wholly neo-Gothic appearance by A. Grotte from 1893–1905; the
building houses a collection of synagogical metalwork but has been
closed for restoration for many years. Just to the S of the synagogue is
Široká, where you turn right, following the southern wall of the Old
Jewish Cemetery. The **Pinkas Synagogue**, which is attached to this
wall, was founded by Rabbi Pinkas in 1479, rebuilt in 1535, and
enlarged and remodelled by Juda Goldsmid de Herz in 1625. The
hall features late Gothic net vaulting, and walls inscribed with the
names of the 77,297 Jews killed by the Nazis in Bohemia and
Moravia during the last war (of this number, 36,000 were from
Prague).

Continuing E along Široká you will come, at the end of the

cemetery wall, to the large riverside square formerly known as the Red Army Square (náměstí Krasnoarmějců), but now renamed after the 1968 'martyr' Jan Palach, to whom there is a small memorial containing a bust made from a death mask. The imposing *Rudolfinum*, on the northern side of the square, was built in the late 19C by Josef Zítek and Josef Schulz as an art gallery and concert hall; the seat of the Czech parliament from 1918–39, the building was later used again for cultural purposes, and is now one of the main venues of the annual music festival known as the Prague Spring.

Turning right as soon as you enter the square from Široká, and walking N from it along 17. listopadu, the next building which you come to is the **Museum of Decorative Arts** (Umělecko-průmyslové muzeum), a French-style neo-Renaissance structure rising up above the western side of the Old Jewish Cemetery. The museum, founded in 1885 with a largely didactic purpose, was housed at first in the Rudolfinum while awaiting its eventual transference to the present building, which was completed by Josef Schulz in 1900; the façade is covered with reliefs by Bohuslav Schnirch and Antonín Popp representing the different branches of the decorative arts in Bohemia, and the coats of arms of the Bohemian towns most renowned for these arts. The museum itself, usually empty, and looked after by a particularly charming group of elderly women, is one of the great little-known attractions of Prague. Its collections, ranging from the Middle Ages up to the present day and with the main emphasis on Bohemia and Moravia, include glass, ceramics, porcelain, woodwork, furniture, metalwork, clocks, textiles, costumes, prints, posters and photographs. Despite the great size of the building, only a small proportion of its objects are on display, the rooms that are at present open being only those on the top floor, which is reached by walking up a monumental staircase adorned with painted decorations. The rooms have ceilings attractively decorated with turn-of-the-century grotesque work, and the display is endearingly old-fashioned and crowded, the overall effect—enhanced by the occasional dramatic lighting—being that of great wealth and variety, as in a Netherlandish still-life painting. Among the finest of the objects permanently on show are the numerous pieces of Bohemian baroque glass, and the superlative collection of Meissen porcelain figurines.

Continuing N along 17. listopadu will take you to the náměstí Curieových, a riverside square standing at the northern end of Pařížská, and bordered to the south by the fussy modern block of the luxurious Hotel Intercontinental (1968–74), and to the west by the *Law Faculty of Charles University*, an Art-Deco structure designed by J. Kotěra in 1919. Head S of the square along Pařížská, and turn left beyond the Hotel Intercontinental to reach, on the eastern side of a small garden, the ulice Elišky Krásnohorské, where, at Nos 10–14, is a remarkable 'Cubist' block, built by Otakar Novotný in 1917–19. Continuing S along this street, you will shortly rejoin Široká, passing on your left just before doing so the *Church of the Holy Ghost*, a single-aisled structure of 1346 remodelled after a fire in 1689; in front of the building stands a statue of St. John of Nepomuk (1727) by F.M. Brokoff. Turn left along Široká, and then turn left into Dušní, where, directly facing the eastern end of the Church of the Holy Ghost, is the *Spanish Synagogue*, a neo-Moorish structure designed by J. Niklas in 1882; the interior, at present closed for restoration, has elaborate stucco decorations inspired by those of the Alhambra in Granada. Walk N along Dušní until you reach the 17C–18C *Church of SS. Simon and Judas*, the choir of which has an organ on which both Mozart and Haydn played. U milosrdných, which runs E of the church, will take you to the present entrance of the former **Convent of St. Agnes** (Anežský klášter), a large and important medieval complex containing the 19C Czech paintings belonging to the National Gallery, as well as a collection of Czech arts and crafts of the 19C.

The Convent of St. Agnes, which is sometimes known by the ridiculous name of the 'Bohemian Assisi', was founded for the Poor Clares by Wenceslas I in 1233, probably on the request of his sister, Agnes of Bohemia, who became the first abbess. The large complex was virtually complete by the end of the 13C, and relatively few changes were to be made to it over the next four centuries, even after 1555 when the place was taken over by the Dominicans. A certain amount of new building work and remodelling was to be carried out in the wake of the Old Town fire of 1689, but with the dissolution of the convent in 1782, the whole complex fell into decay, its buildings being used as crafts workshops and poor people's homes. Extensive restoration work was begun this century, and in the course of this the foundations of a neighbouring Minorite monastery of the early 13C were discovered. Restoration is still slowly continuing.

The museum installed in the convent is centred around a large cloister, which has largely retained its mid-13C appearance, apart from the upper level of the eastern side, which features a Renaissance arcade built by the Dominicans. The holdings of 19C Czech applied art are displayed on the ground level of the cloister, at the south-east corner of which is a door leading into the convent's two adjoining churches, the restoration of which has recently been completed. The earliest of the two churches was dedicated to St. Francis and completed by the mid 13C; however only its presbytery has survived, and this is known today as the Mánes Hall and is used for concerts. Projecting east of this structure is the spacious and elegant *Church of St. Saviour*, which dates from the 1280s, and is a fine example of French Gothic influence. Stairs off the east side of the cloister climb up to the painting collections on the first floor. In these well-modernised upper rooms are displayed in chronological order works by all the major Bohemian artists of the 19C, beginning with classical landscapes by Procházka and ending with the rural genre scenes and cityscapes of Jakub Schikaneder, with whose late works Czech art is brought into the 20C. Among the more important Czech artists working in the early 19C were the painter of romantic Gothic interiors, Ludvík Kohl, the portraitist Antonín Machek, the mythological painter František Tkadlík, and the landscapists August Piepenhagen and Karel Postl, the latter being the first professor of landscape painting at the Prague Academy. Two other major names are Josef Navrátil—the author of a stunningly simple and realistic series of still-lifes—and Antonín Mánes, who is represented here by a number of romantic landscapes imbued with nationalist sentiment, most notably his view of the ruins of Kokořín Castle (1839). Two of Mánes's sons were painters, the most famous being the elder one, Josef, whose work dominates Czech 19C art. The paintings of his on show here reveal his extraordinary variety, and range from such academic canvases as Petrarch and Laura (1845–46) to a series of remarkably fresh landscapes painted in the 1850s and 1860s (for instance Gmunden, and the Mountain Hut); among his other works here are lively portraits of Luisa Bělská (1857) and Anna Václavíková (1862), detailed drawings of national folk costumes, a pair of mysteriously lit nudes (Dawn and Evening, 1857), and two large-scale oil studies for banners (one for the Říp Association at Roudnice, 1863–64, and the other for the Smíchov

Lukes Choir, 1868). Of Mánes's younger contemporaries, the only one to achieve an international reputation was Jaroslav Čermák, who specialised in ambitious scenes of Czech history, such as The Hussites Defending the Pass (1857). Academic landscapists of this period include Bedřich Havránek, Alois Bubák, and Adolf Kosárek, while one of the finest of the genre painters was Soběslav Pinkas, who did numerous scenes of Prague life, such as his Children on Kampa Island (1854). From the 1850s onwards an increasing number of Czech artists spent long period in France, including Pinkas himself, Viktor Barvitius, Karel Purkyně, and Antonín Chitussi. Barvitius was the author of the delightfully detailed and atmospherically lit genre scene, Thursday in Stromovka Park (1865); Purkyně meanwhile was an artist who fell strongly under the influence of Courbet, as can be seen in his powerful portrait of Jech the Smith (1860), and in the boldly painted still-lifes, The Snow Owl (1862) and Onions and Partridges (1862). Chitussi painted many landscapes while staying in and around Paris, and, on his return to Czechoslovakia, did numerous Barbizon-inspired scenes in the region where he was born—the Czech Moravian Highlands. Towards the end of the 19C many of the leading Czech artists were engaged in the decoration of the Prague National Theatre, including the landscapist Julius Mařák, and the specialists in allegorical and classical scenes involving female nudes, Vojtech Hynais and František Ženíšek. The most important of the artists of the so-called National Theatre Generation was the prolific Mikoláš Aleš, among whose works in the museum is a series of cartoons for his series, Legend of My Country, which he painted for the National Theatre; many other of his drawings and decorative designs are to be seen here, as well as numerous historical canvases such as The Meeting of George of Poděbrady with Matthias Corvinus (1877), Milica and the Yugoslavs (1876), and Hussite on the Baltic (1877), a bleak snow-covered landscape featuring a lone rider on horseback in front of the tomb of one of his comrades. The Czech turn-of-the-century artist best known outside of Czechoslovakia, Alfons Mucha, is represented here only by very slight works. In compensation there is a superb group of paintings by Jakub Schikaneder, ranging from the Bastien-Lepage-inspired Autumn (1884) to the large, suggestive and almost monochromatic city scenes of the first and second decades of this century, such as Winter Evening in the Town (1907–09) and Embankment (1916–18).

After leaving the Convent of St. Agnes head S down the short Anežská, at the end of which you will come to the Church of St. Castullus, which dates back to the early 14C. Though the main nave and chancel were remodelled following the fire of 1689, the south aisle has been preserved in its medieval state, as has the remarkable twin-aisled extension which was added to the north side of the church in 1375; the extension features a fine net vault with bosses decorated with masks and leaves. The walls of the sacristy meanwhile are covered with medieval murals, comprising a series of Apostles' heads of c 1400 and scenes of the Crucifixion and the Last Supper of c 1500.

Running alongside the southern side of the church is the Haštalská trída, where at No. 4 is an Art Nouveau house (1905) with a beautiful tree decoration on its façade; next to this is a portal of the same period incorporating an elegant rose window. Parallel to this street to the S is the Dlouhá třída, which follows the early medieval route connecting the Old Town Square with the colony of German merchants at Poříčí (see Route 1D). Turn left along Dlouhá, passing, at No. 37, the House At the Golden Tree (Dům U zlatého stromu), which has a late 16C courtyard dating from the time when the house belonged to the Mayor of the Old Town, Václav Kročín. At the eastern end of Dlouhá you will come to the Revoluční avenue, where you turn right, rejoining shortly afterwards the náměstí Republiky.

B.   The Little Quarter

The Little Quarter or Malá Strana, founded in 1257 by Přemysl Otakar II in the outer bailey of Prague Castle, was known up to the early 14C as The New Town below Prague Castle. Later in the century Charles IV considerably extended this town with the creation of new fortifications incorporating to the south the Petřín Hill. This hill forms today part of a large wooded park, the northern sides of which are fringed by lush gardens attached to baroque palaces. Gardens and baroque palaces, many of which now serve as embassies, are the dominant feature of the Little Quarter, the most genuinely picturesque area of a city steeped in the picturesque, the one least spoilt by modern development, and the one which can most truly be compared to a stage set. Whereas the Old Town is flat and overprettified in its centre, the steeply pitched Little Quarter offers a most variegated profile, and is as yet in a state of evocative decay. If approached from the Old Town along the Royal Route, which crosses the Charles Bridge, the sense of excitement and expectation is particularly acute, the bridge's gesticulating statuary sharply converging on the Little Quarter's turreted entrance gate, behind which rises the massive dome of St. Nicholas, and, higher still, the dramatic silhouette of Prague's castle.

THE CHARLES BRIDGE (Karlův most), one of Europe's most beautiful bridges, is not simply the visual centrepiece of Prague, but has also played a central role in the life and history of the city.

The first bridge to span the Vltava at this point was a wooden construction, first mentioned in 1118 and destroyed by flood in 1157. On the instigation of Queen Judith, the wife of Vladislav I, a 21-arched stone bridge was built in its place between 1158–60, but, in 1342, this too was to collapse after a flood. In 1357 Charles IV entrusted the architect Peter Parler with the construction of a new bridge, which was to be known as the Stone or Prague Bridge up to 1870, and only thereafter as the Charles Bridge. Built out of sandstone blocks, this 16-arched structure runs a slightly irregular course due to the fact that while the bridgeheads of the Judith's Bridge were retained new piers were constructed in the middle of the river, just to the south of the destroyed old ones. The new structure, which was completed in the early 15C, has been damaged a number of times by floods, and two of its arches had to be rebuilt in 1890, but it has never collapsed.

As well as serving as part of the processional route of the Bohemian kings, the Charles Bridge was a place where business transactions took place, tournaments held, custom dues collected, law suits settled, criminals executed, and delinquents punished by being dipped in the Vltava in wicker baskets. The most famous incident in its history occurred on 20 March 1393 when the future St. John of Nepomuk was bound hand and foot and thrown from its parapet into the river, where, according to legend, his body floated for an unnaturally long time, a group of five stars hovering above it. In 1683, at a time when the Jesuits were beginning to promote the Nepomuk cult, a statue to him by J. Brokoff was placed on the bridge, near the supposed point from where he was flung. This led to several religious orders commissioning other statues for the bridge, from J. and F.M. Brokoff, M.V. Jäckel, Matthias Braun, J.O. Mayer, and M.B. Mandl. The baroque statues, which were all in place by 1714, were joined between 1857–59 by works by Emmanuel Max; between 1908–37 a number of other statues were added, and some of the more worn ones removed to the Lapidarium of the National Gallery and replaced by copies. On 9 February, 1911 the bridge witnessed one of the many extravagant incidents in the life of the great hippy hoaxer and comic writer Jaroslav Hašek. A newspaper of the time reported that 'in the small hours of this morning Jaroslav Hašek wanted to throw himself from the parapet of the Charles Bridge into the Vltava ... The theatrical hairdresser, Mr Edward Bräuer, pulled him back. The police doctor diagnosed a pronounced neurosis, and he was taken to a mental home.'

The bridge, which is closed to traffic, is popular with carousing couples and lingering tourists, and at night is a meeting-place for singing and guitar-playing students, whose appearance and behaviour are little different to those of their hippy predecessors who gathered here in the late 1960s. The views on all sides are uninterruptedly beautiful, and the place becomes especially evocative on a winter's night, when, in the dim light of lanterns, a freezing mist rises from the river, and isolated groups of pedestrians glide past and disappear into the gloom. Another of the bridge's attractions are of course its statues, which turn the whole structure into a museum of Bohemian sculpture. On the first pier to the right immediately beyond the Old Town Gate (see Route 1A) stands the Madonna and St. Bernard (1709) by Matěj Václav Jäckel, a sculptor who introduced to Bohemia the dynamic high flown style of the Italian artist Bernini. This style was used to far more expressive effect in the work of Matthias Braun, an Austrian-born sculptor who first came to Bohemia in 1710, invited by the Cistercians of Plasy to execute statues for the Charles Bridge; a copy of the second statue which he did here, representing St. Ivo (1711), can be seen on the left-hand side of the bridge, directly facing Jäckel's Madonna and St. Bernard. The other outstanding Bohemian sculptor of this period was Ferdinand Maximillian Brokoff, an artist noted for his realism, and who carried out several works for the bridge, including the sculptural group of SS. Barbara, Margaret and Elizabeth, which adorns the second pier on the left-hand side. The first monument to be placed on the bridge was a gilded bronze Crucifix, cast by J. Hilger in 1629, and set up on the third pier to the right in 1657; the two stone figures were executed by E. Max in 1861, while the Hebrew inscription on the cross, dating from 1696, is said to have been paid for by a Jew as a fine for mocking this Christian symbol.

Continuing to cross the bridge, you will pass between the sixth and seventh piers a relief marking the supposed spot where St. John of Nepomuk was thrown into the Vltava in 1393; the bronze statue of the saint which was placed on the bridge in 1683, stands on the eighth pier to the right, and was executed by Johann Brokoff after a bozzetto by Matthias Rauchmüller. Towards its western end the bridge crosses the picturesque Kampa Island, which is separated from the left bank by a narrow canal, and is sometimes referred to as the 'Venice of Prague' (see below). Above the steps leading down to it, on the twelfth pier to the left, is a sculpture of The Vision of St. Luitgard (1710), which is the first work which Matthias Braun did in Prague, and in many ways the most powerful and emotionally compelling on the bridge; tradition has it that the work was based on a design by Peter Brandl, and there is certainly something very painterly in its wildly agitated drapery. Two piers further along to the left is another of the sculptural masterpieces of the bridge, a group by F.M. Brokoff of 1714 featuring SS. John of Matha, Felix de Valois, and Ivo, with a Turk guarding a group of captured Christians, the whole carved with Brokoff's characteristic realism (note, in particular the face of the Turk); the work was commissioned as a gesture of thanks to the Trinitarian Order for having redeemed Christians from Turkish captivity. Directly opposite this group is a statue by F.M. Brokoff of St. Vitus (1714), the only marble work on the bridge, the other stone sculptures being all of sandstone.

The bridge ends picturesquely at a gate of 1410 flanked by two towers, the taller of which was built in 1466 at the behest of George of Poděbrady, and is closely similar to the Old Town and Powder Towers; the shorter tower, a survival of the Judith's Bridge fortifications, dates back to 1166 but was remodelled in 1591. Once through the Little Quarter gate the Royal Processional Route headed W along Mostecká, today a busy shopping street featuring a number of fine Renaissance and baroque palaces, most notably, at No. 15, the *Kaunic Palace* (now the Yugoslav Embassy), which was built in 1773–75 by Anton Schmidt, and has a façade richly decorated with stuccoes by Ignác Platzer. The street leads into the sloping **Little Quarter Square** (Malostranské náměstí), which is divided in two by the massive church of St. Nicholas and adjoining buildings. The square, surrounded today by buildings of largely 17C and 18C appearance, formed originally the nucleus of Prague Castle's outer bailey, and in the middle there once stood the Romanesque Rotunda of St. Wenceslas; the site of a market and Town Hall for many centuries after the foundation of the Little Quarter in 1257, the square remains to this day the lively heart of this area, with an important tram junction at its lower, eastern end. The latter half of the square, known as the Lower Square, features on its eastern side (at No. 21) the former *Town Hall*, which was founded in the late 15C, and where in March 1575 a group of Habsburg opponents comprising neo-Utraquists, Lutherans and members of the Union of Czech Brethren formulated the so-called Czech Confession, a plea for legal recognition of Evangelical trends. This meeting is recalled in a plaque on the building's façade, the present appearance of which is due to reconstruction work carried out in 1617–22 by Giovanni Campione de Bossi. The elegant façade, divided by cornices into three main floors, is articulated by pilasters flanking paired windows crowned by broken pediments; the interior is now used for lectures, and musical and theatrical performances. Dominating the northern side of the Lower Square is the imposing *Smiřický-Montág Palace*, which dates back to 1606 but was rebuilt in a late baroque style by J. Jäger in around 1763; the building is famous as the place where on 22 May 1618, Albrecht Smiřický and an invited group of leaders of the anti-Habsburg opposition hatched the plot which was to lead the following day to the 'Second Defenestration', the incident which sparked off the Thirty Years' War. Adjacent to this, on the western side of the Lower Square, is the enormous and rather severe bulk of the former Jesuit College, which is attached to the northern side of the church of St. Nicholas, and was built by D. di Orsi between 1674–91 on a site previously occupied by a group of 20 burghers' houses. In front of the east end of the church, and projecting out into the Lower Square, is the Grömling Palace, another late 18C work by J. Jäger; the interior houses the large, elegant and very popular café known as the *Little Quarter Coffee-House* (Malostranská kavárna), which has its origins in the Radetzky Café of 1874.

Walking up from the south-eastern corner of the Little Quarter Square to the square's upper, western half, you will skirt to your right the southern side of the church of St. Nicholas and to your left a group of tall, narrow-fronted houses of Renaissance and medieval origin, where you will find several long-established places for eating and drinking. No. 10, At the Golden Lion (Dům U zlatého lva), is the only building in the whole square to have completely retained its Renaissance appearance, and houses one of Prague's finest restaurants, U mecenáše; this restaurant, serving excellent food in intimate, Renaissance-style dining-rooms, is on the site of a tavern dating back to the reign of the Emperor Rudolph. The upper and quieter half of the Little Quarter Square is known as the Upper or Italian Square, and has in its centre a Plague Column put up by Alliprandi in 1715 in place of a fountain. Its western side is taken up entirely by the neo-classical façade of the Liechtenstein Palace (1791), while facing this is the west façade of the **CHURCH OF ST. NICHOLAS** (sv. Mikuláš), one of the outstanding baroque buildings of central Europe, and rivalled only by Prague Castle as the dominant element in the city's skyline.

The present Church of St. Nicholas occupies the site of a 13C three-aisled structure which was handed over to the Jesuits shortly after the Battle of the White Mountain of 1620. Later in the 17C the Jesuits built a College alongside the old church, and in 1673 laid the foundations of a new church, the construction of which was not begun until 1703, under the direction of Christoph Dientzenhofer. The church was roofed by 1705, but work was subsequently interrupted through lack of funds, and was only continued between 1709–11, when the west façade was completed and the nave vaulted. Further financial difficulties led to the east end being closed by a provisional, illusionistically painted wooden screen until 1637, when work was resumed under the direction of Dientzenhofer's son, Kilian Ignaz, who between 1737 and 1752 built the chancel and domed crossing; the tower alongside the dome was added by Anselmo Lurago in 1755. The finished church, the largest Jesuit church in Bohemia if not in the whole of central Europe, was to inspire early this century some effusive prose by the French Catholic dramatist Paul Claudel. In the introduction to his religious drama, The Shoe of Satin, Claudel referred to the building as a 'sanctuary where everything is suffused by inner life and eloquence, where the whole structure is an act of grace which immediately draws us in, where everything is peace, joy, and not simply a smile, but an outburst of laughter ...'

Despite the protracted history of its construction, the church of St. Nicholas has an impressive unity, and its undulating west façade, with its remarkably rich play of concave and convex surfaces, is a powerful preparation for the dynamic interior. Once inside the single-aisled building you are astonished by an array of pinks and pastel greens, and exhilarated by an extraordinary sense of movement. The nave walls, with their undulating balconies, and giant, obliquely set pilasters, positively ripple and create a flowing line which culminates in the enormous oval of the crossing. The originality of the nave vaulting, with its intersecting ribs as in a Gothic building, is obscured by the vast ceiling painting by Johann Lukas Kracker representing The Apotheosis of St. Nicholas (1760–61); the dome meanwhile is covered by The Celebration of the Holy Trinity (1752–53) by Franz Xavier Palko, who also executed, along with Josef Hager, the wall-paintings in the chancel. The magnificent statuary was largely the work of Ignác Platzer the Elder, who was responsible for the statue of St. Nicholas on the High Altar, the agitated saints along the nave, and the four overblown figures of the Church Fathers in the corners of the crossing. The remarkable pulpit (1765), a gilded rococo confection in pink marble, is by Richard and Peter Prachner. Of the paintings, special mention should be made of the first chapel to the left, where there is an altarpiece of the Holy Rood by K. Škréta, and one of St. Barbara by L. Kohl; a painting of St. Michael by the Neapolitan painter F. Solimena is in the second chapel to the left, while in the third chapel to the right is The Death of St. Francis by F.X. Balko.

After leaving the church, head to the northern end of the Upper Square, turn right, and, just before entering once again the Lower Square, turn left into the narrow Sněmovní. Among the old palaces and houses on this street, which lies almost under the shadow of Prague Castle, is the gabled and well-preserved Renaissance structure at No. 10 called *At the Golden Swan* (Dům U zlaté labutě), which was built by Ulrico Avostalis in 1589 for one Michal Lagrand. At its upper end the street is continued in the picturesquely shabby and rubbish-strewn cul-de-sac with the inappropriate name of U zlaté studně (At the Golden Well); the peeling, blackened end house, at No. 3, is known as *At the Painters*, for it belonged to the turn-of-the-century artist Karel Klusáček, who painted on its façade a now barely decipherable decoration featuring St. Methodius. After turning back at the end of the street, take the first turning to the left, which leads you into the Valdštejnské náměstí. This narrow square is named after the **Palace** on its eastern side (at No. 4), which was built in 1623–30 for the great Albrecht of Wallenstein, whose family seat it was to remain until 1945. Built by Giovanni Pieroni to designs supplied first by Andrea Spezza and then by Niccolo Sebregondi, it was the earliest of the many grand palaces erected in Prague in the 17C and 18C. Its interior, open to the public for occasional concerts, features a splendid main hall with a stuccoed ceiling incorporating a fresco by B. Bianco representing Wallenstein himself dressed as Mars and riding a chariot; the work was executed in 1630, only four years before Wallenstein's ignominious murder at Cheb (see Route 10). Architecturally the finest feature of the building is the Loggia overlooking the palace's wonderful gardens, the entrance to which is on Letenská (see below). Before making your way to Letenská a number of other important palaces and gardens remain to be seen to the N of the Wallenstein Palace, beginning with the *Ledebour-Trauttmansdorf Palace*, on the north-western corner of the Valdštejnské náměstí. This late baroque palace, designed by I.J. Palliardi in 1787, is remarkable above all for its gardens, which were laid out by Santini-Aichel in 1716 and rise steeply in terraces from a Sala Terrena up to a Belvedere, the whole enlivened by fountains and a statue of Hercules. The gardens, usually open to the public in the summer months, form today part of a public park comprising as well the terraced gardens of two adjoining palaces to the N, on Valdštejnská Street. The first of these palaces, at No. 14, is the early 18C *Pálffy Palace*, the gardens of which feature three terraces linked by a covered staircase and a loggia; on the middle terrace is a sundial bearing a Latin inscription and the date 1751. The entrance to all the gardens, which are known as **The Palace Gardens Below Prague Castle**, are to be found alongside the next palace, the **Kolowrat-Černín Palace**, situated at No. 10. The building was designed in 1784 by Ignác Jan Palliardi, who was also responsible for laying out its gardens, which are perhaps the finest of them all and comprise a luxuriant rococo complex of staircases, terraces, fountains, loggias, balustrades and pools. The last of the great palaces along Valdštejnská is the *Fürstenberg Palace*, which was built in 1743–47 by an unknown architect clearly under the influence of K.I. Dientzenhofer; it is now the Polish Embassy, and its attractive 18C gardens are closed to the public.

Return to the Valdštejnské náměstí and continue S along Tomášská, where you will pass on the left-hand side, just before rejoining the Little Quarter Square, one of Prague's best known Beer Cellars, *U Schnellů*; this friendly and modest establishment, if rather popular with tourists, has a décor dating back to 1787. Turn left at the end of the street into Letenská, where you will find immediately to your left the *Church of St. Thomas* (sv. Tomáše), which was founded in 1285 for the Order of Augustinian Hermits. The medieval church, partially rebuilt in the 16C and 17C, was remodelled by K.I. Dientzenhofer in 1722–31. The main façade, featuring a portal of 1617 and a sandstone statue by Hieronymus Kohl of St. Thomas (1684) was given by Dientzenhofer a dramatic Borromini-inspired appearance through the addition of massive, projecting forms intended both to strengthen the structure and to make the most of the restricted site; the interior, with a presbytery retaining some of the medieval masonry, has ceiling paintings by V.V. Reiner representing scenes from the lives of SS. Augustine and Thomas, and (on the dome) The Four Continents. In the first chapel on the right is a painting of St. Thomas (1671) by K. Škréta, of whom there are two further paintings in the presbytery (an Assumption and a Holy Trinity, both of 1644). Paintings by Rubens of St. Augustine and the Martyrdom of St. Thomas were recently transferred from here to the National Gallery and replaced by copies. The former friary attached to the church is now an Old People's Home, but its cellar (entered at No. 8 Letenská) continues to function as the celebrated ale house which was founded here in 1348, its dark beer having originally been made by the monks. This establishment, known as *U Tomáše*, is today a tourist attraction which tends to be booked up in advance by large groups; earlier this century, however, it was the place to which the rowdy literary club known as Syrinx transferred its allegiance after tiring of the now equally spoilt U Fleků in the New Town (see Route 1C). Across Letenská from St. Thomas is the entrance to the short Josefská, on which stands the former *Church of St. Joseph*, an oval structure which was built by Jean Baptiste Mathey in 1682–92 and modelled on Flemish and Roman patterns.

Continuing to walk N along Letenská, you will skirt to your left the garden walls of the Wallenstein Palace (see above) and eventually come to the entrance to these gardens. The **Gardens**, open only during the summer months, were laid out in the early 17C and have at their centre an avenue of bronze statues copied after works by Adriaen de Vries which were stolen from here by the Swedes in 1648 and are now to be seen outside the Swedish Royal palace at Drottningholm. The avenue leads to a tall and magnificent **Loggia** built by G. Pieroni in 1623–27, and decorated inside with painted scenes by B. Bianco of the Trojan Wars (1629–30), set in a stucco framework. Elsewhere in the gardens are an aviary, grottoes, and a long fishpond which was used in 1816 for the testing of a model of a steamboat designed by J. Božek; the bronze of Hercules standing in the middle of the pond is an original by de Vries. On summer weekends the gardens are used by artists for the display of their works, while the former Riding-School here houses occasional temporary exhibitions organised by the National Gallery.

Letenská Street comes to an end at the broad and busy Klárov, which marks the north-western edge of the Little Quarter. Turning left here will bring you immediately to the *Malostranská Metro Station*, the most elegant in Prague; erected in 1978, it has a small forecourt with fountains and statuary copied from 18C models, and a vestibule containing copies both of rococo vases and of Matthias Braun's statue of Hope from Kuks (see Route 3). In the square in front of the station has been recently placed a plaque commemorating a student, Marie Charousková, who was killed during the protests of 1968.

Turning right at the end of Letenská will bring you into U lužického semináře, which was named after a Seminary (at No. 13) built in 1726–28 for Lusatian–Serbian students. To your right you will skirt the walls of the large Vojanov Gardens, which were founded in the 17C and contain near their entrance (which is also on this street) a statue by I.F. Platzer of St. John of Nepomuk standing on a fish. Discreetly tucked away on the opposite side of the street to the gardens (at No. 38) is the small, simple and very lively beer cellar known as *U dvou srdcí* (At the Two Hearts), a place as yet free of tourists and where a matronly waitress places a large glass of beer on your table almost the moment you sit down. Near the southern end of the street turn right into Mišenská, where you will find, at Nos 1 and 12 two appealing corner houses designed respectively by Kilian Ignaz Dientzenhofer and his brother Christoph. The continuation of Mišenská, Dražického, will bring you back to the Charles Bridge, next to the main entrance of the celebrated *U tří pštrosů* (The Three Ostriches), the exterior of which has fragments of mural decorations of ostrich feathers, as well as a house-sign with ostriches, all dating back to 1606. The building owes both its name and decoration to a merchant called Jan Fux, who rebuilt the house after 1597, and made a living partially by selling ostrich feathers, then a fashion novelty. Functioning already as a tavern in Fux's time, the building was acquired early the following century by the Armenian coffee-salesman Deodatus Damajan (see p 108), who in 1714 opened here the first coffee-shop in the Little Quarter. Between 1972 and 1976, the place was restored and transformed into a luxury restaurant and tiny, exclusive hotel, the latter boasting the best-situated rooms in Prague. The restaurant, patronised almost exclusively by tourists, is reputed to serve the best food in Czechoslovakia, but relies today too much on its past reputation, and lacks warmth and character.

After returning to Mostecká you should turn left immediately into Lázeňská to begin a tour of the southern half of the Little Quarter. On this short street were once situated the workshops of Adriaen de Vries and other foreign sculptors who came to Prague at the time of Rudolph II. Later in the 17C the street came to have a hotel, at No. 6 (At the Baths) which was to host up to the early 19C some of the most distinguished visitors to Prague, including Peter the Great of Russia in 1698, the pioneering balloonist Jean-Pierre Blanchard in 1790–91, and, in 1833, the French writer Chateaubriand; two years after the latter's visit (which is commemorated by a plaque), the hotel was rebuilt in an Empire style. In 1796 Beethoven stayed at the fine late baroque palace at No. 11 (At the Golden Unicorn). At the southern end of the street begins a small area of town originating in plots of land that in 1169 were given over by Vladislav II to the Order of the Maltese Knights (the Johannites). The church which formerly belonged to this order, *Our Lady under the Chain* (Kostel Panny Marie pod řetězem), dominates the area, standing as it does at the junction of Lázeňská and the narrow, connected squares of Malta and the Grand Priory (Maltézské náměstí and Velopřevorské náměstí). The original three-aisled Romanesque structure of the 12C, the oldest church in the Little Quarter, was pulled down in the middle of the 14C, and work was begun on a new building. The latter was abandoned by the end of the century, the only parts to be completed being the western vestibule and its two austere and fortress-like towers which form such an incongruous presence in the middle of this intimate part of town. The former nave of the Romanesque church serves now as a forecourt to a baroque church built largely by Carlo Lurago in 1640–60; within the latter is a high altar of the 1660s by Karel Škréta, representing the Virgin Mary and St. John the Baptist coming to the assistance of the Knights of Malta during the Battle of Lepanto of 1571.

Facing the church, at the north-eastern end of the Maltézské náměstí (at No. 11) is a building dating back to 1531, and known as the Dům U malířů (At the Painters) after the painter Jiří Šic, who lived here in the late 16C; the building, remodelled in around 1690, and restored in the 1930s, now houses one of Prague's most attractive wine bars. A number of fine 17C and 18C palaces line the rest of the square, at the centre of which is a sculptural group by F.M. Brokoff featuring St. John the Baptist, erected as a plague memorial in 1715. On the eastern side of the square (at No. 14) is the arcaded Straka Palace of c 1700 (with fresco decorations inside by the early 18C Swiss painter J.R. Byss), while on the western side (at No. 6) is Jäger's Turba Palace of 1767–68, a beautiful rococo structure articulated with giant pilasters and serving today as the Japanese Embassy. Giant pilasters feature also on the façade of the large Nostitz Palace (No. 1; today the Dutch Embassy), which takes up all of the southern side of the square, and was built in 1660–70 by Francesco Caratti, who was later to perfect such an ordering of a façade in his Černín Palace on the Loreta Square (see Route 1C); the main portal was a rococo addition of 1760 attributed to A. Haffenecker, while the attic was decorated in 1720 with sculpted vases and emperors by M.J. Brokoff (the originals have now been replaced by copies).

Make your way back to Our Lady under the Chain, and turn right into the Velkopřevorské náměstí. Immediately to your left on entering the square is the main façade of the Grand Prior's Palace, which was rebuilt to a design by Giuseppe Bartolomeo Scotti in 1726–28, and has a fine portal with vase decorations from the workshop of Matthias Braun; torchbearers and vases from the same workshop adorn the grand staircase of the richly stuccoed interior. The building houses a section of the Museum of Czech Music, and has an excellent display of old musical instruments, sadly lacking at present the Stradivarius violins, which were stolen in 1990. Facing the building on the southern side of the square, are the late 16C Small Buquoy Palace (at No. 3) and the adjoining Buquoy-Valdstejn Palace (at No. 2; now the French Embassy), the present façade of which dates back to 1719. At the eastern end of the square, also on the right-hand side, is the Hrzán Palace (at No. 1), which despite remodelling carried out in 1760, still retains a largely Renaissance appearance, complete with extensive sgraffito decorations. Another Renaissance structure, directly facing the palace, is the picturesquely gabled Grand Prior's or Stepan's Mill (at No. 7), which was functioning up to 1936, and is one of several mills built on the narrow branch of the Vltava called the Čertovka or the Devil's Stream. This stream, separating the Lesser Town from Kampa Island, was first referred to simply as 'The Ditch', and only acquired its present, more romantic name towards the end of the 19C, when the Straka Palace on the nearby Maltese Square came to be known as 'The Devil's House' after an eccentric woman owner.

Beside the Grand Prior's Mill is a bridge leading over the Čertovka stream to **Kampa Island**, an area once taken up entirely by vineyards, gardens and fields, and which only had buildings from the late 16C onwards. Successive floods changed the shape of the island over the centuries, and the narrator of Jiří Weil's novel Life with a Star (1964) even recalls frequent arguments with his mistress when she 'claimed that Kampa was a peninsula and I said it was an island'. Most of the houses on this so-called 'Venice of Prague' are concentrated in the northern half of the island, on either side of the quiet and tree-lined Na Kampě Street, where, at No. 11, there is a bronze plaque and bust marking the house where the composer Bohuslav Martinů lived. At its northern end the street broadens out into a picturesque square from which steps lead up to the Charles Bridge. A pottery market was regularly held here up to 1936, and this tradition has recently been revived; the square, like the Charles Bridge itself, also attracts numerous singing, guitar-playing students, who seem to have stepped straight out of the 1960s. For the last few years large crowds have assembled here on 14 December to commemorate the death of the singer John Lennon, whose cult in Czechoslovakia appears rather greater today than that of St. John of Nepomuk.

Walk S down Na Kampě to the southern half of the island, which largely comprises a public park. Leave the island at its southernmost point and turn right into Říční, where you will soon pass on your right the *Church of St. John at the Wash-House* (Kostel sv. Jana Na prádle). The homely name of this church is entirely appropriate to this structure of rustic simplicity, which dates back to the 13C, and contains inside fragments of late 14C wall-paintings. On the opposite side of the street, at No. 11, a plaque marks the turn-of-the-century building where the brothers Josef and Karel Čapek moved to after settling in Prague in 1907.

The brothers Čapek were to stay in their Říční house until 1925, Karel writing here in the early 1920s the plays that were to establish his reputation as a dramatist, most notably his science fiction work RUR (1921) and his morality play From the Life of the Insects (1922), which he wrote in collaboration with his painter brother Josef. The Scottish poet and translator Edwin Muir befriended Karel at this time, and published a short memoir of him in his autobiography, The Story and the Fable (1940): 'We saw a great deal of Karel Čapek, who lived a few minutes' walk away from us in a rambling old house with a large garden hidden away behind it. Though he was about the same age as myself, he was already round-backed; the brightness of his eyes and the flush on his cheek showed that he was ill. He knew only a little English, and we only a little German, so we had to converse in an absurd mixture of the two. He was always busy, always merry ... Čapek seemed to be known and loved by every one, and when we walked along the street with him every second or third passer-by would shout, "Oh, Karlíčku!" the equivalent of "Hullo, Charley!" as if the mere sight of him filled them with pleasure.'

From the Church of St. John at the Wash-house head NW along Vsehrdova, passing at No. 14 the *Works Mill* (Mlýn Hut), another of the old mills on the Čertovka. The narrow and slightly run-down Všehrdova will take you to the long and busy Újezd, where you will find, immediately to the right (at No. 40), the *Michna of Vacínov Palace*, a large complex dating back to the late 16C, and with a baroque wing built by Francesco Caratti in 1640–50. This wing, with a grimy, peeling façade overlooking Újezd, is covered both on the outside and inside with Italianate stucco decorations by Domenico Galli. The interior, which is occupied today by the sports Faculty of Charles University, is also worth seeing for its small but very evocative *Sports Museum*, with old bicycles, sports trophies, photographs, and other objects relating to the history of sport in Prague, all incongruously displayed under Galli's stuccoes, in rooms that appear to be as little visited as they are dusted.

Walk N along Újezd into its northern continuation, Karmelitská, on which stands, on the left-hand side, the former Carmelite Church of *St. Mary the Victorious* (Kostel P. Marie Vítězné). Built originally for the German Lutherans between 1611–13, it came into the possession of the Carmelites in 1624, who subsequently had it rebuilt as a thanksgiving for the Habsburg victory at the Battle of the White Mountain. Though generally referred to as the first baroque church in Prague, this would be better described as one of the many dreary European imitations of the Gesù in Rome, and has little of architectural interest. Its singularly dark and depressing interior, however, is much visited on account of a tiny votive image of the Infant Christ displayed in a chapel on the right of the nave.

The celebrated wax image of the Infant Christ lifting his arm in blessing is a Spanish work of the 16C which for some reason—perhaps connected with some confusion between the Spanish and Italian languages—is popularly known by the Italian name of 'Bambino di Praga' ('Child of Prague'). Brought over from Spain in the mid 16C by María Manríquez de Lara, the Spanish wife of Vratislav of Pernštejn, it was later presented by her to her daughter Polyxena on the occasion of the latter's marriage to the High Chancellor Zdeněk Popel of Lobkowitz. The widowed Polyxena gave the work to the Carmelites in 1628, since when the statue, with its numerous changes of clothing, has acquired a growing mythical status, and inspired countless reproductions in dubious taste. The absurd and kitsch qualities of the Bambino di Praga have been wittily exploited by the writer Bohumil Hrabal, whose novel I Served the King of England (1989) includes a fantastical tale of a successful Bolivian plot to replace the work surreptitiously with a copy and take the original back to South America, where it 'was supposed to be tremendously popular ... so popular, in fact, that millions of South American Indians wore replicas of it on chains around their necks and had a legend that Prague was the most beautiful city in the world and that the infant Jesus had gone to school there.'

Of greater artistic interest than the Bambino di Praga itself is the gilded wooden altar on which it has been placed, a rococo structure carved by Petr Prachner in 1776; elsewhere in the church are a number of dramatic canvases of saints by Petr Brandl.

Continuing N up Karmelitská, you will pass on your left, at No. 25, the *Vrtba Palace*, which František Kaňka remodelled around 1720 and endowed with some of the most beautiful if also most hidden gardens in Prague. The **Vrtba Gardens**, reached by way of a passage running through the Palace, form today a small and quiet public park at the edge of a great sweep of verdant parkland covering the Petřín Hill. After passing through a courtyard adorned with statues by Matthias Braun of Atlas and two female allegorical figures, you will come to a Sala Terrena decorated with painted mythological scenes by V.V. Reiner. Further works by Braun, of Bacchus and Ceres (c 1730) are followed by a balustraded double staircase where mythological figures alternate with Greek vases; from the highest of the gardens' terraces there are wonderful views of Prague Castle and St. Nicholas. In his travel book, The Double Eagle (1988), the British writer Stephen Brook relates how during a stay in Prague he soon forsook the Wallenstein for the Vrtba Gardens, preferring the latter for its greater tranquillity and absence of tourists. One can only hope that the present restoration campaign—which has led to the temporary closure of the Gardens—does not deprive the place of its charm, which was dependent to a great extent on its character of quiet neglect.

Karmelitská will bring you back at its northern end to the Little Quarter Square (Malostranské náměstí), from where you begin the steep walk up to Prague Castle, passing through what is in many ways the most attractive part of the Little Quarter. There are three main ways of climbing up to the castle from the square, the shortest and steepest, and the one offering the finest roof-top views, being the ascent up the Castle Steps (Zámecké schody). From the north-western corner of the Lower Square turn right into Sněmovní, and then immediately left into Thunovská, off which stands (at No. 14) the large *Thun Palace*, a building of 17C origin with a façade of 1716–27 by Antonio Giovanni Lurago; at this palace, now the seat of the British Embassy, Mozart and his wife Constance stayed during their first visit to Prague in 1787. Further W up Thunovská there begins on the right-hand side of the street the **Castle Steps**, which pass to the left, at No. 25 Thunovská, the greyish-white and recently restored *Palace of the Lords of Hradec*, which dates back to the late 16C and is crowned by a group of small, Renaissance gables; this building, now connected to the Italian Embassy on Nerudova (see below) was from 1911–28 the house of the artist Alfons Mucha, who is commemorated here by a plaque. The Castle Steps, which lead directly up to the Hradčany Square, were built originally in the 15C on the site of a path of 13C origin. A number of small buildings grew up alongside them, and in the 16C and 17C artists and craftsmen used to sell their wares here (the wide stone ledges of some of the windows were once used for display purposes).

The tourist shops today are not to be found on the Castle Steps but are concentrated instead along **Nerudova**, which is the main and most traditional approach to the castle, and the one which was favoured by the Royal Coronation processions. Nerudova begins at the upper western end of the Little Quarter, and is lined its whole length with 16C to 18C buildings, many of which with shop fronts displaying crafts products and souvenirs. The first building on the right (at No. 2) houses the lively pub *U kocoura* (At the Cat), which sells Pilsner Urquell Beer. Further up the street, on the left-hand side (at No. 5), is the **Morzin Palace** (now the Romanian Embassy), which was built by Santini-Aichel in 1713–14, and has magnificent sculptural decoration by F.M. Brokoff on its façade: its two portals are surmounted by statues of Day and Night, while in between these is a balcony supported by figures of Moors, executed with Brokoff's customary realism. The Italian Embassy, slightly higher up Nerudova on the opposite side of the street (at No. 20), occupies another splendid baroque building by Santini-Aichel, the **Thun-Hohenstein Palace**: built in 1716–c 1725, its portal was decorated around 1730 with two deeply and vigorously carved eagles by Brokoff's great and dynamic rival, Matthias Braun. Santini-Aichel seems also to have been responsible for the portal of the adjoining *Church of Our Lady of Unceasing Succour at the Theatines* (Kostel Panny Marie ustavičné pomoci u kajetánů); the rest of the church, built in 1691–1717, has been attributed to J.-B. Mathey. Further up the street, also on the right-hand side (at No. 34), is the *House at the Golden Horseshoe* (Dům U zlaté podkovy), where you will find the beautifully preserved wooden interior of an early 18C pharmacy, one of the oldest surviving pharmacies in Prague. At the top of the street, on the left-hand side (at No. 47), is the *House at the Two Suns* (Dům U dvou slunců), a building of Renaissance origin with attractive late 17C gables. Attached to its façade is a large memorial plaque—executed in 1895 by F. Houdek after a design by V. Oliva and a model by V.R. Smolík—recording that in this house there lived between 1845–57 the poet and journalist after whom the street is named, Jan Neruda; the everyday life of this part of Prague provided

Neruda with the subject matter of his delightful short-stories, Tales from the Little Quarter (1878). To complete the journey up to the castle, you should turn sharp right at the end of Nerudova and walk up the street named Ke Hradu, which means 'Towards the Castle'. Turning instead to the left you enter Úvoz Street, which climbs up slowly towards the Strahov Monastery and Loreta Square (see Route 1C); the street is bordered to the right by another fine succession of 16C–18C houses, and to the left by a shaded balustrade commanding excellent views of the Petřín Park.

Another way of climbing up towards the castle and the Hradčany from the Little Quarter Square is to follow the streets running parallel to Nerudova to the S, beginning with Tržiště, which starts at Karmelitská, by the side of the Vrtba Palace (see above). By far the grandest palace on this blackened and slightly decrepit street is the *Schönborn-Colloredo Palace* (at No. 15), which was built in the mid 17C on a site previously occupied by five houses, and remodelled in around 1715, probably by Santini-Aichel; the building is now the American Embassy, and its impressive gardens, laid out by M. Lebsche in the late 17C, are not open to the public. Tržiště veers to the right after the palace, and after tunnelling through a group of houses, joins up with Nerudova, at a point directly in front of the Thun-Hohenstein Palace (see above). Alternatively you could turn left at the Schönborn Palace on to Vlašská, or take the second turning to the left, and walk up the narrow street parallel to Vlašská, Břetislavova. The building at No. 2 Břetislavova is an early 18C structure known as At the Child Jesus and attributed to Santini-Aichel. However, those who visited the street in the past generally did not do so for architectural reasons.

Until comparatively recently Břetislavova was known popularly as Corpses' Street, for it was along here that funeral possessions would pass on their way to the now demolished cemetery on St. John's Hill. This was also one of the main brothel streets of Prague, and the poet Jaroslav Seifert recalled in his charming memoirs how as a schoolboy he timidly paid a visit to the street from his faraway home district of Žižkov, his interest in the place having been excited by the report of one of his friends. The street was deserted, and the disappointed Seifert was on the point of leaving when, outside a house to be identified with At the Child Jesus, he heard a soft knock on a window, and was tempted to peer inside. 'The curtains parted, and a girl stood by the window with a dark braid hanging over her shoulder. Surprised, I remained stockstill. When she saw my frightened look she smiled and said something to me, but I did not hear her voice through the glass. The street is so narrow that two steps were enough, and I was on the other side of the street.' Yet, his curiosity now aroused, he felt compelled to return to the window, and was met this time by the sight of the smiling girl removing her blouse and beckoning him inside, a sight—his first of the naked female breasts—which led him to run with heart beating all the way down to the bottom of the Little Quarter. Later he was to evoke the street in his elegaic poem, View from Charles Bridge: 'A few steps from the Royal Road/ was a dark corner,/ where tousle-haired prostitutes appeared/ to walkers in the evenings,/ luring into their dead wombs/ young inexperienced boys,/ as I was then./ Now all is silent there./ And only television aerials haunt/ the ridges of the roofs.'

Břetislavova leads into Jánský vršek, where, on turning right, you will reach the upper end of Nerudova. Turning instead to the left you will come to Vlašská, at a point just below this street's most important building, the **Lobkowicz Palace** (at No. 19; now the German Embassy). Begun by G.B. Alliprandi in 1703 and completed by I.J. Palliardi in 1769, this palace took as its main inspiration Bernini's unrealised plan for the Louvre in Paris, and features an entrance hall leading to a large oval vestibule projecting out on to the palace's gardens. These gardens, which are open to the public, were given after 1793 an informal English look by J.V. Skalník, who is best known for his landscaping of the spa at Mariánské Lázně (Marienbad); the Alpinum which he created here was the first in Bohemia. From the palace you can reach the upper end of Nerudova by walking due N along the narrow Šporkova, which curves around a picturesque group of houses before ending up at Jánský vršek (see above). Continuing instead to walk W along Vlašská you will pass to your left the northern walls of the Lobkowitz Gardens and, to your right (at No. 34), a hospital and chapel founded in the early 17C by Prague's Italian community, which was centred in this area.

At the western end of Vlašská you enter the large area of parkland covering the Petřín Hill, and can either turn right in the direction of the Strahov Monastery (see Route 1C), or else turn left and make your way to the top of the hill, which is crowned by trees. Peering up above the summmit is a slightly decrepit imitation of Paris' Eiffel Tower; this structure, closed at present for much needed restoration, was erected for the Jubilee Exhibition of 1891 and commands a remarkably extensive panorama of the city, with particularly fine views towards the Castle. Immediately to the S of this is another structure created for the Jubilee Exhibition, a crenellated neo-Gothic structure (also closed at present) containing inside a hall of mirrors and a large tableau with waxwork figures representing Czech students defending Charles Bridge against the Swedes in 1648: the hall of mirrors is recalled in Josef Škvorecký's novel, The Cowards as the place where the book's hero, Danny Smiřický, asks to be kissed by the girl he loves so that 'it would be like a thousand kisses all at once'. Just to the S of this, also among trees, is the *Church of St. Lawrence*, a Romanesque structure remodelled in the 18C. Further S still is the upper station of a funicular railway which was built in 1891, and has recently been opened following a long period of closure; it descends down to the long Újezd Street (see above), passing, towards the bottom of the hill, through the so-called Petřín Gardens, where there is a statue to the poet Jan Neruda.

This statue of Jan Neruda held a particular significance for the latter's great Latin American namesake, the Nobel Prize-winning poet Pablo Neruda. The real name of this Chilean poet was Ricardo Eliecer Neftalí Reyes, but he changed his name at the very start of his career, for reasons that have both mystified and irritated Czech writers (including Josef Škvorecký). The Czech satirist Erwin Kisch, whom the Chilean had befriended in Madrid in the 1930s, decided one day to ask him why he had changed his name, but he simply replied: 'My dear Kisch, you who have discovered the mystery about Colonel Redl will never clarify the mystery surrounding my being called Neruda.' The answer was in fact quite simple, as he himself admitted in his autobiography, I Confess to Have Lived. His father, a train-driver, was not at all happy with the idea of his son becoming a poet, and so the young poet searched for another name under which to publish his first collection of verse. 'I happened upon the name Neruda in a Czech magazine without having the slightest idea that it belonged to a Czech writer, worshipped by all his people, author of the most beautiful ballads and romances, and who was commemorated by a statue in the district of the Little Quarter in Prague. As soon as I arrived in Czechoslovakia, many years later, I placed a flower at the foot of his bearded statue.'

South of the funicular the green and wooded slopes of the Petřín Hill are interrupted by the so-called *Hunger Wall* (Hladová zeď), which was erected by Charles IV between 1360–62, and marks the south-eastern boundary of the Little Quarter; it derives its curious name from the fact that the poor of the city were employed in its construction, and were thus able to secure a livelihood. On the bosky slopes that stretch S of the wall into the district of Smíchov can be seen the charming, if rather neglected wooden church of *St. Michael* (sv. Michal), an 18C structure brought here in 1929 from a remote Carpathian village near the Ukranian town of Mukacevo.

C.   Prague Castle and the Hradčany

'A spell hangs in the air of this citadel', wrote Patrick Leigh Fermor in A Time of Gifts (1977), 'and I was under its thrall long before I could pronounce its name.' The enormous citadel, or 'Pražský Hrad', rises up above the Little Quarter like a town in its own right, its elegant classical casing holding together a veritable architectural treasury from which project the fantastical Gothic spires of St. Vitus's Cathedral.

The complex history of Prague's citadel goes back to around AD 870 when Prince Bořivoj, founder of the Přemyslid dynasty and first prince of Bohemia, erected on top of a hill a modest but strategically situated fortified settlement. This became the seat of the Přemyslid princes, replacing the previous one at Levý Hradec, further N along the Vltava. In the early 10C the Church of St. George and the Rotunda of St. Vitus were founded here, and in 973, when the citadel became also the seat of the Prague bishopric, Bohemia's oldest convent was established alongside St. George's. A devastating fire in the early 11C led in 1041 to Prince Břetislav I replacing the former earthen ramparts of the citadel with stone ones, but 26 years later the Princes of Bohemia were temporarily to abandon the citadel in favour of Vyšehrad, where they were to remain until 1139. In preparation for the return here of the Přemyslids, Soběslav I constructed a new palace and rebuilt the fortifications, the line of which is largely preserved in the citadel of today. The importance of the citadel was to reach its zenith in the following century, during the reign of Charles IV, when the place was transformed into an imperial residence and work was begun on the great Gothic cathedral of St. Vitus. Later in the century, though the citadel was to remain the seat of Bohemia's government, its role as a residence of the country's rulers was to be greatly diminished as a result of Wenceslas IV's decision to move to the Royal Court in the Old Town. King Vladislav Jagiello turned the place once more into a royal residence in 1484, and brought Benedikt Ried to Prague to rebuild and extend the castle's palace and fortifications; however, later in his reign, he and his court were to be based mainly in Budapest.

Bohemia's first Habsburg rulers, beginning with Ferdinand I, renewed the building activity in the citadel, and in the course of the 16C, the place was to become an impressive Renaissance complex, with pioneering Italianate structures such as the Summer Palace (Belvedere), and the Tennis Court. With Rudolph I, and the international group of scientific and artistic luminaries that he gathered around him, the castle was once again, if only briefly, the seat of one of Europe's most brilliant courts. His successor, Matthias, vaunted the glories of the Habsburgs through the commissioning in 1614 of the imposing triumphal arch known today as the Matthias Gateway. Yet it was only four years later that the Habsburgs were to suffer here a profound humiliation when two of their councillors were ejected from one of the palace windows. Following this incident, which sparked off the Thirty Years' War, the rebelling Czech Estates made the castle the seat of their government, though they were only to remain here for two years, their cause being momentously defeated at the Battle of the White Mountain in 1620. Reduced subsequently to the status of secondary residence the castle declined, and little important work was to be carried out here until the reign of Maria Theresa, who initiated a major rebuilding campaign which was to give to the complex the late baroque and neo-classical framework which it has largely kept to this day.

The last important building campaign in the castle took place after 1918, when Tomáš Masaryk turned the complex into the presidential seat of the newly created Republic of Czechoslovakia. St. Vitus's Cathedral was finally brought to completion, and the lively and idiosyncratic architect Jože Plečník was entrusted with the relaying of gardens, and the remodelling of courtyards and interiors. Plečník's additions are bright and cheerful, but the castle has acquired this century sinister connotations, thanks partially to the popular identification of the place with the novel of this name by Franz Kafka, who indeed stayed here between 1912 and 1914 in his sister's house on Golden Lane. Kafka's vision of faceless tyranny and monstrous bureaucracy seem at any rate to have been prophetic of the years when the castle served as the seat of Czechoslovakia's Communist rulers.

The late eighteenth-century forecourt to Prague Castle; the guards are wearing the new uniforms issued at the beginning of Václav Havel's presidency

There is so much to see in the castle that the better part of a day is required to begin to do justice to the complex. To conserve their energy, many people prefer to reach the castle by public transport, and save the beautiful walks through the Little Quarter for the late afternoon descent (see Route 1B). The easiest access by public transport is to take the underground to the Malostranská station, and from there catch a No. 22 bus to the junction of Mariánské hradby and U Prašného mostu, where you are left with a five minutes' walk, arriving eventually in the citadel's second courtyard. If you decide to walk all the way up the hill to the castle, the quickest ascent is up the Old Castle Steps (Staré zámecké schody), which begin the climb at a point just to the N of the Malostranská station, and enter the citadel at its narrow eastern end.

Whatever route or means you chose to reach the castle, a tour of the place is best begun at its western end, which faces the Hradčany Square. Railings and a gate flanked by copies of two overblown sculptural groups of battling Giants by Ignác Platzer (1786) mark the entrance to the First Courtyard, which is guarded by soldiers who perform at 12.00 and 3.30am every day a Changing of the Guard ceremony. On the other side of the courtyard to the gate is the *Matthias Gateway*, a large Roman-style triumphal arch inspired if not actually designed by the Mannerist architect Vicenzo Scamozzi, and executed by Giovanni Maria Philippi in 1614. Originally a free-standing structure rising directly above the ramparts of the citadel, it was later incorporated into the palace's monumental west façade, which was built to designs by the court architect N. Pacassi in 1763–71. Further modifications to the courtyard were carried out in 1920–22 by Jože Plečník, who designed the two 25m-high flagpoles (tapering structures made out of pine trees taken, symbolically, from the Czechoslovak frontier), pierced the main block with openings on either side of the Matthias Gateway, and ingeniously reduced the importance of the latter—a symbol of Habsburg dominance—by laying across the courtyard two paths of darker coloured paving stones that direct the eye to the new side entrances. The entrance to the right of the gate leads to a staircase climbing up to the Presidential reception rooms, while that to the left opens up on to Plečník's greatest work for the castle—an enormous hall built in 1927–31 and named today after the architect: featuring a ceiling of copper panels and walls articulated by three superimposed rows of Ionic columns, this room looks ahead to many of the 'Post-Modernist' structures of the 1970s and 1980s. Sadly both this hall and the presidential rooms are open to the public only on special occasions.

To enter the castle's Second Courtyard you can go through either the Matthias Gateway or else the arch just to the left of the First Courtyard; adjacent to the latter, at the northern end of the castle's west façade is a small *garden* laid out by Plečník in 1927, and arranged on two levels that are joined by an ingenious circular stairway. The Second Courtyard, dating back to the late 16C, and given its present unified appearance in the late 18C, is centred around a baroque fountain adorned with statues by Jeronym Kohl (1686). The southern side of the courtyard comprises the western end of a long building known as 'The Municipal Building', which extends all the way up to the Old Palace in the Third Courtyard; its monotonous, uniform façade shields a series of rooms (closed to the public) dating back to 1534. Attached to the south-eastern corner of the Second Courtyard is the *Chapel of the Holy Rood* which was built in 1756–63 by Anselmo Lurago after a plan by Pacassi, and remodelled in 1852–56. Since 1965 the greater part of the **Treasury of St. Vitus's Cathedral** has been installed here.

The treasury was founded by Charles IV, who turned it into one of the most important cathedral treasuries in Europe; many of its objects were brought to him to Prague from the Court of France, many more were given to him as gifts by the leading dignitaries of his time, and others were commissioned from his own jewellers and goldsmiths, including the dazzling Royal Crown of Bohemia, which was made in 1346 out of pure gold, 91 precious stones and 20 pearls (this work is still kept in St. Vitus's Cathedral). After Charles's death, however, the treasury was badly depleted, much of the damage being done by his second son Sigismund, who brought much of the goldsmiths' and silversmiths' work to the castle of Karlštejn, where it was used mainly to finance imperial mercenaries. The treasury was fortunately replenished as a result of later donors and collectors, most notably Rudolph II and Joseph II; the most recent acquisition was the early 13C Záviš Cross, which was brought in 1950 from the former Cistercian monastery at Vyšší Brod in southern Bohemia (see Route 16). Other outstanding items include the 9C Helmet of St. Wenceslas, a 13C French Coronation Cross, the Reliquary Cross of Pope Urban V (1375), the Reliquary Bust of St. Vojtěch (1486), and an 11C Sicilian-Arabic Hunting Horn.

The main rooms on the northern side of the Second Courtyard comprise the Spanish Hall and the Rudolph Gallery, two mirrored and richly stuccoed halls dating back to the late 16C but remodelled in a neo-baroque style by Heinrich von Ferstel in 1866; generally

Key to numbers

1 Matthias Gate
2 Chap. of the Holy Rood
3 Spanish Hall & Rudolph Gallery
4 Klášter sv. Jiří, Convent of St George (Nat.Gallery)
5 Palace of Burgrave
6 Lobkowicz Palace (Nat. Museum)
7 Kostel Všech svatých (Ch. of All Saints)
8 Vladislav Hall

PRAGUE CASTLE

closed to the public they are used today for governmental meetings and receptions. The Rudolph Gallery originally housed the extraordinary art collection belonging to Rudolph II, the sorry remnants of which can today be seen in the ground-floor rooms below, which were formerly the imperial stables.

Rudolph II ranked with his cousin Philip II of Spain as one of the greatest of the Habsburg collectors, but many of his pictures were transferred after his death to Vienna, and others were seized by the Swedes in 1648. In the mid 17C Ferdinand III built up a new collection at Prague, the nucleus of which was made up of works acquired from the Collection of the Duke of Buckingham, which was auctioned at Antwerp in 1648–49. The new gallery remained intact until 1721, when Charles IV began removing many of the better works to Vienna; later in the century Maria Theresa sold off many more of the paintings, as did her son Joseph II in 1782. The dispersal of the collection continued throughout the 19C, and by the end of the First World War it was thought that all the paintings had gone from Prague. Investigations carried out between 1962–64 by the art historian Jaromír Neumann revealed that in fact much had remained in this city, and in 1965 these surviving works were brought together to form the Prague Castle Gallery.

The *Prague Castle Gallery* occupies a series of beautifully modernised rooms, and there are few other collections in Czechoslovakia that are quite so well displayed as this one. The works on show, however, are largely minor ones, and a panel of photographs reconstructing Rudolph II's original collection only emphasises the general mediocrity of what has survived. Works by artists of Rudolph's time include paintings by Bartolomaeus Spranger, Hans von Aachen, Cornelisz von Harlem, and an excellent wooden relief of the Adoration of the Kings by Adriaen de Vries. There are works by the Bohemian artists Petr Brandl and Johann Kupecký, and a painting by Rubens of the Council of the Gods, executed probably in Mantua in 1602. The bulk of the collection is of the Italian 16C and 17C, including a Flagellation by Tintoretto, a Young Woman at her Toilet by Titian (a version of a painting in the Louvre), St. Catherine and the Angel, and Christ Washing the Feet of His Disciples by Veronese, The Centaur Nessus and Deianeira by Guido Reni, and a peculiarly erotic St. Sebastian by Saraceni, with a single arrow placed directly in the groin; among the other Italian paintings are works by Bernardo Monsú, Viviano Codazzi, Orazio Gentileschi, and Leandro, Jacopo and Francesco Bassano.

Entering the third and principal castle courtyard you find yourself directly in front of the west front of **THE CATHEDRAL OF ST. VITUS**, one of the finest and most richly endowed in central Europe.

The cathedral of St. Vitus has its origins in a Rotunda founded by Prince Wenceslas in c 925, and transformed in 973 into the cathedral church of the Prague bishops; in 1060 this was replaced by a three-aisled Romanesque basilica. On the occasion of Prague's elevation from bishopric to archbishopric in 1344, Charles IV ordered the construction of the present Gothic building, for which he summoned from the papal court at Avignon the architect Matthew of Arras. Matthew had laid the foundations of the building and completed its east end up to the triforium level by the time of his death in 1352. In search of an architect to complete Matthew's work, Charles IV turned this time to Germany, and found there Peter Parler, who had been born in about 1330 to a family of Cologne builders and whose father had been responsible for the great town church at Schwäbisch-Gmund. From 1353 up to his own death in 1399 Parler was to be engaged on the building, completing the east end, doubling the chapel of St. Wenceslas on the south-western corner of the ambulatory, constructing the south portal and its adjoining open staircase, and beginning the nave; his work was to be continued by his sons Václav and Jan, who begun work on the south tower. When the Hussites occupied the castle in 1421 the cathedral was greatly damaged and many of its furnishings destroyed; building

Ch. of Our Lady

St John the Baptist

Reliquary Chapel

St Vitus Tomb

Archbishop's Chap.

Tomb

St John of Nepomuk

Cardinal Mon.

St Anne's

Mary Magdelene reliefs

Old Sacristy

Royal Oratory

Holy Rood Chap. (Treasury)

Royal Mausoleum

St Andrew

Wenceslas Chapel

organ loft

South Porch

New Sacristy

New Archbishop's Chap.

E

0 metres 20

ST VITUS CATHEDRAL

activity was subsequently suspended for many years, the completed east end being closed off by a temporary wall.

Work on the cathedral was only to be resumed towards the end of the 15C, during the reign of Vladislav Jagiello: the strange Royal Oratory was put up on the south side of the ambulatory in the 1480s, the upper walls of the Wenceslas Chapel were painted in 1504, and the foundations of the north tower were laid in 1509–11. At the same time Vladislav Jagiello's principal architect, the great Benedikt Ried, formulated grandiose plans for the completion of the nave, but, sadly, lack of funds led to their having to be abandoned in 1511. The main additions to the cathedral later in the century were the work of Bonifaz Wohlmut, who was responsible in the 1560s for the Renaissance organ loft in the north transept and for crowning the Gothic south tower with a Renaissance gallery and bulbous domes (the top part of the tower was later destroyed by fire and rebuilt by N. Pacassi after 1770). A new attempt to complete the nave was made by Domenico Orsi in 1675, but this too was thwarted, and it was not until after the formation in 1861 of the 'Union for the completion of the Cathedral' that work was begun in earnest to try and finish the building. This new campaign was begun by Josef Kranner, and taken over by Josef Mocker, who was Czechoslovakia's answer to Viollet-Le-Duc and someone responsible for the 'restoration' and pseudo-Gothic remodelling of many of Prague's other medieval monuments, such as the Powder Tower. The last architect at work on the cathedral was Kamil Hilbert, who finally completed the fabric of the building in 1929.

The most recent and dullest part of the cathedral is the twin-towered west façade, which features a large rosette window with stained-glass by F. Kysela and three portals with tympana containing carved reliefs executed between 1948–52 to designs by K. Dvořák and L. Pícha. The high point of the exterior is undoubtedly the south façade, thanks to Peter Parler, who wanted to give particular emphasis to the side of the building which both housed St. Wenceslas's tomb and faced the city. This façade is dominated by its 96m-high tower, the tapering Gothic part of which was begun by Parler's sons in the early 15C and has a main window protected by a wonderfully intricate Renaissance grille; the arcaded gallery above this is a mid 16C addition by Bonifác Wohlmut, while the crowning steeple was designed by Palassi in 1770. Immediately to the right of the tower are the three arches of Peter Parler's **South Porch** or Golden Portal, which is decorated on the outside with a much restored mosaic decoration of the Last Judgement executed in the late 14C by Venetian artists; in the spandrels of the central arch are the work's donors, Charles IV and his wife Eliška Pomořanská. One of Peter Parler's main contributions to the cathedral was his inventive vaulting, as can be seen inside the porch, where a skeletal system of ribs is spread out like a fan. Above the porch is a further example of Parler's structural daring—a complex, openwork staircase which was to be imitated in the cathedrals at Ulm and Strasbourg.

Entering the church through the south porch you should note how Parler creates an ingenious progression from three arches to a double doorway, and, finally, to a single portal. Once inside you will find yourself in the south transept, from where one of the best views of the interior can be had. The plan and proportions of the building clearly reflect the work of a French architect, and indeed the arrangement of the east end, with its radiating chapels, seems to have been inspired by that of Narbonne Cathedral, which was completed early in the 14C by Jean Deschamps. Peter Parler provided the choir with its elegant vaulting system of parallel diagonal ribs, and also began the triforium, which runs round the whole building and has inside it a celebrated series of portrait heads representing all those involved in the building of the cathedral, including Parler himself and members of Charles IV's family. Twenty-one of these busts—which are so high up that they can scarcely be seen—were executed by members of

Parler's workshop, but the rest (mainly in the nave) are modern works portraying recent figures such as the sculptors Bohumil Kafka and J. Štursa. The whole west end of the nave is a lifeless imitation of the east end, and bears little relation to the ambitious structure which Benedikt Ried would have created. The finest of the modern contributions to the building are the stained-glass windows, executed mainly by F. Kysela, K. Svolinský and Max Švabinský, the latter's largest work here being the Last Judgement window in the south transept.

To your right, immediately on entering the church from the south portal, is the **WENCESLAS CHAPEL**, which Parler enlarged by pushing out its southern and western walls, the latter at the expense of the transept. The chapel, containing the much restored 14C tomb of St. Wenceslas (d. 929 or 935), has a door of 1370 incorporating a Romanesque lion's head knocker to which Wenceslas is said to have clung when he was attacked and murdered by his brother Boleslav. The interior, reflecting perhaps Charles IV's love of jewellery, is studded on its lower level with around 1372 precious stones; on this same level are also to be found a series of paintings of the Passion by an anonymous Czech artist of 1372 (identified variously as Master Theodoric and Master Oswald). The story of St. Wenceslas is portrayed above these, in elaborately detailed works of 1504 generally attributed to the Master of Litoměřice; the room is further enhanced by Parler's splendid ceiling, comprising parallel diagonal ribs springing from eight corbels to form a star-shaped dome. The Bohemian Crown Jewels (shown to the public only on special occasions) are kept in a room above the chapel.

In the middle of the long east end of the cathedral stands the *Royal Mausoleum*, a large memorial in white marble, executed in 1571–89 by the Netherlandish sculptor Alexander Collin, and surrounded by a Renaissance grille by J. Schmidthammer: on its upper slab are reliefs of the Emperor Ferdinand I, his consort Anne of Jagiello, and his son Maximilan II, while on the sides are shown Charles IV and his four consorts, and the kings Wenceslas IV, Ladislav Pohrobek and George of Poděbrady. The actual tombs of these monarchs, as well as those of Rudolph II and members of the Přemyslids, can be seen in the *Royal Crypt*, the entrance to which lies just to the right of the Mausoleum; within the crypt are also displayed the excavated remains of the cathedral's foundations, including masonry of the 10C and 11C. Behind the Mausoleum is the uninspired High Altar, a neo-Gothic work of 1868–73, designed by J. Kranner and later altered by J. Mocker.

Walking around the ambulatory from its south-western end, you will find next to the Wenceslas Chapel the *Chapel of St. Andrew*, containing the tombstone (to the left, under the window) of Jaroslav von Martinic (d. 1649), one of the two Habsburg councillors thrown out of the Old Royal Palace window in 1618 (see below). The subsequent *Chapel of the Holy Rood*, with fragments of 14C murals, is followed by one of the more remarkable additions to the ambulatory, the **Royal Oratory**—a balcony decorated with characteristic late Gothic fantasy and naturalism, the architectural members imitating the branches of a tree; this highly entertaining work, dating back to the early years of Vladislav Jagiello's reign, is sometimes attributed to the Frankfurt sculptor Hans Spiess. Next comes the *Chapel of the Mary Magdalene*, containing the wall tombs of the cathedral's two main architects, Matthew of Arras and Peter Parler; fragments of late 14C wall-paintings can be seen here, as they can in the following

Chapel of St. John of Nepomuk, which has as well the marble tomb of
Jan Očko of Vlašim, a work of 1370 from the Parler workshop. The
actual **Tomb of St. John of Nepomuk** stands in the ambulatory
passage in front of the last chapel, and is unquestionably the finest of
the baroque furnishings in the cathedral: an elaborate silver structure under a canopy hung with draperies supported by angels, the
tomb was made in Vienna between 1733–36 to the designs of the
great Fischer von Erlach. Tombs from the Parler workshop (1370s) of
prominent members of the Přemyslid family are to be found in the
next three chapels: the tombs of Kings Přemysl I (d. 1230) and
Přemysl Otakar II (d. 1278) are in the *Reliquary Chapel*; those of
Princes Břetislav I (d. 1055) and Spytihněv II (d. 1061) are in the
Chapel of Our Lady (the chapel where work on the cathedral was
probably begun in 1344); and those of Princes Břetislav II (d. 1100)
and Bořivoj II (d. 1124) are in the *Chapel of St. John the Baptist*,
where there can also be seen a statue by J.V. Mylsbek of St. Method
(1869–70) and the so-called *Jerusalem candelabrum*, a fine example
of Rhenish craftsmanship of the early 12C. Behind the High Altar,
and directly in front of the Chapel of Our Lady, is the *Tomb of St.
Vitus*, with a statue of the saint by J. Max of 1840. The northernmost
of the five radiating chapels of the apse is the *Archbishops' Chapel*,
featuring the plain brown marble tomb of Vratislav of Pernštejn, a
work of the late 16C by J. Vredemann de Vries. In the ambulatory
passage in front of this chapel is J.V. Myslbek's over-life-size bronze
statue of the kneeling *Cardinal Bedřich Schwarzenberg* (1891–95),
the most important of the 19C sculptures in the cathedral. South of
this is *St. Anne's Chapel*, displaying on its altar a silver reliquary of
1266, decorated with enamels and precious stones. Further S you
come to the **Old Sacristy**, the vaulting of which (begun in 1356)
shows Peter Parler at his most daring, featuring as it does a dramatically suspended boss supported by four skeletal ribs.

Attached to the north wall of the north transept is Bonifaz
Wohlmut's **Organ Gallery** (1557–61), which curiously combines a
harmonious Renaissance front taken from the pages of Serlio with
Gothic vaulting inside; the stained glass window above this is the
work of Max Švabinský and contains scenes of The Holy Trinity, The
Madonna with Prince Spytihněv II, and St. Wenceslas with Charles
IV (1939–49). The finest of the chapels in the nave is the third on the
left-hand side, the **New Archbishop's Chapel**, which has been the
burial place of Prague's archbishops since 1909, and houses as well
the tomb of the art historian bishop Antonín Podlaha, whose
researches played an important part in the last phase of the cathedral's construction. The chapel is adorned with a vivid stained-glass
window by Alfons Mucha of the Lives of SS. Cyril and Method, and
has next to it a powerful wooden sculpture of the Crucifixion (1899)
by F. Bílek.

Leave the cathedral by its western door, and turn right, touring the
rest of the castle complex in a clockwise direction. Skirting the
northern side of the cathedral is the narrow Vikářská Street, where at
No. 2 is the former Deanery, which was remodelled after 1705 by
Santini-Aichel. In the adjoining buildings at Nos 3 and 4 has been
installed the Vikárka Restaurant, the bar of which is housed in an
early medieval cellar known today as *The Little Cellar of Mr.
Brouček*; this name recalls a popular short story by the 19C writer
Svatopluk Čech which is set in the ale-house originally situated here,
and deals with a man who, under the influence of beer, goes on

a series of imaginative adventures, including to the moon and back to the 15C. A nearby alley leads from the street to the castle's northern bastions, which were renewed by Benedikt Ried in 1485 and include the round tower known as the *Powder Tower* (Mihulka). A small exhibition relating to the castle's fortifications is housed in the ground floor of this building, while on the upper floors (from where there are good views N towards the Summer Palace; see below) are exhibits relating to the scientific and cultural life at the Renaissance Court of Prague: the emphasis is on the time of Rudolph II, of whom there is an elaborately detailed bronze bust by Adriaen de Vries.

Vikářská leads to George's Square (Jiřské náměstí), which faces the apse of the cathedral and is named after the former Basilica of St. George and its adjoining convent. The **Convent of St. George** (Klášter sv. Jiří), in the north-eastern corner of the square, was founded in 937 by Prince Boleslav II and his sister Princess Mlada, who became its first abbess; rebuilt several times—including, most recently, in 1657–80—it was turned into a barracks after its dissolution in 1782 and then converted between 1962–72 into the branch of the **NATIONAL GALLERY** containing Czech art from the medieval to baroque periods. The plain white rooms arranged around the convent's simple cloister provide a perfect setting for the paintings and sculptures, through which you are directed chronologically by arrows. The basement and the ground floor contain the early holdings (up to around 1530), the first important sculpture being the bronze equestrian statue of St. George and the Dragon (1373) by the brothers George and Martin of Kolosvar, a copy of which stands in the Castle's Third Courtyard. An adjoining room is dedicated to the first major Bohemian painter, the anonymous Master of the Vyšší Brod Altarpiece. This altarpiece of the mid 14C, originating from the former Cistercian monastery at Vyšší Brod in southern Bohemia, was probably commissioned by Petr I of Rožmberk; it comprises nine panels of scenes from the life of Christ and the Virgin. A more distinctive personality of slightly late date, and one of the earliest Bohemian artists known by name, was Master Theodoric, who is best known for his panels and murals painted in the Holy Rood Chapel at Karlštejn Castle in 1357–65; he is represented here by six large and luminously modelled heads of saints. A work of great historical interest is the votive picture of John Očko of Vlasim, which portrays the enthroned Madonna flanked by what are sometimes considered as the earliest examples of Bohemian portraiture—remarkably realistic representations of Charles IV, Wenceslas IV and the panel's donor, John Očko himself, Archbishop of Prague. The main sculpture from this period in the gallery is the tympanum of the Crucifixion, which was taken from the north portal of the Týn Church in Prague. The last years of the 14C are dominated by the Master of the Třeboň Altarpiece, whose principal work, from which he derives his name, is to be found here. Only three panels of this work—which was painted in c 1380 for the former Augustinian church of St. Giles in the southern Bohemian town of Třeboň—have survived: these panels, painted on both sides with the most vivid colours and charming naturalistic detail, represent Christ on the Mount of Olives, SS. Catherine, Mary Magdalene and Margaret, SS. Augustine, Giles and Jerome, The Resurrection, and SS. James, Bartholomew and Philip. Of the many anonymous sweetly smiling Madonnas of the early 15C the finest is the famous Vyšší Brod Madonna of 1420. The last of the outstanding Bohemian painters represented in the lower rooms of the gallery is the anonymous Master of the Litoměřice Altarpiece. The altarpiece itself is in the North Bohemian Gallery at Litoměřice (though it seems originally to have come from St. Vitus's Cathedral in Prague), but the National Gallery has a number of other impressive works associated with him, most notably a series of panels from the Strahov Monastery in Prague (c 1505) and a Triptych with the Holy Trinity of 1515–20. Of the later sculptures, special mention should be made of the expressive relief of the Lamentation of Zebrák (early 16C) and a series of five intricately carved reliefs by the artist known as the Monogramist IP, who seems to have come from the Passau or Salzburg region.

The collections of Renaissance and baroque art on the first floor begin with works by artists of the Rudolph Circle, including a bronze of Hercules (1625–26) by Adriaen de Vries and an outstanding painting by Bartolomaeus Spranger of the Risen Christ (c 1590), which was intended for the tomb of the artist's father-in-law, the Prague goldsmith Nicholas Müller (who appears, together with other members of his family, at the bottom of the work). The 17C collections feature an especially large number of paintings by Karel Škréta, of which the most striking are the portraits, in particular a bust of the French painter Nicolas Poussin (whom Škréta met in Rome in 1634–35), an informal group portrait of the gem-carver Dionysio Miseroni and his Family (1653), and a delightful full-length portrait of Maria Maximiliana of Sternberg dressed as a Shepherdess (1665). Among the later paintings of the 17C are the very Rubenesque Liberation of St. Andromeda (1695) by M. Willmann, and a number of rapid oil sketches by Jan Liška. Baroque sculpture is represented most notably by J.G. Bendl's Archangel Raphael of c 1650 (which was taken from the demolished Plague Column on the Old Town Square), several works by F.M. Brokoff (in particular two Moors of 1718–19 from the gates of the Mansion at Kounice, and a polychromed statue of St. John of Bohemia), and Matthias Braun's hysterically posed St. Jude Thaddeus (1712), originally forming part of an altarpiece from the now demolished church of Our Lady in Prague's Old Town. From the latter dismantled altarpiece is also a painting of St. Jude Thaddeus by Peter Bendl, one of the most successful and prolific Bohemian artists of the early 18C: in addition to this and numerous other religious works by him, the gallery has an extensive collection of his portraits, including two self-portraits dating from 1697 and 1703. A more remarkable portraitist than Bendl was Johann Kupecký, who is represented here by two of his greatest works, a seated portrait of the ostentatiously dressed miniaturist Karl Bruni and a portrait of the Artist with his Wife: the latter, a work of uncompromising realism, was painted, unusually, as a token of reconciliation with his wife, whom he had found to be unfaithful and whom he portrayed here in the guise of a penitent. Among the other 18C works are V.V. Reiner's Orpheus with Animals in a Landscape (before 1720), A. Kern's St. Augustine (c 1735), N. Grund's Gallant Scene with a Lady on a Swing (c 1760) and oil sketches for frescoes by F.A. Maulbertsch.

The **Basilica of St. George** (Basilika sv. Jiří), attached to the southern side of the Convent, is the oldest church in the citadel, having been founded in 905. Transformed into a three-aisled structure in 973, it was rebuilt following a fire in 1142, and then again in 1657–80; restoration campaigns undertaken in 1897–1907 and 1959–62 brought back many of the building's 10C to 12C features, making the church one of the best preserved Romanesque structures in Bohemia. The main baroque survival is the vivid ochre west façade (facing George Square) and the adjoining *Chapel of St. John of Nepomuk* (Jan Nepomucký), which was built by F.M. Kaňka and the Dientzenhofer brothers in 1718–22, and is adorned on the outside with a statue of the saint by F.M. Brokoff (the interior, which is rarely open, has a dome frescoed by V.V. Reiner). The south portal of the basilica, facing Jiřská Street, is a coffered classical structure (early 16C) by Benedikt Ried incorporating in the tympanum a late Gothic relief of St. George and the dragon, the original of which is in the National Gallery. The principal Romanesque features of the basilica's exterior are the twin white towers rising up at the eastern end of the church. The cold and heavily restored interior, which is now deconsecrated and used only for the occasional concerts, retains in its nave the original arcades of the 10C and 11C. At the end of the nave, in front of the raised choir, are the tombs of Prince Boleslav II (encased by a baroque grille of 1730), and Prince Vratislav I (in painted wood), the founder of the church. In between the two flights of the baroque staircase which leads up to the choir is the entrance to the remarkable crypt of 1142, featuring columns with cubic capitals. The vault of the choir has scant fragments of wall-paintings of c 1200 representing the Celestial Jerusalem; fragments of 16C painting decorate the vault of the adjoining Chapel of St. Ludmila, which was added in the late 14C and houses the tomb (from Peter Parler's workshop) of the murdered St. Ludmila, one of Bohemia's patron saints.

Jiřská or George's Street, which runs due E of the basilica and slowly descends through the tapering eastern half of the citadel, is the main and oldest street of the citadel, and is lined with a number of Renaissance and baroque buildings. Before reaching the finest of these, you should take the first turning to the left to visit the celebrated **Golden Lane** (Zlatá ulička). This row of tiny houses dating from the end of the 16C runs directly underneath the north-eastern ramparts of the citadel, in between the New White Tower and the Daliborka Tower, both of which formed part of the new fortifications designed by Benedikt Ried for Vladislav Jagiello. The name of the lane is sometimes romantically connected with the alchemists at Rudolph's court, though in fact it derives from the goldsmiths who once lived here alongside the castle's guards. In the 18C and 19C the dwellings here were inhabited by the very poor, and it was only after 1960 that they were to receive their cheerfully-coloured doll's house appearance and tiny shops selling artefacts for the thousands of tourists who daily throng this restricted area. The *New White Tower*, at the western end of the lane, served after 1584 as a prison, among its most famous inmates being the English alchemist Edward Kelley and the leaders of the anti-Habsburg uprising of 1618. The house at No. 22 belonged to Kafka's sister Otla, and Kafka himself stayed here in 1917, reputedly drawing inspiration for his novel, The Castle; the place has recently been acquired by the newly-formed Kafta Society who plan to turn it into a bookshop. The street is also associated with the Nobel Prize-winning poet Jaroslav Seifert, who lived in the late 1920s and early 1930s in a house (now gone) in between the eastern end of the lane and the *Daliborka Tower*, writing here his two collections of poems, Eight Days, and Bathed in Light. The latter tower, another former prison, is named after the first person to be incarcerated here, Knight Dalibor of Kozojedy, whose life was to inspire Bedřich Smetana in his opera Dalibor (1868); a later prisoner was the aristocratic eccentric Count František Antonín Sporck, the founder of the hospital and spa at Kuks in eastern Bohemia (see Route 3).

Returning to Jiřská and continuing to walk E you will pass to your left (at No. 4), the former *Palace of the Burgrave of Prague Castle*, which was built in 1541 by Giovanni Ventura and adapted in the early 1960s to serve as the House of Czechoslovak Children. On the other side of the street is the *Lobkowicz Palace*, which was rebuilt in 1651–68 to the designs of the Italian architect Anselmo Lurago. The building, now housing a branch of the *National Museum*, has a drably arranged display on two floors relating to the history of Bohemia from the arrival of the Slavs up to 1848–49; some of the palace's 17C and 18C ceilings survive, including, in Room 19, a heavily stuccoed 17C ceiling incorporating a clumsy if amusing painted panel of the Triumph of Caesar. Shortly below the palace Jiřská reaches the Citadel's eastern gate, on the other side of which you will come out at the top of the Old Town Steps (Staré Zámecké schody; see above). Make your way back to George Square and bear left, passing to your left immediately on re-entering the square the *Church of All Saints* (Kostel Všech svatých), which was rebuilt after a fire at the end of the 16C and attached after 1755 to the adjoining Theresian Convent for Noblewomen.

On the western side of the Church of All Saints is the **OLD ROYAL PALACE**, which has parts dating back to the 12C but owes its present appearance largely to the rebuilding campaign undertaken by Benedikt Ried in the late 15C for Vladislav Jagiello. Occupying the site of the 9C palace of the Princes of Bohemia, it served from the 13C to the 16C as the palace of the Kings of Bohemia. After the Habsburgs moved their quarters to the western end of the citadel the building functioned up to the end of the 18C as the central offices of the Bohemian state. Thereafter it was neglected and partially used as storage space until 1924, when it was thoroughly restored and taken over for governmental purposes; its main rooms, which have only been open to the public since the 1960s, are still the scene of the occasional important political assembly.

The palace is entered from the castle's Third Courtyard, and as you make your way there from the Church of All Saints you will pass to your left a parapet overlooking the Palace Courtyard, above which rises the **VLADISLAV HALL**, which is adorned on the outside by elegant Renaissance windows that give no hint of the late Gothic fantasies to be found within. When you eventually enter the hall after crossing a dark and austere antechamber adjoining the palace's main entrance, you are confronted with what is architecturally one of the most exciting spaces to be seen in Europe. The vast hall, which is by far the largest room in the palace, was built by Benedikt Ried in 1493–1502 and is dominated by vaulting of breathtaking elaboration: the ribs, likened frequently to the intertwined branches of a forest, have largely ceased to play a structural role, but snake their way around the ceiling in an essentially decorative way, drawing the visitor into the room through their powerful movements, and creating dynamic effects that look ahead to the baroque period. The vaulting, representing an extreme development of the late Gothic style, contrasts markedly with the innovatory Renaissance windows, yet even when handling classical forms, Ried often did so in a highly idiosyncratic fashion, as can be seen in his famous door at the north-eastern end of the room, where a Renaissance arch is supported by twisted pilasters, which are almost a mockery of all that the Renaissance stood for.

Before crossing to the eastern end of the hall, you should go through the door in its south-western corner to visit the room of the *Bohemian Chancellery*, which is famous as the place where the 'Second Defenestration' took place in 1618.

Early on the morning of 23 May 1618, a group of Protestants led by Count Thurn burst into the Chancellery determined to punish the two Catholic councillors Martinic and Slavata, who had been appointed by Ferdinand over their heads. Following a violent row, the councillors, accused of being traitors and worthless followers of the Jesuits, were thrown out of the window. They managed to grab on to the ledge, but Thurn beat their knuckles with the hilt of his sword until they fell. Surprisingly they were not killed, thanks to the unhygienic conditions then prevailing at the castle, whereby the ditch which at that time ran below the whole complex was piled high with sewage which broke the two councillors' fall. This excremental intervention to the course of history was later attributed by Catholics to a miracle.

After returning to the hall walk across to its south-eastern corner, where there is a door leading to a terrace offering a magnificent view of Prague; the helical staircase which descends from here to the gardens below was built by Otto Rothmayer in 1951. Back once more in the hall, and crossing over to its north-eastern corner, you will pass to your right a balcony looking down into the Church of All Saints (see above), which has mainly 17C and 18C furnishings. The extraordinary door with twisted pillars at the north-eastern corner of the hall leads into the **Diet Hall**, which is covered with another late Gothic vault of fascinating complexity. The room, built by Ried in 1500, was destroyed by fire in 1541, and reconstructed nine years later by Bonifác Wohlmut, who provided it with the Renaissance Tribune once used by the supreme scribe. Returning to the Vladislav Hall, and turning right, you will come immediately to a double Renaissance portal. Through the arch on the left a spiral staircase climbing up to the rooms of the *New Land Rolls*, where there is a ceiling decorated with the heraldic shields of the clerks of the Land Rolls; the right-hand arch leads directly to the **RIDERS' STAIRCASE**. Built by Ried in around 1500 it is vaulted in a way which almost surpasses in complexity this architect's achievement in the Vladislav Hall, with ribs that intersect, interrupt and are suddenly truncated, the overall effect being one of suspended movement, a sense of playful abandon being controlled by a rigorous geometrical discipline in a way which would have impressed the baroque architect Borromini.

Patrick Leigh Fermor, in A Time of Gifts (1977), wrote of the vaults that 'they were impossible to describe', and promptly went on to describe them at great length in prose which is almost as difficult to follow as the ribs themselves. To Leigh Fermor 'the marvellous strangeness of the late Gothic vaults enclosing this flight must have germinated in an atmosphere like the English mood which coaxed fan-tracery into bloom.'

Walking down the Riders' Staircase you will reach the palace's northern door, where you leave the building. At present the 14C ground-floor rooms of Charles IV's palace are closed to visitors, as is the cellar below, a survival of the 12C palace of Prince Soběslav. After walking back to the western end of the palace, you should take a closer look at the southern half of the Third Courtyard, in the middle of which stands the famous bronze statue of St. George and the Dragon by the brothers George and Martin of Kolosvar (the original is in the National Gallery at the Convent of St. George). Between 1928 and 1932 the whole courtyard, which at one time was slightly sloping, was relaid and straightened by Jože Plečník, who also designed for it a granite monolith commemorating the dead of the First World War. At the same time Plečník pierced the eastern end of the monotonous 'Municipal Building' on the southern side of the courtyard (see p 134) with a portal and ingenious staircase leading down to the gardens which were laid out originally in the late 17C over the notorious ditch into which the two councillors had been thrown in 1618. The gardens, commanding a magnificent panorama of Prague, were also relaid by Plečník, who divided them into the Paradise Garden and the Ramparts Garden, thus breaking up the monotony of the original formal plan.

From the Third Courtyard you should make your way back to the Second Courtyard, which you should leave through the arch on its northern side. This will take you to the Powder Bridge (Prašný most), which spans the so-called Stag Moat (Jelení příkop), where red deer were kept from the 16C to 18C. After crossing the bridge and continuing to walk N, you will pass on the left an elegantly simple building designed by J.-B. Mathey in 1694 and restored by Pavel Janák in 1948–54; originally housing the Royal Zoo, it now serves as a hall for temporary exhibitions organised by the *National Gallery*, and occasionally shows a selection of the excellent holdings of Czech 20C art intended eventually for Holešovice (see Route 1H). On the other side of the path are the gates to the Royal Garden (Královská zahrada); most of this is now closed to the public, but you can catch a glimpse through its gates of the *Great Ball-Game Court*, an harmonious Renaissance structure built by Bonifaz Wohlmut and Ulrico Avostalis in 1565–69. The path ends at the Mariánské hradby, where you should turn right and follow the northern walls of the garden until you reach the **Summer Palace**.

This structure, popularly and wrongly known as the Belvedere, is one of the purest examples in central Europe of the Italian Renaissance style, the proportions of its arcaded lower level strongly recalling the architecture of Brunelleschi. Begun in 1537 to a design by Paolo della Stella (who executed as well the exquisite mythological and ornamental reliefs on the arcade), it was completed in 1552–69 by Bonifaz Wohlmut, who provided it with the one feature which reveals it as a work situated in Central Europe rather than Italy—the curious copper roof shaped like the inverted hull of a ship. The interior, remodelled in the mid 19C was restored after the Second World War by Pavel Janák, and is now closed for further restoration. The tiny Renaissance garden on its western side contains a celebrated bronze fountain known as *The Singing Fountain* on account of the sounds made by the water dropping from its two basins: the finely detailed work was designed in 1563 by Francesco Terzio. On the eastern side of the building is the small *Chotěk Park*, which was founded in 1833 by the Supreme Burgrave K. Chotěk, and was Prague's first public park; in an overgrown bosky setting at its eastern end stands a delightful memorial by Josef Maudr to the 19C poet Julius Zeyer, whose bronze bust is placed on top of a grotto enclosing a group of white marble figures from his poems.

North of Mariánské hrady begins the verdant district of Střešovice (see Route 1G); within this district, but a few minutes' walk from the Summer Palace, is the *Písek Gate* (on U Písecké Brány Street), which was built by Charles VI in 1721 as part of Prague's new fortifications. Just to the W of this is Mickiewiczova, on which stand a number of interesting buildings of the early years of this century, most notably (at No. 1) the former house and studio of the sculptor František Bílek. Designed and built by Bílek himself in 1911–12, this large and curious brick structure, partially inspired by Egyptian architecture, has been kept to a certain extent as it was in Bílek's day; The garden and studio, both filled with his expressive carvings, are open to the public during the summer months.

Return to the castle's Second Courtyard, and from there make your way back to the Hradčany Square to begin a tour of the Hradčany or

'Castle District'. This district, which stretches to the W of the castle, was made a township in 1320, and enlarged forty years later by the construction of the Hunger Wall (see p 131); the scene after 1541 of intensive rebuilding work, the place was raised to the status of royal town in 1598, and remained as such until the creation of a unified Prague in 1784. The district covers a relatively small area, but is crowded with important monuments, beginning with those on the Hradčany Square (Hradčanské náměstí) itself.

This sloping, wedge-shaped square, lined with imposing palaces, features at its centre a *Marian Column* of 1726 ringed by eight statues of saints by F.M. Brokoff. Adjacent to the western façade of the palace, behind a fine ironwork lampholder, is the *Archbishop's Palace* (No. 16), which dates back to a building of Wohlmut's of 1562, but was rebuilt by J.-B. Mathey at the end of the 17C and given an Italianate baroque façade, with a crowning pediment and statuary, by J.J. Wirch in 1763–65; the interior, closed to the public, is rich in 18C furnishings, including a set of eight Gobelin tapestries of 1753–56. On the left-hand side of the palace is an alley descending to the **Šternberg Palace** (No. 15), a gloomy but impressive structure which is completely hidden from the square. Designed by D. Martinelli, and executed between 1698 and 1707 by G.B. Alliprandi and J.B. Santini-Aichel, it is particularly remarkable for its courtyard, which is dominated on its western side by a large oval pavilion. However, the building is visited less for its architecture than for its paintings, for it houses the Foreign School holdings of the **NATIONAL GALLERY**, an outstanding collection unrivalled in Czechoslovakia.

The rooms of the Sternberg Palace, featuring a number of fine stuccoed and painted ceilings of the early 18C, make an elegant setting for the Foreign School paintings (which have been housed here since 1945), but the display is crammed, old-fashioned and poorly lit. The dingy main staircase adjoining the ticket-office leads up to where the bulk of the collection is shown. On the first floor are the Italian 14C to 16C paintings, which include among the primitives works by Nardo di Cione and Bernardo Daddi and an expressive Lamentation by Lorenzo di Monaco; the quattrocento is represented only by four works, the finest of which are by Benozzo Gozzoli and Pasqualino Veneto. It is on the second floor that the true quality of the gallery is felt, beginning with an excellent group of German 15C to 16C paintings, including Hans Schücklin's Beheading of St. Barbara (1470), monochrome fragments of an altarpiece of 1509 by Hans Holbein the Elder, a portrait by his son of Elizabeth Vaux, Altdorfer's Martyrdom of St. Florian, Baldung Grien's Beheading of St. Dorothy (1516), and a variety of works by Lucas Cranach the Elder, most notably a delightful Adam and Eve of 1537, a Judith and Holofernes of 1550, and fragments from an altarpiece in St. Vitus's Cathedral which was taken down by Protestants in 1619 (the main survival is a panel of the Assumption surrounded by angels and saints). Especially powerful are two large panels by Hans Süss of Kulmbach which originally decorated the organ loft of the Church of Our Lady in the Snows in Prague's New Town; they are vigorous and near-life-sized representations of the Emperor Henry II and the Empress Chunegunda. Süss was an artist greatly influenced by Albrecht Dürer, who is represented here by one of his most famous works, The Feast of the Rose Gardens. Painted in Venice in 1506 for the church of San Bartolomeo (the church of Venice's merchant colony), this work shows the great influence on the artist of the brilliant colouring of Venetian painters such as Giovanni Bellini; in turn the painting made an enormous impact on the

Venetian public, and indeed was their first main contact with contemporary German art. Among the many contemporary personalities that Dürer vividly portrayed on either side of the enthroned Virgin are Pope Julian II, Emperor Maximilian I, Domenico Grimani, Jakob Fugger and Hieronymus of Augsburg; the artist himself, a man not known for his modesty, also included himself among this distinguished company, standing under a tree and holding his signature. The painting was acquired by Rudolph II in 1606, and is the most important of his pictures to have remained in Prague.

A small room tucked away behind the room with the Dürer, contains the small and unimpressive holdings of 17C and 18C French and Spanish art, featuring works by Bourdon, Charles le Brun, Boucher and Mignard, and an indifferent portrait by Goya of Don Miguel de Lardizabal (1815). The best of the French paintings—a dramatically coloured Suicide of Lucretia (1625/6) by Simon Vouet—was painted in Rome under the influence of Caravaggio and is thus displayed in the rooms devoted to the 16th to 18C Italian School. The Italian cinquecento contains good portraits by Lotto and Bronzino, and the so-called Madonna of the Veil, a Holy Family group painted c 1519 by Sebastiano del Piombo, and on loan from the cathedral at Olomouc. The 17C and 18C Italian paintings include Domenico Fetti's Christ in the Garden of Olives, Magnasco's Mary Magdalene in a Landscape, Piazzetta's St. Joseph and Child, an enormous view of London by Canaletto, a head of an old man by G.D. Tiepolo (erroneously attributed to his father Giambattista), a St. Jerome by Ribera, and small oils by Pittoni and Sebastiano Ricci. Of the Netherlandish holdings of the 15th and 16C, there stand out Jan Gossaert's St. Luke Drawing the Virgin and Child (1513–16) and Brueghel the Elder's Haymaking (1565); the former was hung on the main altar of St. Vitus's Cathedral from 1618 up to the end of the 19C, while the latter formed part of a famous series of panels of the Months painted for the artist's Antwerp friend Nicolaes Jonghelinck (the other surviving panels from this series are in the Kunsthistorisches Institut in Vienna). Among the 17C Flemish paintings are a Van Dyck of St. Bruno (1615) and several works by Rubens, including a Cleopatra of c 1615, and two large canvases of St. Augustine and The Martyrdom of St. Thomas which the artist painted between 1637 and 1639 for the former Augustinian Church of St. Thomas in Prague's Little Quarter. The Dutch 17C holdings are extensive and feature genre scenes by Dou, Ter Borch, Ochtervelt, Metsu and David Teniers, still-lifes by Pieter Klaesz and Willem Kalf, and landscapes by Jan van Goyen, Salamon Ruisdael and Aert von der Meer; the two outstanding works in this section are Rembrandt's Scholar in his Study of 1634 and the half-length portrait by Frans Hals of the rather cocksure Jasper Scahde van Westrum (c 1645).

One of the great strengths of the gallery are its holdings of the 19C and early 20C. The works of this period by artists from outside of France are also to be found on the second floor, a number of which being unhappily squeezed into a narrow corridor. The Russian paintings, which deserve a far better display than they have at present, boast evocative forest landscapes by Shishkin (1880s), The Sisters (1922) by Mikhail Nesterov, a futurist Ballet (1912) by Aristarch Vasilevich Lentulov and an excellent group of paintings by Repin from different periods in his long career, beginning with a portrait of his mother of 1867, and ending with a self-portrait of 1915 (especially fine is the portrait of 1896 entitled Artist's Son after his Return, portraying a brooding boy in a brilliantly lit landscape).

Among the German paintings are three works by Liebermann, a self-portrait by Corinth showing the plump and manic artist naked to the waist, Expressionist canvases by Schmidt-Rottluth and Pechstein, and a disturbing work by the undeservedly little known Max Oppenheimer, entitled The Operation: it shows an hysterical group of hands and scalpels. There is a single but highly atmospheric painting by Munch of a group of women dancing by moonlight by a shore (1900). The Austrian holdings begin with small detailed landscapes by the early 19C painter Pettenkofen (including a landscape of the Hungarian village of Szolnok where the artist was garrisoned in 1848), and culminate with superb paintings by Schiele, Klimt and Kokoschka. Schiele is represented by a small townscape of 1911 (a view of Český Krumlov; see Route 16) and a haunting tall canvas of a monk and a woman; the sole painting by Klimt is a large decorative composition in vivid blues and purples, entitled The Virgin and showing an entwined group of female nudes (1913). Kokoschka lived in Prague from 1934–35, and there are several works by him from this period, of which pride of place must go to three large and expressively painted views of Prague from the river, constituting possibly the finest landscapes ever made of this city. Other 20C works on the second floor include paintings by Severini, Guttoso, Carlo Carrà, Oscar Dominguez, Miró and Tapies.

The French 19C and 20C paintings, as well as a small group of French sculptures from this period, are shown in a series of ground-floor rooms on the opposite side of the courtyard to the main staircase. That the French holdings have been separated in this way from the other European schools and given such preferential treatment is irritating and out of line with present art historical thinking, but it has to be admitted that the works in question are of uniformly high standard. Among the artists represented are Corot, Daumier, Courbet, Delacroix, Theodore Rousseau, Pissarro (an excellent view of Pontoise of before 1870), Renoir, Manet (a head of Proust of 1855–56), Degas (Portrait of Lorenza Payese), Van Gogh (Green Rye, 1889–90), Sisley, Cézanne (House in Aix, 1885–87, and a superlative portrait of the Pontoise doctor, patron and friend to the Impressionists, Joachim Gasquet, 1896–97), Gauguin (a wooden relief done in Tahiti, and the famous Pont-Aven parody of Courbet, Good-day Mr. Gauguin, 1889), Rodin, Toulouse-Lautrec (Moulin-Rouge, 1892), the Douanier Rousseau (this artist's only known self-portrait, 1890), Signac, Van Dongen, Matisse, Bonnard, Chagall, Utrillo and Dufy. Many of these works were amassed by Vincenc Kramář, the enlightened director of the Prague National Gallery during the 1920s, who donated his collection to the Gallery in 1960, a few months before his death at the age of 83. Kramář's greatest contribution to the arts in Czechoslovakia was his early championing of Cubism, buying in Paris in the first and second decades of this century works that would profoundly influence a whole generation of avant-garde Czech artists, including Čapek, Filla, Špála, Procházka and the aptly named Kubišta. Thanks to Kramář, the National Gallery has a collection unrivalled in central Europe of the works of Picasso and Braque. The Picassos begin with two paintings belonging to his so-called Negro Period (a Self-Portrait of 1907 and a Female head of the same year) and continue with a large group of 'analytical Cubist works' of 1910 and 1911; there are also some 'synthetic Cubist works' of 1912 and 1913, and later purchases such as his monumental Standing Nude of 1921. The paintings by Braque trace his career from the 'analytical Cubist period' of 1910–11—when his works were virtually identical to Picasso's of these years—to the development of his very lyrical and painterly still-lifes of the 1920s. Among the other Cubist paintings are some early works by Derain, most notably a view of Cadaqués of 1910; Derain's later manner is represented by a sturdy and very classical Seated Woman of 1921.

Leaving the Gallery and continuing to tour the Hradčany Square, you will find on the southern side of the square, at No. 2, the **Schwarzenberg-Lobkowicz Palace**. This large, gabled palace, built by Augustín Vlach for Jan of Lobkowicz in 1543–63, is one of the finest examples in Prague of Bohemian Renaissance architecture, and is covered with restored sgraffito decorations, including on its wide projecting cornice; the interior, featuring 16C painted ceilings on the second floor, now houses a beautifully displayed **Military Museum**, with exhibits relating to early military history throughout the world. The wide, western end of the square is largely taken up by the *Thun-Hohenstein Palace* (No. 5); though known sometimes as the 'Tuscan Palace' (the Duke of Tuscany owned it after 1718), this is in fact a Roman-inspired building, built by J.-B. Mathey in 1689–91, and with an upper balustrade crowned by statues by F.M. Brokoff. At the north-western corner of the square, overlooking Kanovnická Street, is the gabled *Martinic Palace* of 1618–24, its façade sgraffitoed with biblical and mythological scenes.

Walking N along Kanovnická you will come at the end of this street to the *Church of St. John of Nepomuk* (Kostel sv. Jana Nepomuckého), which was built by K.I. Dientzenhofer in 1720–28 and is the first known church by this architect; its dirty, neglected exterior is unremarkable, but the Greek Cross interior, with ceiling paintings of the life of the saint by V.V. Reiner (1728), is richly decorated and stuccoed, and full of movement.

Turning right at the end of Kanovnická, and then immediately left, you will come to the top of what is perhaps the most picturesque of the Hradčany's streets, Nový Svět or The New World (a name which is also applied to this whole corner of town). This narrow, cobbled street, originating in a path leading from Prague to Střešovice, was lined at the end of the 16C with a number of modest houses; the latter, crumbling away over the centuries, came to be occupied by the very poor, but are now showing signs of becoming fashionable homes. At No. 1, on the left-hand side, is the house which belonged first to the astronomer Tycho de Brahe and then to his successor as court astronomer, Johann Kepler (after 1600); further down on this same side (at No. 25) is a memorial plaque by O. Španiel commemorating the house where the violinist František Ondříček was born in 1857. At the bottom of the street on the right-hand side (at No. 10) is a wooden house which has recently been transformed into one of Czechoslovakia's first Bed and Breakfasts.

After turning around at the last house and retracing your steps for a few metres, take the first turning to your right, Černínská, and climb up to the quiet and sloping Loreta Square (Loretánské náměstí). At the narrow northern end of the square, immediately to your right, is the former Capuchin Church of Our Lady, the monastery of which is the oldest Capuchin institution in Bohemia and was founded in 1600; the mid 17C church is very plain in its architecture and decoration, in accordance with the ideals of this Order, but is worth visiting during the Christmas period to see the famous Crib which is assembled here. Rising up above a terrace, and occupying the whole western side of the square, is the **Černín Palace**, which was designed and begun by Francesco Caratti in 1669 for Humprecht Jan Černín of Chudenice, the imperial ambassador to Venice. Domenico Rossi, G.B. Alliprandi and F.M. Kaňka were among the later architects to play a part in the construction of the palace, and the whole structure was extensively restored and remodelled by Pavel Janák in 1928–34. However, the main façade overlooking the Loreta Square remains in its overall conception if not in its detailing essentially as Caratti had planned it, and is not only one of the most monumental façades in Prague, but also the first truly baroque structure in the city, being articulated the whole of its great length (150m) by a giant order of Corinthian columns. Since 1918 the building has served as the Ministry of Foreign Affairs, and in 1948 was the scene of a notorious incident when one of Beneš' ministers, Jan Masaryk (the son of Czechoslovakia's first President), experienced the peculiarly Czech fate of falling out of the window. This incident, proved only in 1991 as a suicide, was the subject of intense speculation, and the Catalan exile Teresa Pamiés related how even years afterwards she was unable to pass 'the beautiful Loreta Square without thinking of the bloody corpse of Jan Masaryk stretched out on the old pavement'.

Facing the Černín Palace on the eastern side of the square is the **Sanctuary of Our Lady of Loreta**, an important place of pilgrimage as well as one of the Hradčany's main tourist attractions. The sanctuary dates back to 1626 when Benigna Kateřina of Lobkowicz, anxious to revive the Marian cult, commissioned a replica of the Virgin's House at the Italian town of Loreta, a house which, according to a 15C tradition, had been transported there miraculously from the Holy Land; at least 50 other copies of this house have been made, but the one in Prague remains the most famous. The Virgin's House is encased by a baroque complex, the main, western façade of which was begun by Christoph Dientzenhofer in 1716 and completed by his son Kilian Ignaz in 1722; in front of it is a balustrade decorated with statues of cherubs by O. Quittainer. The elegant tripartite façade has a frontispiece crowned by a tall tower enclosing an elaborate carillon which was made by Petr Neumann in 1694 and plays various melodies by means of a keyboard, including—at the stroke of every hour—the Marian hymn, 'We Greet Thee a Thousand Times'. After passing through the main portal you come to the cloisters, in the middle of which stands the Virgin's House, which was built by G.B. Orsi in 1626–31, and shrouded in 1664 with a heavy stuccoed decoration featuring Old Testament figures and scenes from the Life of the Virgin; the simple, barrel-vaulted interior in unfaced brick has traces of 17C frescoes. The cloisters themselves date back to 1661 but were raised by a storey by K.I. Dientzenhofer in the 1740s. They are surrounded by small and elaborately decorated 18C chapels, and feature off their eastern side the *Church of the Nativity*, which was designed by J.J. Aichbaurer in 1734, and has a sumptuously gilded interior with ceiling paintings by V.V. Reiner and J.V. Schöpf. After having walked around the cloisters in a clock-wise direction you complete your tour of the sanctuary by climbing up to a room off the cloister's western side, where you will find—displayed under a modern ceiling hung with a glass decoration in questionable taste—a *Treasury* comprising chalices, monstrances and other liturgical objects from the 16C to 18C.

At the foot of the Sanctuary's main entrance is a flight of steps leading up to the southern end of the Loreta Square. Turn right at the top of the square and you will come almost immediately to Pohořelec, a square which has its origins in a suburb of the Hradčany founded

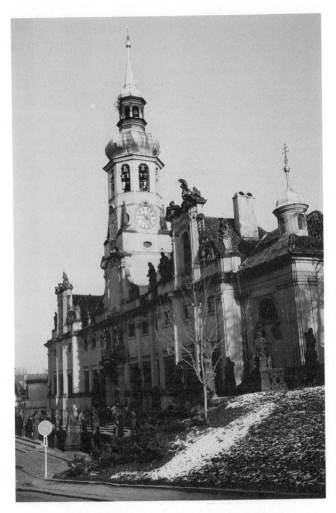

Main façade of the Marian shrine of Loreta, Prague

in 1375; it is lined today with grimy and decayed 17C and 18C buildings. Climbing up the dark and narrow passage through the house at No. 8 (on the southern side of the square) will lead you into the first courtyard of the **Strahov Monastery** (Strahovský klášter); alternatively you could reach this courtyard by walking to the south-western corner of the square, and then turning left, entering the monastery through its elegant gate of 1742, and passing on your left the early 17C Church of St. Roch (which is now used for temporary exhibitions).

The former Premonstratensian Monastery of Strahov was founded by Vladislav II in 1140 on the instigation of the Bishop of Olomouc, Jindřich Zdík, who had first come into contact with the Premonstratensian Order on a visit to Palestine. The monastery, endowed with a formidable library, soon became one of the great centres of learning in Bohemia, and many of the leading personages of the day were educated here. Devastated and plundered by the Swedes in 1648, the place prospered once again after the subsequent Treaty of Westphalia, and acquired so many more books that in 1671 G.D. Orsi began building a new library hall, known today as the Theological Hall. Between 1682 and 1689 the rest of the monastery was remodelled and extended by J.-B. Mathey, and towards the end of the following century a further library hall, the Philosophical Hall, was commissioned from I.J. Palliardi by the enlightened abbot Václav Mayer (1734–1800). Mayer was also responsible for the founding of the abbey's Cabinet of Curiosities (which still survives today, though closed to the public), and it was during his abbacy that the man known as the 'patriarch of Slavic philology', J. Dobrovský, used to stay here. In deference to the monastery's literary traditions, a Museum of Czech Literature was established in the monastery buildings in 1953. Archaeological investigations carried out here during this same decade uncovered extensive remains of the 12C monastery.

Tickets to visit the Strahov Monastery have to be purchased in the passage leading to its second courtyard, situated behind the eastern end of the monastery church of Our Lady. The whole complex (which is slowly being restored) has a dilapidated character, and this is particularly true of its second courtyard, where the entrance to the *Museum of Czech Literature* is to be found. This pleasantly chaotic museum, at present in a more confusing state than ever owing to the re-evaluation of recent Czech writers, is arranged around the monastery's large cloisters, the ground floor area being devoted to the early history of Czech literature, and the first floor area to the 19C and 20C. Three rooms on the western side of the cloisters have been restored to their Romanesque state, while the long *Summer Refectory* (situated off the south-eastern corner of the cloisters) is covered with a wonderful illusionistic ceiling painting by S. Nosecký of the Banquet of Baltasar (1753). To visit the remaining parts of the monastery you have to return to the first courtyard and make your way to the west façade of the *Church of Our Lady* (Kostel Nanebevzetí Panny Marie). This church, which retains its 12C Romanesque basilica plan, was remodelled in the early 17C and again in the middle of the following century; the mid 18C interior has a ceiling decorated with stucco cartouches designed by J. Palliardi, and an organ on which Mozart played. The finest of the baroque additions to the monastery are its two library halls, the entrance to which is adjacent to the church's west façade. The first one which you come to, **THE THEOLOGICAL HALL**, has kept its original wooden shelving and is adorned in its centre with 17th and 18C globes as well as tables displaying a select few of the library's incomparable collection of illuminated manuscripts and incunabula, among which is the Strahov New Testament, an Ottonian work of the 9C–10C constituting one of the oldest written documents surviving in Czechoslovakia; the magnificent ceiling is decorated with late 17C stucco cartouches by Silvestro Carlone framing frescoes by Siard Nosecký celebrating True Wisdom. Grander still is **THE PHILOSOPHICAL HALL** which was built at the end of the 18C around richly gilded and carved walnut furnishings (by J. Lahofer) which were brought here from the dissolved Premonstratensian monastery at Louka outside the South Moravian town of Znojmo (see Route 19). In 1794 one of the greatest fresco painters of central Europe, the Austrian A.F. Maulbertsch, covered the entire vault of this hall with a vast ceiling painting representing the modest theme of The History of Humanity.

A gate at the eastern end of the first courtyard brings you out into the extensive parkland covering the Petřín Hill, and an enjoyable short walk, with beautiful views towards Prague Castle, can be made from here to the Observatory Tower at the top of the hill (see Route 1B). To return instead to the Hradčany Square, go back to Pohořelec and from there head E down Loretánská, which has a number of fine palaces at its eastern end, including, at No. 4, the *Martinic Palace*, which was built by G.B. Scotti in 1700–05 for Jiří Adam II of Martinic—the imperial ambassador to Rome—and was closely modelled on the buildings of the Roman architect Carlo Fontana. At No. 1 is the former *Hradčany Town Hall* (Hradčanská radnice), which dates back to shortly after the raising of the Hradčany to a Royal Town in 1598, and has early 17C sgraffito decorations by Marian de Marianis.

D. The New Town (Nové Město)

The New Town, which was founded by Charles IV in 1348, lies to the S and E of the Old Town. Formed by the construction of a great line of outer fortifications stretching from the foot of the Vyšehrad hill in the S all the way to the Vltava in the N, it constituted one of the most ambitious examples of town planning in 14C Europe. The largest of the four original townships of Prague, it was the main home to begin with of the city's craftsmen and poor, and was later to emerge as the commercial, administrative and social centre of Prague. The medieval street plan has been largely retained to this day, but rapid urban development from the late 19C onwards led to the pulling down of the fortifications in 1875, and the demolition of most of the surviving old houses to make way for large apartment blocks and imposing civic buildings. There are a number of medieval churches to be seen in the district, and numerous baroque monuments; but the appeal of the New Town to the sightseer lies essentially in its great range of exciting monuments from the late 19C and early 20C.

The heart of the New Town, and indeed the bustling centre of the whole city, is the **Wenceslas Square** (Václavské náměstí), a thoroughfare 60m wide and 750m long, which slopes down from the National Theatre to the long boulevards marking the boundary of the Old Town.

Originally a place where horse markets were held, the Wenceslas Square was known as the Horse Market (Koňský trh) up to as late as 1848, when it acquired its present name. The principal thoroughfare of Prague, the square has also been since 1848 the stage of some of the key historic moments in Czech history. A national mass held here in 1848 heralded the revolutionary disturbances of that year, while in 1918, crowds gathered here to celebrate the downfall of the Habsburgs. On 25 February 1948, a popular demonstration in support of the Communist Party of Czechoslovakia took place in the square, and on 16 January 1969, the student Jan Palach set fire to himself near here to draw world attention to the plight of the Czech people. The square also played a major role in the great events of November 1989, beginning with the 17th of that month, when a group of students, officially commemorating the fiftieth anniversary of a Czech student murdered by the Nazis, made their way here from Prague's second district, their numbers greatly swollen in the course of the journey. Greeted by riot police, they burst into chants of 'Freedom' and began singing the Czech version of 'We Shall Overcome', but the police reaction was brutal, and one person was killed and many more injured. This was to spark the whole country into action, and over the next few days crowds gathered in their thousands at the square, chanting 'Freedom', 'Resign' and 'Now is the time'; the statue of Wenceslas was papered with posters and protest leaflets, and in front of it flowers and candles were placed in commemoration of Jan Palach. To the utter disbelief of the crowd, on 24 November, Alexander Dubček, followed by Václav Havel, appeared on the balcony of the Socialist Publishing House to proclaim the imminent success of the 'Velvet Revolution'.

The present-day character and appearance of the Wenceslas Square belie its glorious history, the whole place having something of the tackiness and seediness of London's Leicester Square, or Berlin's Kurfürstendamm. Shopping-arcades, hotels, cinemas, cheap eating establishments and bars and nightclubs with a distinctly dated look surround the square, and at night the place teems with drunken tourists and other more sinister types; muggings have greatly increased here since the 'Revolution', and many Czechs now like to warn you of the dangers of the square late at night, though these dangers remain slight in comparison with those of many western cities.

Tall buildings dating from the late 19C onwards line the whole length of this long thoroughfare and flank a central row of gardens which were laid out in the 1980s and lead up to the vast **National Museum** (Národní muzeum), a pompous neo-Renaissance structure rising up on ramps at the very top of the square, and dominating the whole vista.

The National Museum was founded in 1818 by a group of Czech intellectuals headed by the botanist, geologist and palaeontologist Count Kašpar Šternberg and including Josef Dobrovský, the pioneer of modern Slavonic studies. Thanks largely to the particular interests of Šternberg, the emphasis of the collections was largely on science, but the museum was greatly broadened in its scope from the 1830s onwards, when it became the increasing focus of Czech cultural life and national endeavours; a very important role in developing the scope of the museum was played by the celebrated historian František Palacký, who became the museum's secretary in 1841, and envisaged a place which would reflect every aspect of his country. The involvement of the institution in nationalist political movements, culminating in the insurrections of 1848–49, inspired a growing hostility towards the place on the part of the Austrian authorities, yet the museum was soon to occupy one of the most prominent sites in Prague. The collections were housed at first in the refectory of the Minorite monastery attached to the Church of St. James, but the demolition of the New Town fortifications in 1875 and the consequent removal of the Horse Gate led to a site becoming available at the top of the Wenceslas Square. The opportunity to use a site of such patriotic associations was immediately seized upon by the museum authorities, and in 1883–84 a competition was held for the design of the museum building to be erected here. The competition was won by Josef Schulz, and work on the structure was completed in 1890; its extensive sculptural embellishment involved most of the prominent academic sculptors of the day.

The main façade of the museum features a tall rusticated basement supporting a giant order of Corinthian columns, in the middle of which is a pedimented frontispiece crowned by a gilded dome. The sculptural decoration, like the architecture itself, is very conventional, and includes, at the top of the double ramp which climbs up to the main entrance, a dull group by Anton Wagner representing Bohemia between the Rivers Labe and Vltava. The principal component of the dauntingly large, red marbled interior is the **Pantheon**, a room decorated all over with ambitious historical and allegorical murals by Václav Brožík, František Ženíšek and Vojtěch Hynais; in the centre of the room are six statues and 42 busts—mainly executed between 1898 and 1901—of distinguished Czechs from the 14C onwards, the work of A. Popp. A. Procházka, J.V. Myslbek, M. Havlíček, B. Vlček, L. Šaloun, J. Štursa and K. Dvořák. The National Museum's collections have now been shared out between various buildings throughout Prague, the ones on show in this building comprising those devoted to geology, archaeology, prehistory and coins and medals (all of which are to be found on the first floor), and to zoology and palaeontology (on the second floor). The display is gloomy and unimaginative, and the layman might well agree with the writer Stephen Brook's assessment (voiced in his book, The Double Eagle) that the main emotion which the museum inspires is a sense of awe at the sight 'of so many display cases exclusively devoted to the cockroach'.

Walking down the Wenceslas Square from the National Museum, the first monument you come to, in the middle of the thoroughfare, is the **St. Wenceslas Monument**, the masterpiece of J.V. Myslbek and comprising an equestrian statue of Wenceslas surrounded by four other patron saints of Bohemia—SS. Ludmilla, Procopius and Adalbert and the Blessed Agnes. Originally conceived in 1887, the work was to occupy much of Myslbek's life up to his death in 1922; in the course of the monument's long gestation, the artist's vision of the saint significantly changed, so that the initial romantic representation of a spiritual and temporal leader of the Slavic people became transformed into a sturdy, tightly modelled portrayal of a man embodying the power and authority of the Czech state.

The buildings at the upper end of the square are modern and of little architectual interest, but gastronomes might wish to pay a visit to *The House of Food* at the top right-hand corner of the square (No. 59), a large 1950s with store one of the largest ranges of Czech drinks and food specialities to be found in the country. Further down the square on the right-hand side is the Jalta Hotel (No. 45), another building of the 1950s, with a gallery underneath containing the *Baltic Grill*, Prague's main fish restaurant; this once seedy establishment, which has recently been considerably smartened up, serves occasionally such exotic specialities as whale steak, but more usual fare is overcooked carp. On the opposite side of the square to this begins the dark Ve Smečkách Street, where you will find at No. 6 one of Czechoslovakia's finest small theatres, the *Činoherní Klub*; emerging to prominence in the 1960s, this theatre maintains a great reputation today, and recent successful productions include a lively, erotic dramatisation of Hrabal's novel, I Served the King of England, and Václav Havel's version of the Three-Penny Opera, directed by the famous film-director of the 1960s, Jiří Menzel. The next street off the left-hand side of the square is Štěpánská, at the entrance to which is a corner building centred around a tall, imposing rotunda; this building, with entrances at No. 63 Štěpánská and at Nos 40/38 Václavské náměstí, was erected by Matěj Blecha in 1912–16, and was originally the headquarters of the Moravian Bank. Adjoining it on Štěpánská is the *Lucerna Palace*, an ugly block of 1907–10 featuring a gallery with shops, a cinema, and sleazy restaurants, and, in the basement, a large hall used for concerts and dances; Václav Havel's father, also called Václav, was one of its architects and owners, and joined this establishment with his restaurant at Barrandov to form the lucrative Barrandov-Lucerna Enterprises. Further down Štěpánská, on the other side of the street, is the Hotel Alcron, built in 1929–30 by A. Krofta, and enjoying since then a reputation as one of Prague's most luxurious hotels; its comforts, however, are not quite the equal of its splendid Art Deco interior.

Continuing to walk down the Wenceslas Square, the next building on the left-hand side after the former Moravian Bank is the *Melantrich House* (No. 36), the headquarters of the Melantrich Publishing House and the editorial offices of the newspaper Svobodné slovo (Free Word).

It was to the balcony of the Melantrich House that on Friday 24 November 1989, Alexander Dubček and Václav Havel made their way from the nearby Magic Lantern building to address a vast protesting crowd in the Wenceslas Square. One of those accompanying the two men was the English historian and writer Timothy Garton Ash, who gave a vivid account of this triumphant occasion in his short book, We the People: The Revolution of 89 (1990): 'Protected by Havel's bodyguards ... we emerge from the belly of the Lantern, Dubček and Havel side by side, and scuttle through covered shopping arcades and tortuous back passages to reach the balcony of the Socialist Party publishing house and the offices of Svobodné slovo: the balcony of the free word. Along the arcades people simply gape. They can't believe it. Dubček! It is as if the ghost of Winston Churchill were to be seen striding down the Burlington Arcade ... But when he steps out on to the balcony in the frosty evening air, illuminated by television spotlights, the crowds give such a roar as I have never heard. "DUBČEK! DUBČEK!" echoes off the tall houses up and down the long, narrow square.'

The adjoining building (No. 34) is a gabled structure in a Bohemian Renaissance style designed by A. Wiehl in 1896 and covered with restored sgraffito decorations by Mikoláš Aleš. Facing this, on the other side of the square (at No. 25/27) is a far more remarkable turn-of-the-century building, the **Grand Hotel Europa**. Built in 1903–06 by Bedřich Bendelmayer and Alois Dryák, it features a beautifully ornamented façade crowned by a large ceramic lunette; but its great joy is its perfectly preserved interior, above all that of its bar and restaurant, both boasting stained-glass windows and elegant panelling. Further down on this same side, at No. 19, is a neo-baroque building of 1895–96 now housing the Polish Cultural Centre but originally the Prague headquarters of the Trieste-based insurance company, *Assecurazioni generali*. This is famous as the place where the 24-year-old Franz Kafka began his first job, in October 1907; a medical certificate attesting to 'nervousness and cardiac excitability' allowed him to leave the company the following year, but he continued a career in insurance by joining in July 1908 the Workmen's Accident Insurance Institute, where he was to remain for the rest of his life.

Most of the square's remaining buildings of architectural interest are to be found on the left-hand side of the square, beginning with the *Alfa Palace* (No. 28), a large Functionalist apartment block with shops and a cinema, designed by L. Kysela and J. Jarolím in the late 1920s, and featuring shop-windows of Cubist inspiration. The adjoining Hotel Adria (No. 26) is housed in the oldest surviving building on the square, dating back to the late 18C; just below it, at No. 22, is a hotel of radically different character, the *Hotel Tatran*, a Functionalist work of 1931–32 by Pavel Janák. Further down, at No. 12, is the *Peterka House*, an Art Nouveau former bank built by Jan Kotěra in 1898–1910, when greatly under the influence of the Viennese architect Otto Wagner; the façade is adorned with stucco decorations by J. Pekárek and S. Sucharda. Below an Art Nouveau building at No. 8 is *The House of Shoes* (No. 6), which was originally a department store and studio built by Ludvík Kysela in 1926–28 for the visionary shoe-manufacturer Tomáš Báťa; you should walk through the ground-floor arcade of this pioneering Functionalist building to see its rear façade (overlooking the tiny Jungmannovo náměstí), which features one of the earliest curtain walls of continuous glazing uninterrupted by architectural supports to be seen in Europe. Kysela was also responsible for the adjoining *Lindt's House* (at No. 4), which was built just before the Báťa store, and was indeed one of the first examples of Functionalism in Prague.—Immediately N of here the square broadens to form a large pedestrian area featuring the Metro

Station Můstek and extending into the adjacent boulevards of 28.října and Na příkopě. The last building on the right-hand side (at No. 1) is the *Koruna Palace*, a fine Art Nouveau structure by Antonín Pfeiffer of 1910–14 with a futuristic corner tower and decorative detailing which looks ahead to the Art Deco period.

The southern façade of the Koruna Palace overlooks the busy pedestrian thoroughfare of Na příkopé, which is lined with department stores, banks and bookshops. Turning into this boulevard from the Wenceslas Square you will pass immediately to your left (at No. 1) one of the better examples in Prague of recent architecture: built by Jan Šrámek and Alena Šrámková in 1974–83, it is crowned by a glass and steel gable incorporating the clock of the department store which once stood here. Also to your left (at No. 3) is the *State Bank of Czechoslovakia* (formerly the Bank of Vienna), which was built by Josef Zasche in 1906–08 and is faced with polished granite. Prague's oldest department store, the *House of Fashion* is on the opposite side of the street (at No. 4) and was built in a North Italian Renaissance style by the Viennese architect T. Hansen in 1869–71. The oldest surviving building on the street, and one of the most elegant baroque palaces in the New Town, is further down on the right-hand side (at No. 10). This, the **Sylva-Taroucca Palace** (1743–51), was built for Prince Ottavio Piccolomini by K.I. Dientzenhofer with the assistance of A. Lurago, and is a pedimented structure with a rusticated basement and a main floor articulated by giant order pilasters; the attic is decorated with sculptures of mythological figures and vases by F.I. Platzer, who was also responsible for the putti and vases on the balustrade of the staircase inside. On the building at No. 14—the Commercial Bank of Czechoslovakia (1930)—a bust and plaque by B. Neužil records the site of the house where the writer Bozena Němcová died in 1862. Facing this, across the narrow Panská, is the *Church of the Holy Rood* (Kostel sv. Kříže), a massively built neoclassical structure designed by G. Fischer in 1816. Further down Na příkopě, at No. 18, is the former *Provincial Bank*, an Art Nouveau building of 1911–12 by O. Polívka, attractively decorated on the outside with mosaics by J. Preisler and sculptures by C. Klouček and L. Šaloun. The same architect and sculptors collaborated on the adjoining former *Savings Bank* (No. 20), a building of 1894–96 in a Czech Renaissance style, and incorporating a baroque portal from a palace of 1757; the entrance vestib<u>ule</u> is covered with wall-paintings of 1896 by Max Švabinský. On the opposite side of the street to this (at No. 29) is a modern building featuring on its first floor Prague's principal Russian Restaurant, the *Moskva Restaurant*, and, on its ground floor, an unappealing Russian imitation of a fast food joint, *Arbat*. Rather better food seems once to have been served at the late 18C palace on the other side of the street (at No. 22), a building which was converted in 1945 into the *Slavonic House*, a cultural centre complete with bookshop, cinema, exhibition hall and restaurant.

The restaurant of the Slavonic House became in the early 1950s a great meeting-place for the Spanish political exiles in Prague, thanks to its cook at that time, a Catalan exile called Josep Esquerré who learnt how to adapt Czech and Slovakian food to Spanish tastes. Teresa Pamiès, another exile from Catalonia, fondly remembered his cooking in her nostalgic book on Prague (1987): 'To please our particular (Spanish) palates he would cook succulent beans with pieces of pigs' ears, prepare stupendous rice dishes with Russian trab in place of Mediterranean sea-food, and make some memorable stews that would leave us bloated and fuel our aversion to Czech "knedlíky" (dumplings), potato soup ("bramboračka"), greasy goose with cherries, the ubiquitous bitter cauliflower known as "kyselé" and the equally ubiquitous "párky", grilled sausages that were sold in the street ... as soon as Autumn came.'

Next to the Slavonic House, at No. 24, is the *State Bank of Czechoslovakia*, which was put up in 1929–38 on a site that was occupied in the 19C by two hotels, At the Blue Star and At the Black Horse; a number of distinguished people were guests at these hotels, including the Russian anarchist Mikhail Bakunin, and the composers Chopin (to whom there is a plaque) and Liszt. Across the street, in a site now occupied by the grim 1930s administrative building at No. 33, there once stood Prague's most elegant café, the Café Français, where Liszt was frequently to be seen.

Na příkopě comes to an end at the Powder Tower and the náměstí Republiky (see Route 1A), where you should turn right into Hybernská, a narrow but busy street of 18C and 19C buildings, many in a decrepit condition, and others covered permanently in scaffolding. The first building to your right (at No. 20) was formerly a hotel, and this is where Tchaikovsky stayed in 1888 when he came to conduct the Prague première of his opera Eugene Onegin. Further down on the right-hand side (at No. 10), but at present completely hidden by boarding, is the former *Hotel Central*, a narrow-fronted but lavishly ornamented Art Nouveau structure built by F. Ohmann, B. Bendelmayer and A. Dryák in 1899–1902. On the other side of the street the late 18C Sweerts-Špork Palace (at Nos 3/5) is followed by the beautiful and recently restored *Kinský Palace*, which was designed by Carlo Lurago after 1651 and given a new façade at the end of the 18C. This building, which until recently housed a Lenin Museum, played an important part in the history of the Czech Communist Party, and was the scene in 1912 of the 16th All-Russian Conference of the Social-Democratic Party of Russia (the so-called Prague Conference), chaired by V.I. Lenin. In 1920, after the building had been forcibly occupied by right-wing leaders of the Social-Democratic Party, the left-wing leadership of the party declared a general strike, during which there were violent clashes between workers and police on Hybernská; this conflict led to the formation in 1921 of the Communist Party of Czechoslovakia. Further down the street Hybernská reaches an intersection formed by Havlíčkova to the N and Diážděná to the S; at the corner of Hybernská and Dlážděná is the *Café Arco* (No. 15), today an old-fashioned but unremarkable-looking establishment, but at one time one of Prague's famed Bohemian meeting-places.

The Café Arco on Hybernská came into being at the end of the 19C when the headwaiter of a staid café bearing the same name but in a far more fashionable part of town quarrelled with his employer and spitefully opened his own Café Arco in the rather less salubrious neighbourhood of Prague Central Railway Station. This new establishment, which was to reach the height of its notoriety in the years immediately preceding the First World War, soon attracted most of Prague's artistic and literary élite. Its regulars, who came to be known as the 'Arconauts', included a large proportion of German-Jewish writers, most notably Franz Werfel, Max Brod, Franz Kafka and Egon Erwin Kisch. The writer Karl Kraus, believing that this Jewish group at the Café Arco represented a cabal which besmirched the purity of the German language, penned a violent attack on the café, writing of the place the untranslatable line: 'Es werfelt und brodet und kafkat und kischt'.

The *Prague Central Railway Station* (Nádraží Praha-střed), at the corner of Hybernská and Havlíčkova, was Prague's first railway station, and was opened on 20 August 1845. The building, which has a main hall covered with an interesting roof in iron, wood and glass, is in a most depressing condition and attracts numerous loiterers of seedy and sinister appearance. Walk to the northern end of Havlíčkova, and turn right into Na poříčí, where you will find immediately to your right (at No. 24), the former **Legio Bank** (now the Ministry of Consumer Goods), an extraordinary structure of Cubist inspiration built by Josef Gočár in 1922–25. In this highly sculptural building, featuring a heavy, projecting attic, and a giant order of cubic columns crossed by deeply cut bands, Gočár enjoyed a most successful collaboration with the sculptors Jan Štursa and Otto Gutfreund; above the shop-front Jan Štursa placed four enormous consoles of workers (1922–23) to support a long frieze by Gutfreund (The Return of the Legionaries, 1921), a work of great stateliness and power which is considered by many to be one of the key landmarks in 20C Czech sculpture.

Further along the street, at No. 40, is the *Hotel Axa*, a fine Constructivist building of 1935 by V. Pilec. Just before the hotel, you should cross the street and head N along the short Biskupská, which was where the Merchants' Court of Poříčí's German community was situated up to 1235. At the end of the street is the late Gothic *Tower* belonging to the former German church of *St. Peter na Poříčí*. The latter building, just to the N of the tower, is a triple-aisled structure which dates back to the mid 12C and was originally the parish church of the German Poříčí district; in 1235 the church and surrounding area fell into the hands of the Knights of the Cross. Fragments of the original Romanesque church survive in the west façade and south wall of the main nave, but the rest of the building was much altered over the centuries, and was subject to neo-Gothic remodelling by Josef Mocker in the 1870s. Running behind the church is Petrská: walking W along this street you will come to the small Petrské náměstí, off which runs Soukenická (where you will find on the house at No. 13 a plaque marking the site of the birthplace of the topographical artist Wenceslas Hollar, who is best known for his views of London, where he died in 1677). Walking instead E along Petrská and then taking the first turning to the right you will rejoin Na poříčí at the point where it disappears under the large flyover Wilsonova února, which marks the eastern boundary of the New Town. On the other side of the flyover is the tiny and unpromisingly situated *Šverma Park* (Švermovy sady), which was founded in 1875 on the site of the recently demolished New Town fortifications. On this park's southern side, adjoining today a noisy area occupied by tacky market stalls, stands a grand neo-Renaissance structure built by A. Balšánek in 1896–98 to house the newly formed *Museum of the City of Prague*. On the ground floor of this slightly run-down museum is a fine display of artefacts and works of art from the 6C onwards relating to the early history of Prague, and including Slavonic pots, fragments of 13C frescoes, old Bohemian glass, and Renaissance and baroque furnishings; the second floor, at present being rearranged to take in recent developments in the city's history, is reached by a grand oval staircase, and features an enormous plaster model of Prague, made by Antonín Langweil in 1826–34.

Only a short distance S from the museum along the Wilsonova února is the magnificent Art Nouveau **Central Station** (Hlavní nádraží), but the journey is complicated on foot and best undertaken by taking the metro from Sokolovská (directly in front of the museum) to the following stop, Hlavní nádraží. The metro will take you to the station's modern extension, which dates from the 1970s and is built underneath the Wilsonova února and the narrow Vrchlického Park to the west. The original station (once called the Franz Josef Station) stands above the eastern side of the wide Wilsonova února, and was built by Josef Fanta in 1901–09; its most exciting feature is its twin-towered façade, featuring an ironwork central canopy and large-scale carvings of nudes and other allegorical figures by S. Sucharda, H. Folkmann and Č. Vosmík.

Further S along the Wilsonova února in the direction of the nearby National Museum are the reconstructed late 19C *Smetana Theatre* (originally the main German theatre in Prague) and the modern glass building of the *Federal Assembly*. At the south-western corner of the Vrchlického Park is another of the old luxury hotels of Prague, the *Hotel Esplanade* (with a neo-baroque gilded interior), while directly across the park from the Central Station begins Jeruzalémská. Walking down the latter street, you will pass to your right (at No. 5) the *Jubilee Synagogue*, a neo-Moorish building of 1906 with a vividly coloured façade. At the end of the street turn left on to Jindřišská, where you will find to your left the *Church of St. Henry* (Kostel sv. Jindřicha), which was founded in 1350 but much altered in later periods and given a neo-Gothic exterior by Josef Mocker in 1879; Mocker was also responsible for the neo-Gothic remodelling of the late 15C *Belfry Tower* on the other side of the street. Continuing to walk down Jindřišská you will soon reach its intersection with Panská and Politických vězňů. At the corner of Panská is the *Palace Hotel*, a luxury hotel of the turn of the century which has recently been reappointed in lavish style; on Politických vězňů meanwhile you will find at No. 20 the notorious *Petschek Palace*, a neo-Renaissance building of 1923–25 which served as the Gestapo headquarters during the last war, and was the place where numerous Czechs were tortured and executed, including Julius Fučík. At the end of Jindřišská you will come back to the lower end of the Wenceslas Square.

You can begin a tour of the southern half of the New Town from the bottom of the Wenceslas Square, where you should turn left into the quiet Jungmann Square (Jungmannovo náměstí), which runs parallel to the pedestrian thoroughfare of 28. října. In the middle of this square is a curious Cubist *Street-Lamp* designed by Vratislav Hofman in 1913, while at its south-eastern corner is the entrance to a courtyard leading to the former Carmelite **Church of Our Lady of the Snows** (Kostel Panny Marie Sněžné).

Founded by Charles IV in 1347 on the occasion of his coronation as King of Bohemia, the church of St. Mary of the Snows was intended as a vast triple-aisled structure which would have extended right into the present Jungmann Square. However, work on the building was interrupted during the Hussite wars, in which this church played an important role. The radical Hussite speaker Jan Želivský preached here between 1419 and 1422, and it was from here that on 30 July 1419 a procession set out to carry out the 'first defenestration' in Prague. Želivský was buried in the church in 1422, but the building was later left to decay and its steeple demolished. The abandoned church and convent came in 1603 into the hands of the Franciscans, who embarked on a campaign of restoration and rebuilding.

On entering the church you are immediately struck by its great height and size, though in fact what you are seeing constitutes only the chancel of the triple-aisled structure which was originally conceived. The furnishings are baroque, but the building has otherwise a completely Gothic look despite the fact that the net-vaulting and much of the masonry dates back only to the time of the Franciscan restoration. The former monastery gardens on the south side of the building were relaid in the 1950s and form today a pleasant public park, shaded by trees.

At its western end the Jungmann Square leads to the busy junction of 28. října, Jungmannova třída and Národní třída. The white corner building at the end of 28. října (at No. 1) is a fine Functionalist department store of 1927–31; at No. 30 Jungmannova třída (almost immediately to your left on reaching the street from the square) is Jan Kotěra's *Mozarteum* of 1911–13, one of the earliest modernist buildings in Prague and with a façade decorated with sculptures by J. Štursa. The corner of Jungmannova třída and Národní třída is taken up the bizarre and colossal **Adria Palace**, a heavily ornamented structure built by Pavel Janák and Josef Zasch in 1923–25 and featuring an attic level made up of square, crenellated towers that give the whole building the look of some futuristic urban fortress; the sculptural decoration on the façades was carried out by J. Štursa, Otto Gutfreund and K. Dvořák. Within this fantastical building can appropriately be found the **Magic Lantern**, a place which has played an important role not only in the history of experimental theatre and cinema, but also in the recent political history of Czechoslovakia.

The Magic Lantern was created for the Brussels World Exhibition of 1958 by Alfréd Radok, who, together with the brilliant stage designer Josef Svoboda, and up-and-coming talents such as the film director Miloš Forman, devised a brilliant illusionistic spectacle involving stage-sets, actors and film. Such was its success in Brussels, where it did much to draw world attention to the cultural life of Czechoslovakia, that it was decided afterwards to turn it in Prague into a permanent cultural institution. However, Radok and his collaborators were soon to fall victims to the political situation of the time, and were ousted and replaced by lesser talents. The Magic Lantern has survived to this day as an anodine tourist attraction booked up weeks in advance by large groups, and virtually impossible to get into on your own without recourse to bribery at the door. To anyone who has ever attended one of these shows it might well have come as a surprise to find out that this same place was to serve in November 1989 as the meeting-place of the newly formed Civic Forum, which in a matter of days succeeded in ousting the Communist Government of Czechoslovakia and hoisting Havel to the presidency of the country. The critical discussions that took place in the Magic Lantern were held not only in the dressing and smoking rooms but also on the stage, against the absurd background of a set for a production of the Minotaurus. The only foreigner present for most of the meetings was the Englishman Timothy Garton Ash, who wrote that for nearly two weeks he was 'privileged to watch history being made inside the Magic Lantern'. His short book, We The People: The Revolution of 89 (1990), includes a long and vivid account of these days, days when 'in a sense, all of Prague became a Magic Lantern'.

Národní třída (National Street) is Prague's most important street, and is vibrant with cars and people, and lined its whole length with department stores and monumental civic buildings. As you walk down it in the direction of the Vltava the first major building which you will pass to your right is the *Plateys House* (at No. 37), which was rebuilt and enlarged by Henri Hausknecht after 1813 and turned into the first tenement building in Prague; the main wing contains a hall where concerts were once held, one of the musicians who performed here being Franz Liszt in 1840 and 1846 (a marble bust of the composer has been placed on the building's back entrance). On the other side of the street, at No. 26 (at the junction with Spálená), is Prague's main department store, *Máj*, a light structure in glass and aluminium built in the 1970s by the Liberec architectural firm SIAL 02. A short detour down Spálená can be made to see the first Constructivist building in Prague, the former *Olympic Department*

Store, which is situated on the left-hand side of the street, at No. 16. This eight-storey reinforced concrete structure, with elements derived from transatlantic steamers, was built in 1923–27 by Jaromír Krejcar, who married shortly afterwards the journalist and former mistress of Kafka, Milena Jesenská; the building houses today one of the most interesting of Prague's small theatres, the *Studio Ypsilon*.

Back on the Národní třída and continuing to walk W, you will pass on the left-hand side, just after crossing Voršiliská, the late 17C former convent church of *St. Ursula* (sv. Voršily), which was designed by Marcantonio Canevale. Facing this on the other side of the Národní třída are two remarkable and adjoining Art Nouveau buildings, both designed by Osvald Polívka. The first of these, at No. 9, is the former *Topic Publishing House* (1910), a richly stuccoed building which is now used by the Union of Czechoslovak Writers; the second building, at No. 7, is the former headquarters of the *Praha Assurance* (1905–07), and, though a less decorative structure than its neighbour, has superlative reliefs on its façade by Ladislav Šaloun. Much of the remaining right-hand side of the street is taken up by the *Czechoslovak Academy of Sciences* (at Nos 5 and 3) a grimly impressive neo-Renaissance structure built by V.I. Ullmann in 1858–61 as the headquarters of a bank. The last building on the right, at No. 1, is the elegant and old-fashioned *Café Slavia*, a popular tourist haunt which is also one of the oldest of Prague's surviving literary cafés.

The German poet Rainer Maria Rilke was one of the many artists and writers who frequented the Café Slavia in the early years of this century, and he used the place as the setting of his evocative short stories, Tales of Prague. A later habitué was the poet Jaroslav Seifert, who was one of the stalwarts of Prague's coffee-house culture from the 1950s right up to the 1960s. Since the 1960s the place has held regular jazz concerts, which used to attract many of the city's political dissidents.

The two end buildings on the left-hand side of the street are the *New National Theatre* (No. 4) and the **NATIONAL THEATRE** (Národní divadlo) (No. 2). The former, one of the boldest and most distinguished examples of recent Czech architecture, is arranged around a small square and comprises three shaped blocks coated in glass, the one facing the street resembling a translucent honeycomb; the complex was built in 1977–83 by Karel Prager. The building is used almost exclusively for drama productions organised by the National Theatre Company, the present director of which is Otomar Krejča, who achieved international fame as actor and director in the 1960s, when he ran The Theatre Beyond the Gate (Divadlo Za Branou). Opera and ballet are put on at the adjoining National Theatre, one of the great landmarks of Prague, and by far the most eloquent architectural expression of Czech nationalist aspirations in the late 19C.

In 1845 a group of prominent Czech patriots, including František Palacký, Josef Jungmann, Josef Kajetán Tyl and Jan Evagelista Purkyně, sent a petition to the Emperor Ferdinand V asking for permission to build an independent Czech theatre in Prague. The proposal was also supported by the writers Jan Neruda, Vítězslav Hálek and Karel Havlíček Borovský, the latter making the practical suggestion that the money for the building should be raised through voluntary contributions. A fund-raising campaign with the slogan 'the Nation for Itself' was subsequently begun, but it was not until 1868 that the foundation stone of the building was laid. The architect chosen was Josef Zítek, who was supervising the final details of his work in 1881 when a fire broke out destroying the auditiorium and much of the building's decorations. Within the remarkably short space of six weeks enough money had been raised to rebuild the theatre, a task which was given to Josef Schulz. The theatre was finally opened on 18 November 1883 with a production of Bedřich Smetana's opera Libuše. The painters and sculptors involved in the decoration of the building include almost all the leading Czech artists of the late 19C, a generation which is in fact referred to as 'The Generation of the National Theatre'; among these artists were the sculptors J.V. Mylsbek, Bohuslav Schnirch and Anton Wagner, and the painters Mikoláš Aleš, Václav Brožík, Vojtech Hynais, Josef Tulka and František Ženíšek. In 1977–83 the building was extensively restored by Karel Pragner, and can be appreciated today at its resplendent best.

The grand exterior of the building, which has echoes of the Vienna Opera House and rather more distant ones of Renaissance Italy, is crowned by a Palladian-style roof highlighted by gilding. Some of the finest statuary of the main façade is concentrated on the attic level where there is a row of statues of Apollo and the Muses by B. Schnirch, who also modelled the flanking bronze chariot groups; on the side façade overlooking the Masaryk Embankment is a portal decorated with reclining figures by J.V. Myslbek of Opera and Drama. A bronze figure by Myslbek representing Music presides over the profusely embellished main foyer, where can be seen allegorical ceiling paintings by Ženíšek, fourteen lunette paintings by M. Aleš of scenes from Smetana's opera My Country and a gallery of bronze busts by different artists of the leading figures in the history of Czech theatre and opera. Of the many other decorations in the building special mention must be made of the works of Vojtech Hynais. He decorated the stairs leading up to the presidential box with a painted allegorical frieze, painted vivid representations of the Four Seasons for the ladies' boudoir of the presidential box (note in particular the female figure floating over a snow-covered landscape), and provided the stage with its superlative and celebrated back-cloth; the latter, portraying the unpromising theme of The Origin of the National Theatre, is full of references to Raphael and Renaissance painting and yet is saved from the absurder excesses of academic art through the sheer energy of the composition and execution.

The Národní třída comes to an end by the Vltava river, where you should head S down the Masaryk Embankment (the former Gottwaldovo nábřeží), passing alongside the *Slovakian Island* (Slovanský ostrov). This island, formed by alluvial deposits in the 18C, was strengthened by container walls in 1784, and partially built upon. In 1830 a restaurant was erected in its southern half, and this soon became one of the main centres of Prague's social and political life. Concerts were held in the building—including ones given by H. Berlioz and F. Liszt—and in 1848 the place hosted the inaugural session of the Slovakian Congress. Memorial plaques commemorating both this congress and the distinguished Slovakian writer Ludovít Štúr, one of its participants, are to be seen on the walls of the present restaurant, which was built in 1884 and is now the home of the National Folk Song and Dance Company. The rest of the island is taken up by a wooded public park laid out in 1931 and containing at its northern end a bronze memorial by K. Pokorný to the writer Božena Němcová. Straddling the narrow stretch of water between the island and the southern end of the Masaryk Embankment is the *Mánes Gallery*, the seat of the Mánes Society of Artists, which was founded in 1898 in opposition to the Czech Academy of Arts. Their present headquarters, a simple, white Functionalist building erected by Otakar Novotný in 1923–25, is curiously but picturesquely linked to a Renaissance water tower which once formed part of the Sitka Mills; the Gallery puts on exhibitions by contemporary artists.

Leave the river at the Mánes Gallery and head E down Myslíkova, turning off on to the third street to the left, Křemencova, to visit at No. 11 on the left-hand side Prague's most famous beer-cellar, *U Fleků*.

The origins of U Fleků go back to at least 1499 when the brewer Vít Skřemenec acquired the house which stood on the site of the present building and founded the beer-cellar and small brewery which came to be known for the next 250 years as 'Na Skřemenici' (hence the name of the street). The name U Fleků dates back to after 1762, when the establishment was bought by the Flekovsky family from Počenice, who, during the short time which they owned the place, became celebrated throughout Prague for the quality of their beer. The present neo-Gothic appearance of the interior is due to renovations carried out in 1898–1905, under the direction of the architect F. Sander; the pseudo-medieval wall-paintings were the work of L. Novák. The newly restored ale-house soon became a popular literary haunt, and for years afterwards there would always be a section reserved for writers. In the early years of this century it served as the meeting-place for the literary club known as Syrinx, whose members included a number of future leading Czech writers and dramatists, including K.H. Hilar (later to become director of the Prague National Theatre under the Republic), the poet Opočensky, the playwright Jiří Mahen, and Rudolf Těsnohlídek, who wote the story of Janáček's opera, The Cunning Little Vixen. Another of its members, then experiencing his first taste of Bohemian life, was the future author of the Good Soldier Švejk, Jaroslav Hašek, who doubtlessly enjoyed the rowdiness of many of their meetings, the tone of which can be judged from what one of its sculptor members once told him: 'Come here, you hairy bastard, and let me tear all those lice off you!' Later the Club changed its allegiance to the St. Thomas' Tavern in the Little Quarter, but Hašek himself was soon to tire of the group, finding it not too silly but too intellectual, and having no interest in its occasional serious discussions about 'modern art'.

A picturesque old clock, hung like a tavern sign, marks the entrance to U Fleků, which has a number of attractively panelled rooms, with wooden tables, and neo-Gothic vaulting; the dark beer which they make and serve here is excellent. Unfortunately, however, the place today has mainly been taken over by loud-mouthed carousing tourists (mainly German coach groups), and this is not an establishment where many Czechs would be proud to be seen in. Returning to Myslíkova turn left until you reach the lower end of Spálená, where, on turning left again, you will find shortly on the right-hand side the Cubist corner building known as the *Diamond House*, which was built in 1910–12 by Ladislav Skřivánek and Matěj Blecha; an amusing feature is the Cubist arch (designed perhaps by Antonín Pfeiffer) which joins the building to the neighbouring 18C Church of the Holy Trinity and frames a statue of St. John of Nepomuk by M.J. Brokoff (1717).

Retracing your footsteps and heading S down Spálená you will soon reach the northern end of the long Karlovo náměstí (Charles Square), a square which is even larger than that of Wenceslas, but with a much more sober and less energetic character. Originally Prague's biggest market square, and known as the Cattle Market until 1848, it was transformed in the middle of the 19C into a wooded public park, complete with statues to famous Czechs such as the poet Vítězslav Hálek and the botanist Benedikt Roezl; the buildings that surround the park are set back from it by wide and busy streets and have largely a stately but unremarkable 19C character. The main building at its northern end is the *New Town Hall* (Novoměstská radnice), which dates back to 1367 but has kept little of its medieval structure apart from the tower of 1425–26, the cellars and the double-aisled entrance hall (now used for marriages); the gabled façade overlooking the square is a reconstruction of 1905 of the building as it appeared in the 16C. The town hall is famous as the place where on 30 July 1419 the reformist preacher J. Želivský led by an irate mob demanded from its councillors the release of certain reformist prisoners; after refusing their demands the councillors were thrown out of the windows and killed, thus sparking off the Hussite revolution and inaugurating a long Czech tradition of 'defenestration'. Adjacent to the Town Hall, on the north-eastern corner of the square, is the late

18C *Salm House* (at No. 24) which marks the site of a Renaissance home (of which the portal has survived) owned in the early 18C by the leading baroque sculptor Matthias Braun, who died here in 1738.

Cross over to the western side of the square and walk half-way down it to Resslova, where you turn right, heading back in the direction of the river. On the right-hand side of the street (at No. 9) is a former Priest's Home designed in 1736 by K.I. Dientzenhofer, who was also responsible for the adjoining **Church of SS. Cyril and Methodius** (Kostel sv. Cyrila a Metoděje) to which this institution was attached. This impressive church, built in 1730–36 and originally dedicated to St. Charles Borromeo, is a tightly-composed structure, with symmetrically treated pedimented façades, and a powerful entablature tying the whole building together; the interior is stuccoed by M.I. Palliardi and decorated with frescoes by K. Schöpf depicting the life of St. Charles Borromeo. In 1942 the parachutists responsible for the assassination of the German Protector of Bohemia, R. Heydrich, took refuge in the church's crypt but were killed here while making a last stand against the Nazis. Further down the street, on the left-hand side, is the *Church of St. Wenceslas* (sv. Václava), which was founded in 1170 but rebuilt at the end of the 14C, during the reign of King Wenceslas IV. The building has been much altered over the centuries though fragments of the medieval masonry are to be seen in the façade, and there survives inside a late Gothic vault of 1586–87; the distinguished Art Nouveau sculptor F. Bílek executed the pews and the altar of the Crucifixion (1930).

At the end of the street head S down the Rašínovo nábřeží (the former Engels Embankment) until you come to the Palackého náměstí (Palacký Square). The late 19C *Palacký Bridge*, which spans the river at this point, was once crowned at its corners by large and imposing sculptural groups by J.V. Myslbek representing mythical figures from Prague's early history, but these were transferred in 1945 to the park at Vyšehrad. Their absence is amply compensated for by the presence in the middle of the square of the **Palacký Monument**, one of the most exciting examples of public statuary in Prague, and the masterpiece of Stanislav Sucharda, assisted by the architect Alois Dryák. As with the near contemporary Hus Monument in the Old Town Square, its gestation was a long one, being first planned in 1898, and not unveiled until 1912, by which time it was to seem rather dated and its outstanding qualities not fully appreciated; a romantic and deeply poetic work, it shows an ingenious use of different materials, the real world—including the heavy, seated figure of Palacký himself—being depicted in stone, the allegorical one in bronze, the whole composition culminating in a magnificent, asymmetrically placed bronze group soaring up above the central stone plinth.

From the square head E up Na Moráni, which will bring you back to the Charles Square, at its lower end. The southern side of the square is taken up by a hospital wing of the Charles University, the large building at its western corner being romantically known as the *Faust House*. This late 18C structure marks the site of a house where Edward Kelley—the English adventurer at the court of Rudolph II—carried out his alchemical experiments in the hope of producing gold; later alchemists also worked here, and in the 18C, when a chemist occupied the building, the legend was born that the imaginary Doctor Faust had been another of its occupants until he was carried off through its laboratory ceiling after having sold here his soul to the devil. Whether out of a sense of humour or in respect of the building's tradition, the

Medical Faculty of Charles University has installed here its own pharmacy.

Walking S from the Faust House down Vyšehradská, you will soon see, picturesquely rising above a great double-ramp staircase on the left-hand side of the street, the **Church of St. John on the Rock** (Kostel sv. Jana Na skalce), which was built between 1729 and 1739, and is one of the more remarkable buildings by Kilian Ignaz Dientzenhofer. Extracting the maximum dramatic potential from the restricted site, the architect canted the twin towers of the west façade to create a powerful sense of movement which is continued in the interior, the nave of which comprises an octagon with concave sides. Floating above the white walls inside are ceiling frescoes by K. Kovář depicting the Glorification of St. John of Nepomuk (1745), while on the high altar has been placed a wooden statue of the saint by J. Brokoff (1682), a work which served as the model for the bronze of this subject on the Charles Bridge. On the other side of the street to the church is the former *Na Slovanech Monastery* (popularly known as the Emmaus Monastery), which was founded by Charles IV in 1347 for the Croatian Benedictines. Extensively remodelled and rebuilt during the 18C and 19C, the whole complex was heavily damaged by bombing in 1945, and thereafter restored for the use of the Czechoslovak Academy of Sciences. The finest medieval survival, though heavily restored after 1960, are the frescoes of 1370–75 preserved in the vaulted monastery cloister and representing scenes from the Old and New Testaments; these were the work of three painters, M. Wurmser, Master Osvald and the painter known as the Master of the Emmaus Cycle. The Gothic walls of the monastery church now support a daring but very elegant modern superstructure built by František Černý in 1965–68 and comprising two interlaced sail-like forms soaring up into the sky.

The southern continuation of Vyšehradská, Na slupi, skirts the University Botanical Garden (which is open to the public) and passes to the left, as it nears the Vyšehrad Hill, the *Church of Our Lady Na Slupi*, a building of late 14C origin which was restored by Bern Grueber in 1858–63; a notable feature of the interior is the way the 15C vault is supported by a single pillar. Immediately S of the church turn left into Horská and head E until you reach the large monastic complex known simply as the **Karlov**. This former Augustinian Monastery was founded by Charles IV in 1351, and has a most exciting church, the nave of which is octagonal in emulation of Charlemagne's burial chapel at Aachen. The church was completed in 1377, but its nave was covered by Bonifaz Wohlmut in 1575 with an astonishingly bold star-shaped vault. The furnishings and other elements of the building are additions of the baroque period, including the steep triple-flighted staircase which leads up to the Chapel of the Holy Steps on the southern side of the church; this Scala Santa, up which pilgrims are meant to climb on their knees, was built in 1708–09 and is often attributed to Santini-Aichel. A visit to the church is completed by descending into the crypt, where you will be surprised and delighted to find yourself in an early 18C grotto imitating the cave in Bethlehem where Christ was born; the walls are covered with pastel-coloured stucco decorations by R. Beier, representing classical buildings and giving you the impression that you have taken a wrong turning and stumbled from the Holy Land into Arcadia. The fantasy of the whole experience will soon disappear as you walk from the church to the adjoining monastic buildings (dating from the late 17C), for you will find here the dismal museum dedicated to the Czech Police Force, containing no fewer than 444 pistols confiscated from 'spies and agents'. The museum's most popular exhibit is the stuffed carcass of the Alsatian hound known as Brek, who was famous for capturing an exceptionally large number of fugitives trying to escape from Communist Czechoslovakia.

Heading N from the Karlov up Ke Karlovu, the third street which you will pass to your right is Na Bojišti (at No. 12), a large Beer-House and Restaurant which owes its fame to being mentioned in Jaroslav Hašek's book, The Good Soldier Švejk. To this establishment, known as U kalicha (The Chalice), the congenital idiot Švejk decides to come on the day that the Sarajevo assassination is announced in Prague. He soon enters into an unwise conversation with the only client then present in the bar, a plain-clothes police-officer, and thus unwittingly embarks on his inglorious career in the Austrian army. The landlord described in the book is one Mr Palivec, a notoriously rude man whose every other word is 'arse' or 'shit'. The present-day establishment is scarcely more prepossessing than the place known to Hašek, but with the difference that it is constantly booked up by tour groups. It exploits to the full its Hašek connections, with representations of people from the book covering the walls of its large dining-room, and numerous Švejk souvenirs being sold in its vestibule; the usual drab Czech dishes which it serves are given exotic 'Švejkian' names such as 'Mrs Müller's dumplings' or 'Mr. Palivec's stew'.

Returning to Ke Karlovu and continuing N, you will come almost immediately on the right-hand side (at No. 20) to the elegant Summer Pavilion which was built by K.I. Dientzenhofer in 1715–20 for Jan Václav Michna, but is generally known as the **Villa America** on account of a hotel which existed nearby. This jewel-like building, painted outside a vivid red, is set in a small garden adorned with sculptures from the workshop of Matthias Braun; the main room on the first floor is covered with a delightful illusionistic ceiling painting (c 1730) by J.F. Schors. Since 1934 the building has housed a museum devoted to the composer Dvořák, who lived in the vicinity (see below) and whose writing desk, piano and other personal belongings are exhibited here (the museum has reopened after being closed for many years for restoration). On the other side of the street to the building is a small and rather neglected wooded park, off which stands the former Augustinian Church of St. Catherine (sv. Kateřiny). This building and its adjoining convent were founded by Charles IV in 1354 in thanksgiving for his victory at the battle of San Felice in Italy. Destroyed by the Hussites in 1420, the church was rebuilt in 1518–22, and then again by K.I. Dientzenhofer and F.M. Kaňka in 1737–41. The one survival of the medieval church is its enormously tall tower, which, thanks to its octagonal upper floors, is sometimes known as 'the Minaret of Prague'. The outside of the building is remarkably dilapidated, but the magnificent baroque interior, with ceiling frescoes by V.V. Reiner, has been given added magic and drama through housing today the sculpture collections of the City Museum of Prague, including works by J. Platzer and Matthias Braun, and J.J. Bendl—a wonderful statue in polychromed wood of the Archangel Rafael (c 1650).

At its northern end Ke Karlovu emerges at the wide and busy Ječná, which you should cross and then turn left and enter the first street to your right, Štěpánská. Walking N up Štěpánská you will pass to your right Na Rybníčku Street, on which stands the much restored and altered Rotunda of St. Longinus, which dates back to the beginning of the 12C and is the smallest of Prague's Romanesque rotundas. Further N Štěpánská joins Žitna, another busy thoroughfare, where, if you turn left, you will find shortly on the left-hand side (at No. 14) the building where the the composer Anton Dvořák lived from 1877 up to his death in 1901; he stayed at first in a now ruinous house in the courtyard, but later moved to a more salubrious location at the front of the building (where a plaque to him has been placed high up on the façade). On the opposite side of the street begins Školská, where at No. 16 you will find a plaque recording the house where the writer Jaroslav Hašek was born on 30 April 1883; ironically for the birthplace of the future *enfant terrible* the house belonged at that time to a respected advocate and Prague alderman, Dr Jakub Skarda, a family relative. Near the eastern end of Žitná you will come to the Wilsonova února, where, on turning left, you will soon rejoin the National Museum on the Wenceslas Square.

E. Vyšehrad and Southern Prague (Zbraslav, Hlubočepy and Smíchov)

Below the southern end of the New Town is a great wooded outcrop of rock rising directly and steeply above the Vltava river and supporting the citadel of **VYŠEHRAD** ('The Castle on the Heights'), the history of which is tied to the mythical origins of Prague.

According to legend the castle at Vyšehrad was the home of Princess Libuše, who foresaw from this site the future glories of Prague, and married here the ploughman founder of the Přemyslid dynasty. The truth, however, was that this was not the first seat of the Czech princes, and was preceded both by Prague Castle and Levý Hradec. Founded probably in the early 10C it became at the end of the century briefly the seat of Boleslav II. In the late 11C the Přemyslid princes once again abandoned Prague Castle in favour of the Vyšehrad, and founded here in 1070 a Collegiate Chapter. The latter, headed by a dean whose role came to be analagous to that of Chancellor of Bohemia, was to remain here for centuries afterwards, but the princes themselves were to return permanently to Prague Castle in 1140. The importance of the Vyšehrad declined, though it was to be renewed once more during the reign of Charles IV, who rebuilt the royal palace, erected new fortifications, and established the castle as the starting-point of the Czech coronation processions. In 1420, during the Hussite Wars, almost all the buildings on the Vyšehrad were destroyed, and in their place there was subsequently built up a small town of craftsmen and tradesmen. This town, known as the Town of Mount Vyšehrad, was destroyed in the mid 17C to make way for a baroque fortress, which was to be abolished in 1866, just under twenty years before the Vyšehrad was to be incorporated into the city of Prague. The Vyšehrad's mythical early history, its nationalist associations and, not least, the romantic beauty of its site, combined to make the place in the 19C a great source of inspiration to artists, writers and musicians, and not only to those of Czech blood but also to a number of Germans as well. The German works referring to the rock and its history include C. Kreutzer's opera Libussa, Mendelssohn's sonata, Libussa's prophecy, K.E. Ebert's poem, Vision from the Vyšehrad, and Grillparzer's drama, Libussa. M. Aleš, J. Döbler, K. Postl, E.G. Buquoy and K. Pluth were among the many Czech painters to feature the place in their works, while their compatriot J. Zeyer wrote an enormously popular series of poems entitled 'Vyšehrad' (1879–80). But the Czech who did most to establish the place and its legends in the national consciousness was Smetana, whose opera Libuše (with a libretto by J. Wenzig) was chosen appropriately for the inauguration of the Prague National Theatre in 1883. At the height of all this romantic adulation of Vyšehrad, two deans, V. Šulc and M. Karlach, proposed to convert the original parish cemetery of the Chapter into a national cemetery, a scheme which took root in the 1880s and culminated in the building between 1889 and 1893 of a great pantheon of celebrated Czechs, the Slavín. The rest of the citadel was laid out in 1927 as a public park.

The easiest approach to the Vyšehrad from the centre of Prague is to take the metro to the Vyšehrad station, where you will find yourself on the southern side of a long bridge—a masterly piece of engineering of the late 1960s—which connects the hill with the New Town and the Vinohrady. On the eastern side of the station stands one of Prague's most recent luxury hotels, the bland, American-style *Hotel Forum* (opened in 1989), which overlooks a large prison, the courtyard of which had to be roofed over so that the hotel guests would not be offended by the sight of exercising prisoners. On the other side of the bridge is the similarly characterless *Palace of Culture* (1969–81), which none the less enjoys a wide terrace with extensive views to the N, a panorama dominated by the Karlov Church (see Route 1D). Walking W along this terrace you will come to the quiet Na Bučance Street, which will take you after a few minutes to the western entrance of the Vyšehrad citadel. You enter through the mid-17C Tábor Gate, and, after passing to your right the scant ruins of part of the 14C fortifications erected by Charles IV, reach the monumental *Leopold Gate*, the most impressive survival of the 17C citadel, and protected by a deep ditch once spanned by a drawbridge; it was built before 1678 by C. Lurago. On the other side of this gate you will see to your right the oldest surviving structure in the Vyšehrad, the *Rotunda of St. Martin* (sv. Martina), which dates back to the late 11C, but was heavily restored in 1878–80: the earliest of Prague's Romanesque rotundas, it is also the only one to have kept its original shape. Walking W from here along the lane called K. rotundě, you will pass to your left the former late 18C Deanery, which was built on the site of the Romanesque basilica of St. Lawrence; the foundations of this church (which was destroyed by the Hussites in 1421) can be seen at the back of the building, while inside the building is a small display relating to the history of the Vyšehrad.

Further W, on the right hand side of the road, is the *Church of SS. Peter and Paul*, which though founded by Vratislav II in 1070 in conjunction with the Collegiate Chapter, owes its present appearance to neo-Gothic rebuilding carried out by J. Mocker and F. Mikeš in 1885–1903. Besides the twin-towered western façade of the church is the entrance to the **Vyšehrad Cemetery**, which is surrounded by a neo-Renaissance arcade designed by A. Wiehl in 1887, shortly after it was decided to convert the former parish cemetery into the resting-place of great and famous Czechs. Apart from its historical and sentimental interest the cemetery constitutes a major gallery of sculpture, many of the tombs being executed by leading sculptors who themselves lie buried here, such as J.V. Myslbek, O. Španiel and B. Kafka. Among the tombs to be found in the main part of the cemetery are those of the artists Mikoláš Aleš, Antonín Chitušsi, Julius Mařák, Karel Purkyně, Otakar Španiel and Václav Levý; the musicians Antonín Dvořák, Bedřich Smetana, František Ondříček, Josef Slavík and Zdeněk Fibich; the scientists Jan E. Purkyně, and Josef Heyrovský; and the writers Karel Čapek, Karel Hynek Mácha, Jan Neruda, Vítězslav Nezval and Božena Němcová. Particularly touching is the grave of Němcová, who was treated better in death than she was in life (she died neglected and in poverty), and given a tombstone carved with scenes from her best known work, The Grandmother. A special part of the cemetery (on the eastern side) is taken up by the Pantheon or Slavín, which was built by Wiehl in 1889–93 and is dominated by statues by F. Maudr representing Rejoicing Homeland and Mourning Homeland. Over 50 people have been buried here to date including the artists Vojtěch Hynais, Bohumil Kafka, Ladislav Šaloun, Jan Lauda, Alfons Mucha, Jan Štursa, J.V. Myslbek, and Václav Špála; the architects Josef Gočár,

Kamil Hilbert and Jaroslav Fragner; the writers Julius Zeyer, Josef Hora and Jaroslav Vrchlický; the musicians Jan Kubelík, Jan Heřman, Zdeněk Otava and Vílem Zítek; and the actors Zdeněk Štěpánek and Eduard Kohout.

To the S of the church is a shady park entered through a baroque gate taken from a 17C armoury; standing forlorn and neglected in the middle of this area are J.V. Myslbek's large sculptural groups of mythical Czech figures such as Libuše and Přemysl which once proudly stood on the corners of the Palacký Bridge in the New Town. The most enjoyable feature of the park is the dramatic view down to the Vltava from the western ramparts, from where you will also see, clinging to the rock face, the ruins of an early 15C watch-tower which was given in the 19C the romantic name of Libuše's Baths. After leaving the park turn right down K. rotundě, and then immediately left, skirting the eastern wall of the cemetery. You will soon reach the citadel's 19C northern gate, from where you begin the sharp descent to the heavily built area comprising the former outer bailey of the castle. Most of the buildings are apartment blocks of the 19C and 20C, and at the bottom of the first street to the right, Přemyslova, you will find at No. 98 (on the corner with Neklanova) a tall, angular and exceedingly graceful building articulated by prismatic forms. This remarkable apartment building of 1911–13 is the earliest and largest of three **Cubist Buildings** erected by Josef Chochol at the foot of the Vyšehrad. Turning left at Neklanova, and walking around the hill in an anti-clockwise direction you will come after Vnislavova to Libušina, on which stands, at No. 3, a building by Chochol of 1912–13 intended for single family occupancy and featuring a beautiful façade built up of diamond shapes. At its southern end the short Libušina joins the Rašínovo nábřeží (the former Engels Embankment), where, on turning left, you will find shortly on the left-hand side of the street (at No. 6) the third of Chochol's buildings in the area, a house intended for three families dating also from 1912–13.

Václav Havel lived higher up the Embankment at No. 78, in the top-floor flat of an apartment block designed and owned by his grandfather; the block, closely supervised during the Communist regime, has now become a place of pilgrimage, and is covered with graffiti in praise of the president.

South of the Vyšehrad extends a vast area of suburbs with little of architectural or scenic interest until you reach the outlying district of Zbraslav, which lies on the other side of the Vltava and was not incorporated into Prague until 1974. From the Rašínovo nábřeží you could take trams No. 3, 17 or 21, which go under the Vyšehrad Tunnel of 1902–03 and follow the right bank of the Vltava all the way S to Prague-Braník Station; from there to Zbraslav runs a No. 245 bus.

ZBRASLAV, 12km from the centre of Prague, will give you a first taste of the Czech countryside, and indeed continues to be a popular place for weekend excursionists, accessible in the summer months by a pleasure boat departing from below the Palacký Bridge: it was on a boat outing to Zbraslav organised by the Mánes Association of Artists in 1926 that Kafka's former mistress, Milena Jesenská, met and fell in love with the man who was to become her first husband, the architect Jaromír Krejcar. The beauty of the place lies essentially in the wooded riverside parkland attached to its former **Cistercian Monastery**, one of the best views of which is to be had from the bridge which the No. 245 bus crosses. The monastery, founded in 1292 on the site of a Royal hunting lodge, was entirely rebuilt in the early 18C, first under the direction of Santini-Aichel (from about 1700) and later under that of F.M. Kaňka (from 1724–32). The elegant buildings, with their white-washed roooms, and large ceiling paintings by V.V. Reiner and F.X. Palko, make a most beautiful and restful setting for one of Prague's most enjoyable museums, containing the holdings of 19C and 20C Czech sculpture from the **NATIONAL GALLERY**. This is an area of art which is disgracefully little known outside of Czechoslovakia, and it is to the credit of the English art historian and former museum director, Peter Cannon-Brookes, that a large selection of works from this remarkable museum was brought to the National Gallery of Wales in 1983.

The 19C collections are displayed on the ground floor and include the originals and models of a number of Prague's more celebrated public monuments, beginning with the original stone carving of Václav Prachner's Allegory of the Vltava (1812) from the garden wall of the Clam-Gallas Palace. Among the other early 19C works are Václav Levý's bronze of Adam and Eve (1849) and a bronze bust of Bernard Bolzano by Arnost Popp, who was a designer at the Smíchov porcelain factory. Much of the ground-floor area is taken up by the works of Josef Myslbek, who indeed dominated Czech sculpture of the late years of the 19C, and won even the praise of Rodin. Typical of his grand, heroic style is his bronze group of Záboj and Slavoj (1882), a competition design which won for him the commission to execute the statues for the Palacký Bridge (these are the works which are now in the Vyšehrad). His other works here include a bronze modello for the figure of Music (1892–94) in the vestibule of the National Theatre, portrait busts of the poet Mácha and the composer Smetana, and four huge sculptures of saints intended for the culminating achievement of his career, the Wenceslas Monument in the Wenceslas Square. Other turn-of-the-century sculptures in the collection include a bronze modello by B. Schnirch for one of the chariot-drawn Tigras (1892) from the National Theatre's main façade, a Rodin-like bust of Dvořák (1906) by Josef Mařatka, and works by F. Bílek, Stanislav Sucharda, Otakar Španiel, and Bohumil Kafka. The bulk of the 20C holdings are on the first floor, and feature three famous nudes by Jan Štursa—a standing bronze of Eve (1908–09), a limestone carving of strong Oriental influence entitled Melancholy Girl (1906) and the elongated, daringly poised Wounded Man of 1921. Dominating Czech 20C sculpture in the same way that Myslbek had presided over the preceding century was Otto Gutfreund, who began his career in a Cubist vein (for instance the bronze Cubist Bust of 1912–13), and later went on to develop a very realistic yet highly personal style devoted to the portrayal of the everyday world. These latter works, characterised by their simple, stately forms and complete lack of sentimentality, often made use of colour, for instance in the terracotta Self-portrait of 1919, and in the groups of Industry and Commerce, both executed in 1923, in wood and plaster respectively. They represent a truly Czech style of sculpture and their so-called Objective Realism was to be emulated by numerous other artists such as Karel Pokorný (Earth, 1925 and Ostrava, 1936), Jan Lauda (The Potter, 1923), Karel Kotrba (Portrait of the painter Miloslav Holý, 1924), Bedřich Štefan (Girl Drinking Grenadine, 1924), Otakar Švec (The Motorcyclist, 1924) and Karel Dvořák (The Girl Friends, 1924).—After leaving the monastery buildings you should wander around the gardens and forecourts, where numerous other sculptures are to be found, most notably another version of Otto Gutfreund's group, The Family (1925), the recumbent figures of which look perfectly at ease on the lawn.

There are several buses heading back N from Zbraslav along the left bank of the river (Nos 129, 241, 243 and 245), following a dual carriageway which in its later stages runs directly alongside a train line and other roads to create a polluted thoroughfare of inhuman proportions. To your left, as you enter the suburb of **HLUBOČEPY**, there rises above all this a wooded hill crowned by the spacious residential district of *Barrandov*, which was laid out by Max Urban, Václav Havel and Josef Barek in 1927–37. To walk up to this district you should descend from the bus just before the Antonín Zápotocký Bridge, and bravely make your way across the road and train line until you reach the pleasant path which ascends to the *Barrandov Tower*, at the northern end of the narrow Barrandov Street. This fine Constructivist building, surrounded by trees and with a terrace commanding an excellent panorama of the Vltava, was created by the father of President Havel (with the assistance of Max Urban); originally a restaurant forming part of Havel's Lucerna-Barrandov Enterprises, it is now a Night Club. Numerous Functionalist villas built for the wealthy and enlightened middle classes of the 1930s can be seen in the course of a walk to the upper southern end of Barrandov, three particularly interesting ones being situated at the junction of Skalní (No. 10), Barrandovská (No. 60) and Lumiérů (No. 41). Lumiérů, a straight street running along the top of the ridge, leads at its southern end to the greying buildings of the *Barrandov Film Studios*, which were founded by President Havel's uncle Miloš in 1933. In the wake of drastic economy cuts introduced by Czechoslovakia's new governments, these studios have been forced to reduce the number of films made each year from about 30 to five, which accounts partially for the slightly desolate look of the complex. The first major film to be produced here under the new regime is, inevitably, to have a script by President Havel, and be directed by his old friend, Jiří Menzel; another project at present under way here is an international co-production of a film about Kafka directed by the young American creator of Sex, Lies and Videotape (1989), Stephen Siederberg. Outside the studios you can catch a No. 248 bus, which will allow you to rejoin your route N along the river.

North of the great 'spaghetti junction' which surrounds the Barrandovský most (bridge) you will reach one of Prague's most heavily industrialised areas, **SMÍCHOV**. Most of the buses stop at the Smíchov Station, which though modernised and enlarged after the war, is one of the oldest of Prague's main railway stations, being founded in the 1860s. Smíchov itself, despite its largely bleak look, has several places of interest, but these are all to the N of its station, from where it would be best to take the underground to the following stop, Andel. From here you can walk W along the busy Plzeňská for about 1.5km, and then turn left on to Mozartova, where you will find, at No. 2, the main tourist attraction of Smíchov, the **Bertramka**. This modest and recently restored 18C villa, with a wooden gallery and a quiet, bosky garden, was the home in the late 18C of the composer F.X. Dušek and his wife J. Dušková, a famous singer. They were close friends of Mozart, who stayed with them on his visits to Prague in 1786, 1787 and 1791. The house has now been done up as a delightful small museum to Mozart, with appropriate 18C furnishings, unobtrusive background music, and several mementoes of his stay in Prague, including a piano on which he allegedly played. Another of the mementoes is a curious German painting of c 1800 showing the interior of a former beer cellar near the Powder Tower, and bearing the inscription: 'This is where Mozart ate, drank and composed Don Giovanni in 1787'. Casanova, who was also staying in Prague at this time, later claimed responsibility for forcing Mozart to write this opera. On your way back to Anděl metro station you could make a short detour to your left at the bottom of Mozartova to visit the house at No. 2 Dušková where the Communist journalist and Nazi victim Julius Fučík was born in 1903.

Back at Anděl metro station head N along Stefáníkova (the former S.M. Kirova), where you will pass shortly to your right a large and dark neo-Renaissance church by Antonín Barvitius (1881–85). In the decayed garden on its northern side is the *Portheimka*, a small summer villa built by K.I. Dientzenhofer for his own family, but now in a crumbling condition; this toy-like building, with a first-floor room covered with a ceiling painting by V.V. Reiner, is used today for avant-garde art exhibitions that often clash violently with the faded setting. Due east of here is the small Lesnická Street, where there is a plaque at No. 7 marking the house where the physicist Albert Einstein lived while teaching at the German university in Prague from 1911–12. Continuing N along the busy shopping street of Stefáníkova you will pass to your left *The Realistic Theatre*, the drab appearance of which belies the lively nature of its productions (a liveliness which dates back to the 1920s, when J. Čapek was a director) and the important part which it has played in Czechoslovakia's recent history. For it was here, following a strike of actors and students on 19 November 1989, that a hastily convened late night meeting led to the creation of the Civic Forum Party, which was soon to replace the Communist regime. Just to the N of the theatre the square emerges at the náměstí Sovětských Tankistů, which has a plinth in its centre supporting one of the first Soviet tanks to reach Prague in May 1945.

The tank has recently aroused much controversy, but suggestions that it should be removed have been turned down on the grounds that it is one of the more familiar of Prague's landmarks, as well as being a popular meeting-place. ('See you at the tank', is a remark often to be heard here). As a compromise solution, the tank was given—early in 1991—a more friendly and human aspect by being painted pink, but this led to protests from the Soviet Embassy. The paint was subsequently removed, but has now been put back again, and is likely to remain for some time to come.

On the western side of the square is the entrance to the Kinský Gardens, which form part of a vast area of parkland stretching up the Petřín Hill and into the Little Quarter (see Route 1B). Turning left immediately on entering the gardens and following the path parallel to Holečkova, you will reach the early 19C *Kinský Villa*, where you will find the ethnographic collections of the *National Museum*, with costumes, pottery and other exhibits relating to Czech and Slavonic folk culture.

F. Eastern Prague (Vinohrady, Vršovice, Žižkov and Karlín)

East of the Wenceslas Square extends the district of **VINOHRADY**, a large area of long, straight streets lined with dirty 19C and 20C apartment blocks and offices, some with a decayed splendour. The places of specific interest here, as throughout eastern Prague, are widely scattered, making a walking tour practicable only to the most dedicated sightseer. The main civic buildings of Vinohrady are around the large náměstí Míru, which lies one stop away by metro from the southern end of the Wenceslas Square. In the middle of the square stands the brick neo-Gothic *Church of St. Ludmila* (sv. Ludmily), which was built by Josef Mocker in 1888–93 and has a west tympanum decorated with a relief by J.V. Myslbek of Christ with SS. Wenceslas and Ludmila. The northern side of the square is dominated by the grand façade of the recently restored *Vinohrady Theatre* a neo-baroque building with Art Nouveau elements, built in 1903–06 and crowned by winged allegorical groups by M. Havlíček. East of here begins one of the longest streets of Vinohrady, Slezská, where, shortly on the left-hand side (at No. 7) is an interesting red-brick building by Josef Gočár, built in 1924–26 as an Agricultural College. Nearby, on the parallel Vinohradská, stands the former *School of Commerce*, which is decorated around its entrance by four sculptural groups of workers by Karel Dvořák (1925), a very lively example of so-called Objective Realism.

Further E down Vinohradská, adjoining the Jiřího z Poděbrad metro station (one stop E from the náměstí Míru), is one of the greatest and most original monuments erected in Czechoslovakia between the wars. This, **THE CHURCH OF THE SACRED HEART** (Kostel Nejsvětějšího Srdce Páně), was built by Jože Plečnik in 1929–33, and looms massively over the bleak gardens that have been laid out in the middle of the George of Poděbrady Square. Inspired by a combination of an Early Christian basilica and an Egyptian temple, it handles its eclectic borrowings with a boldness which is uncompromisingly modern. Its glazed brick exterior, studded all over with what seem to be overblown guttae, has walls that project diagonally near the top to form a massive cornice; a great pedimented clock tower, as wide as the building itself, rises high above the east end of the building and supports an enormous clock, glass-fronted on both sides and resembling a rose window. The wide single-aisled interior, with coffered ceiling, unfaced brick walls and marble floors, has an altar made with marble from the Šumava mountains and impressive statuary at its east end by D. Pešan. The whole building, which acquires a particular magic when spot-lit at night, looks ahead to 'post-modernist' architecture of the 1960s and 1970s, but has a grandeur and individuality which is quite unique to Plečnik. There are few other modern churches in Europe which are quite as powerful as this one.

The other attraction in the vicinity of the square is of a rather different kind: at No. 21 Jagellonská (turn left at the western end of the square, and then take the first turning to the right) is Prague's longest established game restaurant, *Myslivna*, a place where you can eat one of the best meals to be had in Czechoslovakia, served in intimate surroundings that have yet to be taken over by tourists. Just

*The main façade of Jože Plečnik's Church of the Most
Sacred Heart of Our Lord, in Prague's Vinohrady district*

to the N of this restaurant, on the Mahler park (Mahlerovy sady),
soars Prague's futuristic television tower of the late 1980s.

At its bleak, easternmost end, Vinohradská Street passes next to
three of Prague's largest cemeteries. Beyond the Flora metro station
the street skirts the southern side of the *Olšany Cemetery*, which was
founded during the big plague in 1680, and soon became the main
burial place serving the communities on the right bank of the Vltava.
Besides the main entrance gates on the náměstí Jiřího z Lobkovic are
photographs of the tombs of some of the famous Czechs who are
buried here, among whom are the writers Josef Jungmann, Pavel
Šafařík and Jan Kollár; the philosopher Bernard Bolzano; the architects Antonín Barvitius and Josef Fanta; the sculptors Josef Max,
Bohumil Schnirch and Josef Mařatka; and the painters Josef Mánes,
August Pipenhagen, Josef Navrátil and Antonín Slavíček. The tombs
are adorned with works by many of the leading Czech sculptors,
including Myslbek, Mařatka, Max, Bílek and Kafka, but perhaps the
most endearing is that of the illustrator to Švejk, Josef Lada, who is
commemorated by a tomb shaped like a bird's house. At present the
most honoured occupant of the cemetery is the student 'martyr' Jan
Palach, whose tomb (just to the right of the main entrance) is
shrouded with flowers and candles; his body was immediately
placed here after his dramatic death in 1969, but then was removed
in 1974 to his country village, and only brought back here in
November 1990.

Immediately to the E of this cemetery is the *New Jewish Cemetery*
(Židovské Hřbitovy), the entrance to which is adjacent to the Prague-
Strašnice metro station: arrows here will direct you to its most visited
tombstone, that of the writer Franz Kafka. Slightly further E

Vinohradská skirts the northern side of the *Vinohrady Cemetery*, which was founded in 1885 and has in its centre the neo-Gothic chapel of St. Wenceslas. One of the greatest Czech painters of the turn of the century is buried here, Jakub Schikaneder, as is the most influential and original Czech sculptor of this century, Otto Gutfreund, who died from drowning in 1926, and is commemorated here by a bust by his close friend Karel Dvořák. In the Functionalist Crematorium to the E of the cemetery lie the ashes of the journalist and writer Egon Erwin Kisch.

Due S of the Olšany Cemetery is a quiet residential street lined with grand suburban villas and named after the brothers Josef and Karel Čapek (bratří Čapků), who spent much of their later life in the ochre-coloured building at No. 30, which was built by L. Machoň in 1923–24. Further S begins the district of **VRŠOVICE**, where you will find, standing on the náměstí Svatopluka Čecha, the Constructivist *Church of St. Wenceslas* (sv. Václav), which was built by Josef Gočár in 1929–30, and is dominated by a tall tower; now turned on the outside a dirty grey, this narrow building clings to the slope of a verdant hill, and is built on different levels that lead up to the apse, a delicate and luminous structure largely composed of stained glass. On a hill to the W of the church is the pleasant *Havlíček Park* (Havlíčkovy Sady), commanding good views of southern Prague, and featuring at its northern end the late 19C *Gröbe Villa* (now a Youth Centre), a large villa of Italian Renaissance inspiration, designed by A. Barvitius.

North of Vinohrady is the district of **ŽIŽKOV**, a traditional working-class district with a long history of revolutionary activity which once earned the place the name of 'Red Prague'. It has also strong associations with poetry, being the birthplace both of the German poet Rainer Maria Rilke and of the Nobel-Prize winning poet, Jaroslav Seifert, who was born here in 1901 and was recently honoured by the changing of the district's main street from Kalininova to Seifertova. Seifert once referred to this place where he had spent both his childhood and adolescence as 'my beautiful and adored Žižkov', though this is not a reaction which is going to be shared by most of the casual visitors here, the majority of whom come simply to climb up to the monument of Jan Žižka. The traditional approach to this monument from the centre of Prague is to walk from the Powder Tower to the eastern end of Hybernská (see Route 1D), and then turn left on to Husitská. Coming instead from Vinohrady's náměstí Míru, you should walk N along Italská, skirting the western side of *Rieger Park* (Riegrovy Sady), a late 19C park with fine views and, in its south-western corner, a monument of the 19C politician František Rieger by J.V. Myslbek; at No. 4 Chopinova, on the other side of the park to Italská, is an interesting brick building by Jan Kotěra, erected in 1909–10 for the Laichter Publishing House. At the northern end of Italská you will reach Seifertova, a junction marked by the náměstí Winstona Churchilla, on which stands one of the pioneering examples of Functionalist architecture of the 1930s, the former *Pensions Institute* (now the Central Trade Unions Council). This vast structure, comprising two great rectangular blocks arranged in cross formation, was described by the architect Martin Shand as 'the white cathedral of Prague', but now is a depressing grey, and, for all its originality in the context of 1930s architecture, is a foretaste of the worst architecture of the post-war period.

After crossing Seifertova and continuing N along Řehořova, you will come to Husitská, where, off its western end, a path begins the climb up the wooded hill to the Jan Žižka Monument, passing to the right a grey block containing a grim display of Second World War mementoes belonging to the *Czech Army Museum*. The monument to the Hussite hero Jan Žižka (after whom the whole district was named in 1877) occupies a site where Žižka defeated the troops of King Sigismund on 14 July 1420. Known officially as *The National Monument*, this structure features a granite-faced building dating back to 1929–30, adorned inside with mosaics by M. Švabinský and J. Obrovský, and relief carvings by K. Pokorný. This building was enlarged and adapted after the Second World War to contain the Grave of an Unknown Soldier from Dukla, as well as the tombs of prominent Communists such as Klement Gottwald, Antonín Zápotocký, and Ludvík Svoboda; this is at present closed for restoration necessitated both by structural and ideological reasons. In front of the building stands an enormous equestrian bronze of Jan Žižka by Bohumil Kafka, a work of 1950 which is certainly impressive from a great distance, but is largely of interest for featuring in the Guinness Book of Records as the world's largest sculpture. The greatest reward of a walk up to the monument is the magnificent panorama of Prague to be had from here, a panorama which used to inspire the young Jaroslav Seifert, who was later to write some of the finest poetry ever dedicated to this city. East of the monument runs a monotonous tree-lined avenue the whole length of the hill's ridge, at the eastern end of which you can turn left and descend a steep path down to the railway line and across to U Invalidovny Street. You have now entered the district of **KARLÍN**, and will see to your right the impressive if rather dilapidated block of a great hospital (now the *Invalid War Veterans' Home*), which was built in 1730–37 by Kilian Ignaz Dientzenhofer; though of enormous size, what you see today represents only a corner of a projected complex of truly monumental proportions. Sokolovská Street stretches W from here all the way back to the Jan Šverma Park, at the entrance to the New Town (see Route 1D).

G. Western Prague
(Střešovice, Břevnov and Liboc)

STŘEŠOVICE, which lies immediately to the W of the Hradčany (see Route 1C), is traditionally the most luxurious of Prague's suburbs, and is a quiet area of attractive modern villas, spaciously laid out. One of these villas, confiscated from a wealthy Jew, gave the name of this district rather sinister connotations for Prague's Jewish community during the Second World War, for it was here that the Central Office for Jewish Emigration was situated, an office which was directly subordinate to the Gestapo, and responsible for the organisation of the notorious 'transports' to Terezín and elsewhere: accounts of the compulsory visits to Střešovice are included in Jiří Weil's disturbing novel, Life With a Star (1964), which was based on the author's war-time experiences. A large part of Střešovice is made up of the so-called *Ořechovka Villa Quarter*, which was planned by J. Vondrák and J. Šenkýř in 1920–23 on the model of England's Garden Suburbs. In the course of the 1920s this quarter was greatly expanded, and, between 1929 and 1931, there was built on its outer southern limits (at No. 14 Nad hradním vodojemem) by far the most distinguished of Střešovice's buildings, the **Maison Muller**. This cube-like structure, with large expanses of bare masonry discreetly pierced by small, irregularly placed openings, is the work of the revolutionary Moravian-born architect Adolf Loos (assisted by Josef Fanta), and is the only one of his buildings to be seen in Czechoslovakia; the interior, characterised by its every space being of different height and shape, is possibly to be opened in the near future as a museum.

The district of **BŘEVNOV**, which extends to the S of Střešovice, and to the W of the Petřín Hill (see Route 1B), begins at its eastern end with the largest Sports Stadium in the world, the *Spartakiáda Stadium*. Designed by Alois Dryák in 1926 for a seating capacity of over 200,000, this ungainly complex looks for most of the time like some stranded folly of megalomaniac scale, but comes to life every five years with an internationally renowned gymnastic display known as the Spartakiáda; the next such event is planned for 1995. Running W from near here is the long Bělohorská Street, which passes though an area of large housing estates, including one of 600 apartments dating from the late 1930s. Further W along the street (at No. 28) is the elegant Empire-style hostelry known as *At the Chestnut* (Dům U Kaštanu), where on 7 April 1878, a secret meeting headed by J.B. Pecka and L. Zápotocky led to the formation of the Czech Social Democratic Workers' Party (plaque).

Just beyond the building the street turns into a wide thoroughfare, which is bordered on its northern side by a neglected corner of countryside surrounding the former **Monastery and Church of St. Margaret** (sv. Markéty) (accessible by trams No. 8, 22 and 23, which run the whole length of Bělohorská). This place, with its decayed, abandoned character, and isolated situation in a generally grey Prague suburb, may induce a sense of great pathos in the visitor, particularly in those who come here in the knowledge that they are visiting the oldest monastery in Bohemia and one of Prague's finer baroque complexes. Founded for the Benedictine Order in 993 by Boleslav II and the Prague bishop, St. Adalbert, the monastery and church were completely rebuilt by Christoph and Kilian Ignaz Dientzenhofer in the early 18C. The monastic buildings, with fine ceiling frescoes by C.D. Assam of 1727, are at present closed while awaiting much needed restoration. But the interest of the place lies essentially in its church, which was built by Christoph Dientzenhofer in 1700–15, and has a powerful and tightly composed exterior with a giant order of pilasters and columns running around its whole length, and a dynamic attic level of gables crowned by undulant pediments. The single-aisled interior is composed of a series of intersecting transverse ovals, with giant piers projecting diagonally into the nave as in Christoph Dientzenhofer's comparably majestic Church of St. Nicholas in the Little Quarter; the ceiling frescoes, by J.J. Steinfels, represent the founding of the monastery by St. Adalbert. The crypt, open on Sundays only, is that of the original Romanesque building of the late 10C. Within the overgrown orchard garden behind the church is a baroque pavilion in deplorable condition surrounding a well where St. Adalbertus is said to have met Boleslav II at the time of the monastery's foundation.

At the westernmost end of Břevnov is the limestone hill associated with one of the most famous and tragic battles in the history of Bohemia, the Battle of the White Mountain (Bílá Hora). It was here, on 8 November 1620, that the Protestant army led by Count Matthias von Thun was defeated by the Habsburg troops under Maximillian of Bavaria; Elector Frederick of the Palatinate, who had been elected King of Bohemia by the Protestants the previous year, was forced to flee, and Bohemia was not to regain its independence until after the First World War. Much of the site is taken up by an English-style park which was laid out in 1797 on a game reserve founded by Ferdinand I in 1530 (to reach its main gates you can continue along Bělohorská on trams No. 8 or 22, and get off at Na Vypichu). Within the park long alleys of trees lead to the remarkable Renaissance building known as the **letohrádek Hvězda** or 'Star Castle'. This star-shaped structure of 1555–58 was built by Hans Tirol and Bonifaz Wohlmut as a hunting-lodge for Ferdinand of Tyrol, and later became the residence of the latter's future wife, Philippine Welser. The exterior, restored by Pavel Janák after the Second World War, is austere and rather dilapidated, but the interior features outstanding stucco ceiling decorations of mythological scenes and grotesques by Italian artists. The building, which was turned after the 16C into a powder-magazine, now houses on it upper floors a museum devoted to the 19C writer of historical romances, Alois Jirásek, and to his painter contemporary, Mikoláš Aleš (who is represented here largely by his book illustrations). In the basement is a large model of the Battle of the White Mountain.

The western continuation of Bělohorská is Karlovarská, on which stands (at No. 6) the early 18C *Church of Our Lady of Victory* (Panny Marie Vitězné), which replaced a 17C chapel commemorating the Habsburg victory at the Battle of the White Mountain; the interior has ceiling paintings by V.V. Reiner and C.D. Assam.

H. Northern Prague (Letná, Holešovice-Bubeneč, Troja and Dejvice)

Rising above the Vltava immediately to the E of the Little Quarter is the large **Letná Park** (Letenské Sady), which was laid out after 1858. Occupying an excellent vantage point at its western end, with beautiful views across the river to the Old Town, is the *Hanavsky Pavilion*, a tentative Art Nouveau structure built by Otto Prieser for the Exhibition of 1891, and used today as a night club. Similarly well-located is the *Praha-Expo 58 Restaurant* (on the eastern side of the park), which originally formed part of the Czech Pavilion for the Brussels World Fair of 1958; the indifferent quality of the food which is served here is partially compensated for by the dining room's panoramic, semi-circular window.

To the W and N of the restaurant extends the largely industrial district of **HOLEŠOVICE**, which was annexed in 1869 to the village of **Bubeneč**, and incorporated into Prague in 1884. A large and grim Functionalist block immediately behind the restaurant houses the *National Technical Museum*, which includes among its extensive collections, sections devoted to astronomy, metallurgy and horology. Of particular interest to children is the guided tour which you can take of a reconstructed coal-mine in the basement; also entertaining is the section labelled in English 'the Centre for Noise Ecology', where you can play around with numerous objects for making and recording sounds. But, above all, you should visit the Hall of Transport at the back of the building, a tall space crammed to capacity with every conceivable form of transport, from the early 19C onwards; the exhibits are arranged in three superimposed galleries around the hall and also in the centre of the room, where old bi-planes and even a hot-air balloon hover above a traffic-jam of old cars and trains, including the luxury train carriage in which the Emperor Franz Joseph travelled in 1891.

A grid of streets lined with blackened apartment blocks of the 19C and 20C begins behind the museum. Head E on Letohradská, and, at the end of this street, turn left on to F. Křížka, which crosses the busy shopping street of Milady Horákové and comes to an end at the wide Veletržní Street, near the 1960s block of the luxury Park Hotel. Directly in front of this hotel, at 45 Dukelských hrdinů, is the enormous former *Trades Fair Building*, which was built by Oldřich Tyl and Josef Fuchs in 1924–28, and was the earliest Constructivist building on such a grand scale in Europe. This pioneering structure, which was badly damaged by fire in 1982, is in the process of being transformed to house the 20C Czech collections of the **NATIONAL GALLERY**. Work on this museum was begun in 1982, and is progressing at a frustratingly slow rate; when the place is eventually opened, visitors to Prague will at last be able to appreciate to the full the extraordinary contribution which Czechoslovakia made to the arts in the early years of this century. Of the museum's holdings—a selection of which can sometimes be seen at the former Royal Menagerie in Prague Castle (see Route 1C)—pride of place must be given to the paintings of Kupka, who began his career in a Symbolist manner, and went on to produce in the second decade of this century large abstract paintings of lush colours and lyrical intensity; towards the end of his life, he developed a more ordered and geometrical abstract style. Czech Cubism will also be well represented in this museum, and include works by Josef Čapek, Václav Špála, Josef Šíma, Emil Filla and Bohumil Kubišta (a beautiful Cubist view of Prague of 1912). Among the experimental works of the 1920s and 1930s are delicate collages by Jindřich Štyrský and bizarre assemblages by Ladislav Zívr; among the later paintings are the haunting surrealist landscapes of the 1950s by Kamil Lhoták.

The Dukelských hrdinů leads N of the future museum to the entrance of the *Park of Culture and Rest*, which was the main site of the Jubilee Exhibition of 1891; between the wars the place was used for trade fairs before being transformed into a park named until recently after the Communist journalist killed by the Nazis, Julius Fučík. The large glass and ironwork structure which faces you on entering the park was the main hall of the Jubilee Exhibition, and was built by Bedřich Münzberger and František Prášil in 1891; the adjoining Prague Pavilion, also closed to the public, houses the remarkable **Lapidarium** of the National Museum, featuring many of the originals of famous public statues that have been replaced *in situ* by copies. Behind the main hall is a large cylindrical structure, containing inside a vast circular canvas by J. Marold of the Battle of Lipany of 1434 (1898); the canvas is displayed in a darkened setting, surrounded by real earth, sticks and other objects, the whole forming a powerful illusionistic recreation of the battlefield. Elsewhere in the park, which is used regularly for folkloric events and an annual reconstruction of battles in the Thirty Years' War, are a Sports Stadium, a Swimming Pool, a Planetarium and the main section of the Czech Pavilion designed for the Brussels World Exhibition of 1958. A gate on the western side of this park leads into the large and wooded *Stromovka* ('Royal Enclosure'), which was laid out as a public park in 1804 on the site of a royal hunting ground founded by King John of Luxemburg in the early 14C.

North of Holešovice-Bubeneč, on the other side of the Vltava, is the suburban district of **TROJA**, which was named after a large baroque country house known generally as the **Troja Château** (the easiest access by public transport is by bus No. 112 from the Praha-Holešovice metro station). This magnificent house, recently re-opened following major restoration, was built in 1679–75 for Count Václav Vojtěch of Sternberg; the architect was Jean-Baptiste Mathey, who introduced a French pavilion plan with projecting wings. Its principal façade is its southern one, dominated by a monumental oval staircase profusely decorated with statues of gods and goddesses battling with Titans. The rooms on the main floor boast one of the most extensive cycles of baroque frescoes to be seen in Czechoslovakia, including, in the side rooms, some amusing allegorical ceiling paintings by Francesco and Giovanni Francesco Marchetti, and illusionistic landscapes on the walls; the enormous Grand Hall is covered all over with frescoes by Abraham Godyn set in an ambitious illusionistic framework featuring fictive architecture and tapestries, one of which is marked by the shadow cast by a Moor plunging head forwards into the room. The building now houses the collections of the *Prague Municipal Art Gallery*, which is composed almost exclusively of 19C Czech painting. Most of the leading Czech artists of this period are represented, though largely with minor works: among these artists are Viktor Barvitius, Alois Bubák, František Ženíšek, Jakub Schikaneder, Maximilian Pirner, Max Švabinský, Jan Preisler, Luděk Marold and Mikoláš Aleš. Particularly numerous are the works of Jaroslav Čermák and Václav Brožík, the latter being the author of the gallery's two most celebrated pictures, Master John Hus Facing the Council of Constance, and The Election of George of Poděbrady as King of Bohemia. The garden below the building's southern façade is one of the earliest examples in Bohemia of a French formal garden, and has terraces adorned with eccentric ornamental vases by Bombelli. Next to the house is the entrance to Prague's Zoo, which was founded in 1931, and can only be recommended to those who might enjoy the experience of riding over an aviary in a chair-lift.

The suburb of **DEJVICE**, which lies to the N of the Hradčany and to the W of Bubeneč is served by the Dejvice metro station (formerly Leninova). The large square on which this station is situated forms the axis of a radiating group of wide, long avenues, one of which, Jugoslávských partyzánů, leads N to the *Hotel International*, a towering block of the 1950s inspired by Moscow University; the gloomy, spacious and oppressively marbled interior is an atmospheric reminder of the heyday of Soviet domination of Czechoslovakia. Immediately to the N of the hotel turn left on to Pod Juliškou and walk up to Na Štáhlavce, which curves its way to the top of the wooded hill on which stands the innovatory suburban estate known as the *Baba Villa Colony*. The idea for this estate came about as a result of the exhibition 'Nový dům' ('New House'), which was organised in Brno in 1928 by the Czech architectural group known as the Werkbund. Nineteen members of the Prague Werkbund, following a general lay-out devised by Pavel Janák, subsequently created on this hill a group of 33 houses built in close consultation with the clients, who had the freedom to chose their own architect. This 'ideal estate', spaciously arranged along the parallel streets of Na ostrohu, Na Babě and Nad Paťankou, comprises an interesting variety of Functionalist houses, including five buildings by Josef Gočár and three by Pavel Janák himself (his own house was at No. 16 Nad Paťankou, at the edge of the estate, and with potentially beautiful views looking E towards Troja).

2   Excursions from Prague

Almost everywhere in Bohemia and even Moravia is within a relatively short distance of Prague, making the possibilities of day excursions from the capital almost endless. Included below, however, are only the major sights that fall within the administrative region of Central Bohemia; other, lesser sights within this same region, not meriting a special journey, are included in the longer itineraries described elsewhere in the guide.

A.   Kutná Hora and Kolín

Total distance 137km. Prague—34km Kostelec nad Černými Lesy—
31km—**Kutná Hora**—16km *Kolín*—56km Prague.

The fastest route to Kutná Hora from Prague is by way of Kolín, but a
quieter and more attractive approach is to take the road which runs
parallel to the S, passing through Říčany (20km SE of Prague) and
Kostelec nad. Černými Lesy. **KUTNÁ HORA**, picturesquely situated
above the northern banks of the narrow and meandering Vrchlice
river, is a place of decayed beauty but rich in monuments testifying to
its medieval heyday, when it was the second most important town in
Bohemia.

The rapid development of Kutná Hora in the Middle Ages is due to the
discovery here, in the late 13C, of rich silver deposits, a discovery which was
soon to make the Czech monarchs among the richest in Europe. Wenceslas II
invited Florentine mintners to found a Royal Mint at Kutná Hora, and, by the
1380s work was begun here on one of the greatest of Bohemia's cathedrals. The
town became at the end of the century the favourite residence of Wenceslas IV,
but it was to suffer greatly in the course of the Hussite Wars, the retreating
Hungarian troops under Sigismund of Luxemburg even setting fire to the place
in 1421. Kutná Hora experienced a brief renewal of prosperity during the late
15th and early 16C, when the townspeople were able to secure for the
completion of their cathedral, two of the most outstanding architects of the time,
Matěj Rejsek and Benedikt Ried. However, by the middle of the 16C the local
silver deposits came to be exhausted, a crisis resulting in the cathedral being
left unfinished in 1558, and the town entering a long decline which was to be
consolidated by the Thirty Years' War, and a severe fire in 1771. Kutná Hora is
today a district capital, with engineering works and a tobacco factory on its
outskirts, but with a quiet and depressed character reflecting the town's many
years of stagnation.

Approaching Kutná Hora from the Prague road, you will find, at the
western end of the old town, fragments of the original fortifications,
in front of which you should take the turning to the right marked
Černiny. The Cathedral of St. Barbara, occupying a verdant south-
western corner of the town, will appear shortly to your left, but, if you
were to continue for a further 1km on this road, you would find to
your right a turning leading to the *Church of the Holy Trinity*, a late
14C to early 15C structure standing in isolation in a field; this small
triple-aisled hall-church, usually closed, has a most elegant interior,
its vaulting supported by four slender columns. You can park your
car facing the west façade of the **CATHEDRAL OF ST. BARBARA**
(sv. Barbora), to which you descend on steps from the road.

The building, founded in 1388, was initially conceived on a model of a French
Gothic cathedral, in emulation of Peter Parler's cathedral at nearby Kolín; by
1421, however, when work was suspended, only the eight chapels in the apse
and part of the aisles had been vaulted. Work on the building was not to be
resumed until 1481, first under the direction of Master Hanuš, and then, after
1489, under that of the great Matěj Rejsek, who was responsible for the vaulting
of the chancel. Six years after Rejsek's death in 1506, the burghers of Kutná
Hora, anxious as always to employ the most fashionable and prestigious
architects of the time, called on the services of the royal architect Benedikt Ried,
who had only recently completed his remarkable work for Prague Castle. The
possibility that funds might run out before the massive structure originally
envisaged could be finished, may have encouraged Ried drastically to change
the plan of the building and transform it into a three-aisled hall church, the side
aisles becoming galleries, and flying buttresses being used to support sheer
walls pierced with enormous, traceried windows. The vaulting of the nave was
completed to his design in 1547, but just over ten years later work on the
cathedral was abandoned, and the west end left as a blank wall; the present
west façade is a dreary, compromise solution of the late 19C.

SEDLEC

KUTNÁ HORA

0 metres 300

Ch.of the Holy Trinity & TÁBOR

The Cathedral of St. Barbara represents one of the most extreme developments of the late Gothic style in Europe, and has a most bizarre and exotic skyline comprising three massive tent-like forms that from the distance give the impression that some fabulous Turkish sultan has encamped here. The fantastical character of the light and spacious interior is due largely to the extraordinary vaulting, comprising stiff rib patterns of exceptional complexity in the chancel, and, in the nave, flowing lines of endlessly fascinating geometrical inventiveness, spreading out like tree branches from the piers before bursting out in the centre into six-petalled flowers. The furnishings of the cathedral include a pulpit of c 1560 decorated with stone reliefs of the Evangelists, 17C confessionals, and an exuberant baroque organ. The most interesting addition to the interior are the anonymous late 15C frescoes to be found in the **Smíšek Chapel** on the southern side of the ambulatory. Michael Smíšek of Vrchovište— a rich mine owner, and the Administrator of the Royal Mines, acquired this chapel in 1485, and was buried here in 1512. The decorations on the walls, executed in c 1496, include a trompe-l'oeil recess in which Smíšek can be seen dressed as a sacristan and preparing for a mass with the assistance of his two sons; the other scenes are of the Crucifixion, Trajan's Justice, the Arrival of the Queen of Sheba before Solomon, and Augustus with the Tiburtine Sibyl. The figurative style of these works, and their perspectival illusionism, suggest a knowledge of North Italian painting of the early Renaissance.

The cathedral once stood isolated from the rest of the town, but in the late 17C the Jesuits built immediately to the N of it their largest seminary outside Prague. The attractive Barborská Street runs in between the long eastern façade of this building and a baroque balustrade adorned with statues by Baugut; from here can be had one of the best views of Kutná Hora, some of the town's finest buildings—including the distant church of St. James (sv. Jakub)—standing huddled around the edge of a curving slope which is covered in gardens and falls steeply down to the Vrchlice river. Just to the N of the Seminary, on the right-hand side of the street, is the *Hrádek*, a structure of 13C origin (with a charming late Gothic oriel window), originally forming part of the fortifications, but later adapted as the home of the Administrator of the Mines; it now houses the town's *Mining Museum*. Behind the building an attractive lane descends through gardens to the entrance of the medieval mines, which can be visited. From the First World war Memorial just to the N of the Hrádek a charming, cobbled lane called Ruthardská heads E towards the Church of St. James (see below).

Continuing instead N on Barborská you will reach at the end of the street the Komenského náměstí, where you should turn left and walk up Rejskova until you come to a remarkable 12-sided *Gothic Fountain*, which was built in 1493–95 and is generally attributed to Matěj Rejsek. Head E of here along Husova, and take the first turning to the left, which joins up with the long Jiřího z Poděbrad. Directly facing you, on the northern side of the street, is the so-called *Stone House* (Kammenný dum), a late 15C structure with a much-restored gabled façade dominated by a box-shaped oriel covered all over with lively carvings; inside is a dreary local museum. Just to the E of this is the náměstí 1. Máje, where you should head S on Šultysova, a beautiful short street which is lined with decayed 17C and 18C buildings and leads to a Marian *Plague Column* of the early 18C; at the end of the street, on the left-hand side, is an excellent old beer-cellar. The exceedingly narrow Vysokokostelecká, which runs S from here, is hemmed in by narrow houses, above which rises the impressively tall Gothic tower of the **Church of St. James** (sv. Jakub). When this triple-aisled hall church was begun in the 1330s, it was conceived on a scale comparable to that of deanery churches such as the one at Plzeň, but work was brought to a halt by the Hussite Wars, leaving even the south tower unfinished; the interior, completed at a much later date, is Gothic in structure, but entirely baroque in its furnishings, which include a high altar of Christ and St. James by Petr Bendl.

Leaving the church by its south portal you will find immediately to your left the most important secular building in town, the former Royal Mint or **Italian Court**, which was built in 1300 for the Italian mintners invited to Kutná Hora by Wenceslas II; in around 1400 the place was enlarged and remodelled as a residence for Wenceslas IV, and, following the closure of the Mint in 1727, was converted into a Town Hall, which it remained until very recently. The interior, which can be visited on a guided tour, features a ground-floor room where a selection of coins are displayed, including the most famous ones to have been minted at Kutná Hora—the Prague silver groschens (the last of these was made in 1547). The most important room is the early 15C Session Hall, which has a panelled ceiling of 1400 and two large wall-paintings of the late 19C, representing The Election of Vladislav Jagiello, and The Decree of Kutná Hora—a decree passed by Wenceslas IV in 1409 whereby the rights of Czechs at Prague University were greatly improved; these late Romantic works were painted by the Spilar Brothers in collaboration with K.J. Klusáček. Another room, The Hall of Revolutionary Traditions, has a bombastic canvas of around the same date by Adolf Liebscher, depicting Jan Žižka outside Kutná Hora. The chapel which Wenceslas IV founded in 1400 was completely redecorated early this century.

At the Havlíčkovo náměstí, which lies on the eastern side of the Italian Court, turn left to reach the large Palackého náměstí, the town's main square, where there are a number of fine old houses as well as a rather bleak modern hotel, the Medínek. Heading E from here on Tylova, you will pass immediately on the right-hand side, at No. 507, the 18C house where the pioneering Czech dramatist and theatre director J.K. Tyl was born in 1808; inside is a small commemorative museum to him. Continuing E on Tylova, and taking the third turning to the left, Brandlova, you will reach the late Gothic *Church of Our Lady 'Na Náměti'*, where the great baroque painter Petr Brandl was buried in 1735. Return to the Palackého náměstí, and head N on Na Sioně, which will take you to the upper end of Jiřího z Poděbrad, where there stands a former *Ursuline Convent*, begun by K.I. Dientzenhofer on a pentagonal plan in 1734 and never finished.

One of the outlying residential districts to the E of the Convent is **Sedlec**, which you can pass through on your way to Kolín. From the large ring road which encircles the old town, head due E on Revoluční, at the end of which you will see in front of you the imposing church of the former **Cistercian Abbey of Sedlec**. The abbey was founded in 1142, but the present church dates back to around 1300, when work was begun on a building modelled on a French cathedral, with a five-sided apse, and seven radiating chapels in the chevet. This church, which was more or less complete by the 1320s, was gutted during the Hussite Wars, and was not to be rebuilt until 1702. This task was first entrusted to the German architect P.I. Bayer, but he was soon replaced by an architect at the very beginning of his career, Santini-Aichel. The new building, completed by 1706, is a masterly example of the 'baroque-Gothic' manner peculiar to this architect, and features vaulting which is as complex as Ried's in the cathedral of St. Barbara in Kutná Hara (to which it clearly owes a debt), but treated with dynamic, baroque fluency. At present, unfortunately, you can neither visit the church—which has been closed for many years for restoration—nor the adjoining monastic buildings (now a Tobacco Factory), which feature a vast refectory of 1752–57, decorated with 16 enormous frescoed scenes by the Moravian painter with the appropriate name of Juda Tadeáš Supper. What you can see, however, is the nearby **Ossuary** (just to the N of the church, along Zámecká), which was formed initially of the bones of 30,000 people killed in a plague of 1318; the chapel to house these was remodelled in the 18C by Santini-Aichel, and again in the 19C. The Schwarzenberg family, who acquired the chapel following the dissolution of the monastery in 1783, commissioned in 1870 one František Rinta to arrange the skulls and bones in a decorative manner, a task which had first been undertaken in the early 16C, by a half-blind monk. The results of Rinta's endeavours, which were to occupy him and members of his family for four years, are morbidly fascinating, and include chandeliers, bones hung like Christmas paper chains, and even the coat of arms of the Schwarzenberg Family.

1.5km E of Sedlec along Road 33 you reach the intersection with Road 38, which will take you after a further 12km to Kolín. Continuing instead E along Road 33 you will come after 4km to the country house of **Kačina**, which was built between 1802 and 1822 for Count Johnann Rudolf Chotek. Designed by the Dresden architect Ch.F. Schuricht, this is a Palladian exercise on a megalomaniac scale, and features an enormous pedimented frontispiece, flanked by exceptionally long Ionic arcades. The excellently preserved interior contains outstanding Empire furnishings, and there is a fine English-style park, with lakes and long avenues of trees.

Kolín, which has been described as 'Bohemia's Crewe', is a heavily industrialised town, and one of the main railway junctions of Czechoslovakia. You should come here, however, if only to see the Deanery **Church of St. Bartholomew** (sv. Bartoloměje), which rises on a small hill just to the S of the main square. Begun in the late 13C, it seems to have been damaged by fire in 1349, and was partially rebuilt after 1360 by the great Peter Parler, who had been called in by the building's patron, the Abbot of Sedlec. The dark and broad nave—built around 1280, and the earliest example in Bohemia of a German Hall structure—is joined awkwardly by steps to Parler's light and elegant chancel. The large main square was rebuilt after a fire in 1734, and features on its western side a group of extraordinary gabled houses by the local baroque architect, Josef Jedlička. From Kolín you can return to Prague on the busy Road 12, which passes through flat and dreary countryside.

B.   Průhonice, Sázava, Český Šternberk and Konopiště

Total distance 140km. Prague—13km *Průhonice*—34km **Sázava**—17km *Český Šternberk*—31km **Konopiště**—45km Prague.

Heading SE of Prague on Czechoslovakia's main motorway, the D1, you will reach after 13km the suburban district of *Průhonice*, which is famous for its golf course, and has recently been endowed with one of the country's most luxurious hotels, the Golf Hotel. The *Castle*, which dates back to the 13C, was rebuilt in a neo-Gothic style at the end of the last century for Count Ernest Emmanuel Silva-Tarouca; it has retained, however, an old chapel with much restored 13C frescoes. Next to the chapel is an entrance to a small and enjoyable *Art Gallery*, largely composed of French-inspired landscapes by Czech artists of the first half of this century, including works by Antonín Slavíček (the delightful Veltrusy Park of 1897), Josef Ullman, Josef Hubáček, Otakar Nejedlý, Jan Slavíček, Vilém Nowak, Otakar Kubín, Josef Kilián, Oldřich Blažíček and Václav Špála. Of a special interest are the castle's extensive *gardens*, which were laid out at the end of the last century, and bought by the Czech state in 1927. The gardens, which are now administered by the Botanical Institute of the Czech Academy of Sciences, are informal in their layout and filled with rare and exotic plants.

Returning to the D1 and continuing to drive S, you should leave the motorway at Ostředek (25km), and head N through forest to the former **Monastery of Sázava** (9km), which is situated by the Sázava river, in an area popular as a summer resort.

The monastery was founded by Prince Oldřich in around 1032, supposedly as a result of a chance meeting in the forest with the hermit priest St. Procopius. Procopius, a Slavonic scholar, became the first abbot of the monastery, which belonged initially to the Basilian Order, a Slavonic order founded by Basilius the Great in the late 4C. Sázava became a great centre of Slavonic culture, and it was here that the Slavonic liturgy was used for the first time in Bohemia; this liturgy was to be banned after 1096 following the expulsion of the Slavonic monks by Břetislav II. The abbey church was rebuilt after 1315, and the whole complex greatly altered in the 17C and 18C. Shortly after its dissolution by Joseph II in 1785, the monastery was sold at auction and converted into a private residence for Emmanuel Tiegel, Knight of Lindenkron. Archaeological excavations carried out after 1940 have revealed fragments of the medieval monastery.

A visit to Sázava is more of historical than of architectural or artistic interest. The interminably protracted guided tour around the monastery buildings is devoted to the ground-floor rooms around the former cloisters, beginning with displays relating to the history of the Great Moravian Empire, and including a collection of archaeological finds from the site. The richly stuccoed early 18C refectory is decorated with frescoes by Jan Kovář, representing the story of the founding of the monastery. The highpoint of the tour is the chapter house, where 14C frescoes of the Life of the Virgin were discovered in 1943. The upper rooms of the monastery have a collection of locally made glass. The Gothic church, begun in 1315, was left incomplete, and its western tower and the arches of its nave stand today exposed in front of the present church, which comprises an 18C remodelling of the 14C east end. The white interior has a high altar of 1755 featuring a dynamic and elaborate sculptural surround by Richard Prachner; the semi-circular crypt with Gothic rib vaults in brick was restored in the 17C and again in 1950. Nearby can be seen the excavated foundations of the original 11C church.

Further S along this beautiful, forested stretch of the Sázava river is the impressive castle of *Český Šternberk*, which rises above the trees on a great outcrop of rock (the easiest approach to the castle from Sázava is to return to the D1, which you then leave after 8km, and drive for a further 2km). The castle was founded in around 1240, but rebuilt and strengthened in the late 15C and early 16C. Crenellations and battlements from the medieval structure can still be seen, though the present appearance of the building is due largely to further remodelling carried out in the 17C and 18C; the interior is remarkable above all for the heavy and extensive stucco decorations executed between 1660 and 1667 by the Milanese artist Carlo Brentano.

From Český Šternberk retrace your way back to the D1, but instead of rejoining the motorway, drive under it and follow the road to Divišov (2km), from where you continue driving W to the small town of Benešov (16km). The castle of **Konopiště** lies 2km W of the town, and is set high in a hilly wooded park, with baroque statuary and strutting peacocks adorning the upper lawns. Dating back to 1300, the castle has prominent medieval features such as tall, crenellated round towers and a moat where bears were kept until very recently. The whole place was in fact completely remodelled after 1889, when the place came into the possession of the ill-fated successor to the Austro-Hungarian throne, the Archduke Franz Ferdinand d'Este. Ferdinand, who was married to a member of the Bohemian Chotek family, stayed regularly at Konopiště right up to the time of his assassination in 1914, and held here in his last year secret meetings with the German Emperor Wilhelm II: Mrs Müller, from Hašek's novel The Good Soldier Švejk, refers to him as 'our Ferdinand ... the fat churchy one, from Konopiště'. The heavy panelled interior of Konopiště is immensely evocative of the last days of the Habsburgs, of whom there are numerous photographs and other mementoes, including portraits of Ferdinand and his family by

František Dvořák. You are shown not only Ferdinand's bedroom but
also his magnificently appointed bathroom; in addition you will see a
school painting by Botticelli presented to Ferdinand by the Kaiser
Wilhelm, fine collections of Meissen and armoury (including an
exquisitely wrought arm-piece of 1598 made for Gesualdo da Venosa
by Pompeo della Cesa), and some of the earliest radiators in the
Austro-Hungarian Empire. But the lasting impression of the building
is of a veritable forest of antlers and other hunting trophies, of which
there are an estimated 300,000.

Drive N from Benešov along the E55, and leave the road after 5km
to visit the village of *Poříčí nad Sázavou*, where there are two
Romanesque churches of the early 13C; one is the tiny cemetery
church of St. Peter, while the other is the parish church of St. Gall,
which was remodelled inside during the baroque period but has kept
its original crypt with cubic capitals. 11km further N along the E55
you will rejoin the D1 at Velké Popovice, a 27km drive from Prague.

C.   Karlštejn and Křivoklát

Total distance 125km. Prague—31km **Karlštejn**—14km *Beroun*—
21km **Křivoklát**—25km *Lány*—34km Prague.

From Prague head S for 10km on the dual carriageway of Road 4,
then take the turning to the right marked Radotín and Černošice, and
follow the Berounka river until you reach **KARLŠTEJN**, a small wine-
growing village lying under the shadow of one of the largest and
most fantastically shaped castles in Bohemia. This castle, which
projects high above the steep and densely forested slopes behind the
village, is by far the most popular sight near Prague, and attracts
daily great coachloads of tourists.

Karlštejn Castle was built by Charles IV in the mid 14C to house the imperial
crown jewels, the Bohemian royal insignia, and a large collection of relics.
Designed by the great French architect, Matthew of Arras, the building was
begun in 1348, and completed in the remarkably short space of seven years.
The imperial jewels were removed to Prague by Sigismund of Luxemburg in
1420, shortly before the castle was besieged for seven months by the Hussites;
the jewels were eventually to end up at the Hofburg in Vienna. As for the
Bohemian royal insignia, these were to be returned at the outbreak of the Thirty
Years' War to St. Vitus's Cathedral, where they can now be seen in a room
above the Wenceslas Chapel. Extensively rebuilt in 1575–97, the castle complex
later lost its importance, and was in a ruinous state when, in 1887, F. Schmidt
and Josef Mocker embarked on a restoration campaign which was to be no less
drastic than that of Viollet-le-Duc at Carcassonne.

Those coming to Karlštejn by car are not allowed to drive up to the
castle from the village, and have to make the arduous ascent on foot,
sharing the narrow, winding road with a virtual queue of other
tourists. Your spirits are at first maintained by the castle's extraordinarily romantic and picturesque profile, but begin to sag the more
you realise that what you see is largely a medieval sham, which seems
almost to have been devised for the tourist market. Gloomy, insensitively restored rooms await you, as well as a guided tour of numbing
boredom; however, a visit to the castle is made worthwhile not only by
the magnificent forest views to be had from the top, but also, and more
importantly, by the outstanding 14C decorations to be found within.

After passing through two gates you will find yourself in the Burgrave's courtyard, beyond which to the W steps descend to a narrow stretch of battlements containing an 80m-deep well which was built in the 14C by mining experts from Kutná Hora. You should return to the Burgrave's courtyard (where the castle's ticket office is to be found) to begin a tour of the main part of the castle complex, which is built up on the slope to the N of here, its highest and furthest point being the Keep. The first part of the castle which you visit is the *Imperial Palace*, where you will find displays relating to the Bohemia of Charles IV as well as a diptych by Tomaso di Modena, which is kept at present in what was once the imperial bedroom. Next you come to **The Tower of Our Lady**, which features on its second floor the Chapel of St. Mary, the walls of which are covered with dark and faded murals (attributed to Nikolaus Wurmser and painted in the 1370s) representing the Apocalypse, scenes in the history of the castle's creation (including the gift from the King and Dauphin of France of two thorns from the Crown of Thorns) and Charles IV himself, who is portrayed with unflattering realism, stooped before a gilded cross. The Emperor's own, private chapel was the adjoining St. Catherine's Chapel, where he would shut himself up for hours in deep meditation, important documents being passed to him through a hole in the west wall. This tiny chapel can literally be described as jewel-like, for Charles had the walls embellished all over with gilded plaster and a dazzling array of coloured, polished stones, leaving uncovered only some murals of saints, of slightly earlier date. The highpoint of the castle tour should be the **Keep**, which is joined to the Tower of Our Lady by a covered, wooden gallery. Sadly, however, this has been closed for many years for restoration, and you are thus prevented at present from seeing the remarkable **Chapel of the Holy Rood**. This chapel, consecrated in 1360, and divided in two by a gilded iron screen, has a gilded ceiling set with glass stars, and walls encrusted with no less than 2200 semi-precious stones as well as 128 painted wooden panels by one of the greatest Bohemian painters of the 14C, Master Theodoric. The relics were once to be found behind the panels, while the jewels and insignia were kept in a niche behind the altar, over which Tomaso da Modena's diptych was originally placed.

From Karlštejn you should head W along the river Berounka to the small town of *Beroun* (14km), after which you continue to follow the river for much of the way to the castle of **Křivoklát**, a further 21km. The landscape after Beroun becomes densely forested, and Křivoklát itself is hidden among trees above a tiny tributary of the Berounka. It is another of Bohemia's royal castles, but a less spoilt one than Karlštejn, and with a pleasantly ramshackle character.

Founded in 1109, the castle was acquired in the mid 13C as a royal residence by Přemysl Otakar II, and was later inherited by Charles IV. Charles spent little of his time here, in contrast to his son Wenceslas IV, who was a passionate huntsman, and came frequently to hunt around Křivoklát; the place provided him with respite from the duties of kingship, and he even burnt down the comfortable dwellings in the castle's outer bailey so that he would not be too troubled by emissaries coming to visit him here. He strengthened the fortifications and undertook much rebuilding at Křivoklát, but the present appearance of the castle is due largely to work carried out at the end of the 15C by Vladislav Jagiello. The Habsburg Emperor Rudolph II stayed here several times, but in 1658 the Habsburgs were obliged first to pawn the castle to John Adolph of Schwarzenberg and then to sell it to the Counts of Wallenstein. After 1685 the building came into the possession of the Fürstenbergs, who were to be responsible for much rebuilding and restoration work in the 19C and early 20C, work which was partially to be supervised by the leading neo-Gothicist Josef Mocker.

The castle at Křivoklát comprises a picturesque and slightly run-down assemblage of structures, dominated at the narrow, eastern end by a tall round tower. The central building is the royal palace, which features on its south façade a delicately carved oriel window, adorned with relief carvings of Vladislav Jagiello and his son Louis. The interior, which has been gutted several times by fire, is remarkable above all for the chapel attached to the eastern end of the palace. Begun in the 13C but altered in the late 15C, it has elaborate late Gothic vaulting to which has been added wooden and brightly coloured skeletal ribs supporting a pendulant boss; the stalls are of the late 15C, as is the splendidly intricate altarpiece, a structure in polychromed wood dedicated to the life of the Virgin and attributed to a Litoměřice artist. The 13C library, once one of the most important in Bohemia, has today a largely 19C appearance. Some rooms off the outer bailey house today a large collection of hunting guns.

The fastest way back to Prague from Křivoklát is to return to Beroun and from there take the D5 motorway. Alternatively you can head NE to join the E48 at Kačice (19km), passing after 14km the village of *Lány*, which has a former Fürstenberg Castle which was used this century by both Presidents Masaryk and Beneš; Masaryk, together with his American wife and their son, lie buried under a simple tombstone in the cemetery on the outskirts of the village. Kačice, a 32km drive from Prague, is situated in the middle of a large coal-mining area incorporating Kladno and **Lidice** (see Route 2D below).

D.   Lidice and Budeč

Total distance 54km. Prague 20km—**Lidice**—9km *Budeč*—25km Prague

Few places in Europe testify so poignantly to Nazi atrocities as **Lidice**, a village and memorial situated 20km NW of Prague, in a grim and flat coal-mining area (2km W of the dual carriageway of Road 7). The present village, a characterless grid of the post-war years, lies just to the W of the extensive memorial marking the site of the previous village, a place which the Nazis had hoped to obliterate completely from all maps, but which is now, ironically, one of the most visited of Czechoslovakia's war monuments.

The destruction of the village of Lidice on 10 June 1942, was the most notorious of the many Nazi reprisals that followed the assassination of the German Protector of Czechoslovakia, R. Heydrich. Lidice appears to have been chosen for no apparent reason other than that it belonged to a coal-mining region with a strong Socialist tradition. The official Nazi explanation was that the villagers were all partisans who had supported Heydrich's assassins, though it was later to transpire that the Nazis themselves had compromised the place by hiding a large cache of weapons in a mill outside the village. On the evening of 9 June 1942, shortly after placing these weapons, members of the Gestapo and the SS surrounded Lidice, rounding up all the village men into a farmyard, and taking the women and young children to the village school. In the course of the night 173 men were executed, the oldest being a man of 84, the youngest being not yet 15; 11 more were killed early the following day after returning from night-shift in the mines. The women were all sent to concentration camp, as were most of the children (the majority being eventually gassed in Poland); the more German-looking children were given German names and placed in German homes. The village was razed to the ground, buried under soil and its name obliterated. The only male villager later to return was a murderer who had been kept in a Prague prison, and went back to Lidice one day hoping to surprise his mother and ask her forgiveness for his crime. The story of his return home has fired the imagination of several Czech writers, most notably Bohumil Hrabal, in his novel, I Served the King of England: 'The murderer sat down, his hands hanging over his knees like two flippers, then stood up again and stumbled through that moonlit landscape like a drunk. He stopped by what looked like a post in the ground, fell down, and embraced it. It wasn't a post at all, it was what was left of a tree trunk with the stump of a single branch on it, as though it had been used as a gallows. This, said the murderer, used to be our walnut tree, this is where our garden was, and here ... he knelt down and felt around with his hands for the crumbled foundations of the house and the farm buildings.'

The decision to rebuild the village and erect a commemorative memorial to the old Lidice was taken almost immediately after the Soviet 'liberation' of Czechoslovakia in May 1945. An architectural competition was subsequently held, the winners of which were the architects, V. Hilský, Z. Jirsák, F. Marek, R. Podzemný and A. Teuzer; the foundation stone of the new village was laid in June 1947. In the summer of 1954, the Chairman of the British Committee 'Lidice Shall Live', proposed to enlarge the memorial with the creation of a 'Rose Garden of Friendship and Peace'; opened in 1955, this was created from rose seedlings sent from all over the world.

Despite being in the middle of an ugly, built-up area, the commemorative memorial itself is spread over a pleasant green slope fringed with distant pines. At the higher end of the hill are the Rose Garden of Friendship and Peace and a large and austere arcaded memorial centred around an eternal flame. At the end of the eastern arcade is a museum containing photographs of the murdered villagers, and other sad mementoes, such as identification cards pierced by bullet-holes; visitors are also shown here an old documentary film which includes an ironic last sequence with a smiling Stalin promising an end to all of Czechoslovakia's troubles. A path below the museum leads down the green slope to the mass grave of the murdered men, adjoining which is the reconstructed wall of the farm where they were shot. Further down are the foundations of the village church and school, the latter once bearing the inscription, 'School, My Happiness'.

The only other place of interest in the immediate vicinity of Lidice is the site of the Slavonic hill-fort of *Budeč*, which can be reached by returning to Road 7 and driving N to Stehelčeves (2km), where you take the turning to the right; the site, which is situated 4km E of Road 7, in between the villages of Kováry and Zakolány, is marked by an isolated church rising above fields. The fort at Budeč, which features in the early Czech legends, seems to have been founded around 900 by Prince Spytihněv, the second earliest known prince in Czech history. It was he who was probably responsible for the building of the much restored Rotunda which forms today the apse of the Budeč church; to this Rotunda, the oldest surviving one in Bohemia, a Romanesque tower was attached in the 12C, and a nave in the 17C.

E.   Roztoky, Nelahozeves, Veltrusy and Mělník

Total distance 79km. Prague—8km *Roztoky*—15km **Nelahozeves**—5km **Veltrusy**—19km **Mělník**—32km Prague

A pleasant excursion N along the river Vltava can be made from Prague's Dejvice Square, where you head N along Jugoslávských partyzánů (see Route 1H) and then follow the banks of the river all the way to Mělník. In the outlying township of *Roztoky* (8km) is a small round castle dating back to the 13C but rebuilt in the 16C, and used in 1945 as a factory for making penicillin; the former moat has been covered over and turned into gardens, while the castle itself has now a modest but interesting historical museum. Standing on top of a ridge just to the N of the town, with views over a railway line down to the river, is an isolated medieval church marking the site of the 9C Slavonic hill-fort of *Levý Hradec*, the first seat of the Přemyslid princes.

The small industrial town of Kralupy, 13km further N along the river, features in the poetry and recollections of Jaroslav Seifert, who had happy childhood memories of the place before the Second World War, and paid a nostalgic return trip there shortly after the town was badly damaged by an Allied air raid in March 1945; on this visit he re-met by chance one of the girls of his childhood dreams, and discovered that she was the sole survivor from her Jewish family, and was on the point of emigrating to Canada. 2km further N is the quiet and attractive village of **Nelahozeves**, where the composer Antonín Dvořák was born in 1841, in an early 19C house marked today by a plaque. Dvořák's father was the local butcher, and, at the back of the house, is an outdoor toilet built in what was once the slaughter house; the house itself is now a commemorative *museum* containing mementoes and furniture from the composer's childhood. Crowning the hill which rises immediately to the S of the house is the village's impressive **Renaissance Castle**, which was built in the 1550s, possibly by Bonifaz Wohlmut, for Florian Griespek of Griespach, a wealthy Bavarian nobleman employed in the service of Rudolph I. Sgraffito decorations extensively cover the exterior of the building, while inside is a large hall with elegant Renaissance fireplaces as well as painted and stuccoed scenes of classical history and mythology. The greater part of the enormous interior is taken up today by the Old Master paintings and sculptures of the *Central Bohemian Gallery*, most of which are from the former Lobkovic Picture Gallery at Roudnice (see Route 7). The gallery is particularly strong on Spanish works, and though the supposed Velasquez painting is obviously a school work, there are fine portraits by Juan Pantoja de la Cruz and Sanchez Coello; the other works are mainly by 16C–18C Flemish and Italian artists, including Conrad Wiertz, Frans Francken, Cornelis van der Voort, Antonio Molinari, G.M. Preti, G.P. Panini, and Canaletto (a large view of a Carnival on the Thames, 1748). The 19C is represented principally by a romantic evocation of a monastery by Granet, suggestive nocturnal scenes by Jakub Schikaneder, and a view of Nelahozeves in 1841 by Carl Robert Croll.

On the other side of the Vltava to Nelahozeves is one of the most beautiful country houses near Prague, **Veltrusy**, a place which inspired the setting of Dvořák's opera, The Jacobins.

This former residence of the Chotek family was built in the 1720s on a marshy, wooded site known as 'the island'. The house, comprising four small wings radiating from a domed cylindrical hall, was inspired by the pleasure palace designs of Fischer von Erlach. The interior was extensively remodelled after 1760 when the then owner, Rudolf Chotek, was made Austria's first Supreme Chancellor; it contains fine collections of porcelain and 18C furniture, much rococo stuccowork, and several painted ceilings, including, in the main hall, an ambitious composition described in the English brochure to the house as 'an allegory of the four periods'. The main façade of the house, featuring a great staircase adorned with statuary, overlooks a French formal garden of the early 18C. Behind the house, however, extends a vast wooded park which was begun shortly after a great flood in 1764, and came to be one of the greatest examples of romantic landscaping in Bohemia, with numerous splendid follies, including a mock medieval mill, a Doric pavilion, a Chinese Pheasantry, a Greek rotunda, and a bizarre Egyptian structure erected during the wake of publicity following Napoleon's Egyptian campaign of 1816–19. The park today, more romantic than ever for being in a slightly dilapidated state, attracts numerous weekend excursionists from Prague.

19km N of Veltrusy along Road 9 is the small town and wine-growing centre of **Mělník**, which is beautifully situated on a vine-covered hill rising above the confluence of the rivers Vltava and Labe; the vines were brought originally from Burgundy by Charles IV. The dominant landmarks are the tall steeple of the 15C–16C *Church of SS. Peter and Paul* and the imposing bulk of the adjoining **Castle**. The castle, which dates back to a Slavonic hill-fort of the 10C, was the occasional residence of the Bohemian queens up to 1475. The present structure—the result of rebuilding and remodelling carried out in the 16C and 17C—houses both a small *Viticultural Museum* and a well and spaciously arranged **Art Gallery** devoted to Czech painters of the 17C and 18C, including Willman, Kupecký, Jan Liška, Václav V. Reiner, Jan Jiří Heinsch and Karel Škréta. Also to be found here is the *Ludmila Wine Bar and Restaurant*, where you can try the local wines while enjoying a steep view over vines down to the river.

The direct route back to Prague (32km) is to head S along Road 9.

EASTERN BOHEMIA

3   Prague to Náchod

Total distance 170km. Prague—E67/D11 48km **Poděbrady**—22km
Chlumec-nad Cidlinou—28km **Hradec Králové**—72km *Náchod.*

The E67/D11 heads due E from Prague through what is at first flat
and dreary agricultural countryside. *Sadská*, 37km E of the city, is a
tiny spa town where Mozart stayed for three weeks on his second
visit to Bohemia in 1787; his stay was paid for by Czech friends who
were anxious about the impoverished musician's health. Czechoslovakia's youngest spa town, **Poděbrady**, is 11km further on, by the
banks of eastern Bohemia's largest river, the Labe. In the main
square is an equestrian statue by B. Schnirch to the town's most
famous son, George of Poděbrady, who was Regent of Bohemia
before becoming king of the country in 1453; his brilliance as a
statesman was comparable to that of his Hungarian contemporary,
Matthias Corvinus, who was likewise elevated from regent to king. A
museum to George is to be found in the town's ochre-coloured
Castle, which stands off the square and projects over the Labe. This
much-restored building, dating back to the 13C, was rebuilt between
1545 and 1582, and further altered in the mid 18C. In its large austere
courtyard is a plaque to a German farmer, Bülow, who, searching for
new sources of drinking water for the town, uncovered in 1905 a
mineral spring within the castle grounds. The curative properties of
the water were soon afterwards recognised by a local physician, Dr
Bohumil Bouček. Poděbrady's *spa*, founded in 1908, is especially
favoured by those suffering from heart diseases; its buildings lie
scattered around a great park just to the N of the main square.

Further E along the E67 the landscape becomes hillier and more
wooded. Outside the village of *Chlumec nad Cidlinou*, 21km from
Poděbrady, is one of Bohemia's most original baroque mansions,
Karlova Koruna. Commissioned by František F. Kinsky to commemorate a visit by Charles VI, it was begun in 1721 to one of the last
designs by Giovanni Santini-Aichel, and completed in 1723 by F.M.
Kaňka; the design, comprising three wings arranged in star-like
fashion around a circular block, was probably inspired by the
fantastical 'pleasure house' designs of the Austrian architect Fischer
von Erlach. The interior, gutted in 1947, now houses a permanent
collection of masters of the Bohemian baroque, including Karel
Škréta, Jiří Heerman, Jan Liška, Michael Leopold Willman, Antonín
Kern, Johann Kupecký, Václav Reiner and Matthias Braun; plaster-
casts of Braun's monumental works at nearby Kuks (see p 200) take
up much of the ground-floor saloon.

The village of Chlumec itself is purely of historical interest, the
place having been the centre in 1775 of one of the largest peasant
uprisings in Bohemia's history: after its suppression, nearly 3000
serfs were brought to a farm near Chlumec and burnt to death.—On
the outskirts of the village, in the direction of Hradec Králové, is a
statue of a rebel peasant by J. Obrovský.

The direct road from Chlumec to Hradec Králové passes 6km S of
the castle of *Hrádek U Nechanic* (3km before reaching Hradec turn

left on to the Nechanice road, and then turn left again at Stezery). The castle was built between 1839 and 1857 for Franz Ernst von Harrach, who had hoped to enlist the services of Franz Beer, the architect of the extraordinary neo-Gothic pile at Hluboká (see Rte 15B); in the end the building was designed in a Tudor Gothic style by the Viennese architect Karl Fischer, who supposedly was inspired by George Lamb's designs for Crewe Hall in Cheshire. Many of the castle's original furnishings survive, though a large part of the interior is also devoted to contemporary Czech history; there is a large deer park in an English style.

An ALTERNATIVE ROUTE from Chlumec to Hradec Králové is by way of Pardubice, which is reached by leaving the E67/D11 3km E of Chlumec, and then driving 27km SE along the D36. 10km before Pardubice is the small spa resort of *Lázně Bohdaneč*, which has innovative spa buildings in a 'Cubist' style by Josef Gočár, designed in 1911 when the architect was 31. **Pardubice**, a large industrial town on the river Labe, has an important history and a small but attractive old quarter.

First mentioned in 1295, Pardubice was elevated to the status of town in 1340; but its greatest period was from 1491 to 1581, when it was owned by the Pernštejn family, among the most important Bohemian patrons of the Renaissance. Heavily damaged by fire in 1507, the town was rebuilt at remarkable speed, with Italian masters working alongside native craftsmen. A Master John from Olomouc was called in to create a unified town plan comparable to those of Renaissance Italy. Sadly most of 16C Pardubice was destroyed during the Thirty Years' War, in particular as a result of a siege carried out by the Swedish army in 1645. From the late 19C the town developed as one of the major industrial centres of Bohemia, with extensive chemical and engineering works. The town's best-known product, manufactured in the outlying district of Semtín, is the explosive known as Semtex, a particular favourite with terrorists owing to its being undetectable by electronic means.

Among those born in Pardubice were the cousins František and Václav Veverka, who invented before 1827 the swing-plough; and Jan Kašpar, who in 1910 became the first Czech aviator. A famous annual event of Pardubice is the Grand Pardubice Steeple Chase, which was first held on 5 November 1874, and is run on what is regarded by some as one of Europe's most demanding racecourses.

The surviving old monuments of Pardubice are concentrated on the small yet excellently preserved Pernštýnovo Square, which comprises almost entirely buildings of the 16C and 18C. The square can be entered through the arch of the Renaissance *Green Tower* (1540), a tall structure rivalled only by the nearby Pernštejn Castle as the dominant element in the old town's sky-line. The castle itself, built between 1512 and 1543 to replace an earlier Gothic building, has been badly damaged over the years, though it still retains an exquisitely carved Renaissance gateway and bridge, and some interesting painted panels of this period, including an allegory of Fortune which is considered to be the earliest painting of a nude in Bohemia; the interior also contains a Regional Museum, and—in what was once the castle brewery—the East Bohemian Gallery (*Východočeská Galérie*), featuring mainly 19C works, including A. Machek, A. Kosárek, Julius Mařák and A. Chitušsi. The church of St. Bartholomew (sv. Bartoloměj) on Pernštýnovo náměstí dates back to 1295 but was rebuilt after 1515 by the Pernštejns, who displayed here their characteristic love of rich sculptural decoration. A house on the south-western corner of the square has a tablet of 1511 recording the legendary encounter of the first Pernštejn with a bison. For an actual representation of a monster you should turn to the house known as *U Jonáše* on the opposite end of the square, which has an extraordinary stuccoed façade of 1797 by Jakub Teplý representing Jonah and the Whale.

In the suburban district of Pardubice known as Pardubický, near the so-called 'Small Château' or Zámeček, is a small memorial museum to those killed by the Nazis in 1942 in retaliation for the town having harboured the parachutists implicated in the assassination of Heydrich (see Lidice).

8km S of Pardubice along the D37 is the town of *Chrudim*, a dull industrial town but with remains of its medieval fortifications, and with a number of old houses, including the Mydlář (Mydlářovský dům) house (1573–77), which contains a museum of puppetry; in addition the town boasts a puppet theatre and an annual international puppet festival.—The main tourist attraction near Pardubice is the stud farm at Kladruby nad Labem, 14km E of the town in the direction of Kolín (see Route 2A); here you can hire horses or go riding in horse-drawn carriages.

North of Pardubice the D37 follows the quiet and attractive Labe Valley, passing 3km outside the town the rebuilt Hussite castle of Kunětická Hora, which rises above the river Labe on a wooded hill of volcanic origin. After 22km, at the confluence of the rivers Labe and

Orlice, you come to **Hradec Králové**, the administrative, cultural and economic centre of East Bohemia.

One of the oldest towns in Bohemia, Hradec Králové was already a fortified settlement and the leading centre in eastern Bohemia before the establishment of the Czech state in the 10C. Turned in the 14C into the seat of the widowed Queens of Bohemia (hence the name 'Hradec Králové' or 'castle of the Queens'), the town soon became one of the most imposing in the country. Badly damaged during the Thirty Years' War, the place was extensively rebuilt during the late baroque period. An imposing new fortress was constructed between 1766 and 1789, but this was destroyed shortly after the crushing defeat of the Austrians by the Prussians at the battle which took place at Chlum Hill, on the eastern outskirts of Hradec Králové, on 3 July 1866. Between 1900 and 1930 the town was considerably enlarged, a large new quarter growing up on the right bank of the Labe. The architects responsible—most notably, V. Rejchl, O. Liška, J. Kotěra and J. Gočár—were leading exponents of Functionalist design, and helped transform Hradec Králové into one of the foremost centres of modern Czech architecture. The town has continued to grow at a rapid pace since the Second World War, but with rather less original results. The place is now a major industrial town, specialising in such diverse products as chemicals, timber, diesel engines for ocean-going vessels, and musical instruments.

The old town of Hradec Králové, surrounded by extensive remains of its fortifications, stands on high ground in between the Labe and Orlice rivers. It is a large area with numerous Renaissance and baroque buildings but with little charm or warmth. The vast Žižkovo náměstí, attached to the smaller Husovo náměstí, is lined at its western end by the Town Hall (dating back to the Gothic period but heavily remodelled first in the Renaissance and then in 1850), the impressively tall *White Tower* (1574–80), and the twin-towered *Cathedral of the Holy Spirit*. The latter was begun in 1360, and much restored after fires in 1484, 1509 and 1536; the brick exterior is virtually unornamented, while the white and similarly austere interior has a very tall nave, low aisles and simple vaulting. On the southern side of the square is the former Bishop's Palace, dating back to the late 18C and today housing the *Regional Gallery*, which has a collection of modern Czech art, including works by Alfons Mucha, František Kupka, Bohumil Kubišta, Emil Filla, Jan Preisler, Jan Štursa and Josef Wagner, and a characteristically ghoulish painting by the Symbolist artist Josef Váchal. Adjoining this is an 18C Jesuit College attached to a church designed by the Italian architect C. Lurago and built in 1654–66; the interior of the church has a striking baroque decoration in white and gold, and a main altarpiece by Petr Brandl framed by painted architecture.

Heading NE of the square along Palackého, you will pass to your left the grimy *Hotel Bystrica*, a work by Jan Kotěra with a charming restaurant decorated with stained-glass by František Kysela and murals by Jan Preisler. At the northern end of Palackého, overlooking the river Labe, is a small park containing another, earlier work by Kotěra. Built in 1909–11 as the *Regional Museum*, it has a curious Secessionist exterior in red brick and concrete, with two massive sculptures guarding the entrance. The simple and unremarkable interior has extensive collections of the applied art of the 19C and 20C. On the other side of the Labe is the New Town or Nové Město, where you will find numerous severe Functionalist blocks of a type which followed on from Kotěra's Secessionist works. One of these is Gočár's *Státní Gymnasium*, which stands off V. Lipách, opposite a church by this architect. Rising on a column placed directly in front of the Gymnasium is a lively and elegant bronze nude by Jan Štursa.

N of Hradec Králové, 14km along the D33/E67, is the village of *Smiřice*, the original home of the Smiřický family. Their former

mansion, in the bosky southern outskirts of the village, has a large
chapel, begun in 1696 or 1699, and consecrated in 1713; its undulate
oval plan has something of the dynamism of Christoph
Dientzenhofer's architecture, but the Gothic-inspired vaulting recalls
the work of Johann Santini-Aichel. *Jaroměř*, 10km further N, has a
15C church with a baroque belfry and a row of late Gothic and
Renaissance burghers' houses. But its principle interest is the fortress
known as the *Josefov* in the southern half of the town: founded by the
Emperor Josef II in 1780, this was a structural complex of considerable
strength and sophistication, but one which never had to withstand a
single siege.

Leave the D33/E67 at Jaroměř and take the road to Dvůr Králové.
After 6km the road passes through the tiny and pretty village of **KUKS**,
outside which you will find the remains of what was once an ambitious
baroque complex. These remains, comprising a chapel and a hospital,
dominate the verdant slopes on the other side of the river Labe to the
village. Though only fragments of a once magnificent whole, and
themselves in a lamentable condition, they—and the nearby and
similarly ruined statuary in the so-called Bethlehem Wood—constitute
among the greatest baroque attractions of central Europe.

The creation of the Kuks spa was due to Count Franz Anton Graf von Sporck, a
man of fascinating contradictions and one of the most enlightened patrons of the
European baroque. Sporck came from a recently ennobled family of German
origin, his father being from a line of modest Westphalian freeholders. The father
had been raised to the nobility and given an extensive estate in Bohemia as a
reward for the active part which he had played both in the Thirty Years' War and
in the wars against the Turks. In 1662, at the age of 65, he had increased his
Bohemian domain through the acquisition of a large property now known as
Choustníkovo Hradiště, in the vicinity of Kuks. Franz Anton Sporck was born that
same year, and was to spend much of his youth on his father's new estate. After
studying law and philosophy, he inherited, when only 17, all his father's
properties and a vast wealth estimated at more than 6000 guilders. Subsequently
he travelled around western Europe, spending much of his time at the court of
Louis XIV. The sight of Versailles under construction must undoubtedly have
nourished Sporck's plans to create something on a comparably megalomaniac
scale in his native Bohemia. He was only too conscious of being from an
aristocratic family of little standing, and was anxious to astound the Bohemian
nobility through a spectacular act of patronage. It says much of his character,
however, that he seems to have despised the very nobility whom he wanted to
impress. He was to lead the life of an autocratic nobleman, determined to have
control over every aspect of his subjects' lives, while at the same time remaining
at heart a life-long rebel. A champion of the poor against feudal exploitation, he
was even to be discovered at one large ball in Prague debating at three o'clock in
the morning social injustices in Bohemia. Though a former law student, he was to
hold all lawyers in contempt, and was even to commission at Kuks an enormous
symbolical sculpture of Herkomanus, the patron of dishonest lawyers. Both
Sporck's rebelliousness and the perverse, contradictory nature of his character
are reflected in his attitude towards religion: schooled at a Jesuit College, he was
to have constant disputes with the Jesuits, attempt to liberate Catholicism from
the rigid influence of the Vatican, belong to a circle of free-thinkers who
advocated religious tolerance, regularly attend the sermons of the Lutheran
preacher Christian Voight, and become involved with Jansenism to the extent of
sympathising with numerous Czech exiles. And yet he was to support the
Catholic authorities in Bohemia and, to their approval, to commission for near
Kuks some of the most moving and powerful biblical statuary in the history of
baroque art, works that were perfectly in accordance with the Jesuit ideal of
emotional directness in religious representation.

The history of Kuks goes back to the early 1690s when Sporck discovered near
his estate at Hradiště a mineral spring reputed to have healing powers. In 1694
these powers were verified by a group of professors from Prague University, and
Sporck decided to turn the place into a spa, the fame of which he hoped would
soon eclipse that of Karlovy Vary. A number of spa buildings, guest houses and
places of entertainment were constructed on the left bank of the Labe, on a site
now occupied by the village of Kuks; alongside these structures Sporck also built

for himself a large mansion intended to replace his family seat at Hradiste. After 1707 construction work was extended to the right bank of the Labe, where there were laid out in ascending order a race course, a summerhouse and garden (complete with maze and fountains), a chapel and hospice, a further garden, a cemetery, and a windmill pumping water to the whole area. The architect of the chapel, and probably of the Sporck mansion as well, was the Italian-born G.B. Alliprandi, one of the pioneering baroque architects of Bohemia and at that time very much in demand in the Bohemian capital. But Sporck's greatest coup was in securing in 1712 the services of the Tyrolean sculptor Matthias Braun, then fresh from his triumphant first commission in Bohemia—the sculptural group of St. Luitgard for the Charles Bridge in Prague. The first biographer of Braun, M. Pelc, suggested that it was Sporck who had had this sculptor brought to Bohemia in the first place. Though this is unlikely, there was clearly a very close understanding between the two men, and Braun was allowed at Kuks a freedom which he would have found in few other places in Europe. By 1712, construction work at Kuks was nearing completion, and attention could be devoted more fully to the decorative embellishment of the place. So far the main sculptural work carried out at Kuks had been by an artist of Flemish descent, Bartholomew Zwengs, and had consisted of a number of dull and mannered works for the hospice garden. Braun's first task was the bizarre one of executing a series of grotesque dwarfs to surround the race course; but even in these minor works he showed himself to be an artist far more suited to convey Sporck's dynamic ideas than was the staid Zwengs. Afterwards he had a commission for a group of Beatitudes to be placed on the terrace in front of the Hospice Chapel. Whereas for these works he was considerably helped by his workshop, for the flanking allegorical figures of Vices and Virtues—his subsequent commission—he appears to have been largely unaided. Braun's final works for Sporck were his biblical scenes for the nearby New Grove at Žireč ('the Bethlehem Wood'), a series of chapels, statuary and hermitages that were brought to completion around 1733 and constituted the last and in many ways most personal of Sporck's plans for the area.

During Sporck's lifetime, Kuks was indeed the thriving social and cultural centre which he had intended. There were great hunting expeditions, fairs in which wells would be filled with wine, Venetian nights on the Labe involving music and cannon salvoes, and knighthood ceremonies for the Order of St. Hubert, a hunting order founded and led by Sporck himself, and boasting the Emperor Charles VI among its members. Sporck was a man of enormous culture, and his house at Kuks attracted numerous artists, writers, musicians and philosophers, including the painter Brandl, the lyric poet Matthias Gunther, and Johann Sebastian Bach. At Kuks Sporck amassed an important library of philosophical works, and set up his own printing press, which brought out numerous tracts of the French Enlightenment. He had a particular love of music, acquiring a private orchestra, and developing a specialist interest both in popular religious songs and—much to Bach's approval—the French horn, with which he had fallen in love in Paris: thanks to Sporck Kuks became the first place in Bohemia to hear this instrument. It was perhaps fortunate that Sporck died in 1738, at the height of Kuks' fame; for it was only two years later that a tragedy was to befall the place from which it was never to recover.

On 22 December 1740, the Labe overspilt its banks, washing away the three bridges, the race course, the summer pavilion, and a number of other structures; more importantly it destroyed for ever the healing spring, thus bringing to an end Kuks' days as a spa. The later history of Kuks is a depressing tale of decay, insensitive alterations and wilful destruction, culminating in 1901 in the pulling down of Sporck's mansion. Not even the Bethlehem Wood was spared, the buildings and statuary becoming so overgrown and neglected that in the late 18C much of the stone was taken away to be used in the construction of the Josefov fortress at Jaroměř. Thoughts on the transience of earthly glory might easily come to the visitor to Kuks today, and yet the sense of pathos which the place emanates is also integral to its haunting and unforgettable appeal.

Virtually nothing of the Kuks known to Sporck is to be seen on the left bank of the Labe, with the exception of the village school, which was formerly the Sun Inn; on the outskirts of the village there has also survived one of a number of timber-roofed cottages built for craftsmen, workers and servants, this particular one being once the home of the engraver M.J. Rentz. The **hospice and chapel** on the other side of the river are reached by a pleasant if steep path through meadows. Finally you come to a grand flight of steps built around the entrance of the chapel crypt, and leading to the terrace which Braun adorned with his statues of Beatitudes and Vices and Virtues (the latter group has recently been replaced by copies, the originals having been taken inside). These wildly gesticulating statues, together with Alliprandi's dynamic and richly modelled chapel façade, enliven the otherwise dreary silhouette of the hospice, the work mainly of Petr Netola.

The whole complex is at present being thoroughly and slowly restored, and only a small part of the interior can now be visited. The guided tour which you are obliged to follow takes you first inside the deconsecrated oval chapel, where a number of paintings have been placed, including a hunting portrait of Sporck by Jozef Ignaz Capon. Of the adjoining hospice rooms that you can at present visit, the most interesting is the Apothecary, which is claimed to be the oldest surviving one in Europe after that of Dubrovnik. Another room contains a fascinating anonymous painting representing Kuks in 1724, featuring the bizarre race course as well as the many splendid buildings on the left bank of the Labe. A number of statues by Braun and his workshop, including some of the 12 surviving dwarfs from the race course, are to be seen in the corridors and derelict courtyard of the hospice; others are in the overgrown garden (closed to visitors), together with works by Zwengs. The intention is eventually to display the choicer pieces in the renovated parts of the hospice, but as yet only the remarkable **VICES AND VIRTUES** from the terrace are on show in the new setting. Occcupying the whole of a long dormitory on the other side of the courtyard to the chapel, these 24 figures, weathered though they are, have a quite overwhelming impact. The influence of the Roman baroque sculptor Bernini is evident, but the pathos of Braun's figures, and the hysterical rendering of their draperies, make Bernini's works seem quite restrained in comparison. Similarly the allegorical details are taken largely from Cesare Ripa's Iconologia (a source book for baroque artists), and yet Braun is remarkably free and inventive in his interpretation of them. He is perhaps at his best in his figures of Vices, for in these he combines drama with savage and satirical naturalistic detail, some of this clearly intended to parody the nobility: the strutting woman representing Pride, for instance, is clearly some society hostess at a ball. Two further works by Braun are shown to you at the end of the tour, when you are taken outside and down into the chapel crypt. This austere chamber where Sporck lies buried has a main altar featuring a stone relief by Braun of the *Resurrection*, and a free-standing **Crucifixion** by the same artist. This latter work, Braun's only known one in wood, portrays the twisting body of Christ with extreme emotion.

A visit to Kuks is not complete without a trip to the nearby Bethlehem Wood (Betlém), where the most moving of all Braun's works are to be found. At one time there was a clearly marked forest path connecting the place with the hospice, but today it is best reached by car from the village of Kuks. Follow the side road in the direction of Dvůr Králové, and turn left at Žireč (3km); after 2km you will come to a car park, from where it is about a 20-minute walk to the site. The various chapels, hermitages and sculptures that Sporck built in the forest here were partly intended as an alternative religious attraction to a large Jesuit College at Žireč; their site was also a reflection of Sporck's hunting interests, and indeed one of the commissioned sculptures was of the patron saint of the hunting order which Sporck had founded, St. Hubert. The end result was like a mixture of a Calvary and some fantastical Renaissance garden such as Bomarzo near Viterbo. All that remains today are some heavily worn carvings and sculptures chiselled directly into boulders and rock formations found in the forest. They are disposed on either side of a long path, and recent sign-posting and tidying of the site have threatened to give the whole the bland character of some Nature Trail; one of the sculptures has already been protected by a ridiculous wooden roof, and the day might not be far off when all the works will have to be covered in this way. None the less there can still be few places in Europe where art of the highest quality merges so closely with Nature as it does here.

The first work to which you come is a near indecipherable Flight into Egypt by Petr Brandl. The following works are all by Braun, beginning with a dramatic free-standing sculpture of the hermit **Garinus**: this, the only known representation of an obscure Egyptian who chose to live like an animal as an act of penance, portrays the hermit emerging from under his cave with a terrified expression (there was once a sculpture opposite of a hound rushing towards him); the life-like quality of this work was originally enhanced by the figure being painted. Next come sculptures of the Czech saint *Jan Krstu*, the Egyptian hermit *Onufrius* (1731) and *Mary Magdalene*. The latter is attached to a large rock on which are to be found the most important works of the site, including the one which gave the area its name of Bethlehem (Betlém) Wood. Adjoining the Magdalene is a powerful and deeply cut relief representing **The Vision of St. Hubert** (1726); on the collar of a dog can be seen the inscription FAGUS, a reference to Sporck's name (Franz Anton Graf von Sporck). Excellently preserved reliefs pf the **Nativity** and **The Journey of the Magi** (both of 1731) come next, divided from the St. Hubert scene by a cave where there was originally a spring which flowed into a quadrangular-shaped pool. Further along the path is the last of the surviving monuments, *Jacob's Well* (1732), a pond once filled with water around which are the ruined figures of Christ and the women of Samaria; the water for this came from a powerful spring behind, which also supplied water for seven nearby fountains, including one which spouted up to a height of 8m. Opposite the well is a stone seat on which Braun supposedly sat while at work here.

Returning to Žireč you can continue to *Dvůr Králové* (3km), which was once the favourite residence of a Bohemian queen. Its main tourist attraction is its zoo, which was founded in 1946 by the African explorer Josef Vágner, who was concerned to save various African species from extinction; the open layout of the place is on the lines of England's Whipsnade. In the centre of the town is an elegant if much restored hall church of c 1400 and, on the main square, a former Town Hall (now a restaurant), designed by U. Avostalis in 1572 but much modified in recent years.

Take the main road back to Jaroměř, and rejoin the D33/E67 in the direction of Náchod. 12km from Jaroměř is the small town and health resort of *Česká Skalice*, well known in Czechoslovakia for its associations with the much-loved writer, Božena Němcová (1820–62). Němcová, Bohemia's first important women writer and a pioneering novelist in the Czech language, attended the wooden village school here between 1824 and 1830 (this much altered building, behind the main square, is now a memorial to her). In 1837 she married in the town, the wedding place taking place in *The Golden Lion Inn* (U Českého lva), which has now been converted into a museum to her; outside is a statue of her by M. Kucová-Uchytilová. Němcová was brought up in a valley 4km to the N of Česká Skalice, in a tiny valley now known as *Grandmother's Valley* (Babiččino údolí) in honour of Němcová's most famous novel, The Grandmother. Many of the places described in this simply written tale of country life can be recognised in the valley, such as the Úpa river, Vitorka's sluice-gate, and the charming, isolated cottage named the Old Bleaching Place. A naturalistic sandstone group of *Němcová's Grandmother* (1922) by Otto Gutfreund stands in front of an old mill, while at the nearby baroque mansion of Ratibořice (remodelled in an Empire style c 1800) are kept souvenirs of Němcová's life; the mansion was the property of the Duchess of Zahan, who employed Němcová's parents in her domestic service.

The poet Jaroslav Seifert (1910–86), a self-confessed urbanite who was rarely happy while staying in the countryside, confessed in his memoirs to have spent in the Grandmother's Valley 'a few dazzling moments, which one apparently can experience only in this country and in this region, hallowed by the reality which we respect and the legends which we love ... The little Ratibořice château in the distance radiated so much artistic colourfulness that it reminded us of the best etchings by Mr Vincent Morstadt ... In a remote valley people were mowing hay, and when the warm wind was blowing gently, we smelled the mingled odours of hay, of freshly cut grass, and of the ripe meadow, from which the sun was drinking morning dew and all the hidden nectars. As we walked slowly along the meadow path, our eyes could not absorb all the colours, the white and yellow daisies, the blue veil of sage and the red poppy. There was also the tenderly pink sainfoin, not to speak of all the constantly shifting and trembling greens...'

Náchod, 8km E of Česká Skalice, is a border town with Poland and a centre of the textile and rubber industries. Rising on a wooded hill above its small main square is a huge Renaissance castle built for the Smiřický family; they had to forfeit the building following their involvement in the Battle of the White Mountain in 1620, and it came into the hands of the Piccolominis, who extended the house to the N, and laid out a formal French Garden; inside is a richly stuccoed chapel of 1654 and collections of baroque and Empire furniture, and Dutch tapestries.

Náchod was the birthplace in 1924 of one of the greatest Czech novelists of today, Josef Škvorecký, who lived here until moving to Prague after the Second World War. During the war Škvorecký worked at the local Messerschmitt factory, and came to know the future film director Miloš Forman, who was staying at Náchod with his uncle. Memories of the town and of his upbringing here are the subject of his charming essay, I Was Born at Náchod, which is included in his collection of prose, Talkin' Moscow Blues (1988). A visit to the town will also be very much appreciated by anyone who has read Škvorecký's so-called 'Smiřický' novels, highly autobiographical works in which the town is thinly disguised as Kostelec. Škvorecký cheekily gave to the narrator of these works the name of Danny Smiřický, whose family is supposed to be distantly related to the famous and powerful owners of Náchod's castle; Škvorecký's adoption of this aristocratic name for his fictional *persona* seems to have been inspired by his uncle's discovery that a 17C ancestor had managed the estates of Count Czernin. The first of these books was The Cowards (1958), while late ones include The Swell Season, The Engineer of Human Souls and The Miracle Game.

4km to the S of Náchod along the D14 to Rychnov is the small and attractively situated town of *Nové Město*, founded in 1501 on a spur locked between a bend of the river Metuje. After a fire in 1526, the lords of the town, the Pernštejns, decided to rebuild the place in a uniform Renaissance style. The main survival of this period is a row of houses on the square, all featuring identical arcades and vaulting. The castle built by the Pernštejns was completely remodelled during the baroque period and then re-altered between 1909 and 1911 by D. Jurkovič; the latter architect was responsible for the Art Nouveau 'Ribbed Hall'.—The most important castle of the area is that of

Opočno, 13km further S (continue on the D14 until you reach Dobruška, and then turn right). This castle, occupying an impressive site above a lake and a ravine, is famous as the place where there was signed in 1813 the treaty of the Anti-Napoleon Coalition between the Russian Tsar Alexander I, the Prussian Chancellor Hardenberg and the Austro-Hungarian Chancellor Metternich. The present-day appearance of the building is due mainly to construction work carried out between 1560 and 1569 for William Trčka of Lípa, a diplomat who had recently taken part in an important mission to Genoa in Italy. The highpoint of the architecture is the magnificent three-storeyed courtyard, inspired in its detailing by contemporary Italian examples, but with tall proportions that are more characteristic of Czech Renaissance architecture. The much-altered interior contains a wide variety of collections, from Venetian and Neapolitan paintings of the 16C to 18C to hunting trophies, Flemish tapestries and African and American ethnographical objects.

North-east of Náchod you enter an enclave of Bohemia which juts out into Polish Silesia. At *Hronov*, 6km from Náchod in the direction of Broumov, is the wooden cottage where the writer Alois Jirásek was born in 1851. Jirásek, one of the most famous Czech writers of historical novels and plays, wrote often of his native region, most notably in his chronicle U nás (In Our Country). He is commemorated at Hronov by a statue to him by Q. Kocián outside his birthplace, and an annual amateur dramatic festival called Jirásek's Hronov. *Police nad Metují*, 9km further N, has a small convent church remodelled by the great baroque architect Kilian Ignaz Dientzenhofer, who worked extensively in this area.

Crossing the modest Falcon Mountains, you come to a broad valley which opens out to the SE into the Polish plain of Klodzko. *Broumov*, in the centre of this valley, is a dull town but with an interesting *Benedictine monastery* founded in 1322, but rebuilt by K.I. Dientzenhofer between 1728 and 1738. Only the church of the monastery is readily accessible, the rest of the complex being now occupied by several orders of nuns; you should try and persuade the nuns to allow you into the splendidly decorated library, and into the inner courtyard, each side of which has a dynamically projecting centrepiece crowned by a pediment. Othmar Zinke, the abbot who had commissioned from Dientzenhofer the reconstruction of Broumov, was also responsible for providing him with work in numerous other places in the area, the intention being to promote the glories of the Catholic Church in traditionally Protestant Silesia. There are churches designed or altered by Dientzenhofer in the surrounding villages of Verneřovice, Ruprechtice, Heřmánkovice, Bezděkov, Vižnov, Šonov and Křinice. But the finest of the commissions obtained for Dientzenhofer by Zinke was that of the abbey church of Swieta Jadwiga at Legnickie Pole (Wahlstatt), which lies some 20km to the N and is now in Polish territory.

4 Prague to Harrachov

Total distance 127km. Prague—D10/E65 19km *Brandýs nad Labem/
Stará Boleslav*—35km **Mladá Boleslav**—31km *Turnov* (**Český ráj**)—
42km *Harrachov*

The popular resorts of the Bohemian Paradise (Český ráj) and Giant
Mountains (Krkonoše) are easily accessible from Prague by way of
the D10/E65, which is a dual carriageway almost as far as Turnov.
Until just after Mladá Boleslav the landscape is flat and of little
interest. *Brandýs nad Labem*, 19km N of Prague and 2km W of the
motorway, is a town dating back to the 14C and which formerly had a
large Jewish population. It was greatly favoured by the Emperor
Rudolph II, who frequently hunted on the game reserve here. The
medieval castle on the left bank of the Labe was transformed by the
Emperor Ferndinand I in the early 16C into a four-wing Renaissance
mansion; the building was further embellished by Rudolph II, who
employed Italian craftsmen and architects in the creation of a fine
series of terraces and gardens. The once separate township of *Stará
Boleslav* on the other side of the river is a smaller and generally more
attractive place than Brandýs. Its quiet main square is entered
through a Gothic gateway, the only survival of the town's fortifications, which were constructed originally in the 10C by the brother of
King Wenceslas, Boleslav. Jealous of Wenceslas' popularity with the
Czech people, Boleslav killed his brother in 929, supposedly outside
the church on the opposite side of the square to the gateway (this
church, now ·named after the murdered king, was rebuilt in the
baroque period). A statue of Wenceslas of 1894 stands in the middle
of the square.

17km further N along the D10/E65 is the exit to *Benátky nad
Jizerou*, a village rising on an isolated wooded hill above the river
Jizera. The place is dominated by its *Renaissance Castle*, which
belonged for many centuries to the Thun family. In the late 16C the
Thuns were patrons to the astronomers Tycho de Brahe and
Johannes Kepler, both of whom stayed and worked at Benátky
immediately after their arrival in Bohemia; an imaginary account of
life in the castle at this time is featured in the novel Kepler (1981) by
the Irish writer John Banville. A later guest at the castle was the
composer Smetana, who was put up here while working as a music
teacher to the Thuns in the early 1840s. The castle is now an old
people's home, and only its courtyard and overgrown gardens can be
seen. The main features of the exterior are a tall tower used by Tycho
de Brahe and Kepler as an observatory, and, in the courtyard, some
extensive and remarkable Renaissance sgraffito work featuring
scenes both from the Old Testament and of hunting; from the
gardens there are panoramic views over the fertile Jizera Valley.

Back on the D10/E65 after 13km you will reach **Mladá Boleslav**, a
town of 13C origin which has grown into a large industrial centre since
the construction in 1895 of the Laurin and Klement factory; this
factory, built at first to produce bicycles, later developed into the
Škoda Automobile works, the most important car manufacturers in
Czechoslovakia. The dirty and poorly maintained old part of town is
spread along a ridge, encircled by fragments of 13C walls; at its
southern end is a medieval castle which was remodelled in the 16C
and unhappily restored in recent years to house a Regional Museum.
North of the castle is a main square containing a Gothic church heavily
altered in the baroque period, and a 16C Town Hall distinguished on

the outside by sgraffito decorations of allegorical figures. On the northern outskirts of the old town is the small baroque church of St. John (sv. Jana) (with an altarpiece of 1727 by V.V. Reiner), while further N, beyond the enormous Škoda factory, you will come to the pleasant wooded suburb of Kosmonosy; in the middle of a bosky public park is an imposing Renaissance mansion which was rebuilt in the 18C and is now a school building in an advanced stage of decay.

The town of *Mnichovo Hradiště*, 10km further N, is associated with the Czech partisan Jan Šverma, who was born at 38 Palacký Street in 1901; he was killed by the Nazis in 1944. Exhibits relating to Šverma's life are contained in the Municipal Museum, which is housed in the 17C mansion on the town's northern outskirts. This enormous and austerely decorated building, at present closed for much-needed restoration, is preceded by an elegant though little cared for formal garden, which in turn is enveloped by a large English-style park. Begun in the early 17C on the site of a 13C fortress, it belonged at first to Kryštof Budovec, one of the Protestant leaders who fought against the emperor Ferdinand II in the Battle of the White Mountain of 1620. The place was subsequently confiscated from him, and, like many such properties, ended up in the possession of General Albrecht von Wallenstein, who by 1725 could boast of being the owner of over 50 castles and villages in Bohemia. Wallenstein himself was by no means consistent in his loyalty to the emperor, and his opportunism and scheming eventually led to his murder in Cheb at the hands of four English mercenaries. His body was afterwards brought to Mnichovo Hradiště, and now lies in a 17C Capuchin chapel to the N of the house.

As you continue N towards Turnov, you will have your first glimpse to the right of the stone monoliths and dense forest that comprise the area known as Český ráj ('the Bohemian Paradise'). *Turnov*, a popular centre for exploring this area, is a small and unremarkable town, but with a pleasant forested setting and a centuries-old reputation for jewellery and semi-precious stones (in particular for red Bohemian garnets); a large collection of such stones, together with panels devoted to the local jewellery industry, are contained in the Municipal Museum. In the northern outskirts of the town is the castle of *Hrubý Rohozec*, a late Gothic structure remodelled in a Renaissance style and containing much of its original decoration, as well as a large collection of weapons.

The bizarre sandstone rock formations of the **Český ráj** constitute one of several such curiosities in eastern and northern Bohemia, most notably in the Adršpach–Teplice area and near Hřensko. During the early Mesozoic era deposits of sand and calcium clay were created here by the sea; when the water receded there remained chalk tables that were later eroded by rain water to form honeycombs, hollows, and fantastical phallic-like projections. It was during the Romantic period that these rocks protruding through the pines came to exert a widespread fascination, those in the Bohemian Paradise having the added Romantic attraction of ruined castles in the vicinity. The first attempts to scale the rocks were made in the early 19C, but it was not until the 1960s that climbers were drawn here in large numbers. The Bohemian Paradise, a relatively small area, is criss-crossed today with footpaths, and it is possible to walk its entire length, from Turnov to Jičín, in a long day.

For those visiting the area by car, take the D35 SW towards Jičín. Just outside the town, hidden among trees to the right of the road, stands the ruined castle of *Valdštejn*, 13C in origin but much altered in the 15C, 18C and early 19C; abandoned later in the 19C, its picturesque wooded setting helped to maintain its popularity with landscape painters and poets, among whom were K.H. Mácha. 5km further on you pass through the village of *Hrubá skála*, notable for its castle and nearby rock formations, the latter being among the most extensive in the area and sometimes described as forming a 'rock town' or 'ghost city'; to see them you should leave the main road and take the turning to the right marked Vyskeř. Back on the D35 continue for 2km and then turn right towards the hamlet of Troskovice; before reaching the hamlet you will come to a car park, from where there is a steep forest path ascending to the ruins of **Trosky Castle**, a landmark visible from far around and one of the most romantic sites in eastern Bohemia. Of this late 14C building (the name of which means 'Ruins'), only two towers survive, both implausibly perched on soaring pinnacles of rock. The pointed, jagged outline of the towers merges almost imperceptibly with the twisted forms of the rock, creating structures resembling those in the fantastical pen sketches of the Romantic writer and artist Victor Hugo. The taller of the two rocks can be climbed up to the base of the tower and is known as 'Věž Bába' or 'Grandmother Rock' to distinguish it from 'Věž Panna' or 'Girl Rock'. The view from the top is quite magnificent , and extends well beyond the surrounding trees of the Bohemian Paradise to embrace an endless undulating patchwork of meadows, cultivated fields and distant woods.

Returning to your car, continue past Troskovice and rejoin the D35 at Újezd, from where it is a 12km drive to Jičín. Alternatively you can turn right at Újezd towards Mladejov and then take the first side road to the left, passing, 3km before Jičín, the *Prachovské skály* rock formations. The latter include not only pinnacles but also a number of rocks perforated so as to form dramatic bridges and gateways; recent archaeological evidence shows that the site was inhabited in prehistoric times and that there was also a Slav settlement here.

The town of **Jičín** is well worth a visit for its arcaded main square, the best preserved in this part of Bohemia, and lined almost entirely with Renaissance and 17C houses. Its dominant building is the palace of Albrecht von Wallenstein, occupying the site of a medieval castle and transformed between 1630–34 into a ducal residence; the interior now houses a Regional Art Gallery of little interest, but the elegant Italianate courtyard should be seen. The architect, the Italian Nicolo Sebregondi, was also commissioned by Wallenstein to undertake the replanning and reconstruction of much of the town, but building work was terminated after Wallenstein's murder in 1634. Assisted by his compatriots Spezza and Pieroni, Sebregondi was none the less able to complete, in a very short space of time, a relatively large number of buildings, including the new town church of *St. James* (sv. Jakub), one of the first centrally planned structures of its type in Bohemia. The same team was also responsible for the large Cartusian Monastery at nearby Valdice (this is now a prison and inaccessible).

Return to Turnov along the D35 and continue on the D10/E65 to *Harrachov* (42km), a popular centre for touring Krkonoše (the Giant Mountains; see Route 5).

5 Harrachov to Trutnov

Total distance 60km. Harrachov—D14 (to Trutnov, then side-roads)—31km *Vrchlabí*—29km **Trutnov**.

The Giant Mountains (known in Czech as Krkonoše) mark the northernmost frontier of eastern Bohemia, and are by far the most popular tourist attraction of this region, drawing large numbers of Czech and German visitors both in summer and winter. The mountains are not as spectacular as their name suggests, having gently rounded summits, and being largely obscured by dense forests. Yet they include the highest mountain in Bohemia (Mt Sněžka, 1600m), and give birth to one of the main rivers of Europe, the Labe. Though mild in appearance, the mountains are also famous for their extreme and very changeable weather conditions, and indeed have average temperatures and snowfalls comparable to those of much higher peaks in the Alps.

Dating back to the palaeozoic age, 400 million years ago, the Giant Mountains seem to have acquired more or less their present shape in the Tertiary era. Their first mention in history is a Slav document of 1110 referring to them as Krkonoše. Already by the 13C their natural resources were being exploited: gold and other metals were mined, trees cut down, and glassworks founded. In the 15C and 16C the activity of the area was greatly increased by the arrival of prospectors from Italy, who went further and further afield in their hunt for minerals and metals. The population of the area was at this date still concentrated almost entirely along its four river valleys, the only other habitations being isolated wooden huts used occasionally by shepherds. The Italian prospectors, with characteristic Italian exaggeration and fantasy, appear to have given colourful accounts of their excursions into the mountains, and the area soon developed a reputation for its wild aspect and supernatural occurrences. It was not so long after the arrival of the Italians that the mountains came to be known by the Latin name of 'Montes Gigantum', a reference not to their size but to a mysterious giant on whom responsibility was placed for the sudden and violent storms that are typical of this area. This giant, now called Krakonoš (Rübezahl in German), is today the tourist mascot of the area, and features in countless postcards and other souvenirs, resembling not so much a terrifying monster but rather an elderly and hirsute German hiker, complete with green jacket, hunter's hat, pipe and wooden stick.

Mining activity in the Giant Mountains declined with the Thirty Years' War, and was soon superseded by cattle breeding and pasturing: the primitive shepherds' huts, known as 'Boudas', were transformed by the 18C into large farmsteads. With the rapid development of tourism here after 1800, the name 'Bouda' came to be applied to tourist chalets and eventually to hotels—an idiosyncrasy of the area. Skiing was first practised in the Giant Mountains in the 1880s, and today the whole range has more ski-tracks and chair-lifts than any other part of Bohemia. The interests of tourism have frequently run counter to those of ecology, and the fate of the area arouses growing concern in Czechoslovakia. It is an area famed for its botanical life, and is often regarded as a transitional zone between the vegetation of northern and southern Europe. Alpine plants grow in the ravines, rare flora dating back to the post-ice age are to be found in the upper peat-bogs, while on the meadows on the middle slopes are endemic plants such as the bell-flower (*Campanula Bohemica*). In 1963 an area of 40,000 hectares was turned into the Krkonoše National Park, the first and as yet only such park in Bohemia, and—together with the park on the Polish side of the mountains—the largest natural reserve in central Europe. However, though this has done something to check commercial exploitation of the area, there still remains the daunting problem of pollution, coming not only from nearby industrial works in Bohemia, but also from ones in Poland and eastern Germany. Acid rain has affected the Giant Mountains more severely than any other part of Europe, and large stretches of forest have a pitiful desiccated look; among the wild life casualties has been the lynx, killed off through the destruction of its main food sources.

Harrachov, the main resort in the western half of the Giant Mountains, is a long, sprawling place which was formed in the early 18C by the joining together of three separate settlements along the Mumlava Valley. The name of the town is derived from that of the former lords of the area, one of whom, Count Ferdinand Bonaventura of Harrach, founded a glass factory here in the early 18C which is still functioning; the art of the Harrachov glass manufacturers can be seen in the showroom of the factory, in a chandelier in the church of St. Wenceslas, and in the modest Museum of Glass which is situated at the very centre of the town. As a winter resort, Harrachov boasts the largest ski-jump platform in Czechoslovakia. One of the finest walks in the vicinity is up to the tourist chalet of Vosecká bouda (2½ hours). This walk follows for most of its length the narrow, wooded banks of the Mumlava, and passes after 20 minutes a small waterfall, a popular beauty spot; shortly before the river's source the path divides into two, the path to the right taking you to Labská bouda (see below), the one to the left to Vosecká bouda. At Vosecká bouda, you will find yourself above the tree level and just below the western end of the Path of Czechoslovak–Polish Friendship. This latter path, swerving in and out of Polish and Czechoslovak territory, follows the ridge of the Giant Mountains for 28km, up to the Pomezní boudy chalets. It is certainly the best introduction to the area, though until recently was out of bounds to westerners.

Most of the main viewpoints in the Giant Mountains are accessible either by car or chair-lift. To reach these you have to make a number of turnings off the D14, which runs parallel to the entire range of the mountains while never affording any extensive panorama of them. You join the road 3km to the S of Harrachov, and follow at first the pleasantly wooded upper valley of the Jizera. After 21km you come to the hamlet of Hrabačov, where there is a cross-road: turning right here you will soon reach the village of Jilemnice (outside of which is a museum of folk costume housed in a mansion of 18C origin), while on turning left you will begin the steep 18km climb up to the tiny tourist chalet of Vrbatova bouda, on the ridge of the Giant Mountains. The views from this lonely spot are among the most dramatic in the area, and include, to the E, the rounded, forlorn peak of Mt Sněžka. You will also find around here a number of bunkers that were put up in the 1930s with the intention of warding off a Nazi invasion. Another sorry memorial—and one which serves as a salutary reminder of the potential dangers of the Giant Mountains—is to Bohumil Hance and Václav Vabata, two champion Czech skiers who were killed here in 1913 while skiing in adverse conditions. Northwest of this monument an unasphalted track leads to Labská bouda, a large, isolated and dramatically-situated modern hotel, almost literally hanging over Poland.

A short walk to the W of Labská bouda brings you to the source of the Labe, around which are placed the coats of arms of the major towns which the river later passes, including the one at its estuary, Hamburg. To the E of Labská bouda runs a beautiful footpath which follows the Labe down to the resort of Špindlerův Mlýn (2½ hours), passing on the way a couple of waterfalls. To reach this resort by car from Labská bouda, you have to return all the way to the D14, and then follow this for 7km to *Vrchlabí*. This quiet town is worth a short stop to see its Regional Museum, which is taken up almost entirely by a permanent exhibition pretentiously called 'Stone and Life'. This didactic exhibition, displayed in a former Augustinian convent founded in 1705 by Count Maximilian Morzin, is devoted largely to the ecology of the Giant Mountains National Park, and features a taped commentary, slide projections and illuminated panels: the ground-floor rooms deal with the main vegetation belts of the mountains, while in the basement is a tank representing a cross section of a typical mountain brook, and including live birds and fish.

Leaving the D14 at Vrchlabí head N to *Špindlerův Mlýn* (17km), which is the most central of the Giant Mountains' resorts, and in many ways the most pleasant. Leisurely laid out among trees and meadows sloping down to the Labe, it has a range of homely hotels which is rare for Czechoslovakia: among these are the expensive Hotel Savoy, the cheap and humble Starta and the privately-owned Humbertus, three timber-framed structures dating from the turn of the century, the last one having originally been a pub. Špindlerův Mlýn has also the advantage of being virtually traffic-free, as all visitors' cars have to be left in the car park on the southern outskirts of the resort. A special permit is needed for drivers intending to drive from the resort up to the ridge of the Giant Mountains (8km), where there is a large tourist chalet (Špindlerova bouda). 2km along this road is the Koliba Myslivna, where you can eat excellent game (served with a juniper berry sauce) in a rustic setting. 3km further up is a track to the right leading precipitously down to what must be among the most attractive of the Giant Mountains' tourist chalets: these, the Jelení boudy, include a number of timbered 19C farm buildings with beautiful views over woods and mountain meadows.

It is possible to walk from Špindlerův Mlýn to the summit of Mt Sněžka in 3½ hours. To make the ascent by a combination of road and chair lift, you have to drive back to Vrchlabí, drive E for 20km along the D14, and then turn left towards Pec pod Sněžkou. 8km before the turning is a road marked to *Hostinné*, a leading paper-making centre and the birthplace of the graphic artist K.V. Klíč (1841–1926), the inventor of collotype and photogravure printing techniques; in a former monastery church here, you will now find the Museum of Antique Art, a collection of casts from famous Greek and Roman statues. An alternative route to Pec is along the side-road through Janské Lázně (turn left 8km after Vrchlabí). *Janské Lázně*, hidden among trees on the lower slopes of Mt Černá (1290m), is a small spa resort, with a number of elegant buildings from the mid 19C; the popularity of the spa greatly increased after the First World War, with the discovery that its waters were beneficial for those suffering from polio. The main tourist attraction of the place is the funicular climb up to Mt Černá; the funicular, completed in 1928, is the oldest in Czechoslovakia. 3km beyond Janské Lázně you come to the main road connecting the D14 with Pec.

Pec pod Sněžkou, the main resort on the eastern side of the Giant Mountains, is dominated by a tall hotel block inappropriately named the Hotel Horizont. Those intending to take the chairlift to the summit of Mt Sněžka, Bohemia's highest mountain, are obliged to leave their cars outside the hotel and walk from here to the chair-lift station (1.5km). The popular ascent up to *Mt Sněžka* is made in two stages (near the half-way point is an excellent small restaurant serving local specialities). The chair-lift is a very old one and inadequate for the large number of people who daily queue to use it; a new one is planned, but this is being strongly opposed by environmentalists, who are worried that the unique ecology of the mountain will be damaged even further. Crowds have been attracted to Mt Sněžka since at least 1880, when the first Czech guidebook to Bohemia described the scene as 'comparable to an ant hill: tourists with their rucksacks, salesmen with half barrels of beer or water, sedan chair porters to carry delicate ladies or stern people up and down...' The bare summit of the mountain is not for lovers of sublime, solitary places, and is covered with a dense accretion of ugly, decaying structures: the oldest of these is a circular 16C stone structure which has served both as a chapel and a pub. Matters are not helped by the summit being on the Polish border: menacing signs warn you not to cross a particular line, and there are soldiers with machine guns to reinforce these instructions.

9km E of the junction of the Pec road and the D14 is **Trutnov**, a district capital and a place sometimes referred to as 'the Gateway to the Giant Mountains'; its imposing main square features a number of recently restored Renaissance and baroque houses. Trutnov is a popular centre of excursions both to the Giant Mountains and to the curious rock formations in between Ardšbach and Teplice, 14km NE of the town (follow the side-road to the Polish frontier, turn right to Chvalec, and then left to Ardšbach). These rocks, comparable to those of the Bohemian Paradise (see Route 3), were visited by Goethe in 1770.

6   Harrachov to Děčín

Total distance 120km. Harrachov—E65, then Road 14 23km
Jablonec nad Nisou—13km *Liberec*—E442 45km *Zákupy*—30km
Benešov n. Ploučnici—9km *Děčín*.

South from Harrachov (see Route 5) the E65 descends sharply
through forests to Tanvald (10km), where you turn right on to Road
14 to *Jablonec* (13km), a small, industrial town set in the valley in
between the Giant and Jizera mountains. Jablonec is today a place of
bland and exclusively modern appearance, but it has had an international reputation over the centuries for its glass and costume
jewellery.

Documents attest to glass being made in the Jablonec area as early as the 14C,
but it was not until the second half of the 16C that the trade became firmly
established here, the then virtually untouched surrounding forests providing
the large amount of wood necessary for the furnaces. The Renaissance glass-
makers of this area improved on the greenish 'sylvan' glass of the preceding
period, but as yet were unable to emulate the clear glass produced at this time
in Venice; the shape and decoration of the vessels created here were distinctly
German, with crudely painted and engraved heraldic motifs and genre scenes.
By the late 17C extensive experimentation had led to the creation in North
Bohemia of a new type of glass involving potash and a high proportion of chalk.
This glass was not only of far greater brilliance than that of before, but also had
many of the properties of rock crystal and thus made possible intricate and
sophisticated engraving—the hall-mark of 'Bohemian glass'. The fame of
Bohemian glass spread widely, helped by the efforts of itinerant traders from
the area, whose journeys established trade links with places as far apart as
Moscow, Constantinople and Stockholm. However, from c 1725 the main centre
for the manufacture of such glass shifted from Bohemia to Silesia, where most of
the finest glass of the German rococo was produced. The one unrivalled
speciality of the Jablonec area from the early 18C onwards was the manufacture
of costume jewellery, an industry which developed after c 1711 with the
invention of the so-called 'Turnov paste', a pot metal of special composition
which was capable of imitating many types of precious stone. Despite a serious
slump in the 1930s, costume jewellery has become once again the main industry
of Jablonec, and one of Czechoslovakia's most important exports.

An interest in glass and costume jewellery is the only good reason for
stopping at Jablonec, which is a town almost devoid of architectural
or historical monuments. The only buildings worth remarking date
from the early years of this century, and the largest and finest of
these—in the very centre of the town—houses the *Glass and Costume Jewellery Museum* (Muzeum Skla a Bižuterie). This tentative
Art Nouveau construction of c 1900, dark and dirty on the outside,
but with a completely modernised interior, was originally the export
house of a large fashion jewellery company. Its clearly arranged
collections have an excellent chronological display of glass and
jewellery from the Middle Ages right up to modern times, including
exquisite examples of Bohemian cut glass, and bizarre Art Nouveau
works; among the jewellery on display is 'ebony glass', which
enjoyed a particular popularity in Victorian England owing to the
mourning fashions of that time. Fashion and costume jewellery is
made today at the Jablonex factory on the outskirts of the town. The
work produced here might not be to everyone's taste, but should you
want to see it, you should visit the export showrooms, at 2777

Opletalova. The setting is at least pleasant—a handsome if over-restored Art Nouveau building.

A short drive W of Jablonec, along Road 13/E442, leads you shortly into *Liberec*, the largest town in North Bohemia. This sprawling, amorphous place dating back to the early Middle Ages, rapidly expanded in the late 19C, thanks largely to its thriving textile industry. Its most impressive monuments are largely of this period, including the eclectic former *Town Hall* (now the seat of the local council), which rises to an extraordinary height above the large and pompous central square. It was built in 1893 by the Viennese architect Neumann, who was also responsible for the rebuilding of the Altes Rathaus in Vienna. The most salient features of its exterior are its tall and steeply pitched roofs, its pointed Flemish-style gables, and its three remarkably elongated towers with complex piles of ornament tapering out to needle-like spires; beautiful stained-glass windows adorn the stair-case well inside. Of the same period, but in attractive parkland surroundings, is the imposing German Renaissance style building housing the most important of the town's several museums. This, the *North Bohemian Museum* (Severočeské muzeum) has objects relating to local history and natural history, as well as a fine collection of applied arts objects, most notably porcelain.

Dominating the skyline to the W of Liberec is Mt Ještěd (1012m), which is crowned by an enormous spaceship-like object which functions as a hotel, revolving restaurant and television tower. Another excursion can be made to the Jizera mountains (Jizerské hory), which stand to the N of the town, occupying a narrow wedge of land between Germany and Poland. The outstanding monument in this area is the castle at *Frýdlant*, 23km due N of Liberec on the main road to Poland. The castle, projecting romantically above a dense forest of pines, dates back to the mid 13C, but was largely rebuilt in a Renaissance style by the late 16C Lombard architect Marco Spazzio. One of the many Czech properties appropriated by Albrecht von Wallenstein at the beginning of the 17C, it was later acquired by the Clam-Gallas family, under whom extensive rebuild-ing was carried out in the 19C. The courtyard is distinguished by its extensive sgraffito decoration, while inside are a series of 19C panelled rooms of pseudo-medieval appearance. There is a gallery of works by the leading Czech baroque artists, including a Portrait of Count Sporck by P. Brandl.

The village below the castle has a faded charm of its own, with a quiet main square on which can be seen (at No. 7) a pale blue 18C house decorated with stuccoed scenes of an amorous nature. Nearby stands the 16C Church of the Holy Rood, containing the *Sepulchre of Melchior, Catherine and Christopher of Redern* (1605–10). This work, the masterpiece of Gerhard Heinrich from Amsterdam, is one of the finest tombs to be seen in Czechoslovakia outside Prague. Though closely similiar to Venetian altar tombs of the Renaissance, it has elements that look ahead to the baroque, such as the dynamic poses of some of its figures, and the clustering of columns in its centre.

You can continue a tour of the Jizera district by heading E from Frýdlant to Hejnice (10km), and from there take the turning to the right to nearby *Lázně Libverda*, a tiny spa-town in a verdant valley. Known for its healing springs since at least the 16C, this pleasantly old-fashioned place attracted in the 19C a number of famous visitors, including the writer Božena Němcová, the scholar and Czech nationalist Josef Jungmann, and the composer Carl Maria von Weber, who conceived here part of his opera, Der Freischutz. The present spa buildings are of the early years of this century, and include a delightful promenade overlooking a small garden. A curiosity behind the village is the Obří sud, a restaurant taking the form of a gigantic beer barrel. The road E of Hejnice will take you into the heart of the Jizera mountains, though as a result of military installations is at present officially closed to western visitors. The devastation caused by acid rain resulting from unchecked industrial development in Czechoslovakia, Poland and eastern Germany is pitifully apparent in the burnt-out forested landscape which you have to pass through.

Continuing your journey W from Liberec along the E442, turn S at Lvová (26km) until you reach Mimoň (12km). The small town of *Zákupy* lies 7km to the W, along the road to Česká Lípa. The parish church is of the 16C, but the main interest is the sprawling castle on the outskirts, a construction with a mainly baroque exterior and a formal terraced garden in a French style. Napoleon's son was made Duke of Zákupy in 1818, but never took up residence here. In 1850–53, the castle was adapted as a residence for Archduke Ferdinand, and the interior was redecorated by artists such as Josef Navrátil, who painted some rooms with rococo motifs; the castle can today be visited on a guided tour, but the place has suffered greatly from a recent fire.

From Zákupy you can make a short detour S to what is now known as *Mácha's Region* after the Czech romantic poet of the last century, Karel Hynek Mácha. Take the side road which joins Zákupy to Road 38, and then head S for 4km in the direction of Mladá Boleslav. You will then come to Lake Mácha (Máchovo jezero), a large lake used for swimming and sailing, and with densely forested hills coming directly down to the water's edge. Mácha, a native of North Bohemia, was enamoured of the lake and its surroundings and found inspiration here for his most popular poem, May (1836). From the village of Doksy, on the southern shores of the lake, you can retrace one of the poet's favourite walks by following the 8km path to the ruined medieval castle of *Bezděz* (those wishing to do the journey by car can continue S along Road 38 for a further 7km and then turn off to the left). Built in 1264–78 by King Přemysl Otakar II, Bezděz was made a royal residence in 1350 by Emperor Charles IV. After the Thirty Years' War the castle, once one of the most important in Bohemia after Karlštejn (see Route 2C), fell into ruins. The combination of ruins, pine trees and a formidable history later made it a great place of pilgrimage for romantics and nationalists, attracting the likes not only of Mácha but also of the composer Bedřich Smetana, who set here one of the scenes in his opera, The Secret (Tajemství).

Driving W from Zákupy in the direction of Česká Lípa, you come shortly to the banks of the river Ploučnice, which you follow all the way NW to Děčín. 22km after Česká Lípa is the very attractive small town of *Benešov nad Ploučnici*, which has a sloping and toy-like main square surrounded by old buildings. Among these are the upper and lower castles, both built by Friedrich de Salhausen in the early 16C. The lower of the two, intended for Friedrich's oldest son, is the only one which can be visited at present (the upper one is expected to reopen in 1992 following extensive restoration). Recorded early music accompanies you as you walk around its simple and tastefully restored Renaissance rooms, one of which is a well preserved kitchen; there are collections of armoury from the Thirty Years' War, 16C and 17C furniture, and—in a room above the entrance gate—a group of mainly Empire clocks.

The large industrial town of *Děčín* is attractively situated at the junction of the rivers Ploučnice and Labe, hemmed in by wooded hills. On its SE outskirts, dwarfed by flyovers, is a small and neglected baroque footbridge with a sculptural group in the middle by J.M. Brokoff; these sculptures are shortly to be sent to the Lapidarium in Prague, and replaced by copies. Dominating the centre of the town, and occupying a lofty position above the Labe is a vast castle dating mainly from the baroque period, and preceded by formal, terraced gardens; Chopin was a guest here in 1835. The building is at present a school for Russian children, and cannot be visited.

7   Prague to Děčín

Total distance 116km. Prague—E55 to 45km *Roudnice nad Labem*—19km **Terezín**—2km **Litoměřice**—26km *Ústí nad Labem*—24km to *Děčín*.

The most direct route to North Bohemia from Prague is along the E55, a road which takes you through a predominantly flat landscape. The one prominent natural landmark comes into view a few kilometres N of Veltrusy (see Route 2E). This, the Říp Mountain, is a basaltic cone rising in isolation to a height of 459m above the surrounding fields. According to legend, Čech, the first Bohemian to arrive in the country, stood on top of this hill and was so impressed by the beauty of the surrounding landscape and abundance of game that he decided to found Bohemia. On top of the hill is a chapel founded by the 12C king Soběslav I in commemoration of a victory over the German emperor Lothair.

North of the Říp Mountain, and a 4km drive E of the E55, is the town of *Roudnice nad Labem*. This small town, built on a bend of the river Labe, is huddled around its monumental baroque *castle*. Erected between 1653–65 over the foundations of a 13C fortified residence belonging to the Archbishops of Prague, the castle was designed by the Italian-born architect Francesco Caratti. This 16-bay structure, articulated by giant Doric pilasters, is impressively grand, though it seems a tentative work in comparison with Caratti's subsequent Černín Palace in Prague, where the pilasters are replaced by a giant order of columns. The building has served for a long time as a military musical academy, and its art collections—amassed by the Pernštejns and the Lobkowicz—have been taken to Prague and Nelahozeves. However in the former stables near the palace has been tastefully installed a small but select *Gallery of 20C Czech Art*. There are Cubist works by Emil Filla and Jaroslav Král, but the highpoint of the museum is a large collection of Impressionist-style works by Antonín Slavíček: the latter were acquired by a friend of the artist, August Švagrovský, who came from Roudnice and of whom there is a portrait here by Miloš Jiránek. Among the other attractions of Roudnice are two buildings by Octaviano Broggio, an Italian baroque architect who settled in Litoměřice and produced much work in northern Bohemia. One of his buildings at Roudnice is his reconstruction of the 14C church belonging to the former Augustinian monastery: this is of interest largely for its decorative detailing, in which he gives a baroque interpretation to Gothic forms. His small chapel of St. William, built in 1720, is decorated by colourful *frescoes* by V.V. Reiner, painted in 1729 and representing the Holy Trinity surrounded by Virtues.

Regaining the E55 and continuing to head N, you will soon pass on the left the former convent of *Doksany*. Founded as a Premonstraten-sian nunnery in 1144 by Vladislav II's queen, Gertrude, it was the scene in 1619 of a peasant revolt against the absolute authority of the Church; completely rebuilt after 1679, it was dissolved at the end of the 18C and converted into a château. The entrance gate to this vast complex is of undulating design, while inside the church is a painting by Petr Brandl of the Birth of the Virgin Mary and—in the dome—illusionistic frescoes by a Bohemian follower of A. Pozzo, Jan Hiebel; there are biblical frescoes by F.A. Palko in what was originally the refectory of the convent.

Some 9.5km beyond Doksany, on the banks of the river Ohře, is the so-called **Small Fortress of Terezín**, the sturdiest and best-fortified section of a defensive complex founded in 1780 by Joseph II and which included the adjoining town of *Terezín*. This grim and once impregnable complex is a fascinating example of neo-classical military architecture, but it is essentially its terrible history, first under the Austrians, and then the Nazis, which draws visitors to the place today.

The small fortress of Terezín, known originally as Theresienstadt, was one of the more notorious political prisons in the Habsburg Empire, acquiring especial fame after 1914 when Gavrilo Princip was imprisoned here for his part in the assassination of Archduke Ferdinand at Sarajevo. At the end of the First World War he was joined here by 560 soldiers who had participated in an anti-military rebellion in the North Bohemian town of Rumburk. Though Theresienstadt was a place with a frightening reputation, conditions under the Habsburgs were as nothing in comparison to what they were to be under the Nazis, who in 1940 established in the Small Fortress a police prison headed by the infamous Heinrich Jöckel. The following year the townspeople in Terezín itself were cleared, and the town turned into a ghetto numbering c 250,000 Jews, of whom 80,000 were eventually deported to Auschwitz, Treblinka and Majdanek, and many others died of hunger. For crimes committed in the ghetto Jews were imprisoned in the Small Fortress, which though officially a place for political prisoners rather than for extermination, assumed the character of a concentration camp. In April 1945 an epidemic of both enteric and spotted fever broke out here, and spread quickly owing to the appalling conditions. Soon afterwards the advancing Russian army forced the Nazis to abandon the place and its prisoners. Jöckel fled to Bavaria, but was eventually caught and imprisoned in the Small Fortress before being tried at Litoměřice and sentenced to be hung. The Jewish ghetto at Terezín occupies an important place in the history of Czech culture, owing to the large number of musicians, artists and writers who were interned here. Probably for propaganda reasons, the Nazis permitted a flourishing cultural life at Terezín, and the scores of at least 50 musical pieces composed here have survived, including works by Pavel Haas (1899–1944), Egon Ledec (1889–1944) and Hans Krasa (1899–1944); there was even an active jazz band known as 'The Ghetto Swingers', the members of which were largely drawn from the Jazz Quintet Weiss, a celebrated group from Prague. The internees were also allowed a studio for drawing, and a powerful group of drawings portraying ghetto life has been preserved in the State Jewish Museum in Prague; the two men in charge of this studio were Bedřich Fritta (1906–44) and Karel Fleischmann (1897–1944). Some of the writers who survived the ghetto later wrote vivid fictionalised accounts of their experiences here, most notably the short-story writer Arnold Lustig; one author, J.R. Pick, even managed to write a humorous novel about Terezín called The Society for the Prevention of Cruelty to Animals, the plot of which involves a group of Jewish youngsters who catch and eat the pets of SS guards to protect the beasts from exposure to their masters. The opening story of My First Loves (1985) by Ivan Klíma (1931–) is a childhood impression of life in the ghetto, while both the ghetto and the Small Fortress feature in the novel A Change of Skin by the Mexican writer Carlos Fuentes, who visited Terezín in 1961 and 1963.

The Small Fortress is today a memorial to Nazi atrocities, and a symbolic cemetery commemorating those whom they murdered has been laid out in front of its main entrance. There are excellent and very informative English-speaking guides to accompany you on the harrowing visit to the fortress, which has been little altered since Nazi times even to the extent that the chilling and ironic words *ARBEIT MACHT FREI* ('Work makes Free', the slogan of the concentration camps) have been left above the entrance gate to one of the yards. Among the many cells that you are shown is one intended originally for 40 prisoners but which was filled with over 100 people by the Nazis; grimmer still is a small damp cell into which 60 Jews were crammed and forced to sleep standing up. You are shown too the cell in which Princip was incarcerated, a space containing today mementoes both of him and the Sarajevo assassination; Princip was condemned to 20 years imprisonment, but died here of tuberculosis after only four years. An underground passage leads from the Small Fortress to the former Ghetto of Terezín, which is surrounded by defensive canals, and is taken up today by a great barracks.

The large industrial town of **Litoměřice**, once the third or fourth city in Bohemia, rises up on the right bank of the Labe 2km to the N of Terezín and just above the confluence of the Ohře. Founded in 1230, it has kept today parts of its mighty original fortifications. However, much of the medieval town was destroyed in the Thirty Years' War, and most of the old buildings that survive today are of the baroque period. Polluted and with an overall covering of grey, Litoměřice might not be one of the most cheerful places in Bohemia, but it has much of architectural interest, as well as an excellent art gallery. The architects who left the greatest mark on the town were Giovanni Broggio and his son Ottavio: the former, an Italian immigrant, settled in around 1668 at Litoměřice, where his son—the more important of the two—was born that same year. At the SE corner of the large and dirty main square, the náměstí Míru, is the Church of All Saints (sv. všech svatých), a late Gothic foundation remodelled by O. Broggio in 1718, and containing rich stucco decorations inside. The narrow Jesuitská Street, leads S from here to the Jesuit Church of Our Lady, a large red ochre building built by O. Broggio between 1704–31; a bridge connects the church with the former Jesuit College where the leading Czech nationalist and compiler of the first Czech-German dictionary, Josef Jungmann, taught between 1799 and 1815. Heading off from the north-eastern corner of the main square is the Velká Dominikánská, on which stands O. Broggio's church of St. James (sv. Jakub), distinguished by a tall and powerful façade now in a deplorable condition.

The main monuments of Litoměřice lie W of the main square, beginning with the *Regional Museum* on the Michelská. Housed in the former Renaissance Town Hall, it was founded in 1874 and is one of the oldest museums in North Bohemia. On the ground floor is to be seen the museum's greatest treasure, indeed one of the finest and most famous cycle of Renaissance paintings in Bohemia—the six remaining panels of the so-called **Litoměřice Altarpiece**.

The panels, representing scenes from the Passion and the Life of the Virgin, were probably painted around 1500. The unknown artist, sometimes identified with the German Hans Elfelder, is always referred to as the Master of Litoměřice, and is also thought to have been responsible for the celebrated frescoes in the upper level of the St. Wencesclas Chapel in St. Vitus's Cathedral, Prague. The artist, who was a far more sophisticated painter than his contemporaries in Bohemia, was almost certainly a court painter to Vladislav Jagiello, and probably executed the Litoměřice Altarpiece for the All Saints' Church attached to the Royal Palace in Prague Castle. It is likely to have been removed from this church after 1541, when the building was damaged by a severe fire; the surviving panels are generally identified today with a group of scenes of the Passion documented as being presented in 1633 to the Church of All Saints in Litoměřice by the Imperial magistrate of this town, Herold of Stod.

In the same room as the powerfully realistic panels by the Master of Litoměřice is an expressive Crucifixion by Wolfgang Katzheimer (d. 1508). The rest of the ground floor mainly comprises mediocre local works of recent times, but upstairs is a good representative collection of Czech art from the 15C to 20C, including works by Brandl, Škréta, Braun, Mánes, Slavíček and Mucha. You can ask one of the staff of the museum to take you to the Mácha memorial room at Máchova ul. 10 (a good five minutes' walk away): this small museum to the poet Karel Hynek Mácha, has been set up in the house where this popular romantic poet died in 1836. In 1938, when this part of Bohemia was seized by the Germans, the Czechs were allowed to move the tomb of their beloved Mácha from Litoměřice to Prague's Vyšehrad.

If you turn N at the western end of Michelská you will reach the scant ruins of the town's castle, converted in the 19C into a brewery and now being made into a cultural centre. Turning instead to the S you will begin the climb along the quiet Dómské Street up to the cathedral, passing as you do so the small, jewel-like church of *St. Wenceslas* (sv. Václav): built in 1714–16 by O. Broggio, this oval structure with a lively undulating profile, is similar to Christoph Dietzenhofer's chapel at Smiřice (see Route 3). This whole area of town has the quality of a sleepy suburb, and the cathedral itself stands on a large shaded and overgrown square surrounded—as in a cathedral close in England—by houses that once all belonged to the clergy. The *Episcopal cathedral of St. Stephen* (sv. Štěpán) was founded in 1057 but rebuilt after 1655 to designs supplied by J.D. Orsi and G. Broggio. The light and simple interior contains several fine works of art, including an altarpiece of St. Peter by K. Škréta (2nd chapel to right), and two paintings by Cranach (3rd chapel to right). The high altar has a splendid gold and black frame encasing a dark and warped canvas by Škréta representing the Stoning of St. Stephen.

From Litoměřice a short EXCURSION can be made to the large country house of *Ploskovice*, 6km NE of the town (take the Žitenice road). This building, the secular masterpiece of O. Broggio, was designed in 1720, but extensively redecorated inside in the 19C. The interior, featuring an amusing grotto flanked by atlantes, has various rooms in a rococo style by Josef Navrátil; the gardens were laid out in 1850.

The journey from Litoměřice to Děčín can be made by winding your way along the banks of the Labe. The valley narrows shortly after leaving Litoměřice, and steep verdant hills roll down directly into the river, calling to mind certain stretches of the Rhine Valley. High above the river, on the southern outskirts of Ústí nad Labem, looms a castle which appealed to the Romantic generation with the same fervour as did the famous Rhineland sites, and which had a name in German which could have been taken from a Gothick novel—Schreckenstein. *Střekov*, as this place is more prosaically known in Czech, was begun in the 14C, rebuilt two centuries later and destroyed at the end of the 18C. Its Romantic appeal, based partly on the beauty of the castle's site, was certainly heightened by the numerous legends attached to the building, such as the story of Mathilde of Schreckenstein being discovered here with her lover by the dreaded huntsman Kuba: the enraged Kuba had her thrown from the battlements, and her cries are still said to echo around the ruins on dark summer nights. Many of the great Czech Romantics such as the poet Mácha visited the site, but the most famous visitor was Wagner, who came here in 1842 and was inspired to begin work on his opera Tannhauser. Today the beauty of the place is somewhat marred by the ever encroaching town of Ústí nad Labem, a river port and large chemical centre. Ústí was one of the North Bohemian towns to suffer most during the last war, but it has kept its Gothic cathedral—a hall-church rebuilt in around 1500 with star vaulting. The town was the birthplace in 1728 of one of Europe's leading neo-classical painters, Anton Rafael Mengs.

Děčín (see Route 6) is 24km to the NE, on the E455.

8   Děčín to Karlovy Vary

Total distance 146km. **Děčín**—E442—34km **Teplice**—8km **Duchcov**—22km *Most*—25km Chomutov—15km **Kadaň**—42km **Karlovy Vary**.

The E442 extends the whole length of northern Bohemia, from Jablonec (see Route 6) to Karlovy Vary (see Route 10). After Děčín (see Route 6) it runs in between the now polluted Central Bohemian Highlands and a series of mining towns and industrial centres that make this whole area one of the most built up in Czechoslovakia. It was not so long ago that this area was renowned for its great beauty, the spa town of **Teplice** being once the most popular of all Bohemia's spas, and inspiring Wagner to write to his sister: 'Oh this town of Teplice with its endless vistas; it is really the most beautiful place I know'.

The spa at Teplice was founded by King Vladislav II's queen, Judita, as early as the 11C, and its curative waters had supposedly been discovered three centuries earlier by a shepherd. The fame of the spa was well established by 1793 when a disastrous fire destroyed much of the town. In the end, however, the disaster turned out to be beneficial, for, on the instigation of the local aristocrat Prince Johann Nepomuk von Clary und Aldringen, a major building programme was begun which soon was to turn Teplice into one of the smartest spas in Europe. Wagner, Chopin, Liszt, Pushkin and Ibsen were among the many celebrities who took the waters here in the 19C, though the two whose names are most closely associated with the place are Goethe and Beethoven. In 1812 both Goethe and Beethoven found themselves together at Teplice, and Beethoven gave an account of one of their meetings in a letter to the writer Bettina Brentano, an account which throws much light on the respective personalities of the two men. Apparently they were both walking in the park when the young third wife of the Austrian Emperor Franz I passed by. Goethe politely bowed and stood aside, but Beethoven walked resolutely on, later reminding Goethe of their own superiority in relation to the royal party.

If 1812 was a cultural landmark in the history of the town, 1813 was a political one, with Franz I, Alexander I of Russia and the Prussian king, Friedrich Wilhelm III signing at Teplice a famous treaty against Napoleon. The spa continued to prosper until the 1880s when the flow of the spring waters was badly affected by flooding in the nearby Döllinger mine. Since that time the waters at Teplice have had to be pumped, but it was only in recent years, with the digging of wells over 1000m deep, that the curative waters have come to be available again in significant quantities. However, the reputation of Teplice with foreign visitors has never recovered, due largely to the rapid industrial growth of the town since the end of the last century.

The extensive, noisy and polluted modern town of Teplice should not deter visitors from coming here for it shields a quiet and delightful

Plague column of the Holy Trinity (1718) by Matthias Braun, Teplice

spa town, spaciously arranged and with numerous fine old buildings, in particular from the neo-classical period. At the centre of the old spa town is the Castle Square or Zámecké náměstí, dominated by a 20m-high *plague column*, one of the finest in Bohemia, and the work of Matthias Braun. The castle itself, of medieval origin, was completely transformed during the neo-classical period, and has housed since 1897 a regional museum featuring period rooms, archaeological, historical and natural history collections, and rooms devoted to Beethoven and Pushkin; its enormous gardens, now a public park, contain two lakes and various temples and other follies. The chapel adjoining the castle is one of the earliest examples in Bohemia of the neo-Gothic style, while adjacent to this is the baroque parish church of c 1700. Directly in front of the castle, on the opposite side of the square, is a narrow pedestrian street (Lázeňská) running between the buildings that comprise today the J. Fučík Sanatorium. The pale blue building with the Palladian-inspired double colonnade is a reconstruction of the Municipal Baths (Městské Lázně) of 1838–39; opposite is the yellow Zlatá harfa house, where a plaque commemorates Beethoven's stay in 1811.

8km W of Teplice is the small mining town of **Duchcov**, which is built around a château formerly owned by the Wallenstein family. The château, which once formed part of a great complex featuring a theatre, riding-school, and a hospice, has frequently been compared with the East Bohemian castle of Kuks (see Route 3), an analogy reinforced by its important picture gallery founded in 1723, and its once incomparable collection of statuary by Matthias Braun. However, if Kuks today is only a shadow of its former self, Duchcov is a paler reflection still, and its present dilapidated condition, and shabby surroundings, testify to an especially poignant history of decline.

The original castle at Duchcov was a late 16C structure belonging to the Lobkovic family and designed by the Italian architect U. Aostalli. The property was acquired by the Wallenstein family in 1642, and remained in their hands until 1921. Between 1675 and 1685 the property was rebuilt and extended by the French architect J.B. Mathey, whom Jan Bedřich of Wallenstein had summoned from Rome. In 1722 Jan Ferdinand Schor laid out the castle garden in a baroque style, and six years later Ottavio Broggio brought to completion in the garden's western half a large hospice containing frescoes by V.V. Reiner and statuary by Matthias Braun. Braun was summoned again to work at Duchcov in 1735–38, when he created almost 60 sculptures for the garden, many of which were placed—as at Kuks—along the terrace in front of the hospice. The château was remodelled between 1812 and 1818, and the garden relaid in an English style, a transformation which led to the selling off of many of Braun's statues; those that remained rapidly fell into ruin. A fire in May 1945 gutted the large castle chapel, destroying an altarpiece featuring a painting by Reiner and statues by Braun; the hospice was pulled down in 1959 to make way for a coal mine. The sad history of Duchcov was compounded in 1988 with the robbery of most of its important paintings, a fact of which you are not informed when purchasing your tickets for the obligatory guided tour.

The castle forecourt, facing the town's main square, contains the surviving statuary executed by Braun for the garden and hospice; the rebuilt castle chapel stands adjacent to the main block of the château. The tour of the interior is long and tedious, and the most impressive of the rooms that you are shown is the first one, with its ceiling decorated by Reiner with scenes representing the military glories of the Duke of Wallenstein. The other rooms have a stripped, desultory quality, and display odd pieces of furniture on loan from the Fine Arts Museum in Prague, a collection of porcelain, and the sad remains of the Wallenstein picture gallery, most notably a curious picture by Paul Troger of Adam and Eve and their Children, and a painting attributed to G.D. Tiepolo of the Rape of Europa; the missing pictures include works by Spranger, Cranach, K. van Mander, Škréta and Liška. The rooms scarcely evoke the atmosphere of the house in former times, and it is difficult to imagine that such luminaries as Schiller, Goethe, Beethoven, Chopin and Tsar Alexander I were once guests here. The one person whose stay at Duchcov is remembered here today is Giacomo Casanova, whose life is the subject of a series of historical panels arranged in the rooms in the wing where he lived from 1785 to his death in 1798. A visit to Duchcov will be appreciated by anyone seriously interested in Casanova's life, for though the building has changed greatly since his day, the whole place highlights in its starkness and shoddiness the sense of desolation and abandon which the celebrated lover is known to have experienced in his last years.

Born in Venice in 1725, Giacomo Casanova was brought up virtually as an orphan, and learnt from an early age how to live off his wits, in particular from the gullibility of the aristocracy. As a lover his career began when he was 16 or 17, reputedly initiated by two girls in the same bed; his passion for sexual intrigue soon equalled that of his other life-long loves, gambling and eating macaroni. By 1755 news of his increasingly scandalous sexual doings reached the ears of the Inquisition, and he was thrown into the notoriously damp and rat-infested prison of Venice's Ducal Palace; his remarkable escape from this was to provide him with a dinner-party story which was to win him invitations from many of the leading aristocratic families of the time. After 1757 his life and sexual adventures became ever more complex and took him to every corner of Europe. Eventually, in 1785, he befriended Count Wallenstein, who offered him token employment as librarian at Duchcov.

While at Duchcov, Casanova published various unreadable books on history and philosophy, and also wrote his delightful Memoirs, for which he was best to be remembered after his death. In one passage of these he referred to the continual mist which appeared to hang over Duchcov, and how he longed for some rays of sunshine to come through it and cheer him up. Elsewhere in this book he referred to his writing as 'the only thing which has kept me from going mad, or dying of grief in the midst of the discomfort and pettifoggying annoyances daily caused me by the envious wretches who live with me, in this castle of Dux [Duchcov]…' His particular enemy at Duchcov was the house steward, Master Faulkircher, to whom he addressed a series of acrimonious letters at the back of his Memoirs. Matters came to a head on 11 December 1791, when Faulkircher supposedly arranged for one of his men to beat up Casanova in the streets of the town. Casanova died in the château in 1798, reputedly saying on his deathbed, 'I have lived as a philosopher and die as a Christian.'

A tour of Duchcov is completed by wandering into the gardens, which have now been turned into a public park; a hideous modern pavilion has been erected to display the frescoes by Reiner that decorated the dome of the destroyed hospice.

From Duchcov an EXCURSION could be made to the important convent of **Osek**, which lies 8km to the W, directly under the shadow of the wooded hills that mark the border with Germany. Osek was a Cistercian community founded at the end of the 12C. Its earliest surviving part is its chapter house of c 1240, joined by steps to a 14C cloister and featuring richly carved columns and other detailing that suggest links with the Cistercian architecture of Burgundy. The present convent church was begun in 1712 and is the ecclesiastical masterpiece of Ottavio Broggio. Its dynamic ground-plan, a variant of one by Fischer von Erlach, is matched by a tall and superb undulating façade, profusely decorated, and with a rich play of contrasting shapes and surfaces.

Regaining the E442 S of Duchcov, you will soon reach the small spa and mining town of *Bílina*, which has a 17C castle and late Gothic parish church. *Most*, 10km further W, lies at the very centre of North Bohemia's coal mines, and has a modern and largely unappealing look; the town is so polluted that the local school children have been provided with respiratory masks since November 1990. However, the place has retained a magnificent *parish church*, which was built in the form of a Saxon hall-church by Jakob Heilmann of Schweinfurt in the early 16C; the great Benedikt Reid is known to have been invited in 1519 to settle a dispute over Heilmann's work here, and he might well have had an influence on the graceful and elaborate vaulting.

West of Most the E442 turns briefly into a dual carriageway before reaching, after 25km, the town of *Chomutov*, a large mining town and centre of iron and steel industries, but with a number of buildings from the late Gothic, Renaissance and baroque periods; late Gothic cellular or diamond vaulting (a peculiarity of Bohemia) can be seen in the parish church (in the space under the tower) and in a room of the Town Hall. After Chomutov the landscape becomes hillier and more wooded, and continues to do so all the way to Karlovy Vary. At Vernéřov, 15km W of Chomutov, turn left to **Kadaň**, a quiet town raised above the Ohře river, and with perhaps the best preserved old centre in North Bohemia. A thriving town in the middle ages, Kadaň was destroyed by the Swedish army in the Thirty Years' War, but rebuilt in the 18C, and not much changed since then. The long main square, with its arcaded houses and central plague column, has a particularly harmonious appearance. From here a wide pedestrian street (J. Švermy) leads to the tall Mikulovicka Gate, the oldest remaining part of the town's fortifications.

You can regain the E442 by taking the road which follows the Ohře to Klášterec nad Ohří. Suspended above the river, in a wooded, isolated spot on the outskirts of Kadaň, is a former Franciscan monastery dating from the end of the 15C; the small complex, at present boarded up and rapidly decaying, has in its cloisters and chapter house what is reputed to be some of the earliest cellular vaulting in Bohemia (c 1480). The tree-lined stretch of the Ohře valley W of Kadaň is especially attractive and can be appreciated to the full from the terrace of the small baroque château at *Klášterec nad Ohří*. The surrounding gardens, now a public park, were once adorned with statues by J. Brokoff. The ones that have survived have been haphazardly assembled outside the château, the interior of which now contains a collection of porcelain made in the local Thun factory, which was founded in 1794. The village church of the Holy Trinity was built in 1665–70 to the designs of C. Lurago.

The E442 snakes its way along the Ohře almost all the way to Ostrov (22km), a small town in the administrative region of West Bohemia. A plaque on the town's former monastery (now a school) records that the first concentration camp in Czechoslovakia was established here; nearby, in a wooded park, is an 18C château serving as a small art gallery and local museum.

For Karlovy Vary see Route 10.

9   Prague to Karlovy Vary

A.   Via Louny and Žatec

Total distance 147km. Prague—Road 7/E442 59km *Louny*—23km *Žatec*—65km **Karlovy Vary** (see Route 10).

Leaving Prague on Road 7 to Slaný you pass through featureless built-up countryside. After Panenský Týnec, with its ruins of a Clarissine convent begun in 1532, the landscape improves, and you are offered a sweeping vista over the valley of the middle Ohře and across to the distant hills marking the Saxon frontier. *Louny*, 10km further W, is situated on the Ohře and has retained sections of its fortifications as well as a number of medieval and Renaissance buildings. Its chief treasure is the Deanery Church of St. Nicholas (sv. Mikuláš), built after 1518 in replacement of an earlier structure which had burnt down the year before. The architect was the great Benedikt Ried, whose hand is immediately apparent in the triangular tent-shaped roof which dominates the exterior. But the great joy of the church is its wide and elegant pale yellow interior, which takes the form of a great hall divided into three naves of four bays each. From slender concave-sided piers ribs are sprung in tree-like fashion to form the playful and elaborate vaulting characteristic of Ried's work. The one incongruous element in this light and harmonious space is the heavy baroque high altar of 1700–08.

Continue W along Road 7 for another 13km and then turn W to *Žatec*, a further 10km drive. This is famous hops country, and everywhere you look there are poles supporting what is sometimes referred to as 'green gold'. Žatec, the main hop-growing centre in Czechoslovakia, rises on a spur of land above the Ohře, and has an excellently preserved centre, with a chain of old squares lined with Gothic, Renaissance and baroque buildings; the Renaissance Town Hall was rebuilt in 1770 and given its onion-shaped dome. From Žatec you can either head straight to Kadaň (22km) and join up with Route 8 to Karlovy Vary, or else make a loop to the S to take in the country house at **Krásný Dvůr** (see Route 9B).

B. Via Lubenec

Total distance 123km. Prague—E48 47km Řevničov—38km Lubenec—38km **Karlovy Vary** (see Route 10).

The direct road from Prague to Karlovy Vary, the E48, runs through dull gently rolling countryside and goes through no town or village of any great interest. At Lubenec, however, it is worth making a detour 17km to the N to visit the country house at **Krásný Dvůr** (take the road to Podbořany and, just before reaching there, turn left towards Buskovice, and then take the first road to the right). Nearing Krásný Dvůr you enter the flat hop-growing landscape which extends towards Žatec (see Route 9A). Your first view of the property is of a wooded hill from which peeps what seems like a Gothic spaceship: this is not the house itself but one of the many follies in the extraordinary park.

Though the park is the main attraction of Krásný Dvůr, the house itself is by no means without interest. The present structure, commissioned by František Josef Czernin, was built in 1720–24 by František Maximilian Kaňka; it remained the property of the Czernin family until 1939, when it was commandeered by the Nazis. The pale yellow exterior, altered slightly in the late 18C, has an elegant French look. The interior is excellently preserved and is filled with fine 18C furniture, porcelain, stoves and clocks; among the paintings are works by Brandl, Škréta and Vigée-Lebrun, and a curious set of pictures of dogs by the baroque artist P.V. Berger.

The **park** at Krásný Dvůr, laid out between 1783 and 1793 by the forester Jan Wachtl and the gardener Franck of Červený Hrádek, was the brainchild of Jan Rudolf Czernin. Czernin, a keen botanist, respected the existing trees in the grounds (such as an oak reputed to be over 1000 years old), and insisted also that all the new trees and shrubs to be planted were indigenous or semi-indigenous. As for the park's eclectic range of follies this might well reflect the interests formed by Czernin in the course of a Grand Tour of Europe undertaken in 1779. Many hours could be spent wandering around the huge park and coming across unexpected delights at every corner, such as lakes, a rotunda, an obelisk, temples, a red house in a Dutch style, and a Chinese pavilion. The highpoint, both literally and architecturally, is the neo-Gothic belvedere, a soaring octagonal structure with an upper room supported by buttressing, and from which a good view can be had over the park and out towards the surrounding plains and distant Ore Mountains.

WESTERN BOHEMIA

10 Karlovy Vary to Mariánské Lázně

Total distance 84km. Karlovy Vary—E49/Road 21 46km **Cheb**—38km **Marianské Lázně**.

KARLOVY VARY, lying picturesquely along a deep forested valley at the confluence of the rivers Teplá and Ohře, is perhaps the most visited town in Czechoslovakia after Prague. Described since at least the 19C as the 'Queen of the spas', it is better known under its German name of Carlsbad, a name which conjures up memories of a vanished aristocratic Europe.

The town of Karlovy Vary, founded in 370, grew up around a series of 12 hot mineral springs lined along the banks of the narrow river Teplá and discovered, according to tradition, by the Emperor Charles IV while on a hunting expedition. For over two centuries the place had little more than 100 buildings, but by the end of the 16C it had already begun to attract a distinguished aristocratic clientele; the international reputation of its curative waters spread rapidly after the Thirty Years' War. The first bathing establishment was erected in 1704, bathing being at first the only way in which the waters were used: a popular treatment of the day was to be immersed in the hot water until the skin was sore, a barbaric practice which gave rise to the term 'flaying-baths' (Hautfresskur). By around 1766 the fashion for bathing was temporarily abandoned, to be replaced by a scarcely more appealing drinking cure which involved the taking of between 50 to 70 cups of the hot sulphurous liquid every day. Such excessive drinking was later to be heavily criticised by the local physician, Dr David Becher, who in 1789 carried out the first scientific analysis of the waters.

Building activity at Karlovy Vary intensified in the early 19C, and the town spread up into the surrounding hills as well as northwards towards the Ohře river, where it gradually merged with the villages of Bohatice, Drahovice and Tuhnice. The opening up of the railway to Karlovy Vary in 1870–71 increased yet further the flow of visitors to the town and led to the construction of majestic turn-of-the-century apartment blocks with names such as Venezuela, Brasilia and America that served to emphasise the international character of the place.

The full list of famous people who have visited Karlovy Vary over the centuries could extend for pages, but among the most celebrated visitors are Albrecht von Wallenstein (1630), Augustus of Poland (1691), Peter the Great (1711 and 1712), Frederick I of Prussia (1732), Leibnitz (1712), Maria Theresa of Austria, Goethe (14 seasons), the Prussian Field Marshal General Blücher (1812–13), Schiller (who spent his honeymoon here), Bismarck and Karl Marx (1874–76). The town has played an especially important role in the history of music, and its distinguished musical visitors have included Bach, Beethoven (who delighted the public by the playing of a free fantasia at a charity concert here), Liszt, Brahms, Paganini, Smetana, Janáček and Dvořák (who conducted here the first performance of the New World Symphony). A guidebook to the town of 1871 recorded that 'there is scarcely a piece of classical music of any recognised merit which does not figure in the programme at some concert during the seasons.' The practice of regularly performing classical music in the town's colonnades continues to this day, and in recent years a number of other important musical activities have been instituted, most notably the annual Dvořák Music Festival held in the autumn. The local symphonic orchestra is one of the oldest in Europe, and in 1984 celebrated its 150th anniversary.

In terms of sheer numbers of visitors, Karlovy Vary is perhaps more popular now than ever, though it is customary among travel writers to look back nostalgically to bygone days and bemoan the decline of the place today. Certainly the present-day visitors are neither as aristocratic nor as international as before, and are taken to a great extent from the German middle classes, whose presence here in large numbers have made Karlovy Vary one of the more expensive Czech towns to stay in. The spa cure today—considered to be effective for the treatment of diabetes, duodenal ulcers, and digestive and intestinal diseases—is based largely on a combination of bathing and drinking. As at

CHEB

Railway & Bus Stations

Ohre

Chebský most

VÍTĚZNÁ

ONDŘÍČKOVA

KVAPILOVA

VARŠAVSKÁ

BULHARSKÁ

MASARYKOVA

NÁBŘ. A ZÁPOTOCKÉHO

BEZRUČOVA

I.P. PAVLOVA

AMERICKÁ

RUMUNSKÁ

BEZRUČOVA

Poštovní Bridge

HAVLÍČKOVA

JEDNOTNÝCH ODBORŮ

MÁCHOVA

LIDICKÁ

Hotel Thermal

I.P. PAVLOVA

BEZRUČOVA

HŘBITOVNÍ

Dvořákovy Sady

PODĚBRADSKÁ

Sadová Colonnade

SADOVÁ

I.P. PAVLOVA

NA VYHLÍDCE

SS.Peter & Paul

Muhlbrunnen Colonnade

SADOVÁ

ONDŘEJSKÁ

KŘIŽÍKOVA

PETRA VELIKÉHO

ZÁMECKÝ

St Luke

Czech-Russian Colonnade

K. MARXE

Astoria Hotel

SADOVÁ STEZKA

Diana Tower

Findlater Memorial

Trži Colonnade

TRŽIŠTĚ

NA VYHLÍDCE

Haus Zawoski

Yuri Gagarin Colonnade

St Mary Magdalen

DUKELSKÝCH HRDINŮ

MUSKIVO NÁM.

MORAVSKÁ

KOLMA

Theatre

MORAVSKÁ

Hotel Pupp

Museum

VOLGOGRADSKÁ

Charles IV. Park

POŠKOVÁ

Hotel Imperial

CHEB

Findlater Chapel

JINDŘATÉRKA

STEZKA

SLOVENSKÁ

U IMPERIÁLU

U IMPERIÁLU

N

Art Gallery

PEŠINA

PRAGUE

SLOVENSKÁ

KARLOVY VARY

0 metres   400

Mariánské Lázně one of the more bizarre sights at Karlovy Vary is that of hundreds of people slowly walking up and down the colonnades with specially shaped porcelain jugs that allow the water to be sucked through a long spout.

In addition to remaining an active spa town, Karlovy Vary has had an extensive industrial quarter along the banks of the Ohře since the beginning of the last century. Two of the traditional industries are porcelain and glass-making, the most famous factories being the Pirkenhammer Porcelain factory (founded in 1803) and the Moser Glassworks (founded in 1889). Another traditional industry (established in 1807) is the making of the popular herb-flavoured liquor known as becherovka. Bearing the name of the great Dr Becher, it is often jokingly described as the town's thirteenth spring, and the only one which works.

By far the most attractive approach to Karlovy Vary is from the S, along the side road which branches off the Mariánské Lázně road and winds its way along the Teplá. A more usual approach, however, is from the adjoining train and bus stations, situated in the drab and industrialised northern half of the town, where turn-of-the-century gloom competes with socialist functionalism of the 1950s and 1960s. The beauty of Karlovy Vary is concentrated around the banks of the Teplá, which can be reached from the stations by walking the whole length of the broad Masarykova. You will end up at the Poštovní bridge, which marks the northern entrance to the spa town, and from which point onwards Karlovy Vary takes on the verdant picturesque aspect so familiar from photographs and paintings. The narrow, steep and restlessly winding valley in which the spa town is set is covered in its upper reaches with a dense covering of firs, pines, oaks and beeches, rising above which are numerous splendid monuments of the *belle époque*. The way in which the town is snaked around the river creates an ever-changing sky-line and is liable also to make you lose your sense of direction, an experience known even to those who have stayed in the town for a long time.

When you reach the Poštovní bridge head S along the Teplá, keeping the river always to your left. As you walk S towards the Dvořák Park you will note on the other side of the river a large modern complex: this is the spa Hotel Thermal (1975), the most luxurious modern hotel in town and the venue today of the important annual Film Festival which has been held in Karlovy Vary since 1958. On the southern side of the small but elegant Dvořák Park is the *Sadova Colonnade* (1881–82), an elaborately decorated wrought-iron work in white and grey by the prolific Viennese architects Fellner and Helmer. Further to the S is the **Mühlbrunnen Colonnade**, a long and sober classical structure designed in 1871 by the Prague architect Josef Zítek. It overlooks a square adorned with potted palms, beyond which is a diverse row of buildings standing on the opposite side of the Teplá (which at this point disappears briefly under the pavement). Directly in front of the northern section of the colonnade, where concerts are held, is a half-timbered and very Germanic-looking building housing a bar and restaurant called *Petr*: this was originally the House of the Golden Peacock, where Peter the Great is meant to have stayed. Further S along the same row is the popular Café Astoria and the adjoining hotel of that name, a 1920s construction with a splendid ceramic decoration.

The busy pedestrian street running between the Colonnade of Czech-Russian Friendship and the Teplá is named after Karl Marx, whose stay at Karlovy Vary is commemorated in a small museum at No. 29/9 of this street. K. Marx Street turns to the S into the Tržiště Street, where at No. 29, overlooking the river, is the Art Nouveau *Haus Zawojski*, one of the finest buildings in this style in western Bohemia.

Designed by the Viennese architect Karl Haybäck, the Haus Zawojski, was built between 1899 and 1901 under the supervision of the local architect Karel Heller. The man who commissioned it, Felix Zawojski, was a successful tailor who had trained in Paris and Vienna and had worked in India, North America and on the French Riviera before deciding to settle at Karlovy Vary; his social prestige had been enhanced by marrying an academic Hungarian painter called Marie Stennpier. On the ground floor was a luxury glove shop, while above was a tailor's workshop, a doctor's surgery and—in the attic—a chemical laboratory. The building was sold to a bank in 1911, and divided into flats after 1945. At present there are plans to restore it for use as a spa administration office.

On the opposite side of the road to the Haus Zawojski is the entertaining *Tržní Colonnade* (1883): this elaborate wooden structure by Fellner and Helmer, now closed while awaiting much-needed restoration, resembles the casing of a Swiss cuckoo clock. The colonnade is at the very centre of Karlovy Vary, facing the oldest and most important spring in town, and underneath the town's castle—a baroque structure which replaced Charles IV's hunting lodge, and is now joined to the lower town by an old lift. The Teplá is once again covered at this point, and over it has been built a square supporting on its eastern side a colonnade incorporating the famous Sprudel spring. The original structure, another work by Fellner and Helmer, was dismantled in 1939 by the Nazis, who used its copper roof for making armaments. It was replaced in 1975 by the fussy and uninspiring *Yuri Gagarin Colonnade* (1975), named after the well-known Soviet cosmonaut, who stayed in Karlovy Vary in 1961 and 1966. The *Sprudel Spring* is not only the oldest in town, but also the hottest and most productive, attaining temperatures of 72° centigrade, and producing daily over two million litres of water; at regular intervals throughout the day it spurts up to a height of over 10m, watched by an admiring crowd.

The Tržiště Street joins at its southern end the Dukelských hrdinů, which runs alongside the now exposed Teplá; at the junction of the two streets is the Čedok office, while next to this is the Hotel Atlantic, a building of the early years of this century which has kept many features of its original interior, including a dark-panelled staircase. The western side of the Dukelských hrdinů is lined all the way down to the Hotel Pupp with restaurants, shops and cafés. Retracing your steps to the Yuri Gagarin Colonnade you should now walk S along the other side of the river, beginning at the church of *St. Mary Magdalene*, which stands on a raised site to the E of the colonnade. This important work by Kilian Ignaz Dientzenhofer, built in 1732–36, takes the form of an elongated oval, and has an exterior featuring a convex west façade and concave sides. South from here is Mukivo náměstí (formerly Lenin Square), on the southern side of which is the town's imposing *Theatre* (1884–86), a neo-baroque edifice by Fellner and Helmer and closely similar to their Theatre at Odessa: it was here that Dvořák gave in 1893 the première of the New World Symphony, and it was also here that Hitler made a speech in 1938. Further S, and almost opposite the Hotel Pupp, is the Karlovy Vary Museum (ul. manželů Rosenbergových č. 23), containing collections relating to the history and geology of the town, as well as a large collection of local porcelain and glass. Before crossing the river and visiting the Hotel Pupp, you could continue heading S until you cross the Charles IV Gardens and reach the former *Kaiserbad* (or Bathhouse I, as it is less glamorously known today), another grandiose structure by Fellner and Helmer (1892–95). Inside this oppressively marbled building has recently been installed the first Casino in Czechoslovakia since the war. The interior is memorable largely on account of its wall decorations by Wilhelm Schneider

(1914), one of which is a gigantic representation of all the celebrated visitors to have come to Karlovy Vary.

The vast, dazzlingly white **Hotel Pupp** represents the ultimate in wedding-cake architecture, and is surely one of the most impressive-looking Grand Hotels in Europe. The longest-running hotel establishment in town, it reverted back after the 1989 Revolution from Grandhotel Moskva to its original name of Hotel Pupp, the name by which it has always been affectionately known.

Founded by the (Konditorei) Johann Georg Pupp in 1793, the hotel was rebuilt in the late 19C, the principal architects involved being the ubiquitous Fellner and Helmer. It was shortly before the First World War that the infamous Colonel Redl—the subject of John Osborne's A Patriot for Me and of a film by the Hungarian director István Szabó—handed over in this hotel Austrian military secrets to the Russians. In 1938 the hotel was extended, and further additions and modernisation were carried out in a questionable taste in the 1970s. Though renovated in 1981, further restoration is intended, and it is hoped eventually to remove the modern additions and bring back as much as possible of the building's turn-of-the-century character.

A remarkable amount of the original interior has survived, for instance the mirrored and exuberantly stuccoed Small Hall (Malá Dvorana), and the adjoining French Restaurant, an elegant neo-rococo space where recently the Spanish king Juan Carlos ate. But the great surprise of the interior is the unexpectedly large **Concert Hall**, a white and neo-baroque stucco concoction constituting the most heavily ornamental work by Fellner and Helmer in Karlovy Vary. On its stage—flanked by busts of Smetana and Dvořák—is an organ comprising 66 keys and 4788 pipes, while on the staircase leading up to the upper gallery are two large paintings by Willhelm Schneider (1907). Before leaving the hotel you should ask to see Room 167, a large suite built for the emperor Franz Josef (who never came here) and which has been left virtually unchanged since then: reserved today for important guests or honeymoon couples, it contains a huge bathroom equipped with all the most up-to-date appliances of the turn of the century.

Continuing walking S along the Teplá from the Hotel Pupp, you will find yourself skirting extensive and densely wooded parkland which spreads up the hilly ground behind the hotel. As you walk along the riverside Puškinova stezka towards the Town's *Art Gallery*—the last monument of importance on the western banks of the Teplá—you will see high on the hill on the other side of the river the Hotel Imperial, an establishment even more monstrous in size than the Hotel Pupp, and intended when built to supersede the latter in luxury; built just before the First World War by the French architect Ernest Hebrard, it never recovered from being converted into a hospital during the last war. The Art Gallery is devoted exclusively to 20C Czech art, and has works by Jakub Schikaneder, Jan Preisler, Antonín Slavíček, Václav Špála, Otakar Kubín and Emil Filla; of particular interest is a Cubist Circus by Bohumil Kubišta, and a Cubist Head (1914) by Josef Čapek, the brother of the writer Karel.

The paths on either side of the museum will lead you up into the wooded hills above the town, where numerous fine and celebrated walks can be taken. It is in the upper reaches of Karlovy Vary, away from the main tourist thoroughfare along the Teplá, that the most poignant memories of old Carlsbad are to be found. Within the vast forested park into which you climb you will come across numerous memorials to celebrities who have stayed in the town, as well as several chapels now mainly in an abandoned state. One of the latter is

the wooden *Findlater Chapel*, paid for by the Earl of Findlater, a great
benefactor of the town. Behind this is a look-out tower, now called the
Diana Tower: an extensive panorama can be had from the top. Nearby
is an obelisk to the same Earl of Findlater ('Nature's Friend'), from
where you can make your descent back into the town by way of the
Sovova stezka. This will take you to Zámecký Street, next to the
Evangelical church of *St. Luke*, a red brick, neo-Gothic relic of
Victorian England. From here you could descend directly down to the
Tržní Colonnade, passing on your left (at No. 618/41) the house where
Marx stayed (plaque). Alternatively you could turn left at the church
and then right into the splendid but shabby Sadova Street, which is
lined by an impressive group of residential buildings. Steps at the top
of the street lead up to the recently restored Russian Orthodox Church
of *SS. Peter and Paul* (1897), a gilded bulbous-domed apparition.
Descending the street you will pass in turn (respectively at Nos 729/32,
956/28 and 239/4) plaques recording the visits to Karlovy Vary of
Janáček, Karel Čapek and Dvořák. Eventually you will find yourself
back at Fellner's and Helmer's Sadová Colonnade.

Leave Karlovy Vary on the E48 to Cheb. Just off the road, on the
western outskirts of the town, is the Moser Glassworks, a building
dating back to the late 19C, and with a much visited showroom, where
you can not only buy modern examples of Moser ware but also look at
the models made for distinguished clients of the past. At its most
extravagant Moser ware features a delicate combination of gold and
glass, examples of which are the models prepared for such monarchs
as Alfonso XII of Spain, Victor Emmanuel of Italy, King Carol of
Romania, and Edward VII of England.

Shortly before N. Sedlo, you should briefly leave the E48 to visit the
small town of *Loket*, romantically situated above a green and wooded
bend of the Ohře river. Its impressively fortified castle, dating mainly
from c 1400, is best seen from the old bridge across the Ohře, perched
as if in some illustration of the Picturesque above a steep and verdant
bank. On the other side of the building is a small town resembling an
ageing toy, and with a narrow main square lined with old buildings.
One of these is the Hotel Bílý kůň, where a plaque records numerous
visits by Goethe; Goethe's stay in the town is documented in a small
museum installed within the castle, where you will also find displays
of local porcelain and glass. You can regain the E49 by following the
Ohře river in the direction of Sokolov, a modern town happily
bypassed and with billowing smoke from its chemical industries
which helps to explain much of the pollution both at Loket and Karlovy
Vary.

Cheb, raised on a spur of land above a flat, wide stretch of the Ohře
Valley, is an industrial, agricultural centre which has also managed to
keep over the centuries a large and evocative medieval quarter.

Since earliest times Cheb has occupied a border position between Bohemia and
Germany. Archaeological evidence has been used by the Czechs to show that the
original settlement was a Slavic one, but the first document to mention the
place—of 1061—indicates a large and growing German population in the area. In
1167 the town became an eastern outpost of the Holy Roman Empire after
Friedrich Barbarossa founded a fortress here. It was not until 1322 that the town
was definitely acquired by the Czech crown, but even so the German element in
the population was to remain a large and powerful one. Significantly the place
remained a strongly Catholic town during the Hussite Wars, and had several
bloody conflicts with the Hussites. The strategic position of Cheb at the entrance
to Bohemia led to a highly insecure period during the Thirty Years' War, with
both fighting sides using it as an important base for their military operations.
Taken by the Saxon armies in 1631, it was retaken the next year by Albrecht of

Wallenstein, and then occupied by the Swedes in 1647. In Czech history Cheb is known above all as the place where the great Wallenstein lost his life, murdered in 1634 after having been betrayed by his colonels.

Cheb took many years to recover from the devastation of the Thirty Years' War, and a full recovery was not to take place until the 19C, thanks to the wealth brought in by the newly founded spa resort at Františkovy Lázně, and to rapid industrialisation. After the First World War the Germans in the town had sufficient influence to make Cheb part of the ill-fated Deutsches Böhmen province, an independent region which managed to survive only for one month. The fate of the German population in Cheb was sealed once and for all after the Second World War, when most of the Germans fled, leaving the town for many years seriously underpopulated.

Cheb was the birthplace of one of Germany's greatest baroque architects, Balthasar Neumann (1687–1753). The son of a local cloth-maker, Neumann rose from his humble origins to become the favourite architect of the Schönborn Prince-Bishops of Würzburg and the consultant to virtually every prince in southern Germany.

*The 'Špalíček', a group of sixteenth-century merchants'
houses on the main square of Cheb; to the far right is the
sixteenth-century building (now housing the Regional
Museum), where Wallenstein was stabbed to death in 1634.*

As with Karlovy Vary, Cheb does not appear at its best when approached from the railway station, an ugly red-brick building situated in an area of the town filled with large and grimy buildings. The attractive part of town is its northern half, beginning with the outstanding **náměstí krále Jiřího z Poděbrad**, which is named after the Czech king who did most to secure the political and financial security of the town, George of Poděbrady. The sloping wedge-shaped square, which widens as it descends to the N, is lined on all sides with a superlative series of 15C to 18C houses. Near the top of the square, at the crossing with Březinová, is the yellow, 18C House of the Two Archdukes (who are depicted on a medallion), Cheb's oldest surviving inn, and an establishment much-vaunted in pre-First World

War guides. Lower down, on the opposite side of the square, is the baroque former *Town Hall* (1728), a building designed by G.B. Alliprandi and with a fine interior recently converted to house the regional art gallery (containing Czech 20C works). Attached to a gabled Gothic house further down on the same side is an 18C palace grandly decorated with a giant order of pilasters and exuberant rococo stucco. But the buildings that leave the most lasting impression are a group of tall, free-standing and tightly packed houses at the lower end of the square: known collectively as the *Špaliček*, these half-timbered structures, used by Jewish shopkeepers in the 16C, give to this square a predominantly medieval and Germanic character. A large Renaissance house behind them, at the very end of the square, is famous as the place where Wallenstein was stabbed to death by a soldier acting under the orders of the Irish commander of the town garrison. The building now has the more placid function of *Regional Museum*, where, in addition to the usual collections of local history, is displayed a large and rare group of old bicycles.

Immediately to the N of the square is the large parish church of St. Nicholas (sv. Mikuláš), a 13C foundation rebuilt as a hall-church in the 15C, and much altered and restored since then, including by Balthasar Neumann in the 18C. A medieval church of more genuine appearance is the nearby *St. Barbara* (sv. Barbora), on Mlýnská, a few minutes' walk to the W; this 15C hall-church, containing fragments of wall-paintings, now serves as a small museum of Gothic statuary. The street on which it stands leads down to the river, through a bosky, and rather neglected, part of town. Projecting above the river's wooded banks is the *castle* founded by Friedrich Barbarossa in 1167, the entrance to which can be reached by turning left from Mlýnská into Hradní.

It was at a banquet given here on 25 February 1634 that Wallenstein's loyal officers were killed, an event which immediately preceded the murder of Wallenstein himself. The castle and this tragic event were featured in Schiller's drama Wallenstein (1799), for which the author came to Cheb to research in 1791. Schiller's contemporary, Goethe, a frequent visitor to the town, befriended the castle's executioner.

The castle, strengthened in the 13C and again in the baroque period, is now in a ruinous state, but has kept extensive sections of the early medieval walls. Of particular interest is its much restored late 12C *chapel*, a two-storeyed structure in a transitional Romanesque style with a crypt featuring crudely carved capitals and corbels. The surrounding overgrown forecourt is now used as an outdoor cinema, while in the rooms adjoining the sturdy entrance gate is a museum containing prehistoric finds and other items of local interest.

At the end of Hradní turn left into Dlouhá, off which stand the town's two remaining churches of interest. One is the monastery church of St. Francis (Františkánský kostel), remarkable above all for its 14C cloister. The other is the *Church of the Poor Clares* (1707–11), a work generally attributed to Christoph Dientzenhofer, and featuring this architect's characteristic system of intersecting vaults: of the two buildings this one is usually the easiest to get into, serving as it now does as an exhibition and cultural centre. Behind the Franciscan church is the town's modest neo-classical theatre of the early 19C.

The spa town of **Františkovy Lázně** (Franzensbad) lies just 4km to the N of Cheb and was only made an independent township in 1852.

The second oldest of West Bohemia's three most celebrated spas, Františkovy Lázně does not enjoy the beautiful surroundings of its two rivals: instead of being hemmed in by a densely wooded valley, it is encircled by marshes and flat parkland. None the less it is by far the quietest of the two places, and has been little disturbed by modern development. To Goethe, the place was a 'paradise on earth'.

The curative effects of the local water—known initially as 'Cheb water'—were known back in the Middle Ages, and it is even said that in 1196 the water was drunk for medicinal purposes by Prince Jindřich Břetislav, brother of the Czech king Přemysl Otakar I. Cheb mineral water was recommended in the 16C by the great scientist and physician Paracelsus, and in the following century was exported to Saxony. Profits from the sale of the water helped pay for the restoration of Cheb's fortifications in 1670.

The decision to create a spa community around the mineral springs was not taken until 1793, the main person behind the scheme being the local doctor Bernhard Adler. The first season was inaugurated later that year, and in the following year the place was named 'Village of Emperor Francis' in memory of a visit paid by Francis II of Austria; in 1803 it was renamed 'Francis' Spa'. Twenty-four boarding houses had been constructed by 1810, and from 1829 onwards the surroundings of the spa were landscaped by Martin Soukup and his son Antonín. Among the distinguished visitors in the 19C were J.G. Herder, Goethe, Beethoven (1812), and Božena Němcová (1846/47), the latter staying here at the same time as Goethe's last great love—Ulrica von Lewetzow.

The spa treatment, involving both a drinking cure and mud baths, is used for limb, heart and circulatory disorders, but is especially renowned for its success with female sterility and other female problems.

Františkovy Lázně is a small place, having as its nucleus a a square grid of streets surrounded by parkland on all sides. The main spring, the *Francis Spring*, is on the southern end of the grid and encased in a 1963 reconstruction of one of the spa's original neo-classical buildings. This small and engagingly simple Greek Doric rotunda of 1793 reflects the clean and peaceful character of the town. Inside are shiningly bright bronze pipes carrying what might possibly be one of the world's largest supplies of free mineral water—the townspeople of Cheb frequently come here to take it away in large jerry cans. Next to the building is a Doric colonnade of 1844, equally modest in its architecture, and also coloured—as are so many of the buildings here—the deep yellow known once as *Kaisergelb* or 'imperial yellow'. In the gardens in front of the spring is a hideous modern bronze of a seated naked boy holding a fish, a work which for some reason has come to be regarded as a symbol of the spa: the penis shines like a holy relic thanks to the popular belief that those who touch it will become pregnant, presumably a desperate last resort if the spa waters fail.

North of the spring runs the town's main street, Národní, where you will find what little there is of animation in Františkovy Lázně. The first building which you come to on the left is the former Casino, a late 19C structure in the style of a Palladian basilica; a street behind it leads towards the Luisa Spring, which is covered by a round and wide arcaded structure of c 1800 resembling an open umbrella. Continuing northwards up Národní, the next building on the left is the *Three Lilies* (Tři Lilie) Hotel and restaurant, which dates back to 1808 and has attractive 19C furnishings. Further up the street on the same side is the house (No. 4) where Beethoven stayed in 1812 (plaque). The avenue leads into a small park with a lake and turn-of-the-century bandstand. Turning right before the park into Ruská you will come after a few minutes to the *Božena Němcová Theatre*, a good example of Czech 'Cubist' architecture of the 1920s. The street which runs S of the theatre, Dr Podhoreckého, represents the eastern side of the town's grid, and skirts the Smetana Gardens, in the middle of which is the grand turn-of-the-century Hotel Imperial. On the other side of the street, at No. 8, is the local museum, which has exhibits relating to the history of Františkovy Lázně, including a group of old bath-tubs.

In the gardens to the S of the Francis Spring are the *Glauber Springs*, discovered in 1919 by Dr Glauber and housed in a building representing a wonderful Art Deco interpretation of the classical style; the bright interior is particularly fantastical and appealing, with its ceramic tiled floor, bronze and marble furnishings, and ethereally light colonnade. A building in a similar style covers the Natalia Spring, a good 15 minutes' walk to the E, in a wooded setting on the edge of marshland.

After returning to the outskirts of Cheb on Road 21, you continue following this road for another 27km to **MARIÁNSKÉ LÁZNĚ**. Better known as Marienbad, this was the favourite spa of the British monarch Edward VII, and is idyllically set in a landscaped valley hemmed in by pine-clad slopes.

The local cold springs—of which there are 40—have been known since at least the 16C, but the wooded area in which they are situated remained wild and barely disturbed up to the beginning of the 19C. The land belonged to the Premonstratensian Monastery of Teplá (18km to the E), and it was an abbot of this institution, K.K. Reitenberger, who, together with a doctor called J.J. Nehr, was eventually to found the spa of Mariánské Lázně in 1809. Its popularity grew rapidly, and by the second half of the century its hitherto neglected site had been transformed into a complex of some 90 hectares of parks and gardens, laid out mainly by the landscape architect Václav Skálnik (d. 1861). As with all the main Bohemian spas, the list of famous people who stayed here in the 19C and early 20C is formidable, and there are monuments to many of them scattered around its parks. Goethe, inevitably, was one of them, and it was here that the old man fell in love with the sixteen-year-old Ulrike von Lewetzow, the muse behind his Marienbad Elegy. Gogol wrote Dead Souls here, and Wagner composed Lohengrin. Chopin came here, as did Weber, Goncharov, Turgenev, Ibsen, Lehár, Mark Twain, Maxim Gorky, Jan Neruda and Franz Kafka. But the final seal of approval was the popularity which the place enjoyed among monarchs, in particular Edward VII of England, a frequent visitor. Mariánské Lázně was not simply a centre of convalescence and entertainment, but also the scene of much diplomatic activity, culminating in a famous meeting in which Edward VII attempted to persuade Franz Josef to sever Austria's alliance with Germany.

The formidable, nostalgic associations of the name Marienbad lived on well after the collapse of the Austro-Hungarian Empire and were exploited by the French film-maker Alain Resnais in the title of his pioneering, hallucinatory film, Last Year in Marienbad. Needless to say, this film has absolutely nothing to do with the real spa, but its repeated image of static, isolated figures in a formal French park has strongly influenced the perception of Mariánské Lázně of those who have never come here. The lush and informal English gardens to be found instead might come as a surprise to many.

The side road which descends into Mariánské Lázně from the wooded hills to the N brings you directly into the spa section of the town, and shows off the place and its surroundings to their best advantage. However the more usual approach is from the S, where the bus and railway stations, as well as the main parking area, are to be found. It is an exceptionally long town, and from the two stations you would be best advised to take a No. 5 trolley bus, which will lead you along Husova and into the Hlavní Třída. This long avenue, together with its northern continuation Odborářů, constitutes Mariánské Lázně's main thoroughfare and runs along the whole N–S axis of the town. Bordered to the E by parkland incorporating the Ušovický river, it is lined on its western side by grand and rather

Bus & Rail Stations & PLZEŇ

decayed late 19C residential blocks and hotels. Shortly after entering Odborářů, you will note rising behind the buildings to your left the gaudily painted *Russian Orthodox Church* (1901), the interior of which has an unusual iconostasis made with ceramics from Loket. Just to the N of this building along Ruská (a street parallel to Odborářů) is the neo-Gothic Anglican Church, the sad condition of which inspired the *Times* correspondent Richard Bassett to write in his nostalgic Guide to Central Europe (1987): 'Where once a monarch [Edward VII] and his entourage regularly worshipped, there remains only dust and decay'. At the northern end of Odborářů is a small and sparse museum relating to Chopin's stay at Mariánské Lázně.

Turning right at the end of Odborářů you will find yourself in the historical centre of town. The original spring, the *Křížový* or Cross Spring, is surrounded by a rectangular neo-classical colonnade of 1818 and surmounted by a dome crowned by a cross—a reference to the spring's original ecclesiastical owners. Adjacent to it to the S is the long *Maxim Gorky Colonnade*, a grandly embellished and recently restored cast-iron colonnade of 1889 cast in the Blanské

ironworks. At the other end of the colonnade is the modern 'Singing
Fountain', a wide fountain with jets syncopated at every odd hour of
the day with music (and with coloured illumination at night) to create
popular water spectacles. East of here is the náměstí J.W. Goethe,
containing on its southern side a large and ungainly neo-Byzantine
Catholic church of 1844–48. Among the pompous turn-of-the-
century buildings on the upper side of the square is the thermal Hotel
Kavkaz, once named the Hotel King of England in honour of the stays
here of King Edward. The hotel which it replaced was owned by the
mother of Ulrica von Lewetzow, whom Goethe met and fell in love
with while staying here in 1821–22. When Goethe returned to
Mariánské Lázně in 1823, he moved into the adjacent 18C house
which is now the *Town Museum* (in Goethe's day it was a hotel
known as 'At the Golden Grape'). The ground floor of this museum is
devoted to local history, while on the upper floor is a suite of 18C
rooms restored to the state in which they were when Goethe used
them.

Following the Karlovarská E of the náměstí J.W. Goethe you will
reach a street which climbs up to the Hotel Esplanade (Wagner
stayed in a house just below this hotel). In the wooded hills higher up
is the turn-of-the-century *Krakonoš Hotel* where there is a terrace
with broken statuary representing fairy-tale figures, including a
statue of the giant Krakonoš; at one time there were statues lining
the whole length of the attractive woodland path which descends
from the hotel straight down into the town. The nearby and luxurious
Golf Hotel, on the side road leading to Prameny, is popular with
foreign golfers and even has a head porter—the charming Tunkl
Boris—who was one of Czechoslovakia's leading golf players. The
hotel's celebrated golf course, one of the best in this country, was
founded in 1905 by Edward VII, who is commemorated here by a
plaque attached to one of the trees; the Golf Club pavilion is a half-
timbered English-style building of 1908. Beyond the hotel is a side
road to the left which descends through the forest to the tiny spa of
Lázně Kynžvart. The lords of the village were the Metternichs, and it
was the famous Chancellor Metternich who in 1833 had the baroque
ancestral home rebuilt as a three-winged neo-classical construction
by the Vienna-based Italian architect Pietro Nobile; the building, at
present closed while awaiting much-needed restoration, stands in
the middle of a large English park, and has fine Empire furnishings,
as well as a collection of gifts presented to the Chancellor.

Another EXCURSION from Mariánské Lázně is to the former Premonstratensian monastery of *Teplá*, on the outskirts of the village of
that name (take the Karlovy Vary road for 6km and then turn off to
the right).

The monastery was founded in 1193, and soon rose to become one of the
wealthiest in Bohemia. However, from the late 14C onwards it was troubled by
a series of misfortunes, beginning with plagues, and culminating in the looting
and razing of the monastery following the ex-communication of its monks in
1467. Rebuilding was begun in the early 16C, but the monastery was soon to
suffer further extensive damage as a result of a series of fires, local peasant
uprisings, and the Thirty Years' War. At the end of the 17C Kilian and Christoph
Dientzenhofer were brought in to rebuild much of the complex, and further
work was carried out here in the early years of the present century. Dissolved
after the Second World War, the place served until recently as a barracks.

Today the monastery has a sad and shabby look, its buildings lining
an unkempt forecourt. The church, which was consecrated in 1232, is
by far the oldest part of the surviving complex, and has kept its

original Cistercian Gothic fabric, even if heavily disguised by later restorations and a series of baroque altars. The important library of the monastery, containing numerous illuminated manuscripts produced here from the 16C onwards, occupies a neo-baroque building of 1902–10, the large interior of which has a stuccoed and frescoed ceiling in the manner of the great artists of the Bohemian baroque.

11 Mariánské Lázně to Domažlice

Total distance 73km. Mariánské Lázně—Road 21 36km Stříbro—27km Horšovský Týn—10km Domažlice

Take Road 21 to Stříbro and then the side road S from here to the village of Kladruby, pleasantly situated on the peaceful river Úhlavka. Looming fantastically above the wooded, hilly banks on the other side of the river to the village—off the road which leads towards Ostrov u Stříbra—is the former Benedictine **MONASTERY OF KLADRUBY**, containing one of central Europe's most striking and original baroque churches.

The monastery was founded by the Czech Prince Vladislav I in 1115 on an ancient merchant route linking Prague with Bavaria. Generously endowed by Vladislav and subsequent members of the Přemyslid family, the place became in the 14C Bohemia's richest monastery. On the death of Abbot Racek in 1393, King Václav IV attempted to use the monastery's vast revenues to create a new Episcopal See in Bohemia, the idea being to undermine the power of his chief political adversary, Jan of Jenštejn, Archbishop of Prague. The Archbishop thwarted this plan by encouraging the monks at Kladruby to elect a new head, an appointment which was later endorsed by the Archbishop's Vicar-General, Jan of Pomuk (Jan Nepomucký). Eventually the enraged king had the latter tortured, quartered and flung into the Vltava river.

Though badly damaged during the Hussite Wars and again during the Thirty Years' War, the monastery regained its former importance in the course of the 17C. The emergence at the end of the century of John of Nepomuk as patron saint of Bohemia and the centre of a flourishing Jesuit cult, coincided with the magnificent baroque reconstruction of the monastery. The main architect involved was Santini-Aichel, who brought the monastery church to completion in 1726. In 1765 reforms instituted by the Emperor Joseph II led to the dissolution of the monastery, which later passed into the hands of the Austrian Field-Marshal Prince Windisch-Grätz; it remained the property of this family until 1945.

Brian Knox, in his pioneering architectural guide to Bohemia and Moravia of 1952, described Kladruby as a 'dream made stone', but wrote that it 'is hardly mentioned in the guides, and the organised parties pass it by. It is a little damp; a few windows have been broken. But I do not feel that it can ever be forgotten'. His comments still hold true today, and your first impression on passing through the entrance gate of the monastery is one of neglect and abandon. Turning right you enter an inner courtyard bordered to your left by the New Monastery Building, which was built by Kilian Ignaz Dientzenhofer between 1729 and 1739 and later adapted for use as a library by Prince Windischgrätz: featuring a main portal flanked by atlantes, it is now in a lamentable state, and is closed to visitors. The official tour of the monastery begins with the Winter Refectory in the adjacent Old Monastery Building, where a small art collection has been assembled, including a portrait of Count Nostic by Škréta and a painting by Tischbein. Along the north side of the large cloister has been placed a group of statues by Matthias Braun and his school,

*Interior of the former monastery church at Kladruby, one
of the most outstanding examples of Santini-Aichel's
'Baroque Gothic' manner*

taken from Valec château near Karlovy Vary. On the east side,
meanwhile, leading to the church entrance, can be seen four 16C
wooden reliefs from southern Germany.

As soon as you reach the church, all the other attractions of the
monastery, interesting though they are, become of incidental significance. An extraordinary example of the adaptation by a baroque
architect of the Gothic style, the church was begun by Santini in 1713

and made to incorporate the ground-plan of the original three-aisled Romanesque basilica, the longest in Bohemia and completed and consecrated in 1233. From the outside the church has a largely conventional Gothic appearance, with the exception of the bizarre crossing lantern—a ring of exuberant ogee-arched windows with a pinnacled superstructure supporting the crown of the Prince of Bohemia (the abbot of the time, Abbot Finzguth, described it as being *more Gottico nondum viso*, in a hitherto unseen Gothic manner). A less spectacular but no less original feature is the glazed staircase well attached to the north side of the apse. The exhilarating interior of the church, in vivid pistachio green, is notable above all for its elaborate, fantastical vaulting—worthy in its complexity of Bene-dikt Ried's at Kutná Hora—and for its furnishings. The latter, designed also by Santini, include an inlaid wooden pulpit in the form of the prow of a ship, and culminate in a quite remarkable high altar situated at the end of an undulating chancel. The altar, a perfect synthesis of baroque movement and Gothic fantasy, comprises white and dynamic marble figures by Matthias Braun set against an openwork Gothic structure spiked with nodding crocketed pinna-cles. Below the crowning sculpture of the Crucifixion are the symbols of the Evangelists, while lower down is a statue of the Madonna (the only work not by Braun) flanked to the left by St. Benedict and to the right by St. Wolfgang. Of great iconographic interest is Braun's tiny statue of Christ in the golden tabernacle underneath the Virgin: this is unique in showing the crucified Christ with only one hand attached to the cross, the other one touching instead his right thigh. The frescoes in the lantern vault and along the sides of the nave are by the celebrated Bavarian artist Cosmas Damian Assam, and feature scenes from the lives of the Benedictine saints.

After leaving the monastery continue on the Ostrov road for a further kilometre, then turn right to Zhoř and *Horšovský Týn* (23km). Commanding extensive views over flat wooded and agricultural countryside, Horšovský Týn is an attractive small town centred around a sloping *square* lined with colourful and recently restored Gothic, Renaissance and baroque houses. A bridge links the upper part of the square with a large castle dominating a wooded public park comprising the former moat and castle gardens. The castle itself was built originally between 1260 and 1270, then extended after a fire in 1547 into a four-winged mansion by John the Younger of Lobkovice and his son Christopher, major-domo to Rudolph II; confiscated from the family in 1623 after Vilém of Lobkovice had been sentenced to death for his part in the Battle of the White Mountain, the estate was then acquired by Count Maximilian Trautt-mansdorf, whose family were to keep it until 1945. Behind the gabled Renaissance façade and entrance gate is a courtyard with fine Renaissance sgraffito decoration. A surprising amount of the original medieval interior has survived, and the highpoint of the obligatory guided tour is the *chapel* of c 1275, a tall rib-vaulted structure containing fragments of Renaissance frescoes. Later in the tour you come to a series of rococo rooms, some of which are hung with paintings optimistically described as being by Canaletto.

Horšovský Týn marks the northern boundary of a small region famed for its folklore and quaintly called in English the *Chod Region*.

The Chods, an ancient ethnic group, were entrusted in the middle ages with guarding the Bohemian border with Germany. The Bohemian monarchy rewarded them in 1325 with special privileges, the loss of which after the Thirty Years' War was to result in 1692 in a Chod uprising led by Jan Sladký-Kozina.

In the 19C the history and strong folkloric traditions of this people came to have a romantic attraction to a number of Czech writers, most notably the novelists Jindřich Jindřich and Božena Němcová. Until comparatively recently the women of the region could be seen on Sundays dressed in their traditional folk costumes featuring low black shoes, brilliant red hosiery and elaborately decorated bodices and silk aprons; the men meanwhile had white shirts and broad-brimmed black hats. Ceramics and other crafts objects in a traditional Chod style continue to be produced today, but in factories rather than in the typical wooden houses of old, of which few survive.

The capital of the Chod Region is **Domažlice**, a well-preserved town in verdant surroundings and with a long, narrow and particularly beautiful arcaded main square. The houses date back mostly to the Gothic and Renaissance periods, but have baroque or Empire gables. One of the houses at the western end of the square has a plaque to Božena Němcová, who worked here as a teacher. Half-way down the square stands the town's most prominent landmark, the round and slightly leaning 13C tower attached to the church of *St. Mary*; an excellent panorama of the town and surroundings can be had from the top. The church itself was rebuilt in the early 18C to the designs of Kilian Ignaz Dientzenhofer, and has frescoes inside by the baroque painter F.J. Lux. Opposite St. Mary's is the neo-Renaissance Town Hall of 1891, while at the eastern end of the square is a tall, heavily restored and steeply gabled gatehouse of c 1270, the main survival of the town's medieval fortifications. The town's castle, just to the S of the main square, was founded in 1284, but was completely transformed in the 18C; it houses today the drearily old-fashioned *Chod Museum*, devoted to local history and folklore. Further folkloric items, collected by the writer Jindřich Jindřich, can be seen in the museum named after him just below the town's medieval gatehouse.

A 28km tour around the Chod Region could be made by driving 5km S along the main road to Germany, and then turning right to Újezd (a further 5km), the birthplace of the leader of the 1692 Chod uprising, Jan Sladký-Kozina; there is a small museum to him at the so-called Kozina's farm, and a tall statue of him in traditional Chod costume on top of the hill of Hrádek, behind the village. 8km further W, at the foot of hills popular with skiers, is the small town of *Klenčí pod Čerchovem*, known for its ceramics (which can be bought at the Chodovia Cooperative) and for being the birthplace of the Chod Region's most famous native writer, J.S. Baar (1869–1925), who is commemorated here by a memorial room. From here you can return to Domažlice via Draženov (5km), where there are three rare surviving examples of traditional Chod farmsteads (Nos 2, 5, 8).

12 Domažlice to České Budějovice

Total distance 168km. Domažlice—Road 22 37km *Klatovy*—30km Sušice—38km Vimperk—20km **Prachatice**—43km **České Budějovice**.

The SW frontier of Bohemia, bordering on Germany, is marked by the Šumava mountains, a range of about 120km which you follow for almost its entire length while driving from Domažlice to České Budějovice by way of Sušice. Gently contoured, relatively little populated, and covered with one of the largest and most dense forests in Bohemia, the area is popular both as a summer and winter resort, and has formed since 1963 a protected landscape region of 1630 sq km. The river Vltava—the longest river in Czechoslovakia and the inspiration of innumerable poems—has its source in these mountains, as does its left tributary, the Otava. The route which you take is roughly that of the medieval trading route known as the Golden Path, along which malt was exported and salt imported.

Head E from Domažlice (see Route 11) on Road 22, passing after 11km the village of *Kdyně*, dominated by the ruins of 13C Rožmberk Castle (destroyed by Ferdinand III in 1655). *Klatovy*, 21km further E, is sometimes known as the gateway to the Šumava region, and is one of the most important towns in the area. Founded in 1260, it had become by 1547 the seventh wealthiest town in Bohemia. Though retaining its medieval chessboard plan, sections of its fortifications and a number of fine monuments, the town centre never lives up to the expectations aroused by the magical silhouette of spires and towers which the place presents from a distance. Almost everything of interest is to be found around the lively main square, where Renaissance and baroque monuments vie with uninspiring development of more recent years. At the SW corner of the square stands the town's tallest and most distinctive monument, the Black Tower, begun in 1547 by one Master Antonín and restored in 1295; you can climb up to the gallery to enjoy a wonderful view S over the Šumava range. Adjoining it is the Renaissance Town Hall of 1557–59, decorated with modern sgraffiti. Adjacent to the tower on the western side of the square is the twin-towered *Jesuit church*, begun to designs by Giovanni Domenico Orsi in 1656, but rebuilt by Kilian Ignaz Dientzenhofer in 1703–22 following a severe fire. The interior is interesting primarily on account of the Pozzo-inspired illusionistic frescoes over the east end, the work of the Jesuit painter Ignaz Raab and František Palko.

The most popular tourist attraction in Klatovy lies underneath the Jesuit church, but can only be reached from a door outside the building. This, the Klatovy *catacombs*, was used as a burial place from 1676 up to 1783, when the Emperor Joseph II forbade the practice of church burial. Thanks to a system of ventilating air-holes that allow dry air to circulate freely within the crypt, the 40 corpses that remain here (out of an original 200) are in a mummified condition. A taped commentary in English, beginning jovially with the words 'Welcome to Kladruby', provides an historical distraction while you gape morbidly at the corpses, most of which are of people associated with the Jesuit College to which the church was attached. Among the mortal remains you can admire are those of one of the founders of the College, Albert Chánovský, the mathematician Benjamin Schleier, and a certain foreigner named Jok Fabricius, whose career began auspiciously as a bachelor of philosophy, but ended as college shoemaker.

A more cheerful sight is that of the neighbouring *Baroque Pharmacy*, situated on the W side of the square, at No. 149. It was originally to be found inside the Jesuit College, but following the suppression of the Jesuit Order in 1773 was acquired by a local apothecary and transferred to his own premises; it functioned as a pharmacy up to 1964, but now forms part of a small museum. The beautiful rococo panelling was completed in 1733 by John Geschwent, a cabinet-maker who was born in Allgau in Schwaben in 1701 and died in Silesia in 1745. A carved unicorn's horn (the apothecary's trademark) hangs in the room, though unquestionably the most spectacular work here is a baroque centrepiece featuring a statue of St. Michael (patron of apothecaries) trampling over the devil, the symbol of disease; below these figures are two black men holding vessels which probably once contained 'Therial' and 'Mythridatum'. In a backroom can be seen 18C distillation and grinding equipment. Off the NE corner of the square stands the White Tower, which was built in 1581, redecorated in 1687, and again in 1898. Behind this is the *Archdeacon's Church*, which conceals behind a 19C west façade an attractive hall-church with a chancel of c 1400 and a nave completed by Master Antonín in the 1550s; the nave has elaborate net vaulting. 11km to the N of Klatovy on the Plzeň road is the impressive castle of *Švihov*, begun in c 1480 by Puta of Rýzmberk, chief justice of Bohemia, and completed in around 1520 following the intervention of Benedikt Ried. The eastern half of this once massive castle was razed on the orders of the Habsburgs, and the remaining parts suffered much damage after being transformed into a granary in the 18C. The most eloquent survival is the late Gothic chapel of 1515, decorated with an amusing painting of St. George and the Dragon; also of interest is the hall, which has a a fine coffered ceiling of 1578 taken from the château at Dobrovice.

Those intending to stay a while in the Šumava could take the E53 S from Klatovy to *Železná Ruda* (39km), passing through a landscape which becomes progressively hillier and more forested. Železná Ruda, the most popular of the Šumava resorts, is 2km from the German border, just to the N of the highest peak in the range, Grosser Arber, the summit of which (1456m) is in Germany. 2km to the N of Železná Ruda on the road to Nýrsko is the resort of Špičák, from where you can take a chair-lift (in three stages) to the summit of Pancíř (1214m). From the car park at Špičácké sedlo, 1km further N along the road, a bus will take you up to the Black Lake (Černé jezero), a potentially beautiful spot encased in a wooded mountain hollow, but until recently spoilt by restricted access imposed by its being in a sensitive border area.

Continuing E from Klatovy, you should stay on Road 22 for a further 13km, then head S for another 17km to *Sušice*. Sušice is a tiny industrial town with the slightly incongruous reputation of being the leading manufacturer of matches in central Europe; this industry was established here in the early 19C, and soon gave the place an international renown. The main tourist attraction is the **Šumava Museum**, situated in the beautiful Veprchovský House on the main square. The house itself, of medieval origin, immediately attracts attention with its Renaissance façade, featuring an extraordinary gable made up of superimposed rows of blind arcading, the end result looking more Indian than European. As for the museum, this is one of the oldest in Czechoslovakia, having been founded in 1879 on the instigation of a local schoolteacher with a passion for preserving the relics of the past: at the time of its foundation there were only 26 other museums in Bohemia and Moravia. The collections are small but excellently displayed in a homely and lovingly restored interior, including rooms in Renaissance, baroque and Beidermeier styles. Apart from items relating to local history, ethnogaphy and archaeology, there is a good collection of traditional Šumava glass, a 15C woodcarving of the Madonna and Child, and a superlative set of pewter which had been hidden for three centuries in the masonry of a local house, where it had been left by one Adam Cech, a local citizen who had fled the country after the Battle of the White Mountain.

From Sušice you could make a short DETOUR to see the ruined castle of *Rabí*, which lies 10km to the N in the direction of Horažďovice. Belonging to the powerful Rožmberk family and one of the largest castles in Bohemia, Rabí was besieged and conquered in 1421 by the Hussite leader Jan Žižka, who lost here his second eye; the complex, of 14C origin, was rebuilt in the 1520s with the assistance of Benedikt Ried.

Returning to Sušice continue driving in a south-easterly direction towards Vimperk. A winding drive of 17km through an attractive forested valley will take you to *Kašperské Hory*. A gold-mining town in the Middle Ages, this is now little more than a large village with a cheerful looking main square, one side of which is taken up by the baroque Town Hall, a three-gabled structure in dazzling white and yellow. Peering over a pine-forested hill to the N of the village are the extensive ruins of the *castle* erected by Charles IV in 1356 to guard the local gold mines. These romantically set ruins can best be reached by driving E out of the village, and then taking the turning to the left marked Nezdice; after 2km you come to two houses, alongside which is a path leading up into a forest; follow the green markings, and after 1.5km you will arrive at the castle (only the exterior can be seen).

East of Kašperk Castle you cross into the administrative region of South Bohemia. The village of *Vimperk*, 21km further on, lies in the shadow of a 13C castle reconstructed in the 19C and used today as a local museum with documents relating to local history and industries, and to the flora and fauna of the Šumava mountains; at Sudslavice, 4km to the N, is a 600-year-old lime tree, one of the oldest in Czechoslovakia, and measuring nearly 12m in diameter. 20km to the E of Vimperk, in the direction of České Budějovice, is *Husinec*, the birthplace of Jan Hus (1369–1415), who is commemorated by a statue by Karel Lidický (1958) in the village square, and a small museum in the house where he was born. As a youth Hus frequented the market at *Prachatice*, situated high on a hill 4km to the S and encircled by extensive surviving sections of its medieval walls. It is the most attractive town in the Šumava region, and a foretaste of the so-called Rose Towns to the E.

Founded as a trading post in 1325, Prachatice received at the end of the century a royal charter from Wenceslas IV which gave it the Bohemian monopoly of the salt trade. The town prospered as never before, though its golden age is generally considered to have been the 16C, when it came into the possession of the Rožmberk family. A severe fire in 1507 led the Rožmberks to rebuild most of the town, and the old centre today has an essentially Renaissance character.

The town is especially rich in sgraffitoed Renaissance buildings, many of which are to be found on the beautifully preserved main square. At the top of the square is the *Old Town Hall* (c 1571), with monochrome scenes by both Czech and Italian artists of the Dance of Death, and allegories of Justice; the New Town Hall (1903), further down on the same side, is in a neo-Renaissance style, and covered with sgraffiti. At No. 169 is the Princes' House (Kníšecí dům), built by the Rožmberks in 1572 and decorated with much-worn biblical scenes; under one of the arcades of the adjoining Custom House is a representation of the Rožmberk rider. Among the finest of the sgraffiti decorations are the battle scenes on the 16C Rumpál House, a house owned by the Rumpál family up to 1671 and later becoming for a while a brewery and pub.

Towering behind the NE corner of the square is the imposing, fortress-like mass of the 14C *St. James Church* (sv. Jakub), the interior of which has net-vaulting of 1410. The picturesque narrow street which leads down to it from the square is lined the whole

length with old buildings including—just below the church—the
richly decorated Hejdlův House. The street ends at the sgraffitoed
Písek Gate, which is attached to the longest surviving section of the
town's 14C and 16C fortifications; a long and narrow park lies below
them, offering a fine view of the town rising above its defensive
walls.

Leaving the town on the road marked Vodňany, you will regain
4km to the N the main road to České Budějovice. 10km along this is
the Renaissance summer palace of *Kratochvíle*, situated at the
western end of a marshy lake, and with its moats now silted, and
gardens planted with vegetables rather than flowers. Commissioned
as a pleasure retreat by Vilem of Rožmberk (the brother of Petr Vok),
it was built in 1583–90 by Baldassare Maggi da Vomio. This same
architect was responsible for the extensive stucco decorations that—
together with the much damaged frescoes by Jiří Widman of 1589—
constitute the chief interest of the interior. The greatest of the rooms,
the Golden Hall, runs along the whole western side of the house, and
has a remarkable ceiling stuccoed all over with scenes from classical
history. After Netolice, 2km to the E, continue driving E for a further
13km, until you join the E49, which will take you after 12km to České
Budějovice (see Route 16).

13   Prague to Plzeň

Total distance 78km. Prague—D5/E50 18km Beroun—44km
Rokycany—16km **Plzeň**.

The main road from Prague to Plzeň runs through gently rolling
countryside with dense areas of forest. A dual carriageway for the
first 28km, the D5 bypasses the town of Beroun, and, 14km later,
goes through *Žebrák*, where there is a ruined royal castle dating
back to c 1280; remodelled by Wenceslas I at the end of the 14C, the
building was further altered during the Renaissance period. The
more important royal castle of Točník, founded by Wenceslas IV in
c 1400, stands 2km N of the road, but is closed to visitors. The town
of Rokycany, 26km further W, is one of the oldest in Bohemia, though
the few surviving traces of its past—such as remains of its medieval
fortifications—have now been surrounded by iron foundries and
other industries. More extensive industrial development awaits you
at **Plzeň**, known for its Škoda works, but, above all for its beer.

Founded in 1295 by the banks of the river Radbuza, Plzeň enjoyed many royal
privileges and soon flourished as a commercial centre, its drapers acquiring an
international reputation. Commercial prosperity continued into the 17C, and
many foreign merchants, craftsmen and artists settled here, in particular from
Germany and Italy. A strong bastion of Catholicism since Hussite times, Plzeň
suffered terribly during the Thirty Years' War, the ravages of war being also
compounded by a series of plagues. However, the town began to revive at the
end of the 17C, with a new wave of immigrants, and the establishment here of
the iron, steel and textile industries. The industrialisation rapidly intensified in
the course of the 19C, with the creation in turn of the first tannery (soon to be
the third largest in Bohemia), the Burgher Brewery (which was to make the
name of Plzeň perennially linked with beer), and the Škoda engineering works.
At the same time Plzeň emerged as an important centre of the Czech National
Movement, and many important theatrical productions in the Czech language
were brought here from Prague by the famous playwright and director J.K. Tyl,
who died in the town in 1856.

Plzeň is not one of Czechoslovakia's more beautiful towns, its industrial growth having led in the last century to the destruction of many of its older houses, and to the pulling down after 1828, of the remaining sections of its medieval walls; further devastation was caused by heavy bombing in 1944–45. None the less a number of interesting monuments have survived, as well as the town's original chessboard layout. The greatest concentration of old buildings is on the blackened and enormous main square (*náměstí Republik*y), which takes up two large blocks of the chessboard. Occupying an isolated position on the northern half of the square is the *Cathedral of St. Bartholomew* (sv. Bartoloměj), built between the 14C and 16C, and crowned by the tallest steeple in Bohemia (103m; you can climb up to the gallery). The interior of this triple-naved hall-church, at present closed for major restoration, has vaulting sprung from massive round piers; there are traces of wall-painting, and a delicately

poised marble Madonna and Child of the 14C. The late Gothic
Šternberk Chapel (Šternberská kaple), attached to the south side of
the chancel, has interesting vaulting with pendulant bosses supported by free-standing ribs.

Adjacent to the cathedral's west façade is a Plague Column of 1681
with sculptures by K. Widman, while behind this, on the north side of
the square, is the Renaissance Town Hall. Built in 1555–58 by the
Italian architect Giovanni Stazio, this building, with its rusticated
ground floor, has elements of a Tuscan cinquecento palace; however,
the gabled attic storey—probably an addition of the 1570s—gives the
structure an unmistakably central European look. The pseudo-
Renaissance sgraffito work dates from the time of the building's
restoration in 1907–12; elsewhere in the square are late 19C sgraffito
decorations by M. Aleš. Among the other surviving old houses on the
náměstí Republiky is the baroque Archdeacon's House (1710) directly opposite the cathedral's west façade. North from here runs
Dominikánská, where, at No 25, stands the modest but elegant early
18C Mestl house. The finest of all the town's secular baroque
buildings is that at No. 251 on the parallel street to the W, Sedláčkova. Crowned by a gable in the form of a broken Borrominesque
pediment, it is named after the architect who built it, Jakub Auguston
(d. 1735), the son of Italian immigrants to the town. Another of
Auguston's works can be seen by walking to the southern end of
Sedláčkova, and then turning left into Bezručova. This work, the
Dominican church of St. Anne (sv. Anny), is at the junction of
Bezručova and B. Smetany, and was Auguston's major Plzeň commission; the convent to which it was attached was converted in 1804
into a school (now the State Science Library), where the composer
Bedřich Smetana was to study between 1840 and 1843.

The old centre of Plzeň is surrounded today by a series of gardens
marking the site of the medieval walls. In the Smetana Gardens,
immediately to the S of the former Dominican Convent of St. Anne, is
a memorial to Smetana (1874), as well as an imposing turn-of-the-
century theatre named after J.K. Tyl. The theatre stands at the SW
corner of the old town, and from here a detour could be made into an
ugly modern district to see the Škoda Museum (Korandova 4), a good
20 minutes' walk to the E (walk or take No. 34 bus along the busy
Tylova to Husovo náměstí, then head south).

The history of the Škoda works goes back to the foundation in 1859 of the
Waldstein engineering works, a company which was purchased by the Plzeň-
born Emil Škoda ten years later. Under Škoda the company rapidly expanded,
particularly after 1890, when it began manufacturing arms. Today the name
Škoda is generally associated with cars, which have in western Europe a
reputation as bad as the Russian Ladas, and are likewise the subject of many
English jokes, e.g.: Question: 'What is a Škoda without a roof?'. Answer: 'A
skip'.

The museum has much photographic documentation relating to the
history of the Škoda works, as well as many working models of
engines, cars, and other products.—Returning to the old town head E
of the St. Anne's church to the Františkánská, where you will find a
former Franciscan church and monastery (Františkánský klášter s
kostelem) dating back to the late 13C; the church itself was rebuilt in
the baroque period, but the former chapter house (now the Chapel of
St. Barbara) has not been altered since medieval times, and is
extensively covered with interesting frescoes of c 1460. Behind the
monastery, at the SE corner of the old town, is a grand eclectic
structure of 1886, designed by Josef Škorpil and housing today both

the *West Bohemian Museum* and the more recently formed *West Bohemian Gallery*. The former has historical, natural history and applied arts collections, while the latter specialises in Czech art of the 19C and 20C, including works by M. Aleš, J. Navrátil, K. Purkyně, J. Preisler (the Symbolist triptych, Spring), A. Slavíček, B. Kubišta, E. Filla, V. Špála, J. Čapek and J. Šíma. Walking N from the museum along the gardens that border the eastern edge of the old town, you will pass on your left (in between Dřevená and Pražská Streets) a curious long building known as the *Meat Hall* (Masné krámy): though dating back to the founding in the early 14C of the Plzeň Guild of Butchers (the oldest guild in the city), it was much altered in the 19C, and is now used for concerts and temporary exhibitions. Opposite it, on the northern side of Pražská, is a tower of 1532 which served both as a water-tower and as part of the town's fortifications. The parallel street to the N of Pražská is Veleslavínova, where at No. 6 a building of 14C origin houses the *Brewery Museum* (Pivovarské Muzeum), a fascinating collection relating to the history of beer-making in the town, and incorporating the building's medieval beer-cellars and malt-house.

After retracing your footsteps S to Dřežvěná, head E along M. Škardové and cross the river Radbuza. The continuation of M. Škardové on the other side of the river is the wide and bleak u Prazdroje, off the left-hand side of which you will come after a short walk to the entrance to the **Pilsner Urquell Brewery** (Plzeňský Prazdroj), the major tourist attraction of the town. Visits to the brewery are normally possible only for groups, and should always be reserved beforehand with Čedok.

The rights to brew beer were granted to the Burghers of Plzeň from the time of the town's foundation in 1295; these rights, later restricted to those who had houses within the old fortifications, were to be kept right up to the 19C. The beer was brewed in the cellars of the burghers' homes and then sold after having been stringently tested by inspectors appointed by the Town Council: beer of low quality could be sold at a lower price only to the poor of the town, while beer considered a complete failure was publically disposed of in front of the Town Hall, this being the biggest disgrace a burgher-brewer could suffer. The way in which the beer was tested is not known, though there is a popular and fanciful tradition which has it that the inspectors sat with their leather trousers on an oak bench on which the brew was poured: if, on rising, the beer stuck to the trousers, it was thought to be of sufficent density and thus a good brew.

In 1842 the Plzeň citizens holding the beer-brewing right decided to pool their resources into a single enterprise, so as to profit from new and improved methods of production. The success of the Burgher Brewery was immediate, the taste for the beer produced here catching on immediately in Prague, and then spreading by the 1850s to Vienna and the West Bohemian spas; by the 1860s the beer was being exported to Paris and London, and in 1873 the first shipment of it was made to the United States of America. In 1898 the beer was given the label 'Pilsner Urquell' (in Czech, 'Prazdroj Plzeň'), meaning 'the ancient spring of Plzeň'. The original 'Pils', and as such the prototype of pale beer throughout the world, its popularity continues to increase, and there are many who regard it as the finest of all beers. The key to its success lies partly in the care taken in the proper drying of the malt, in the use of the excellent hops around Žatec in North-west Bohemia, and in the maturing of the beer in the traditional oak wood casks.

Beside the entrance to the brewery is a lively turn-of-the-century Beer-Hall (*Prazdroj*), where you can drink the beer to the accompaniment of suitably copious and hearty fare. The entrance itself takes the form of a triumphal arch erected in 1898, and celebrating 56 years of the brewery's existence. Beyond it extends an industrial landscape which can have changed little since the beginning of the century, with red-brick chimneys, ageing rails and pseudo-medieval

Stuccoed façade of beer-hall in the Pilsner Urquell Brewery, Plzeň

towers. The interesting guided tour starts off with a short film show, and then takes you down into the cold and evocative 19C cellars, where warm clothing is advisable. At the end of the tour you finally get round to tasting the beer, and do so in a gabled turn-of-the-century building with a delightful white stucco façade decorated with scenes of beer-making; the intimate interior has an Impressionist-style painting by Blažíček representing a Beer-Garden (1924).

From the brewery it is a 20 minutes' walk S along Nádražní and Mikulášská to the *Church of St. Nicholas* (sv. Mikuláš) (the same journey could be undertaken in a No. 1 or 2 tram). This simple, modest building dates back to 1410 but was remodelled during the baroque period; in its shaded cemetry you will find the graves both of Emil Škoda and J.K. Tyl, the latter commemorated by a statue of an angel mourning over a representation of the masks of comedy and tragedy. In the north-eastern suburb of Doubravka, and best reached from the brewery by car, is the church of *St. George* (sv. Jiří). Standing isolated among fields in a bend of the river Berounka, this church dates back to the Ottonian period, and though extended in the Gothic and baroque periods, has retained a much-restored 9C apse.

SOUTHERN BOHEMIA

14 Plzeň to České Budějovice (via Strakonice)

Total distance 141km. Plzeň—E49 36km *Nepomuk*—24km *Blatná*—25km *Strakonice*—56km **České Budějovice**.

Leave Plzeň on the E49, making a short detour if you wish at the south-eastern suburb of Černice to visit the Church of All Saints at Starý Plzenec (3km to the E of the road), a pre-Romanesque rotunda heavily restored over the centuries. Continuing along the E49 you will pass shortly on the left the ruined hill-top castle of Radyně (10km S of Plzeň), a 14C structure largely hidden by pines. *Nepomuk*, 20km further to the S, is famous as the birthplace of Jan Nepomucký, the insignificant 14C prelate who was to be transformed 300 years after his death in 1393 into the patron saint of Bohemia. This quiet hill-side village, just off the main road, has on its main street a parish church with a Gothic façade of c 1380 shielding a baroque structure built by Kilian Ignaz Dientzenhofer between 1733 and 1738; the interior, undecorated by frescoes, is notable for its simplicity. At *Lnáře*, 15km further on, is an early 17C château preceded by a bridge adorned with 18C statues.

You are now officially in South Bohemia, and beyond Lnáře pass the first of the small lakes that are so characteristic of this region. *Blatná*, 9km further E, has a celebrated example of one of South Bohemia's many 'water-castles'. Fringed by trees and surrounded on three sides by a great expanse of water, Blatná, was the principal seat of one of the most important Bohemian families, the Rožmitáls. It was Zdeněk Leo of Rožmitál, Supreme Burgrave of the Kingdom of Bohemia, who between 1523 and 1530 had the medieval castle transformed into a formidable Renaissance residence, with a modern system of water defences; Benedikt Ried is known to have been involved in the planning. The picturesque profile of the castle today, complete with steeples, turrets and a half-timbered tower, is largely the result of extensive remodelling carried out in the early 19C. The interior—at present closed for restoration—contains some late 15C wall-paintings featuring naïf views of Blatná and Rožmitál, and exhibits relating to the 19C Czech physicist J.E. Purkyně, who was a a tutor here to the Hildprant family between 1810 and 1813. The village church has an elegant two-aisled interior of 1515 covered with the curious cellular vaulting peculiar to Bohemia. Rising directly above fields outside the tiny village of *Paštiky*, 2km NE of Blatná, is the undulating west tower façade of St. John the Baptist (1747–51), a late work by K.I. Dientzenhofer. The plan of this single-aisled church is longitudinal, though the rounded corners inside give the impression of a centralised one.

9km SE of Blatná, leave the E49 and head S along a side road to Osek and *Strakonice* (16km). Situated on the river Otava, the town of Strakonice derived its wealth initially from gold found in the river; from the 18C onwards it developed into a small industrial centre which from 1812 onwards mysteriously concentrated on the making of fezzes, in which field it has—perhaps, not surprisingly—few rivals in Europe. Another of its curious traditional industries is the making of bagpipes: the dramatist Tyl wrote a play entitled The Bagpiper of Strakonice, and every year a bagpipe festival is held in the grounds of its castle. The castle, one of the first in Bohemia to be surrounded by water, stands on a verdant island in the middle of the Otava. Founded in 1260, it comprises an attractive jumble of medieval buildings, including a machiolated round tower, several half-timbered burgher houses, and a church. There is a small museum with tools and other objects relating to the gold-sifting industry.

East of Strakonice follow Road 22 to Vodňany (23km), where you will regain the E49; a drive of 33km though a landscape of lakes and marshes will take you to České Budějovice (see Route 16).

15 Prague to České Budějovice

A. Via Příbram and Písek

Total distance 235km. Prague—Road 4 62km Příbram—17km
Březnice—18km *Orlík*—18km **Zvíkov**—16km *Písek*—52km **České Budějovice**.

The main route from Prague to České Budějovice by way of Příbram and Písek runs parallel to the river Vltava, though, after Zbraslav (see Route 2) always at some distance from the river. There is a small road which follows the Vltava from Zbraslav to Štěchovice, 16km to the S, but afterwards the river winds unaccompanied through dense forest; pleasure boats from Prague also turn back at Štěchovice, for between here and Zvíkov lie a series of major dams that have turned the river into a sinuous series of connected lakes, the shores of which are popular with swimmers anglers and campers.

Road 4, the main road running SW of Prague, is dual carriageway almost all the way to Příbram (62km). After 54km the road passes next to the industrial town of *Dobříš*, where there is an important rococo château designed by the French architect Jules Robert de Cotte in 1745, and completed in 1765; the large English garden once attached to the house is now a public park, but the house itself, together with its surrounding French Garden (containing statuary by I.F. Platzer), is reserved for members of the Czech Union of Writers, and cannot be visited; it was at a meeting of young writers held in Dobříš in the autumn of 1956 that the future playwright and Czech president Václav Havel (1936–) first drew attention to himself, making a controversial speech on the ambiguous relationship between official and suppressed literature. One of the most famous of all Czech writers this century, Karel Čapek (1890–1938), acquired in 1935 a country cottage 3km SE of Dobříš at *Strž*. He and his wife (whom he had married that year following a long friendship dating back to the early 1920s) devoted an enormous amount of energy to improving and looking after the 22 hectares of land which came with the house. However, he was to die only three years later, literally heartbroken by Chamberlain's betrayal of Czechoslovakia. He was at Prague at the time, and had been eagerly awaiting the spring, when he hoped to return to Strž; as he lay dying he reputedly asked the doctors, 'What's the weather like outside? Is there ice on the ground? In ninety-one days we'll go to Strž together. All of us. In Strž the trees and the grass will be green by then. In ninety-one days...' Čapek's cottage, beautifully situated by a small lake, houses today a memorial museum to him.

6km S of Dobříš, Road 4 passes the village of Obořiště, where the former Pauline Convent (now an agricultural college) has a church designed by Christoph Dientzenhofer; built in 1702–11, it was this architect's first work in Bohemia, and, with its concave façade and undulating interior, one of the earliest examples in this country of the influence of the Italian architect Guarino Guarini. After a further 6km along Road 4, the dual carriageway comes to an end, and you should turn right to *Příbram*, a 6km detour to the east. Příbram itself—an industrial town where silver was mined up to the end of the 19C—is of little architectural interest, but above its western suburbs rises a hill (the so-called *Svatá Hora* or 'Holy Mountain') crowned by one of the largest pilgrimage churches in Czechoslovakia. The church (1658–75), towering above terraces decorated with statues of angels and saints by Matyáš Hueber (d. 1702), was designed by two of the leading architects associated with the early baroque in Bohemia, Carlo Lurago and Domenico Orsi; inside there are frescoes by the first baroque artist to employ this technique in Bohemia, Jan Jakub Steevens.

Head S from Příbram along Road 30, and after 5km (just before regaining Road 4), turn right to *Březnice*, a further 12km. The town's church (1637–42), attached to a former Jesuit College, is a large and forbidding work by Carlo Lurago; the interior contains altars by Škréta and Franz Xavier and Ignaz Raab. More interesting is the château, situated in a wooded public park on the edge of town, and creating beautiful reflections in the small lake below it. The original medieval castle was transformed into a Renaissance residence in the mid 16C, at around the time that Ferdinand, the son of the Emperor Ferdinand I, was married here to Philippine Welser of Augsburg. In front of the building is a sculpture by the locally born artist Ludvík Kuba (1863–1956), more of whose works can be seen in the gallery installed inside. Leave Březnice on Road 19, which heads in a SE direction towards Tábor, crossing Road 4 after 11km, and, 7km later, the Vltava. On the western shores of the river—which widens here into a wide and long lake created by the largest of this river's dams—stands the castle of *Orlík nad Vltavou*. Huddled between water and forest, this former Schwarzenberg property, dates back to a 13C castle, built, strategically, near what was once a ford across the Vltava; altered and extended at the end of the 16C, it was reconstructed after a serious fire in 1802, and then remodelled in a neo-Gothic style by B. Grueber between 1849 and 1860. The interior includes a well-preserved series of Empire rooms filled with furniture of that period, and a second-floor gallery crammmed to capacity with hunting trophies and a collection of arms dating from the 17C to 19C. Also on the second floor is the *Teska Hall*, so-called on account of a remarkably elaborate and deeply carved coffered ceiling executed in 1882–84 by Jan Teska, a relative of the painter Mikoláš Aleš.

Numerous canoists and a summer boat service ply the Vltava in between Orlík and Zvíkov. The journey between the two places is rather less easy by car, and involves a short detour away from the river: the quickest route is to drive due S from Orlík, past Starý Sedlo and Nevězice, then turn right towards Smetanova, and finally left and left again. The castle of Zvíkov, one of Bohemia's most important medieval sights, occupies a magnificent isolated position, thrust up high on a wooded spit of land at the confluence of the Vltava and the Otava; forests extend as far as the eye can see. Built for the Přemyslid kings, it was begun in around 1234, and its walls completed by 1270; though never taken by force, it was mortgaged in the 14C to the Rožmberks, who in later years were badly to neglect it. Unlike most other Czech castles it was not added to or remodelled in later centuries, and the parts that survive today, scattered around their sylvan setting, give a good idea of how the former royal residence originally looked. You enter through a gate adjoining a tall round tower comprising the oldest part of the complex. North of here—to the E of a large courtyard—is the royal palace itself, centred around an unusual hexagonal-shaped courtyard comprising two superimposed rows of arcading, the upper of which is decorated by simple tracery. A room on the ground floor has exhibits relating to the construction of the castle, while upstairs is a terrace with a superb panorama over the Vltava. On the upper floor are also to be found the **Royal Chapel** and the so-called *Bridal Chamber*, the two most exciting remaining parts of the palace interior. Both places are decorated with fascinating if over-restored wall-paintings by an anonymous master of c 1480 (the restoration was carried out at the end of the 19C). One of the walls in the Bridal Chamber shows courting couples in contemporary dress being entertained by a jester and musicians; above, keeping a watch on the proceedings, are the figures of four Bohemian kings. The entrance to the Royal Chapel has a tympanum with sculpted fragments (restored in 1977) representing the Adoration of the Magi. A row of blind trefoiled arcading runs round the lower walls of the chapel, each arch containing paintings of saints by the anonymous master of c 1480; the same artist was also responsible for the paintings above, among which are an Adoration of the Virgin and one of the earliest representations in western art of Purgatory. On the high altar is a fine woodcarving of the Deposition of Christ by an anonymous artist of c 1520.

The road S from Zvíkov joins after Road 33 9km, where you turn right to *Písek* (a further 7km.). Attractively situated on the Otava, Písek is both a holiday resort and a small industrial town which rose to prosperity in the Middle Ages through the sifting of gold-bearing sand from its river (the word 'Písek' means sand). The old centre of the town is best seen from the opposite side of the Otava, from where it presents a little-spoilt profile of 13C to 18C structures rising directly above the water. In the foreground is a late 13C bridge claimed to be the oldest in Czechoslovakia and adorned in the middle with anonymous baroque statues of 1754–57. The most prominent of the riverside buildings is the former *Royal Castle*, commissioned by Otakar II in 1254 but much altered in later centuries. The outstanding feature of the interior is the 13C Knight's Hall, decorated with anonymous wall-paintings dated 1479. The paintings, like those at Zvíkov, are in a fanciful and decorative late medieval manner, and feature battle and tournament scenes, as well as over-life-size figures of George of Poděbrady and of his predecessor Ladislav the Posthumous. By this date the castle had for 20 years been the property of George of Poděbrady's brother-in-law, Leo of Rožmitál (d. 1485).

At Písek you join up with the E49, which will take you after 52km to **České Budějovice** (see Route 16).

B.   Via Tábor and Bechyně

Total distance 149km. Prague—D1/E55 36km Benešov—43km
Tábor—18km *Opařany*—10km **Bechyně**—42km **České Budějovice**.

Take the D1 motorway to V. Popovice (21km), then head S on the E55
past Benešov and **Konopiště** (See Route 2B) until eventually, 43km
later, you approach **Tábor** from its north-western suburbs. The old
centre is seen from this part of town looming above a large lake,
which was created in 1492 by the oldest dam in Bohemia, and given
the biblical name of Jordan. To the S Tábor rises above luxuriant
slopes falling steeply down to the river Lužnice. The beauty of
Tábor's situation, its numerous Renaissance buildings, and its strong
associations with the Hussite movement, make the town one of the
great tourist attractions in South Bohemia.

Following the martyrdom of Jan Hus in 1416, his followers came to be divided
into two distinct groups, the 'Calixtines' being the more aristocratic of the two,
and the 'Utraquists' having both a more popular appeal and a more radical
outlook. Later a third and yet more radical party came into being, which
rejected the Mass, and indeed all but two of the Sacraments, and insisted on the
Bible as the sole authority in all matters of belief. This new party held open-air
meetings throughout Bohemia, but their main centre was at Ústí, a small town
to which they gave the name of the mountain where Christ was transfigured,
Tábor. In 1420 the charismatic leader of the so-called Táborites, Jan Žižka,
founded the present Tábor, 4km to the N of the former one, and on a site
occupied by a castle built in 14C over a Celtic oppidum. The blind Žižka
died of the plague in 1424, and his supporters henceforth called themselves the
'Orphans', feeling that they would be unable to find a new leader equal to him.
The Táborite movement died out in the 1430s, but the town which Žižka had
founded lived on as a Royal town after 1437. The castle was later converted into
a brewery, and the visionary settlement of the Táborites is today a small
industrial town known for its manufacture of sparking plugs for cars.

Surrounded on three sides by its defensive walls, the old centre of
Tábor has been remarkably little spoilt. From the Jordan Lake follow
Palackého tř. into its continuation Pražská, the town's main commercial street, but picturesquely narrow and lined with old buildings; the
finest of these are at Nos 12 and 13 (on the left-hand side), which are
covered with lively sgraffito decorations of battle scenes (1570).
Pražská leads into the town's main square, which is named after Jan
Žižka, who is commemorated by a memorial on the square's north
side. The square, which has been given by recent restoration a bright
and cheeful look, is the town's main showpiece, and contains most of
Tábor's more interesting monuments. In the centre is a Renaissance
fountain, while all around are houses crowned with a remarkable
variety of gables. One of the more fantastical of these gables belongs
to a popular tourist restaurant on the north side of the square
(adjoining the old U Lichviců ale house); it comprises elaborately
intertwined blind arcading, and open-work motifs on the sides.
Occupying the north-western corner of the square is the now
glisteningly white *Church of the Transfiguration of Our Lord on
Mount Tábor*, begun in 1440 on the site of a Hussite church and
largely completed by 1512. You enter through the south side, with its
three Renaissance gables, and find yourself in a a bright and
spacious three-aisled structure, the nave of which was given cross-
and net-vaulting by Master Staněk in 1512. Of slightly later date, and
more remarkable, is the 'cellular' or diamond vaulting in the chancel,
the effect of which, in the words of Brian Knox (1952), is like standing
'inside some huge intricately pleated white skirt'.

The west side of the square is dominated by the **Old Town Hall**, a triple-gabled structure flanked by a tall tower. The heavily restored building, built between the late 15C and early 16C, contains an excellent museum devoted to the history of the Hussite Movement, featuring medals, manuscripts, armoury and applied arts objects connected with the movement, as well as more recent works of art of Hussite subject-matter. The beautifully vaulted and starkly impressive *Hall* contains the model of Bohumil Kafka's dynamic equestrian portrait of Žižka (1935) which now crowns Prague's Žižkov Hill. From the museum you can undertake a tour of the extensive series of tunnels that extend underneath the square. Begun after 1420 and completed 100 years later, they were used at first to store beer, but later acted as shelters during the frequent fires that swept through the town in the 16C; subsequently they were used for prisoners.

Behind the Town Hall lies an empty and neglected part of town with roughly cobbled streets leading to the attractive náměstí Mikuláše, on which stands a 17C former Augustinian Monastery. The 14C Kotnov castle (300m from Žižka náměstí along Klokotská) is on the south-western corner of the town, and has functioned as a brewery since the 18C; it is attached to the 15C Bechyně Gate, which has a high-pitched roof of toy-like appearance. The view from the other side of the gate down to the river is over trees and hanging gardens.

Leave Tábor on Road 33 in the direction of *Písek*. On the outskirts of the town take a turning to the left to *Klokoty*, a tiny pilgrimage church and cloister (1710–30), given an exotic oriental profile through a series of eight onion domes. The place stands above a particularly wooded stretch of the river Lužnice, and commands an excellent view towards Tábor. Continue on Road 33 to *Opařany*, which has a remarkable Jesuit Church built in 1732–35 by K.I. Dientzenhofer. The interior, with a complex and dynamic plan based on two interconnected tranverse ovals, features tangential three-dimensional ribs and the broken segmental pediments so characteristic of this architect's work.

At Opařany leave Road 33 and head S to **Bechyně** (10km), passing after 5km the ruins of Dobronice castle. Bechyně, which is linked to Tábor by the oldest narrow gauge railway in Bohemia (built by František Křižík in 1903), is a small town and peat spa impressively situated above a wooded gorge thrust above the river Lužnice. The sloping and very attractive main square is a quiet and shaded place, more appropriate to a village than a town. Off a street near the top of the square is the former *Franciscan Church and Cloister*, built in the late 15C, but revaulted in the late 16C: the 'cellular' vaulting in the nave is perhaps the most extraordinary of its kind in Bohemia, and seems less an example of late medieval architecture than a German expressionistic fantasy of the 1920s. The former Franciscan monastery hangs directly above the gorge, as does the other important monument in the town—the *Castle*. The Castle, at the bottom of the main square, is a building of 13C origin which was given its present look in the late 16C. The slightly shabby interior, now used for conferences organised by the Czech Academy of Sciences, has a Hall decorated c 1590 with Old Testament figures and representations of virtues and vices; these amusing works, surrounded by a fictive framework in a North Italian style, are comparable to paintings produced at the court of Rudolph II. Bechyně has a long-standing ceramics tradition, and a gallery putting on exhibitions by modern ceramic artists adjoins the castle.

Spanning the Lužnice gorge below the castle is a pioneering parabolically arched concrete bridge. On the other side of the river head S to the pretty village of *Týn nad Vltavou* (10km) where there is a small museum with archaeological, numismatic and ceramic collections. After crossing the Vltava drive S for 21km to **HLUBOKÁ NAD VLTAVOU**, a sprawling village at the foot of a wooded hill crowned by one of the most famous and spectacular country houses in Czechoslovakia.

The origins of Hluboká are in a castle probably founded by Wenceslas I in the early 13C; it remained officially a royal property until 1562, when it was sold to the Lords of Hradec, who had it entirely rebuilt. The work was no sooner over than it was sold again, this time to the Malovec family, who were to be its last Czech owners, keeping it until 1622. In 1661 it became one of the several South Bohemian properties owned by the Bavarian Schwarzenbergs, whose official architect, P.I. Bayer, was to remodel the building in a baroque style between 1707 and 1728. Only after 1830 did the Schwarzenbergs decide to make this their principle Bohemian residence, and at the same time to create a new building which would amply reflect their high standing at the Viennese court, their vast wealth and the progressive outlook which they had recently shown in a series of imaginative industrial and agricultural enterprises. The fantastical turreted showpiece which you see today is due to the rebuilding campaign carried out after 1841 by the Viennese architect F. Beer, and completed in 1871 by F.D. Deworecky.

The house at Hluboká is frequently described as in an English Gothic style, and W.S. Monroe in his Bohemia and the Czechs (1902) even makes the curious assertion that the building is 'a replica of Windsor Castle in England'. However the house bears as much relation to a real English building as Mad Ludwig of Bavaria's Neuschwanstein bears to German medieval architecture. The enormously tall white-stoned structure looks like the work of a demented pastry chef, and all that it has in common with Windsor are its machiolated towers, which are here piled up in profusion to create purely decorative effects: it is a vision of England as exprienced by someone with the imagination of a Walt Disney. As you pass through the main entrance note the bronze handles on the doors, which represent a crow pecking at the eye of a Moor—the grotesque heraldic symbol of the Schwarzenberg family and a motif to be repeated constantly throughout the house. Around the larger of the two courtyards inside are a series of stag heads carved in stone. The entrance hall beyond overwhelms by the sheer quantity of intricate woodcarvings (by local artists), and indeed the hallmark of the whole interior is the abundance of decorative woodwork. Almost everywhere there are marquetry floors, and elaborate wood panelling, both on the walls and ceilings. Crammmed with characteristically Victorian *horror vacui* into this already congested setting is a wealth of furniture and other applied arts objects, including Czech baroque glass, Italian Renaissance tables, Bohemian 18C porcelain, Kreussen jugs, an outstanding collection of 17C to 18C tapestries, and an inlaid baroque wardrobe left by the writer A. Stifter. The paintings, featuring several dubious attributions, are less impressive, though among them are many interesting family and other portraits, including one by Reynolds.

If the lover of fine arts is less than satisfied by a visit to the house at Hluboká, there is always the consolation of the **South Bohemian Aleš Gallery**, which was transferred in 1956 from České Budějovice to the former riding stables adjoining the house; it bears the name of Mikoláš Aleš (1852–1913), one of this region's greatest painters. The building itself, also designed by F. Beer (1845–47), is entered through a magnificent and very innovative iron and glass construction in an elaborate Gothic style. The collections largely originate from the former Diocesan and Municipal Museums at České Budějovice, and from the monastery at Vyšší Brod. The works include 20C Czech masters such as Václav Špála, Josef Čapek and Antonín Hudeček, and the largest collection of Dutch paintings in Czechoslovakia (the latter comprises mainly minor works, but note the portraits by Cornelis van der Voort and Paulus Morelsee, and the still-lifes by Pieter Claesz). By far the most distinguished aspect of the gallery is the large collection of Bohemian paintings and sculptures of the 14C and 15C, most notably a series of characteristically sweet Madonnas and Child, including the sculpted *Rudolvov Madonna* (c 1300, the oldest work in the gallery), the painted Madonna of the Trinity of České Budějovice (before 1410) and the charming *Hluboká Adoration* (c 1380), a work generally attributed to the Master of Třeboň, one of the finest Bohemian artists of the 14C.

Within the extensive grounds of Hluboká are various lakes and canals, and much statuary. 2km SW of the house, by the edge of the Munický Lake, is the *Ohrada hunting Lodge*, built by Bayer for the Schwarzenbergs in 1709–15. The interior, featuring a large ceiling painting of the Enthroned Diana, has been a Museum of Hunting and Forestry since 1842 and is oppressively decorated with hunting trophies, some of the antlers even being used for table legs and candelabra.

South of Ohrada you join the E49, which will lead you after 6km to **České Budějovice** (see Route 16).

16 Prachatice to Jindřichův Hradec via Vyšší Brod

Total distance 189km. Prachatice—18km Volary—68km **Vyšší Brod**—9km **Rožmberk nad Vltavou**—18km **Český Krumlov**—24km **České Budějovice**—24km **Třeboň**—28km **Jindřichův Hradec**.

Instead of driving directly from Prachatice to České Budějovice you could make a detour through the southern half of the forested Šumava, ending up at Vyšší Brod, from where you can begin one of the most exciting architectural itineraries through Czechoslovakia.

Head due S of Prachatice to Volary (18km), where you can see some of the last surviving examples of the traditional Alpine-style folk architecture of the Šumava, featuring wooden galleries and wide saddle roofs. 11km W of Volary is the glass-making village and holiday resort of *Lenora*, where there is a 19C covered wooden bridge across the Vltava. The place makes a good centre for excursions up Mt Boubín (1362m), on the slopes of which is a primeval forest which has been protected since 1858. The trees are mainly spruce, and include bizarrely shaped fir and beech trees; a nature trail has been set up along the edge of the forest. Lenora is also exceptionally popular with canoists, who can start from here a memorable trip along the Vltava, the source of which is nearby to the west.

Continuing S from Volary you follow the river all the way to Vyšší Brod. After Želnava (12km) the river turns into an artificial lake, the largest in Czechoslovakia, and much frequented by holiday-makers.

The dam is at Lipno, 36km further south. From Lipno the journey to Vyšší Brod is completed by winding along the river's banks through dense forest.

The village of **Vyšší Brod**, in forested surroundings only 7km to the N of the Austrian frontier, grew up around its Cistercian monastery, one of the most famous in Czechoslovakia.

In 1259 Vok of Rožmberk, high officer at the Royal Court, summoned 12 monks from the Cistercian monastery at Wilhering in Austria to found a monastery in the vicinity of his residence at Rožmberk nad Vltavou; the idea of creating such an institution here was part of an attempt to colonise the South Bohemian borderland. The foundations of the monastery church were laid in the 1260s, but the chancel was not begun until 1292; the nave was commenced in the 1360s and vaulted in 1385. At the time the nave was conceived, a member of the Rožmberk family, Petr Vok of Rožmberk, was serving under Charles IV in Prague as Dean of the Chapter of the royal chapel of All Saints, and it is likely that through this connection the royal architect Peter Parler came to influence the construction of the Vyšší Brod church. When completed the church was one of the largest in Bohemia, an indication of the wealth and prestige which the monastery then enjoyed. Heavily fortified owing to its position on the Bohemian border, Vyšší Brod survived two sieges during the Hussite Wars in the early 15C, but then was severely damaged in 1526 by fire. After the death in 1611 of the last of the Rožmberks, Petr Vok, the monastery came under the protection first of the Eggenbergs, and then, after 1719, of the Schwarzenbergs. The monastery was not to be dissolved until 1950.

The former monastery at Vyšší Brod, though still surrounded by its fortifications, has suffered greatly over the years, not only on account of the fire of 1536, but also because of drastic restoration over the centuries, and the taking away of most of its important art treasures. A visit here is largely of historical rather than of architectural or artistic interest. The official guided tour of the monastery begins with the church, which was much altered during the baroque period and given a modern look as a result of restoration carried out in the 19C and 20C. The painting on the high altar is a poor and late imitation of Titian's Assumption in the Frari in Venice, but it has a magnificent baroque framework of 1644–46. In the course of 19C restoration, medieval frescoes on either side of the high altar were damaged irreparably, and in their place were put oil paintings representing the same subject-matter: one, painted in 1840 by Josef Hellich, shows the monastery's founder being miraculously saved from the flooded Vltava river; the other, a work of 1879 by Bartoloměj Čurn, is of Vok of Rožmberk and his wife Hedvika of Schaumburg consecrating the church to the Virgin Mary and St. Wenceslas. In the second chapel on the west side of the south transept is a copy of the famous Vyšší Brod Madonna (now in the National Gallery of Prague), one of the major works of Czech medieval art: the painting's donor, Vok of Rožmberk, is shown kneeling in the left-hand corner.

Off the cloister is the *Chapter House*, the oldest surviving part of the monastery. Built between 1280 and 1285, though heavily restored in recent times, it is a unique example in Czech medieval architecture of vaulting being supported by a single central sheaf pillar; the tracery of the central rosette window is original, but the stained glass dates from the 19C. Afterwards you are taken to see the library, which was founded at the same time as the monastery and contains 70,000 volumes, as well as an important collection of manuscripts and incunabula. The present building dates from 1757, and constitutes the highpoint of the tour. You are first shown the Small Library Hall—with a ceiling of the Judgement of Solomon by Lukáš Vavra—where you will find displayed the first official map of

Bohemia (by Jan Kryštof Müller); later comes the *Large Library Hall*, dazzlingly gilded, filled with furniture made by one of the monks (Josef Raffer), and with a ceiling fresco by Vávra of Christ in the Temple. The tour ends with the small art gallery founded by Abbot Valentin Schoper in 1838, and containing a largely dismal collection of paintings, with the exception of a beautiful head by the Bolognese painter Mauro Gandolfi (1764–1834), and some landscapes by Norbert Grund.

Separate to the tour is a museum installed in the former residential part of the monastery. It is difficult to conceive of the prosaic mind who had the idea of establishing here, in one of the more sacred spots in Bohemia, a museum devoted to the Czech Postal Service.

From Vyšší Brod to Jindřichův Hradec stretches a land known frequently as the Rose Country after the symbol of the former lords of the area, the Rožmberks. The first important member of the family, Vítek z Prčic, was chamberlain to Vladislav II, and had a son called Jindřich who founded in 1220 the castle later named after him at Jindřichův Hradec; the last of the Rožmberks, Petr Vok (1539–1611), lies buried at his ancestral monastery at Vyšší Brod. The land over which the family ruled is virtually unrivalled in Czechoslovakia for its concentration of outstanding towns and monuments. It is also a region of great natural beauty: up to České Budějovice you follow a narrow, wooded and little-spoilt stretch of the Vltava valley, while afterwards you travel through a haunting area of lakes and marshes.

From Vyšší Brod you follow the Vltava for 9km to **Rožmberk nad Vltavou**, an exceptionally pretty village with crumbling old houses and a 15–16C Deanery Church standing directly above the mossy, tree-lined banks of the river. This quiet, semi-abandoned place was once the main residence of the Rožmberks, whose castle stands imposingly in the wooded upper slopes of the village. Approached from Vyšší Brod, you will notice to the right of the castle, and at a higher level to it, an isolated round tower almost lost among the trees. This is all that survives of the original castle founded here by the Rožmberks in the mid 13C.

The 13C castle lost its importance after 1302, when the Rožmberk family decided to transfer their main residence from here to Český Krumlov. None the less the Rožmberks by no means entirely neglected their ancestral seat, and later in the 14C built here a two-storeyed lower palace with a square tower. When the upper castle burnt down in 1522, the family devoted all its attention to the lower building, which they transformed into a Renaissance residence. In around 1600 Petr Vok had part of the palace magnificently redecorated for his nephew and heir Jan Zřínský, whose death in 1612 spelt the end of the Rožmberk succession. The castle passed first into the hands of the Schwarzenbergs, and then into those of the Boucquoys, who were awarded the building for the part which they played in the Battle of the White Mountain. Under the Boucquoys—who were to keep the building until 1945—the castle was subjected to extensive alterations, first in a baroque style and then in a neo-Gothic one.

The tour of the castle begins with the neo-Gothic Crusader's Gallery, a long panelled space lined with romantic historical portaits; afterwards comes the so-called Bower of the White Lady, filled with mementoes of the Rožmberk family, and of the legendary woman known as the White Lady, who had a monster of a husband, and whose ghost is still said to haunt Český Krumlov. A subsequent room, devoted to the military commander Charles Bonaventura (the father of Albert Bucquoy), has an interesting painting by Jacob Grimer of the Feeding of the Five Thousand (1560), in which Ferdinand I and his wife Anne of

Austria are represented. After the Bedroom, with its 16C Dutch bed and chandelier, comes the Picture Gallery, where there are paintings by Václav Reiner, Johann Kupecký and Škréta. By far the most distinguished room is the following one, **The Banqueting Hall**, which formed part of the redecoration programme commissioned by Petr Vok for Jan Zřinský in c 1600. Zřinský had spent much time with his mother and step-father in Mantua, and the artists who worked for him in this room were either Italian or at least well acquainted with North Italian art of the late 16C. Almost every part of the room is painted, including the wooden ceiling, which has panels covered with

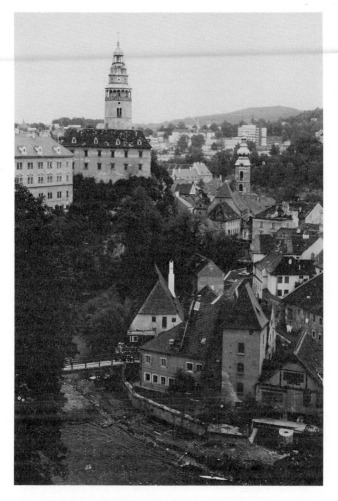

General view of Český Krumlov from the castle gardens; the vista is dominated by the castle's Renaissance tower

grotesques. In the recesses of the windows there are curious frescoes of the Ten Stages in Human Life, while between the windows hang seven paintings of the Planets; by the sides of the doors are trompe-l'oeil figures as in Veronese's frescoes in the Villa Maser. At the end of the hall, and separated from it by a Renaissance grille, is a small space reserved for the musicians. Here, in an illusionistic setting featuring a ceiling supported by caryatids is the most extraordinary of all the castle's frescoes, a representation of musicians which incorporates actual jewels (the real jewels were stolen in the Thirty Years' War and have been replaced by copies). The remaining rooms include an Armoury and rooms in an early baroque style devoted to later members of the Bucquoy family.

From Rožmberk nad Vltavou to České Budějovice you drive alongside the Vltava for a further 24km, passing through wooded countryside with hardly a single house. **ČESKÝ KRUMLOV**, crammed in and around a dramatic loop of the river, seems to have slumbered since the 18C, acquiring a dirty and decaying look, but at the same time keeping one of the most beautiful and evocative old centres in Czechoslovakia. The town is dominated, both literally and in terms of its history, by the massive and sprawling **castle** complex, the largest in Czechoslovakia after Prague Castle.

The castle of Český Krumlov is first mentioned in a document of 1253, when it belonged to the Vítek family. The Lords of Krumlov, as the Víteks are often known as, died out in 1302, and their estate was inherited by their distant relatives, the Rožmberks. The Rožmberks turned Český Krumlov into the administrative, and cultural centre of their vast domains, and extended and radically altered the castle. To the 13C lower castle they added an upper castle in the 14C, and then remodelled the entire complex in the 16C. The last of the Rožmberks, Petr Vok, sold the castle in 1602 to Rudolph II, but the place was only to remain in Habsburg hands until 1622, when it was resold to the Eggenbergs. In 1715, on the extinction of the Eggenberg family, the castle was inherited by the Schwarzenbergs, who remained the owners until 1947. Much building work was carried out here in the 17C and 18C, but little was done subsequently either to the castle, or indeed to the small town which had grown up at its feet. The Austrian painter Egon Schiele lived in the town in 1911, and did several paintings of the place, one of which is in the National Gallery in Prague.

A tour of Český Krumlov is best begun at the *České Budějovice Gate*, which stands at the northern edge of town, on the left bank of the Vltava: next to the gate is a lane leading down to the town's main car park, which stands between the river and the largest surviving section of the town's medieval ramparts. The gate itself is an impressive structure of 1598, designed by the Italian architect Domenico Cometa and copied almost directly from an engraving after Serlio; it is painted on its inner side. Once through the gate you find yourself in a world of narrow streets squeezed between tall irregularly shaped houses with high-pitched roofs, some of which cluster like limpets around the rock on which the castle is built. The street due S of the gate leads into Latrán, the town's picturesque main thoroughfare, which curls around the foot of the castle rock and down to the river. Half-way down Latrán on your right is a lane leading to the Red Gate (1861), through which you enter a large courtyard forming the castle's outer bailey. Among the buildings here are a former Salt House first mentioned in 1511 (to the right of the gate) and (on the left-hand side of the courtyard) a former residence of the chief officer of the castle. Looming in front of you is the lower castle, above which a round tower rises to a height of 72m, creating the most prominent landmark on the Český Krumlov sky-line. The base of the tower is the main survival of the original 13C castle, but what gives the structure its distinction is the arcaded upper gallery and elaborate crowning-piece, a 1580s addition which makes the tower resemble some 16C astronomical instrument. Joining the outer bailey to the lower castle is a bridge spanning a moat where bears have been kept since the 16C. Across the bridge and through the gate on the other side you enter a second courtyard, adorned with cannons, and lined with walls that were given painted rustication in the 16C (restored in 1842); the buildings here include a former mint and agricultural college, the latter (founded in 1800 and dissolved in 1850) being one of the first of its kind in Bohemia. A passage of the late 16C will take you from the second into the third courtyard, where the obligatory guided tour of the main and upper castle begins.

After such a build-up, the tour of the building comes as somewhat of a disappointment. Many of the rooms are at present closed for restoration, and those that are not have a sparse, forbidding look, the result of years of neglect. The tour begins with the Chapel of St. George, which dates back to 1334, but was given a stucco facing between 1750 and 1753 by a Viennese craftsman called Matthias André. Afterwards comes a Renaissance Hall (a remodelling of 1574–77 of the upper castle's 14C Hall), and a further series of rooms decorated in the late 16C, all containing portraits and other souvenirs of the Rožmberk family. The Renaissance Grand Hall was destroyed in the late 17C to make way for the present staircase, up which you climb to the second landing, from where there is an excellent view of the town. The upper rooms are all of the baroque and rococo periods, and include an early 18C dining room containing two tapestries after cartoons by Rubens, and a rococo cabinet of 1755 with pastel-blue chinoiserie decorations. The last upstairs room which you visit is the Castle Picture Gallery, founded in 1733, and featuring a good portrait by Gerhard Seghers, rather lost among a host of lesser Flemish and Dutch works of the 17C, including numerous contemporary copies and studio pictures. Finally you descend to the **ball room** (at present being restored), by far the most appealing room of the castle. In 1748 an artist of Swabian origin, Josef Lederer, decorated the long room with among the most entertaining rococo frescoes to be seen anywhere in central Europe. These comprise a Venetian-inspired illusionistic framework of balustrades and theatre boxes, behind and in front of which parade a whole series of colourful musicians, spectators in contemporary dress, masked figures, musicians, harlequins, and other types taken from the *commedia dell'arte*; the artist himself makes an appearance, drinking a cup of coffee.

At the end of the tour you should make a visit to the castle's gardens (now a public park), situated to the W of the castle's fourth courtyard, and reached by a long covered bridge suspended high between the castle rock and a wooded hill. The view at the end of the bridge looking back towards the castle is one of the finest to be had of the town, with only some modern buildings in the distant wooded hills interrupting a scene virtually unchanged since the 18C. The large gardens, laid out in the 18C, are themselves a great treat, and contain a terrace and balustrade covered with mythological figures, and several fine buildings, including the dainty Bellaria Summer Palace, and a garden pavilion with an illusionistic rococo ceiling. Best of all is the building which you come to immediately after entering the gardens from the castle, the **Castle Theatre**. The present structure, commissioned by Josef Adam of Schwarzenberg, was built in 1766–67, and has been left untouched since then, complete with all its original stage mechanism, including a set of 12 backcloths in the style of the Bibienas. As an intact 18C theatre it is rivalled in Europe only by Drottningholm in Sweden.

Leaving the gardens it is best to retrace your long way back through the castle's four courtyards and down to the Latrán Street. On the opposite side of the street to the castle is the Pivovarská ulice, a lane leading past the former Convent of the Minorites and the Poor Clares (a mid 14C foundation almost completely rebuilt in the baroque period and now partially used as an Old People's Home), and down to a brewery which has been created out of the former armoury of the Rožmberks, a work by the Italian architect Antonio Cometa. Back on the Latrán continue walking down to the river, noting to your right the medieval wall-paintings at No. 15, and, to your left, the riverside late medieval church of St. Jošt. Crossing the river by the Lazebnický Bridge, you enter the part of town which is squeezed into the near circular loop of the Vltava. The main street here, Radniční, connects the bridge with the town's main square, where you will find a plague column of 1716, the Renaissance Town Hall (with an attic of 1580), and a 19C Art school and Music Academy. From the eastern side of the square the Horní ulice climbs steeply up to the *Kaplanka House* (No. 139), which has been virtually unchanged since 1520. Immediately behind it, almost at the highest point of town, is the *Parish Church of St. Vitus* (1407–39), with terraces on its southern side falling directly down to the river. The graceful triple-aisled interior boasts the remarkable *Sepulchre of William of Rožmberk*, which extends to the height of the vaulting, and is surmounted by a statue of the Rožmberk rider; made out of marble, terracotta and copper, it was executed between 1593 and 1597 by the sculptor Georg Bendel and the goldsmith Jan Dorn.

Continuing E along Horni ulice you will pass on your right a former Jesuit College built in 1586 by Maio da Vomio, and housing since the 19C the Hotel Růže; on the other side of the street, in the former Jesuit Seminary, is the well-displayed *Regional Museum*, with archaeological and historical collections, and much Gothic to baroque statuary. You can return to the Lazebnický bridge by following the semi-circular line of streets to the W of the main square; among the fine buildings that you will pass are the House of Jakub Krčín of Jelčany (No. 54 Na Louži), and the House of the alchemist Michael of Ebersbach (Široká).—4km W of Český Krumlov is the notable pilgrimage church of *Kájov*, which was largely rebuilt in 1471–85: the plainly vaulted chancel contrasts with the two-aisled hall nave, the ceiling of which is a veritable forest of delicate ribs.

Leaving Český Krumlov on the road to České Budějovice, turn off after 5km to visit the quiet village of **Zlatá Koruna**, which is famous for its former **Cistercian Monastery**. This walled complex, standing in isolation between fields and the beautiful verdant banks of the Vltava, was founded by King Přemysl Otakar II in 1263 and given the name 'Golden Crown'. Ruined by the Hussites in 1420, the building was restored after 1609, and extended in the 18C; further restoration work was carried out after the Second World War. The oldest surviving part of the complex is the severely vaulted chapterhouse of c 1280. The church interior, despite baroque additions and a glistening coat of white paint, is essentially that which was built between c 1340 to c 1360; Parler was at work here in 1359, and the nave shows clearly the influence of Prague cathedral, being one of the first spaces in Europe where the vaulting springs directly from the walls and piers instead of from capitals. Of the 18C additions the great jewel is the gilded and frescoed library of c 1770.

At the confluence of the rivers Vltava and Malše, 19km further N of Zlatá Koruna, stands the regional capital of South Bohemia, **ČESKÉ BUDĚJOVICE**. Though much rebuilt in the 19C and early 20C, and surrounded now by extensive industrial suburbs, the old centre of České Budějovice has retained its original medieval town plan, and has a spacious and solemnly impressive character.

Founded by Otakar II in 1265, and laid out by Otakar's engineer Hrz of Zvíkov, České Budějovice boasted a town plan which for sheer scale and ambitiousness was not to be rivalled until the creation of Plzeň 30 years later. The manufacturing of beer and the storing of salt transported from Austria contributed to the town's early prosperity, which reached its highpoint in the 16C with the revenue derived from the exploitation of the nearby fish-ponds. Devastated during the Thirty Years' War, and by a serious fire in 1641, the town subsequently stagnated, and its fortunes were not to improve until the 19C, when it developed into a major industrial centre. The town today has an important engineering industry, and large enamelware and pencil factories, the latter founded in 1847. But its best known institution is the Budweis Brewery, which has been functioning since 1894, and produces one of the finest of Czech beers (the original 'Budweiser' or 'Bud', as it is known to its American enthusiasts).

The medieval grid-plan of České Budějovice is contained within an oval area encircled by rivers and a long canal. At its centre is the

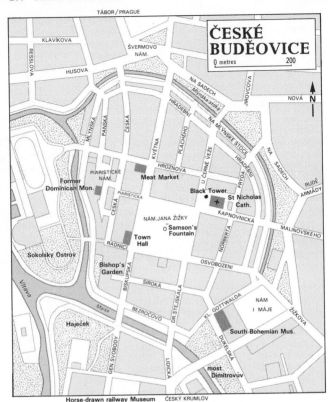

Horse-drawn railway Museum   ČESKÝ KRUMLOV

Žižka Square (Žižkovo náměstí), one of the largest not only in
Czechoslovakia but also in Europe. This vast and traffic-free quadra-
tic space is empty save for the impressive *Samson's Fountain* at the
centre: executed by Josef Dietrich in 1727, it comprises a statue of
Samson rising above a large basin supported by struggling atlantes.
The arcaded buildings lining the square are mainly of the 18C and
19C, the finest being the Town Hall in the south-west corner:
crowned by three baroque steeples this originally Gothic structure
was rebuilt in 1727–30 by Antonio Martinelli, who had come from
Vienna to Bohemia to replace Bayer as the Schwarzenberg architect
at Český Krumlov; note, on the left-hand side of the façade, a metal
stick used for checking the length of materials.

The town's cathedral, off the north-eastern corner of the square, is a
13C foundation which was rebuilt in 1641–49 and heavily restored
since then. Of greater interest is the *Black Tower* next to it, a structure
72m in height which was designed by Vincenz Fuggeral in the early
16C; you can climb up to its gallery, from where you can best
appreciate the medieval layout of the town. The oldest monument in
České Budějovice lies off the north-western corner of the square and
can be reached by walking E along Piaristická. This, the former
Dominican Monastery of St. Mary, was founded at the same time as
the town, but was extensively remodelled at the end of the 18C when it

*The Žižkovo náměstí in České Budějovice, the largest
square in Czechoslovakia; in the centre in the Samson
Fountain of c 1727, while behind rises the early sixteenth-
century Black Tower*

passed into the hands of the Piarists; the dreary late baroque interior of
the church retains fragments of medieval frescoes. The street leading
N off the north-western corner of the square, Květná, will take you
after 50m to the former *Meat Market*, a curious long structure dating
back to 1554 and now functioning as a restaurant.

Running S from the Town Hall is Biskupská, where at No. 132 is
the late 18C Bishopric, with a very plain exterior. Turn right into
Široká to see at No. 39 a private house containing traces of wall-
decorations painted in 1653; at the end of the street, in a squalid alley
adjoining the neglected Bishop's Garden, is one of the towers from
the medieval fortifications. Continue S along Biskupská and cross the
river Malše. Further S, near the junction of General Svoboda and the
main road to Český Krumlov, is a tiny museum commemorating the
first horse-drawn railway in continental Europe. Built in 1827–30, it
linked České Budějovice with the Upper Austrian town of Linz, and
functioned up to 1830; the museum is installed in the original station.
Return to the north side of the Malše and turn right down Bezručovo.
Off the gardens at the end of this street is the *Regional Museum*
(Jihočeské Muzeum), a pompous eclectic building of the turn of the
century housing extensive historical, numismatic and archaeological
collections.

One of the most distinctive features of the South Bohemian
landscape is its chain of some 270 artificial lakes or fish-ponds, which
extends to the W and E of České Budějovice. The best base for
exploring this lakeland scenery is the charming small town of
Třeboň, which lies on the northern shore of Lake Svět, 24km E of
České Budějovice along the E49.

The channelling of water from the marshy expanses of South Bohemia dates back to at least the 12C, though the present sophisticated system of interlocking lakes held by dams and linked by narrow canals and conduits, was esentially the creation of the Rožmberks in the 16C. The first engineer whom they employed, Štěpánek Netolický, was responsible for the construction in 1506–20 of the Zlatá Stoka, or Golden Canal, which feeds water to most of the large ponds around Třeboň; in the second half of the century Jakub Krčín of Jelčany built a number of new ponds, as well as the Nová Řeka canal, which diverted flood waters from the Lužnice to Nežárka rivers. The ponds have always been used for the breeding of carp, a statutory Christmas dish in Czechoslovakia, as well as one of the staples of Jewish cuisine. Every three years the ponds are drained, and the fish brought in by a wide sweep of drag-nets. The Rožmberks, and later the Schwarzenbergs, employed a 'water-bailiff' or 'fish-master' to protect each of the main ponds from poachers and to regulate the water level; these men lived in log cabins near the ponds.

The maternal grandfather of the writer Jaroslav Hašek was the water bailiff of a lake near Protivín, some 40km NW of České Budějovice. His life inspired Hašek's Stories from the Water-bailiff's Lodge at Ražice, which were published in 1908 in the humorous weekly, Merry Prague (an English translation appears in Sir Cecil Parrot's Hašek anthology, The Red Commissar, London, 1981). The last of these stories tells how one day, when the grandfather was out fishing on another lake, a miscreant opened the sluices of his pond, leaving the carp high and dry. With great presence of mind the grandfather revived the fish by bringing in horse-drawn tanks of water. However, his superior continued to blame him for the incident, whereupon the grandfather flung his fishing-boots on the ground below the man's feet, thus losing his job and showing a disregard for authority which was to be inherited by Hašek himself.

Another writer associated with the lakes of South Bohemia is Ivan Klíma, who spent childhood holidays near Lomnice, just to the N of Třeboň; the idyllic if rather haunting calm of the area is memorably captured in his short story, My Country, which appeared in the semi-autobiographical collection, My First Loves (1985).

Třeboň, a quiet town and small spa, has a tiny but beautifully preserved old centre, bordered by parkland and water and encircled by its medieval fortifications. Acquired by the Rožmberks in the mid 14C, the town was extensively developed in the 16C, at the same time that the South Bohemian fish-ponds were being created; the last of the Rožmberks, Petr Vok, made the castle here his permanent home from 1602 to his death in 1611. Enter the town through the impressive 16C Svinenská Gate, on the other side of which (to the right) is an old brewery installed in a former store house belonging to the Rožmberks (beer has been made at Třeboň since 1379). To the left of the gate is the entrance to a complex of 15C–18C buildings comprising the Castle. The main building here, standing in a shaded courtyard, dates back to 1379, but was rebuilt several times, including in 1599, when the Rožmberk architect Domenico Cometa gave it a white Renaissance facing. The interior, containing a number of 16C rooms, now houses a small history museum, with interesting displays relating to the local fishing industry. The northern gate of the castle complex will take you out on to the narrow and exceptionally attractive J. Fučík náměstí, where there is a fountain of 1569 and a Plague Column of 1780. Among the 16C–18C buildings that line the square is a Town Hall of 1566 and (on the north side of the square) the house belonging to the 16C water engineer Josef Štěpánek Netolický. Behind the square, adjoining the town's north-western fortifications, is the former Austin canons' convent of St. Jiljí, which was founded in 1369. The convent buildings are of the late baroque period (and have been converted into offices and apartments), but the church and cloister are the original late 14C structures. The church, begun in 1370, has an outstanding interior, divided into two by a line of very slender columns, sixteen times as high as they are thick; the fresco decorations are of the 15C. Beyond the northern fortifications, on the north side of the Zlatá Stoka, is the toy-like 18C house where the dramatist Tyl briefly lived.

South of the Svinenská Gate is a landing stage from which you can make a pleasant trip by steamer around the large Svět lake, which is surrounded by extensive wooded parkland. West of the landing stage, along the lakeside Světská hráz, is a sandy beach popular with bathers. Set back from the lake, a ten minutes' walk NW of the beach, is the Sanatorium Aurora, the main building of the Třeboň spa; the surroundings are delightful, but the building itself resembles a large modern factory. The treatment here, used in particular for rheumatic diseases and disorders of the spine and joints, is based on mud baths, the mud being taken from the local peat marshes.

On the southern shores of Lake Svět is a large neo-Gothic Mausoleum erected by the Schwarzenbergs; nearby is an important fish-farm. Much of the land surrounding Třeboň is now a protected nature reserve, the area being of great interest both to ecologists and ornithologists. A nature trail through the peat bogs has been established at Červené blato, 15km to the south. 4km to the N of the town is the largest of all the Bohemian fish-ponds, *Rožmberk*, covering an area of 489 hectares, and constructed by Jakub Krčín of Jelčany in 1584–89; the view from its wooded north-western shores over this vast still expanse makes a powerful impression, and embraces a distant glimpse of Třeboň rising above trees. The hamlet of Ruznice, further N on the Lomnice road, has a group of traditional farm buildings in a style known as 'rustic baroque'. The nearby ponds of Velký Tisý and Malý Tisý form part of a large bird sanctuary.

Jindřichův Hradec, 28km NE of Třeboň, was a most important town in the Middle Ages, though a series of severe fires in 1435, 1773 and 1801, reduced the place to the small and run-down textiles centre of today. Its main interest is the great complex comprising its **Castle**, which stands at the lower end of town on a tongue of land projecting picturesquely over a great pool formed by the river Nežárka.

The castle was built c 1220 by Jindřich, the son of Vítek of Prčice, Chamberlain to Vladislav II. Descended from this early member of the Rožmberk family were the powerful Lords of Hradec, under whose rule (between the 14C and 16C) the castle was greatly extended, and the town behind it rose to become one of the largest in Bohemia. The main additions and alterations were commissioned in the late 16C by Adam II of Hradec—Lord Chancellor of Bohemia, and nephew of Lord Zacharias, the creator of the Renaissance Palace at nearby Telč. The most important architect employed by Adam was Baldassare Maggi (Maio da Vomio), who came from the village of Arogno near lake Lugano, and entered the service of the Lords of Hradec in around 1575.

The last Lord of Hradec, Jáchym Oldřich, died epileptic and deformed in 1604, only seven years before the death of the last Rožmberk, Petr Vok.

The castle, potentially one of Bohemia's major tourist attractions, is in a most depressing condition, and is likely to remain closed for restoration until at least the year 2000; among the highpoints of the interior is a hall covered with gruesomely realistic wall-paintings relating the story of St. George and executed in 1373. The visitor today is only able to visit the main courtyard, the finest feature of which is the three-tiered *Large Arcade*, built by Maggi between 1586 and 1591. Through the gate in the arcade you have a tantalising glimpse over an untended garden to an extraordinary pavilion known as the **Rondel**. This rotunda, designed by Maggi, but executed in 1591–93 by his assistants and compatriots, Giovanni M.

Faconi and Antonio Cometa, is a bizarre mixture of Italian and central European elements. The main ground-floor window is straight out of Palladio, while the steeply pitched conical roof ringed by gables is a flight of pure Bohemian fantasy. The interior is decorated all over with a remarkable stucco decoration carried out between c 1594 and 1600 by Georg Bendel and Giovanni P. Martinola.

A narrow street ascends from the main castle gate up to the town square, which is lined with 18C and early 19C houses, and is dominated in the middle by Matthias Strachovský's Trinity Column of 1764–68. Svatojánská leads from the square up to the church of St. John the Baptist, the most interesting of the town's several churches, and occupying the highest point in town. Built over a recently excavated Romanesque rotunda, this much altered 14C structure (at present undergoing further extensive restoration) has early 14C wall-paintings.

The most enjoyable EXCURSION to be made from Jindřichův Hradec is to the castle of **Červená Lhota**, which lies 18km to the N of the town, in between the villages of Dirná and Deštná. This pale pink gabled structure, more like a toy than a real building, stands in the middle of a lake ringed by pine trees, and is one of the more enchanting sites in Southern Bohemia. Of 12C foundation, it was rebuilt in 1530 for Jan Kába von Rybňany, then remodelled after 1641, and further restored in the 19C and 20C. Its main façade, reached from a 17C bridge, rises above a miniature formal garden squeezed between the masonry and the water; the interior has a mainly Empire look, and is notable for its simplicity. The composer Karl Ditters von Dittersdorf (1739–99) spent the last years of his life here, and is buried in the nearby cemetery at Deštná.

MORAVIA

17 Prague to Brno

A. By the motorway

Total distance 213km. Prague—D1 91km Humpolec—29km
Jihlava—93km **Brno**.

The D1, Czechoslovakia's main motorway, efficiently links the three
main cities of Czechoslovakia, reducing the journey from Prague to
Brno to 2½ hours, and from Brno to Bratislava to 1½ hours. The
landscape as far as Brno is remarkably unchanging, and comprises
endless rolling vistas of fields interrupted by patches of dense forest.
For much of the journey the road runs parallel with the narrow and
wooded valley of the Sázava, along which are some of the finest sights
to be seen in the vicinity of the road, including the monastery of
Sázava and the castle of *Český Šternberk* (see Route 2B). Nearer the
Moravian border is the former Premonstratensian monastery of *Želiv*,
which stands on a tributary of the Sázava, 10km to the S of the D1 (turn
off at Koberovice, 81km SE of Prague). Apart from the beauty of its
position, impressively perched above the forested banks of the river,
Želiv is notable above all for the interior of its church, a 14C hall-
church remodelled in a 'Gothic-baroque' style by the great Santini-
Aichel after 1712. Santini created within the nave curious projecting
galleries, but his most original contribution here was his characteristically elaborate and very expressive vaulting.

You can extend your detour to Želiv by heading S from here to
Pelhřimov (a further 13km). This small town belonged in the 13C to the
Prague Bishopric, which used it as a base for colonising the Moravian
borderland. Two of the gates from the medieval fortifications have
survived (Rynárecká and Jihlavská), but the rest of the medieval town
was largely destroyed by fires between the 16C and 18C. Late
baroque and neo-classical buildings today make up most of the old
centre, which, thanks to the town's economic decline in the last
century, has been left remarkably untouched. You can regain the D1
at Komorovice (17km) by driving N from Pelhřimov along the E551.

The present-day border of Bohemia with Moravia comes near the
village of Větrný Jeníkov, 12km further down the D1 from Komorovice
and 10km before Pávov, where a branch of the motorway leads after
7km to the large industrial town of **Jihlava**.

Founded in 1240 in the vicinity of silver deposits, Jihlava became for a short while
the most important silver-mining town in Europe after Freiburg in Germany; the
Royal Mint was situated here until the early 14C, when it was transferred to
Kutná Hora by Václav II. In the 1730s the imperial post road from Vienna was re-
routed N from Jindřichův Hradec to Jihlava, much to the detriment of the former
and to the advantage of the latter. Numerous industries were established in the
town in the 19C, and today the place is a major engineering and textiles centre.

The Austrian composer Gustav Mahler (1860–1911) was born in the neighbouring village of Kaliště (Kalischt); soon after the birth his father—a brewer and
publican—moved the family to what is now Malinovského in Jihlava itself, where
the future composer studied at the German Gymnasium.

The main interest of the town is its vast square, the equal in size if not in beauty to that of České Budějovice. The medieval houses were gutted by fire in 1523, and most of the buildings lining the square date from the late 16C to the early 19C; one of the finest (No. 58) is a late 16C building housing the Museum of the Bohemian-Moravian Highlands, the collections of which relate largely to the natural history of the area. The appearance of the square is hardly enhanced by the prominent Prior department store, a characterless modern building. The plague column is of 1690.

Return to the D1 at Pávov and continue for a further 87km to Brno (see Route 20).

B. Via Žďár nad Sázavou and Pernštejn

Total distance 218km. Prague—D1 68km Loket—Road 18 49km Havlíčkův Brod—31km **Žďár nad Sázavou**—37km **Pernštejn**—33km **Brno**.

Those not wishing to rush all the way from Prague to Brno on a motorway should leave the D1 (see above) at Loket (68km SE of Prague), and then head N on to Road 18, which after Ledeč nad Sázavou (17km) runs parallel with the D1, following for over 60km the attractively wooded Sázava valley. At Světlá, 17km E of Ledeč, enthusiasts of the writer Jaroslav Hašek (1883–1923) could make a detour 10km to the S to see the village of *Lipnice nad Sázavou* (follow the Humpolec road for 7.5km, then turn left at Dol. Město). In this quiet village, surrounded by woods and dominated by a 14C castle (extended in the 16C), Hašek spent the last 15 months of his life, engaged on his never to be completed work, The Good Soldier Švejk.

Hašek moved from Prague to Lipnice in August 1921 on the recommendation of a painter friend, Jaroslav Panuška, a well-known landscapist who came from the Bohemian-Moravian Highlands and frequently painted at Lipnice. Panuška thought that the move would be beneficial to the ailing writer, who was now reaping the consequences of a lifetime of gluttony and alcoholic abuse. The two men arrived at the village together and put up at an inn called the Czech Crown. Invald, the landlord of this inn, after being initially suspicious of the shabbily dressed and penniless writer, later became totally devoted to him, and even gave him a credit of 500 crowns. Hašek was delighted with his new circumstances, and was pleased, as he put it, to be living 'bang in the middle of a pub. Nothing better could have happened to me'. A favourite haunt of both Hašek and Panuška was the castle at Lipnice, which enjoys beautiful views over the lush Sázava valley. After befriending the custodian they were given a key to the building, and would come here of an evening to light a fire in the courtyard, grill sausages and sing old Austrian songs. Once they held a notorious drinking party here, in which the local school-teacher was left drunk in a corner. Hašek decided to play one of his characteristic pranks, and locked up the building with the teacher inside. Later that night frightened villagers claimed to have seen a ghost running along the battlements. Hašek shouted out that this was none other than the White Lady of Rožmberk, and that in her interests it would be best to shoot and 'liberate' her. The poor teacher was finally released in a trembling state.

In the summer of 1922, after securing a contract for The Good Soldier Švejk, Hašek bought a ramshackle house on the slope below the castle, but occupied only one of its rooms. He now weighed over 24 stones, and his health was causing serious concern. Eventually he consented to be examined by a doctor, who told him that he would never be able to complete *Švejk* unless he took greater care of himself. Hašek replied that he would have to kill off Švejk before allowing himself to die, and this would never happen as Švejk would always live on among the Czech people. He fell into a coma on the night of 3 January 1933, waking up only to beg the doctor for a sip of cognac. He was given milk instead, which prompted his last words: 'But you're cheating me'. For his funeral, attended by few of his friends and none of his family, his swollen body had to be taken out through the window rather than down the stairs. Shortly afterwards his debtors came round and loaded all that they could find on to a cart. He was buried in the local churchyard.

The house where Hašek spent the last months of his life has now been turned into a small museum to the writer. The gravestone of the writer in the local cemetery was initially a simple one, but it has since been replaced by a granite monument in the form of an open book, bearing the gilt inscription: 'Austria, never wert thou so ripe to fall, never wert thou so damned.' In deference to Hašek's memory a Festival of Satire and Humour is held annually at the village.

From Lipnice take the side road E to Okrouhlice (8km), where you will regain Road 18. The industrial town of *Havlíčkův Brod*, 9km further E, was founded by German miners in the 13C, and is named after the 19C radical journalist Karel Havlíček Borovský (1821–56), whose house here (at No. 19 ČSLA náměstí) is now a museum to him. The town, which has retained fragments of its medieval fortifications, also has an art gallery devoted to Czech illustrations and satirical drawings from 1918 onwards, including works by Hašek's illustrator Josef Lada. Continuing along Road 18 you will come after 31km to *Žďár nad Sázavou*, a small industrial town which grew up by the side of a former **Cistercian Monastery** founded in 1252. The abbot in the early 18C was one of the most important patrons of Santini-Aichel, who spent large periods at Žďár from 1706 almost up to his death in 1723, producing here some of the more bizarre works of a very eccentric career. His remodelling of the medieval abbey church—his first task here—is difficult fully to appreciate owing to the main vaults having been damaged by fire in 1784; the interest of the interior lies primarily in the transepts, which are spanned by low arches support-ing dynamically-shaped organs featuring solomonic columns and curiously bent piers. The high altar (1735) is the masterpiece of Řehoř Thény, a Tirolian pupil of Matthias Braun; he used his own features for the face of St. Luke.

Santini's plans for the rest of the abbey complex were never to be fulfilled (an exhibition relating to Santini's work can be seen in the stables), though what he completed includes a number of symbolically-shaped buildings such as a court in the shape of a lyre, and outbuildings in the form of the abbot's initials. Both Santini's and the abbot's love of symbolism is further revealed in the delightful cemetery on the other side of the street to the monastery. Beyond the entrance pavilion (a later addition) you find yourself in an enclosure of undulating walls containing three simple chapels representing the Trinity; a statue of an angel by Thény stands in the middle, waiting to wake up the dead.

Symbolism of an unrivalled complexity in Bohemian architecture characterises Santini's last and most fascinating work at Žďár, the **PILGRIMAGE CHAPEL** (1720–22) which sits on top of an adjacent hill. The idea of building this chapel followed the discovery in 1719 of the miraculously undecayed tongue of Jan Nepomucký, who had been murdered supposedly for his refusal to betray the secrets of the confessional. It so happened that the finding of the tongue coincided with the fifth centenary of the coming to Žďár of a Cistercian community originating from the monastery at Nepomuk. To celebrate the two events, and to play his own part in the growing Nepomuk cult, the abbot not only commissioned the chapel from Santini, but also had the hill on which it was to be built renamed Zelená hora (Green Hill) after the hill on which the monastery's mother institution had been

established. Virtually every detail of the plan and every architectural
form of the chapel refers either to Nepomuk's tongue or else to the
figure five, which was both an allusion to the fifth centenary and to the
halo of five stars which hovered around the martyr's head after he was
thrown into the Vltava. The chapel stands at the centre of a precinct
contained within a ten-pointed cloister housing five other chapels. It
takes the shape of a five-pointed star, and represents Santini's most
imaginative fusion of the Gothic and baroque styles. The bizarre
exterior has the angular character more typical of the former style,
while the white-washed interior makes a baroque play of concave and
convex forms. The use of Gothic lancet windows has a symbolical as
well as an aesthetic significance, for they echo the tongue-shaped
forms that are everywhere to be found, and allude also to the saint's
tongue having been compared in its steadfastness to the Sword of the
Lord. Such obsessive symbolism and complex planning are worthy of
comparison with Borromini's church of San Ivo de la Sapienza in
Rome, a building to which Santini may indeed have been paying
hommage.

At *Obyčtov*, 10km S of Žďár, is another work commissioned from
Santini by the abbot—a chapel dedicated to the Virgin and planned in
the shape of a tortoise, the symbol of constancy. To the N of Žďár
extends a large area of protected forest embracing the highest point in
the Bohemian-Moravian Highlands (Devět skal, 836m), and the large
Velké Darko lake; the latter, 10km due N of Žďár and near the source
of the Sázava river, is used for swimming and water-sports.

Continue E from Žďár along Road 18 until you reach the small town
of Bystřice nad Pernštejnem (27km), from where you head S on a side-
road to the castle of **Pernštejn**, a further 10km. The castle, rising over a
sea of pines on a rocky spur above the river Nedvědička, has a
picturesque profile rivalling that of Karlštejn (see Route 2C, and seems
likewise to be taken straight out of a fairy-tale illustration. The seat of
the Pernštejn family up to 1596, the castle was first mentioned in 1285,
and soon came to be regarded as unassailable; the oldest surviving
parts are the round tower and the ramparts. The building was
reconstructed after a fire in 1457, and further extensive remodelling
took place in the Renaissance. The Mitrovie family, who succeeded
the Pernštejns and retained the building until 1945, did little to alter
the castle's exterior. The cold and rather inhospitable interior, however, was largely redone in a rococo and Empire style, and rather
spoils the expectations raised by the memorable first impression of the
building.

Driving E from Pernštejn alongside the Nedvědlička for 2.5km (note
the fine 18C wooden bridge below the castle) you will come to a main
road leading SE towards Brno. 4km after the turning is the village of
Doubravnik, where there is one of the last Gothic hall-churches in
Czechoslovakia, constructed in 1539–57, possibly by Mert Hübel, the
architect then in charge of the Church of St. James in Brno. At *Tišnov*,
10km further S, is a Cistercian convent founded in 1233; of particular
interest is the west portal or Porta Coeli, an early 13C work richly
adorned with carvings. The remaining 24km to Brno (see Route 20)
continue to be through wooded hilly landscape, but with increasing
signs of industrialisation.

18 Jindřichův Hradec to Brno

Total distance 137km. Jindřichův Hradec—Road 23 41km **Telč**—
36km *Třebíč*—60km **Brno**.

Head E of Jindřichův Hradec on Road 23, crossing the Moravian
border shortly after Studená. The landscape of marshes and chains of
large fish-ponds characteristic of South Bohemia extends well into
this part of Moravia and provides **TELČ** with an enchanting setting.
The old town of Telč, one of the most beautiful and best preserved in
central Europe, floats above water like the North Italian town of
Mantua. Its long western and eastern sides are lapped by water from
two great ponds that are joined together at the N by a canal running
through the wooded grounds of the castle. Coming from Jindřichův
Hradec you should leave your car in the car park just to the N of the
canal, off České armády Street. A 17C bridge, at the junction of the
canal and the northern end of the Štěpnický pond, leads you to a 16C
gate (the Small Gate) marking the northern entrance to the old town.
On the other side of the gate unfolds before you a world which has
little changed since the early 18C. Before walking around the
remarkable main square which opens up to your left, turn right and
enter the **CASTLE**, the interior of which contains some of the finest
Renaissance rooms in Czechoslovakia.

The original castle at Telč, an early 14C structure centred around a tiny
courtyard, was acquired in 1339 by the Lords of Hradec from Charles IV in
exchange for the strategically important castle at Bánov, situated on the former
border with Hungary. The present appearance of the castle is due largely to the
16C Governor of Moravia, Zacharias of Hradec (d. 1589), who, following a stay
in the Italian town of Genoa in 1552, decided to turn Telč into his principal
residence. At first he limited himself largely to redecorating both the exterior
and interior of the old building with sgraffito decorations, but from the 1560s
onwards he undertook ambitious architectural extensions, including the building of two new wings; his principal architect seems to have been the Italian,
Baldassare Maggi (Maio da Vomio), the man responsible for the Renaissance
work at Jindřichův Hradec. The building came into the hands of the Liechtenstein family after 1712.

The official tour of the castle begins with two of the rooms which
Zacharias of Hradec had decorated in the old building. The first of
these rooms, the *Small Banqueting Hall*, comprises fascinating
monochrome decorations after engravings by the southern German
artists H. Aldegrever and V. Solis; the subjects are Orpheus Playing
to the Animals, the Banquet of Herodotus and female figures person-
ifying the Seven Sins. The adjoining room is the *Treasury*, covered all
over with further monochrome sgraffito work, and featuring the
earliest surviving examples in central Europe of fictive perspectival
decorations. Next comes the *Chapel of St. George*, a tall space of
Gothic proportions coated in elaborate Renaissance stucco decorations; in the centre, surrounded by an elegant Renaissance grille, is
the marble tomb of Zacharias and his wife Kateřina of Valdštejn. In
the nearby former Armoury is a cellular vault adorned all over with
Renaissance grotesques. The long Wedding or *Theatre Hall*, opposite
the Armoury, has a splendid wooden coffered ceiling, and—covering
what was originally a stone fireplace—a frescoed decoration with
scenes representing Judith and Holofernes and Hercules capturing
the Hind of Artemisia (the freshness of these works is due to their
having been hidden by plaster up to 1950). Moving from this room to
the adjoining African Hall is like going from the sublime to the

ridiculous, the latter room comprising an absurd and rather surrealist display of tiger skins, ostriches, hippotamus and zebra heads, and other gruesome trophies collected by the last owner of the castle in the course of safaris undertaken between 1903 and 1914.

An elegant Italianate loggia connects the oldest part of the castle with the *Marble Hall*, which was used by Zacharias of Hradec as an Audience Chamber. The Deeds of Hercules are portrayed in the panels of its amusing coffered ceiling (c 1570), which bizarrely features sculpted reliefs and even real antler horns attached to a painted sky. Gilded and witty reliefs of mythological figures set against a blue background are to be found in the 30 octagonal panels comprising the magnificent coffered ceiling of the *Golden Room*. This room, originally the castle's ballroom, has walls lined with portraits of the Liechtenstein Family, and a Musician's Gallery decorated with Allegories of the Five Senses. The last important room which you visit is the *Blue Hall*, with another splendid ceiling in gold and blue, this one comprising the coat of arms of the Hradec family flanked by four painted reliefs of the elements. Separate to the tour is a small historical museum and art gallery installed in rooms off the delightful Renaissance garden to the right of the main entrance. The gallery is dedicated to the painter Jan Zrzavý (1890–1977), who was born near the Moravian town of Havlíčkův Brod, and specialised in naïvely simplified figures in haunting settings; his art was an influence on both the naïf and Surrealist painters associated with the group Devětsil.

In between the castle and the adjacent and rather severe late 17C Jesuit College is a covered passage leading to the parish church of St. James, a late 14C foundation completed in 1443; there is a wonderful view of the town from its tower. Extending like a funnel to the S of the castle is the **náměstí Míru**, one of the most beautiful squares in a country celebrated for its squares. There is not a single modern building to spoil the arcaded rows that run, like the backcloths of a stage set, the whole length of the square's immensely long sides. The houses are mainly of the 15C and 16C, though with gables dating from the baroque period. Wholly of the Renaissance period, and the most striking of all the square's many charming buildings, is the house at No.61 (dated 1555 and today housing the tourist office), which has a most fanciful gable and comparably playful sgraffito decorations. The Town Hall, on the opposite side of the square, is distinguished by a giant order of pilasters. Beyond a plague column of 1716–17, near the top of the square, is a street (Palackého) leading to the so-called Big Gate, which forms part of the extensive surviving stretch of fortifications on the town's southern side.

The next important town along the main road to Brno is *Třebíč* (36km), today a centre of engineering, footwear and other industries, and boasting—next to the parish church of St. Martin—a tower with the largest clock in Czechoslovakia (the diameter of its dial is 7.1m). Of greater interest is its former *Benedictine Abbey*, around which the town had originally grown. Founded in 1101, it stands on a hill above the town, and has a church which is potentially one of the more important early medieval monuments in Moravia. Sadly this mid 13C structure, in a transitional Romanesque style, has suffered badly from a combination of neglect and heavy-handed 18C restoration and remodelling. Of the exterior the finest surviving parts are the power-fully carved north portal (Porta Paradisi) and the galleried apse; the best preserved part of the interior is the chancel, the nave having been spoilt by lifeless, unimaginative revaulting by Kaňka in the

Telč, view looking up the náměstí Míru, one of the best-preserved squares in Czechoslovakia

18C. The adjoining monastic building was converted into a private residence in the 16C, and today houses the West Moravian Museum, of interest largely for its collection of traditional cribs or Bethlehems.

Náměst nad Oslavou, 21km further E, is a small town with a long-established tradition in carpet-weaving. It stands on the banks of the river Oslava, which is here spanned by an 18C bridge decorated with 20 baroque statues dating from 1730 to 1740. Rising high on a steep hill above the river is an important Renaissance castle, commissioned in around 1573 for Lord Chief Justice Jan of Žerotín and completed in the 1580s by his son Karel the Elder.

The Žerotíns, the most prolific builders in Moravia, were a leading Protestant family. Karel the Elder, in the course of his remarkably extensive travels around Europe, had actively supported the French king Henry IV and had befriended some of the more important personalities of the Protestant courts, as well as the Swiss reformer and successor to Calvin, Theodor de Bèze. Both Karel and his father Jan were members of the Unity of Bohemian Brethren, one of the printing centres of which was established at Náměst in the 16C and published here in 1533 the first Czech Grammar Book.

The castle at Náměst has been tentatively attributed to the Italian architect Leonardo Garvi and is at any rate one of the main Moravian buildings in an Italianate Renaissance style. Especially notable is the Bramante-inspired double flight of steps on the exterior, and the arcaded courtyard inside; the interior has been much altered, and now contains a collection of 16C to 18C tapestries. The architect of Náměst might also have worked for the Žerotíns at their castle at *Rosice* (a further 20km along Road 23), where you will find one of the most elegant of the Moravian Renaissance courtyards. Built in around c 1580, this courtyard comprises three superimposed arcades, the spandrels and balustrades of which are covered all over with delicate Renaissance reliefs: this extensive use of sculptural decoration is one of the hallmarks of Moravian architecture of this period. 4km E of Rosice, Road 23 joins up with the D1 motorway, leaving you with a further 14km of to Brno (see Route 20).

19 Telč to Brno via Vranov and Znojmo

Total distance 163km. Telč 12km *Dačice*—12km *Slavonice*—32km *Bítov*—22km **Vranov**—18km **Znojmo**—28km *Moravský Krumlov*—39km **Brno**.

The most rewarding route from Telč to Brno involves making a large loop S through the quiet unspoilt countryside bordering with Austria. Leave Telč on the road which heads due S to *Dačice* (12km), where you will find an uninspired cube-shaped memorial on the sloping main square. This is not a provincial attempt at abstract art but rather a work commemorating Dačice's main claim to fame as the village which introduced the world in 1843 to the sugar cube. The inventor was a man of distant Swiss origin appropriately called Jakub Kryštof Rad, who manufactured the cube in a building on the square now occupied by the House of Culture. If you descend to the bottom of the square and cross the river, you will come on the other side to a former Franciscan monastery, the 18C building of which has been drably converted into a museum and art gallery. The collections, unsurprisingly, deal in part with Krystof and his crystal sugar, but there is also a small group of erotic engravings by the turn-of-the-century Moravian artist Max Švabinský, and a room devoted to the locally born F. Bilkovsky, a sugary sweet artist working in a Dufy-like style.

Return to the main square and head W for 3km on the road to Jindřichův Hradec, then head due S to Slavonice, a further 9km. The town of Slavonice, once part of the fiefdom of the Lords of Hradec, was founded in 1277, and reached the height of its prosperity in the mid 16C after it had been chosen as a staging post on the imperial road to Vienna. The Thirty Years' War left 73 of its 164 houses deserted, and its fate was finally sealed in the 1730s with the re-routing to the N of the imperial road. Slavonice has preserved much from its days of 16C glory, but in a sad, decayed state. There are two market squares, both of which are lined with arcaded, gabled houses dating back to the Renaissance. The western and larger of the two has at No. 46 (on the N side) a house featuring a ground-floor room with a quite extraordinary cellular vault which has been likened to a cluster of half-opened fans; this plaster work was executed in the 1540s by Master L.O. (Leopold Österreicher). The western end of the square is bordered by a plain and much-restored Town Hall of 1599, rising behind which is the Parish Church; the latter, founded in the late 14C and completed in 1521, adjoins a tall bell-tower of 1549. To the E of the church extends the smaller and more appealing of the town's two squares, this one boasting on its southern side a beautifully sgraffitoed house of the late 16C. At the far end of the square is the medieval Jemniče Gate.

Leave Slavonice on the Jemniče road, and then turn almost immediately right to Písečné. The journey E from Slavonice to Bítov (32km) is on a series of tiny meandering roads across rolling agricultural countryside spoilt only—until recently—by the sinister fencing marking the Austrian border. After Písecné (9km) turn left and then immediately right to Dešná (6km), which you cross and continue to head eastwards for a further 7km. Turn right on to the road marked Police and Vysočany and continue driving east. Shortly before Bítov (8km) you enter a dense forest encasing the long and winding Vranov reservoir, a popular place for swimming, fishing and water sports. The road follows the reservoir for 2km, and, after passing underneath the ruins of the medieval castle of Cornštejn (abandoned in the 17C), crosses the water just in front of Bítov. The castle of *Bítov*, towering over the reservoir, was built in the 13C for the Dukes of Lichtenberg, who remained the owners until 1576; its present romantic appearance is due to neo-Gothic remodelling in the 19C. **VRANOV** lies at the eastern end of the reservoir, and can be reached from Bítov by boat. The journey by car is more circuitous and involves driving N for 7km, then turning right and following the road E to Šumná (8km). 2km beyond Šumná turn left through forest to Vranov (5km), which, when approached from this direction, offers an outstanding view of its castle, a vast and dramatic baroque edifice poised in sublime isolation above trees and sheer cliffs that rise high above the deep and narrow valley carved by the river Dyje.

The castle at Vranov, first mentioned in 1100, was once a royal castle guarding the southern borders of Přemysl territory. Following a long succession of subsequent owners, and a troubled history devastated by fire in 1665, the castle was acquired in 1680 by Michal Jan II of Althann. In 1688 Michal Jan made the inspired and enlightened decision to employ at Vranov an up-and-coming Viennese architect who had spent 16 years with Bernini in Italy and of whom the Liechtensteins had spoken very highly. The man was Fischer von Erlach (1656–1723), one of the most brilliant architects of the central European baroque. Fischer, with great boldness, did away with the original castle chapel and replaced this with an enormous oval hall, The Hall of the Ancestors. In 1698, three years after the latter's completion, Fischer designed a family tomb for Michal Jan II, and in the following year began work on a chapel to house it. This was largely finished in time for Michal's death in 1702, though the two belfry towers of the west front were not to be added until 1710. Plans for rebuilding the rest of the castle were suspended for many years and it was not until 1723, when Vranov came into the hands of Jan Michal's ambitious and highly cultured daughter-in-law, Marie Anna Althann, née Pignatelli, that they

*View of Vranov Castle from the north-west; the remains of
the medieval ramparts are to the right, while to the left is
Fischer von Erlach's Trinity Chapel, begun in 1698*

were to be finally resumed. The re-construction was entrusted to one of
Fischer's sons, Josef Emmanuel (1693–1742), and was still incomplete by the
time of Marie Pignatelli's death in 1755. Her son, Michal Antonín Althann,
inherited her castle and estate, but not her cultural interests, and neglected all
work at Vranov in favour of a passion for hunting; by stocking the estate with
deer and boars to satisfy this passion he succeeded in destroying many of the
crops, and reducing greatly the value of the land. A new interest in the house
was shown by his successor, Michal Josef, whose particular contribution was
the sumptuous neo-classical decoration of the second-floor rooms; however his
excessive spending on the house, combined with a passion for gambling and
high living, eventually forced him in 1793 to put the house up for auction.

The new owner—Josef Hilgartner of Lilienborn, Attorney of Bohemia—pulled
down some of the remaining parts of the medieval castle, reconstructed the
stables, and landscaped the surroundings in a romantic style. His principle
contribution, however, was to set up a pottery in the castle grounds in 1799. This
pottery, later specialising in what came to be called Vranov Wedgeware, was
enormously successful, and by 1839 was employing 80 workers to create
products that were exported to different parts of the world; it continued to
function until 1882. The castle, owned by a variety of families after Josef
Hilgartner, was seized by the Nazis in 1942 and by the Czech State in 1945.
Careful restoration work is still in progress.

After crossing the bridge which leads to the main entrance of the
castle, you will pass on your left steps descending to Fischer von
Erlach's *Trinity Chapel*, a small oval construction clinging dramatically right above the cliff face. Beyond the gate is a small courtyard
around which are administrative buildings comprising all that
remains of the old castle. You walk through a second gate into the
Court of Honour, which is bordered to the left by landscaped terraces
affording magnificent views over the surrounding landscape. At the

far end of the courtyard are two massive sculptural groups (c 1727) by Antonio Mattielli representing *Hercules fighting Antaeus* and *Aeneas saving Anchises*. They were presented to Marie Pignatelli by her imperial admirer Charles VI in 1732, and placed on either side of a grand limestone staircase built that same year. The steps lead up into the main part of the house, where the official tour begins.

Adjacent to the entrance hall is Fischer von Erlach's dynamic **HALL OF ANCESTORS**, which in its architecture, sculpture and frescoed decoration is one of the most exciting baroque spaces to be seen anywhere in Europe. The oval, one of Fischer's most characteristic forms, is here given a particularly dramatic power not only through being spectacularly placed on a cliff edge, but also through being used on an enormous scale, a feat which required remarkable engineering skills for the vaulting: it is above all this oval which gives the castle from a distance such a dynamic and exhilarating profile. Thanks to Fischer's growing fame, he was able to secure for the painted and sculptural decoration of the interior two of the leading central European artists of the day, the painter Johann Michal Rottmayr and the sculptor Tobiáš Kracker. The former covered the ceiling with a great illusionistic representation of the Apotheosis of the Althann family (1695), while the latter produced for the niches along the walls a series of over-life-sized figures representing some of the ancestors of Michal Jan II of Althann (installed in 1694). As an example of self-promotion on a megalomaniac scale, the hall is rivalled only by G.B. Tiepolo's glorification of the Schönborns in the Würzburg Residenz.

The hall might be the highpoint of the castle tour, yet the other rooms that you are shown comprise a beautiful series of intimate and lavishly furnished late 18C interiors, including a Pompeian Room, an Oriental Room, a Swiss Room, a superb circular marble bathroom, two rooms adorned respectively with embroideries and coloured engravings by Mengs, and a room which Josef Hilgartner used as one of the first Freemasonry Lodges in Moravia.

Leaving Vranov by the same road on which you entered the town, head due E to **Znojmo** (23km), which lies at the point where the river Dyje leaves its narrow wooded valley and enters a great plain stretching S to nearby Austria. Znojmo, which rises on rocky ground above the river, has had a long and distinguished history.

The original settlement in the area was the Great Moravian citadel of St. Hippolytus, situated 2km W of the present town, and founded as far back as the 9C. A later citadel was established at present-day Znojmo by Prince Břetislav I in the 11C, and occupied an important position on an international trade route. The apanage Přemyslid princes made it their seat, and the Přemyslid king Otakar II was buried in its Minorite monastery; the Emperor Sigismund died here in 1437, and a Diet proclaimed in the town in 1628 strengthened the position of the Habsburg family on the Czech throne. Znojmo's subsequent history is less glamorous, the place developing into a quiet market town and centre of light industries; today it is known less for its royal and imperial associations than for the fame of its pickled cucumbers, a speciality introduced here from Hungary in 1571.

Much of the old town of Znojmo has survived, including extensive sections of its 14C–16C fortifications, but the town as a whole has a run-down, untidy quality. The life of the town is concentrated in the upper square (náměstí Kosmonautů), where late baroque and ugly modern buildings jostle uncomfortably together. Descending S from here on Obroková, you will pass near the end of the street the *Town Hall Tower*, a pinnacled and fantastical structure built in 1445 by

Mikuláš of Sedlešovice. South of the tower extends the náměstí Míru, the largest square in town, but with a sad and neglected character. The square slopes down the hill to the former Capuchin monastery, which has an uninspired late baroque church. Return to the upper town by heading W off the square on the Velká Mikulášská, at the top of which you will reach the town's well-preserved western ramparts, which enjoy an excellent view down the wooded banks of the Dyje and over the flat fertile country stretching to the south. The large and impressive hall-church which stands above the ramparts is the parish church of *St. Nicholas* (sv. Mikuláš), dating back to the 14C but largely rebuilt in the late 15C by Mikuláš of Sedlešovice; behind the building is the late Gothic church of *St. Wenceslas* (sv. Václav) (vaulted in 1521), which has the curious feature of having its lower windows actually incorporated into the ramparts. Walking N from here along the ramparts you come to the castle, which has been converted into the Sladovna Brewery and is thus officially closed to visitors. You are thus prevented at present from seeing the oldest and most interesting monument in Znojmo, an 11C round chapel (sv. Kateřina) decorated inside with frescoes commissioned in 1134 by the Přemyslids and constituting one of the most extensive surviving series of Romanesque frescoes in Czechoslovakia. Adjoining the castle, and near a terrace with good views W over wooded hills to the Citadel of St. Hippolytus, is the former Minorite monastery, which now contains the South Moravian Museum, featuring a small gallery of Habsburg portraits, a lapidarium, and archaeological and natural history collections. Přemyslovců Street will lead you back from here to the náměstí Kosmonautů.

To visit the *Citadel of St. Hippolytus* leave Znojmo at the northern end of town and drive for 2km on the Mašovice road; the old fortified church of St. Hippolytus was pulled down to make way for the present late baroque edifice, the interest of which lies primarily in the eloquent dome frescoes by the expressive Austrian artist F.A. Maulbertsch (1768). By the river on the southern outskirts of Znojmo is the former Premonstratensian monastery of *Louka*, which was founded in 1190. The baroque monastery buildings have been used as an army barracks since the time of Joseph II, and the valuable library which was once here is now in the Strahov Monastery in Prague. However you can still see Louka's much-restored and altered church, which dates back to shortly after the monastery's foundation.

The fastest way from Znojmo to Brno is along the straight and flat Road 54, but a more peaceful route through rolling countryside is by way of *Moravský Krumlov* (leave Znojmo at the southern end of town and head NE on the road marked Suchordly). The small town of Moravský Krumlov (32km), badly damaged in the Second World War, is famous for its castle, which was rebuilt after c 1560 for Pertold of Lipá, hereditary marshal of the Kingdom of Bohemia. The unknown architect—possibly to be identified with the builder of Náměstí and Rosice—created an elegant Italianate structure centred around a three-tiered arcade courtyard. The much altered interior contains an interesting cycle of paintings devoted to Slavonic subject-matter, and painted between 1910 and 1928 by Alfons Mucha, an artist best known for his *fin-de-siècle* posters executed in Paris. At Ivančice, 10km further N, turn right to Modřice (20km), which lies on the main road to Brno. A detour 4km to the S along this road will take you to the former Benedictine abbey of *Rajhrad*, founded in 1048 and the oldest in Moravia. The present abbey church was begun in 1722 by Johann Santini-Aichel, and is one of his finest works in a strictly baroque style. The surprisingly large interior is particularly splendid, and comprises three interconnected oval spaces, the domes of which are covered in illusionistic frescoes. Typically for this architect the three spaces have a symbolic significance, as is indicated by the inscription on the arch over the altar: *Faciamus hic tria tabernacula*, the words spoken by St. Peter at the Transfiguration. On the left-hand side of the church is a tablet commemorating George James Ogilvy, who defended Brno against the Swedes in 1645. Return to Modřice, from where the remaining 9km to Brno (see next route) are on dual carriageway.

20 Brno

Brno, the capital of Moravia and the third largest town in Czechoslovakia, is spaciously laid out between gentle wooded hills. Though of ancient origin, and with numerous monuments from different periods in history, its present character was acquired from the late 18C onwards, with the rapid development of its textile mills and other industries. Known sometimes as the Manchester or Leeds of Czechoslovakia, it is a city of a remarkably progressive character which has played an important role in the development of 20C architecture.

The origins of Brno are seen by some to go back to the Celtic stronghold of Eburodunon, mentioned by Ptolemy; others trace the town back to a Slavic citadel, or 'brniti', established in about the 5C AD. A seat of the apanage Přemyslid princes by the 11C, Brno was raised to a town in 1243, and became the centre of the Moravian Margraves after 1349; it emerged as capital of Moravia in 1641. The town prospered to begin with as a result of thriving trade relations with Venice, Genoa, the Hanseatic ports, and numerous towns in eastern and central Europe. Over the centuries Brno successfully withstood sieges by the Hussites, the Swedes and the Prussian armies of Frederick II, and was only captured once—by Napoleon in 1805. The town's industrial development dates back to the foundation in 1766 of a textile factory comprising 120 looms; within the space of 14 years 19 other such factories had been established, thus earning the place the name of 'rakouský Manchestr' (the Austrian Manchester). After 1818 locally built machinery began to replace English imports, thanks to the creation of the Salms ironworks at nearby Blansko. A further great boost to the town's economy was provided in 1839, when the railway line was completed between here and Vienna; later in the century, it developed into a considerable engineering centre, which it still remains.

One of the most outstanding periods in Brno's history followed the creation of the Czechoslovak Republic in 1918. The local industrialists, many of whom were Jews, were anxious that their town should reflect the progressive and revolutionary spirit of the new country, and became patrons to some of the greatest figures of the European avant-garde. It was at Brno that the German architect Mies van der Rohe built the Villa Tugendhat, one of the pioneering modernist constructions of this century. Less well known today outside of Czechoslovakia, though no less deserving of attention than the work of Mies van der Rohe, were the achievements of the Brno-based group of artists, architects and intellectuals known as BLOK, which was founded in 1920, and included among its prominent members the painter Kalab, and the architects Bohuslav Fuchs (1895–1972) and Bedřich Rozehnal. A symbol of the new Brno was the vast trade Exhibition ground which was opened in 1928 and designed by the city's most adventurous architects.

After suffering from the dispersal of its Jewish community in the late 1930s, Brno was then badly affected by heavy bombing in the Second World War. The architecture of post-war Brno bears little comparison to that of the inter-war years, though an active cultural life has continued to flourish here. Furthermore the Exhibition Ground, revived in 1955 after the closure of the one in Prague, has been the scene since 1959 of an International Engineering Trade Fair, an event which helps to sustain in the town a cosmopolitan and dynamic atmosphere.

Among the famous people to have been born in Brno are the botanist and founder of the modern theory of heredity, Johann Gregor Mendel (1822–84); the inventor of the Kaplan water turbine, Viktor Kaplan (1876–1934); the Austrian architect Adolf Loos (1870–1933), and the writers Bohumil Hrabal (1914–) and Milan Kundera (1929–).

A.   Central Brno

Brno is not the best preserved of Czechoslovakia's towns, and its old monuments are widely scattered and enveloped by extensive 19C and 20C development. The greatest concentration of these monuments is around the Zelný trh, which has kept the shape of the original 13C market square, and indeed bears the name of Cabbage Market. In the middle of this, the largest square in Brno, is the *Parnassus Fountain*, built in 1693–95 to a design by Fischer von Erlach. The *Old Town Hall*, the town's most important surviving secular building from the medieval period, lies off the northern side of this square, and functioned as a town hall from the 13C up to 1345.

The main entrance to the building, off Radnická, is marked by a tall tower built in the 13C but heavily remodelled in later periods. At its base is a fancifully elaborate late Gothic portal executed c 1510 by the Austrian sculptor and architect Anton Pilgram. This colourful and belligerent personality spent much of his life in Vienna, where in 1513 he was to quarrel with the local mason's guild, on whom he was to take his revenge by caricaturing their leading members in his sculptural decoration of the pulpit in St. Stephen's Cathedral. According to tradition he committed a comparably vindictive act at Brno: considering himself to have been underpaid for his work on the Town Hall portal, he is said to have destroyed its central pinnacle on his last night in the town and to have replaced it with the present bizarrely drooping form, a comment on the bent character of the Brno burghers. Behind the entrance portal is the suspended corpse of a creature said to be the infamous Brno dragon, a monster which lived in the river Svratka, and terrified early travellers to the town; in fact it is the mummified remains of a crocodile presented as a gift to Matthias Corvinus by a Turkish delegation on their way to Poland. Hanging alongside it is a 16C wheel recalling the story of a young wheelwright who bet a good barrel of wine that in the space of twelve hours he would fell a tree in the forest, make a carriage wheel from it, and roll it all the way from Mikulov to Brno Town Hall. He won the wager, and the wheel has become a symbol of the town, an indication of how work is done well and quickly here; the irony is that the young wheelwright gained little from his achievement, for he was considered to be in league with the devil, and died in poverty. Exhibitions are now held in the Old Town Hall, and, in the summer months, you can walk up to the gallery of the entrance tower.

Returning from Radnická to the Zelný trh, walk round the square in an anti-clockwise direction, and you will pass at Nos 12 and 13 two reconstructed houses of medieval origin forming what is known as the Malý Špalíček or Little Block. On the southern, upper side of the square is the vast *Dietrichstein Palace*, a much-restored structure of the early 17C built as the palace of the Bishops of Olomouc in Brno, and taken over in 1805 by Marshal M.I. Kutuzov, Commander-in-Chief of the Russian troops fighting Napoleon; today it houses the historical, archaeological and natural history collections of the extensive *Moravian Museum*. The elegant late 18C *Reduta Theatre*, on the south-eastern corner of the square, is the town's oldest theatre, and was where Mozart performed in 1767; today it specialises in operettas put on by the Brno State Theatre. On the southern side of the building extends the triangular-shaped Kapucínské náměstí, originally the Coal Market, and a place where charcoal was sold from the 14C onwards. The *Capuchin Monastery*, which gives the square its name, is a mid 17C structure of interest largely for its crypt, where a specially designed air passage has preserved the corpses of Capuchin monks and distinguished benefactors of the monastery in a mummified state; the corpse of Brno's leading baroque architect, Mořic Grimm, provides the crypt with one of its grim attractions, as does that of the belligerent Austrian commander Baron von Trenck who died in Brno's notorious Špilberk prison in 1749.

From the Dietrichstein Palace the narrow Petrská Street climbs up to the attractive Petrov Hill, where the town's citadel was situated before being re-sited to the Špilberk. As you climb you will pass the site intended for the Divadlo na Provázku (literally the Theatre on a String), a reconstruction of an avant-garde youth theatre which was founded in 1967 and named after a leading minister of the time.

The *Cathedral of SS. Peter and Paul*, occupying the site of the former citadel, was begun in the 14C over a Romanesque structure; partially burnt in the 16C, it was remodelled by Grimm in the baroque period, and given a neo-Gothic presbytery by A. Prokop in 1889–91, and its two tall towers and steeples in 1904–05. You enter through a neo-Gothic portal attached to a 14C/15C west façade; the main interest of the interior is to be found in the first chapel to the right, a *Madonna and Child* of c 1307, one of the most important surviving medieval statues in Moravia. The cathedral, which dominates the Petrov Hill, overlooks to the S the verdant Denis Park (Denisovy sady), in which remains of medieval and 17C walls have been preserved, as well as a classical obelisk, erected in 1818 to commemorate the end of the Napoleonic Wars. Brno is a place where wine is drunk almost as much as beer, and on the southern slopes of the hill can also be found a number of privately owned wine cellars, where families and friends get together occasionally for wild drinking sprees.

You can descend to the lower town from the cathedral by way of the Biskupská and its continuation Dominikánská, two streets lined with much restored 16C–18C buildings comprising the Velký Špalíček or Big Block. Of especial interest is No. 9 Dominikánská, where is to be found *The House of the Lords of Kunštát*, a medieval palace transformed in the Renaissance period and again at the beginning of the 18C; it is now an exhibition hall and cultural centre. The street ends up alongside the former *Dominican Church of St. Michael*, which rises on a terrace fringed by baroque statuary above the small náměstí Družby národů, the town's former fish market. The church, remodelled by J.K. Erna in the late 17C, was attached to a monastery founded in the 1330s; the Estates of Moravia used to meet in the latter's main cloister, which has retained fragments of its medieval masonry. The baroque monastic buildings which extend north of the cloister were designed by Grimm after 1690 and now form the present Town Hall.

Panenská leads N from the náměstí Družby národů to the unprepossessing Hotel International (1960–62), which overlooks to the W the verdant Špilberk Hill. On Husova, adjacent to the western entrance to the hotel, is the neo-Renaissance *Moravian Gallery*, which was built by a Jewish textile merchant in the 1880s as a museum of the applied arts; there is a choice and excellently displayed collection of objects from the 16C onwards, including numerous Biedermeier and Secession works. Walking N from here up Husova you will come to the late 19C Besední dům, which was once the main Czech cultural centre of the town, and is now the home of the Brno State Philharmonic Orchestra. Turn right here into Solniční and walk along this street until you come to the pedestrian shopping street of Česká, where you turn right again and head south. As soon as you enter Česká, you will pass on the left-hand side the most distinguished-looking of Brno's modern hotels, the *Hotel Avion*, which was designed in 1927 by Bohuslav Fuchs, who created a narrow and impressively simple street front in glass and steel (the hotel has subsequently been expanded). Among the other buildings you will notice as you walk S down Česká is Stopka's Beer Hall (No. 5), the exterior of which was covered in sgraffiti decorations by L. Novák in 1919.

The street leads into the náměstí Svobody, the oldest and second largest square in Brno. This square, at the heart of Brno's pedestrian district, has an overall drab and 19C character, and yet it preserves monuments from earlier periods. At its centre is a plague column of 1680 designed by J.K. Erna, while at No. 13 is the late 16C Schwartz House, a Renaissance palace boasting an arcaded courtyard built in 1589–96 by A. Gabri and J. Gialdi; the building was heavily restored in 1938, and the once plain exterior given a sgraffito decoration by E. Hrbek. At the eastern end of the square, and entered at No. 1 Gagarinova, is the former Foundation for Noblewomen (Ústav Šlechtičen), founded in the 1670s as a home for orphaned girls from aristocratic and burgher families; the building, remodelled in the 18C and 20C, now houses the ethnographical collections of the Moravian Museum.

Brno's pedestrian district continues S and to the E of the square, but for the moment you should head N along 9 Květná, reaching after a few minutes the finest of the town's medieval monuments, the **Church of St. James** (sv. Jakub). Founded in the 1220s for the German burghers of Brno, it was rebuilt from the late 14C onwards, Anton Pilgram intervening in the construction around 1495; a fire in 1515 delayed the completion of the building until 1592, when the tower was erected. An amusing and curious feature of the exterior is the obscene figure placed high on the south side of the tower. It apparently shows a smirking man gesturing with his anus in the direction of the distant Czech church of SS. Peter and Paul. Traditionally this figure has been interpreted as an indication of German attitudes towards the Czechs, but recent investigations, involving a photographer and a fireman's ladder, has revealed in fact that the man is not alone, but is accompanied by a woman with whom he is engaged in activities not normally associated with a church. Inside the building you find yourself within a great hall-church of great lightness, height and elegance, and with elaborate Gothic vaulting of c 1585: at least one architectural historian has described this as the last great masterpiece of the Gothic in Czechoslovakia. The high altar and other furnishings are neo-Gothic works of the 19C, but there is an outstanding pulpit of 1525, containing baroque reliefs of the life of Christ. Among the Gothic, Renaissance and baroque tombs in the ambulatory is the tomb of Field Marshal Count Radwit de Souches (d. 1697), the defender of Brno against the Swedes.

Further N along 9 Květná, at the junction with the náměstí Rudé armády, is the pale yellow façade of *St. Thomas* (sv. Tomáš), originally attached to a 14C Augustinian monastery. The Gothic church was remodelled in a baroque style by J.K. Erna in the mid 17C, and further altered by M. Grimm in the following century; inside is an altarpiece by F.A. Maulbertsch. The náměstí Rudé armády marks the northern border of the old town, and has in its landscaped centre a large sculpture of a Red Army soldier representing the Victory over Fascism, a work by V. Makovský of 1955. Parkland, following the line of the former medieval fortifications, takes up the whole NE corner of central Brno. Turning right at the náměstí Rudé armády on to Rooseveltova, you will skirt the Osvobození Park, on the edge of which stands the *Janáčkovo divadlo* (Janáček Opera House), erected in 1960–65, and specialising in both opera and ballet. The first main turning to the right down Rooseveltova is Chorázova, off which stands the *Church of the Assumption of Our Lady*, a Jesuit church built in 1666 and lavishly remodelled inside by M. Grimm in 1735. Back on Rooseveltova continue heading S into Divadelní, which passes alongside the *Mahen Theatre* (1881–82), the main dramatic theatre of Brno and apparently the first in Europe to have had electric lighting. The small building behind

it—an originally Art Nouveau structure rebuilt in 1946—is the House
of Art of the City of Brno, a centre for art exhibitions. After passing
the Mahen Theatre, cross the Malinovského náměstí, and turn right
until you reach Novobranská, which leads to the Měnín Gate, the
only remaining gate from the town's fortifications. Heading SW from
here along Orlí, the first street which you come to is the attractive
Minoritská, one of the pedestrian streets that extend S from the
náměstí Svobody. At the junction of Orlí and Minoritská is the
Technical Museum, with collections ranging from hunting weapons
and mechanical musical instruments to computers, microscopes and
hydro-electric generators. Heading N up Minoritská you will come to
the *Minorite Church*, a building of 14C origin which was given after
1716 a lively and richly ornamented façade by M. Grimm, who was
also responsible for the attached *Loreto Chapel*. At the southern end
of Minoritská is a former Franciscan monastery, the cellars of which
have been converted into a stylish and animated Wine Bar. The
street finishes up at the south in front of the Grand Hotel, an early
20C establishment with the shabby look characteristic of places with
this name. South from here is the náměstí České armády, and further
S is the town's main *railway station*, a superb 19C ironwork construction which has recently been lovingly restored. From here you
can return to the old town of Brno by walking N along the wide Třída
Vítězství (Victory Avenue), the main shopping street of the town.
Turning left from here into Květinářská or Orlí will take you back to
the náměstí 25 Února.

B.   Western Brno

West of the Hotel International you can climb up through parkland to
the **Špilberk Citadel**, which was put up in the late 13C, and
reconstructed at various times in history, most notably in the 17C. A
large network of underground tunnels is said to lie underneath the
complex, one of which apparently led to a village 18km away, from
where fresh produce was supplied to the fortress in times of siege.

Gaining a reputation for being impregnable during the Thirty Years' War, the
Špilberk later acquired considerable notoriety on account of its prison, which
was established here in the 17C. In the 18C and early 19C many of the leading
miscreants of the Habsburg Empire were incarcerated here, including numerous Italian, Polish and Hungarian revolutionaries. Among the best known
prisoners was Colonel Trenck, the leader of the half-savage group of Austrian
soldiers known as the Pandours; he died here in 1749. But it was above all for
the Italian poet and revolutionary Silvio Pellico that the prison was to be best
remembered. He, together with fellow members of the secret society called the
Carbonari, was a prisoner here between 1822 and 1830, an experience which
left his health ruined and led him to write in 1832 *Le mie prigioni* (My Prisons).
This moving and shocking account of conditions in the Špilberk horrified liberal
Europe, and apparently inspired Chancellor Metternich to say that the book
had done more damage to Austria than a lost battle; the name of Pellico is today
recalled in a street underneath the citadel.

The citadel can at present only be appreciated for its extensive views,
its buildings being closed for restoration until at least 1994. When
work is completed, there will be a museum devoted to the history of
Brno housed within the former prison cells, and also an important
art gallery, featuring a good collection of 20C Czech art, including
many works by the Czech Cubist, Alfred Justitz. Descending the

western side of the citadel hill you reach the busy Úvoz Street, at the southern end of which is Mendlovo náměstí (Mendel Square). Rising above the square is the former convent church of the Assumption of Our Lady, which has a baroque high altar of 1734–35 containing an Italian-Byzantine icon. The former *Convent of the Poor Clares* to which the church was attached was founded in 1323 by Queen Eliška Rejčka. Of the original structure, there remains only the chapter-house and a fragment of the cloister, the rest of the convent being largely reconstructed between the 15C and 18C. Of great interest is the mid 18C *Library*, which has elaborate baroque shelving, and close associations with several of the best-known Moravian scientists and musicians of the 19C. The composer Křížkovský worked in the library, as did his famous pupil Leoš Janáček; the place is remembered above all for the genetician Mendel, who was a monk at the monastery, and to whom a small museum is dedicated adjoining the library. The wine bar installed in the convent cellars rivals that of the Franciscan monastery as a popular and elegant place to eat and drink.

Heading W from Mendel Square along Klášterská and its continuation Vystavní you will come to Brno's celebrated **Výstaviště Exhibition Ground**, the most important in Czechoslovakia. Founded in 1928, and originally laid out by the architect Emil Kralík, it has been the venue since 1959 of an International Engineering Trade Fair, and, since 1965, of Intercanis Brno, an international dog show which now attracts up to 12,000 dogs to the city; these events are held respectively every September and July. But an interest in either dogs or engineering is not essential to a visit to the Exhibition Ground, which is well worth seeing for the architecture alone. The main hall today is a vast domed structure of 1960, but of greater beauty are the original buildings of 1928, in particular **Hall A**, a pioneering white and glazed construction supported by rows of massive parabolic arches; the architects were Kalous and Valenta, working under Kralík's supervision. Other fine works of this period include Bohuslav Fuchs' red-brick and glass *Brno-Moravian Pavilion*, and a *Tower* by Bohumír Čermák, a stunning glass structure built around a staircase well and resembling a futuristic fantasy. Many other outstanding buildings of the 1920s are to be seen in the suburban districts of Žlutý Kopec and Jiráskova čtvrť, which spread over the green and shaded hill rising up to the N of the Exhibition Ground: in these suburbs were once the homes of many of the more enlightened of the town's industrialists. You can ascend the hill on Lípová Street, where at No. 18, at the junction with Neumannova, is one of Fuchs' greatest buildings, a *Nursery* designed in 1929 and having the simple, abstract qualities of a painting by a Constructivist such as Mondrian. Lípová continues into Tvrdého, which descends into Úvoz, at the foot of the Špilberk Hill.

C.   Northern Brno and the Moravian Karst (Moravský Kras)

Head N from the náměstí Rudé armády along Kouvicova. On the right-hand side of the road, beyond the tall block of the Hotel Continental (1961–64), is a neo-classical 19C building which was formerly the

School of Organists where Janáček taught; it is now the *History of Music Department* of the Moravian Museum, and includes a large collection of photographs, documents and other items relating to the history of music in this region; its extensive manuscript collection, founded by Professor Vladimír Heifert in 1919, has autograph works by Liszt, Brahms, Dvořák, Martinů and Beethoven. In 1910, after being appointed to the staff of the School of Organists, Janáček moved to an adjacent house at 14 Smetanova, and lived there until his death in 1918. The house, incorporated into the garden of the museum building, now forms a museum to the composer, where you can see numerous photographs documenting his life, as well as listen to recordings of his music; the highpoint of the visit is the well-preserved study, in which the master's piano is to be found. Continuing N up Leninova you will come eventually to Bohuslav Fuchs' largest building in the city, the Provincial Army Headquarters of 1937. Further N you come to the housing estates of Tábor and Králové Pole, where, in the middle of grim socialist blocks of the 1950s and 1960s, can be seen innovative co-operative housing of 1928.

It is a modern building which provides Brno with its greatest if also most neglected attraction. This, the **VILLA TUGENDHAT** by Mies van der Rohe, stands in the hill-side suburb of Černé Pole, a short distance NE of the Janáček House. Continue until the end of Smetanova, cross the wide Lidiká, and then follow Lužanecká, skirting to the S the large Lužánky Park. At Drobného turn left, and then take the first right into the steeply ascending Schodová, which you climb until you reach Černopolní, where you turn right again. The entrance to the villa is 50m down the road on the right-hand side.

The garden façade of Villa Tugendhat, Brno

The Tugendhats were a Jewish family which had settled in Brno in 1864, and had risen in the late 19C from being drapers to owning important textile mills. Fritz Tugendhat, the grandson of the first Tugendhat to have moved to Brno, was born on 10 October 1895, and, on 30 July 1928, was married in Berlin to

Greta Weis, née Löw-Beer. Greta was the daughter of another textile manufacturer, and on this, her second marriage, received as a gift from her father a plot of land on Brno's Černé Pole Hill. Even before marrying, Fritz and Greta had met Mies van der Rohe in Berlin and had asked him to design a house for them. Mies (as he came to be known to his friends and to architectural historians) first came to Brno in September 1928 to inspect the proposed building site, and by 31 December of that year had already drawn up a project for the house. Work was begun in June of the following year and was complete by December 1930; Mies designed not only the architecture but also all the furniture of the villa. The Tugendhats lived here until 1938, when they fled from the Nazis, and eventually moved to Venezuela, where they remained after the war. The Nazis occupied the house after 15 March 1939, and confiscated it from the family on 4 October 1939; ownership fell officially to the German Reich on 12 January 1942. After plundering the house and devastating the garden, the Germans abandoned the place in 1949. The badly damaged villa served for a short while as a private ballet school, but then was appropriated by the Czech State, who used it at first as a home for the National Institute of Physiotherapy, and then, after 1955, as the department of rehabilitative physiotherapy of the Pediatric Teaching Hospital of Brno. The latter department only moved out of the building in 1969, six years after it had been declared a cultural monument, and immediately prior to a restoration campaign based partially on a report drafted by an architect from the Chicago studios of Mies van der Rohe, Dirk Lohan. Ownership of the building reverted in 1986 from the District National Health Authority to the National Committee of the City of Brno. By July 1989, however, the building was occupied only by a caretaker with strict instructions to turn all prospective visitors away. The future of the building remains uncertain, though it is hoped that the Brno authorities will have the good sense to open it shortly to the public.

The Villa Tughendat, one of the key works in the history of the modernist movement in architecture, occupies a sloping site with magnificent views towards the old centre of Brno. From the much-altered street-side (sadly, the only part of the building which can at present be seen by the public), the villa appears as a single-storey horizontal structure; seen from the large and steeply inclined garden, however, it is a three-storey block. The main entrance is at street level, and on this level were once to be found bedrooms, bathrooms and a garage; on the floor below were the kitchen and main living quarters, while on the lowest floor were storage-rooms, service rooms and bedrooms for occasional use. The architecture clearly reflects the ideals of the Dutch Constructivist group De Stijl, which believed that modern architecture should be based on a system of right-angled planes, perpendicular and parallel to each other. Decorative details were abolished, and space was conceived as flexible as possible, delineated by white carpets and chrome-plated cruciform columns, and with a minimum use of walls. The main room of the house was a space of 235 square metres, which was intended as a study and library, and as a place for resting, listening to music and receiving visitors. On two sides it was bordered by great sheets of glass, and it was directly connected to a garden terrace: Mies brilliantly exploited the panoramic situation of the house and also broke down the rigid division between interior and exterior, as he did in the German pavilion which he designed at the same time for the Barcelona Exhibition of 1929/30. The interior of the villa is now stripped (some of Mies' furniture is kept in storage in the Moravian Gallery), and hung with dust-sheets; the garden is being dug up. Yet the place inspires in those lucky few who manage an entry a sense of serenity and timelessness.

One of the most popular excursions from Brno is to the *Moravian Karst* (Moravský kras), a round trip of some 60km. From the Villa Tugendhat head S down Černopolní until you reach the wide

Merhautova, where you turn left, following the signs for Adamov and Blansko; much of the journey is along the Svitava river. *Blansko* (25km) is a small industrial town set among wooded hills and with an iron industry dating back to medieval times; many of Czechoslovakia's bronze memorials, and much of the ironwork from the country's old monuments were cast in the foundries here. The local castle, remodelled in a neo-Renaissance style in the late 19C contains the Museum of the Moravian Karst, with exhibits relating to the local iron industry. The Moravský Kras is a name given to the limestone area 3km to the E of Blansko: 6km wide and 25km long, it is an area densely covered in forests, intercut with gorges, and pitted with caves, many of which have been formed by the underground river Punkva. Important archaeological finds have been made in a number of the caves, and in those known as Sloupsko-Šošůvské jeskyně (in the vicinity of the village of Sloup, 14km NE of Blansko) can be seen traces of prehistoric wall-paintings.

By far the most visited of the caves is the *Punkevní jeskyně* (Punkva Cave) which can be reached by heading E from Blansko on the Jedovnice road, and then turning off after 2km in the direction of Sloup; at the Hotel Skalní Mlýn (a further 2km and a popular base for those wishing to spend a long time in the Kras), the road forks, and you should take the turning to the left, continuing to drive along the bottom of a small wooded gorge formed by an overground stretch of the Punkva river. The entrance to the cave lies 1.5km further on, at the point where the Punkva disappears into the rock. The popularity of the cave is such that there are generally large queues to get in it, and in the summer months it might be necessary to book a visit several hours ahead. While waiting you might have to avail yourself of the nearby toilet complex, which is of interest in being one of the earliest examples of privatisation in Moravia (an enterprising family bought it back in 1987): as a guide was heard to say in 1989: 'In England you privatise your heavy industries; in Moravia we privatise our toilets'. The visit to the cave lasts about an hour and a half, and is by a combination of foot and boat, an altogether claustrophobic experience. Perhaps the most enjoyable moment comes half-way through the trip when you emerge into daylight, at the bottom of the **Macocha Abyss**: suddenly you are confronted with steep and rocky slopes streaked with rich vegetation of an intense green. The 138m-deep abyss, one of the deepest in Europe, appears to have created by the collapse thousands of years ago of the ceiling of an enormous domed space. This dramatic and sinister mark on the landscape has naturally given rise to many abysmal local stories, at least one of which is supported by documentary evidence.

In 1560 a woman from the nearby village of Vilémovice was told that her ill young son would die if she did not kill her older stepson, who was said to be draining the former's health away. Believing unquestioningly in this superstitious nonsense, she took the stepson to the Macocha Abyss, and threw him into it. Fortunately—though not for her—he managed to cling on to the vegetation on the sides, and was shortly afterwards saved by a group of foresters. When the latter heard of what the stepmother had done to him, they did the same to her, though she was not to be assisted by the vegetation, and was thus to become probably the first person to reach the bottom of the abyss. It was not until 1734 that a more leisurely descent was to be made into the abyss, led by a monk from the Augustinian monastery at Brno. The Punkva Cave itself was only explored after 1909, five years before part of it was opened to the public.

Returning to the Hotel Skalní Mlýn, turn left on to the Ostrov road, and you will begin climbing up the Punkva gorge; after 2km another turning to your left will take you after 1km to a forest car park and restaurant at the top of the Macocha Abyss. Back on the Ostrov road turn right after 50m to nearby Vilémovice, and from here descend to Jedovnice. The road back to Brno heads S from here, but you could make a detour 3km to the E to visit the village of *Senetářov*, where, in 1972, all the villagers pooled their resources to build their own church; this appealing structure, rising on steps above a pool, is distantly indebted to Le Corbusier's church at Ronchamp. The village of **Křtiny**, 8km to the S of Jedovnice and pleasantly situated among rolling meadows fringed by woods, has one of the most impressive baroque churches in Moravia. This soaringly tall pilgrimage church, so unexpectedly large for its rural setting, has its origins in a chapel of 1237, and attracts numerous pilgrims each year on St. Anne's day. The present structure, designed c 1710 by Santini-Aichel, has the plan of a Greek cross and is an example of Santini's work in a strictly baroque as opposed to baroque-Gothic style. The interior, revealed by recent and still incomplete restoration to be dazzlingly bright, has domes frescoed in 1728–50 by Etgens, Ignác Raab and Winterhalter. Of great ingenuity is the way in which the Greek Cross is joined to an oval cloister belonging to the former convent attached to the church. Driving SW of Křtiny by way of Babice and Bílovice you will reach Brno after 16km, entering the town on the same road on which you left it.

21   Brno to Ostrava

A.   Via Olomouc

Total distance 179km. Brno—E462/Road 58—36km Vyškov—41km **Olomouc**—25km Lipník nad Bečvou—19km Běloton—20km *Fulnek*—38km *Ostrava.*

Heading due E of Brno you soon reach the E462, which is now a dual carriageway almost all the way to Olomouc. Almost immediately after leaving Brno you enter a chain of fertile and much built up valleys that extend all the way to Ostrava and form the backbone of Moravia. The landscape along this, the main Ostrava road, becomes increasingly industrialised, and the towns you pass are of little interest. *Vyškov*, 36km E of Brno, has in its main square a Renaissance Town Hall of 1569–1613. The industrial north-western suburb of Dědice was the birthplace of Klement Gottwald (1896–1953), the first Communist president of the Czechoslovak Republic, and a person whom most Czechs would now prefer to forget (the museum to him in the house of his birth has recently been closed). Of far greater interest is the town of **OLOMOUC**, which remained up to the 17C the second most important town in the kingdom of Bohemia. Impressive even today in its scale, this polluted, heavily industrialised and much damaged town, has a fascinating if very scattered range of monuments.

A Slavic settlement on a spur above the Morava river dates back to the 7C AD, though there is no evidence that this place was one of the main centres of the Great Moravian Empire. On the contrary, the settlement seems to have increased in importance following the collapse of the Moravian Empire in the early 10C and the annexation of Moravia by the Přemyslid king Boleslav I in 955. In the early 10C it became a seat of the apanage Přemyslid princes following the construction of a fortress here by Břetislav I. Made a bishopric in 1063, Olomouc continued to prosper, and knew one of the greatest periods in its early history under its fifth bishop, Jindřich Zdík, who had been educated in the Prague court, and was a loyal supporter of the Přemyslids; holding office between 1126 and 1150, Zdík was reponsible for the consecration of the unfinished Basilica of Saint Wenceslas (sv. Václav), and for the building of a Bishop's Palace, which constitutes today, even in its fragmentary state, one of the most important Central European palaces from the Romanesque period.

The capital of Moravia from 1187 to 1641, Olomouc was made a royal town in 1248. The last of the Přemyslids, Wenceslas I, was murdered here in 1306, but the town was subsequently to receive the support of the Luxembourgs, Charles IV making frequent stays in its castle. It was at Olomouc in 1469 that King Matthias of Hungary proclaimed himself king of the Czechs. In the 16C, despite tensions between the Lutherans and the Catholics (the town had a large and powerful German minority), the economic and cultural life of Olomouc experienced a period of remarkable vitality, leading in 1573 to its Jesuit College being raised to a University, which was to survive until the mid 19C. Only during the Thirty Years' War, when Olomouc suffered severe damage, was the town's importance seriously diminished. Occupied by the Swedes between 1641–50, Olomouc was replaced as the Moravian capital by Brno, and was never to regain its former supremacy. An extensive rebuilding campaign was conducted after 1709, but the construction by Maria Theresa later that century of a large fortress not only put a halt to this, but also led to an order to pull down all buildings within a radius of 1.5km from the fortifications. The imperial court of Vienna, fleeing from the revolutions of 1848–49, took refuge at this fortress, and it was here that Emperor Ferdinand I handed over power to Franz Josef. But the fortress constituted a severe obstacle to the town's commercial development, which in consequence benefited little from the construction of a railway here in 1841. The fortress was finally abolished in 1888, and only then did industrialisation rapidly take hold, a process which has continued up to the present day. The University, which had survived up to the middle of the 19C, was revived after the Second World War, and contributes to much of the liveliness of the town; it bears today the name of the great Czech historian Palacký. Despite the town's extensive industries (ironworks, a distillery, soap, chocolate and engineering factories, and so on), the place has a reputation for the fertility of the surrounding countryside, and every year since 1966 has held an important Flower Show.

The wedge-shaped historic centre of Olomouc is separated from the extensive surrounding development by a ring of parks, the southernmost of which (the Smetanovy sady) being the venue of the town's flower show. On the town's wide, western side the line of the old fortifications is marked by the spacious Leninova Boulevard, while on the other sides are to be found long stretches of the original fortifications; immediately below the fortifications, and running from the south-western corner of the town to the north-eastern spur of land where the original citadel was sited, is a canal of the Morava river. The lively centre of Olomouc is the western side of town, where you will find the town's largest square, the vast náměstí Míru. This square typifies the character of the town, having numerous monuments of interest spread around an overall grim space with a predominance of tall turn-of-the-century and modern buildings. The *Town Hall*, a whitish free-standing structure in its centre, dates back to the 1348, though it was remodelled in the late Gothic, Renaissance and baroque periods, and was much restored after the Second World War. On its southern side there projects the apse of its late 15C chapel, while on its eastern side is a Renaissance loggia rising above a flight of steps of 1564. The building's most popular feature is the clock on its northern side, which was rebuilt by Karl Svolinský in 1945 and features a hideous mosaic of workers, peasants and intellectuals, and has figures that are supposed to move around in

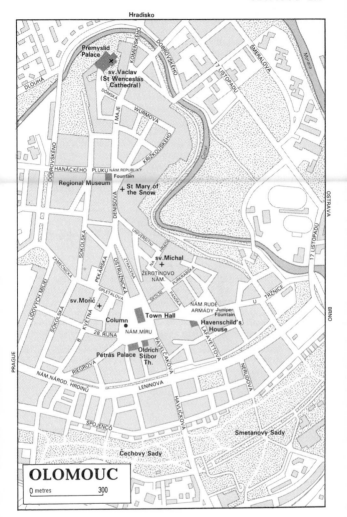

Hradisko

Přemyslid
Palace

sv.Václav
(St Wenceslas
Cathedral)

DLOUHÁ

DÓMSKÁ

I MÁJE

WURMOVA

HANÁCKÉHO PLUKU NÁM.REPUBLIKY
Fountain

Regional Museum
St Mary of
the Snow

Canal

DENISOVA

UNIVERSITNÍ

sv.Michal

ŽEROTÍNOVO
NÁM.

ZÁMEČNICKÁ

SOKOLSKÁ

PEKÁRSKÁ

TŘÍDA

ÚDOLNÍ

OPLETALOVA

LAZECKÁ

PURKRABSKÁ

ŠKOLNÍ

PANSKÁ

NÁM.RUDÉ
ARMÁDY Juniper
Fountain

sv.Mořic

KVĚTNÁ

28.ŘÍJNA

Column

Town Hall

Havenschild's
House

LAFAYETTOVA

NÁM.MÍRU

SOKOLSKÁ

LIDOVÝCH MILICÍ

Oldřich
Stibor
Th.

PAVELČÁKOVA

Petráš Palace

RIEGROVA

HRDINŮ

NÁM.NAROD.

LENINOVA

HAVLÍČKOVA

NERUDOVA

SPOJENCŮ

Smetanovy Sady

Čechovy Sady

OSTRAVA

BRNO

DOBROVSKÉHO

COMENSKÉHO

DOBROVSKÉHO

17 LISTOPADU

ŠMERALOVA

Morava

17 LISTOPADU

KŘIŽKOVSKÉHO

OLOMOUC

0 metres   300

procession every hour. On the western side of the square are two
other buildings of interest, the baroque Petráš Palace (at No. 410)
and the elegant Oldřich Stibor Theatre, built in 1830 by Josef Kornhäusel; Mahler was appointed Kappelmeister at this theatre in 1883,
but a combination of local anti-semitism and his own autocratic
behaviour led to his dismissal three months later.

Olomouc is one of the Czech towns richest in public statuary, and it
is above all the statuary on the square which holds the visitor's
interest. The 35m-high **Plague Column**, executed by Václav Rokytský
between 1716 and 1754, is the largest of its kind in Czechoslovakia,
and is bursting with baroque statuary celebrating, according to a Latin
inscription, 'the divine Trinity': eight rows of steps, containing eight

rows each lead up to eight doors that open into an eight-sided chapel surmounted by a mighty superstructure tapering to a column to which sculpted angels acrobatically cling; one 19C traveller wondered how such a monument could possibly have been thought suitable for 'the noble simplicity of Christianity'. Near the monument, and also to the N of the Town Hall, is a massive statue of Hercules (1688), executed by Michal Mandík to a design by V. Render; opposite the eastern steps of the Town Hall is an equestrian statue by Jiří Schaumberger of Gaius Julius Caesar (1725), who is considered by legend to have been the founder of Olomouc.

28 října leads N of the square to another fine baroque monument, a staute of Mercury (1727), executed by Filip Sattler, also to a design by V. Render. East of here, along the busy shopping street named 8 května, is the Olomouc parish church of *St. Moritz* (sv. Mořic), the oldest part of which is the 13C south tower. The north tower was begun in 1412, and the whole church gradually rebuilt from west to east, the work still continuing in 1540; the furnishings inside the wide and graceful triple-naved hall are mainly of the baroque period, including an organ of 1745, the largest in Moravia. Returning to the náměstí Míru along Opletalova, make your way S to the adjoining náměstí Rudé armády, the second largest square in town. At its funnelling northern end is a fountain of Neptune (1683) by Michal Mandík, while behind is the town's second plague column, this one executed by V. Render in 1716–23. Among the several fine houses surrounding the square are the late 16C Hauenschild's House (No. 25) and the Renaissance house at No. 22 known as Zlatý jelen (At the Golden Stag). On the southern side of the square is V. Render's Jupiter Fountain of 1707, which stands in front of the former Capuchin church of 1655–61.

Leave the square on Panská, which heads off in a north-easterly direction from the Neptune Fountain and will take you to the former Dominican Church of *St. Michael* (sv. Michal), which was founded in 1230; the whole church was rebuilt by Giovanni Pietro Tencala, and all that remains of the original medieval building is the late 14C chapel of St. Alexis, attached to the north aisle. Universitní heads N from here to Denisova, which forms part of the town's main axis. As you walk along Universitní, you will pass on your right the late baroque buildings (1701–08) of the former Jesuit College, which enjoyed the status of a University from 1576 to the mid 19C. The former university church of *St. Mary of the Snow*, at the junction of Denisova and the náměstí Republiky, is the most important creation of the Czech Jesuits after the church of St. Nicholas in Prague; this heavy but dynamically planned structure was built by Josef Pirner in 1712–19, and is extensively covered inside with frescoes. On the other side of the náměstí Republiky to the church is a former Clarissine Convent of 1773, converted by the Emperor Joseph in 1785 into the library and north wing of the university; the building (at present closed for restoration) now houses the *Regional Museum*, containing archaeological, historical, applied arts and natural history collections, and a baroque globe from the Jesuit University.

In the middle of the náměstí Republiky stands the Triton's Fountain, a work by V. Render of 1709. The continuation of Denisova N of this square is 1. Máje, another of the town's straight and very long streets lined with shabby apartment blocks of the early years of the century. Walking to the northern end of 1. Máje will take you almost outside the cathedral of St. Wenceslas. A longer and more interesting route to the cathedral is to turn right after the náměstí Republiky into

Křížkovského, and then turn left at the end of this into Wurmova; the triangular-shaped part of the town which you are now in was laid out after the Thirty Years' War, and contains baroque buildings now appropriated by the Palacký University, as well as the vast but curiously unmonumental Archbishop's Palace, designed by Filiberto Lucchese for Archbishop Liechtenstein in 1664. Wurmova will lead you back into 1. Máje, at a point directly in front of the short Domská, which ascends to the cathedral square. The *Cathedral of St. Wenceslas* (sv. Václav), standing in what was once the town's citadel, was originally a Romanesque structure consecrated during the rule of the fifth Bishop of Olomouc, Jindřich Zdík. Rebuilt after 1265, and then altered once more between 1616–19, the structure was turned by Gustav Merett into the present soaring but dreary neo-Gothic structure in 1883–90; within the crypt is a collection of ecclesiastical bric-à-brac, including a painting of Christ by Ignáz Raab. Of far greater interest than the cathedral is the adjoining building known as the **Přemyslid Palace**, which in fact was the Bishop's Palace built by Jindřich Zdík after 1141. The fragmentary but eloquent remains of the original Romanesque palace lay hidden for centuries under later medieval work, but a series of arches from this building were revealed in 1867, and more of the structure has been uncovered in the course of a recent archaeological and restoration campaign. You enter the building through a 19C door, and will find near the entrance a model of the 12C palace. Before going upstairs and seeing the Romanesque fragments, you have to walk around a Gothic cloister of the late 14C, the north side of which has an interesting group of early 16C murals. Above the vaults of the built-in cloister runs a magnificent Romanesque arcade of paired and tripled columns belonging to the second and best preserved floor of the former palace. The rich sculptural decoration of this arcade is unlike that of any other Romanesque building in Czechoslovakia, though it can be paralleled with certain decorative details in the Holy Roman Emperor's Cathedral at Speyer in the Rhineland; it is possible that Bishop Zdík, in the course of one of his diplomatic missions to the Rhineland in the 1130s, contracted builders at Speyer to come and work with him in Olomouc.

The palace occupies the north-eastern corner of town, and from its second-floor windows you look out over gardens and fields. Back on the 1. Máje continue walking E, and you will come to Komenského, which crosses in turn first the canal of the Morava river, and then the river itself. From the wooded banks of the latter is an excellent view N towards the former Premonstratensian monastery of *Hradisko*, which was founded in 1078, and transformed after 1661 by Giovanni Pietro Tencalla, Domenico Martinelli, and others, into the largest Premonstratensian monastery in the world; since the late 19C it has served as a rather grim hospital. On this same, eastern side of the river, adjoining the bridge, is a sleek Russian Orthodox Church of the early 20C. From here you could make an excursion by car to the Pilgrimage Church of *Kopeček*, which can be reached by driving 3km NW on the Šternberk road, and then turning off to the right on to the road marked Samotisky and Kopeček (a further 5km). The church, built in 1669–79, is another work by Tencalla, and dazzling above all in its scale and inflated architectural detail.

Continuing on your drive to Ostrava, head E of Olomouc on the E442. 2km E of Lipník nad Bečvou (25km), you will see peering above a wooded hill on the right of the road the impressive ruins of Helfštejn Castle, dating back to the 13C and constituting the largest castle ruins in Moravia. You remain on the road for a further 15km, bypassing the small industrial town of Hranice, and turning off to the N on Road 47 at Bělotín. North and E of Hranice begins one the most industrialised parts of Czechoslovakia, though Road 47 largely avoids the worst industries, and indeed skirts the southern edge of attractively rolling countryside. The village of *Fulnek*, 20km N of Bělotín, is a pleasant surprise. Though damaged by bombing during the Second World War, it has been well restored, and has a charming main square surrounded on three sides by 17C and 18C buildings and backed on the fourth side by a wooded hill crowned by a baroque castle. Steps lead from the square to an early 18C church half-way up the hill. Next to this is the rebuilt *School of Lutheran Brethren* famous as the place where the great pedagogue and Czech nationalist Jan Comenius taught between 1618 and 1621 (plaque). From Fulnek Road 47 heads NE past Bílovec (11km), entering the polluted surroundings of Ostrava shortly after Klimkovice (a further 10km). The centre of *Ostrava* (see Route 22) lies a further 17km NW of here.

B.   Via Kroměříž

Total distance 174km. Brno—19km **Slavkov**—52km **Kroměříž**—53km *Valašské Meziříčí*—17km *Nový Jičín*—11km *Příbor*—22km *Ostrava.*

The greatest attraction of the surroundings immediately to the E of Brno is the site of one of Napoleon's most famous battles, fought in 1805, and named after the nearby baroque castle of Austerlitz (Slavkov in Czech). Slavkov lies 19km due E of Brno, but the battlefield itself lies 10km before this, and can be seen to your right as you drive due E of Brno on the dual carriageway of the E462. The battle was directed by Napoleon from the top of the hill of *Žuráň*, which you can reach by leaving the motorway just beyond the turning for Šlapanice, about 500m E of the motorway restaurant and snack-bar known unromantically as the Non-Stop Motel. Films re-enacting the battle have always featured a savage, densely pine-forested landscape, while in fact the eastern surroundings of Brno comprise flat countryside which has been extensively cultivated for centuries. A tiny road leads to the top of the gentle Žuráň Hill, which is distinguished by two solitary trees, next to which is a bronze plaque inscribed with a diagram indicating the respective positions of the troops that took part in the battle. From this commanding site you can see rising above fields to the N the hill which Napoleon's troops named Santon after a mountain in Egypt; to the S meanwhile are the distant Pratzen heights (Pracký kopec), which were also to play a crucial role in Napoleon's victory.

The Battle of Austerlitz was fought between Napoleon and the combined armies of the Russians and Austrians. Whereas the French troops numbered only 35,000, the Alliance had 80,000; at the end of the battle French losses amounted to 7000 as opposed to 35,000 killed in the Alliance. The reasons for Napoleon's astonishing victory are given in Leo Tolstoy's famous description of the battle in War and Peace, one of the most vivid accounts of war in 19C fiction. The battle began early on the morning of 1 December 1805. It was a foggy morning, and the confused Russian and Austrian troops made their way from the Pratzen heights in the direction of the Santon Hill, where they imagined that the greater part of Napoleon's army was entrenched. Though unseen by them

Napoleon and his troops were able to watch their movements from the top of the Žuráň Hill, which by a great stroke of luck stood up above the fog. The scene from the hill was memorably evoked by Tolstoy: 'Napoleon, in the blue cloak he had worn throughout the Italian campaign, sat on his small grey Arab horse a little in front of his marshals. He gazed in silence at the hills which seemed to rise out of the sea of mist, and the Russian troops moving across them in the distance, and he listened to the sounds of firing in the valley. Not a muscle of his face—still thin in those days—moved; his glittering eyes were fixed intently on one spot. His forecasts were proving correct. Part of the Russian force had already descended into the valley towards the ponds and lakes, part were abandoning the Pratzen heights which he had intended to attack and which he regarded as the key to the position. He saw through the fog, in a hollow between two hills near the village of Pratzen, Russian columns, their bayonets gleaming, moving continuously in one direction, towards the valleys, and disappearing one after another into the mist.'

Napoleon was in a confident mood, not only because the weather was on his side, but also because the day of the battle happened to be the anniversary of his coronation as emperor. He bided his time, waiting for the perfect moment to attack the now dangerously extenuated Russian forces. Finally, in the words of Tolstoy, 'when the sun had completely emerged from the fog, and fields and mist were a dazzling brilliance—as though he had only been waiting for this to begin the action—he drew the glove from his shapely white hand, made a sign with it to the marshals and gave the order for battle.' After capturing the Pratzen heights, Napoleon was able to attack the remaining Alliance forces from the rear, thus achieving a swift victory. His vantage-point on the Žuráň Hill was to be used with equal success in the Second World war by the Russian Marshal Marikovsky, who directed from here a battle with the Germans.

Instead of immediately rejoining the E462 after descending from the Žuráň Hill, you should take the first turning to the right and follow for a few hundred metres the side road which runs parallel with the motorway; take the next turning to the right marked Pracký and drive to the top of the Pratzen heights, where there is an outstanding Art Nouveau memorial (1911) by J. Fanta, which instead of celebrating Napoleon's victory, represents a plea for Peace. It is a monumental tapering structure in stone and bronze, surrounded by statues symbolising the four continents, crowned by the Crucifixion, and with a chapel at its base dedicated to Peace; the idea for this 'Peace Memorial', the first of its kind in the world, was that of the historian Alois Slovak (1859–1930). In the small museum adjoining the memorial is a bust of Slovak, together with mementoes of the battle and several of the numerous finds that continue to this day to be dug up in the surrounding fields; the most interesting item is the table on which Napoleon played chess with his officers shortly before the battle.

Return to the E462, which you follow for a further 3km before heading SE on to the E50. The village of *Slavkov*, 6km E of the turning, is dominated by its imposing baroque château, built c 1700 for the Kaunitz family. It was designed by the Italian architect Domenico Martinelli, who seems to have derived inspiration for the main façade, with its massive convex centrepiece, from Bernini's unexecuted design for the Louvre. The interior of the building has retained, if in a rather shabby state, much of its original baroque decoration, but is visited usually on acccount of the worthy Napoleonic Museum which is installed here; the beautiful, but rather unkempt gardens, have much baroque statuary. 10km further E along the E50 is the moated castle of *Bučovice*, which, despite numerous insensitive alterations, remains one of the finest of Moravia's Renaissance châteaux. Built in 1566–87 for Jan Šembera Černohorský, it was executed by Pietro Gabri of Brno to designs supplied by Pietro Ferrabosco di Lagno (1512–96), a Como-born architect who worked for the Habsburgs. The oustanding feature of

*View of the garden façade of the baroque château of
Slavkov (Austerlitz)*

its exterior (which originally had battlements rather than the present
high-pitched roof) is its central three-storeyed courtyard, of an
elegance and lightness quite unusual for Czechoslovakia, and wholly
Italian in character; in the middle stands a baroque fountain of a man
embracing the Golden Fleece, a work apparently commissioned from
Paolo Materna by one of the Liechtensteins in c 1635. Of the
Renaissance rooms inside special mention must be made of the
Imperial Room, which has a richly painted and stuccoed ceiling
(dating from after 1583), featuring lunettes with gilded and richly
worked statues of Mars, Diana, Europa and Charles V.

Continue for a further 7km along the E50, and then take the side-
road to the N marked Zdounky and **KROMĚŘÍŽ**. The latter, 25km
from the E50 and in the middle of a very fertile district known as the
Haná, is sometimes referred to as the 'Hanák Athens', a rather
absurd comparison given that all that the two places have in common
are their pollution. None the less this small town, the closest Czech
equivalent to the former principalities of Germany, has played a vital
role in the history of the arts in central Europe.

The origins of Kroměříž are in a fortified Slavic settlement of the 9C. In c 1107
the place was acquired by the Bishopric of Olomouc and rapidly grew in
importance. A key period in its early history was the mid 13C when Bishop
Bruno of Schauenburg endowed it with municipal privileges, built a large
market square (on the site of the present main square), and encouraged so
many settlers to move here that he is sometimes identified with the Pied Piper of
Hamelin. Little survives of the medieval or indeed Renaissance town of
Kroměříž, the place having been devastated by the Swedes (led by General
Tortenson) in July 1643. The bishops lavishly rebuilt the town, turning it into
one of the great baroque ensembles of Czechoslovakia. A particularly important
role was played by Prince-Bishop Karl von Liechtenstein-Castelcorno, who in

1690 commissioned from Giovanni Pietro Tencala the present Bishop's Palace, and was also responsible for the Italianate Květná or Flower Garden, with its breathtakingly grand colonnade by Tencalla. But the Prince-Bishop's involvement with the arts was not limited simply to patronage: he dabbled in architecture himself (one of the early plans for his palace was drawn up by him) and, more importantly, assembled an extraordinary collection of old master paintings. His 18C successors maintained his enlightened interest in the arts, and when the palace was badly damaged by fire in 1752, one of the leading rococo artists of the day, F.A. Maulbertsch, was called in to redecorate two of the rooms.

The Empress Maria Theresa and the Russian Tsar Alexander III were among the many distinguished visitors to the Bishop's Palace; more significantly, between November 1848 and March 1849, when the Austrian Imperial family were in exile in Olomouc, the Austrian Imperial Parliament held their meetings here, and drafted a famous constitution which included the statement that 'all power comes from the people'.

Kroměříž today is a sleepy small market and industrial town, with a grimy and slightly run-down look but with an undeniable charm. Its excellently preserved old centre is still encircled by extensive stretches of the original fortifications. At the northern entrance to the old town is the náměstí Dukelských Hrdinů, dominated on its northern side by the twin-towered and oval-domed *Piarist Church of St. John the Baptist*, a grand and harmonious baroque structure begun in 1737 by the obscure Italian architect Cirani. From the back of the church Pilařova Street leads in a north-easterly direction towards the Bishop's Palace. The first important building which you come to is the former collegiate church of *St. Maurice* (sv. Mořic), which was built by Bishop Bruno of Schauenberg after 1260; the simple, light and much-restored interior constitutes the main survival of medieval Kroměříž, and features the tombs of a number of the Bishops. Running along the western side of the building is the tiny Probošství, which is lined with elegant baroque houses, one of which (No. 5/7) has a garden with an excellent view towards the apse of the Piarist church. On the other side of the church is the massive 18C bulk of the former College and Archbishop's Seminary, which is linked by the Mill Gate of 1585 to the **Bishop's Palace**. Tencala's monumentally proportioned palace, built over medieval and Renaissance structures, can only partially be visited, and many of the numerous rooms centred around its grey and rather forbidding courtyard seem to have been abandoned. The surviving rooms with the finest decorations can only be seen in the course of an obligatory guided tour, and include a richly stuccoed ground-floor room of c 1700, and the first-floor Sněmovní sál, a vast rococo hall (now used for concerts) adorned with chandeliers, and with gilded plasterwork set against a glisteningly white background. On the second floor is the unappealingly named **Fief or Vassalage Hall**, where the enthroned Prince-Bishops would hold meetings. The interest of this room is its spectacular and vividly painted ceiling painting by F.A. Maulbertsch representing the Apotheosis of the Bishops of Kroměříž; this work, which owes a clear debt to the dazzling propaganda scenes of the Venetian artist G.B. Tiepolo, features a portrait of Maulbertsch himself, standing under an umbrella. A pupil of Maulbertsch was responsible for the rather clumsier and less brightly coloured Triumph of Bishop Egkla adorning the ceiling of the neighbouring and beautifully panelled *Library*; the library has an outstanding collection of coins, as well as a musical archive containing autograph scores by Haydn and Mozart. The famous **PICTURE COLLECTION** of the Prince-Bishops is also to be found on the second floor, and can fortunately be visited without the distracting presence of a guide. Though badly displayed in large, poorly lit and depressingly decorated rooms, the collection is unquestionably the finest in Czechoslovakia outside of Prague, and alone justifies a visit to Kroměříž.

The bulk of the collection was brought together by Prince-Bishop Karl von Liechtenstein-Castelcorno, and was largely made up of works from private collections that he had acquired, including those of Provost Josef Seragli de Contis, an unknown nobleman from Prague, and the Imstenraed brothers from Cologne. The most important of the Bishop's paintings, most notably the 16C Italian works, had once formed part of the fabled collections amassed by Charles I of England, Count Arundel and the latter's brother-in-law, the Duke of Pembroke; 238 works from these collections were put on the market by Banker Jabach in 1673, and ended up not only in Kroměříž, but also in Prague Castle, the Imperial collections in Vienna and the Louvre in Paris. The collection of the Prince-Bishop was supplemented in the mid 18C by paintings amassed by Bishop Egkla.

Among the earliest paintings in the collection are a Martyrdom of St. Catherine, a Diptych of St. Catherine, and a superlative **Martyrdom of St. John the Baptist**, all by the German artist Lucas Cranach, and commissioned in the early 16C by one of the Bishops of Kroměříž; the latter painting, a richly detailed work mingling fantasy with intensely realistic observation, features the coat of arms of the Kroměříž bishops, and is signed and dated 1515. Other early Northern School works include The Virgin and St. Anne by an anonymous Nuremberg master of 1487, a Dürer-like Portrait of a Young Man (1505) by Hans Kulmbach, a portrait by Quentin Matsys of King Christian II of Denmark, and a Portrait of a Man (1558) by Bartholomaus Brujn. The oldest of the Italian School paintings is an Adoration by Neri di Bicci. Among the 16C Italian paintings are a series of works by Jacopo Bassano, a Samson and Delilah by G.A. da Pordenone, and a work by Veronese featuring the Apostles, a fragment of a much larger painting cut down in size to make it more saleable. The most famous of the 16C paintings, indeed the great glory of the collection, is Titian's **FLAYING OF MARSYAS**, a signed work of 1570/71, which was cleaned in 1986 prior to being shown at London's Royal Academy: dating from the artist's late period, and possibly unfinished, it is one of the artist's most personal and mysterious works, sombre in tonality, the paint boldly applied in places by the artist's fingers, and with a touch of the most grotesque black humour in the detail of the foreground dog happily lapping up the blood of the unfortunate protagonist. Of the 17C Italian paintings, mention should be made of a dark and dramatic Annibale Carracci of *Latona and the Farmers*, and an excellent Domenico Fetti of *Christ in the Garden of Olives*. The highpoint of the Northern School paintings of this period are Van Dyck's Portrait of a Man with a Glove and his double portrait of **King Charles I and Henrietta Maria**. Also of interest are a vivid *Vision of St. Jerome* by Jan Liss, Alchemist at Work by David Ruckaert III, a trompe-l'oeil Still-life by Samuel von Hoogstraten, and a gruesome work by Johann Heinrich Schönfield showing Cato committing suicide by tearing out his entrails.

Once you have left the palace, you should visit its *gardens*, which now form a public park, and can be reached by heading W of the building down Ztracená, turning left into Vodní, and then left again. Within the gardens is a baroque colonnade adorned with mosaic lunettes (1945–51) by the locally-born artist Max Švabinský; the greater part of the gardens was relaid in the early 19C in a romantic English style, and features among its woods a lakeside Chinese pavilion, and a Pompeian Colonnade. Return in the direction of the

Palace, and turn left at the end of Ztracená into the adjacent Main Square. This large and slightly decayed square, with a Marian Plague Column of the early 18C, retains its medieval shape, but is lined with buildings mainly of the baroque period; the main survival from the Thirty Years' War is the Town Hall of 1611, in the square's north-western corner. On the eastern side of the square is a small well-arranged museum dedicated to one of Czechoslovakia's most celebrated artists of recent times, *Max Švabinský*. Born in Kroměříž in 1873, Švabinský died in Prague in 1962, at the age of 89. Though in later life he received such prestigious commissions as the design of the stained-glass windows in St. Vitus's Cathedral in Prague, his most striking works are nearly all from the first decade of the century, and are characterised by their brilliant colouring, and heavy symbolism. One of the largest and most vivid works in this museum is The Yellow Umbrella (1909), which features two female nudes in a sensual outdoor setting painted with broad areas of pure pigment. The large Studio of 1914 illustrates the more conventional development of his later work, but is of interest as a psychological study of the artist. It shows the artist absorbed in his work, surrounded by members of his family, including his first wife Ela—who looks away from him—his brother, and his sister-in-law; the latter, whom he was shortly to marry, features also as the muse whom he is painting.

You can return to the Dukelských Hrdinů by walking N from the square along Jánská, which is lined by elegant 18C buildings; near the end of the street, opposite the Piarist Church, is Švabinský's birthplace (No. 15/16; plaque). Leaving the old city centre and walking N from the Dukelských Hrdinů, you will come to the broad Kojetínská Boulevard; turn right along this, and then left into Gen. Svobody, passing on your right the gabled Bishop's Granary of 1711. At the end of this street is the **Květná** or Flower Garden, a rectangular Italian Garden commissioned by Karl von Liechtenstein-Castelcorno in 1665 over what had previously been the episcopal vegetable garden. Long narrow vistas converge on an oval pavilion designed by F. Lucchese in 1668; the northern end of the garden is bordered by an exciting 200m-long colonnade (1675), one of G.P. Tencalla's most successful works, and adorned with classical busts and statues.

After seeing Kroměříž head E of the town to Hulín (6km) and then from here follow the road to Holešov, Bystřice pod Hostýnem and Valašské Meziříčí. The towns that you pass though on your way to Ostrava become increasingly industrialised, but from Holešov onwards you skirt to your right the attractive wooded hills that belong to one of the Moravian districts most famed for its folklore, Wallachia. The Wallachians were shepherds who came to this part of Moravia in the 16C; their origins are disputed, and have been sought for in places as far apart as Poland, Slovakia, the Ukraine and Romania. *Valašské Meziříčí* was one of the main cultural centres of Wallachia, and it was here, in 1871, that the first grammar school in the district was founded. A centre of the cloth industry from the 16C onwards, and now with extensive chemical, electrical engineering and glass industries, it is a largely ugly town, but with a pleasant main square featuring a number of 16C–18C buildings, including an early 17C Town Hall and, at No. 10, a former Pharmacy known as At the Red Eagle; elsewhere in the town is a partially wooden church of the 16C. Head N of the town on Road 57, passing through after 9km the village of *Hodslavice*, where there is a tiny wooden church of

1551 and the house where the historian and politician František Palacký (1798–1876) was born. The sprawling industrial town and district capital of Nový Jičín, 8km further N and a well-known centre of hat production, has a particularly fine main square, lined on all sides with colourful arcaded houses from the 16C to 18C; one of these is the former Post House of 1563, famous as the place where General Suvorov and Tsar Alexander I were put up in 1805. An interesting *Hat Museum* (Kloboučnické muzeum), said to be the only one of its kind in the world, has been installed in the town's château, and includes hats worn by such famous personages as Masaryk.

From here take the E462 dual carriageway to *Příbor*, a small town with another pleasant square, but of interest largely on account of its associations with the founder of psychoanalysis, Sigmund Freud (1857–1939).

Sigmund Freud was born at Příbor (known in German as Freiberg) on 6 May 1856, and spent his early childhood here; he was the first son of Amalie Freud née Nathanson, the second wife of Jakob Freud, a Jewish textile manufacturer. Even during his lifetime the house of his birth was commemorated by a plaque, and in a letter of 25 October 1931 to the Mayor of the town, Freud expressed his certainty that 'deep within me, although overlaid, there continues to live the happy child from Freiberg, the first-born son of a youthful mother, the boy who received from this air, from this soil, the first indelible impressions'. On another occasion he wrote: 'When I was seventeen and at my secondary school, I returned for the first time to my birthplace for the holidays ... I know quite well what a wealth of impressions overwhelmed me at that time ... I believe now that I was never free from a longing for the beautiful woods near our home, in which ... I used to run off from my father, almost before I had learnt to walk.'

The modest house of Freud's birth is at No. 117 Zámečnická, and there is talk at present of turning it into what would be the third Freud Museum in the world (the other two are in Vienna and London); for the moment visitors to the town with an interest in Freud will have to content themselves with the small collection of mementoes installed in the former Piarist College.—Another famous personality of the area, and a contemporary of Freud, is the composer Leoš Janáček (1853–1928), who was born at *Hukvaldy*, 8km to the E of Příbor (take the main road to Frýdek-Místek for 6km, and then turn right). The composer was born in what is still the village school (plaque); in later life he often came to stay in a nearby house called Podobora, where there is a small museum to him. The latter is situated at the foot of Hukvaldy's large and impressive medieval castle, which was founded by Arnold von Hückeswagen in 1240. 6km to the S of Příbor is **Kopřivnice**, an industrial town of unmitigated ugliness, but of interest to those excited by old cars.

The industrial development of Kopřivnice dates back to 1812, with the foundation by Ignác Raška of a pottery works which soon began exporting earthenware to Vienna, Germany, France, and England. Of greater importance was the founding by Ignác Šustala in the summer of 1850 of what was to become the Tatra Engineering Works. In 1882, a year after the railway had come to the town, the Tatra Engineering Works began producing freight wagons, and later became one of the main world suppliers of luxury saloon cars intended for heads of state in Europe and Asia. But the real breakthrough came in 1897 with the creation of the so-called President, the first automobile of the Austro-Hungarian Empire; on 21 May of the following year this car set off on a trial journey from Kopřivnice to Vienna, a journey of 328km which it accomplished in 14½ hours of driving time. From that time onwards car production developed as the main speciality of Tatra, though today the firm produces only lorries and the heavily built black limousines once used to transport important dignitaries of the Communist party. The research for this present guide was largely undertaken in a Tatra, kindly put at the author's disposal by the Czech government.

In a small garden adjoining the Tatra Works is a large glass and steel hangar housing the *Tatra Technical Museum*, which is packed to capacity with old cars, including the famous President of 1897. Incongruously tucked away on a wooded slope just to the S of Kopřivnice is the delightful village of *Štramberk*. At the top of this village, rising above trees, is the solitary round tower of its medieval castle, while the village centre below comprises a remarkable group of 18C to 19C traditional Wallachian folk houses, mostly semi-timbered and featuring beautiful carving, low wooden gables and balconied fronts.—Return to Příbor, and head due N to Ostrava (see Route 22), another 22km, passing next to Ostrava's airport.

C.   Via Uherské Hradiště and Zlín

Total distance 223km.Brno—71km *Uherské Hradiště*—26km **Zlín**—33km *Vsetín*—17km *Rožnov pod Radhoštěm*—45km Frýdlant nad Ostravicí—31km *Ostrava.*

This, the longest and most complex route from Brno to Ostrava, is also scenically the most attractive, taking you to the forested heart of Wallachia; none of the towns that you will pass has the wealth of old monuments which you will find, say, in Olomouc or Kroměříž, but for enthusiasts of modern architecture there is the compensation of Zlín, the most interesting modern town in Czechoslovakia.

Head due E of Brno on the E462 and continue as for Route 21B up to the turning for Kroměříž. East of the turning you remain on Road 50 up to as far as Uherské Hradiště (a further 41km), passing after 14km the early 18C château of *Buchlovice*, which is distinguished by a most lively main façade featuring a concave and balustraded central block; built for the Berchtold family, the architect is unknown, though there is an implausible family tradition that he was none other than the great Roman architect Carlo Fontana. From Buchlovice you could make a DETOUR 6km NE to the former Cistercian abbey of *Velehrad*, founded in 1201 over a Slavonic site; though transformed following a fire in the early 18C, the abbey church still retains its Romanesque apse.

Numerous finds from the period of the Great Moravia Empire have been dug up in and around the small industrial town of *Uherské Hradiště*, which was founded in 1257 by Přemysl Otakar II, and retains fragments of its medieval fortifications and a number of burghers' houses of the 17C and 18C. The *Moravian-Slovak Museum*, in the Smetana Gardens, contains archaeological finds from the area, including Romanesque stones from the nearby monastery at Velehrad; of special interest is the folklore collection, which reflects the rich folklore traditions of the eastern borders of Moravia. Next to the museum is an art gallery, largely devoted to 19C local masters. 16km further E is the smaller town of *Uherský Brod*, also with remains of its medieval walls; in the late 17C stables of the town's castle (a Renaissance structure remodelled in the 17C) is a small museum to the scholar and teacher Jan Comenius (1592–1670), who is thought by some to have been born in the vicinity. The town stands at the edge of the South Moravian Lowlands, and by the foothills of the White Carpathians, which mark the border with Slovakia. The highest peak of these mountains, Velká Javorina (970m), lies only 18km to the S of the town; however, the most direct crossing into Slovakia is to continue along Road 50, which will take you after an attractive 37km drive to the outskirts of the Slovakian town of Trenčín (see Route 27).

Head N from Uherské Hradiště on Road 55, and turn right after 16km on to Road 49 to **Zlín** (a further 10km). Zlín lies in the south-western corner of Wallachia (see Route 21B), an area of wooded hills and low mountains, which you will be travelling through for most of the remaining journey to Ostrava. 'Here bread ends and stone begins' was how this traditionally poor area was once characterised. Industrial and agricultural growth since the last century have radically changed this image, and the green, spacious and pleasantly situated town of Zlín was seen at one time as a projection of the ideal city of the future.

The town of Zlín, which was known as Gottwaldov from 1949 to 1990, was first mentioned in the early 14C, but its importance dates from after 1894, when Tomáš Baťa founded a footwear factory, which was to prosper during the First World War through the supplying of boots to the army; soon Baťa footwear was to develop an international reputation, with a chain of retail outlets throughout Europe. Tomáš Baťa was a man of vision and enlightened tastes, and his shops and factories became a hallmark for the latest in modern design, architecture and technology. During the optimistic years following the establishment in 1918 of the Czechoslovak Republic, Baťa envisaged a model city for the workers employed at his Zlín factory. The French architect Le Corbusier was called over to draw up a plan for this city, but in the end most of the work was entrusted to the locally born architect František Gahura (1891–1958), who had gone to Prague initially to study sculpture and had subsequently become an architectural student under the celebrated 'Cubist' architect Kotěra. The new town which Gahura built with the assistance of his two pupils Lorenz and Karfík was damaged during the Second World War. Renamed in 1949 after the Socialist president Klement Gottwald, the model town which Baťa had envisaged was transformed by later architects into an example of Socialist architecture at its most drab. The town continues to develop industrially but its remaining vitality as a cultural centre is maintained largely by its well-known film studios, which specialise in animated films, and were formed by one of Czechoslovakia's most adventurous animators, Karel Zeman (1910–). The British dramatist Tom Stoppard (1937–) was born in Zlín, but his father left shortly afterwards for Singapore, and Tom and his mother ended up in England.

The town of Zlín is a narrow and sprawling place, its ramshackle old centre being situated at its eastern end, where you will find a Renaissance château (remodelled in the baroque period) now housing the Regional Museum of South-East Moravia: the museum has a permanent exhibition relating to the animated films of both Karel Zeman and Hermína Týrlová. The modern centre of the town lies just to the W of this, one of the principal squares being the náměstí Práce (Work Square). Around both this square and the adjacent long and verdant avenue which runs S up a forested hill (Masarykovo náměstí), are spaciously disposed the main surviving buildings from Gahura's visionary Zlín. On the north side of the square is the former Baťa Factory's main office building, a multi-storeyed structure in which Tomáš Baťa had installed for himself a moveable glass office on an elevator, so that he could inspect what was happening on every floor, and also be accountable for his own activities; a footwear museum is now to be found in this building, which is called today the Svit National Corporation. On the opposite side of the square are a cinema, a department store and a hotel, all dating from 1931 and the work of Karfík; facing the store, across the upper end of the long avenue, is Gahura's School Building of 1929, named after the first president of the Czech Republic, Tomáš Masaryk. The avenue, a sloping lawn bordered by trees and four- and five-storey blocks of flats, leads up to Gahura's House of Culture of 1932, which served once as a memorial to Tomáš Baťa and featured the private aeroplane in which he died in 1938 on a fog-bound trip to Dresden; today the building has an excellent small *Gallery* devoted to 20C Czech painting and sculpture, and including works by Bohumil Kubišta, Emil Filla, Václav Špála, Jaroslav Král, Jan Štursa, Otto Gutfreund, and Karel Lidický.

Head E from Zlín on Road 49, and follow the built-up banks of the Dřevnice river until *Vizovice* (14km), which is widely known in Czechoslovakia for its distillery, where one of Czechoslovakia's best plum brandies (Jelínek slivovice) is produced. For the cultural tourist there is a baroque château built in 1750–66 for the Brno nobleman F.A. Grimm; inside is a frescoed hall, a fine collection of china and Louis XVI furniture, and a picture gallery featuring paintings questionably attributed to masters such as Magnasco, Jan Breughel the Younger, D. Teniers and V. Liberi. At Vizovice you should leave Road 49 and head NE through forest to the small industrial town of **Vsetín**. This town, first mentioned in 1309, became in the 17C a major centre of the Wallachian resistance to the Habsburg programme of Catholicisation; today the place is sometimes referred to as Partisan Town owing to the activities in the surrounding forest of the Jan Žižka brigade during the last war. The history of the town, and the rich folklore of the area are commemorated in the Museum installed in the castle on the main square (a Renaissance building remodelled in the 18C and 19C); also on the square is the former Town Hall of 1721. Vsetín and its surroundings are popular with holiday-makers, and there are a number of attractive villages with Wallachian timber-framed houses to be seen along the narrow valley of the Vsetínská Bečva, which runs to the E of here. Continuing your journey to Ostrava, the shortest if not the quickest route from Vsetín to Rožnov pod Radhoštěm is the side road which heads NE of the town, climbing the western slopes of the wooded Cáb Mountain (842m); there are several fine walks to the summit, where there is a tourist chalet). After 10km you descend to a small lake, and then turn right, passing after 3km the village of Valašská Bystřice. *Rožnov pod Radhoštěm*, a further 4km, is a popular holiday resort, with, in its lushly wooded outskirts, one of the best and most extensive of Czechoslovakia's Skansens (open-air museums of folk architecture). This particular **Skansen** displays in its spacious forested setting a wide range of reconstructed Wallachian timber-framed buildings, including the delightful former Town Hall of Rožnov (1770), shepherds' huts, a small wooden church, a belfry, taverns, farmsteads, a forge, and so on; you can go inside most of the buildings, where appropriate furniture, utensils, and garments are arranged.

Rising to the N and E of Rožnov are the Beskid Mountains, which form the north-western part of the Carpathian Massif. Sadly, pollution from the industrial developments around nearby Ostrava have taken away much of the charm of this area which once inspired the music of Janáček; the sky is often hazy, and acid rain has destroyed large parts of the forest. None the less there are pleasant walks to be had in the area, for instance from Rožnov to the summit of Radhošt (1129m). For those wishing to stay a while in the mountains, there is a group of fantastically shaped timber-framed tourist chalets on the ridge at Pustevny (head E out of Rožnov on Road 18, and then turn left after 7km, climbing the mountain for a further 5km); 2km further on in the direction of the ugly Frenštát pod Radhoštěm is the timber-framed Hotel Vlčina, a picturesque old building depressingly revamped in recent times.

The most direct route from Rožnov to Ostrava is to drive N along Road 58 past Frenštát pod Radhoštěm and Příbor (see Route 21B). A longer but more attractive route, taking you through the finest parts of the Beskids, is to follow Road 18 E of the town for 19km, then turn left to Bílá. Just beyond Bílá turn left again and you will find yourself driving alongside a large reservoir and in between two of the highest of the Beskid peaks—Smrk (1276) and Lysá hora (1323). After Ostravice (13km N of Bílá), you emerge into the vast industrial area which stretches towards Ostrava. *Frýdek-Místek*, 16km further N, mainly along dual carriageway, appears from the road to be merely a featureless industrial sprawl, yet it has a pleasant old centre almost resembling that of a village. At its heart is a 17C castle, with an excellently displayed museum relating to the history and folklore of Wallachia, and containing souvenirs of Janáček and the Silesian poet Petr Bezruč (1867–1958), who spent many years here. Back on the dual carriageway you are faced with a depressing 22km drive from here to the centre of *Ostrava* (see Route 22).

22 Hradec Králové to Ostrava

Total distance 253km. Hradec Králové—Road 11 121km Šumperk—61km *Bruntál*—38km *Opava*—33km *Ostrava*.

Driving E from Hradec Králové along Road 11 you will approach the chain of the Orlické hory or Eagle Mountains, which mark the border with Poland. At *Kostelec nad Orlicí* (30km) is an elegant Empire château (1829–35), built by J. Koch for a member of the Kinsky family. 6km further E, at *Doudleby nad Orlicí*, is another fine château, this one dating back to the late 16C and remodelled between 1670 and 1690; it features a charming courtyard of 1585 covered with elaborate sgraffito work of flowers and hunting scenes, and a series of baroque rooms decorated with mythological scenes. *Vamberk*, 2km further on, has a long tradition in lace-making, examples of which can be seen in the local museum. From here you can make a short DETOUR N to the small industrial town of *Rychnov nad Kněžnou*, which lies at the foot of the Eagle Mountains, and has been a centre of the cloth industry since the time the town was founded in 1258. The place is dominated by the pompous mass of its château, which was built for Karel Kolowrat in 1676–90, and remodelled in 1722, possibly by Santini-Aichel, who was responsible for the undulating façade of the adjacent church. Inside the château can be seen the Kolowrats' extensive picture collection, which is particularly strong on Czech works of the baroque period, including K. Škréta's The Arrival of Jacob in Laban (signed and dated 1643), a portrait by P.C. Bentum of Jan František Kolowrat (c 1730), and still-lifes by Isaac Godyn (c 1700) and J.A. Vocásek (c 1740); among the foreign school paintings are works by A. Magnasco, H. Rigaud, J.G. Hamilton, H. van Aachen, and A.R. Mengs. 12km NE of Rychnov is Ricky, the main winter and summer resort in the Eagle Mountains, an area which is relatively scant in tourist accommodation.

Continuing E from Vamberk, you skirt the southern slopes of the Eagle Mountains, sharply climbing a few km W of Červená Voda (50km) before descending into Moravia. 33km further E is the district town of *Šumperk*, which has been a textile centre since the 18C; the main square has some baroque houses and a Plague Column of 1719. Šumperk lies in the southern foothills of the Jeseníky Mountains, a large protected area forming a popular winter and summer resort, and featuring waterfalls, caves, curative springs and great pine forests. Following Road 11 from Šumperk you head N for 5km and then turn sharply E, crossing the southern end of this range. If you want to spend more time in these mountains you could take the left turning at the point where Road 11 swerves to the right, and continue in a northerly direction towards the town of Jeseník. *Velké Losiny*, 3km N of the turning, is a small spa town which makes a pleasant base for mountain walks. The paper mill here dates back to 1515 and is one of only seven remaining places in the world where paper continues to be made by hand. The town is also celebrated for its castle, which was built in the 1580s for the powerful Žerotín family, and has three storeys of arcading overlooking its open courtyard; in the 17C the building became notorious as the scene of witch trials that resulted in the deaths of numerous innocent women.

Jeseník, 41km further N along a winding road through dense forest, dates back to a prosperous mining community of the 14C, and features a Town Hall of 1610 and a Renaissance castle (now a local museum) surrounded by a moat. 1km N of the town is a spa founded in 1826 by a local farmer, Vincenz Priessnitz, who was the first to discover the curative properties of the local waters, which he tested at first on himself and then on his family and friends. The fame of the Priessnitz-Gräfenberg cold water cure (Gräfenberg was the German name for the town) soon spread widely, and in 1845 one of the patients here was the Russian writer N.V. Gogol. Most of the surviving buildings, including the main Spa Building, are of the early years of the century; the cold water cure is still recommended for those suffering from nervous complaints, respiratory diseases and metabolical disorders, but the spa today has the faded character of a place past its heyday. Similarly pleasant and old-fashioned is the tiny spa of *Lipová Lázně*, situated 4km due W of Jeseník, cosily set between trees and lush rolling meadows; founded in 1830 by a man called Schroth, its waters have been used since then for the treatment of obesity and rheumatism.

Back at Jeseník you can rejoin Road 11 at a point 61km E of Šumperk by going back 8km down Road 44 and then turning left in the direction of *Karlova Studánka*, a further 18km through forest. Karlova Studánka, situated at an altitude of 800m, and hidden among pines, is another small spa, but slightly earlier in date than those of Jeseník and Lipová Lázně: the waters have been used for the treatment of respiratory disorders since 1780, and the spa buildings are all of the 19C. A most enjoyable walk can be made W of here, following to begin with the upper reaches of the Bílá Opava river, which forms here a series of waterfalls; above the river's source are the tourist chalets of Ovčárna and Baborka, and further up is the summit of the highest peak of the Jeseníky Mountains, Praděd (1492m). After leaving Karlova Studánka, drive in a south-easterly direction to Bruntál, where you will regain Road 11.

At *Bruntál*, an industrial district town dating back to a thriving mining community of the early 13C, you near the built-up plains that stretch towards Ostrava. The chief interest of the town is its château, which has a monumentally grand main façade designed by F.A. Neumann in 1766 and articulated by giant pilasters. Behind this, and coming as quite a surprise, is an arcaded courtyard of the 16C centred around a well which is protected by delicate Renaissance ironwork; the interior of the building, at present closed for restoration, is all of the baroque period, and includes a main hall decorated by large landscape frescoes. 21km NE of Bruntál is the border town of *Krnov*, which is known internationally for the making of organs. Described misleadingly in at least one guidebook as a 'charming old town', Krnov has in fact been insensitively developed since the late 19C, and has little to commend itself to tourists other than its *Hotel Morava*. In contrast to the dreary modern blocks that comprise most hotels in provincial Czech towns, the Hotel Morava is a place of character installed in a Minorite Monastery founded in the 14C and rebuilt after 1730; the cosy dining-room of the hotel, situated off the former cloisters, is decorated with appealingly clumsy frescoes by the 18C master Josef Sterna.

Opava, 38km E of Bruntál along Road 11, and 25km SE of Krnov on Road 57, is a large and rapidly expanding industrial town, its architecture being characterised by the use of red brick. The main centre of Czech Silesia (the greater part of Silesia fell to Prussia in 1742 and now forms part of Poland), Opava is the birthplace of the leading Silesian poet Petr Bezruč (1867–1958); the town has a long and important history dating back to the late 12C, but repeated raids in the Thirty Years' War and heavy bombing during the last war have ensured that its surviving old monuments are few and scattered. Its main attraction is the excellent *Silesian Museum*, housed in a building of 1893–94 (at Tyřsova 1), and containing extensive natural history, archaeological architectural, historical and ceramics collections. A popular excursion from Opava is to *Hradec nad Moravicí*, 8km due S of the town on Road 57. Here stands a large country house in the middle of a beautiful English-style park rising above the river Moravice. At the entrance to the park, and just above the village of Hradec, is a neo-Gothic red-brick building, built originally as the stables of the mansion, and now occupied by a restaurant. The house itself, dating back to 1600, was rebuilt in 1795, and further altered in a neo-Gothic style after 1880. Its heyday was the early 19C, when a number of leading musicians came to stay here, including Beethoven in 1806 and 1811, and Liszt in 1846 and 1848; the place has unfortunately been threatened in recent years by erosion of the surrounding land, and will be closed for restoration until at least 1997.

33km E of Opava the sight of smoking chimneys and coal slags welcomes you to **Ostrava**, the largest industrial town of Czechoslovakia, and this country's leading source of coal and iron.

Ostrava was founded in 1267, but only began to develop its present importance after 1767, when coal deposits were discovered here. Both the Rothschilds and the Habsburg Těšín archdukes speculated in the early mining activities here, and the town received a further boost in 1828 with the opening of the Vítkovice Ironworks; the building of a railway to Vienna in 1847 consolidated the town's rapid growth. The playwright and future President Václav Havel spent in 1980–81 the worst period of a four-year term in prison at a camp near Ostrava; he described his guard here as 'a genuinely dangerous person' who once said to him that 'Hitler did things differently—he gassed vermin like you right away!'

Until recently pollution was so bad in Ostrava that a permanent black cloud seemed to hang over the town. This situation has now greatly improved, and the centre is relatively clean and with its fair share of green spaces. None the less, apart from a lively cultural life, the town has little to offer the tourist, having virtually no old monuments and few interesting modern ones. The *Municipal Museum*, with natural history, musicological, archaeological and historical collections, occupies the former Town Hall, a structure of 1556 rebuilt in 1859. The local *Art Gallery*, housed in the Palace of Culture (Jurečkova 9), has works by 20C Czech artists, including A. Slavíček, J. Preisler, B. Kubišta, O. Kubín, V. Špála, and E. Filla.

23 Hradec Králové to Olomouc

Total distance 154km. Hradec Králové—E442—57km **Litomyšl**—19km *Svitavy*—42km Mohelnice—36km *Olomouc.*

The E442 follows for much of its length an ancient route from Bohemia to Moravia. Its greatest attraction, the town of **Litomyšl**, lies 57km SE of Hradec Králové (see Route 3) and was once a great road junction. The town's declining fortunes in the 19C, when the railway was routed to the north of it, had the beneficial result that its beautiful old centre was left relatively unchanged.

The town of Litomyšl was founded in 1260 around a 10C castle and a 12C Premonstratensian monastery; made a bishopric in 1344, it remained one until 1421 when the town was captured by the Hussite leader Jan Žižka. In the 19C the town became associated with many of the leading figures in the history of Czech culture. The scientist Jan Purkyně taught at the Piarist School here and the historical novelist Alois Jirásek worked at the local secondary school; Božena Němcová lived here in 1860–61, and Jan Neruda's Pictures of Life were first printed at the shop called Augusta's. The town's most famous association was with the composer Bedřich Smetana, who was born here in 1824. In his honour, every year in July an Opera Festival is held here bearing the name Smetana's Litomyšl.

The long main square of Litomyšl is one of the most beautiful in Bohemia, and is lined with arcaded houses dating back to medieval times, but with gables and stuccoed fronts mainly of the 16C–18C; one of the finest of the houses is U rytířů (At the Knights; No. 110), which has amusing Renaissance decoration sculpted by a Master Blažek in 1546 and featuring a squat and clumsy group of knights. Off the northern end of the square is a green avenue leading up to the remarkable château built for Vratislav Pernštejn by the Italian architects Giovanni B. Aostali and Ulrico Aostalli in 1568–81. A series of sgraffitoed gables crown this building's main block, which is attached to an arcaded three-storeyed courtyard; the courtyard façade of the main block is covered all over with an exuberant wealth of sgraffito decoration, featuring ancient battle scenes. Today, the château houses a museum devoted to the *History of Czech Music*, one of the chief protagonists of this history, Bedřich Smetana, having been born in the 17C living quarters of the adjoining Litomyšl brewery, of which his father had been the director (plaque). Also next to the château is the two-towered façade of the Piarist church, begun by Alliprandi in 1714 and attached to the college where Purkyně taught. 18km S of Litomyšl is the small town of *Polička*, which was founded in 1265 as the seat of the Bohemian queen. The town has a few remains of its medieval fortifications, and a main square with a baroque Town Hall and a Marian Plague column of 1727–31. As with Litomyšl, Polička boasts a celebrated composer, Bohuslav Martinů, who was born here in 1890 in surroundings even more distinctive than those in which Smetana had been born: his birth took place in the tower rooms of the neo-Gothic parish church, his father having been the town watchman. Whereas Smetana ended up in the Pantheon of Czech Heroes in Prague's Vyšehrad, Martinů, after a lifetime away from his native town, was buried in the local cemetery in 1959; some of his work recollects his native region, in particular his composition, The Opening of Wells, a glorification of this area.

Continuing to drive SE from Litomyšl on the E442 you pass after 17km the northern outskirts of the industrial town of Svitavy. 18km further on is *Moravská Třebová*, a textile centre which has kept its medieval grid plan of c 1265, stretches of its old walls, and a number of late gothic and Renaissance buildings, most notably the Town Hall, which was remodelled between 1550 and 1565. Shortly to the E of the town the E442 enters a forest and crosses into Moravia, the first Moravian town you come to being Mohelnice (24km), from where there is a is dual carriageway all the way to Olomouc (36km; see Route 21). 8km to the S of Mohelnice, at Bouzov, you could turn off to the right to visit the castle of *Bouzov* (a further few km). This castle, founded in c 1300, came later into the possession of the 15C Bohemian king, George of Poděbrady. In 1699 it was acquired by the Grand Masters of the German Teutonic Knights, a military Order which bitterly oppressed the Slavic peoples under the pretext of spreading Christianity. The appropriately sinister-looking building seems to have been created for some wicked fairy, a look which is in fact due to neo-Gothic remodelling carried out for the Grand Masters in 1895–1912.

24 Brno to Bratislava

Total distance 121km. Brno—D2—49km Břeclav—72km **Bratislava**.

South-east of **Brno** (see Route 20) the D2 Motorway crosses the flattest part of the Moravian Lowlands, the monotony of the landscape broken only by distant glimpses to the right of the gentle Mikulov Hills, which mark the border with Austria. At Hustopeče (26km S of Brno), you could leave the motorway to make a detour to the border town of *Mikulov* (a further 17km via the village of Strachotín). This pleasant small town once had a large Jewish population, and in the 18C the Supreme Rabbi for the whole of Moravia lived here; in what was originally the ghetto can be seen an old Jewish synagogue and cemetery. On the small and sloping main square is a Town Hall of 1606, and a number of Renaissance houses; the town's principal landmark is its castle, which dates back to the 13C and was greatly altered and extended in the 17C and 18C centuries; the castle complex, heavily restored after the last war, now contains a small hotel, a theatre, a restaurant, a local museum with exhibits relating to viniculture, and extensive wine cellars. Mikulov is at the centre of a small but well-known wine-producing district, and it is essentially the town's excellent white wines rather than its monuments that make the place popular among excursionists from Brno.

The principal tourist attraction of this south-eastern corner of Moravia is the house and gardens at **LEDNICE**, which lies in the middle of the flat plain 15km to the E of Mikulov. The place can be reached from Mikulov by heading S for 4km on the Valtice road and then turning left; if coming from the D2 you should turn off at Podivín (15km S of Hustopeče), and drive in a SW direction for 5km.

The house at Lednice dates back to an early 13C estate which was acquired in 1371 by the Liechtensteins, who remained the owners until the Second World War. The medieval castle was replaced by a Renaissance one, which in turn was followed by a large baroque structure built at the beginning of the 17C; in 1688–90 the great Austrian architect J.B. Fischer von Erlach created stables here, as well as terraces and fountains. Further remodelling of the main house took place between 1766 and 1772, and again between 1845 and 1856, the latter building campaign lending the structure its present neo-Gothic appearance.

The pinnacled and battlemented neo-Gothic skyline of the house is most picturesque, if not as grand or exciting as that of Hluboká near České Budějovice (see Route 14). Part of the interior, with its heavily panelled rooms, can be visited on a guided tour; another part forms a museum dedicated to agriculture, hunting and fishing (some of the outbuildings at Lednice are at present occupied by the Institute of Agriculture and Horticulture, a department of Brno University). Among these outbuildings are Fischer von Erlach's monumentally grand **Stables**, which are arranged around an enormous courtyard and articulated by giant piers and columns. Adjoining the house is a magnificent **Greenhouse**, designed by the English architect G. Devien in 1843–45, but later overlaid with filigree neo-Gothic ornamentation by the Viennese architect G. Wingelmüller. The real pleasure of a visit to Lednice comes from the vast and beautifully landscaped grounds. Three lakes to the S of the house were created c 1600, but the first major landscaping took place towards the end of the 18C, the park being laid out at that time in the shape of an enormous star, with follies and summerhouses placed along the axes; between 1805 and 1811 an Italian architect called Fanti devised a new park in an English Romantic style, its principal feature being the enormous lake to the N of the house, featuring no less than 15 islands. The most celebrated of the many follies to be seen in the grounds is the 60m-high **Minaret** to the N of the house, built by J. Hardmuth in 1798–1802; to the E of this, by the southern shores of Fanti's large lake, is a purpose-built ruined castle, *Hansenburg Castle*, designed by J. Kornhäusel in 1815. The same architect was also responsible for *The Temple of Apollo* (1816), which stands next to the Mill Pond to the S of the house.

Back on the motorway at Podivín continue heading S, the next exit being that for Břeclav (8km), an important railway junction and the main town of the Podluží district, which is the part of South Moravia most renowned for its folklore. The great centre here for folk arts and traditions is the lowland town of **Strážnice** (30km NE of the Břeclav exit along Road 55), where even the railway station is decorated with pseudo-folk designs. The town is known for its hand-painted ceramics, but above all, for its annual folk festival which is held usually in the last week of June, and features singing and dancing in traditional costumes. Good examples of local folk art are on show at the castle here (a medieval structure rebuilt in the 19C), and there is also a large Skansen on the outskirts of the town.

Continuing S on the motorway from the Břeclav exit you reach the Slovakian border after 10km, from where it is a 58km drive to **Bratislava** (see Route 25). As you near Bratislava, the wooded southern slopes of the White Carpathians come into view to your left, and, during the last stages of your drive, rise directly above the road.

SLOVAKIA

25 Bratislava

The capital of Slovakia lies by the Danube, hemmed in to the north by the verdant vine-covered slopes of the Lesser Carpathians, and overlooking to the south a great plain which stretches over three countries. Bordered by both Austria and Hungary, and situated on a river which has served since ancient times as one of the great thoroughfares between eastern and western Europe, Bratislava is a city which has occupied literally a position of central importance in European history. The Italian writer and literary historian, Claudio Magris, in his brilliant philosophical and poetical travelbook *Danube* (1986), identifies the city as 'one of the "hearts" of Mitteleuropa, with layer upon layer of centuries forever present, unresolved conflicts and lacerations, unhealed wounds and unreconciled contradictions.' Despite the complex legacy of its past, modern Bratislava exudes liveliness and optimism, the result to a certain extent of Slovakian culture asserting itself following centuries of Hungarian and Austrian dominance. The difference in mood between Bratislava and Prague is very noticeable, and was especially so at the time when Magris compared the two cities. 'Ever since the events of 1968', Magris wrote in 1986, 'the splendid city of Prague has given an impression of being under the spell of neglect and death, while Bratislava, in spite of everything, is sanguine and cheerful, a vital world in an expansive phase, looking not to the melancholy of the past, but to growth and the future.'

The rocky outcrops on which the castles of Bratislava and nearby Devín were built were occupied as far back as prehistoric times and became in the 1C BC the site of fortified settlements founded by the Celtic tribe of Boyes. After the 1C AD, the Romans, gradually shifting the northern frontier of their empire to Slovakia, created the settlement of Posonium, from which was to be derived the Hungarian name for Bratislava, Pozsony. The Slavs settled in the area in the 5C and 6C, and between 623 and 656 revolted against the rulers of that time, the Avarians, and founded a state of their own; this was later incorporated within the Great Moravian Empire, which came into being after the unification of the countries of Nitra and Moravia in the 9C. The castle at Bratislava is first documented in 907, when it is referred to as Presslauspurch or 'Pressalas' castle' (hence both the Slovakian name 'Bratislava' and the German one, 'Pressburg').

Nomadic Hungarian tribes had first arrived in the Danubian lowlands in 895, and by the 10C had turned the castle of Bratislava into an important stronghold on the north-western borders of the Hungarian Empire; the Slavonic population none the less stayed on, and was to remain under foreign domination until 1918. A settlement on the eastern slopes of the castle hill grew up in the 12C and in 1291 was granted a Borough Charter by the Hungarian king Andrew III. The town developed as one of the most prosperous in Hungary, thanks to its importance as a trade and crafts centre, and also to its viniculture, which had been established here by the Romans. The growth of the town intensified in the 14C and 15C, and a second line of fortifications was put up. The Emperor Sigismund of Luxemburg had the castle rebuilt in 1423, and shortly afterwards granted the town the privilege of minting its own coins, and having its own coat of arms; in 1439 Albrecht of Habsburg allowed a bridge to be built across the Danube, and in 1465, King Matthias Corvinus founded here the 'Academia Istropolitana', the first university in Slovakian territory.

The heyday of Bratislava came after the defeat of the Hungarians by the Turks at the Battle of Mohács in 1526. Queen Mary, the widow of the Hungarian king Lewis II, took refuge at Bratislava, and from that time onwards the Hungarian

Diet was to hold its sessions here, electing in one of its first meetings Queen Mary's brother, Ferdinand of Habsburg, as Hungarian king. The official proclamation of Bratislava as capital of Hungary, seat of the Hungarian Diet, and Coronation City, came ten years later, in 1536; in the course of three centuries nine kings and eight queens were to be crowned in the city. During the 17C and 18C, the twin Hungarian townships of Buda and Pest stagnated and produced little of architectural interest, but Bratislava became one of the great baroque cities of central Europe, and, with a population of 26,845 by 1773, emerged also as the largest city in Hungary. A period of particular prosperity was during the reign of Maria Theresa of Austria (1740–80), who gave the title of Hungarian viceroy to her son-in-law Albert of Teschen, and designated Bratislava Castle as his seat. Maria Theresa and her court regularly took up residence at Bratislava, and in consequence the leading aristocratic families at nearby Vienna had palaces built here. Musical life flourished in Bratislava, and numerous important compositions were performed here following their premières in Vienna and Esterházy. The court orchestra of Prince Nicholas Esterházy of Eisenach gave frequent performances in the Grassalkovich Palace, and the orchestra's leading composer and conductor, Joseph Haydn, even premièred in this city his opera La Canterina. Mozart came several times to Bratislava, his first visit being in 1762, fresh from his triumph at the age of six at the Viennese court; this and subsequent visits were organised by an acquaintance of his family, Count Charles Hieronymus Pálffy. The librettist of Mozart's opera The Magic Flute, Emmanuel Schikaneder, worked in the city from 1782–84, and Mozart's widow Constanza settled here after her second marriage. The composer Johann Hummel was born in Bratislava in 1778, and was active for a short period in the most celebrated of the city's orchestras—that of Count Grassalkovich. Beethoven was also associated with Bratislava, and in 1796 met up again up with a former pupil, Countess Babetta Keglevich, to whom he subsequently dedicated a number of works, including his Sonata in E sharp, op. 7.

A thriving cultural life was to persist in Bratislava long after the reign of Maria Theresa, but the city was to lose its dominant role in Hungarian affairs after 1783, when the Emperor Joseph II had the central Hungarian offices transferred to Buda and the Crown jewels to Vienna; as a result of this action, the city's population soon fell from 33,000 to only 11,000. The early 19C is marked in Bratislava by the growth of the Slovakian Movement, one of its leading protagonists, Ľudovít Štúr settling here in 1829 and issuing in 1845 the first Slovak political paper—Slovenskie národnie noviny. In 1848, at the last session of the Hungarian Diet held in Bratislava, Štúr successfully presented his plea for the abolition of serfdom. Two years later Emperor Franz Josef proclaimed Bratislava as district capital of the five Hungarian counties comprising western and central Slovakia, and made Slovak the official language; he was to abrogate his decision ten years later, and the political importance of the city was to decline yet further.

After the Dual Compromise of 1867, Bratislava became the seat of a number of secondary government institutions, and, like Budapest, was subject to rapid industrialisation, with many large chemical, engineering and textile works being set up here. At the same time the city continued to play a major role in the musical life of central Europe, becoming closely associated during this period with most of the leading Hungarian composers. In between 1822 and 1885, Ferenc Liszt made no less than 15 visits to Bratislava, and in 1881 and 1855 performed here with the Russian composer and pianist Anton Rubinstein; the composer and pianist Ernö Dohnányi was born here in 1877, and both Ferenc Erkel and Béla Bartók were students in the city.

By the late 19C the journey between Vienna and Bratislava was reduced to little more than an hour, and the Viennese tended to look on the city as a suburb of their own and, up to 1918, would regularly come here to enjoy the good local wines. On 1 January 1919 Bratislava became part of the Czechoslovak Republic, though the district of Petržalka, on the southern side of the Danube, was to remain occupied by Hungarian troops until August of that year. In 1946 the city was joined to the surrounding communities of Petržalka, Prievoz, Vajnory, Rača, Lamač, Dúbravka and Devín to form Greater Bratislava, which had a population of 190,544. The Act of the Czechoslovak Federation was signed at Bratislava Castle on 30 October 1968, and the city was made capital of the Slovak Socialist Republic.

Bratislava has been unfairly neglected by foreign visitors to Czechoslovakia, most of whom limit their city sightseeing largely to Prague, and tend, ignorantly, to think of Bratislava as a provincial town rather than as somewhere with the character and attractions of a capital city.

BRNO

Slavín Monument

PUŠKINOVA

Former Archbishop
Summer Palace

V.L.Lenin Mus.

ŠTEFÁNKOVA

SPOJNÁ

NA

SLAVÍNE

MIŠÍKOVA

LERMONTOVOVA

NONOSVETSKA

MOŠKOVA

DONOVALOVA

VICKOVA

KUZMÁVYHO

Janko Král Mus.

SOMOLICKÉHO

MOYZESOVA

Grassalkowich
Palace

NA
MA

ŠULEKOVA

TIMRAVINA

PALISADY

PALISADY

ŠTETINOVA

MIEROVÉ NÁM.

PANENSKÁ

BRADLJANSKA

LYCEJNÁ

POŠŤ

Protestant Lyceum +

ŠMERALOVA

KONVENTNÁ

DREVENA

PARTIZÁNSKA

ZOCHOVA

STAROMESTSKA

Trinity Ch.+

SUCHÉ MÝTO

HURBANOVO
NÁM.

OKTOBROVÉ
NÁM

Michalská
brána
Gate

ZAMOCNICA

Francisc
Ch.

PALISADY

ZÁMOCKÁ

KAPUCINSKA

BAŠTOVÁ

sv. Anny

K.LARISKÁ

MICHALSKÁ

Mirbach
Pal.

DIBROVO
NÁM

ZAMOCKÁ

Ch.of the Poor Clares

FARSKA

SEDLARSKÁ

NÁM.
4.APRIL

MUDRONOVA

STAROMESTSKA

KAPITULSKA

Univ.
Library

WOLKROVA

ZELENA

RYBÁRSK

DEVIN

Castle

Ho.at the
Good Shepherd

ZAMOCKA SCHODY NEBLAVBOD

JIRASKOVA

Acad.
Istropolitana
St Martin's
Cath.

NALEPKOVA

Mus.Galle
of Bratislav

Gate

VODNY

VRCH

RUDNAYOVO
NÁM.

HUIEZDOSLAVOVO
NÁM.

Carlt
Hot

N

ŽIŽKOVA

Fisherman's Guild

NÁBR ARM GEN.L.SVOBUDU

Slovak Nat.Mus.

RÁZUSOVO NÁBR

BRATISLAVA

0 metres   200

most SNP

Ideally Bratislava should be included in any tour combining Vienna and Budapest, for it is a city which can boast many of the more enjoyable features of its two neighbours, but without the latter's oppressive tourism. Its situation is as beautiful as that of Budapest, and its baroque and rococo palaces are as elegant as any in Vienna. The local wines are excellent, and a trip to the wine-cellars on the outlying slopes of the Lesser Carpathians is as pleasurable as a visit to the Vienna Woods, particularly at the time of the autumn grape harvest when for a period of two to three weeks the delicious young wine known as 'Burciak' is available. Furthermore Bratislava maintains a reputation for its lively musical life, with musical peformances put on not only at the city's outstanding turn-of-the-century Opera House and Concert Hall (the Reduta), but also in historic buildings throughout the old city centre. Since 1950 an international music festival, now called the Bratislava Music Festivities, has been held every spring, and there are also a Jazz Festival (which has been running since 1956), a Popular Song Festival called the Bratislava Lyre (held in either May or June), and a Summer Arts Festival covering the months of July and August. Every odd-numbered year in September and October the city's House of Culture (near the Námestie SNP) organises an important International Biennial of Book Illustrations.

At least two days are needed for a leisurely tour of Bratislava's main sights, which include the castles of both Bratislava and Devín, the Cathedral of St. Martin, the Church of St. Clare, the Mirbach, Pálffy and Archbishop's Palaces, the Old Town Hall, the St. Michael's Tower and the neighbouring Pharmaceutical Museum, the Clock Museum, 'At the Good Shepherd', the Tower of the SNP Bridge, the Memorial on the Slavín Hill and the Slovak National Museum and Gallery. With the exception of Devín and Slavín, all these sights are within easy walking distance, and it is not advisable to take your car to the city centre.

A.   Central Bratislava

A tour of Bratislava could begin at the Hurbanovo námestie, at the southern end of which is **St. Michael's Bridge**, which is surmounted by baroque statues, and spans what was formerly a moat where travelling players performed in the 18C. Within the moat can be seen the main surviving section of the town's fortifications, which date back to the 13C and 14C and were pulled down in 1775 on the orders of Maria Theresa. After crossing the bridge, you pass through a 15C gate known as the Powder Gate and enter the narrow and pedestrian Michalská, which, together with its southern continuation Jiráskova, is one of the most beautiful of the old city streets, and is lined its whole length with 16C–18C buildings into which the occasional antiques shop and second-hand bookshop have been incorporated. No. 15 on the right-hand side of the street is the narrowest house in Bratislava, while on the other side of the street (at No. 28) is one of the city's oldest pharmacies, known as **At the Red Crayfish** (U červeného raka), and now forming part of a fascinating Pharmaceutical Museum. In the first room of this museum can be seen the original late 18C decoration of At the Red Crayfish, comprising elegant black and gilded furnishings, and a trompe-l'oeil painted ceiling featuring Chronos, the God of Time. An evocative description of this room forms the opening passages of the chapter on Slovakia in Magris' book, Danube (1986): 'That eighteenth-century shop...gives the impression of a military parade in its rigid symmetry, of an unassuming yet determined art of war displayed against Chronos. The pots on the shelves, in cobalt, emerald green and sky blue, embellished with floral designs and biblical quotations are like the ranks of tin soldiers in museum reliefs of famous battles; the tinctures, balsams, balms, allopathics, purgatives and emetics are there at their battle stations, ready to intervene according to the requirements of strategy. Even the labels, with their abbreviations, are reminiscent of military contractions: Syr., Tinct., Extr., Bals., Fol., Pulv., Rad.' Within the other rooms of the museum are objects relating to the history of pharmacy in Bratislava from the Middle Ages onwards, including a 15C Gothic mortar, Italian majolica pots of the 16C and 17C, an amusing 17C copper mortar supported by the mournful figure of a Turk, prescription books dating back to 1644, and a reconstruction of a baroque pharmacy originally attached to the Convent of the Order of St. Elizabeth's sisters (in the middle of this is a wooden statue of St. Elizabeth, the patron saint of herbalists). The eagle eyes of Claudio Magris, always on the lookout for the culturally significant, fall, in his book Danube, on a hefty volume entitled Taxa Pharmaceutica Posoniensis, written by Ján Justus Torkos, and published in 1745 in four languages: Latin, Slovak, Hungarian and German.

Built across the Michalská, and rising high above the Pharmaceutical Museum, is **St. Michael's Tower** (Michalská brána), which gives this street its name. One of the most distinctive landmarks in old Bratislava, the tower was originally connected to a church of this name, which fell into disrepair after the Battle of Mohács (1526) and was pulled down. The lower part of the tower dates back to the 14C and features a Gothic gate which originally led through the inner walls of the city's fortifications, and is today the main surviving city gate; the upper part of the tower was added in 1511–17, and was given its onion-shaped copper steeple in 1758. The small rooms within the tower contain a well-displayed museum devoted to weaponry and the history of the town's fortifications. Bratislava was renowned for its gunsmiths, and among the objects on show—which range from medieval armour to Second World War machine guns—are firearms dating from the time of Master Heinrich, who is the earliest known of the city's gunsmiths, being first mentioned in 1414; a curiosity is a painting of fighting soldiers (1840) which is riddled with bullets and was originally used for shooting practice. From the highest room in the building you can walk outside to the gallery which encircles the tower and from which an excellent panorama can be had of the town.

Walking through the gate and heading S down Michalská, you will pass on the left-hand side of the street (at No. 8) the white-washed façade of the small Gothic church of St. Anne (sv. Anny), built in 1311 and remodelled on the outside in 1845. On the other side of the street, at No. 7, is a house dating back to 1648; this was the birthplace of Johann A. Segner (1704–77), the inventor of the turbine engine and of the so-called Segner's Wheel. Lower down on the same side (at No. 3) is a baroque palace built in 1730 for Count Pavol Jesenák, and, below this, at No. 1, is the monumental late baroque façade of the palace now housing the University Library of Bratislava, which is the largest library in Slovakia and the second largest in Czechoslovakia. The palace, featuring a main portal flanked by atlantes, was built to a design by the Italian architect G.B. Martinelli in 1753–56, and functioned up to 1848 as the seat of the Hungarian Diet: it was during the last meeting to be held here that Ľudovít Štúr made his impassioned plea for the abolition of serfdom in Hungary. The University Library extends into the palace attached to the southern end of this building, at the entrance to the continuation of Michalská, Jiráskova. Built between 1775–78 for Count Leopold de Pauli, this palace has in its courtyard a charming *Musical Pavilion*, where concerts are still given, and which bears a plaque to the composer Ferenc Liszt. It was here that the nine-year-old Liszt gave his début performance to a group of five magnates who, on the strength of this concert, decided to finance the prodigy's studies abroad.

Further S down Jiráskova, on the left-hand side of the street (at No. 10), is another palace associated with an infant musical prodigy: this, the recently restored palace built in 1747 for the Pálffy family, was where the six-year-old Mozart gave a concert in December 1762 on the invitation of Count Charles Hieronymus Pálffy, the elder son of the court chancellor Leopold Pálffy. Facing it across the street at No. 3 is *Academia Istropolitana*, which was founded by Matthias Corvinus in 1465 as the first University in Slovakian territory.

During the 25 years of its existence, the Academia Istropolitana attracted a number of internationally renowned teachers, including the astronomer, mathematician and physicist Johannes Müller Regiomontanus and his successor the Polish astronomer Martin Bylica from Olkusz. The Vice-Chancellor was the Bratislava provost Schomberg, while the Chancellor was the renowned humanist and archbishop of Esztergom, Ján Vítéz. Sadly, however, the institution did not outlive the death in 1490 of its founder and benefactor, Matthias Corvinus, who was not only a brilliant monarch and statesman, but also one of the great scholars of his age. In later years the building was adapted for a number of different educational institutions, and is now the Drama Department of the Academy of Fine Arts.

The buildings of the Academia Istropolitana, erected on a site originally occupied by the 14C Royal Mint, have been completely remodelled and restored over the centuries and retain little of their original late Gothic and Renaissance elements. At the southern end of the street, at No. 1, is the rococo palace built in 1770 by M. Walch for Count Erdödy, and, behind this, running in a north-easterly direction from the south-western corner of the old town, is a long pedestrian and shopping thoroughfare comprising the Nálepkova and its continuation Leningradská. The former, into which the Jiráskova leads, was known originally as the Langestrasse or Long Street, and features a great number of elegant 18C palaces. Turning left into Nálepkova from Jiráskova you will find on the opposite side of the street (at No. 27), the Keglevich Palace, another of the important centres of musical life in the 18C: Beethoven, a teacher and protegé of Countess Babetta Keglevich, was one of the many who gave concerts here. On the same side of the street, a few houses further to the E, at No. 19, is another of the palaces belonging to the Pálffy family. This particular one shields behind its austerely classical façade fragments of a building dating back to the 13C and incorporating Roman bricks; altered extensively in the 14C, it was acquired by the Pálffys in the mid 18C, and rebuilt by them in the middle of the following century. Excellently renovated in 1981–87, the palace has housed since 1988 part of the **Municipal Gallery of Bratislava**. On the ground floor are shown Slovakian paintings of the late 19C and early 20C, among the most interesting of which are some landscapes by Ladislav Mednyánsky (in particular the delicately coloured A Foggy Autumn Day, and Dominik Skutecký's much reproduced genre scene, Market Day at Banská Bystrica. There are also some interesting Post-Impressionist landscapes of 1913–14 by

Anton Jasusch and some early works by one of the leading Slovakian painters of this century, Martin Benka. You pass through a medieval arch as you walk up to the first floor, where are to be found a group of minor medieval panels which had been housed until recently in the former convent church of St. Clare. The greater part of this floor is devoted to the pioneering Slovakian painters of this century, including characteristically Fauve-like landscapes by Ľudovít Fulla (Piazza San Marco, Venice, 1930, and Madonna and Child, 1935), a further work by Martin Benka (In the Sliac Valley) and paintings by Janko Alexy, Josef Sturdiak and Cyrian Majernik. On the second floor are the gallery's rather dismal foreign school holdings, comprising dull 17C Dutch works, and 16C–18C Italian paintings that are largely school works, copies, anonymous, or wishful attributions; there is also a painting by the obscure Scottish artist William Darling Mackay, representing a ruined castle by the seashore absurdly identified as Edinburgh castle. Temporary exhibitions are held on the third and top floor of the building.

After leaving the Pálffy Palace, continue to walk along the Nálepkova in the direction of Leningradská, and you will pass on this same side of the street, the Bállasy Palace of 1762 (No. 15), the Esterházy Palace of 1743 (No. 13) and, at No. 11, the *Chapel of the Brotherhood of Christ's Body*. The latter (now a store and closed to the public) was originally a Gothic chapel of 1390; damaged during the Bethlen Uprising in 1620–22 it was altered in 1627 and remodelled in 1772, when it was frescoed by followers of Maulbertsch. Return to the junction of Nálepkova and Jirásková, and continue to follow the former in a south-westerly direction, gradually ascending towards St. Martin's Cathedral. On the left-hand side, at No. 33, is the Csáky Palace of 1775, designed by M. Walch in a Louis XVI style and recently restored and given a vivid coat of yellow paint. Adjoining it is a splendid turn-of-the-century pharmacy, which is still functioning and features its original neo-baroque exterior and furnishings. The street ends in Rudnayovo námestie, a small shaded square in which are to be found three commemorative busts, one of these being of Ferenc Liszt (by V. Tilgner, 1911), and another (by J. Pospíšil) of the priest Anton Bernolák, the author of the first standard Slovakian grammar. The third bronze, unveiled in 1888 on the occasion of the 200th anniversary of the subject's birth, is of the great Austrian baroque sculptor Georg Raphael Donner, who lived in Bratislava for ten years and executed works for **St. Martin's Cathedral**, which rises on steps above the square.

The first stone of St. Martin's Cathedral was laid at the beginning of the 14C, on the site of the Romanesque church of the Holy Saviour, which had been transferred here in 1221 from its position on the castle hill. Work on the cathedral continued into the 16C, when the place became the coronation church of the Hungarian kings and queens, which it was to remain until 1830. Between 1863–77 the building was subject to extensive restoration and remodelling.

The cathedral, modest in size in relation to its importance, was attached on its northern side to the town's fortifications, the ruins of which can be seen below. The building's tower, which had a defensive function up to the end of the 15C, has an 85m-high steeple supporting a gilded copy of the royal crown of St. Stephen. Entering the building through the early 16C south portal (with Renaissance features) you find yourself in a three-aisled hall-church, with an essentially late Gothic character. None of the medieval furnishings, however, have survived, and the stained-glass windows, the high altar, and the ceiling paintings in the long 16C chancel are all of the 19C. The outstanding work of art here is a bronze group of **St. Martin Giving Away his Cape** (1733–35), by Georg Raphael Donner, one of the leading figures of the Hungarian baroque; this dynamic work, apparently showing the saint dressed in the uniform of a Hussar, stood originally on the Cathedral's high altar, and was flanked by angels that are now to be found in the Hungarian National Gallery in Budapest. Further works by Donner can be seen in the baroque St. Johann Capistran Chapel, most notably the marble *funerary statue* of Archbishop Emmerich Eszterházy. On the wall on the left-hand side of the chancel is a list of the nine Hungarian kings and eight queens who were crowned in this building.

Dividing today the old town from the castle hill to the W is a wide flyover, Staromestská, built on what had remained up to as late as the 1960s of the town's Jewish Ghetto, a district which had deteriorated in its later days into what was little more than a slum. Running N from the cathedral and parallel to the Staromestská, is the atmospherically decayed Kapitulská, at one time inhabited largely by members of the town's clergy. At No. 26, on the left-hand side of the street, is the former Jesuit College, built in 1629–35 and housing after 1855 the Law faculty at which the Slovak writer and patriot Svetozár Hurban Vajanský studied between 1867 and 1870. The building is now used as a seminary, as is the palace on the opposite side of the street (at No. 19), which was built for Bishop Juraj Draškovič in 1632. Towards the end of the street, on the right-hand side, is a small projecting stone house said to be the oldest surviving house in Bratislava. Turn right into Farská, where you will see to your right (at No. 3) a well-preserved late medieval house with Renaissance sgraffito decoration. Opposite this is the former convent *Church of the Poor Clares*, built in the 14C and dominated by an elaborate early 15C steeple; the interior, occasionally opened for concerts, is a pleasingly simple single-aisled structure. At the end of the short Farská, turn left into Klariská, on which were once situated the convent buildings of this mendicant order. The convent, founded by Cistercian nuns in the 13C, and taken over by the Poor Clares at the end of the following century, was burnt down 200 years later, and rebuilt in the 17C to designs supplied by Jacob Rava. Following the abolition of the Order of the Poor Clares in 1782, the buildings were used first as the library of Trnava University, and then as a Catholic grammar school; a plaque records that the composer Béla Bartók studied here in 1892–99. The buildings today house the library of the Faculty of Pedagogy.

At the northern end of Klariská, besides steps leading back up again to Kapitulská, turn right on to Bastová, which will take you back to the St. Michael's Gate. Cross Michalská into Zamocnícka, which is the eastern continuation of Bastová, and likewise used to run below the city's northern walls; the street was lined in earlier times with locksmiths' workshops. Turn right at the end of the street into the narrow and sloping Dibrovovo námestie. To your left, at the north-eastern corner of the square, is the former *Franciscan church and monastery*. The church, consecrated in 1297 in the presence of King Andrew III, was damaged by earthquake in the 17C, and largely rebuilt; of the original Gothic buidling only the chancel remains, a structure which can claim to be the oldest surviving one in Bratislava. Apart from a 15C stone Pietà, the furnishings of the church are all of the 18C, as are the nave, and the adjoining monastery buildings; the medieval tower of the church can now be seen in the Janko Král'Park in Petržalka. Just to the S of the church is the *Chapel of St. John the Evangelist*, which was built as the burial chapel for the family of the powerful magistrate Jacob. Facing the monastery on the north-western side of the square (at No. 11) is one of the city's finest rococo palaces, the **Mirbach Palace**, which was built for Michael Spech in 1768–70, and excellently restored in the 1980s. The elegant period rooms contain a further selection of old master paintings and other works of art from the Municipal Gallery of Bratislava. Of the paintings the most striking are two large canvases of the *Annunciation* and *St. Clare*, painted by the baroque artist Franz Anton Palko for the church of the Poor Clares. There is a bronze bust of 1780 by the Austrian artist Messerschmidt and, in the courtyard, a bronze fountain of a Nymph and Triton, executed by a pupil of the 19C Hungarian sculptor Viktor Tilgner, and located previously in the courtyard of the Slovak National Gallery. Also on show in the palace are four of a set of renowned Northlake Tapestries made in c 1630 and representing the story of Hero and Leander. Of the palace's original furnishings mention must be made of a panelled room covered all over with 18C French prints.

Immediately below the Mirbach Palace, at No. 10, is a house dating back to the early 15C; a drinking establishment since the Middle Ages, the place is now an appealing wine bar called the Velkí Františkáni. Further down the square, past another house of medieval origin (at No. 9), is the entrance to Wolková Street; turn left into this to visit the house at No. 3, which was rebuilt in 1794 by the tobacco merchant Habermayer, and boasts a fire extinguisher of 1820, one of the earliest of its kind. Return to the Dibrovovo námestie, and turn right into the southern half of the square, which is built around a small garden. Within this garden is a memorial of 1907 (by A. Strobl) of the Bratislava-born Hungarian archaeologist Florián Romer, and, below this, a 1933 memorial to A. Kolísek, the architect of the Slovak National Theatre. Further down still is a Marian column of 1675, the oldest such column in central Europe, and put up to commemorate the victory of Emperor Leopold over the rebellious Hungarian aristocrats. Facing the column, on the south-western side of the square, is a small *church* originally built for the German Protestants in 1634–38; after being taken over by the Jesuits in 1672, it received lavish decorations and furnishings, including paintings by F.X. Palko, and a pulpit with reliefs by L. Gode, a talented pupil of G.R. Donner.

The Dibrovovo námestie leads at its southern end into the adjoining námestie 4. apríla, which, despite its relatively small size, was once the main square of Bratislava, a place were markets, popular assemblies and even executions were held. The garden in its middle is dominated by the city's oldest public monument, a *Fountain* executed by O. Luttringer in 1572 to celebrate the coronation of King Maximilian; this tall, tapering work is surmounted by a statue of the knight Roland, the traditional protector of municipal rights. Walk in an anti-clockwise direction around the square, which is surrounded mainly by pompous buildings of the 18C and 19C. At No. 7, adjoining Sedlarská, is a palace—built in 1762 for Count Esterházy—where the Russian pianist and composer Anton Rubinstein stayed in 1847. After crossing Sedlarská turn left into the adjacent Zelená to see the house at No. 1, where there is an elegant baroque fountain in the 18C courtyard. Return to the námestie 4. apríla and turn right, passing after a few metres a magnificent Secessionist building in brilliant yellow (originally a Bank), perhaps the finest building in this style in the city. On the opposite side of the square to this is the most important building on the square, the **Old Town Hall**. Built originally as the private house of the wealthy 14C merchant and civic dignitary Jacob (whose funerary chapel stands in the Dibrovovo námestie), this was adapted after being acquired by the town authorities in the early 15C. Some of the masonry of the 14C structure survives in the façade facing the square, a façade graced by a bay window of 1496–97; the tower was rebuilt after a fire in 1733. A passage on the other side of the Gothic entrance portal leads into a charming courtyard, with a two-storeyed Renaissance loggia on its northern side. A number of the former civic chambers can be visited, including the *Council Hall*, which has a splendid coffered ceiling of 1577; next to this is a room exuberantly decorated in 1695 with stuccowork by the Italian Bastiano Orsati and frescoes by the Augsburg artist J. Drentwett. Also to be seen is a room with Pompeian-style decorations painted in 1862 by the Bratislava painter E. Engel. Most of the Old Town Hall is now taken up by the well-displayed historical collections of the *Municipal Museum*, which was founded in 1868, and is one of the oldest museums in Slovakia.

Beyond the Old Town Hall's courtyard you pass through a neo-Gothic wing and come out into a quiet square (Primaciálný námestie) dominated by the massive *Primatial Palace*, which was built in 1777–81 as the winter seat of the Bishops of Esztergom (the Primates of Hungary); the architect of this French-style neo-classical structure, articulated by a giant order of pilasters, was Melchior Haeferle. The building is famous as the place where the Bratislava Peace Treaty was signed by Napoleon and the Austrian Emperor Franz I in 1805, following the Battle of Austerlitz (two plaques in the courtyard commemorate the event). Functioning as a Town Hall between 1903 and 1947, it has been until recently a branch of the Municipal Museum (the building is at present closed for restoration). In the former Primate's Rooms there used to hang the famous set of six 17C Northlake Tapestries of Hero and Leander (four of which are now in the Mirbach Palace, the disputed ownership of which resulted in a legal battle between the Church and Civic authorities. The architectural highpoint of the interior is a great Hall of Mirrors, where the Hungarian Diet would occasionally hold its assemblies. A 17C statue of St. George stands in the palace's courtyard, off which is a chapel decorated with frescoes by Maulbertsch. On the opposite side of the square to the Palace is the austere and monstrous New Town Hall, built in 1947 over a fine Secessionist building; the original intention was simply to modernise the latter's interior and keep its façade, but the façade mysteriously fell down one night.

East of the square, on the other side of Uršulinská, runs Klobučnícka, where at No. 2 a plaque records the birthplace of the pianist and composer Johann Nepomuk Hummel (1778–1837). Behind the uninspired early 20C apartment block on which this is placed is a courtyard where the actual house of his birth has incongruously survived.

Born on 14 November 1778, Hummel moved to Vienna when still a child, but was frequently to return to Bratislava in the course of his professional life. A pupil of Mozart for two years, he was *Kapellmeister* to Prince Esterházy from 1804 to 1811, acting for the first five years for the aged Haydn. His peripatetic life led him to Brno, Prague, London, Stuttgart, Eisenstadt and, finally, Weimar, where he died on 17 October 1837. One of the great virtuoso pianists of the 19C, he was influential more on account of his piano playing and technique than for his compositions. Among the many whom he inspired were Ferenc Liszt and Anton Rubinstein, both of whom donated the proceeds from a dual recital which they gave in Bratislava in 1885 to the creation of the Hummel Memorial in the Klobučnícka.

The enchanting small house now forming the Hummel Memorial dates back to the 16C, and has intimate rooms filled with 19C furniture as well as documents, photographs and paintings relating to Hummel's life and times. Return to Uršulinská, and walk S down this street to Leningradská, a lively shopping street forming the eastern continuation of Nálepkova, and originally named the Laurensgasse (there is talk at present of bringing back its former name). Turn right into Leningradská and you will shortly pass to your right the Apponyi Palace (1761–62), which is attached to the southern end of the Old Town Hall and was acquired by the city authorities in 1867; inside is a *Museum of Viticulture and Vine-Growing*, featuring 6C–7C documents on viticulture (the oldest in existence), decorative wine barrels, old wine presses, vintners' costumes and so on. At the end of Leningradská turn left into Rybárska brána, which will take you to the avenue marking the southern line of the old town's fortifications, the Gorkého; this skirts the northern side of the impressively long square known as the Hviezdoslavovo námestie. You are now in the cultural heart of Bratislava, and to your left, at the eastern end of the square, stands one of the more flamboyant of the city's public buildings, the *Slovak National Theatre*, built between 1884 and 1886 by the ubiquitous F. Fellner and H. Helmer in replacement of an earlier, wooden structure. In front of this white neo-Renaissance building is a playful *fountain* executed in 1888 by the local sculptor V. Tilgner, and originally intended for the first Bratislava Savings Bank; it is surmounted by a bronze group of Ganymede being carried away by Jupiter disguised as an eagle. Adajacent to the square, on the southern side of the square is the Carlton Hotel, which is formed out of three hotels joined together in the 1920s; its gilded neo-baroque café is one of the most stylish of the city's few surviving traditional coffee-houses. A shaded garden lined with imposing 19C buildings comprises the western end of the Hviezdoslavovo námestie. In the middle of this garden is a commemorative statue of 1937 (by J. Pospíšil and V. Ihrisky) of the man after whom the square is named, P.O. Hviezdoslav, a leading Slovakian poet and playwright who spent much of his life in Dolný Kubín, where he worked as a lawyer.

Return to the Hotel Carlton, and turn right down Mostová, which will take you past the *Reduta*, a neo-baroque structure built between 1912–14 by Komor and Jakab, and intended originally as a casino, dance hall and general place of entertainment. The main hall of this building is today the concert hall of the Bratislava Philharmonic, while the former café attached to the southern side is now used, less romantically, as the head office of Czech Airlines. The Reduta looks S across the small triangular-shaped Ľudovít Štúr námestie down to the Danube. This area marks the site of the so-called Coronation Hill, where the kings on horseback would swear to defend their country against its enemies. In place of T. Bártfay's modern memorial in stone and bronze to the Slovakian patriot and codifier of the Slovakian language, Ľudovít Štúr, there once stood a great bronze statue of Maria Theresa, executed in 1893–95 by one of the most powerful Hungarian sculptors of the last century, János Fadrusz; its artistic qualities, however, were not recognised by the Slovakian patriots who in 1919 blew the work up, thus ridding the city of one of its most eloquent symbols of Habsburg oppression.

At the southern end of the Ľudovít Štúr námestie turn right and walk towards the *Slovak National Museum* (Slovenské narodné muzeum), a pompous classical-style building rising up at the eastern end of a

Bratislava. A view of Reduta with T. Bártfay's monument to Ľudovít Štúr in the foreground

riverside garden, at the junction of Vajanského nábr and Fajnorovo nábr. In front of the building is a memorial of a lion on a column, intended to celebrate the coming into being on 28 October 1918, of the Czechoslovak Republic. Executed in 1938, it was originally put in front of the Reduta and was surmounted by a 4m-high statue of Milan Štefánik, shown in pilot's dress.

The son of a Slovak Lutheran pastor, Štefánik fell foul of the Hungarian authorities on account of his nationalist tendencies when he was still in his teens. Later he went to Paris, and found a post at the Observatoire, which led him on astronomical expeditions to Tahiti and the Sahara. At the outbreak of the First World War he enlisted as a pilot in the French airforce, and earned a reputation for his daring exploits on the Italian and Balkan Fronts. Already he had access to leading French political circles, and through this was able to introduce his fellow Czechoslovak exile, E. Beneš, to a number of key figures in French politics such as Aristide Briand. With the creation of the Czechoslovak Republic, he joined forces with Beneš and Masaryk to form the new country's leading triumvirate. In May 1919, flying home to Slovakia from Italy, he crashed within sight of Bratislava, where a large crowd had come to greet him. This was the first great tragedy in the history of the Republic, and the situation was hardly improved by vindictive rumours that he had been shot down deliberately by Czech machine-gunners. For being the bourgeois son of a clergyman, Štefánik became a *persona non grata* at the height of the Stalinist era, and the large statue to him in Bratislava was taken down. His rehabilitation had begun even before the recent political events in Czechoslovakia, and it is now highly possible that he will once more be commemorated here.

The original Slovak National Museum was founded in the town of Martin, and only in 1924 was work begun on the one at Bratislava. The building, completed in 1928, was the work of M. Harminc and today houses only the scientific, natural history, and geological collections of the museum, the historical, archaeological and numismatic ones being now at Bratislava Castle. The dreary, old-fashioned display features a permanent exhibition of mushrooms, the collecting of which comprises one of the great national pastimes; as a result of numerous Slovaks falling ill from poisonous mushrooms that they have gathered during their weekend break, the Museum offers every Monday a useful 'Mushroom consultation', a service offered in other countries by the local pharmacy. From the pier in front of the museum, you can take a boat trip lasting from between one to two hours along the Danube. One of the bridges which you will pass under is the one just to the E of the museum, the Red Army Bridge; this, the oldest bridge in Bratislava and originally named the Franz Josef Bridge, dates back to 1888–89, but was rebuilt following its destruction by the Germans in 1945.

Heading E from the museum along Vajanského nábr., you will soon reach the Šafárikovo námestie, which marks the south-eastern boundary of the old town. The main building here is the Jan Ámos Komenský University, an austere geometrical structure completed in 1938 to a design of F. Krupka. In the garden on the north side of the square is one of Bratislava's most popular fountains: executed by Robert Kühmayer in 1914, it features an exuberant scene of naked boys playfully tormenting some ducks, and is generally referred to by the people of Bratislava simply as 'The Ducks'. Return to the Ľudovít Štúr námestiealong Vajanského nábr., and continue along the Danube embankment on the Rázusovo nábr.

Immediately to the W of the square, overlooking a narrow riverside garden containing a memorial (by Fraňo Štefunko) to the 19C Slovak painter Peter Bohún, is Bratislava's most important art gallery, the **Slovak National Gallery** (Slovenská národné gáleria). The façade of this building is most striking, consisting as it does of a bold and diagonally projecting modern frontage raised on bricks so as to afford a rectangular vista of what is in fact the remaining half of a white arcaded courtyard belonging to a former army barracks of 1775–63. Such a radical adaptation of an old building has inevitably been much criticised, but this none the less seems to be far preferable to the heavy and reverential classical settings in which national collections are usually displayed. Furthermore the gallery's courtyard fragment—decorated with sculptures from the gallery's collection—has been planted with grass and trees to form a most pleasant small garden; the gallery's interior is light and spacious.

Founded in 1948, the Slovak National Gallery brings together a comprehensive selection of paintings and sculptures produced in Slovakia from the Middle Ages up to the present day; the collections are arranged in a roughly chronological way, the earliest works being on the ground floor, and the most recent on the second floor. By far the most distinguished of the medieval paintings are two panels of c 1480–90 representing **The Death of the Virgin** and **The Tree of Jesse**; painted by an anonymous artist known as the Master of Spišská Kapitula, they have something of the angular expressiveness and incisive realism characteristic of Master Pavol of Levoča, and reflect the high quality of art produced in the Spiš region in late medieval times. Among the baroque works are sculptures by G.R. Donner and his pupil J. Gode, oil sketches by F.A. Palko, J.L. Kracker, F.A. Maulbertsch, and J. Winterhalter, a portrait by J. Kupecký of c 1700, and three works by Jakub Bohdan, an artist who is more widely known as Jakub Bogdani. Of the late 18C sculptures special mention must be made of two grimacing physiological studies in bronze (1770) by F.X. Messerschmidt. Two of the best-known

Slovakian artists of the Romantic period are the expressive landscapist K. Marko and the endearingly naïve J. Czauczik, the former represented here by three works (including a Roman landscape of 1838), the latter by two portraits and a landscape with figures (*Založení rudňanských baní*, The Founding of the Rudnanski Spa, 1815), generally considered to be his masterpiece. Some of the stiff and naïve qualities of Czauczik's art are to be found in the works of Peter Michal Bohún, whose eminence among Slovakian painters of the 19C is due in part to his political activities: Bohún was one of the organisers of the Slovak Uprising of 1848–49, and one of his works in the National Gallery was actually painted during that period and features a scene from the rebellion. His other six paintings here are all portraits, including a well-known one of a woman in blue called *Davidovej-Revickej* (1853–55). Genre scenes by the Banská Bystrica painter D. Skutecký, and suggestively painted landscapes and figure studies by Medňanský, feature among the turn-of-the-century works in the gallery. Josef Hanula, a specialist in peasant genre scenes, is represented by the much reproduced *On Native Earth*, showing a seated peasant. There are two landscapes (including a *View of Kremnica*, 1890) by Vojtech Angyal, a Hungarian painter from the Spiš region who is now usually considered a Slovak artist. The works of Gustáv Mály, Ľudovít Fulla, and Martin Benka—artists who all painted Slovakian landscapes and rural scenes in vivid colours and bold compositions—feature prominently among the 20C holdings. A more original artist than any of these is Anthon Jasusch, of whom there is a Delaunay-like *Yellow Windmill* of 1922. Other painters include Mikuláš Galanda, Konstantín Bauer (an expressionistic, satirical work entitled *The judged Woman*, 1927), Josef Kollár, Jan Hála, Josef Bendík, Elemír Halász-Hradil, Zolo Palugyay, Janko Alexy, Cyprían Majerník, Eugen Nevan and Peter Matejka. One of the more recent artists in the collection is the painter of surreal scenes A. Brunovsky, who also designed the present Czech banknotes, a commission which gave rise to the joke that he was paid in his own works. Among the 19C and 20C sculptures in the museum are bronzes by V.O. Tilgner, Ján Koniarek, Fraňo Štefunko, Jozef Pospíšil, Július Bártfay, Rudolf Hornák, Rudolf Pribiš and Jozef Kostka.

After leaving the museum continue walking W along the Danube embankment, passing on your right the luxury Devín Hotel, which boasts one of the most elegant of the city's traditional cafés and restaurants. In between the hotel and the modern SNP Bridge there is at present a large car park commanding an excellent view of the castle hill; sadly this view is shortly to be obliterated by a projected hotel. From here you could walk N to the nearby Hviezdoslavovo, and then regain from here Jiráskova, which will take you back to the Hurbanovo námestie. Alternatively you could walk underneath the Staromestská flyover, and ascend the castle hill.

B. Bratislava Castle and Devín

The ascent to Bratislava Castle from the old town is made on the Zámocké schody, a path which begins below the Staromestská flyover, near St. Martin's Cathedral. After climbing some steps you should turn to the right on Beblavého to visit the surviving houses on the lower slopes of the castle hill. An 18C house at No. 2 Beblavého has been turned into an intimate café, U zlatého slnka (At the Golden Sun); next to this, at No. 1, an austere building of the same period houses an *Applied Arts Museum*, filled mainly with 19C furniture and furnishings. Adjacent to the museum, at No. 1 Židovská (Jew Street), is the most charming of the city's rococo houses, a narrow yellow structure with a gabled side façade, and projecting bay windows decorated with rococo plaster swirls. Called **Dom U dobrého pastiera** (At the Good Shepherd) on account of a wall chapel featuring Christ carrying a lamb, this toy-like building contains a *Clock Museum*, where you can see examples from over four centuries of the art of Bratislava's celebrated clockmakers, who were first documented in the 15C.

Return to the Zámocké schody, and continue your ascent, looking back occasionally to admire the ever more extensive views towards St. Martin's Cathedral and the Danube. You enter the citadel through the early 15C *Corvinus Gate*, which is surmounted by a large ogee arch.

The history of **Bratislava Castle** goes back to a fortified Celtic settlement of the 1C AD, on which was later built the Slavic hill-fort of Presslauspurch, which is first mentioned in 907. The Hungarian king Salomon rebuilt the castle in the 11C, and in the following century his great successor Stephen III lived here. In 1189 the place became an assembly point for those taking part in the Third Crusade, which was led by the Emperor Frederick Barbarossa. Between 1431 and 1434 the castle was entirely rebuilt by Sigismund of Luxemburg, who established the present square ground-plan. Further alterations and extensions were carried out between 1552 and 1570 (to prepare the place as a base against the Turks) and again between 1635 and 1646, following damage caused during the rebellion of Prince Gabriel Bethlen. The latter remodelling gave to the building a third storey and its distinctive corner towers; in 1673 the Emperor Leopold added three artillery embrasures and a new western gate, called today 'Leopold's Gate'. The present look of the building, however, is due largely to the extensive work undertaken here during the reign of Maria Theresa, when the castle became the seat of the Empress' son-in-law, Albert of Saxony. After Maria Theresa, the castle fell out of favour as a Habsburg residence, and in 1783 Joseph II turned the place into a seminary. Those who worked and studied at this seminary were none too enthusiastic about the castle either, finding it cold and uncomfortable; in 1802 it was converted into a barracks, which survived until 1811, when the building was severely damaged by fire. Left slowly to decay after 1811, the castle further suffered during the Second World War, when bombing left only the outer walls standing. The restoration of the castle was begun in 1954 and completed by 1968, just in time for the signing here in October of the Act of the Czechoslovak Federation, which made Bratislava the capital of the Slovak Socialist Republic. The building now serves both as a branch of the Slovakian National Museum and as the seat of the Slovakian State offices (the latter will eventually be transferred to a new building in the vicinity).

On the eastern side of the castle the scant excavated foundations of the 10C Slavonic hill-fort have been transformed by rebuilding and restoration into what looks like an over-sized group of children's building blocks, neatly arranged on the lawn. The castle itself is a chillingly austere building in which has been chronologically arranged a museum with objects, documents and photographs relating to the history of Slovakia from prehistoric times onwards. The main surviving part of the medieval building is the south-east tower, which is known as the Crown Tower owing to the Hungarian crown jewels having been kept there until 1783, when they were transferred by Joseph III to Vienna (at the end of the Second World War they were taken by Hungarian Nazis to Germany, from where they were retrieved by the Americans and removed to Fort Knox; not returned to Hungary until 1978, they can now be seen in the National

'At the Good Shepherd', a rococo house in yellow plaster on Bratislava's Castle Hill; the building now contains a clock museum

Museum at Budapest). Though the castle no longer has these jewels there is the consolation of a *Treasury* which was opened here in 1988 and contains dramatically-lit objects mainly from the period of the Great Moravian Empire; the oldest piece, displayed in a glass pyramid at the entrance, is the tiny prehistoric fertility figure known as the *Venus of Věstonice*, which is carved on a piece of mammoth tusk and is an estimated 25,000 years old. The Representative Halls of the Slovak Government are on the first floor, but are closed to the public.

Leave the citadel by the western Leopold's Gate, and turn left, descending down to the Danube on the steps named Schody pri st. vodárne. At the bottom of the steps is the former *Fisherman's Guild*, an attractive house dating back to the Renaissance and now containing what is perhaps the city's finest fish restaurant, the Rybársky cech. From here you can take Bus 29 almost all the way to Devín Castle, 10km to the west. The journey is along the Danube, largely through a bosky suburban landscape, the idyllic properties of which have been spoilt until recently by a formidable fence preventing people from jumping into the Danube and swimming across to Austria. The suburb of Devín, at one time well known for its red and blackcurrant wines, has the character of a village (in contrast to the ugly modern urban sprawls of Devínska Nová Ves to the W and Dúbravka to the N). The ruins of its castle picturesquely crown a rocky outcrop jutting dramatically above the confluence of the Danube and Morava rivers.

The fortifications at Devín have their origins in a Celtic settlement, on which a Roman camp of the 14th Legion was established in the 2C AD. Although it is now known that Devín was not, as was previously thought, the capital of the Great Moravian Empire (which has been identified as being near Mikulovice in Moravia), the place was clearly an important Moravian settlement, and has a name derived from an old Slavonik word for maiden. The Hungarian king Arpád is said to have come here at the end of the 10C, and, recognising the strategic importance of the site, to have exclaimed 'To here and no further'; whether true or not, Devín became the westernmost point of the Hungarian empire. The present castle was begun in the 13C and extended in the 15C, during the reign of Sigismund of Luxemburg. In the 16C, faced with a potential attack from the Turks, the then owners, the Bathorys, had the castle further strengthened and enlarged. When the Turkish threat had passed, the place lost its strategic importance, and, from the 18C was left to decay; in 1809 Napoleon hastened its decline by blowing up its surviving parts. The ruins of the castle acquired great significance later in the 19C, not so much because of their obvious romantic appeal, but because of their associations with the Slavic past. The castle became a popular meeting-place for Ľudovít Štúr and many other Slovakian nationalists, to whom the Great Moravian Empire represented a Golden Age.

One of the great attractions of a visit to Devín is the view from the ruins down to the wooded banks of the two rivers and across to distant fertile plains; at the point where the waters meet the muddy browns of the Moravia sharply clash with the more translucent hues of the Danube. Squeezed between the rock on which you stand and the river is an abandoned amphitheatre where outdoor plays and performances were put on until 1950, when it was decided that it was dangerous to bring crowds so near to the frontier of capitalist Austria; furthermore the proximity of this border made it prohibited until 1989 to take photographs from this magnificent vantage-point. The castle's walls have gradually been restored and in a reconstructed hall has been installed a small museum of finds from the site. Elsewhere there is a memorial plaque to Ľudovít Štúr and a monument to the legendary Moravian Maiden after whom the place is named. The wooded hill behind Devín is a protected nature reserve forming part of the Bratislava Forest Park, which was created in 1953.

C. Northern Bratislava and the northern environs

North and E of the wide ring of boulevards encircling the old town of Bratislava you come to extensive urban development dating mainly from the post-war years. There are a number of interesting monuments to be seen here, both old and modern, yet these are scattered over a wide area. The bleakness of much of this part of Bratislava is fortunately alleviated by large areas of green and the consoling presence of the nearby wooded slopes of the Carpathian foothills.

Taking as your starting-point the Hurbanovo námestie, begin by visiting the early 18C *Trinity Church* on the western side of the square. The interior features a spectacular illusionistic decoration commissioned in May 1744 by the Hungarian Archbishop, Imre Esterházy, from the great Bolognese specialist in architectural painting, Antonio Galli Bibiena; the decoration, comprising a fictive coffered dome and completed in the remarkable space of a year, is one of the most important examples of *quadratura* or architectural painting in central Europe. Head due E of the church along the boulevard which marks the northern limit of the old town, and you will soon come to the unappealingly named námestie SNP, which commemorates the Slovakian National Uprising. In the wooded garden in the middle of the square stands a modern memorial to the uprising comprising three large bronze figures executed by Ján Kulich in a setting devised by the architect Dušan Kuzma. The figures are of a distraught mother and daughter, and of a man, who, with rifle at hand and at some distance from the women, stares in the other direction; for obvious reasons this absurd group is popularly referred to as the 'Angry Family'. Continue heading E until the neighbouring Kyjevské námestie, and turn left on to the long and broad Československej armády. After a few hundred metres you will come on the left-hand side of this street (at the junction with Hollého) to the former *Convent Church of St. Elizabeth's Sisters*, which was built in 1734–43 by the Viennese architect A. Pilgram; the interior of this imposing building is decorated with frescoes by the great Viennese painter Paul Troger.

The walk further N up Československej armády becomes increasingly tedious, and you would be best advised to take one of the numerous buses and trams that ply its length. Get off at at the Americké námestie, which is at the junction of Československej armády and Mickiewiczova. On the southern side of this square is the enormous palace built in 1768–70 by I. Thalherr for Count Aspremont; the building today houses the Dean's office and administrative staff of the Medical faculty of Comenius (Komenský) University, while the large garden, laid out in a formal French style in the late 18C, is now an attractive Public Park called the Medical Garden (Medická záhrada). The small Sovietske námestie adjoins the northern side of the Americké námestie, and is dominated by a a neo-Gothic church designed by V. Rumpelmayer in 1885–88 as the parish church of the once separate township of Blumenthal; more interesting than the church is the magnificent *Florian Column* in front of it, a busy and dynamic baroque work of 1732–38.

Head NW from the church along Fazulova, turn right at the end of this on to Slovenska, and then left, reaching eventually the long avenue called Mytná. Walking S along this you will pass on the right-hand side one of Bratislava most distinctive modern buildings, the black inverted pyramid forming the headquarters of the *Czechoslovak Radio*. Further S along Mytná is the monstrous Slobody námestie, which was intended in the 1950s as a monumental new main square for Bratislava, but ended up as a grim memorial to the failure of totalitarian town planning. This singularly lifeless space is made pleasant only by its trees and greenery, which, however, have also the effect of detracting from the intended monumentality. At the lower, southern end of the square is an exploding metallic object scattering water known as the Fountain of Friendship (by T. Bártfay among others); Bártfay was also responsible for the heavy stone sculptural group above this—showing a morose Klement Gottwald apparently sprouting wings—and for the monument at the top of the square, another metal ball, this one reasonably intact and representing Peace. The buildings lining the southern and western sides of the square are depressing blocks belonging to the Slovakian Technical College, while on the eastern side is the vast Post Office building, supposedly the largest in the world, and certainly one of the ugliest (work on this structure was begun before planning permission had been given). At the northern end of the square, cowering behind trees from the accumulated horrors all around it, is the former *Summer Palace of the Bishops of Esztergom*. Dating back to the 17C, but remodelled in the 18C, it was used by the Bishops during the Turkish occupation of Hungary, and abandoned by them shortly afterwards. Its ownership later reverted to the state, and the building served as a garrison hospital during the First World War; heavily restored after 1968 it houses today the Government Offices of Slovakia.

By the western side of the building runs Spojná, which will take you to the Štefánikova, directly in front of the *Lenin Museum* (at No. 25), a threatened institution in the new political climate of today. Virtually unvisited, like most Lenin Museums in Russian and eastern Europe, it is worth coming to if only for the splendid neo-rococo 19C palace in which it is housed. North of the museum turn left on to Puškinova, where steps will start you off on your climb through pleasant suburbia up the Slavín Hill. Turn left at the top of Puškinova, and then first right, and you will come finally to steps leading up to the massive monument which dominates the hill.

The **Slavín Monument** is a monument to the estimated 6000 Soviet soldiers who died in 1945 in the course of 'liberating' Bratislava. Much of the memorial, which was designed in the 1950s by the architect Jan Svetlik, comprises a large formal garden incorporating a cemetery; from its terraces there are wonderfully extensive views over the city and the distant Danube. At the very centre of the memorial, rising up on steps, is a Hall of Remembrance supporting a gigantic tapering pillar crowned by a bronze statue of a Soviet soldier breaking a swastika in half. This centrepiece is unquestionably one of the most powerful of its kind in Europe. The austerity of the architecture, featuring geometrical, unadorned arcading is offset by the wealth of statuary surrounding it, executed by the leading Slovakian artists of the day, including L. Snopek, J. Kulich, T. Bártfay and Rudolf Pribiš; the hall is decorated inside by the painter J. Krén, while on the outer walls are inscribed the names of the Slovakian battles in which the Soviet soldiers took part. The crowning bronze of the Soviet soldier is by A. Trizuljak, who subsequently fell out of favour when it was discovered that he regularly attended Catholic Mass.

Descending the hill turn right into Mišikova (rather than left if you were returning by way of Puškinova), Alexander Dubček lives at

No. 46. Take the first street to the left (Donovalova), cross Vickova and continue descending on Kuzmanyho. On the next street which you cross, Somolického, there stands at No. 2 the charming early 20C house which belonged to the Slovakian poet and translator *Janko Jesenský* (1874–1945); the building, which was made into a museum in 1952, has been kept exactly as it was in the writer's lifetime. Continue descending down Kuzmányho, turn right on to Moyzesova and left on to Palisády, then first right on to Stetinova. The latter leads into Panenská, a street lined with distinguished palaces of the 19C, including, at No. 25, a building where the great Hungarian poet and revolutionary Sándor Petőfi once stayed. Lycejná leads S from here to Konventná, passing alongside the *Small Protestant Church*, built by Römisch in 1778 for Hungarian and Slovakian Protestants. On Konventná, at Nos 13 and 15, is the *Protestant Lyceum*, a building associated with many of the leading figures of the Slovak national revival, including Ľudovít Štúr; within the Lyceum can be found the large Protestant Church, built by M. Walch in 1776. Konventná will take you into the large and rather bleak Mierové námestie, dominated on its southern side by Bratislava's latest and most luxurious hotel, the Hotel Forum (1989). On the northern side of the square is the much-altered *Grassalkovich Palace*, built in 1765 by Mayerhofer and now the temporary seat of the youth movement known as the Pioneers; there is a bronze plaque recording Haydn's performances at the palace and, in front of the building, a modern fountain by T. Bártfay of frolicking nude women (The Joy of Life).

The forests and vine-covered slopes of the Lesser Carpathians make for the most popular excursions in the vicinity of Bratislava; much of this gently mountainous area forms part of the vast Bratislava Forest Park, which extends N almost all the way to Modrá. The most accessible place from the city is the hill of *Kamzík*, which can be reached from the Mierové námestie on a No. 13 bus. At the end of the bus route you have a 1.5km walk to the car park adjoining the *Koliba Expo*, a wooden restaurant created for the Montreal World Exhibition of 1968; it is the prototype of the many 'Kolibas' throughout Czechoslovakia—places where you can eat charcoal-grilled meat in intimate and would-be primitive surroundings. There are numerous walks in the surrounding forest, but the great attraction here is the nearby Television Tower, which has a restaurant from which you can observe a breathtaking panorama.

A car is really needed to visit the wine-growing villages at the foot of the Lesser Carpathians' eastern slopes. Leave Bratislava on the dual carriageway which heads NE towards Pezinok. After 15km you pass next to the pleasant small village of *Jur*, which has in its upper part a church of 13C origin commanding views down to the fertile plains to the E; the once German-dominated village has a tradition of wine-growing going back at least to the 13C, when its inhabitants supplied wine to the Hungarian kings. *Pezinok* (a further 6km), is one of the main wine centres of the area, and there are few more stylish places to try the local wines than the town's castle, a building of medieval origin remodelled in 1718: inside are a restaurant and a complex of wine bars. Pezinok was also the childhood home of the leading baroque artist, Jan Kupecký (1667–1740), who is commemorated here by a small museum in the house where he lived. The road to the W of the town takes you across the forested ridge of the Carpathians and to Pernek; 13km along the road is the Baba Hotel, a good base for walks into the mountains. Continuing N from Pezinok, after 8km you will reach one of Czechoslovakia's most famous wine centres, *Modrá*, a small town which has retained a 17C gate-tower (within which a wine bar has been installed) and other fragments from its original fortifications. On the main square, where there is another good wine bar, stands a statue of Ľudovít Štúr, who lived here from 1850 until his death in 1860; he is buried in the local cemetery. As well as being a wine centre, Modrá is well known for its ceramics, which are characterised by colourful floral patterns set against a white background.

North-west of Modrá a small road climbs up through forest to Zochova chata (6km), a complex of wooden buildings comprising a hotel, a Koliba (see above), a restaurant, and a lively small bar (Furmanská krčma); this is a place geared in its appeal to those with a longing for log cabins and the 'simple life' of a forester. 8km due N of Modrá is the castle of *Červený Kameň*, standing in a beautiful wooded setting at the eastern edge of the mountains. This building of medieval origin was acquired by the Fuggers of Augsburg in 1533 and converted by them into a great storehouse; it is said that the ingenious defensive system which the Fuggers installed (involving a novel way of extracting gunpowder smoke) was designed by the painter Albrecht Dürer. In 1588 the place passed into the hands of the Pálffy family on the marriage of Nicholas Pálffy to Maria Magdalena Fugger. The former fortress was subsequently converted into a splendid château, featuring a sala terrena in the form of a grotto. The interior was adapted in 1962 to house a collection of the applied arts, but has been closed since 1982 for further restoration. A further 20km drive N through wooded gently rolling countryside will take you to *Smolenice* a former royal castle dating back to the 13C and given a most picturesque pseudo-medieval look by the Pálffys at the end of the 19C; it now belongs to the Slovak Academy of Sciences, and is used for conferences.

D. Petržalka and Rusovce

The modern *SNP Bridge*, which spans the Danube at a point between the castle hill and the Cathedral of St. Martin's, is one of the most distinctive features of the Bratislava skyline. This bold yet graceful structure is held up by enormous lengths of British-made cable swung from a tall tower formed of two massive pillars supporting high above the ground an oval structure resembling a flying saucer. The latter contains a restaurant which should have been revolving had not the funds run out; the view is at any rate impressive, and worth the queue to get into the small lift which makes the vertiginous ascent. The tower is on the southern banks of the river, in the largely residential district of Petržalka. The other main attraction of this district is the large and wooded riverside park which adjoins the tower. Named today after the 19C Slovakian poet and revolutionary Janko Kráľ, it was founded in the late 18C and as such is one of the oldest public parks in Europe. You will find here the Gothic tower from the Franciscan church on the Dibrovovo námestie, a statue of Kráľ executed by F. Gibala in 1964, and another by A. Rigele of the singer O. Trebitsch (1922). The most impressive of these memorials is that devoted to Kráľ's Hungarian contemporary and fellow poet,

Sándor Petőfi, a powerful work by J. Fadrusz, a leading Hungarian sculptor of the late 19C.

Bus 101 will take you S of Petržalka to Zrkadlový háj (5km), where a large pond forms a nudist swimming pool. 4km further on is the riverside village of *Rusovce*, featuring a 19C château in an English neo-Gothic style, now used by the Slovak Folk Art Ensemble.

Nearby there was accidentally uncovered in 1961 the scant remains of the Roman trading settlement of *Gerulata*; the main interest of the site is its small museum of Roman finds, including a relief sculpture of the mid 2C AD representing Attis.

26 Bratislava to Zvolen

A. Via Komárno

Total distance 266km. Bratislava—100km *Komárno*—44km Štúrovo—122km **Zvolen**.

South and E of Bratislava extends a vast featureless plain, characterised by its ugly small towns and the endless expanses of wheatfields that give to this area its reputation as the 'Granary of Czechoslovakia'. The landscape strongly recalls that of neighbouring Hungary, and indeed this is the part of Slovakia with the largest Hungarian minority.

Leave Bratislava on Road 63, which has little of architectural let alone scenic interest for at least 100km. However, at Nové Košariská, 8km SE of Bratislava, you can make a short detour to the S to visit the tiny village of *Hamuliakavo* (6km), which has a charming Romanesque church in a green and wooded setting. Built at the beginning of the 13C, and restored in the 19C, this white-washed building has a fine Romanesque tower and an apse featuring blind arcading. Besides the nearby marshy banks of the Danube is a cormorant sanctuary. Rejoin Road 63 at Šamorín, 6km to the E, and continue driving for a further 24km to *Dunajská Streda*. This is an ugly industrial town which has, isolated among modern buildings in its centre, a 14C church (remodelled in the 18C), with small fragments of 14C wall-painting on the left-hand side of the chancel. The flatlands N of the Danube have a number of thermal pools, around which holiday resorts have grown up; one of these, congested at weekends in the summer, is to be found on the southern outskirts of the town. Another such resort is outside the dull small town of Calovo, 21km futher south.

Road 63 finally reaches the Danube at *Komárno*, 33km SE of Calovo, and by far the most interesting town in this little visited corner of Slovakia.

The town of Komárno grew up beside a celebrated fortress, situated near the confluence of the Danube and the Váh, on the site of the Roman military camp of Kelemantia. First mentioned in 1075, the fortress successfully withstood Tartar invasions in the 13C, and became in the 16C one of the most important Hungarian centres in the struggle against the Turks. The Turks, who first besieged the town in 1529, finally destroyed the place in 1594. Between 1663–73 a new fortress with a star-shaped plan was built by the Emperor Leopold alongside the old one, and at the time of the Napoleonic Wars a system of bastions and walls known as the Palatine Line was put up in between the Danube and the

Váh. A thriving commercial centre in the 18C, Komárno is today a lively market and industrial town, with large shipyards. The place holds an important position in the cultural history of Hungary being the birthplace of both the writer Mór Jókai (1825–1904) and the composer Franz Lehár (1870–1948).

The remains of Komárno's celebrated fortress lie neglected and decaying on the western outskirts of town, undisturbed other than by the odd gypsy encampment. Komárno itself cannot be described as a beautiful town but it is a place with an enormous vitality belying a faded, turn-of-the-century character. The population is mainly Hungarian, and the street-signs are in two languages. On the square directly in front of the bridge which leads into Hungary is a modern bronze statue to the composer Franz Lehár, Hungarian by birth (despite attempts to claim him as Slovak), but whose charming operettas such as The Merry Widow (1905) belong essentially to the world of *fin-de-siècle* Vienna. West of the square, at No. 32 Gábora Steinera, is a small and dusty *museum* devoted both to Lehár and to the writer Jókai, whose romantic historical novels such as Midst the Wild Carpathians enjoyed an international vogue in the late 19C, and were brought out in numerous English editions; the museum contains photographs and other mementoes of the two Hungarians, and even has two writing desks which belonged to Jókai. In the 16C Serbians fleeing from the Turks formed a small Serbian community at Komárno, and in the courtyard adjoining the museum stands a fascinating *Serbian Orthodox Church*. The original church, filled with 16C icons that the Serbians had taken with them from their native land, was burnt down and replaced by an early 18C structure. Some of the icons from the earlier building can be seen behind the magnificent rococo iconostasis; the rococo stalls meanwhile are from the Camaldensian Monastery of Majk in Hungary, which was dissolved by Joseph II and its furnishings sold off. The church functioned up to 1953, the services conducted by a Hungarian priest who came up once a month from the Hungarian town of Szentendre.

Returning to the riverside square head along the eastern continuation of Gábora Steinera. On the left-hand side you will come shortly to the elegant building of the local museum, in front of which stands a powerful late 19C bronze statue of the seated Jókai, at whose feet wreaths and flowers still continue to be placed. Beyond is the late 19C Town Hall, and further along, on the right-hand side of the street, is the former Officer's Casino, a decayed and very evocative neo-Gothic monument from the last days of the Habsburg Empire (the building is now a restaurant).

From Komárno, Road 63 follows the Danube (Dunaj) all the way to Štúrovo (44km). *Patince*, 10km to the E of Komárno, has mineral springs that were known to the Romans and is today the largest of the thermal resorts in this part of Slovakia; there are two large swimming pools fed from the springs, and numerous ungainly bungalows spread out over a large area of grass and trees. Štúrovo is in itself a place of little interest, but there are tantalising views over the Danube to the town of Esztergom, dominated by the hill on which rises the massive neo-classical cathedral of the Hungarian primates. At Štúrovo you leave the Danube and head due N on Road 76, following for 41km the winding river Hron. The quiet small town of *Želiezovce*, 29km N of Štúrovo, has an 18C château which belonged to the Esterházys who invited here on two occasions the composer Franz Schubert.

Schubert, the son of a Moravian peasant schoolteacher and of a Viennese cook, was an impoverished 21-year-old living in Vienna when in 1818 he was invited to Želiezovce to teach the daughters of J.K. Esterházy. He arrived here on 7 July and remained until 19 November; six years later, in 1824, he was here again, staying from 25 May to 17 October. His best pupil was Karolina Esterházy, who accompanied him daily at the piano, and for whom he composed several works. While at Želiezovce, Schubert took a keen interest in the life of the villagers, and also made a number of important friendships, most notably with the singer K. Laczná, the actress Z. Müller and Baron Schönstein, who sang his songs. Among the numerous piano duets that he wrote here were his German dances (D618), Polonaises (D618A), Divertissements à la Hongroise (D818), and two works that he dedicated respectively to Beethoven and Karolina Esterházy, Variations (D624) and the four-hand Fantasy (D 940).

The château at Želiezovce was built in 1720 but remodelled towards the end of the 18C. Schubert himself stayed in a small late 18C classical building in the park; this charming place, known as the Owl's Lodge, has housed since 1970 a small commemorative museum devoted to the composer's life. 12km N of Želiezovce, turn right on to Road 75, which crosses the Hron and passes through Demandice (13km). 8km E of Demandice turn left on to Road 66, which you follow for the remaining 62km to **Zvolen** (see Route 28), the landscape becoming progressively hillier and more wooded.

B.   Via Nitra

Total distance 196km. Bratislava—96km **Nitra**—62km Žarnovica—15km **Banská Štiavnica**—27km Zvolen.

Head E from Bratislava on the E571, passing through dull, agricultural countryside, which is unrelievedly flat until you reach **Nitra**, a large town sprawled underneath a prominent citadel, and with the pleasing sight of vine-covered slopes rising to the north.

Nitra rose to prominence in the 9C AD, when it became one of the most important centres of the Great Moravian Empire. In 820 the Moravian Prince Pribina made the town his seat, and founded here shortly afterwards the first Christian church in Slovakia; in 880 the town was raised to a bishopric. After the fall of the Moravian Empire, Nitra became the residence of the Hungarian apanage princes, which it was to remain until the end of the 11C. Subsequently it suffered from a brief period of subjugation to the Bohemian Přemysl king Otakar II, and was much damaged in the course of Tartar raids, the Hussite Wars, and the Hungarian rebellions led by the Zapolys, the Bethlens and Ferenc Rákóczi. The greatest damage of all was caused by the Turks, who repeatedly raided the castle in the 16C and 17C and in 1663 managed finally to conquer the town, which they afterwards destroyed. Nitra today has developed into a prosperous industrial town, and leading wine-growing and agricultural centre. The Agricultural University of Slovakia is situated here, and hosts every year an important agricultural fair with the Freudian-sounding name of AGRO-KOMPLEX.

The main monuments of interest in Nitra are concentrated in the town's **Citadel**, the earliest surviving parts of which date back to the 11C; new fortifications were erected in the Middle Ages and again in 1603, and most of the buildings to be seen today within the walls are largely of the 17C and 18C. You enter the complex through a gate on the northern side of the námestie Osloboditelov, and climb up the Samova Pribinova until you reach a green and sloping square. The heavy baroque houses which line the Samova Pribinova and the southern side of the square were once used exclusively by the clergy, but today have been appropriated by local government offices and drab museums, including an Agricultural Museum. This whole part of town has an empty forsaken character. At the upper northern end of the square stands an exuberant *Marian Plague Column* executed

by Fogerle in 1750 (restored in 1956), and behind this rise the walls of
Nitra's castle, entered through a *Renaissance Gate*. Immediately
inside the castle grounds are the *Cathedral* and the adjoining *Bishop's
Palace*. The latter, was built in 1732–39 above the basement of a
medieval palace; it has rich baroque decorations inside, but is not
usually open to the public. The cathedral's history is a complex one,
and the present building, entered through the south portal, comprises
in fact three separate churches. After turning right as soon as you enter
the building you will find a modern door leading to the old cathedral,
which was built in 1064 over the church founded by Prince Pribina in
c 833: this tiny white-washed space was rebuilt in the 13C and 14C
and renovated in the 18C, but it still retains its Romanesque apse. The
main body of the cathedral features an upper and lower church, the
former dating back to 1333–55 (but remodelled in the 18C), and the
latter to the early 17C; these two structures, separated by a sacristy,
form together a dark and oppressive whole, with gloomy baroque
frescoes.

Returning to the Námestie Osloboditelov at the foot of the citadel,
you should visit the large Art Nouveau building at No. 3, which was
built in 1874 as the County Hall, and today houses the *Regional
Gallery*, containing an important collection of 19C and 20C Slovakian
artists, including works by Jozef Kollár, Janko Alexy, Martin Benka,
Gustáv Mallý, Jozef Šturdík, Julius Bártfay and Rudolf Pribiš. There is
in addition a permanent exhibition of the paintings of František
Studený, who was born in 1911 in the nearby village of Nová Ves nad
Žitavou, and died in Bratislava in 1980; his paintings mainly comprise
expressively painted still-lifes and landscapes. Of the other old
buildings in the uninspiring lower town of Nitra, the most prominent is
the twin-towered 18C Franciscan Church, which stands below the
eastern slopes of the citadel, and has a richly frescoed interior belying
a drab façade. North of the citadel is the *Zobor Hill*, a pleasant
suburban district with vines growing on its upper slopes; there are
several popular wine-bars here, most notably the Zoborská pivnica on
Dobšinského.

After Nitra continue driving E along the E571, which, 16km beyond
Zlaté Moravce (25km), turns sharply N and follows the narrow,
wooded valley of the upper Hron, approaching ever closer to the
mountains of Central Slovakia. At Žarnovica, 62km NE of Nitra, leave
the E571 and turn right to **Banská Štiavnica** (21km), a small town lost
today among high wooded hills but with a fascinating and important
history, and with the potential to be one of the major tourist sights of
Slovakia.

The historical importance of Banská Štiavnica is due to its silver and gold mines,
which were exploited from at least the mid 13C onwards, when the place was
made a royal free town. The local mining activity reached a peak in the late 15C,
and then briefly declined in the following century; in 1526 there was organised
here what was probably the first mining strike in history. The Turkish capture of
Buda in 1541 led to further anxiety in the town, and to the construction of the so-
called 'New Castle' and other fortifications. The mining industry was revived in
the early 17C, and in 1627 the use of gunpowder in mines was first tried out here;
a further innovation occurred in 1732 with the use of a steam engine to pump out
water from the mines. By the 18C the town's population had grown to 24,000 (as
opposed to only 10,000 today), and in 1760 the world's first Mining Academy was
opened here. The seams were finally exhausted in the early 19C, and though a
forestry school was founded here in 1807, the town slowly stagnated.

Banská Štiavnica, a town little spoilt by modern development, is
spread meanderingly along the slopes of a hill, and its layout is at first
rather baffling. The place has a decayed character, but at present is

undergoing major restoration, the scaffolding throughout the old centre adding to the general confusion. The main square is the narrow and sloping Trojičné námestie (Trinity Square), at the bottom of which is the *St. Catherine's Church* (sv. Katerína), a hall-church dating back to 1488–91, and with wall-paintings of c 1500 inside; facing it is the belfried Town Hall, an originally Gothic building remodelled in the mid 18C. Half-way up the square, on the right-hand side, is the *Hellenbach House*, a 16C structure built originally as the seat of the Court of the Hungarian Mining Towns; it now houses a museum with geological finds from the mines. The adjacent building, also of the 16C, but with traces of murals on the outside, is an art gallery putting on temporary exhibitions. Further up the square is another museum, containing a display of Slovakian mining lamps. After walking back to the Town Hall and turning right you will soon reach the *Old Castle*, the present appearance of which is due largely to the work carried out between 1546 and 1559 in anticipation of Turkish attacks; the building, now undergoing major restoration, is destined as a museum devoted to the history of mining in Slovakia.

To reach the *New Castle*, you have to return to the Trojičné námestie, and head S in the direction of Štiavnické Bane, leaving the old town through the 18C Piarg Gate (Piargska brána). The New Castle, standing in trees high above the town, was built in 1564–71 as a guard tower against the Turks. This simple, harmonious structure, comprising an unadorned and white-washed central rectangular block buttressed by round towers at each corner, has been entirely modernised inside to house an interesting museum documenting the Turkish presence in Slovakia. The upper floor, dominated by a bewildering relief map of 17C Slovakia, has excellent views from its low windows down to the town. Further along the road to Štiavnické Bane is what is described as a *Miners' Skansen*, an area of 20 acres in which numerous old mining houses and other structures have been assembled, and where you can even visit a mine.

20km N of Banská Štiavnica you rejoin the E571, and head E along dual carriageway to **Zvolen** (see Route 28).

27   Bratislava to Žilina

Total distance 199km. Bratislava—E75 46km **Trnava**—33km **Piešt'any**—42km *Trenčín*—78km *Žilina*.

Drive NE of Bratislava on the dual carriageway of the E75, passing in succession on the city's outskirts a large group of chemical works and the lake of Zlaté Piesky, a popular place for bathing and boating. 46km beyond Bratislava is the exit for **Trnava**, a large lowland town which has played an important role in Slovakia's ecclesiastical history, and is sometimes referred to as the 'Slovak Rome'.

First mentioned in 1205, Trnava was made by Bela IV of Hungary in 1238 the first royal free town in Slovakia. Only four years later the place was devastated by Tartar hordes led by Peta Khan, the nephew of the infamous Ghengis. Further royal privileges helped the town rapidly to recover and to develop as a thriving commercial and agricultural centre. Following the Battle of Mohács in 1526 the Hungarian archbishopric at Esztergom was transferred here, thus making the town the main religious centre of Hungary, a position which it was to retain for over 200 years. In 1635 Archbishop Petr Pázmány founded here a Jesuit Academy, which was later raised to the status of university. The transference of this large and influential institution to Buda in 1777, and the return to Esztergom in 1820 of the archbishopric, led to the town's diminished importance in

Hungarian affairs. At the same time, however, the place emerged as a major centre of the Slovak national revival, for it was here, in 1792, that Anton Bernolák, the first codifier of the Slovak literary language, founded the first Slovakian Learned Society. From the mid 19C onwards the town was extensively industrialised. The Hungarian composer Zoltán Kodály (1882–1967) spent much of his childhood here, his father being the local stationmaster.

The description of Trnava as the 'Slovakian Rome' gives a misleading impression of the appearance of the town today, a sprawling and decayed place where the surviving old parts are unhappily combined with tasteless modern development. There are remains of the old fortifications, a parish church dating back to 1380, and a charmingly preserved theatre of 1838, though the main interest of the town is its 17C–18C university complex, which is dominated by the massive *University Church of St. John the Baptist*; the austere twin-towered façade of this church, built in 1637 to the designs of the Italian architect Pietro Spazzo, belies a richly stuccoed single-naved interior featuring a gilded altarpiece reaching right up to the ceiling. The other university buildings, like the nearby 16C Archbishop's Palace, are remarkable more for their scale than architectural elegance. Of the town's squares the least spoilt is the Svätoplukovo námestie, featuring an 18C Plague Column, and a group of crumbling 18C houses that once belonged to the clergy. 17km NW of Trnava is *Dolná Krupá*, a château built for the Brunswick family in 1793–94. Beethoven, a friend of the family, stayed frequently in the rococo house in the château grounds and composed here in 1801 his Moonlight Sonata; the château now belongs to the Slovak Union of Composers.

As you continue N from Trnava along the E75 you join the valley of the river Váh, which you follow all the way to Žilina. **Piešťany**, 33km N of Trnava, stands at the northernmost edge of the plains of SW Slovakia, within sight of wooded foothills. It is Slovakia's largest and most famous spa town.

The earliest mention of the thermal springs at Piešťany dates back to 1113, and the fame of the waters had spread widely by the 16C, when a number of distinguished doctors began recommending them for their curative properties, including Johann Grato de Craftheim—physician to the Emperors Ferdinand I, Maximilian II and Rudolph II—and Baccius Elpidianus, physician to Pope Sixtus V. The first detailed scientific analysis of the waters was carried out in 1642 by the Benešov doctor Adam Trajanus, and a further study was included in *Taxa Pharmaceutica Posoniensis* (1745) by the renowned Ján Justus Torkos from Bratislava. The Piešťany springs, which reach temperatures of 69C, are rich in gypsum and sulphur, and are much used by sufferers from rheumatism and other diseases of the joints; treatment today involves a combination of water and sulphuric mud baths.

The lively centre of Piešťany is situated on the W bank of the Váh, and features a number of imposing turn-of-the-century buildings, most notably the Hotel Slovan, and the adjoining former *Kursalon*; the latter, designed by Alpár in 1894 and boasting an immense central hall, includes today a museum documenting the history of the spa. North of these two buildings extends the riverside Gottwald Park, in which are to be found a cinema, an art gallery and an amphitheatre for musical and other performances. The main spa buildings are spread spaciously over a vast island park in the middle of the Váh, and can be reached by the Colonnade Bridge, just to the S of the Hotel Slovan. All' the old buildings of interest are concentrated in the southern half of the park, beginning with the Thermia Palace, a vast Art Nouveau structure set among gardens coloured by decoratively shaped flower beds; the beautiful interior features a staircase well with a stained-glass decoration of a peacock, and a restaurant with a painting executed in Nice in 1932 by the daughter of the great Alfons Mucha. Just to the E of this building are the Art Nouveau *Irma Baths* (1910–12), where a plaque to the physician Adam Trajanus can be seen, as well as a discreetly placed 19C bust of the Empress Elizabeth. Further E are the *Napoleon Baths*, a group of three neo-classical buildings dating back to 1816–21, and as such the oldest surviving structures in Piešťany; these elegant low buildings are used today by the severely handicapped visitors to the spa. Beyond them is the Sanatorium Pro Patria of 1916. North of here runs a wide and enormously long promenade, bordered on its eastern side by the large blocks of the modern spa. The spa is very popular today with Arab sheiks and their families, whose robes lend an exotic quality to the park; a cultural dimension is provided by the many modern sculptures that are shown here in competition every summer.

Beyond Piešťany, the Váh valley narrows and runs between increasingly wooded and hilly countryside, the range to the W of the river being that of the White Carpathians, the northern continuation of the Lesser Carpathians. At Nové Mesto nad Váhom, 20km N of Pieš tany, you should make a short detour to the ruined castle of *Čachtice*, which lies in the foothills of these mountains. To get there from Nové Mesto drive S for 5km to the village of Čachtice, where, next to the parish church, there is a fine Renaissance building housing a museum of local history and folklore; from the village take to Vaďovce road for 2km, and walk along a ridge for the remaining 1km (an alternative and longer walk is to climb up to the castle from the village of Višnové, directly below the ruins). The castle ruins occupy an isolated hill-top site of great beauty, with extensive views over forested hills and mountains; but many of the people who come here are attracted less by the site than by the place's ghoulish reputation.

This border fortress dating back to the mid 13C, acquired its notoriety in the late 17C, when it was the home of Countess Elizabeth Báthori. The countess believed that she would be able to preserve her beauty through bathing in the blood of virgin girls, and a number of her young domestic staff were apparently used for this purpose. On many other of her female servants she practised sadistic rites of a kind that the much-maligned Marquis de Sade might have fantasised about but would never have indulged in. In 1611, after killing a reputed 600 hundred women, she was finally brought to trial and sentenced to life imprisonment within her own castle; those with a taste for 'Dracula' stories have taken a particular interest in her story, and she was the subject of a book, Dracula was a Woman, by R. McNally. In 1708 the building was captured by soldiers of the rebellious Hungarian aristocrat Ferenc Rákoczi and burnt down.

The ruins of Čachtice, though extensive, retain few of the building's architectural features. Enthusiasts of military architecture will find more of interest at **Trenčín**, a riverside town 22km N of Nové Mesto, and dominated by the second largest castle in Slovakia.

Trenčín, which is marked on Ptolemy's map of the world of the 2C AD, was the site of a battle in AD 179 between the Romans led by Marcus Aurelius and the Germanic tribe of the Kvads; the Roman victory is recorded in what is one of Czechoslovakia's oldest Roman inscriptions, hewn on the castle rock. The castle, first documented in 1113, was a royal property until the end of the 13C, after which it came into the possession of Matúš Čák, who was the undisputed lord of practically the whole territory of present-day Slovakia, which he governed independently of the king; in 1302 Čák began remodelling the castle and constructing within it a new residential palace. After Čák's death in 1321, the castle became once again a royal possession, and rebuilding work was carried out here both by Louis the Great and Sigismund of Luxemburg. In the 16C the castle came into the possession first of the Zapolyas and then of the Thurzos, and the place was greatly strengthened by Italian engineers in preparation for Turkish attacks. From 1597 right up to 1835 the property belonged to the Illesházys, who between 1704–08 were responsible for the last building campaign here. The castle was destroyed by fire in 1790, and was only to be restored after 1956, following over 150 years of abandon. In the meantime the town which had grown up below developed into a prosperous industrial centre, known today for its clothes manufactures, and for having the bottling plant of one of Slovakia's finest plum brandies, made from yellow plums from the nearby village of Bošáca.

The town of Trenčín extends today on both sides of the Váh, but the original settlement is on the E bank of the river, below the wooded hill on which the castle rises. Most of the many 16C and 17C buildings that once made up the old town were destroyed in the course of 19C expansion, and the present-day centre, though pleasant and cheerful, has been greatly modernised. One of the main survivals is the 16C Town Gate, near which steps lead up through the wooded Brezina Park to the *castle*. Within the citadel is a heavily restored 16C church with a Renaissance portal; further up is a bastion dating back to 1540 (remodelled in the 17C) and now housing temporary exhibitions. At the very top of the hill stands the reconstructed castle itself, within which are the *Barbara's Palace* (built in c 1430 and containing fragments of early 15C wall-painting) and the Matthias Tower, which has an upper wooden gallery commanding magnificent views, and from which the complex defensive system of Trenčín is best appreciated.

North of Trenčín, the E75 runs between the White Carpathians and the Strážov Hills, and, after Považská Bystrica (44km), passes near two sites of great natural interest and beauty. 4km N of Považská, underneath the romantic ruins of a castle, turn right to drive through the nearby *Manín Gorge* (Maninska tiesňava), where giant cliffs of limestone fall down dramatically to a fast-flowing stream. Return to the E75, and you will find 9km further N another turning to the right, this one leading after 4km to the *Súlov Rocks*, a group of bizarrely shaped rock formations thrust above the forest. As the E75 nears *Žilina* (20km beyond the Súlov turning; see Route 29) the road follows the Váh as it turns sharply to the E and heads towards the range of the Little Fatra.

28 Trenčín to Banská Bystrica

Total distance 157km. Trenčín—13km **Trenčianské Teplice**—56km Prievidza—37km **Kremnica**—14km Žiar—17km **Zvolen**—20km **Banská Bystrica**.

Head N of Trenčín (see Route 27) on the E75, then turn right after 9km and follow the narrow Teplička valley into the Strazov Hills. **Trenčianské Teplice**, 4km E of the turning, is a delightful small spa town stretched out along the Teplička river, in between steep forested slopes.

The springs at Trenčianské Teplice, first mentioned in 1247, were described at length in 1580 by the chief physician of the Moravian County, Thomas Jordanus of Klausenburg. Fourteen years later the spa was purchased by the Hungarian nobleman, Count Stefan Illesházy, whose family were to own it for two and a half centuries. In 1835 it was bought from them by Juraj Sina, a Viennese financier and banker of Greek origin who had grown rich through the importing of indigo dye. A true entrepeneur, Sina soon turned the spa into a highly profitable enterprise, which it remained under the management of later members of his family. Up to the First World War, the place proved especially popular with the Hungarians, who found that it had a rather more down-to-earth character than most of the other celebrated spas of central Europe. The Hungarian writer Mór Jókai was a frequent guest and described the spa as the 'pearl of the Carpathian mountains'. Other famous visitors included the brothers Čapek, whose father worked here as a doctor. As with Piešťany, the place specialises in diseases of the limbs, and has a lively cultural life, including an annual Musical Festival which has been held here since 1938.

The charm of Trenčianské Teplice lies both in its setting and in its cheerful, informal and exceptionally friendly character, which makes the place so different to most Bohemian spas, over which an atmosphere of gloom and decay seems perpetually to hang. The architecture is modern and largely uninteresting, but there is one jewel which no one interested in the history of 19C orientalism should miss. This, the **Hammam Bath**, is situated right in the centre of the spa, next to the Sanatorium Sina.

In 1885 the then owner of the spa, Iphigenia de Castries—the grand-daughter of Juraj Sina—visited the World Exhibition in Paris and was most taken by a model of a Turkish Bath (or Hammam) which had been built in Egypt for the Egyptian viceroy Izmail; the court architect responsible for the building had, ironically, not been an Arab but a Czech, František Schmoranz (1845–92), who came from Prague and was later to be regarded as one of the leading central European practitioners of the neo-Moorish style. Iphigenia subsequently set off for Egypt to ask the viceroy for permission to build such a Hammam at Trenčianské Teplice; she returned not only with the permission but also with Schmoranz, who began work on the Hammam immediately and completed it by 1888. The Bath attracted the wealthiest and most aristocratic elements at Trenčianské Teplice, including the Countess Paulina Metternich, grand-daughter of the Austrian chancellor, and a friend and confidante of Iphigenia.

The Hammam Bath, used today not as a bath but as a place for relaxing in afterwards and being given massages and mud packs, has a magnificent blue-tiled interior suggestively illuminated by rose-windows in the side walls and a series of glazed openings in the vaulting; built on two storeys, it has an arcade of sandstone columns on the lower floor and, above this, a traceried gallery. The Sanatorium Sina, to which the Hammam is connected, was built in the 1870s following the discovery of the warmest of all the spa's thermal springs (40.2°C); a special feature of this sanatorium is that it is one of only two places in the world where patients are treated directly in the spring. North of the Hammam Bath extends a long riverside park, where there is a path climbing up to the left to the so-called *Green Frog* (Zelená žaba), a popular swimming-pool in a sylvan setting.

From Trenčianské Teplice head SE through forest to the village of Dežerice (20km), where you will join Road 50. Turn left and follow the road for 6km to Bánovce nad Bebravou, which was the home town of Jozef Tiso, a priest and educationalist who served during the Second World War as President of independent Slovakia; this fascist cleric, who was responsible for the deportation of more than 60,000 Jews from Slovakia, was later executed as a war criminal.

In 1990 a national outcry was caused when members of the Slovak Christian Democratic Party decided to honour Tiso's memory in Bánovce with a plaque placed above the Catholic teacher training college which he had founded here in 1934 (the institution was the first in Slovakia). The memorial was soon splattered with paint, and was heavily condemned both by President Václav Havel and the Mayor of the town, Jan Turčan, who ordered it to be removed until 'historians have decided what sort of man Tiso was'.

Beyond Bánovce turn left again, and follow the side road to Uhrovec, a further 7km. The village of *Uhrovec*, is the birthplace of Ľudovít Štúr (1815–56), one of the leading figures in the Slovak national revival; the son of a Protestant teacher, Štúr later codified the Slovak grammar and became the only Slovak in the Hungarian Parliament after being elected deputy for the town of Zvolen in 1847. The fine mansion of 1613 where Štúr was born is now a small museum devoted to the Slovak National Uprising.

Another distinguished native of Uhrovec, who presumably will shortly be commemorated here, is Alexander Dubček. One of the earliest advocates of *perestroika*, and the leader of Czechoslovakia during the heady months leading up to the Russian invasion of 1968, Dubček was subsequently demoted to being Deputy Director of State Forests, and has lived since then in Bratislava; awarded an Honorary Doctorate at Bologna University in 1980, he was finally able to return in triumph to Prague in November 1989, appearing in public with Václav Havel to declare the imminent victory of the 'Velvet Revolution'.

The forest road S from Uhrovec to Dol. Vestenice passes after a few kilometres *Jankov Vršok*, a large memorial dedicated to the Slovakian partisans who, in 1943–44, took refuge in the surrounding forests, where they gathered arms; in January 1945 they were rounded up by the Germans, who afterwards set fire to the forests to burn alive those that who had remained there. The particular partisan group which was based at Jankov Vršok was named after the Hussite leader Jan Žižka. The main part of the memorial here comprises a large amphitheatre where on 29 August each year commemorative festivities are put on, including the occasional folkloric event; above the amphitheatre rises a great column commanding an extensive panorama of the surrounding wooded hills.

Rejoining Road 50 at Dol. Vestenice (7km), continue E along this to Prievidza (21km), and then turn left in the centre of the town to **Bojnice**, which lies just beyond the town's north-western suburbs. This small spa town is dominated by the picturesque profile of its castle, a great battlemented and pinnacled structure looming above a forested park.

Dating back to c 1300, the castle of Bojnice was first owned by Matúš Čák of Trenčín, who kept it until 1321. From the 16C to the mid 17C it belonged to the Thurzo family, who altered the building in a Renaissance style. After coming in 1649 into the possession of the Pálffys, the residential part was extended and the fortifications strengthened. The castle withstood the Turks but was briefly held by Count Rákóczi at the beginning of the 18C. The building acquired its present appearance at the end of the 19C, when Count Ján Pálffy (1829–1908) called in the French architect J. Hubert, who had the whole place remodelled in a style inspired by the châteaux of the Loire.

Parts of the outer 14C ramparts have survived, but the essential look of the building is a pseudo-medieval one of the turn of the century. The tour of the interior is enjoyable largely on account of the eccentric old man who takes you round, but the place itself has little of intrinsic value. The heavy rooms are sparsely furnished and contain as their principal interest some badly labelled minor paintings on loan from Slovakian galleries, including the East Slovak gallery at Košice. The most impressive of the rooms is the *Gold Room*, which has a gilded coffered ceiling copied after one in the Accademia in Venice; in its centre is a portrait of Ján Pálffy by Francesco Silvestri. Also of interest is the *Chapel*, which was built in the mid 17C out of one of the bastion towers, and has a baroque stuccoed and frescoed ceiling.

Return to Prievidza and continue along Road 50 for a further 24km; shortly after Nová Lehota, take the turning to the left marked Janova Lehota and **Kremnica** (15km). Kremnica, one of the most beautiful small towns in Slovakia, owes its former importance to the gold and silver deposits that were once to be found in the surrounding hills.

Silver was mined in Kremnica as far back as the 11C, and gold from the 13C. Awarded royal privileges in 1328, the by now prosperous community of Kremnica began minting silver coins the following year and gold ones in 1335. Commemorative coins and medals are still minted here, though the town has been in gradual decline since its heyday in the 15C and 16C.

Of the fortifications built in the 15C to guard the town's wealth, there are extensive remains, including, just below the main square, the town's principal gate. Around the long, green and sloping main square are arranged a number of fine houses from the 15C and 16C, including at No. 7 a building now housing a *Museum* documenting the history of the town's mint; the mint itself, a 19C building of 14C origin, is at Nos 24/25. In the middle of the square's grassy slopes is an elaborate baroque *Plague Column*, executed by M. Vogerle and D. Stanetti in 1765–72. Rising high above the square is the late 15C parish church, which forms the centrepiece of an excellently preserved **fortified complex** where there is also to be found the Romanesque rotunda of St. Andrew; this whole walled area is unfortunately closed at present for restoration, which will probably not be completed until well into the 1990s.

Drive S of Kremnica on Road 65 and you will reach after 14km the E571, at a point just below the impressive hill-top ruins of *Šašov Castle*, which was first mentioned in 1235 and was abandoned at the beginning of the 18C; the parts that are still standing include a section built in 1424, when the castle was a royal one belonging to the Emperor Sigismund. The town of *Žiar*, 2km to the W, has a palace which was once a residence of the Bishops of Banská Bystrica; rebuilt in 1631 on medieval foundations, it was heavily altered in the 19C and 20C, and is now a school containing a memorial room to Stefan Moyses, the first chairman of the Slovak cultural association, Matica Slovenská (see Martin; Route 29).

17km E of Šašov on the E571 is the town of *Zvolen*, with extensive timber industries and a large and severe **Castle** rising above above the river Hron. Built originally in 1370–82 for Louis the Great, this four-winged block was strengthened and remodelled after 1541 in preparation for Turkish attacks; the building today houses an Art Gallery largely composed of a deposit from the Slovak National Gallery at Bratislava. On the ground floor are copies of the figures from the famous altarpiece of Master Pavol at Levoča, and some murals of c 1452 taken from a church in Zvolen. The first floor is entirely taken over by the Slovak National Gallery's foreign school holdings. Among the Italian 15C and 16C paintings are works by Bonifacio Veronese, Francesco Rondani, and Domenico Beccafumi (Christ in Limbo); the Italian 17C and 18C paintings include a version of Annibale Carracci's Laton Defending His Children (a finer version of this is at Kroměříž), The Taking of Christ by Cecco del Caravaggio, and a Baptism of Christ by Giulio Cesare Procaccini. The German holdings date from the 16C to 18C and feature an interesting Christ before Pilate by an anonymous Westphalian Master of the early 16C. Of the Dutch and Flemish Schools there are still-lifes by Joachim Beukelaer, a Head of Christ from the circle of Albrecht Bouts, a Judgement of Solomon by Nicolaus Knupfer, and a beautiful River Landscape by Salomon van Ruysdael. A great surprise are the English holdings, which boast a portrait by Hogarth of Miss Collot, an excellent double portrait by Raeburn, and a large oil by Sir Godfrey Kneller showing Michael and John Richardson at the Battle of Belgrade. One of the rooms on the first floor contains also the finest survival of the castle's baroque decorations—a panelled ceiling of 1700 adorned with quaintly provincial paintings of famous kings from ancient times up to the 17C. The second floor is taken up by 20C Slovakian medals and small sculptures, including works by Ján Koniarek, Ladislav Majerský, Rudolf Pribiš and František Gibala.

A dual carriageway section of Road 66 heads N from Zvolen along the Hron to **Banská Bystrica**, the capital of Central Slovakia.

Another of the former mining towns of Slovakia, Banská Bystrica was made a
Free Royal Mining Town in 1255. Silver had been mined here since at least the
11C, but from the 14C to the 16C, the town specialised in the mining of copper,
and indeed briefly became the leading copper-producing centre of Europe. In
1525 the local miners went on strike, and for a while occupied the town;
economic decline set in at the end of the following century. An important centre
of Communism between the First and Second World Wars, Banská Bystrica
later played a critical role in the Slovak National Uprising; for two months after
the Uprising, which broke out on 29 August 1944, the town was the seat of the
Slovak National Council, and there were numerous broadcasts transmitted from
here by members of the resistance. The Nazis occupied the town on 27 October
1944, and they were followed by Soviet troops on 26 March 1945. The town has
been extensively industrialised since the last war, and is today a centre of the
timber, engineering, textile and cement industries.

Banská Bystrica, with its forested, mountainous surroundings, and
views to the N of the Large Fatra and Low Tatras, often inspires
nostalgic memories among older Slovaks, who remember the town
for its clean, bracing air and colourful markets. The recent construction on the eastern outskirts of the town of a large cement works
has rather diminished this idyllic vision, yet the place still retains a
character which is both lively and pleasantly old-fashioned. The
historic centre of the town lies off the námestie Červenej armády, and
comprises a group of buildings which once formed the town's
fortified inner citadel. Of the actual fortifications, there remains today
only three bastions and the *main gate tower*, a 15C structure to which
a baroque steeple has been added. At the centre of the citadel is the
parish church, which is dedicated to St. Barbara (sv. Barbora), the
patron saint of miners. This originally Romanesque structure was
extended and remodelled in 1478–1516, and features on its exterior a

sculptural group attributed to Master Pavol of Levoča, who seems also to have been responsible for the altarpiece of St. Barbara, in one of the building's side chapels; on the high altar there was once a celebrated medieval painting of the Death of the Virgin, but this was destroyed by fire in 1761. To the N of the church are the so-called Parish Bastions and a cluster of structures composed of the Miners' and Pisárska Bastions, the late Gothic *Matthias House*, and the small *Church of the Holy Rood*, which dates back to 1479. South of the parish church, and adjoining the main gate tower, is the former *Town Hall*, the southern and eastern walls of which were once attached to the fortifications. Built in 1564–65, but restored and altered at various times since the 18C, this essentially Renaissance structure features an arcaded loggia on its northern and western walls. After suffering fire damage in 1761, it no longer functioned as a Town Hall, and became a school after 1803; between 1945 and 1970 it was the home of the museum documenting the Slovak national Uprising. Since 1970 it has been the seat of the *Regional Art Gallery*, which puts on temporary exhibitions mainly culled from a large permanent collection of 20C Slovak artists, including works by Martin Benka, Miloš Bazovsky, Mikuláš Galanda, Ľudovít Fulla, Zolo Palugyay, Jozef Kollár, Július Szabó, and Fraňo Štefunko. Also represented here is the town's principal native artist, Dominik Skutecký (1849–1921), who after a long period spent in Vienna, Venice and elsewhere in Europe, settled permanently in Banská Bystrica in the 1880s, and painted numerous local scenes, including a series of interiors of blacksmith workshops and copper kilns. Skutecký's main work in the Gallery is his detailed and delightful Market Scene at Banská Bystrica, featuring a well-to-do woman and her daughter set against a background of colourfully dressed peasants.

The market which Skutecký painted used to take place on the square adjoining the western side of the námestie Červenej armády, the námestie SNP. This long and cheerful square, the main square of Banská Bystrica, features a number of buildings from the 16C to the 18C, including, to your left as you enter the square, the late baroque Jesuit Church, which is glimpsed in the corner of Skutecký's painting. Further down on the left-hand side of the square is the 16C Thurz's House, which now houses the Central Slovak Ethnographical Museum; opposite it are the 16C *Benicky's House* (now a cultural centre) and the former *Bishop's Palace*, a baroque structure of the 18C. Heading S on the street adjoining the Jesuit Church (Š. Moyzesa), and then taking the first turning to the left you will come to the *Memorial and Museum of the Slovak National Uprising* (Múzeum SNP). This boldly modern structure built by Dušan Kuzma in 1969 takes the form of two large concrete segments, the appearance and meaning of which have inspired much frivolous comment. The architect's own explanation of the monument—which most closely resembles the bun of a hamburger—is that the dividing line between the two segments symbolises the great breakthrough which the Slovak National Uprising represented in the history of the Slovak People. In the middle of the monument is an eternal flame marking the tomb of an unknown soldier, while within the segments is an excitingly arranged museum which includes a reconstructed guerrilla bunker and a Soviet IL-2 aeroplane. The monument stands in a large formal park which comes down to the river Hron: just to the S of the monument are the scanty remains of the town's outer walls, while at the eastern end of the park is the unprepossessing modern block of the Hotel Lux.

*The controversial hamburger-shaped Museum of the
Slovak National Uprising, Banská Bystrica*

Banská Bystrica is a convenient base for visiting the *Large Fatra*
(Velká Fatra) and *Low Tatra* (Nízké Tatry). Running between these
two ranges, and following for a while a densely forested gorge, is the
beautiful E77, which connects the town with *Ružomberok* (53km; see
Route 29). 7km N of Banská Bystrica along the E77 is a road to the left
crossing the southern end of the Large Fatra; above it twists the
railway line to *Martin* (see Route 29), one of the more spectacular
stretches of railway to be found in Slovakia. Continuing N along the
E77 for a further 7km take the turning to the left just before Staré
Hory and drive to Turecká (2km). From here there is a chairlift up to
Mount Krížna (1574m); at the top an exhilarating hour's walk can be
made over flower-filled meadows to the summit of Ostredok (1592m),
the highest peak in the Large Fatra. The views the whole length of
the walk are quite breathtaking, and, on clear days, you can even see
as far as the snow-capped peaks of the High Tatras. 10km N of Staré
Hory along the E77 is *Donovaly*, a small but popular summer and
winter resort, renowned for its wealth of flowers during the spring.

29 Ostrava to Liptovský Mikuláš

Total distance 194km. Ostrava—E75 31km Český Těšín—48km
Čadca—30km Žilina—E50 25km *Martin*—39km *Ružomberok*—
21km *Liptovský Mikuláš*.

From *Ostrava* (see Route 22) drive SE through heavily built-up
landscape, passing quickly through the Polish border town of Český

Těšín (31km), and entering shortly afterwards a valley of the wooded Beskydy; the Slovakian border is just beyond the village of Mosty u Jablunkova, 40km SE of Český Těšín. The first Slovakian town which you come to is Čadca (a further 8km), a small and uninteresting centre of the textile and timber industries. Beyond Čadca, however, the landscape greatly improves, and you drive through a short stretch of beautiful forest; the first turning to the left will take you to Oščadnica, a most pleasant small and little-known skiing resort lost in the woods. Further small industries await you as you continue S along the E75 to **Žilina** (23km S of the turning), a town of largely modern appearance, but attractively situated on the river Váh and within sight of the Little Fatra (Malá Fatra).

A Slav settlement from the 5C onwards, Žilina was first mentioned in 1208, and became a town in 1312. Though the town was occupied by the Hussites from 1429–34, and devastated by fire in 1521, its prosperity was to grow right up to the end of the 16C, when some 2000 drapery workers were employed here. Repeatedly plundered and pillaged during the Thirty Years' War, Žilina went into a long decline from which it was to be rescued only after the coming of the railway in the late 19C. Extensively industrialised since then, Žilina is today one of the most important railway junctions in Czechoslovakia, and a centre of forestry and the chemical and engineering industries. Discovered here this century was the oldest surviving manuscript in the Slovakian language: known as the Žilina Book, and dating back to 1370, it is a statement of the rights of citizens belonging to a free town.

Just before crossing the Váh and visiting the centre of Žilina, it is worth stopping off at the northern suburb of *Budatín*, where there is a 16C castle standing in extensive parkland and housing the charming *Považká Museum*. The interest of this museum lies in its collection of over a thousand artefacts such as baskets and naive figurines made in wire and tin by the numerous tinker craftsmen who originated from the Žilina area, in particular from the villages of Dlhé Pole and Velké Rovné; these craftsmen once peddled their wares not only throughout Europe, but also in America and even Australia.

Žilina was badly damaged during the Second World War, and its few remaining buildings are concentrated around the arcaded Dukla námestie, which has a number of houses dating back to the 16C. Tolstoy, on visiting this square at the end of the last century, is said to have exclaimed, 'Look, Hungarian Nuremberg', though it is unlikely that visitors today will have such a reaction: heavily restored, and arranged around a small garden adorned with a modern fountain, this is a pleasant but unremarkable space. Nearby is the parish church of the Holy Trinity, a building of medieval origin, but reconstructed on numerous occasions. In the south-eastern suburb of Zavodie is the late Romanesque church of *St. Stephen* (take a No. 1 bus from the centre), which has traces of medieval wall-painting.

Though architecturally uninspiring, Žilina is popular as a holiday resort and makes a good base for EXCURSIONS into the Little Fatra. One such excursion is to head S down the narrow Rajčanka valley, which runs parallel to the eastern slopes of this modest range, through a beautiful landscape of meadows bordered by forests. Follow the main road to Prievidza for 7km, then take the road to the right marked Liet. Svinná. After 2km you will see rising above a densely wooded outcrop to your right one of the largest and most impressive of Slovakia's many ruined castles. The castle of *Lietava*, a strenuous 20 minutes' walk from the road, was built between the late 14C and early 15C, and abandoned in the 18C. Its unprotected walls, still crumbling into the forest, create a most picturesque silhouette, and blend in with the surrounding pines and rock pinnacles in a way which would have greatly appealed to travellers of the Romantic generation; there are wonderful views of the valley. Returning to the Prievidza road continue S for a further 26km, then turn right shortly after Fačkov on to the road which follows the Rajčanka river to Čičmany, a further 7km. The small village of **Čičmany** is lined with some of the most famous surviving examples of Slovakian folk architecture. A village living traditionally off the raising of sheep and cattle, Čičmany was first mentioned in 1272, and later acquired a reputation for the making of felt slippers. A fire destroyed the lower half of the village in 1921, but the place was later lovingly restored by the Institute of Ethnography. The village's attractive wooden houses, featuring galleries and wide eaves, are remarkable above all for their white painted decoration: imitative of lacework, this style of decoration dates back to the 18C, and is unique to Slovakia. One of the houses (*Radenov Dom*) is now a small and charming ethnographical museum, featuring a taped commentary in English about the history of the village, and examples of local crafts, most notably some of the village's celebrated folk costumes, which are characterised by their very sophisticated design and predominance of white.

Wooden house in Čičmany, with the white-painted decoration unique to this village

Another EXCURSION from Žilina is to Terchová and the Little Fatra National Park, which extends over the northern half of the range. Return to the northern suburb of Budatín, and head E along the Váh to Varín (12km), where the road turns NE to follow the narrow Varínka river to *Terchová* (a further 15km). Terchová is famous as the birthplace of one of Slovakia's greatest heroes, Juraj Jánošík, commemorated here by a shining memorial in chrome rising prominently on a hill to the S of the village.

Born in 1688, Jánošík took part in the uprising against the Habsburgs led by Ferenc Rákóczi in 1707–11. He is best known, however, as a bandit chief, in which capacity he earned a reputation as the Slovakian Robin Hood. According to popular tradition he embarked on a life of virtuous crime as an act of vengeance following the death of his parents. Returning to Terchová too late to see his dying mother, he had found his father to be mortally ill instead; the father had been beaten up by his employers for taking time off work to go to his wife's funeral. Arrested in March 1713 at the nearby town of Liptovský Mikuláš, Jánošík was tortured, but refused to reveal the whereabouts of his fellow bandits. Offered a royal pardon on the condition of joining the imperial army, Jánošík refused, saying, 'now that you have roasted me, you can eat me.' He was condemned to be strung up by a hook attached to one of his ribs, and took over a day to die.

From Terchová head S, passing below the statue of Jánošík, and driving though the narrow Tiesňavy Pass. At the southern end of the pass is a landscape of dramatically projecting rocks, at the other end of which you come to an enchanting, little-spoilt valley which is popular both as a summer and winter resort. The first turning to the left will take you after a couple of kilometres to the isolated Hotel Boboty, the perfect base from which to explore the Little Fatra, and with good views towards the highest mountain of the range, Velký Kriváň (1709m). Back on the Tiesnavy road continue S for another 2km to Vrátna Chalet, where the road comes to an end and from where there is a chair-lift taking you up to to Snilovské Sadlo (1520m), which is on the saddle of the Little Fatra range, within a short walking distance of the summit of Kriváň. Returning to Terchová you can either go back from here to Žilina or else turn right and drive for 10km to the Zázrivka river, where there is a road to your right which follows the river all the way to the Orava Valley (a further 13km; see below).

Back at Žilina, head E on Road 18, skirting the southern banks of the Váh. After 11km you will come to the ruined castle of *Strečno*, which rises up on a mound against a dark green background of forested mountains. Begun in the 14C on the foundations of an earlier structure, the castle has a 14C to 15C chapel, and 16C outer fortifications; burnt out in 1678 to prevent its being used by rebels in an uprising against the Habsburg emperor, it has been slowly restored since 1977. Facing the castle, directly above the river, is a plinth of impressively stark simplicity commemorating the French partisans who took part in the Slovak Uprising between September and October 1944. Immediately beyond Strečno, the Váh cuts right through the middle of the Little Fatra Range, creating a beautiful wooded gorge. Rising above trees on the other side of the river to Road 18, and virtually inaccessible, are the romantic ruins of *Starý-hrad Castle*, the oldest part of which is a 13C tower. Once through the gorge, Road 18 comes out into a wide fertile valley known sometimes as the Turiec Garden, which separates the Little Fatra from the Large or Velká Fatra. The main settlement of the valley is *Martin* (14km from Strečno), a town of uninspiring modern appearance, but with an attractive position and a central importance in the history of the Slovakian nation.

Though dating back to 1340, Martin was an insignificant, provincial town until 1861, when there took place here a meeting at which a call was made for an autonomous Slovak nation, with Slovak rather than Hungarian as the official language. Two years later, on 4 August 1863, there came into being the Matica slovenská, an institution dedicated to the promotion of Slovakian culture and education. In 1867 the first Slovak school was founded at Kláštor pod Znievom, just to the S of Martin, and in 1906 work was begun at Martin itself on the

Slovak National Museum. The main branch of the museum has now moved to Bratislava, but Martin—today a centre of forestry and engineering—still retains its cultural importance. The Matica slovenská continues to function, and is now divided between three buildings, within which are the Slovak National Library and institutions dedicated to scientific and literary research.

Among the distinguished natives of Martin is the painter of colourful Slovakian landscapes and rural scenes, Martin Benka (1896–1967).

Martin is a town of interest more for its history than its architecture, its principal monument being the pompous neo-baroque building constituting the first seat of the Matica slovenská (1865). The original National Slovak Museum, a neo-classical building of 1906–07, is now a museum devoted to the natural history of the Turiec region. The new building of the *National Slovak Museum* (1928–32) is now devoted exclusively to the ethnography of Slovakia, and has an extensive collection of folk objects and costumes. A branch of the museum is situated in the house and studio of the painter *Martin Benka*, and displays a large group of this artist's cheerful works.

Just to the S of Martin, off Road 65 to Žiar, an important *Skansen* is being assembled, with folk buildings taken from villages throughout Slovakia. Due W of the town is a tiny road which winds its way up the slopes of the Little Fatra to the modest skiing resort of *Martinské Hole*, which is renowned for its snow conditions, and lies just underneath the peak of Veľka lúka (1476m).

East of Martin Road 18 continues to follow the Váh river, skirting the northern slopes of the Large Fatra. After 20km you reach the confluence of the Váh and Orava, and can make an interesting detour N up the latter valley, following Road 59, which leads eventually into Poland. The modern, unprepossessing town of *Dolný Kubín* (17km N along Road 59) is the administrative capital of the Orava region and is associated with two leading figures of Slovak culture, the composer Janko Matuška, who wrote under the name of Hviezdoslav (1849–1921). The latter, born at the nearby village of Vyšný Kubín, is commemorated at Dolný Kubín—where he spent most of his life—by a memorial museum attached to the town's important library. 11km further N on Road 59 is one of Slovakia's most photographed buildings, **Orava Castle**, perched on a rocky outcrop above the wooded banks of the Orava in a way such as you would only expect to find in the illustrations of Walt Disney. First mentioned in 1267, and enlarged and remodelled at various times between the 13C and 17C centuries, it changed hands repeatedly, and was owned at one stage by the son of Matthias Corvinus. Destroyed by fire in 1800, it was heavily restored between 1813 and 1834 and again in the 1970s. The building has a generally pseudo-medieval character, and is best seen from below, where you can enjoy to the full its picturesque profile and spectacular position. The dreary interior has collections of armour and local history.

Continue along Road 59 to Podbiel and then turn right along the tiny Studený river to Zuberec (15km). 2km due E of Zuberec, in the direction of the Roháče Mountains, is the *Orava Village Museum*, a skansen founded in 1965 and featuring a collection of traditional wooden buildings set in the middle of a dense pine forest. Returning to Podbiel and continuing N along Road 59, you will come after 9km to *Tvrdošín*, where—in the local cemetery on the northern outskirts of this small town—there survives in its original setting a wooden church dating back to the late 15C. A narrow road NW of Tvrdošín leads to a large lake which was formed after the construction of a dam over the Orava in 1954. Five villages were destroyed during the creation of the lake, though the mid-18C parish church of the former village of Slanická survives, standing in isolation on an island which can be reached by boat from Slanická osada (10km NW of Tvrdošín); the church has an amusing collection of Slovak folk painting and sculpture. The lake itself is a popular summer resort, and is much used for swimming and water sports.

Returning to the Váh and Road 18, continue heading E towards Ružomberok, passing after 7km *Ľubochňa*, a small and old-fashioned health resort on the wooded lower slopes of the Large Fatra. This pleasant and bosky spot was, incongruously, the place where the Slovakian Communist Party was founded on 16 January 1921; the building where the critical meeting took place is a half-timbered turn-of-the-century structure known as *Kollárov Dom*. The small industrial town of *Ružomberok*, 12km further E, is of interest largely for its small gallery devoted to the paintings of one of the leading Slovak painters of this century, Ľudovít Fulla, who lived and worked in the town. East of Ružomberok along Road 18 you enter a wide valley, offering you your first view, to the S, of the Low Tatras (Nízké Tatry), Czechoslovakia's second highest mountain range. As you near *Liptovský Mikuláš* (21km; see Route 30), the road turns into a dual carriageway, and you pass to your left a large reservoir; in the far distance you can make out on clear days the snow-capped peaks of the High Tatras (Vysoké Tatry).

30 Liptovský Mikuláš to Prešov

Total distance 157km. *Liptovský Mikuláš*—44km **Štrbské Pleso**—17km **Starý Smokovec**—12km *Poprad*—26km **Levoča**—15km **Spišské Podhradie**—43km **Prešov**.

Liptovský Mikuláš is a small industrial town with few surviving old buildings. These few are centred around the tranquil main square, most notably the much restored church of St. Nicholas (sv. Mikuláš), a Gothic structure of Romanesque origin; it was on this same square that the bandit chief Juraj Jánošík met his gruesome end in 1713, condemned to be hung from one of his ribs. By far the most interesting building in the district is to be found at the hamlet of **Svätý Kríž**, 7km SW of the town (take the road marked Ľubeľa, and then turn left after 6km). Standing in isolation surrounded by pines is a large wooden **Evangelical Church**, which was built originally outside the village of Paludza to the W of Liptovský Mikuláš and then transferred here between 1979 and 1982 following the creation of the large reservoir in that area.

In 1681 the Austrian emperor Leopold passed a law which allowed Protestants to build churches in Catholic lands but according to strict conditions. The church had to be in open countryside, have no belfy, have its main door turned away from the township, be built within the course of a year, and so on. The church now at Svätý Kríž was built initially in the 1680s, but later proved too small for its needs, and was replaced by a much larger structure in 1774. In 1782 the Emperor Joseph II issued an edict of tolerance which did away with most of the conditions previously imposed upon the Protestants; the belfry at Svätý Kríž dates from later that year.

The interior of the church (if closed ask at the nearby pastor's house) comprises a vast galleried space covered with a depressed barrel vault, and apparently held together by nót a single nail; such is the

The wooden Evangelical church at Svätý Kríž

size of the building that a reputed 6000 people gathered here for the reopening ceremony in 1982. The organ, the altars, the pulpit and the choir are all from the original 17C church; the incongruous chandeliers meanwhile are from Murano, and date back to the late 18C.

Though of little intrinsic interest Liptovský Mikuláš does have the advantage of a superb position, in between the Low and High Tatras. The road due S of the town climbs after 7km into the most beautiful valley of the Low Tatras, Demänovská dolina, the entrance to which is marked by a landscape of pines and jagged limestone formations. Shortly after entering the valley you come to the *Demänovská ľadová jaskyňa*, or Ice Cave, which is reached by a chair-lift. Discovered in August 1921, it features extensive ice formations alongside the stalagmites and stalactites (be sure to bring warm clothing); one of the early visitors was the composer Janáček, who once spent a night here listening to the 'music' of the water dripping. Another popular and larger cave, the *Demänovská jaskyňa slobody* (Freedom Cave), is situated 4km further up the road. The road ends at the small summer and winter resort of Jasná, where there are a number of hotels and chalets shrouded by the forest, most notably the Hotel Liptov (within the woods surrounding the hotel is an especially attractive Koliba; see p 334). From Jasná you can ascend by chair-lift to Chopok (2024m), on the bleak and exhilarating ridge of the Low Tatras. Energetic walks, with magnificent views towards the High Tatras, can be made W along the ridge to Chabenec (1955m) or E to the summit of the highest peak of the range, Ďumbier (2043m). Alternatively you can descend by cable car to the resort at Srdiečko on the southern slopes of the range, and join from there the road which heads S to Banská Bystrica (see Route 28).

Returning to Liptovský Mikuláš, head E on the E50. After 17km,

there is a forest road to the right (Road 72) which crosses the Low
Tatras by way of the *Čertovica Pass*, from the top of which you can
take a path to the left for a superb panorama over pines towards the
snow-capped High Tatras. To visit the latter—the most spectacular
area of natural beauty in Czechoslovakia—continue heading E along
the E50 to Tatranská Štrba (35km E of Liptový Mikuláš), from where
there is a road to the left which climbs up to the popular resort of
Štrbské Pleso (9km). A rack railway constructed in 1896 also connects the two places, while a single-track electric railway—the oldest
in Czechoslovakia and in operation from before the First World
War—runs from Štrbské Pleso to Poprad by way of the principal
resorts of the High Tatras.

The High Tatras, the highest mountain range in Czechoslovakia, are composed
largely of granite, though the eastern peaks known as the Belianské Tatry are of
limestone. The mountains, featuring a main ridge 26km long, are fissured by 35
valleys concealing about a hundred mountain lakes. Forests, mainly of spruce,
extend up to around 1800m, after which there are Alpine meadows with rich
and varied high-mountain flora (especially in the Belianské Tatry, which has a
number of protected areas inaccessible to tourists during the summer months).
The last belt of vegetation (above 2300m) comprises isolated growths of grasses
and plants growing in rock crevices and hollows; the highest peaks are covered
in snow throughout the year. Among the wildlife are chamonix, lynx, wild cat,
marmot, wolves, bear, rock eagle and grouse.
    One of the first travellers to explore the Tatras was David Frölich, a student
from nearby Kežmarok who came to the area in 1615. But it was not until the
following century that tourism began slowly to develop here. Among the 18C
visitors was the Bratislava scholar Matej Bél, who, together with Jonas Andreas
Czirbesz, made on August 4 1772 the first recorded climb up the fourth highest
of the Tatra peaks, Kriváň (2494m); soon afterwards Kriváň was to become a
symbol of the Slovak Nationalist Movement, the theme of numerous Slovak
poems, and the object of a nationalist pilgrimage, first undertaken in 1841. An
extensive scientific study of the area was carried out in 1793 by the Edinburgh
naturalist Robert Townson, who was also the first to climb the Tatras' second
highest peak, Lomnický štit (2632m); an account of his experiences was
published in his Travels in Hungary in the year 1793 (London, 1794). Despite all
this early interest in the Tatras it was only with the creation of the Košice-
Bohumín railway line in 1871 that the founding of the first resorts became a
real possibility. The earliest to be established was Starý Smokovec, followed
shortly afterwards by Štrbské Pleso. The clientele was at first exclusively
aristocratic, but today the resorts are the most popular in Czechoslovakia, and
attract great crowds of Germans.

The summer and winter resort of **Štrbské Pleso**, the highest in the
Tatras, developed around its lake, on the shores of which there had
grown up by 1879 a restaurant, a café and a bath-house; in the 1970s
a spa was established here, which is particularly renowned for the
treatment of chest and breathing complaints, and has a special
sanatorium devoted to children with asthma. Most of the buildings at
Štrbské Pleso are modern and concentrated on the lake's southern
shores. The rest of the lake is lined entirely by trees, and, from the
pleasant path which surrounds it, there are much-photographed
views of snow-capped peaks rising above forests. Behind the Hotel
Patria—the main building on the northern side of the lake, and the
one distracting element in the mountainous backcloth—is a path
leading to a large ski-jump and the neighbouring Hotel FIS, both
built in connection with a world skiing championship which was held
here in 1970; in front of the Hotel FIS are three pines of a type
endemic to the region, the *Pinus limba*. Near the hotel is a chair-lift
which will take you up to the Solisko chalet, where refreshments are
available; from here you can ascend either straight to the summit of
Predné Solisko (2093m) or take the blue-marked path to the left,
which will take you into the haunting Furkostká valley, where there

are three lakes. Another excursion from the Hotel FIS is to head N along the red-marked path to the beautiful Poprad lake (Popradské Pleso), an hour and a half's walk. The energetic can continue N from here along a blue-marked path, and then turn right on to another red-marked path, this one zigzagging its way to the summit of Rysy (2499m), on the Polish border; on the way you will cross a snow field and pass the Chata pod Rysmi, the highest mountain hut in Czechoslovakia. From the south-western side of the lake at Štrbské Pleso there is a red-marked path which will lead you after an hour to the Jamské lake, from where it is a two-and-a-half-hour steep climb to the summit of Kriváň (2494m). There are numerous other alternative walks, most of which require at least a day and are only practicable between June and November; the paths, as throughout Czechoslovakia, are extremely well-marked, but can become over-congested at the height of the summer.

16km due E of Štrbské Pleso along a forest road is **Starý Smokovec**, the oldest of the Tatra resorts (on either side are the newer resorts of Nový Smokovec and Horný Smokovec). It has a pleasantly old-fashioned character, with numerous alpine-style, half-timbered buildings of the turn of the century; the one most evocative of past splendours is the *Grand Hotel*, which was built in 1912, and has kept some of its original panelled interior, alongside Art Deco and more modern additions. A funicular of the early years of this century will take you from the resort to Hrebienok, where there are good views looking towards the dramatic Lomnický štít (2632m); among the walks you can do from here is to continue to the top of Slavkovský štít (2452m), a good 3½ hour ascent (turn left at the top of the funicular on to a red-marked path, and then turn right after 20 minutes on to a blue-marked one). *Tatranská Lomnica*, 7km NE of Starý Smokovec, is another old-fashioned resort, this one boasting the Grand Hotel Praha, which stands in extensive wooded grounds, and was built in 1900–14; some of the rooms are still decorated with their original heavy furnishings. A cable-car, dating back to 1940, makes the dizzying climb in two stages from Tatranská Lomnica up to the summit of Lomnický štít, where there is an old astronomical and meteorological station; the half-way station is besides the tiny, spectacularly situated lake of Skalnaté pleso (1751m). 3km SE of Tatranská Lomnica is the Eurocamp FICC, the best-appointed camp site in Slovakia, but not a place for those who appreciate peace and intimacy. *Tatranské Matliary*, 3km NE of the resort, is the site of the sanatorium where Franz Kafka stayed between December 1920 and August 1921, when he was already in an advanced stage of turberculosis.

Continuing to drive NE through the forest you will come after 6km to Road 67, where you should turn left to **Žiar** (a further 9km), a most attractive and little-spoilt village with beautiful views over meadows to the protected Belianské Tatry. The village, rich in folk traditions and a place which resisted in the socialist period the setting up of collective farms, is traditionallly the home of the 'Gorals', an ethnic group derived from the interbreeding of Poles and Slovaks, and named after the Polish word for 'mountain people'. The main street, running parallel with Road 67, is unasphalted and lined with traditional wooden farms, some with cheerful blue and white decoration; many of the buildings are now used as holiday homes by Germans. Adjoining a popular wooden restaurant is a small museum devoted to local ethnography.

Return to Starý Smokovec, and head S to the largest town of the district, *Poprad*, which lies on the western edge of rolling agricultural countryside extending E towards Prešov. This area, with its views over undulating wheatfields to the ever more distant High Tatras, is known as the Spiš, and is of exceptional cultural interest, bearing the mark of many centuries of German dominance. The towns were founded in the 13C by the Hungarian King Béla, and populated with Saxons, who were offered tax exemption and other privileges in return for colonising this area which had recently been ravaged by the Tartars; the Germans represented the majority race until the Second World War. Poprad itself is today largely an ugly industrial town, but it is now joined to the N by the quiet and once separate township of *Spišská Sobota*, which features a most attractive if rather run-down main square, shaded by trees and lined with Renaissance and baroque houses, some with picturesque gables. The main monument on the square is a church of mid 13C origin which was rebuilt in 1468, and given 40 years afterwards a late Gothic chapel (remodelled in the 18C). The high altar of St. George (sv. Juraj; 1516) was the work of pupils of the greatest artist to have worked in the Spiš region, Master Pavol of Levoča, who himself was responsible for the sculptures on the two flanking altars. The free-standing belfry adjoining the church dates back to 1598, but was reconstructed in 1728 and restored in 1956.

Drive E of Poprad on the E50, and, after 14km, you will see, rising above fields to the right of the road the medieval church of *Spišský Štvrtok*. The main body of the church dates back to early Gothic times, but has suffered great damage over the centuries; more interesting is the large chapel attached to its southern side and built in the late 15C as the burial place of the powerful Hungarian family, the Zapolskys. The interior of the chapel, reached through a door on the right aisle of the church, was heavily restored in the late 19C by Ladislaus Steinhausz and given vivid stained-glass windows; the anonymous altarpiece, however, is original, and shows in its main panel the Virgin holding the body of the dying St. John Zapolyas, who was buried at Spišská Kapitula, but whose body was later transferred here. From the crypt underneath the chapel is an underground passage leading to a former Franciscan Monastery, which is now a psychiatric hospital.

LEVOČA, 12km further E and beautifully set among rolling fields has an old centre wholly surrounded by its 14C–15C walls. It is the great architectural jewel of Slovakia, and a place which rivals in its little-spoilt character some of the German colonies of Transylvania.

The history of Levoča goes back to a Moravian settlement which had flourished between the 5C and 9C. However, the town was destroyed in the early Middle Ages by the Tartars, and only renewed after the 13C with the arrival of German settlers. In 1231 it became the capital of the semi-autonomous Spiš region when it was made the seat of the union of the 21 Spiš towns. In 1323 it broke with this union and became a Royal Free Town allied with Bardejov, Košice, Prešov and Sabinov. Though no longer enjoying its previous tax-free status, the town prospered as a result of its position on important trade routes, and enjoyed the greatest period in its history between the 14C and 16C. Printing-works were founded here in 1624, but already the town's decline had set in, a decline which was to be compounded in the 19C, when this by now remote and out-of-the-way place was bypassed by the railway.

A quiet town for most of the year, Levoča comes alive on the first weekend of July, when up to 250,000 Catholics descend on the place to take part in Slovakia's most celebrated Marian pilgrimage. Their pilgrimage to the Shrine of Marianska hora (2km to the N) is comparable to the festive pilgrimages of Spain known as *Romerías*, and is accompanied by much singing and dancing, and an enormous amount to drink. The celebrations begin with a six o'clock mass on Saturday evening, and continue all night, climaxing with a High Mass on Sunday.

A narrow ring of modern development today encircles the old town of Levoča, but once through the medieval walls you will find yourself in a slumbering, slightly decrepit place barely touched by the late 20C. Entering through the Košice Gate on the north-eastern side of town, you will see to your left the *New Minorite Church*, which was built in the middle of the 18C, and has a single nave articulated with elaborate altars, and a profusely rich baroque ceiling decoration. Head W from here along Košická until you reach the main square, where most of Levoča's monuments are concentrated. Surrounding the square are 50 merchants' houses, many with Gothic stone portals, and all originally only one storey high; numerous fires led to most of the medieval houses being rebuilt between the 15C and 17C. One of the finest of the Renaissance houses is the *Thurzov dom* on the NE corner of the square, immediately to your left when entering the square from Košická: it has a wonderful gabled attic, though the sgraffito decoration below this dates back only to 1903. Continuing to walk down the eastern side of the square, you will come first to the town's information office, and then, alongside this (at No. 20), to the house which was used as a studio by the celebrated 16C artist Master Pavol of Levoča; inside is a small didactic museum devoted to artistic practice in Slovakia in the Middle Ages and Renaissance. Most of Master Pavol's known work is to be found in the parish church of **St. James** (sv. Jakuba), which faces the artist's former workshop and stands in the verdant centre of the square, along with the town's other major attraction, the Renaissance Town Hall.

The church of St. James, completed by 1400 though added to and much restored since then, is the largest in Slovakia after the cathedral at Košice; its exterior is dominated by a neo-Gothic tower of 1852–57. The three-aisled interior, entered through the south portal, is remarkable above all for its wealth of polychromed statuary by Master Pavol and his workshop. Above the south door is a Crucifixion group by him, while a studio work of his of 1515 is the altarpiece of St. Anne, attached to the penultimate pier of the right aisle. Behind this, besides the entrance to the chancel, is the altarpiece of St. John (1520), also by Master Pavol and with a central panel featuring both St. John the Baptist and St. John Chrysonomos; its companion-piece on the other side of the chancel is the altarpiece of SS. Peter and Paul of 1500, yet another of his works. In between is Master Pavol's most outstanding achievement, the **HIGH ALTAR**, an elaborate late Gothic structure crowned by a forest of pinnacles, and which, at 2.5m high, is reputedly the largest wing altar in the world; executed in 1508–17, it was restored in 1552–54. The three central figures are of the Virgin and Child flanked by St. John the Baptist and St. James dressed as a pilgrim. Scenes from the lives of these saints are portrayed on the four panels executed in relief on the altar's two wings, which open up to reveal scenes from the Passion. The realism and liveliness of Master Pavol's art is shown above all in the predella of the Last Supper, a witty and unorthodox representation of the scene, with the apostles apparently unconcerned about Christ's message, and shown instead absorbed in their eating and drinking, and even dozing off. Such is the realism of the faces that popular tradition has it that they were portraits of members of the town's council, including one particularly mean member whom Master Pavol decided to take revenge on by portraying him as Judas, an act for which the artist had to leave the town. Continuing walking around the church in an anti-clockwise direction you will come to another work by Master Pavol, this one placed in front of the penultimate pier of the left aisle: this, the altar of St. Nicholas, was executed in 1507 but incorporated a central figure of the 14C. The walls of the left aisle have curious wall-paintings of 1370–1400, showing moralising and apocryphal scenes from the life of St. Dorothy. At the western end of the left aisle, encased in a baroque framework, is a delightful Nativity group of 1494, with a most realistically depicted kneeling shepherd on the left which is clearly by the hand of Master Pavol.

In between the Church of St. James and the **Old Town Hall** (Radnica) is a belfry of 1656–61. The old Town Hall dates back to the 15C, but was rebuilt in 1550–99, and given the two-storeyed loggia on its west side in 1615; the high-pitched roof is of 1893–95. You enter the building through its eastern side, in front of which stands a late medieval cage originally used as a punishment for women. The well-preserved interior of the building features some finely sculpted doors, cellular vaulting, and a Council Chamber adorned with a Renaissance ceiling; the objects on display relate mainly to the history of the town. The neo-classical Evangelist Church of 1825–37 is a free-standing building just to the S of the Old Town Hall, while on the south-western side of the square is an exceptionally well-preserved group of Renaissance buildings comprising the Spillenberg House (Spillenbergov dom; No. 45; built for a distinguished medical family), the Krupek House (Krupeckov dom; No. 44; with a late 16C façade restored in 1979–80) and the former *Levoča School* (No. 40). The latter, belonging once to the Renaissance chronicler of the town, Gaspár Hain, served as the town school in the 18C and 19C; today it houses the Art Gallery of the Spiš region, and includes numerous medieval works from local churches.

Leaving the square by its south-western corner turn immediately to the right and you will come shortly to the attractive Bernolákova ulica. Turn left down this and, beyond a neo-baroque College of the early years of this century, you will pass on the right the former *Monastery Church of the Minorites*, which dates back to the late 15C but was completed in the 17C; inside there are late 14C murals on the north wall. Continuing S down Bernolákova, passing the baroque buildings of the former monastery, you will end up at the Polish Gate, on the other side of which are views over gardens down to a narrow river.

10km S of Levoča is *Spišská Nová Ves*, a former mining-town which was under Polish rule between 1412 and 1472. Encased by modern and industrial development, this bustling small town has kept little of its old centre. The main monument is the Gothic *parish church*, which was begun in 1395, given a tall steeple between 1771–72, and remodelled in the mid 19C; inside are carvings of the Station of the Cross by Master Pavol of Levoča. Facing the north side of the church is a *Municipal Museum* (Gottwaldova 57/50) housed in a building of medieval origin which received in 1765 a lively and amusing rococo facing.—5km SE of Spišská Nová Ves is the château of *Markusovce*, a structure of 1645 remodelled in the 18C; the place was once a furniture museum, but has now a derelict appearance and gives the impression of having been closed for many years. South-west of the town extend the wooded ravines of the Slovak Paradise (see Route 33).

Heading E from Levoča on the E50, you continue driving through the fertile hills of the Spiš, and soon come to two further major attractions of this region, both of which are in the surroundings of *Spišské Podhradie*. 12km E of Levoča, take the turning to the right marked Spišské Podhradie and you will come after 2km to **Spišská Kapitula**, a completely walled township—the only one in Czechoslovakia—standing isolated among fields like an abandoned film set. Officially this citadel is the seat of the Spiš bishopric, though for many years during the period of Socialist rule, there was no bishop to occupy the modest palace within. The other buildings inside once all belonged to the clergy, but now many of them are abandoned, lining cobbled lanes overgrown with grass and weeds; the ugly grey block built built between the wars as a Seminary is now a Police College. Though the interior of the citadel has been much

Inside the small and neglected citadel of Spišská Kapitula

altered over the centuries and does not have the picturesque medieval appearance which the exterior would lead you to believe, it has a hauntingly run-down and deserted character, and you can only be thankful that attempts to transform the whole into a medieval theme park for tourists have so far been resisted. The principal monument is the **Cathedral**, the key to which can be had from the old caretaker in the Bishop's palace opposite the west façade. The building dates back to the 11C, but was heavily remodelled following a fire in the 13C, and extensively restored in the 1870s. The twin-towered west façade is an unsatisfactory mixture of Romanesque, Gothic and Renaissance elements overlaid with heavy-handed 19C restoration. Inside, the main survival of the original 11C church are the Romanesque capitals underneath the organ gallery at the west end. The white-washed, three-aisled interior is otherwise in a Gothic style, the most modern-looking part being the chancel, which was redecorated in 1889 by a member of the Csáky family who was Bishop of the Spiš.

There are notable furnishings, including some locally carved pews of
1630, and various altars of the late 15C and early 16C. The main
altar, a work which has been constantly restored over the centuries,
is an anonymous work dating back to the late 15C and featuring a
central panel of the Crucifixion and two side panels showing the
saints of Hungary and of western Europe. The altar at the end of the
right aisle has a main panel of the Death of the Virgin and is by the
School of Veit Stoss; a carved Coronation of the Virgin, surrounded
by painted scenes of the life of the Virgin, is to be found in a chapel in
the south transept and is by the School of Paul of Levoča. An
anonymous late 15C carved group of the Adoration of the Magi is in
the last chapel of the left aisle. A 14C mural of the Coronation of
Charles of Anjou can bee seen above the north portal, while the coats
of arms of the Hungarians who helped in the wars against the Turks
are hung on the west wall.

From Spišská Kapitula you make a short descent into Spišské
Podhradie, a small town which developed from the 12C underneath
the castle of **Spišský hrad**, a great ruined mass rising on a dramatic
limestone spur 2km to the E (to reach the castle rejoin the E50, take
the first turning to the right, and then turn right again, climbing up
through a stretch of beautiful open countryside). The ruins of the
castle are the largest and most impressive in Czechoslovakia

The limestone spur on which Spišský hrad is situated seems to have been
inhabited as early as the 5C BC, and there is also evidence of a fortified
settlement having existed here in the 2C AD. The present castle—a foundation
of the Hungarian kings—dates from the early 13C, and in 1241 successfully
repelled a Tartar siege; shortly afterwards a keep and palace were built here. In
the late 1430s the widowed queen of King Sigismund, opposing the Polish king
Vladislav's claims to the Hungarian throne, secured the help of Jan Jiskra of
Brandýs, who built the lower fortifications at Spišský hrad, and transformed the
place into the largest castle in central Europe. Later in the century the castle
was donated by the Hungarian throne to the Zápolsky brothers, who abandoned the lower fortifications but extended and remodelled the upper ones.
Further rebuilding was undertaken by the subsequent owners, the Thurzos, and
again by the Csákys who came into the possession of the castle in 1636. The
Csákys were to own the castle up to 1945, but only lived here for about 100
years, moving in the early 18C to Bratislava. In 1710 the castle experienced its
last military action when it was occupied by the Imperial army following the
capitulation of the Rákóczi forces. Destroyed by fire shortly afterwards, and
again in 1780, the castle was then left to ruin; restoration work was only begun
in 1969.

Entering the castle through a Romanesque gate built in 1249, you
find yourself in a reconstruction of the mid 13C palace (of which only
fragments have survived). Within the reconstruction are numerous
finds from the castle, from prehistoric times onwards, and a large
collection of torture instruments loaned from a number of local
museums. There are good views of the restored walls of the lower
fortifications. After leaving the castle, you could head S for 3km to
the tiny village of Žehra, where there is a church dating back to 1275,
but much altered in later centuries. It stands on top of a small verdant
hill, its cheerful white-washed exterior dominated by a black onion
dome; the 17C interior contains a 13C baptismal font, some 15C
carvings, and a series of 13C–15C murals, in a touchingly naïf style.
Return to the E50, and drive the remaining 30km to Prešov (see
Route 32).

31 Poprad to Svidník

Total distance 191km. Poprad—15km **Kežmarok**—45km **Červený Kláštor**—24km *Stará Ľubovňa*—61km **Bardejov**—46km *Svidník*.

Road 67 N of Poprad runs at first through the north-western corner of the Spiš region (see Route 30), with distant views over rolling agricultural countryside to the High Carpathians. After 8km, the road bypasses to the right the small town of *Veľká Lomnica*, where there is an impressive parish church (being restored) built in 1412 over the foundations of a 13C building. **Kežmarok**, 7km further N, is one of the most interesting of the Spiš towns colonised by Germans in the 13C. Though the town has developed considerably following the introduction of textile factories in the 19C, it has kept extensive stretches of its medieval fortifications, several medieval and Renaissance houses, and an old-fashioned Germanic character. Outside the town walls, on Hviedoslava Street, is one of the finest of Slovakia's *Evangelical churches*, built entirely in wood in 1716 but plastered on the outside. The recently restored interior takes the form of a broad, aisleless hall originally containing 1460 seats that have now been removed to make way for a local museum. Next to the building is the *New Protestant Church*, a neo-Moorish structure of the early years of this century. This is a place of great emotional significance to Hungarians, for it is here that their outstanding military commander of the 17C, Imre Thökoly, is buried. Duke of Transylvania and Upper Hungary, Thökoly was born in Kežmarok in 1652 and died in the Turkish town of Izmid Nicomedi in 1705, his remains being subsequently taken back to his native town; his tomb stands in a chapel

The white-washed walls of the town castle of Kežmarok; the gable-like crenellations are typical of the sixteenth-century architecture of the Spiš region

on the right side of the church, bedecked with garlands and other tributes left by Hungarian visitors.

The quiet and tiny Poziarnikov námestie in the town centre is dominated by the *parish church*, which was built in 1444–98, and partially altered in the 16C. Entering through the finely carved south portal, you find yourself in a hall-church with late 15C vaulting; the high altar of the Crucifixion, and the two side altars, are all by the School of Pavol of Levoča. Facing the church is its delightful, free-standing belfry of 1591, of a type which is very characteristic of the Spiš region: covered in white plaster, and sgraffitoed with exquisite Renaissance decoration in its upper level, it is crowned by a fanciful parapet made up of gablets (decorative forms taking the shape of small gables). The church square adjoins the town's long main square, which contains several late Gothic and Renaissance houses, though is mainly 19C in appearance. The most prominent monument is the former Town Hall, a tall pedimented structure dating back to the Renaissance, but rebuilt in the late 18C. On the northern side of the old town, attached to the best preserved stretch of the medieval walls, is the *town castle*, which was built in 1433 and transformed into a sumptuous residence at the end of the 16C. As with the belfry of the parish church, its architecture is unmistakably of the Spiš region, with white plastered walls and small gable-like forms acting as crenellations. Badly damaged by fire in 1787, the building has housed since 1930 a museum containing exhibits relating to the history and archaeology of the town.—6km S of the town is the attractive village of *Vrbov*, with a Spiš-style belfry of 1644, and, on its outskirts, some tiny lakes popular with bathers.

Continue N of Kežmarok on Road 67, which, at Spišská Belá (8km), turns due W towards Ždiar (see Route 30). Leave the road 2km W of Spišská Belá, and take the forest road NW to Spišská Stará Ves (27km). At the crossing 2km N of the latter village turn right and follow the fast-flowing Dunajec river, which marks the border with Poland, and enters the *Pieniny National Park*. In the middle of the forests and low mountains forming this small park is the beautifully situated former monastery, **Červený Kláštor**, which looks N into Poland to the highest peak of the Pieniny range, Trzy Korony (992m), a jagged rocky outcrop densely covered with pines.

Červený Kláštor was founded as a Carthusian monastery in 1319, and appropriated by the Camuldensian Order in 1704; its name, meaning the 'red monastery', might derive from its red-tiled roof. The place acquired a great reputation for its garden of curative plants, particularly during the rule as abbot of Brother Cyprian, the 18C author of a famous Herbarium of 36 pages, and a man with a passionate interest in science. What might well have been Brother Cyprian's most extraordinary achievement—as well as one of the great breakthroughs in Western technology—is sadly unsupported by written evidence. In 1768 he is said to have invented a flying apparatus, which he used to glide from Trzy Korony to the High Carpathians.

The walled and much restored monastery complex has a simple 14C church, and a grass-covered enclosure with a group of one-roomed hermits' dwellings; the famous herbarium can still be seen, as can—in front of this—the laboratory belonging to Brother Cyprian. Most of the surviving buildings are of the baroque period, and are used today as a catering school, the headquarters of the Pieniny National Park, and a historical and ethnographical museum. The main tourist attraction of the place are the trips by raft down a wooded gorge of the Dujanec river from a landing site just below the monastery (the return journey is by bus); the trip can also.be done from the Polish side of the river, which has the added fun of raftsmen in traditional folk costume and a musical send-off. Should the trip by raft not appeal to you, you can do the same journey by walking along the beautiful riverside path.

The road which passes through Červený Kláštor continues SE to *Stará Ľubovňa* (24km), a town on the southern banks of the river Poprad. The town itself is of little interest, but above the river's northern banks there rises up in isolation an imposing castle, built in the 13C to guard the border of the Hungarian kingdom. The castle, in gradual decay from the early 19C onwards, was purchased in 1883 by the Polish Zamojski family, who restored the residential quarters in the lower half of the complex, but left the upper half in ruins. These residential quarters, retained by the family until 1945, now house a district museum.

At Stará Ľubovňa turn E on to Road 77, following the Poprad valley in the direction of Bardejov (51km), passing after 16km the scant ruins of the 13C Plaveč Castle. A slightly longer route to Bardejov is to leave Road 77 13km before the town, and head S on a side road to Kružov (2km), where you turn left to *Krivé*, a further 2km. In an exposed hillside setting just above the latter village is one of the many wooden churches that are to be found throughout eastern Slovakia. As with many of these churches, this one was built by Greek Catholics, a sect which combines elements of Roman Catholicism and the Greek Orthodox Church and is very widespread on the eastern confines of the former Habsburg Empire. Dating back to 1826, this small and simple structure resembling an upturned boat was dedicated to St. Lucas. Continuing to follow the same side road in a south-easterly direction, and turning right after 10km you will come to one of the most remarkable of all Slovakia's wooden churches, that of **Hervartov**. Hidden in a densely wooded grove (high trees were generally planted next to wooden churches to serve as lightning conductors), this Catholic church built out of red spruce, was originally constructed in 1593–96, and renovated at various times since then. It is fascinating above all for the painted decorations inside, which date back to 1594 and were restored in the 1660s and again in 1969–70. They are concentrated mainly on the south wall of the nave, where you will find representations of Adam and Eve, St. George and the Dragon, and engagingly naïf scenes of the Wise and Foolish Virgins, the latter portrayed in contemporary costume and blissfully asleep. Returning from Hervartov to the side road S of Road 77, turn right and then almost immediately left, approaching Bardejov from the south.

BARDEJOV, situated in wooded, gently hilly countryside, is one of Slovakia's best-preserved medieval towns. A royal free town from 1376, Bardejov reached the height of its prosperity in the 15C and 16C, thanks to its situation on an important trade route, its cloth factories, printing works and other industries. Populated at one time by numerous Armenian merchants, the town today has a large Ruthenian or Rusin minority (non-Catholic Slavs of Ukranian origin), with the street signs in both Slovak and Russian.

The old centre of Bardejov is surrounded by extensive stretches of its remarkably well-preserved 14C–15C fortifications, the northern ones having at their foot a long wooded garden containing the Hotel Dukla. Entering the old town from the street on the eastern side of this hotel, you will find yourself immediately in Bardejov's wide and long main square, one of the most beautiful in Czechoslovakia, and surrounded almost entirely by steeply gabled pastel-coloured houses of the 15C and 16C. At the northern end of the square is the *parish church*, built in the 14C on the site of a Cistercian foundation, and restored following a fire in 1878; inside are 11 wing altars of the 15C and 16C, the most notable of which is that of the Nativity, situated just to the left of the neo-Gothic high altar of the early 1890s. Facing the church, in the centre of the square, is the free-standing old *Town Hall*, a recently restored structure dating back to 1505–11 and now housing a museum featuring the largest collection of icons in Slovakia. Two further museums are to be found in two neighbouring houses at the southern end of the square. Between these, running S of the square, is the attractive Rhodyho Street, which leads to the largest surviving area of the town's fortifications, comprising two parallel lines of walls, a gate and bridge, and numerous turrets and bastions. Turning left on to Na hradbách and following the line of the inner walls will take you to the most imposing of these bastions, the *Malá bašta*, a massive structure (later converted into a granary) with a rounded eastern end, and an upper gallery underneath a high-pitched roof with wide eaves. From here the sloping Veterná Street, with numerous fine old houses (including one which belonged to to the town's executioner), will take you uphill to the south-eastern corner of the main square.

Leaving Bardejov on Road 77, you will find 2km to the N of the town a turning to the left to *Bardejovské kúpele*, a quiet small spa which in its heyday was one of the more renowned in Hungary.

The curative properties of the Bardejov waters were recognised in the 13C, but the springs were not be exploited until the 17C. In 1767 Armenian merchants constructed a group of wooden cabins around the springs, and shortly afterwards the place developed as an exclusive and predominantly aristocratic resort, visited, among others, by Napoleon I's wife Marie Louise in 1809, Tzar Alexander I in 1821 and, in 1895, by Empress Elizabeth, in whose honour a row of lime trees was planted. The resort, essentially a summer one, was built mainly in wood, and was severely damaged by fires in 1910–12. Only with the construction of a series of modern buildings in the 1960s was the popularity of the spa revived, but it still remains a very modest place in comparison with others in Slovakia; the waters are used above all for the treatment of digestive orders.

The spa is attractively and spaciously arranged alongside a narrow park bordered by gentle pine-covered slopes. There are a number of turn-of-the-century buildings, including, at the western end of the park, the Hotel Dukla, in front of which is a bronze statue of the Empress Elizabeth. South of this is a small *museum* with a rare collection of icons and, in the sloping woods behind this, Slovakia's first village museum or *Skansen*: founded in 1955, its oldest and most interesting building is a wooden Orthodox Church of 1706.

Return to Road 77, and continue E to *Svidník* (34km), another town with a large Ukranian minority, whose culture is documented here by a small museum. The town, entirely rebuilt after the last war, was destroyed during the Battle of Dukla, which lasted between October and November 1944 and led to what later came to be known as the 'Soviet Liberation' of Czechoslovakia. Red Army troops, led by Ludvík Svoboda, entered Czechoslovakia on 4 October 1944 by way of the Dukla Pass, 15km NE of Svidník along Road 73. Eighty-four thousand members of the Red Army were killed, 9000 of whom were buried at Svidník, at a site marked today by an enormous obelisk. In a field near this monument is a display of tanks, planes and other weapons used in the conflict, and there are more of these arranged at regular intervals the whole length of the wooded valley leading up to the pass. At *Vyšný Komárník*—3km before the pass, and the first

Czechoslovak village to be liberated—is a large Monument to the Unknown Soldier, next to which is a line of bronze busts of the Czech and Soviet officers who took part in the conflict. Along the same valley is the largest concentration of *wooden churches* to be seen in Slovakia, including at Ludomirova, Hunkovce and at Vyšný Komárník itself. Two of the finest are at the neighbouring villages of *Bodruzal* and *Miroľa* (leave Road 73 at Krajná Poľana, 9km N of Svidník, and head in a south-easterly direction): both these churches have three picturesquely shaped steeples crowned by bulbous forms.

32 Svidník to Košice

Total distance 93km. Svidník—57km **Prešov**—36km **Košice**.

43km S of Svidník on Road 73 you come to Road 18, where you can either head W to Prešov or else head E to visit the narrow east-ernmost extremity of Slovakia, driving in between gentle wooded hills to the N, and agricultural plains to the south. Apart from a number of wooden churches, this latter area of Slovakia offers little of architectural interest, and no spectacular scenery such as you find in the centre of the region. The principal attraction is the enormous *Zemplínska šírava reservoir* (70km E of the junction of Roads 73 and 18), Czechoslovakia's most popular water resort, and impossibly crowded during the summer months.

The large industrial town of **Prešov**, situated in flat and built-up countryside, is a bustling place of no great beauty, but with a number of fine monuments around its main square.

A Slovakian settlement existed on the site of present-day Prešov by the end of the 8C, but the first document mentioning the town date only from the early 13C. Granted royal privileges in 1299, Prešov was made a Royal Free Town in 1374, and rapidly developed as an important centre of trade and commerce. The place was a centre of anti-Habsburg uprisings in the 17C and 18C, and as a result suffered badly, in particular after the suppression of Count Thököly's revolt in 1684. Made district town of Šariš County at the end of the 18C, Prešov experienced an economic revival, but this was not sufficient to prevent widespread emigration from the town in the late 19C and early 20C. On 16 June 1919 the short-lived Slovak Republic of the Proletariat was declared here, inspired by the example of Russia's October Revolution. The town today, an important centre of the food, textile and engineering industries, is also the cultural capital of the Ruthenians or Rusins (see Bardejov, Route 31).

The main square of Prešov takes the form of an enormously long avenue dominated at its northern end by the parish church of *St. Nicholas* (sv. Mikuláš), which was begun in the late 14C, and altered in 1502; the medieval furnishings within the light and spacious interior have been replaced by late baroque ones, including several altars and a dynamic pulpit. One of the finest of the old houses on the square is *Rákociho dom*, a double-fronted Renaissance structure housing a museum documenting the Slovak Republic of the Pro-letariat; near this is the Town Hall of 1511–20, from the balcony of which the Republic was declared. At the southern end of the square is the former monastery church of *St. John the Baptist*, built by Gaspar Urlespacher in 1753–59, and featuring an elaborate baroque façade; the monastery belonged originally to the Minorite Order, but with the abolition of this Order by Joseph II in 1787 its buildings were used as a military store before being handed over to the Greek Catholics in 1821. Walking back in the direction of St. Nicholas along the western side of the square, you will come at No. 326 to an *Art Gallery* which puts on temporary exhibitions of Slovakian artists; the permanent collection, rarely on display, contains works by the leading Slovakian artists of this century, including Jozef Bendík (who was born in Prešov), Ľudovít Fulla, Jan Želibský, and Jozef Fabini. An arch through the western side of the square leads into the 29 Augusta ulica, where, on the left-hand side, is the so-called *Caraffa Prison*, built in 1624.

Heading S from Prešov on the E50, you pass alongside the southern suburb of Solivar, an old salt-mining town (the name of which means 'the place where salt is boiled'), where a number of 17C salt works have survived. Shortly afterwards the E50 turns into the D1 motorway, which speeds through flat and built-up countryside almost all the way to Košice (36km).

The second largest town in Slovakia, **KOŠICE** is encircled by extensive industrial development, including the most important foundry works in Czechoslovakia. Its unprepossessing surroundings and remote position have helped to ensure that the town is relatively little visited by tourists, and yet there are few places in Czechoslovakia with such a lively and dynamic character. The combination of animated street life and monumental turn-of-the-century architecture that make Budapest such an exciting city to visit is also to be found here, together with a cathedral which is rivalled only by that of St. Vitus in Prague as the finest in central Europe.

It is not known when the original settlement at Košice was established, though German settlers moved in here following Tartar invasions in the early 13C. First mentioned in 1248, Košice received royal privileges in the 1340s, and became a Royal Free Town in 1347. Trade and commerce flourished from the 14C onwards, with the town acquiring a particular reputation for its furriers, bell-founders and goldsmiths. Enjoying a leading position within the league of East Slovak towns known as the Pentapolitana, Košice became by the 15C the third largest town in the kingdom of Hungary. The Turkish invasion, and the re-aligning of the trade route which once went through the town led to a great decline in the 16C which was only briefly halted towards the end of the following century. Rapid industrialisation led to renewed prosperity in the 19C, and in 1907 the first workers' newspaper in Hungary was published here. After being under Czechoslovak rule for only 19 years, Košice was handed back to the Hungarians as a result of the Treaty of Munich of 1938. At the end of the Second World War it became the temporary seat of the Czechoslovak Government immediately after their return from exile. The town today still has a strong Hungarian minority, though tensions between Hungarians and Slovaks have eased somewhat in recent years, and been largely replaced by a common hatred of the town's large gypsy population.

The centre of Košice is traversed from N to S by a long and broad avenue which swells out in the middle to form two adjoining squares separated by the town's cathedral. There are Czech towns with more beautiful and better preserved main squares, but not even Prague can boast a central thoroughfare with so monumental a character and so suggestive of a major city. Of all the many monuments worth visiting here it is naturally the **CATHEDRAL OF ST. ELIZABETH** (Dom sv. Alžbety) which immediately attracts the tourist's attention.

Work on the cathedral, the largest in Slovakia, was begun c 1380 on the site of a former parish church which had been destroyed by fire in 1378. Sigismund of Luxemburg and later Matthias Corvinus gave much help in the construction of the building, which was supervised until 1420 by the royal architect Master Peter, and until 1477 by Master Stephen of Košice. Badly damaged in 1491, when Košice was besieged in the course of the struggle between Vladislav II and his younger brother John Albert, the cathedral was finally brought to completion in c 1508. A serious fire devastated the interior in 1556, destroying most of the medieval furnishings, including 18 of the original 22 altars.

West façade of the Cathedral of St. Elizabeth, Košice

Following further damage by flood and earthquake, major repairs were carried out in 1857–67, and in 1877—1896 neo-Gothic remodelling of the interior was undertaken by Franz Schmidt, the restorer of St. Stephen's Cathedral in Vienna. A renewed restoration campaign has been in process since 1985.

The exterior of the cathedral, with its crocketed and dramatically tapering crossing tower, and steeply pitched roofs covered in coloured tiling, has a west façade framed by two towers, one tall and octagonal, the other squat with late Gothic detailing; in the tympanum of the west portal is a carved representation of Christ in the Garden of Olives, above which is a group of the Lamentation. The most elaborately shaped and richly carved of the cathedral's portals is the northern one, which has a tympanum portraying the Last Judgement. The dark interior, lit by 19C stained-glass, has at its western end a raised choir supported by arches adorned with intricate late Gothic statuary, the colouring of which was renewed in the last century. Perhaps the most striking architectural feature of the interior is the openwork and minutely carved stone staircase attached to the north side of the presbytery and leading up to the Royal Gallery in the Triforium; executed in 1468–77 it is the masterpiece of Master Štefan of Košice. Of the furnishings special mention must be made of the late gothic pulpit (another remarkably elaborate structure, crowned by a soaring wooden canopy) and of the high altar of St. Elizabeth of Hungary, a vast wing altar containing 48 panels painted on a gold ground, executed in 1474–77 and attributed by some to the German master Michael Wolgemut. In the crypt is to be found the tomb of the great Hungarian challenger to Habsburg rule, Ferenc Rákóczi II, whose remains, together with those of his fellow exiles, were brought over from Turkey in 1906.

In the garden on the south side of the cathedral is the late 14C chapel of *St. Michael* (sv. Michal), which faces to the E the pedimented palace of 1779 which served in 1945 as the first seat of the newly returned Czechoslovak government. In front of the cathedral's north portal is the former belfry tower known as the *Urban's Tower*, a 15C structure surrounded by arcading at ground level and remodelled in the 16C. Adjacent to this, on the western side of the square at No. 40, is a neo-Gothic building of 1849 housing a branch of the *East Slovak Museum* devoted principally to the applied arts. Across the garden to the north of the tower is the majestic *Opera House* (Štátne divadlo) of 1899 (at present under restoration), one of the more lively and imposing works by that ubiquitous Viennese pair, Helmer and Fellner; in the gardens on the northern side of this building is a Marian column of 1723. Continuing to walk N on the western side of the town's principal thoroughfare you will come at No. 72 to a yellow neo-classical palace housing the main branch of the *East Slovak Gallery* (another branch, containing mainly 19C works, is at 22 Strobárova, which runs to the W of the cathedral). The gallery has a representative selection of East Slovak art from the late 18C to recent times, including works by the 18C portraitist Bogdany (who settled in England and is often considered English) and the naïf landscapist and portraitist Jozef Czauczik. Other artists in the collection include Ján Rombauer, Anton Stadler, František Klimkovic, Ladislav Medňanský, Ferdinand Katona, Jozef Hanula, Ľudovít Cordák, Max Kurth, Elemir Halász-Hradil, Anton Jasusch, Konstantín Kövári, Konstantín Bauer, Jozef Bendík and Jozef Fabini. Further N, at No. 88, is the neo-classical Rákóczi Palace, featuring the *Slovak Technical Museum*, the only museum of its kind in Slovakia. The avenue comes to an end at the námestie Maratónu mieru, on which stands the enormous and pompous turn-of-the-century building containing the main branch of the *East Slovak Museum* (Východoslovenské múzeum), with a fascinating range of objects documenting the history of East Slovakia from prehistoric to modern times, including an extensive numismatic collection, and a famed group of goldware.

Returning to the central avenue, and walking down its eastern side, turn left on E. Adyho, and you will pass on the left the *Miklos Prison*, a white-washed 16C structure, inside which you can see much of the original interior, a torture chamber, and a network of secret passages. Adjoining this, at the western end of the street, is the *Executioner's Bastion* (Katova bašta)—a part of the medieval ramparts and containing in its verdant courtyard a picturesque half-timbered tower known as the Rákóczi house. Back on the central avenue, you will find just to the S of E. Adyho (at No. 65) the much-restored *Levoča House*, a building of 15C origin with an attractive white-washed courtyard and an excellent Hungarian restaurant; attached to its southern side is the *Café Slavia*, a splendid Art Nouveau building with polychromed decoration on its exterior. Further S you will come back to the cathedral.

33 Košice to Banská Bystrica

Total distance 214km. Košice—69km Rožňava—53km Švermovo—49km *Brežno*—43km **Banská Bystrica**.

Head S of Košice (see Route 32) on the E571, following to begin with a short stretch of dual carriageway, which comes to an end just before the industrial community of Šaca (16km), and turns sharply to the west. The road, which passes at first through flat countryside, soon enters a green and beautiful valley running between the hills of northern Hungary and the southern slopes of the Slovakian Ore Mountains (Slovenské Rudohorie). At Moldava nad Bodvou, a turning to the right will bring you after 9km to *Jasov*, where there is a former Premonstratensian Monastery, founded in the 12C. The original foundation was destroyed by Tartar invasions in the early 13C, and the present structure is an impressive late baroque building executed in 1750–66 to designs by F.A. Pilgram (the frescoes and the high altar are by J.L. Kracker). The village stands on the eastern edge of the *Slovakian* (Slovenský) *kras*, the largest karst area in central Europe, and extending well to the west of Rožňava; geographically a part of the Slovakian Ore Mountains, it features numerous gorges and caves, in one of which—on the outskirts of Jasov—footprints of neo-palaeolithic man have been discovered. Return to the E571, and continue heading W, passing to the right after 10km the scant, hill-top ruins of *Turna Castle*. 26km later, on the eastern outskirts of Rožňava, the imposing mass of one of Slovakia's most famed castles, **Krásna Hórka**, provides a glowing white crown to a tall, steep mound ringed with wild meadows.

Founded in 1320, the castle was acquired in the 16C by the Andrássy family, who between 1578 and 1586 remodelled the medieval building, and at great expense extended the fortifications in preparation for a possible Turkish attack. Inhabited up to 1812, the castle was partially renovated in 1903 by its last owner, Count Dionysius Andrássy, who transformed it into a family museum (opened to the public in 1910), and built at its foot an extraordinary family mausoleum. In 1989 the castle was re-opened following further extensive restoration.

Shortly before leaving the E571 and climbing up to the castle, you will pass on the right-hand side of the road, the gates of the *Mausoleum* which was built by Count Dionysius Andrássy in 1903–04, and contains the tombs both of himself and of his father Stefán: shaded by a wooded grove it is a lavish temple-like structure in a Secessionist style, with a resplendent marbled interior, the apse of which is highlighted in gold mosaic. At the end of the long climb up to the castle you are offered an outstanding view over fields and wooded hills. In the entrance courtyard is a section of Budapest's Chain Bridge, which was founded in the Andrássy ironworks. The western part of the castle was destroyed by fire in 1817 and has recently been re-opened with a modern display of armour, portraits of the Andrássy family, 17C and 18C furniture, traditional costumes of the Hungarian aristocracy and items relating to the history of the building and of the Thirty Years' War. The series of rooms created by Dionysius Andrássy in 1903 as a family museum have baroque to Empire furnishings and decorations, and include paintings and drawings by Dionysius himself and a fine collection of old European glass assembled by Stefán Andrássy. Among the castle's other attractions are a traditional kitchen and an early 18C chapel housing the mummified and lace-covered remains of Stefán's wife, Zsofía Sereghy.

Rožňava, 5km to the W, is a medieval mining town with an early 18C Bishop's Palace and a main square containing a number of old buildings, most notably a tower of of 1643–54. 14km SW of the town is another of the well-known caves of the Slovenský kras, the *Gombasek Ice Cave*, with ice-covered stalactites as long as 3m; even larger is the *Domica Cave*, which lies 15km to the S (leave the E571 at Plešivec, and turn left), and is linked to the Aggtelek Cave in Hungary (the border between the two countries is marked by a grille).

Continuing on your journey to Banská Bystrica head N of Rožňava on Road 67, and you will come after 6km to *Betliar*, another of the many properties that belonged to the Andrássy family. The present appearance of this château, which dates back to a 16C building remodelled in the 18C, is due to drastic reconstruction carried out in 1880–86. The rather heavy interior (at present closed for restoration) has numerous hunting trophies and collections of china, ceramics, furniture and armour. More appealing are the magnificent gardens, laid out in an English style at the end of the 18C and featuring numerous waterfalls, grottoes, temples and other follies. North of Betliar Road 67 climbs up into the Slovakian Ore Mountains, entering after the small village of Dobšiná (19km) the popular summer resort of the **Slovakian Paradise** (Slovenský ráj), an area of densely forested mountains intercut with deep, rocky chasms. 7km beyond Dobšiná is a turning to the right to Dedinky, where there is a small reservoir and a chair-lift leading up to the wooded plateau of Geravy (a popular place for cross-country skiers). North of the turning Road 67 descends into the narrow Stratená Gorge, the road hemmed in by steep faces of rock. The first turning on the right will take you along a most beautiful if poorly surfaced road right through the heart of the Slovakian Paradise and all the way to Hrabušice (18km). From Hrabušice an hour's walk to the E leads to the finest place from which to explore the Paradise, **Kláštorisko**, a clearing in the forest featuring a restaurant, a group of tourist chalets and excellent views towards the snow-capped High Tatras (see Route 30). It was to Kláštorisko that the inhabitants of the region took refuge in the wake of the Tartar invasions of the early 13C, and in memory of this representatives of the 24 Spiš towns founded here a Carthusian Monastery in 1305; conquered in the 16C by the cruel bandit Matthias Baso, and used by him as a base for his various savage forays, the place was later demolished, and now only a few scant ruins can be seen. Kláštorisko stands above the spectacular gorge of the Hornád, and a short walk can be made from here to the *Tomášov Balcony* (Tomášovsky výhlad), a dramatic overhang with a sheer drop down to the river. There are numerous other walks of a more adventurous kind to be done in the area, most notably along the gorge, and up a series of interconnecting ones; these walks involve climbing up ladders along the side of waterfalls, and skirting sheer rock faces with the aid of chains and climbing irons.

Continuing to Banská Bystrica along Road 67 you will pass, 2km W of the turning to Hrabušice, the *Dobšiná Ice Cave*, the largest such cave in Czechoslovakia, and filled with a massive iceberg 145,000 cubic metres in size. Shortly beyond the cave you leave Road 67, and

Monument at Nemecká commemorating the nine hundred Slovak partisans murdered by the Nazis in a lime-kiln

turn left on to Road 66, which descends through attractive countryside into the valley of the Hron, a valley bordered to the S by the
Slovakian Ore Mountains and to the N by the Lower Tatras (see
Route 30). 14km after the turning there is a small dead-end road to
the right leading after 3km to one of the least-spoilt and least-visited
villages in Slovakia, *Šumiac*; composed almost entirely of traditional
19C wooden houses, the villagers continue to wear the old folk
costumes, particularly on Sundays and public holidays. 14km further
W along Road 66, you pass through the large village of *Helpá*, a place
of no great character but with a number of wooden houses on the
left-hand side of the road, and with a reputation for its folk traditions;
a folklore festival is held here every summer. At *Brežno*, a further
29km W, an old town hall dating back to the 1780s houses a museum
devoted to local history and ethnography. 6km beyond Brežno there
branches off to the N Road 72, a beautiful road crossing right over the
ridge of the Low Tatras. Continuing on Road 66, one of the few sites
of interest before reaching Banská Bystrica (33km; see Route 28) is
Nemecká, the site of a Nazi atrocity during the last war. You will see
on the right-hand side of the road (12km E of Banská Bystrica) a lime
kiln in which around 900 Slovak partisans involved in the Uprising
were killed by the Germans, a crime which was only discovered
much later; a nearby small museum and a modern bronze of a
woman with outstretched arms commemorate the incident.

INDEX

KEY TO ROUTE MAPS

2

GERMANY

Děčín

8

7

6

Ústí nad Labem

Teplice

Csek

Strekc

Duchcov

Litoměřic

Bílina

Terezín

7

Most

Doksany

Chomutov

Roudnic

Klášterec

Verněřov

Louny

Kadaň

9A

9A

Žatec

9A

Ostrov

Krásný Dvůr

Lidice

8

Karlovy Vary

9B

9B

Revničov

Kačice

2D

Františkovy Lázně

10

Lány

Cheb

9B

Lubenec

Křivoklát

2C

Berounka

Beroun

10

Mariánské Lázně

Žebrák

Karlštejn

B O H

Dobříš

11

13

Obořiště

St

Plzeň

Rokycany

Příbram

15A

Kladruby

14

Březnice

11

Horšovský Tyn

Lnáře Paštiky

Orlík na Vltavo

Ujezd

Domažlice

Blatná

14

Zvíkov

Kdyně

Klatovy

15A

Horažďovice

Písek

12

Rabi

Strakonice

Špičák

Sušice

14

Vodňany

Železná Ruda

Kašperské Hory

12

Husinec

Netol

Vimperk

Prachatice

GERMANY

Lenora

Volary

Želnava

1 Route numbers in text

■ Towns with plans in text

0 kilometres   50

Krnov
Bruntál
Opava
Hradec nad Moravicí
Ostrava
Bilovec
Fulnek
Novy Jičín
Přibor
Hukvaldy
Kopřivnice
Štramberk
Frenštát pod R
Hodslavice
Ostravice
Bělotin
Hranice
Lipník nad Bečvou
Valašské Meziříčí
Rožnov pod Radhoštěm
Bystřice pod Hostýnem
Vsetin
Holešov
Kroměříž
Vizovice
Zlín
Velehrad
chlovice
Uherské Hradiště
Strážnice
Čachtice
Nové Mesto nad Váhom
Trenčín
Trenčianske Teplice
Dežerice
Bánovce nad Bebravou
Piešt any
Modra
Pezinok
Jur
Trnava
Nitra
Dunajská Streda
Čalovo
Komárno
Patince
Samorin
muliakov

Český Těšín
Frýdek-Mistek
Mosty u Jablunkova
Čadca
Bilá
Žilina
Varín
Strečno
Martin
Lietava
Považská Bystrica
Fačkov
Čičmany
Bojnice
Uhrovec
Dol.-Vestenice
Prievidza
Kremnica
Nové Lehota
Žiar
Sasov
Žarnovica
Zlaté Moravce
Želiezovce
Demandice
N. Zamky
Šturovo

Slanická Osada
Orava
Terchová
Vrátno
Dolný Ku
Lubochňa
Ružomberok
Donovaly
OSTRENOK
Staré Hory
Nem
Banska Bystric
Banská Štiavnica
Srdieč
S L O

Mostu
Prerov
ulin
Vrátno

21 A
22
21 B
21 C
21 A
21 B
21 C
27
28
26 B
26 A
29
33
26 A

HUNGARY

Dunaj (Danube)
Vah
Morava

6

Český Těšín
Frýdek-Místek
ukvaldy
ivnice
berk   Ostravice
nštát
R   Bílá
v pod
ěštěm

Mosty u
Jablunkova

Čadca

Slanická
Osada   Tvrdošín
Orava   Podbiel
               Zuberec

Spišská
Stará Ves   Ždiar

31

Tatranská
Lomnica
Starý
Smokovec

27   Žilina
            Varín
Lietava   Strečno
Považská
Bystrica
            Martin

Terchová
Vrátno
            Dolný Kubín
Lubochňa

Liptovský
Mikuláš   30

Štrbské
Pleso   30

Tatranská
Štrba

Velká
Lomnica

Poprad

29
Fačkov
Čičmany

Ružomberok

Jasná

Srdiečko

Donovaly
OSTRENOK
Staré Hory
Nemecká

Čertovica
Pass   Helpa   Šumiac

33

Trenčianske
Teplice
28
ežerice   Bojnice   Prievidza
Uhrovec
ovce nad   Dol.-
ebravou   Vestenice

28
Kremnica

Nové Lehota

Žiar

S L O V A K I A

Banska Bystrica

28

33
Brezno

Zvolen
28
Sasov

Žarnovica

Banská
Štiavnica

26A

Zlaté Moravce   26 B

Nitra

Demandice

Železovce

N. Zámky

26A

árno   Patince

Šturovo

1 Route numbers in text
■ Towns with plans in text

0 kilometres   50

POLAND

Vyšný
Komárnik○ ○Bodružal
Svidník ○Mirol'a
‚31'
○
Bardejov ‚32'
Stará Plavěc Krulov
Lubovňa ‚31' Krivé
Hervartov

Spišská Belá
ežmarok
‚30'
Levoča ‚30' Prešov
Spišská○ Spišské ‚32'
išský Kapitula Podhradie
vrtok ○Spišská Nová Ves
ušice ‚32'
edinky
obšiná
Zemplínska Otava

Košice○
Betliar ○Jasov ‚33'
Krásna Horka Šaca
žňava○
‚33' Moldava nad
Bodvou

HUNGARY